THE AMERICAN ALPINE JOURNAL
2003

Above: John Millar and Conor Reynolds with the sunny west face of Swachand (6,721m), India. Guy Edwards
Cover: Arwa Tower, as seen from the summit of Arwa Spire Central Peak in evening light, after
the ascent of Fior di Vite, Garhwal Himalaya, India. Stephan Harvey

Nothing like a change of latitudes to bring out a different face of mountaineering.
Brad Barlage hiking up the Bronco Couloir, with Iceberg Camp #2 beneath him. Andrew McLean
The José Pereyra chillin' at the Macaw Bivy on Autana Tepui, Venezuela. Tim O'Neill

Corporate Friends

OF THE

AMERICAN ALPINE JOURNAL

We thank the following for their generous financial support of the 2003 American Alpine Journal

Marmot

THE NORTH FACE

MSR

MOUNTAIN HARD WEAR

patagonia

MOUNTAIN GEAR
mountaingear.com
800.829.2009

BACKPACKER
The Magazine Of Wilderness Travel

ROCK&ICE

Valery Rozov launching from the top of RUbikon, Great Sail Peak, Baffin Island. Alexandr Ruchkin

The Wichman Tower keeps Robert MacKinnon company in the Arrigetch Peaks of Alaska's Brooks Range. Jeff Pflueger

Friends
OF THE
AMERICAN ALPINE JOURNAL

WE THANK THE FOLLOWING FOR THEIR
GENEROUS FINANCIAL SUPPORT:

Ann Carter
Yvon Chouinard
Gregory Miller
Louis Reichardt
Cascade Section, AAC
New York Section, AAC

The H. Adams Carter Endowment Fund
for The American Alpine Journal

THE AMERICAN ALPINE JOURNAL
710 Tenth St. Suite 140, Golden, Colorado 80401
Telephone: (303) 384-0110 Fax: (303) 384-0111
E-mail: getinfo@americanalpineclub.org

ISBN 0-930410-93-9

Bruno Hasler on the summit needle of Arwa Spire's Central Peak, Garhwal Himalaya. Stephan Harvey

The American Alpine Journal

Volume 45   2003   Issue 77

CONTENTS

CLIMBS AND EXPEDITIONS

American Safe Climbing Association, *by Greg Barnes and Chris McNamara;* Kilimanjaro Porter Assistance Project, *by Ken Stober;* International Year of the Mountains, *by Bernadette McDonald;* The Mountain Institute, *by Alton Byers;* Success and Death on Mt. Everest, *by Raymond Huey and Richard Salisbury*

Including: Evidence of Things Not Seen, *by W.H. Murray;* Fatal Mountaineer, *by Robert Roper;* Detectives on Everest, *by Jochen Hemmler;* The Second Death of George Mallory, *by Reinhold Messner;* Tigers of the Snow, *by Jonathan Neale;* On High, *by Brad Washburn;* Escape from Lucania, *by David Roberts;* The Horizontal Everest, *by Jerry Kobalenko;* Extreme Landscape, *by Bernadette McDonald;* Wizards of Rock, *by Pat Ament;* Climbing Free, *by Lynn Hill;* The Flame of Adventure, *by Simon Yates;* Anderl Heckmair, *by Anderl Heckmair;* Over the Edge, *by Greg Child;* The Fall, *by Simon Mawer;* Women On High, *by Rebecca Brown;* Climb!, *by Jeff Achey;* The Shoes of Kilimanjaro, *by Cameron Burns;* The Hard Way, *by Mark Jenkins;* To Good, the Great, and the Awesome, *by Peter Croft;* Under the Midnight Sun, *by John Jancik, et. al.;* Every Other Day, *by A. J. Ostheimer.*

Remembering RD Caughran, Earlyn Dean, Ken Henderson, Andy Kauffman, Bill Robins, André Roch, Galen Rowell, and Harold Walton.

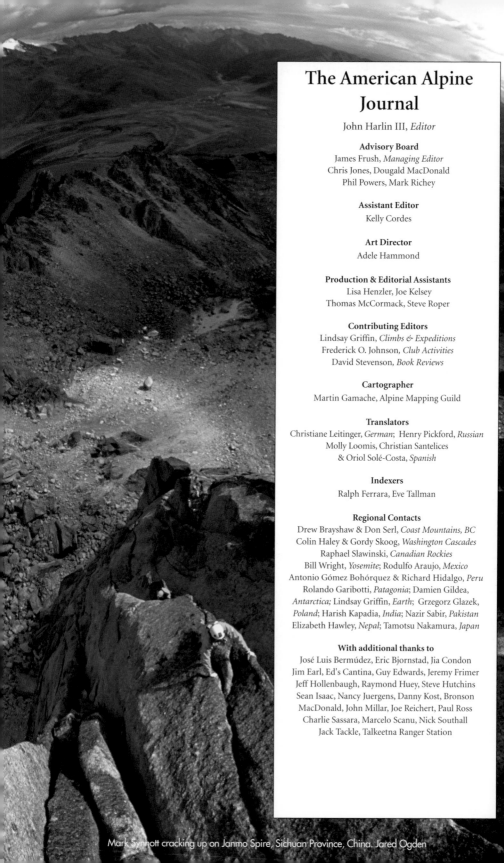

The American Alpine Journal

John Harlin III, *Editor*

Advisory Board
James Frush, *Managing Editor*
Chris Jones, Dougald MacDonald
Phil Powers, Mark Richey

Assistant Editor
Kelly Cordes

Art Director
Adele Hammond

Production & Editorial Assistants
Lisa Henzler, Joe Kelsey
Thomas McCormack, Steve Roper

Contributing Editors
Lindsay Griffin, *Climbs & Expeditions*
Frederick O. Johnson, *Club Activities*
David Stevenson, *Book Reviews*

Cartographer
Martin Gamache, Alpine Mapping Guild

Translators
Christiane Leitinger, *German*; Henry Pickford, *Russian*
Molly Loomis, Christian Santelices
& Oriol Solé-Costa, *Spanish*

Indexers
Ralph Ferrara, Eve Tallman

Regional Contacts
Drew Brayshaw & Don Serl, *Coast Mountains, BC*
Colin Haley & Gordy Skoog, *Washington Cascades*
Raphael Slawinski, *Canadian Rockies*
Bill Wright, *Yosemite*; Rodulfo Araujo, *Mexico*
Antonio Gómez Bohórquez & Richard Hidalgo, *Peru*
Rolando Garibotti, *Patagonia*; Damien Gildea,
Antarctica; Lindsay Griffin, *Earth*; Grzegorz Glazek,
Poland; Harish Kapadia, *India*; Nazir Sabir, *Pakistan*
Elizabeth Hawley, *Nepal*; Tamotsu Nakamura, *Japan*

With additional thanks to
José Luis Bermúdez, Eric Bjornstad, Jia Condon
Jim Earl, Ed's Cantina, Guy Edwards, Jeremy Frimer
Jeff Hollenbaugh, Raymond Huey, Steve Hutchins
Sean Isaac, Nancy Juergens, Danny Kost, Bronson
MacDonald, John Millar, Joe Reichert, Paul Ross
Charlie Sassara, Marcelo Scanu, Nick Southall
Jack Tackle, Talkeetna Ranger Station

Mark Synnott cracking up on Janmo Spire, Sichuan Province, China. Jared Ogden

THE AMERICAN ALPINE CLUB

OFFICIALS FOR THE YEAR 2003
*Directors ex-officio

HONORARY PRESIDENT
Robert H. Bates

President
Mark A. Richey*

Vice President
C. James Frush*

Secretary
Dougald MacDonald*

Treasurer
Charles J. Sassara, III*

DIRECTORS

Terms ending February 2004	*Terms ending February 2005*	*Terms ending February 2006*
James Ansara	Renny Jackson	Conrad Anker
Brent R. Bishop	Steve M. Furman	Jim Donini
Natalie Ann Merrill	Linda McMillan	Michael J. Lewis
Theodore (Sam) Streibert	Kim Reynolds	

SECTION CHAIRS

Alaska	*Blue Ridge*	*Cascade*
Harry Hunt	Jeanette K. Helfrich	Peter Ackroyd
New England	*New York*	*Oregon*
William C. Atkinson	Philip Erard	Bob McGown
Central Rockies	*Sierra Nevada*	*Southwest*
Greg Sievers	Steve Schneider	Michael Brown
Southeast	*South Central*	*Midwest*
Jeff Botz	Andy Jones	Benjamin A. Kweton
Northern Rockies		*North Central*
Douglas T. Colwell		Scott Christensen

EDITORS

The American Alpine Journal	*Accidents in North American Mountaineering*	*The American Alpine News*
John Harlin III	John E. (Jed) Williamson	Lloyd F. Athearn
		Candace Horgan

STAFF

Executive Director	*Climbers Ranch*	*Deputy Director*
Charles S. Shimanski	Paul Nash	Lloyd F. Athearn
Library	*Controller*	*Legislative Liaison*
Fran Loft	Jerome Mack	Caine Cortellino
Maria Borysiewicz		*Development Director*
Elaine Perkins	*Communications Coordinator*	Chris Chesak
Membership Coordinator	Jessica Meinerz	*Membership Services*
Erin Byerly		Jennifer Podolak

PREFACE

When Mark Jenkins drew three circles on a map of Tibet and proposed we climb something inside them, we knew nothing about the peaks within. Nothing, that is, beyond what the 1:500,000-scale U.S. Air Force Tactical Pilotage Chart told us: valleys 10,000-12,000 feet, peaks 18,000-21,000 feet, and "Aircraft … may be fired on without warning." The thought of those unknown 20,000-footers within an unfathomable sea of unclimbed 20,000-footers was more than I could bear. We set the date for April, 2002. Somehow, we'd reach those mystery peaks.

I did a little research and soon came on the trail of Tamotsu Nakamura, author of "East of the Himalaya" in this issue of the *Journal*. It turns out he had been there, photographed the peaks within the magic circles, and attached them to his e-mail to me. I didn't know whether to smile or cry. On the one hand, the thrill of discovery had been snatched away. On the other, those stunning photos redoubled our desire to climb the peaks. When April came around, Mark and I went, reached no summits (blame it on the weather), and determined to return to finish the job. We also had a firsthand sampling of the breadth of Nakamura's wanderings.

Tamotsu "Tom" Nakamura is the climber's guru for that 700-mile expanse between Lhasa and Chengdu. In 1996 he wrote a book, *East of the Himalayas* (alas, only in Japanese), and by the end of 2002 had accumulated 25 exploratory expeditions to the region. When I learned that he was working on a special submission to the *Japanese Alpine News (JAN)* on "East of the Himalayas," I asked him to develop a story for the *American Alpine Journal* as well. As the scope of the region gradually became clear, as well as the virginity of its peaks (99.9% pure?) and the scale of Nakamura's knowledge, there seemed no choice but to do the place justice. This 30-page exposé may be the longest ever contained within the *AAJ*. You'll also notice it's the first time we've used color photos so extensively. Admittedly, such a broad survey of a vast region leaves out many details of the human scale. For a feel of what it's really like to climb here, read the companion stories of first ascents: Carlos Buhler's "Sepu Kangri" in the west, Pete Athans's "Jarjinjabo," and Mick Fowler's "Siguniang" in the east. In between, various attempts and explorations were made, which can be discovered in Climbs & Expeditions. All in all, a significant percentage of this year's *Journal* takes place "East of the Himalaya." Fortunately, such opportunities should last for generations

Coming generations were the point of the "Conference on the Future of Mountains Sports" last September. Some 100 climbers arrived in Innsbruck from around the world in order to sculpt an ethical code to assist climbers as well as the people, cultures, and environments associated with climbing. My invitation came with a string attached: I was to ride herd on one of the working groups, steering it toward consensus in the fields of "Style and Excellence" and "First Ascents." I pictured bolts a-flying. And that was before I had any idea of the explosions to come.

On Saturday morning after breakfast, just before we split into working groups, the delegates were digesting pep talks from Reinhold Messner, Tom Frost, and conference-organizer Nicholas Mailänder, when Etienne Gross stepped to the overhead projector and sketched a detonating bomb. His stated objective was to sabotage the conference on behalf of the Swiss Alpine Club. His reasoning was that this was a gathering of elites attempting to impose their views about style and ethics upon the masses. The masses, in his estimation, are family-climbers who want a fun, safe, sporting experience—"plaisir" climbers, to use a term that was new to me, meaning "pleasure" climbers. The source of controversy was, you guessed it, the bolt. Gross stated that no mountains should be monuments, that everything should be equipped for safety, and that the Swiss Alpine Club would stand firm against the tyranny of the elites. Gross then came to join my group of not-so-shrinking violets.

Somehow, the organizers salvaged the conference, and our group managed to reach some strong (and very carefully worded) statements, as you may read in Articles 8 and 9 of The Tyrol Declaration. Despite the majority's passionate feeling that too many and rappel-placed bolts steal opportunities for adventure from future generations of climbers, we were able to accept that different regions could have different traditions, and that we could tolerate our differences, depending on those local circumstances. Publicly, anyway, all the parties agreed to the basic principles in the final Declaration. Interpreting these guidelines in the field, however, is another matter.

Not long after returning from Tyrolia, I learned that "the world's longest sport route" had been installed by rappel on the face of Mexico's tallest cliff, El Gigante (2,900 feet). Kelly Cordes, the AAJ's assistant editor, proposed a package of lead stories on El Gigante to highlight differences in perspective on such a climb. The three authors we selected had turned in their stories when we learned of a movement to erase the route—i.e., to chop its bolts. For me, the bottom line of the Tyrol Declaration had been its emphasis on dialogue and negotiation over rash action on the part of individuals—in other words, the rule of civil society. Ideally, such dialogue would take place before any controversial action—in the case of bolts, this would be before they're placed, not merely before they're removed. El Gigante seemed like a perfect test case to watch such dialogue in action, which explains the discussion, "A Logical Dilemma," following the various El Gigante articles.

Arguments over style and tools are as old as climbing, with pitons being the big issue of the mid 20th century: "Supposing it was the regular thing for all mountaineers to use pitons on their climbs, would it not be a sign of the degeneracy of man?" (Frank Smythe, 1940s.) I won't hash through the debate on El Gigante here, since you're better off reading it directly. Just remember that the issues are bigger even than El Gigante. As one pro-chop protagonist wrote me privately, "I personally don't give a damn if there is a line of glistening bolts in some Mexican gorge. However, I think it would be very bad for climbing if a 'new school' of international climbing-potential-robbers were established." But is intimidation through chopping more effective than education through dialogue? As an editor, I prefer words to chisels. As an empathizer, I respect the toil that my fellow humans put into their creation and I'm repulsed by the violence of destroying it. As a climber, I'm torn between drawing a line in the sand and recognizing that a limited number of bolted big-wall climbs hurts no one and opens great routes to many. If I sound conflicted, blame it on an excess of tolerance.

One thing is clear, however: old fashioned life-risking adventure is alive and well, and will continue to be the staple of the *American Alpine Journal*'s lead stories. Witness Sean Easton on Mt. Dickey, Brian McMahon on The Flame, Alexander Huber on the Cima Grande. Consider Dieter Klose's proposition that America's biggest wall, the 6,500-foot northwest face of the Devil's Thumb, will never be climbed. And then ponder the fate of Guy Edwards and John Millar, who tried to beat the odds and lost. Mountains are big and don't care. Humans are small and vulnerable. That much will never change.

JOHN HARLIN III, *Editor*

BLOOD FROM THE STONE

If it weren't so big, it would almost have been fun. Five-thousand feet of vertical winter on the east face of Mt. Dickey, Alaska.

SEAN EASTON

Ueli Steck, the east face of Mt. Dickey, and Blood From The Stone. Sean Easton

Our plane spiraled in descent beside the east face of Mt. Dickey. My face was plastered to the window and my hopes were plummeting. I could not see the line of ice I had suspected would be running up this mile-high face. Coupled with the forecast of a huge storm system due to plow into the Alaska Range the next day, our chances to climb were dropping as fast as the barometer. Our K2 Aviation pilot set the plane down, making the first tracks of the year in the Ruth Gorge. No other climbers had yet arrived; alone and without any radios we felt the isolation of the place. Dickey's shadow soon swept across the glacier and covered us as we pitched camp. The temperature instantly plummeted. It was March 12 and still Alaskan winter.

Ueli Steck had spent his savings to fly halfway around the world in the hope of climbing a route he had never seen on a mountain he had never heard of. I apologized for talking him into coming out here. It appeared as if we would have a better chance of squeezing blood from a stone than climbing this mountain. We set up base camp watching the clouds roll in from the Pacific. At bit of Scotch eased us into reconciling ourselves to the fact that this would likely be one of those trips spent shoveling snow and working through our stack of novels.

Mt. Dickey soars to the unimpressive elevation of 9,545 feet. What is impressive, however, are the southern, eastern, and northern flanks of the mountain, which all rise nearly vertically 5,000 feet from the Ruth Glacier. The southeast pillar was climbed by Roberts-Rowell-Ward in 1974; the Wine Bottle Route (northeast pillar, Bonapace-Orgler, 1988) offers 51 pitches on the buttress bordering the right side of the face. The south face is home to some horrendous rock and hosts a few routes. The north face remains unclimbed, and the massive serac band towering over it leaves some clue as to why.

The east face begins steepening in earnest shortly above the Ruth Glacier. About 3,000 feet of near-vertical granite leads to a final section of snow-and rock-bands. A small cornice guards the summit. Anyone willing to expose themselves to the elements could find crack systems in quality rock for a summer big-wall ascent. Additionally, it would be possible to deviate to the right halfway up our route and climb a super-cool ice finish through the headwall.

And the white plumb-line falling top to bottom between our line and the Wine Bottle Route? It begins as frost and powder stuck to a featureless vertical wall. Maybe it will form up fatter in the right year, though.

In May 2001, Dave Marra, Conny Amelunxen, and I had started up the east face. We began at 9 p.m., planning to climb at night and sleep during the warmer daylight hours. The initial pitches were plastered with ice, but it was melting out as we climbed. We decided that no matter how bad we wished otherwise, the conditions weren't right to be on such a large undertaking, so we turned back.

In 2002 I returned with Ueli, hoping that the early season cold temperatures would make conditions more favorable. We had run into each other a few times over the years and got along well. Ueli had recently finished a new direct line on the Eiger's north face, and at age 26 he is the most talented alpine climber I have yet tied into a rope with.

We planned for three to five days round trip. Bivy sacs, isobutone hanging stove set, a pair of rock shoes, Ueli's toothbrush, and two cameras came with us. The face looked like it would offer varied types of climbing, including some aid pitches, so our rack reflected this. We carried a triple set of cams, a double set of nuts, and eight ice screws. Fortunately, a European and an ex-big-wall climber did not have to go through the ethical dilemma of whether or not to take bolts. About 20 8.8mm Petzl self-drive bolts with aluminum hangers went onto the rack.

Ueli Steck on the first M7+ pitch, almost halfway up the headwall.
Sean Easton

To climb as fast and hard as possible, we decided the leader would go without a pack and the second would carry both. The fastest and most practical way to second was by jugging, meaning the anchors would have to be solid. We would lead in blocks, since with only 12 hours of light we wanted to get the most distance out of each day.

Even with clouds rolling in we decided to head up and take a look. Our first day of climbing ended five pitches up, and from there we fixed some ropes and headed back to camp to wait out a two-day storm. We had each taken one fall, my first ever in the mountains, and it looked like the difficulties increased above. I had fallen on relatively easy terrain, pulling out instead of down on my tool as it hooked over a rock, and I dropped a few feet onto a cam. I took a minute to promise myself to climb better and not be lobbing off when it counted.

Ueli whipped pulling a roof. He had climbed vertical snow until it was only an inch thick. Clipping into both tools, he hung and drilled a bolt. The snow ended just under a small roof. Choking up on the head of his tool let him reach over the roof and snag some more snow. Weighting it, his tool ripped and he was off. Without the bolt, that would have been the end of the trip. Ueli was hardly fazed, explaining that he occasionally fell in the mountains. He went back at it and finished the pitch without any other pro.

The storm ended, as they always do. With its passing we returned to our task, heading up onto the gray and white face.

From our high point I led a block of pitches up through a narrow, winding chimney system. Ice and hard snow with smooth granite walls—the climbing was dreamy, leading us higher through the sheer headwall. Ueli led the last two pitches of the day, then we rapped two ropelengths to a bivy. Out of the Alaskan winter ice we hacked a platform that was almost big enough to lie down on and thus passed a long night.

About as thin as ice gets before it becomes mixed. Ueli Steck leading out above the first M7+ pitch, two pitches above the first bivy. Sean Easton

Three-fifths of the way up the headwall, five pitches above the first bivy, Ueli Steck runs it out on yet another serious pitch. Sean Easton

On our second day we made good time trending up left on a narrow ramp system. Serious run-out leads alternated with pitches of ice that would take screws. Ueli led this block, ending each pitch only when the 60-meter rope was tight against the lower anchor. We switched leads late in the day, only a few pitches below the top of the headwall. Here I battled upward in a bottomless, snow-filled chimney until deciding further effort was futile. I came down and drytooled off right toward a more promising line. After 35 feet of aid—the only sustained aid of the route—I left the line fixed and rapped to help chop another bivy. This bivy brought a smile to my face. This was the real stuff, one of the typical miserable alpine bivvies that you read about in the *American Alpine Journal*: chopped-out ice ledge, not big enough to properly lie down on, complete with spindrift and chilly toes. And, as Ueli noted, your partner's spot always looks better.

Buzzing after a breakfast of chocolate-covered coffee beans and a hunk of beef jerky, Ueli was getting fired up for the pitch above. The deal was this: if he got us through then I would take us to the summit. Relieved, I belayed, thinking that whatever came afterward couldn't be harder than this pitch looked. Ueli dispatched it proudly, grading it M7+. Two bolts for protection helped mitigate the poor pro opportunities and made the sustained climbing on crumbly rock and rotten snow somewhat sane. This pitch brought us over the headwall.

After crossing some icefields we reached an imposing black rock band. There was no way to end-run it. We both imagined that this would be hideous vertical shale, so I racked up mentally preparing to meet my maker. After a few feet of climbing I was amazed: I was getting in good gear. Cracks and solid edges accepted metal points. If I hadn't been this high up, I swear I would have been having fun climbing an enjoyable mixed pitch.

The final roped pitch was a thin, detached curtain of faceted AI6. Note to self: bring a file on these routes. It felt like climbing with two sledgehammers as my blunt picks smashed apart the ice. Our final anchor was one bolt in the only protruding rock. Our lead line had a good core shot in it by this point, so we left it clipped and soloed up the snow face, over the cornice, and onto the summit.

Here we spent half an hour feeling the euphoria, brewing water, sorting gear, and checking out the surrounding peaks. The continuity of the line, the stability of the weather, and the knowledge that our abilities were a match for the difficulties—all were in our thoughts. With moments of doubt, we had ventured forth without certainty, open to the possibility of an alpine line tracing its way up the east face, and the path had unwound before us.

Descending via the Dickey-Bradley Col, we raced into camp five hours later as clouds rolled in from the Pacific. Our tracks weaved drunkenly along the rolling glacier. But we had been granted the weather window we needed. We now focused on eating as much of our food as

possible before being flown out. Stamping "OUT" in the snow in front of our tent, we hoped it would be spotted by a pilot flying overhead who would notify K2 to come pick us up. Luckily, this happened the following afternoon.

Arriving in Talkeetna, we found a town that hadn't awakened from its winter slumber; there was no sign of the hordes of the climbers who would fill the streets in the following months. Boarding my return flight home only 12 days after arriving in Alaska, I realized that this seemed far too short a trip to have climbed such an awesome mountain.

I suspect that the Alaska Range will see heavy action as international political instabilities make many other ranges of the world less attractive destinations—and the Ruth will become one of the main attractions.

SUMMARY OF STATISTICS

AREA: Alaska Range

ASCENTS: Blood From The Stone (5,000', A1 M7+ WI6+X), Sean Easton and Ueli Steck, March 18-20, 2002.

Leading out from the second bivy, Sean Easton has eyes for the whipped cream dollop. Ice, dry tooling, snow, and more ice: this pitch had all the goods. Above: Sean Easton on the left, with Ueli Steck, enjoying the summit. Ueli Steck

THE VIKING'S SHIELD

A solo fantasy in eastern Greenland.

MIKE LIBECKI

Mike Libecki at his base camp, with a random peak across the fjord and not another human on any horizon—nor on uncounted horizons beyond. Mike Libecki

Eastern Greenland (remote fjord, Southeast Greenland) Fantasizing is one of my favorite pastimes. The beauty of fantasizing is that you can do it, anytime, anyplace, about anything. You can fantasize about battling sinister, fire-breathing dragons, rescuing sweet, voluptuous maidens from the dragon-guarded dungeons, or about the possible, quite pleasurable reward given by the beautiful, virgin maiden for performing such a dangerous and heroic rescue. In the last several years, though, I have found new favorite fantasies, usually about seeking out tall, luscious, virgin big walls, then climbing them, completely alone, for weeks at a time. And what could be better than actually making such a fantasy real? Isn't that one reason that God put us on this planet, to make our deepest fantasies come true? I like to think so. After all, since we are all going to die anyway, why not live life in the most amazing way we can? Every day I remind myself that this is not only just life, but the chance to choose the highest quality of life. My Grandmother taught me that. And thanks to Grandma's advice, another fantasy of mine came true last year.

When I received the package postmarked Greenland, I knew what it contained, my smile gleaming. My friend Hans Christian, a surgeon in eastern Greenland, had sent me rare Danish military photos of Greenland's east coast taken from an airplane flying at 30,000 feet. When I was in Greenland the year before to climb the Fox Incisor, I inquired about the possibility of finding such photos. I wanted to find never-before-seen, world-class big walls to climb. Since Greenland is governed by Denmark and Hans Christian is a doctor for much of the Danish military in eastern Greenland, the photos turned out to be rather easy to acquire. These photos would change my life.

At a nearby hobby shop I found the perfect five-inch-diameter magnifying glass to start the fantasy research. With photos covering my furniture-less living room floor like a lush growth of lily pads in a pond, I hunched over the photos like Sherlock Holmes hot on the trail of an evildoer. I focused intently on every detail, searching for clues that would lead me to the secret, virgin big walls. Several eye-straining hours later I had pinpointed four small areas on the map, each about the size of a dime, that appeared to be families of steep, massive, granite walls. These areas were 250 miles apart from one another, spread out along Greenland's majestic eastern coast. The minuscule, jagged-edged shadows around the snowy, sawtoothed peaks suggested that the walls were quite steep, perhaps vertical, but it was not for certain. These shadows could be the clues to the ultimate walls I was looking for. "My dear Watson, I think I've got it!" (I was reminded that Holmes' last case was in the high Alps of the Bernese Oberland.) Further research showed that these areas were very remote, possibly untrodden except by the local Greenlandic Inuit people and early Viking explorers.

One of the four areas became an objective for my Year of the Horse Expeditions—2002. The next thing I knew I was dragging seven huge 69.5-pound haul bags (an overweight fee is added for bags over 70 pounds) into the airport. As I often have done, I decided to go alone on a grand expedition, alone on my horse in full armor to battle the fierce and evil dragon. Alone to rescue the sweet maiden from the dragon's dark dungeons. Alone to seek out ultimate adventure on possibly one of the greatest expeditions of my life.

My stallion reared back high and proud into the air, his whinny roaring into the night like a freight train's whistle trumpeting fathomless courage and irresistible victory. Dust exploded off the earth from his thundering hooves as we sped into the night under the eerie, yellow moon. Well, actually, I tucked my airplane pillow under the back of my head, pulled up my little blue airplane blanket, opened my new Stephen King book, and sipped tomato juice with lemon. The airplane rose off the tarmac at sunset. We headed east toward the dragon's lair, hidden somewhere among the huge walls on the eastern coast of Greenland.

After several unexpected, bad-weather days in Iceland, the wind and rain stopped long enough to allow my plane to continue its journey to Kulusuk, Greenland. From there a helicopter shipped me fifty miles to Tasiilaq, a small town populated mostly by Greenlandic Inuit, Greenlandic Huskies (there are almost as many sled dogs as humans), and a handful of Danes. Tasiilaq was the nearest town to my final destination, and I hoped to find someone with an Arctic-worthy fishing boat to take me over 300 miles through ice-laden seas. After talking with several of the locals, my hopes were short-circuited. I was told that it was simply too dangerous to take boats where I wanted to go. This was, to say the least, a less-than-ideal situation. But I remembered that patience and optimism always rule, and that a situation would present itself, as it always does.

I bought a six-pack of Carlsberg, a couple of pieces of fish jerky, and proceeded to hydrate while pondering my options. Halfway through the tasty Pilsners, a Danish friend of mine walked up with one of the local Greenlanders. He translated my needs to the local man, as he spoke no English. This Inuit fisherman decided he would try to take me where I wanted to go, for quite a fair price, of course. He made it very clear, however, that it would be at my own risk. As we talked, I learned that the fisherman, along with the friend who would accompany us, were known as the most experienced seamen in these harsh Arctic seas. Rapid communication now took place through my translator friend, details were settled, such as where I would be dropped off, how long it might take to get there, and what hunting we would do on the way. I

Lost in a maze of sea ice and icebergs during Libecki's journey to the mysterious fjord. Mike Libecki

Going my way? A polar bear shares the sea in eastern Greenland. Mike Libecki

received more warnings of how dangerous the ocean would be. I caught the message that huge sea swells and sea ice could easily lead to suffering and disaster.

Two days later, at 3 a.m., we started out to sea. The 24-hour sun circled above the fishing boat. Myself, the two fishermen, and ultimate enthusiasm occupied the boat as I watched Tasiilaq fade away. We disappeared into a maze of bright sea ice. As I gazed out over the ocean, I could not even see water: it looked to be completely frozen over. Neon turquoise glowed from under cracks in the ice. The ice was so thick that we had to literally push our way through shattered ice pieces with the boat, moving at the pace of a slow walk. Icebergs as big as apartment houses teeter-tottered up and down in the sea. Every once in a while, with sounds like buildings crashing to the ground, massive icebergs crumbled and exploded, while thundering white waves large enough to excite a surfer crashed in every direction. Most of the time the endless maze of sea ice and giant icebergs turned us around, pushed us miles and miles in the wrong direction, and hinted at the impossibility of reaching our destination. We saw many different kinds of seal, huge whales bursting out of the water to breathe, and breathtakingly beautiful polar bears dog-paddling through the frigid mazes. It was one fantastic moment of awe-stricken reality after another. Did I mention something about fantasies coming true?

In this area of Greenland the local people still rely on hunting as a major source of food. I have great respect for other cultures and their ways of living, especially since I have had the opportunity of being close to so many in my travels around the world. I have to admit, though, that I was a little torn watching them hunt the whale, and polar bear; this is something that I am just not used to. The two fishermen respectfully acknowledged that their people have

Iceberg climbing anyone? Near the mysterious fjord. Mike Libecki

survived because of these animals; most of the meat would be taken home to their families. The skins would be utilized for warmth, the bones made into traditional carvings and jewelry. This has been a way of life in Greenland for well over a thousand years.

The men and the fishing boat did not give up the struggle against the stubborn sea ice, and after 100 hours without stopping, we were only a few hours away from my destination. It was nearing the end of summer, so the 24-hour light started to hint at darkness for about an hour each day. There was still enough light for the fishermen to work rotating shifts, one driving the boat while the other slept. Less than thirty miles away from my destination, my map noted an old Inuit ghost town. As we neared the ruins we could see old wooden homes that seemed to fall apart in front of our eyes. We stopped to take a closer look. I found remnants of old toys, broken-down dog sleds, rusty fuel barrels, clothing, pots and pans, rustic wood burning stoves, and even several gravestones. It looked like the people literally up and left without taking anything with them. I later found out that this small village disappeared during the mid-1900s.

Up until this point we had been traveling along the coast on the open ocean. We now turned west and headed deep into a winding fjord no more than a couple of miles wide in most spots. Steep granite walls rose higher as we went deeper into the fjord. Good God, not one climber had ever seen this place! Was this really happening? The walls were, at minimum, 4,000 to 5,000 feet high. Ominous ice caps peered over the top of the granite formations. Countless waterfalls crashed to the ground from thousands of feet above. It was like a fantasy birthday party, and all of these monstrous granite walls and towers were giant pieces of birthday cake topped with white, creamy frosting.

Shuttling loads to the base of The Viking's Shield. Mike Libecki

Half way up the Viking's Shield, with a huge snow storm on the way. Mike Libecki

At the end of the fjord it was not hard to decide where to make my base camp. Giant granite towers loomed in every direction. Just a quarter of a mile away, a river flowed out of the lush green valley that I would call home for the next 30 days. As soon as I got my bags ashore, the two fishermen immediately vanished up the river, returning an hour later with four huge salmon. We ate two of them raw—Greenlandic sashimi.

From the time we left Tasiilaq—100 hours earlier—the two fishermen and I had not spoken a word to each other. Instead we laughed, gestured, and looked into each other's eyes for communication. Just before they left me, one of them pointed to the seals that lounged nearby on the broken sea ice and started to mimic a polar bear. He was warning me that where there are seals, there are polar bears. My only defense would be to use my 30–06 rifle, my 12-gauge shotgun with slugs, my bear spray, or to get on one of the towering granite walls as quickly as possible. If a bear came while I slept on the ground, I would be a very easy, tasty meal.

Absolute utter aloneness. Solo. Silence. I started sobbing like a small child who has lost his parents in an amusement park. Frightened, but excited and curiously free and completely alone, I was happy. I felt an overwhelming joy, ultimate enthusiasm, and magical emotion. The fantasy I dreamed about was really happening! I continued to cry like I hadn't in years. I soaked myself with tears. I was feeling the awesome presence of being alive. I thought about how several months ago I hunched over the aerial photographs taken of this exact area. I now stood in front of the walls I had fantasized about. I cried and screamed and yelled and jumped and threw my arms in the air, howling like a mad werewolf. I was enjoying myself! I continued to cry. I don't know if I have ever cried so hard in my life. I could not stop. I had forgotten how good it felt to cry. Then I started to laugh, so hard that it hurt. Absolute utter aloneness. Solo. Silence. I slept like a baby for the next 18 hours.

I spent several days reconnoitering the area. Serpentine glaciers, neon-blue glacial pools, flowers and plants of every color of the rainbow, and, of course, huge granite walls and towers surrounded me. My base camp was about 40 feet from the ice-laden ocean. Seals sunbathed on the sea ice a stones-throw away. I decided to attempt a route on a

The 4,200-foot Viking's Shield. Mike Libecki

prominent tower a couple of miles from my base camp. With a nod toward the rumors of early Viking exploration in the area, I called this tower the Viking's Shield. It took me six days to shuttle my loads to the base. The wall was much bigger than I thought and ended up being just over 4,200 feet high.

The first 1,800 feet consisted of splitter cracks and dihedrals, no harder than 5.10. From this point a 1,500-foot steep headwall demanded delicate aid climbing, pushing what I usually call A3+, or in other words, very spicy. For example, some of the pitches called for expanding

Getting worked during the second day of the big storm, half way up.
Mike Libecki

beaks, hooks of uncertainty, and, of course, rotten madness. The headwall led me to an 800-foot snow and ice-ridge, with consistent 5.6 climbing to the ice-capped summit. I climbed capsule style, fixing no less than 1,000 feet at a time. Of course, my Year of the Horse costume was present for the summit photos. I spent 22 days making the first ascent of this beautiful virgin tower.

In the Arctic, storms can attack at any time. A sweet bluebird day with sun warming your face and a breeze that would make you think of Yosemite on a summer afternoon can literally turn into a raging-maniac-storm-from-hell in a matter of minutes. I have seen it happen. Fortunately, I love this kind of spice. There is no doubt it is high on the list of the important variables on a fantasy expedition. What sweeter ultimate reality is there than being above the Arctic Circle, alone, on the middle of a 4,200-foot wall, shivering in your fragile, hanging-nylon-condo-tether, while a sinister storm threatens to leave you, freezing to death, dangling by nothing more than your back-up rope? Did I mention that during this you are praying/begging to God out loud, that you will never do anything wrong again if He will just get you out of this alive? Well, it happened once again, the threat of doom, that is. It was the second-most frightening time in my life. When the storm hit, it was after I had reached the summit and was on the way down. I waited out that storm for three days with only enough sleep to have nightmares. Over four feet of snow fell in those three days. All of my anchors below were frozen over when I reached them on rappel; some I could not even find. All of my equipment was soaked through, including my clothes and my skin.

Suffering is an important part of any wonderful journey. That weather made me appreciate appreciation once again. I had experienced only minor storms on the ascent; it seemed too easy and it just did not feel right not to get worked by the weather. Of course, at the time I wished it was not happening. If the huge storm that slapped me in the face on my way down hadn't stopped when it did, it is hard to say what would have happened. It could have turned into one of those stories of the human will to survive. As it worked out, I lost only seven pounds on the whole climb and ran out of food for only one day. My last bit of fuel ran out while heating water for breakfast on the same day I got back on the ground.

The boat picked me up right on time. My two Inuit friends arrived six hours after I had shuttled my last load back into base camp. We all smiled, shook hands, and loaded my gear into the boat. They disappeared again to catch more salmon from the nearby river. Greenlandic sashimi once again. On the way back to Tasiilaq we camped on the shore because the 24-hour light had decreased to about 20 hours. Fall had arrived. We hunted wild duck and seal for our meals. We laughed, gestured, and looked into each other's eyes for perfect communication without words.

Before this expedition, when I was at home studying the Danish military photos, I had found four areas of fantasy big-wall lands waiting to be explored. Three are left to fantasize about. The experience I had with the local Greenlanders filled me with a joyous emotion I can barely describe. 51 percent of the obsession/addiction to go on grand expeditions is to climb beautiful walls and mountains, frolic in alien flora and fauna, and live a life in utter sanctuary and solitude for as long as the adventure lasts. The other 49 percent is to experience other cultures and make new friends from new lands. The percentages may stay the same, but the reasons are changing. I cannot imagine any fantasy more real, emotional, or intense than meeting and making friends with such magical people who have nothing more in common with me than breathing the same air. Good God, life itself is a fantasy in the making.

SUMMARY OF STATISTICS

AREA: Eastern Greenland (remote fjord, Southeast Greenland)

ASCENT: The Vikings Shield, Giving Birth to Reason (4,200', VI 5.10 A3+). Mike Libecki, solo. August 1-September 8, 2002, with 23 days of climbing.

A NOTE ON THE AUTHOR

This was Libecki's third expedition to Greenland, during each of which he made a first ascent. He is planning four more expeditions to explore unknown facets of Greenland's climbing potential. This was also his eighth major Arctic expedition, in addition to expeditions to such places as China, Venezuela, and Madagascar. Libecki, 30, is proud to announce that he has just begun his most amazing and wonderful expedition yet: fatherhood. Lilliana Taylor Libecki was born on March 27, 2003. Mike would like to thank The American Alpine Club's Lyman-Spitzer

Grant and The Mugs Stump Award for help in making The Viking's Shield possible. He lives by the motto: Pursue Passion (why ration passion?).

On the summit, celebrating the Year of the Horse. Mike Libecki

THE FICKLE FACE

The northwest face of Alaska's Devil's Thumb—Could it just be unclimbable?

DIETER KLOSE

The unclimbed (and unclimbable?) 6,500-foot northwest face of Devil's Thumb. The northeast face is in sunshine, and Cat's Ears Spire stands proud. Dieter Klose

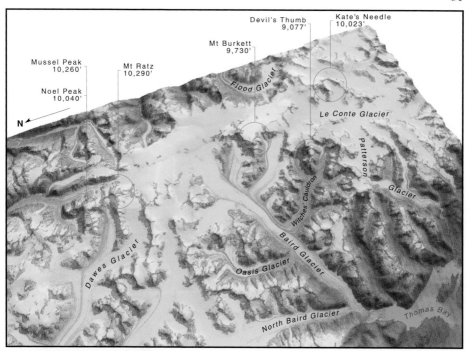

Devil's Thumb
9,077'

Kate's Needle
10,023'

Mt Burkett
9,730'

Mussel Peak
10,260'

Mt Ratz
10,290'

Noel Peak
10,040'

N

Flood Glacier

Le Conte Glacier

Patterson Glacier

Witches' Cauldron

Baird Glacier

Dawes Glacier

Oasis Glacier

North Baird Glacier

Thomas Bay

Source: Landsat TM, September 9, 1989 Bands 3,2,1 as RGB
Place names and elevations from USGS 1:250,000 Sumdum & Petersburg Sheets.
Scale varies in this perspective.

Stikine Icefield
Boundary Ranges
of the Coast Mountains
Southeast Alaska/Canada

Like the Sirens who lured Ulysses to a blissful yet certain death, the northwest face of the Devil's Thumb continues to tempt the alpinist onto her flanks. Yet those who approach this beckoning alpine maiden should have themselves strapped to the mast, as did that wise fellow of yore, and sail on by.

Soaring at an average angle of over 65° and standing 6,500 feet tall, the great northwest face of Devil's Thumb may well be the steepest wall of such size in all of North America. It is a dangerous and difficult face that rarely, if ever, comes into condition. It is the epitome of Fickle. Its direttissima is probably the prize of the continent. But this big, bad, beautiful plum could well happen to be one that never gets picked. Involving an international cast of suitors who have whispered its name for more than 25 years, this wall has repulsed all attempts. It is looking like it may well be The Unclimbable. Imagine: a face that, for whatever reasons, will not be climbed.

In this era of destination consciousness, where obscure new routes and faces are being discovered and ticked off, this face of the Devil's Thumb remains an anomaly. This secreted wall in the Stikine Icecap of southeast Alaska dominates a glacial basin called the Witches' Cauldron. The wild face, discovered well over two decades ago, ends on a very specific summit. Here are all the makings of both post-modern and futuristic alpinism, yet it simply has not, does not, and seems not to be do-able.

Philosophically, the time may be nigh for a reference point, the absolute limit of what a mountain will allow to a simple human. Perhaps this is what the state-of-the-art of alpinism needs: a place where no person will willingly go the distance. A place that simply by its own

John Millar on a rest break during the 2002 approach to the Devil's Thumb. Guy Edwards

nature will remain unwanted by all humans, by choice; a refuge of alpine purity; a sanctuary where only the birds may alight, and then only so long as the avalanches deign. Nothing is allowed or welcomed here, for nothing will survive. Imagine.

The zero success rate has not been for a lack of strong climbers. The list of suitors reads like a who's-who of alpinists. The late, great Mike Bearzi, whose name became synonymous with the northwest face, thought he had cracked the code. He really wanted it, and went there on a total of four month-long expeditions. Along with the author, he made a big dent, but that was shy of even halfway up. Since then, the likes of Alex Lowe, Jack Roberts, Bruce Miller, Randy Rackliff, and Sean Easton have paid empty-handed tribute to the monstrosity.

Last spring two Canadians, Guy Edwards and John Millar, went to have a peek. They were the fourteenth party to do so. Of those fourteen unlucky ones, only five actually set foot on the face. The rest never saw anything close to it being in nick—and didn't even venture onto it.

THE PROBLEM

Several factors lend to the difficulty of finding the face in condition. As a rock climb it's a perfect place to commit suicide, for reasons I'll discuss later. "In condition" means fully iced-up, move-fast terrain. This appears to be possible only during the spring transition, when just the right amount of storms and thaw-freeze conditions coat the face in white and a touch of blue. For a justified attempt, these conditions must then be followed by a promise of at least two days of clear skies in order to quickly climb through the 4,000-plus vertical feet of avalanche-prone zones. Sadly, this springtime period is usually one of unsettled weather, where an apparent clearing is usually just a brief tease. Making a bad call on the weather at this point could leave one stranded up high for weeks, if not avalanched off the wall entirely.

The crux of the diretissima, the steep band at half-height, is concave; any precipitation causes lethal avalanches here, which continue onto the lower face (which is also threatened by a hanging glacier). The steep band is generally the last portion to properly ice-up.

Due to the rather atrocious weather in the region, the face has been seen to ice-up splendidly, only to be melted off by a following period of rain, described by Guy Edwards as "a stage of molt." Lastly, as Alex Lowe put it, scoffing, the face is simply "too low." Starting at an elevation of a mere 2,500 feet and ending at the 9,077-foot summit, the route is indeed low by alpine standards, even taking into account a latitude of 57 degrees north. After icing-up, the lower wall tends to fall apart in short order while the upper portion still beckons. Or, vice-versa. When I was on it, the lower half was in perfect nick, whereas the upper half was out. Perhaps it had fallen apart and needed to get itself back together. Quite the neurotic little über-wall.

THE CONSTANTS

Having lived within sight of the Devil's Thumb for 19 years, I have had the opportunity to either be on the mountain or doing aerial reconnaissance during every month of the year. The change in the demeanor of the northwest face through the seasons is drastic. There are, however, five constants:

1) An average annual rainfall of 10 feet accompanies the Patagonianesque weather.

2) If there is any precipitation, the entire face will be constantly riddled with avalanches.

3) The sun hits the top of the wall at 2 p.m., causing frequent avalanches and/or rockfall.

4) There is a hanging glacier at half-height, which Bearzi dubbed "Sammy Serac." Sammy looses a lethal sweep of the lower part of the route every six days, on average.

5) Avalanches from the massive hanging glaciers and seracs bordering the face sweep the approach at irregular intervals.

In mid-summer the face is almost devoid of snow and ice, with the exception of Sammy Serac. Waterfalls are common. As a rock climb, the slow-going on the rotten gneiss would be sheer suicide, given Sammy's threat and the inherent short spells of clear skies. The summit becomes heavily rimed in any season when the wet southwesterly storms blow through. This rime adds to the otherwise high avalanche hazard as it falls off.

In winter the face is generally bare with occasional dustings of snow, though things are basically too cold to promote a thaw/freeze pattern which forms ice. In all seasons avalanches are commonplace due to the five constants listed above. Hence, siege tactics are not a realistic option.

Springtime, specifically the

Bob Rugo in the Witches' Cauldron during the 1981 approach. Mike Bearzi

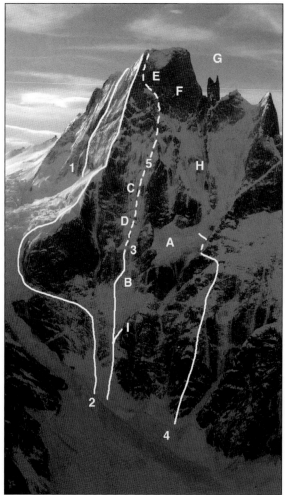

The northwest face of Devil's Thumb, showing (A) Sammy Serac, (B) ramp, (C) steep band, (D) overhang—should be great bivy, (E) exit chimney, (F) overhanging headwall, (G) Cat's Ears, (H) bowling alley couloir, (I) last seen point of Guy Edwards and John Millar. Routes and attempts: (1) northeast face, Bebie-Pilling, 1991, (2) north pillar, Stutzman-Plumb, 1979, (3) Bearzi-Klose highpoint, 1982, (4) Cole-Rouner-Rouner, 1977, (5) Klose's interpretation of the direttissima line. Dieter Klose

months of April and May, is the only time that the face has been observed to be fully iced-up. However, this does not happen every year. Yet, when it does ice up, a reliable fair-weather window must follow for a justified attempt. This combination, although appearing to be a variable, has historically become a constant, in that it constantly *does not happen*.

THE ROUTE

Sitting below the face, one is dwarfed beyond perception. The scale is so vast that I was never able to truly reconcile it in my mind. The word "huge" is not big enough to describe it; "mind-boggling" works better. As the mountain rears overhead, the upper face, so far away, actually looks small, but, as Bearzi described it after a fly-by, "What struck me was how very vast the upper face was. There were canyons and spires, and ridges, as if a whole other mountain range had sprouted out of this face. A person could get lost up there. Yet, here is the paradox. With the wall either being devoid of any specific features representing lines of weakness down low, or having too many up high, and being as extensive as it is, there really is only one line up it. All the myriad parameters cancel each other out, leaving but one choice."

The northwest face direttissima, though not the plumb-line of the proverbial drop of water that Comici would let fall to describe his perfect climb, strikes a sequence of arcs creating a potential alpine masterpiece.

The lower snow and ice bands lead to a short ramp that bisects the first steep section. Next, the "fluff band" is a mix of steps and slabs upon which the avalanches apply a layer best described as fluff-snow. The imposing 800-foot steep band (apparent crux) lures the mixed-master with a choice of three distinct ice-smears. Several hundred more feet on milder-angled mixed terrain lead to a prominent rib on the upper face, where avalanche danger is much reduced. Thence up and leftward toward an Eiger-esque exit chimney, the 300-foot entrance to which appears to be another crux area. Runnels of water-ice linking the stepped buttresses have been observed here at times. A tantalizing alternative would be to tackle the overhanging upper headwall directly, though this would appear to require extensive nailing.

The top of the exit chimney, creating a notch in the summit ridge, is also the start to the normal descent down the southeast face (Beckey Route). The true summit awaits just three or four rope-lengths westward.

THE STRATEGY

The strategy of assault developed by Mike Bearzi in 1981 still holds as the most logical approach, as if logic were a factor in even going there in the first place. A stable, cloudless, and cold northerly weather pattern is a prerequisite once the face is properly iced. Free-solo absolutely whenever and wherever possible, during the hours of midnight to 2 p.m. Swift, ultra-light alpine style is crucial.

The end of the first day should find the party bivying in the prominent cave just above the base of the steep band by 2 p.m, when the daily avalanches start. Here one would also be well above the threat of Sammy Serac. On day two the steep band is passed, and progress speeds to a bivy somewhere in the labyrinthine upper face. Day three sees one moving up

Mike Bearzi and Dieter Klose at the mouth of the Witches' Cauldron on the approach in 1982, with the Devil's Thumb still 10 miles away. Dieter Klose

Bearzi, Steve Monks, and Damian Carroll wining, whining, and waiting for colder skies below the northwest face in 1982. Dieter Klose

toward and through the exit chimney and onto the summit ridge. After one descends the southeast face, the steep, torturous icefall south of the Thumb gives access back into the Witches' Cauldron and the eight-mile hike back to base camp. A previously placed food cache here, or at the base of the southeast face, would provide welcome relief. Three days up, two days down. Piece of cake.

THE AUTHOR'S ATTEMPT

Thomas Bay, April 18, 1982. For some obscure reason Mike Bearzi and I decided to attack the route from sea level, completely unsupported, on our 40-day effort. With some 600 pounds of gear between us (including potatoes and an iron skillet), we humped three loads through the broken snout of the Baird Glacier in a blinding snowstorm. Just as we shouldered our last load, a floatplane landed and expectorated two Brits. The plane flew off and halted introductions commenced. We were, after all, going for the "secret" and coveted northwest face of the Thumb. Steve Monks and Damian Carroll, from Bristol, were going for the northwest face as well, thank you very much. Shit! We had 600 pounds, and they had maybe 200. They'd have had more, but U.S. customs confiscated all of their food containing meat, including the freeze-dried stuff. On a shoestring budget, they hadn't enough cash to replenish their stocks. They also had but one pair of snowshoes between them, whereas we had skis, sleds, and food to eat like plunderous kings. And, we were one whole camp ahead of them. The race was on.

In the two intermediate camps enroute to base, Mike and I did the usual routine: cook tea and meals in the tent and dump the dregs of potato peels and tea outside the tent. At night, rather than don shoes to relieve our swollen bladders, we'd just kneel at the door and let go into the pile of dinner dregs. Due to the daily soakings from the audacious weather, I had repeated dreams of meeting a woman who had a clothes dryer in her tent.

We arrived at base camp on the 24th, a scant mile from the incredibly imposing brutality of the northwest face. It was not yet in shape, so the wait began. By evening the Brits arrived, one postholing behind the leader's snowshoes. They were actually quite fun lads, and over the next few days we shared many a cup of tea (our tea; they had only one bag per man-day, whereas we could have thrown a Boston Tea Party).

As we waited for the face to ice up, the kinship grew. We tried to dig down to the ice of the glacier like kids making a fort, and had ice-climbing comps in crevasses. Eventually, Steve and Damo felt comfortable enough to admit that they had found and cooked-up our potato peels and tea which we'd dumped in front of our tents on the approach. We, on the other hand, didn't feel comfortable telling them what we'd done to those dregs at night.

The days of waiting turned to weeks. Storm after storm blew through, coating the face in ice, or so we hoped. The monotony was broken often by the spectacular avalanches from the mountainsides (including our intended route) that would engulf our camp in temporary, swirling blizzards. Eventually, the Brits had had enough, and they buggered off. On the next day an apparent clearing lured Mike and me onto the wall. We left camp at 2 a.m. with three days of food, five days of fuel, 300 feet of 8mm rope, a super-light rack, a stove, and a sleeping bag. After scurrying through a half-mile of avalanche debris, the bergschrund was easily

passed, for it was filled with snow from above. The difficulty started immediately on a 65° slab covered by six inches of loose snow. Spooky. We stopped and chopped a ledge below the first ice band to wait for daylight. The apparently go-anywhere terrain turned out to require more than headlamps to show the way.

After an hour of eating and watching the weather, we headed up, Mike trailing the rope. Sparrows chirped in the twilight below. We soloed side by side, the ice varying between 60° and 70° for 600 feet. We flew. The ice was excellent, with rarely a bad placement, yet just as rarely a rest step. The 50° snow-band was soft enough to get the feet in halfway. Ice chunks zoomed by frequently despite the early hour. The second ice face dropped under our crampons at a consistent 65°–75°. Nearing the right-angling "ramp" at the beginning of the fluff-band, the thinning ice reclined to 70° and we had a short rest on chopped footholds. We had soloed 2,500 feet in three hours and were basically beyond the threat of Sammy.

Klose squirreling through verglas and fluff near the turnaround point in 1982. Mike Bearzi

Bearzi racing the clock on the rappel in the avy zone in 1982.
Dieter Klose

After 500 feet up the ramp, the angle steepened further as the snow-ice thinned, so we roped up. Mike's lead was outrageous, terrible tool placements topped by a near-vertical 30-foot section of thin, fractured ice, 150 feet out, all without protection. I arrived at his belay to find a very manky anchor. Above us was the first truly vertical section, which consisted of a hundred feet of fluff and sketches of verglas. I led right and up, scouring for something to put my tools on or into. Nothing. Our coating of ice had turned into insubstantial fluff, the backwash of avalanches sailing over these drop-offs. A brief discussion had us in agreement that even if we could somehow make this section go, tomorrow's steep band would yield more of the same. The mountain wasn't ready for us yet. Our attempt came to an abrupt halt.

I unclipped from the silly anchor while Mike led the first rap. I looked around and took in the view. We were way up there, it was way cool what we had done. I was happy. I tried to forget about the hour. It was 10 a.m. At 2 the shit would hit the fan, and we were the fan.

After an hour "off rappel" wafted up; something was wrong. When I arrived at Mike's perch I started to worry. He had gone straight down instead of angling left back to the ramp. The single anchor he'd found was a runner around a 3-inch icicle, and it was virtually a hanging stance. Mike looked tired; he hadn't slept a wink the night before, in anticipation. He pointed out that continuing to rap would get us into overhanging terrain, and that traversing left back to the ramp was the ticket. After a few more minutes, we backed up the icicle with a tied-off knifeblade I'd taken out of the first anchor. Mike led left onto 80° mixed terrain.

Here my psyche began to buckle. I was looking straight up into 3,500 feet of concave wall, with the steep band rearing over me like a monster with fangs bared, ready to drool. Any saliva that came down would surely take me. I was a sitting duck, hog-tied to an icicle and a spindly flap of steel, waiting for Mike to finish his goddamn lead and get us to some shelter. Finally, I couldn't take the pressure any more. I lost it, breaking the rule of maintaining an optimistic morale: "Mike, you have to hurry."

"I know, I know," came his focused yet stressed reply. A few more hour-long minutes and he was on the ramp. His only anchor was his bum on the snow and two axe-plants, with a single tied-off screw between us. The 60-foot traverse had taken him an hour and a half. Following was desperate. His meager footholds of snow had crumbled after his use, leaving me scraping for purchase, way too hurried for the required technical moves. It was a phenomenal lead that somehow I managed to mimic. The hour was 1pm. We had wasted a lot of time on the raps and traverse, and had only one hour left before the afternoon avalanches would begin.

Mike belayed me up the ramp and then down, maniacally looking for a place with enough snow to dig a cave. Finally I found a spot. Mike came down and we started digging. We were tied to the only good anchor we'd found during our time on the wall. After digging in just two feet we hit rock. We dug sideways, swallowing our desperation. By 2 we crawled inside the little hole and sardined with our legs sticking out. To our great relief the short but steep section of wall above us let the avalanches soar over us, just a few feet from our ditch.

We rose at 2:00 a.m. to a cold yet overcast sky. Rather than stay put and potentially be stranded there for weeks, we hoped to get to the bottom before the precipitation and its attendant avalanches would begin. We rapped on the happy cave anchor, then an A2 anchor got us to the snow-ice. From there we performed time-trials in bollard production and virtually flew down the rest of the face. Ice and rocks flew by as well, but we escaped any real avalanches. Those didn't start until we were back at camp, a lullaby for two very tired dogs.

HISTORY

Mid July, 1976: A note in the B.C. *Mountaineer*, Volume 54, mentions a party "under the north face of Devil's Thumb." No details are available.

Early August, 1977: Peter Cole, Nichols Rouner, and Rainsford Rouner. Finding the wall virtually devoid of snow or ice and with no obvious lines up the apparently rotten rock, the trio opted for a line heading to the west buttress, along the couloir that forms the right-hand margin of the face. Starting on an adjacent buttress below the Witches' Tits, they continued across a hanging glacier. While the three were soloing, tragedy struck: Nichols died from rockfall.

Mid-August 1977: Bob Plumb and Dave Stutzman approached from Scenery Lake with an airdrop, planning to go up the lower northwest face via an hourglass couloir, then proceed directly to the north pillar. On the northwest face portion of the climb, Stuzman reported poor rock, waterfalls, and rockfall. The crux of their 60-pitch climb was found in the initial cliff band. Due to the poor nature of the rock and conditions on the lower face, they traversed left into the adjacent icefall, onto the icecap, and thence onto the north pillar. In four days they completed a hammerless first ascent of the north pillar, all under clear skies. They descended via the southeast face and south icefall.

April 30-June 3, 1981: Mike Bearzi and Bob Rugo approached from sea level with an airdrop. The face was in condition when they arrived but, as Bearzi described it, "A three and a half week rainstorm drowned our hopes. A false start or two as a clearing degenerated while the wall degenerated as we degenerated into frustration would sum up the remainder of our stay." As a consolation, they attempted the Beckey route but were turned back by a storm. They completed a 38-mile circumnavigation of the massif on skis and on foot.

April 17-May 23, 1982: Mike Bearzi and Dieter Klose approached from sea level, unsupported. See above story. At the same time, Steve Monks and Damian Carroll approached from sea level, unsupported. See above story.

April/May, 1983: Mike Bearzi and Art Wiggins approached from sea level with an airdrop. Bearzi: "Ten days of clear weather replete with warm easterly winds and nothing even close to nighttime freezing temperatures. The lower 3,000 feet fell apart rapidly and we had no opportunity to make an attempt." At one point the winds were so extreme as to blow their tent down-glacier, with both of them in it. An attempt on the nearby Aiguille du Stikine was thwarted by avalanche hazard and weather.

Ten years elapsed between attempts on the face. It appears that a reputation of futility began to take hold before Bearzi once again grasped the torch, one last time.

April/May, 1994: Mike Bearzi and Barry Rugo approached from sea level with an airdrop. The face appeared to be coming into shape, but a prolonged spell of warmer, wetter weather began to sow doubt. Their only attempt stopped at the end of the first steep section as a result of constant sluff avalanches and non-existent protection. The following day, a warm two-week storm moved in. The team moved around to the west buttress but quit in the face of torrential rain and high winds. Rugo: "My feeling is that someone will, through a combination of luck and manic resolve, get up the thing. They'll be moving light, non-stop, and not placing much gear because there won't be much to place. The upper headwall should nonetheless stimulate some ass-clenching pauses."

May 5-May 18, 1995: Bill Belcourt and Randy Rackliff. Helicopter round trip. Rackliff: "The face looked fantastic with eye-catching runnels streaking down the mid-section. However, in the morning we found that the snow on the glacier hadn't frozen and as if we couldn't have figured out what that meant, a colossal section of serac left of the face broke off, sweeping the entire approach. The timing was fortuitous, as half an hour later we would have been right under it. Avalanches and sloughs fell continuously, day and night throughout the Cauldron. The roar reminded me of camping in the middle of a railyard." As the face fell apart, the pair turned their attention to the virgin West Witches' Tit, summitting after 15 pitches in a continuous push. They then skied around the Thumb, hoping to make a quick ascent of the Beckey route, but were stymied by days of whiteout.

April 20-April 30, 1997: Alex Lowe and Randy Rackliff. Helicopter round trip. Rackliff, the only person other than Bearzi to go to the face more than once, had these observations: "Alex and I left earlier than my previous trip hoping to get a little better freeze. We did; on the second morning the snowpack on the glacier was solid enough to walk on. And that was it. Conditions then returned to Depth Hoar Purgatory and there was never any question of getting on the northwest face. Your real nemesis is the peculiar nature of freeze/thaw dynamic—or should I say thaw/thaw dynamic? It just doesn't freeze the way you'd expect in other areas. One of the fascinations of the face, for me, is that it seems to *demand* a really fast and light style. With the vagaries of weather, thaw, rock/ice fall, etc., I'd want to be racing up this thing and off it fast. Personally I wouldn't go back to the northwest face. But that may have more to do with my current interest level in such things. If you've been winning the lottery a lot lately, and really want to tag a major unclimbed face it's definitely a great one to try. It's SO big and SO cool looking it's hard not to want to be the one who finally gets lucky. Just don't expect Prom night when you get in there."

After climbing to a pass to make radio contact for an early pick-up, the pair descended unroped. Alex went ahead and, just when out of sight, was swept, tumbled, and pummeled down 2,000 feet in an avalanche, unbeknownst to Randy. Moments later, when Randy got over the edge and saw Alex dusting himself off on the glacier 2,000 feet below, he thought, "Wow, I knew Alex was fast, but I didn't think he was that fast!"

April 18-May 3, 1998: Bruce Miller and Jack Roberts. Helicopter round trip. Roberts: "The northwest face appeared to be coated with rime ice over a layer of more substantial ice. How wrong we were. Six days of on-again off-again temps in the 70s, with only one, maybe two nighttime lows around 30 degrees dramatically altered the appearance of the face from being a reasonable objective to simply becoming objectionable to climb due to its altered state. *Unreasonable*." Miller: "The face is conditionally challenged. Avy right down the middle as soon as the sun hits. A trip I'm trying to forget." A slight attempt was made, only to find sodden snow on wet rock coupled with avalanches and rockfall. The trip was aborted early.

Exposure! Looking down the NW face from the summit ridge. It's so steep, after the upper few hundred feet the next thing you see is the glacier 6500' below. Note shadow of Cat's Ears and Devil's Thumb summit. Dieter Klose

Sammy Serac cuts loose a lethal sweep. This and many other avalanche clouds engulf base camp 1.5 miles away. Dieter Klose

March 18-April 5, 1999: Conny Amelunxen, Sean Easton, Keith Reid. Helicoptered in and skied out to tidewater. They waited for two weeks below the face in weather so bad they could only see the face on three days. Temps from 5° to 60° brought snow, rain, and sun in no discernable order. Easton: "An immense wall, requiring just the right combination of weather conditions to set up a face that spans a huge range of temperatures and climbing mediums. Someday a lucky party will be sitting at the base and hit the jackpot."

April 24-June 3, 1999: Lionel Daudet and Sebastian Foissac. Round trip from sea level, unsupported. The face was out of shape, so the pair skied to Burkett Needle. Before starting on their ascent of the Needle, per Daudet, "We had a terrible snowstorm that destroys our base camp, and we had to dig a snowcave in a hurry...." Besides shredding their tent, the winds blew away their sleds, never to be found again. The duo lived out the remaining 24 days using their portaledge for shelter on the successful third ascent of Burkett Needle.

May 16-June 5, 2002: Guy Edwards and John Millar. Round trip from sea level, unsupported. The face was out of shape. During the 20 days, 15 gave continuous rain or snow; five were without precipitation, with only two of these in actual sunshine. No attempt was made on the face. Edwards: "One of the largest prizes that I know of. We watched the face...with lots of objective hazard. The face starts at such a low altitude—you certainly need cold weather to climb the lower part safely. The face is so big there's always a lot of threatening snow, ice, and rock above you. The Devil's own face." The pair instead climbed new lines on both the West Witches' Tit and on Cat's Ears spire, making the second and third ascents, respectively.

SUMMARY

Of all the individuals who have visited the northwest face, not a single one was lacking the technical expertise and determination that the wall would require. The extreme avalanche danger alone has kept many at bay. However, as I have shown, either the conditions on the face, or the weather, or a combination of both were the final culprits in halting all suitors. Some of those lads think it will one day be climbed by a "lucky" party. I doubt it. I believe that the wisdom of Ulysses is the best approach: look and listen, but don't touch. Don't waste your time.

As a result of all this trying, and perhaps because of that trying, we have one big beautiful wall that stands as an even purer virgin, an enduring monument to the tantalizing mystery that forever leads man into the unknown. It is the very nature of this wall to keep it that way. As irony has it, climbers don't embrace that kind of idea, and owing to human nature they are going to keep coming, trying.

EPILOGUE

When my story went to the editor in April, 2003, Guy Edwards and John Millar returned to the Thumb. They skied in with their friend, Kai Hirvonen, under stellar skies. The face was in nick when they arrived. After a day of rest and observation, this trio of hardy alpinists set off for the face during the last hours of Easter. Just before reaching the avalanche debris at the base of the face, Kai followed his gut feeling, told his pals it wasn't worth the risk, and turned around.

From base camp, Kai watched their headlamps ascending into the night. That is the last anyone has seen of them. An exhaustive search by helicopter has revealed no clues as to their fate. It is believed that Guy and John are buried by avalanche at the base of the monument.

A NOTE ON THE AUTHOR

Raised in the flatlands of Germany and the U.S., Dieter Klose, 44, discovered the mountain realm in 1973. A life-long passion for places wild and remote drew him to Alaska, where he lived for 20 years. He has two children, Wrenna (17) and Dylan (15). With dozens of forays into the Devil's Thumb region, and having long-served as a hub for visiting climbers, he's been coined the "Manager" of the Stikine Icecap. He is now based in Colorado between travels, where he works as a home designer and builder, though he continues to visit the Stikine area on an independent study of glacier bears.

EL GIGANTE

A chronicle of early climbing on the giant of
Parque Nacional Cascada de Basaseachic, Mexico.

LUIS CARLOS GARCÍA AYALA

With 660 meters of air underfoot, the exposure and clean rock made this a memorable pitch. Chris Giles

In the state of Chihuahua, a small corner of Tarahumara land conceals countless wonders, some of which have only recently been revealed. Many more await discovery. Between 1994 and 1997 the GEEC—the spelunking and exploration association of the city of Cuauhtémoc and a government agency of Chihuahua—organized a series of expeditions aimed at exploring the Barranca de Candameña. The purpose of these expeditions was to document the canyon and then promote its natural attractions to the world of adventure sports and to the development of eco-tourism. Carlos Lazcano Sahagún, a noted Mexican geologist, explorer, and spelunker (whom we thank for sharing his findings), led the expeditions.

The explorers discovered many attractions, in some cases immediately upon the start of their travels. One of these is the important Duraznos River; its waters plunge to earth at the Basaseachic Waterfall, the starting point of the canyon. This became an expedition objective, and expedition members rappelled its full height, recording it at 246 meters.

They likewise rappelled another waterfall, the Piedra Volada; with its freefall of 453 meters it is the eleventh highest in the world. Near Piedra Volada they discovered the impressive Peña del Gigante (or Rock of the Giant) and, to add spice to their explorations, they decided once again to descend on rappel. To this end they set up rappel stations using natural anchors and Hexentrics and other nuts. All of this was done with respect for ethics and style; they recovered their ropes and left few traces of their passage on the wall. They recorded a descent of 885 meters, making El Gigante the highest known cliff in Mexico.

The explorers of the GEEC brought back important information about the site, as well as obvious evidence of its enormous potential for adventure sports. At this juncture Carlos Lazcano set out to find a Mexican climber interested in making the first ascent of El Gigante.

THE MEETING

Higinio Pintado and Bonfilio Sarabia have been my friends and climbing partners for a number of years and have helped guide my development as a climber. Higinio has climbed on El Capitan and in other big-wall venues. Bonfilio, the younger of the two, was invited to participate in his first big-wall experience, including the logistics accompanying this project. They made up the second rope team gathering to challenge El Gigante.

At the time this photo of El Gigante was taken, it had been rappelled but not climbed. Carlos Garcia

Cecilia Buil, from Huesca, Spain, and I first met in Mexico City, where we climbed together. Soon after, we resolved to climb Yosemite's El Capitan, and so we made the pilgrimage to the famous park. In a month's stay we climbed three routes, Mescalito, Zenyatta Mondatta, and Lurking Fear. Through this we became solid as a rope team, as well as learning a great deal about protection, style, logistics, and ethics of both free and aid climbing on big walls.

On our return to Mexico City we heard rumors circulating within the small climbing community about the existence of an as-yet unclimbed big wall in Chihuahua; we were captivated by the prospect. In mid-February of 1998 we traveled to the city of Chihuahua. Once there we were welcomed by Carlos Lazcano, who briefed us on the logistics of accessing the now-famous Barranca de Candameña. Finally, we gathered the necessary food and equipment and saw to last-minute details.

We left Chihuahua and headed toward Hermosillo, Sonora. At kilometer 272 we came to Basaseachic, at 2,160 meters in the Sierra Occidental. As mentioned earlier, the town is known for the famous waterfall that forms the beginning of the canyon.

THE APPROACH

Six kilometers before the town of Basaseachic lies the sparse settlement of Las Estrelllas. This place marks the beginning of a paved road leading to the ranch of San Lorenzo, a beautiful spot owned by Sr. Fernando Domínguez, who dresses like a rancher from high up in the hills. Don Fernando welcomed us and put us up in two of his comfortable cabins. He was put in charge of transportation, lodging, porters, and communications.

Within two days we were on our way down from a gap that opens out from the village of Huajumar. Soon we were stuck by our first view of the enormous rocky hulk of El Gigante. Although the view from this spot is misleading and makes the colossus seem smaller than it is, it still manages to stand out tall and proud in hues of brown, orange, and yellow.

Some 15 porters led by Don Santiago Pérez and our climbing foursome soon arrived at the foot of the Giant. Our base camp was established near a spring, in lush woods. There, we all gathered around a huge bonfire to nervously celebrate our coming together to pioneer the first virgin big wall in our personal experience.

While constantly stoking the fire, our porters related many legends about this place. One of these was of the famous "Sierpe," an aquatic snake that inhabits the depths of the river. Whenever anyone crosses the river too close to it, the Sierpe coils itself around the victim in order to drag it to the depths, where it is devoured.

After studying the wall Cecilia and I decided we would climb up its center. Higinio and Bonfilio, meanwhile, decided on the section of the huge wall to the left of its prominent rib. It was time to go into action.

Over the next 15 days, we fixed five difficult pitches. We thus became acquainted with the rock's hardness and quality, the difficulties awaiting us, and the likely time frame for completing the ascent. But our food ran out and we decided to come out of the canyon.

In the meantime, Higinio and Bonfilio also abandoned their objective because their chosen route consisted mostly of rotten rock; they also lacked a few pieces of hardware needed to continue.

We made our way up the river toward the Basaseachic Waterfall. As we gradually put distance between the colossus and us, we gained the perspective of our five rope-lengths as mere scratches about the heels of the Giant. Our trek along the Candameña River took us past huge walls and blocks of orange-colored stone. In all, it took us nearly seven hours to walk back to Rancho San Lorenzo, where we spent five days resting among its meadows.

After agreeing with Don Fernando to make radio contact every third day, we headed back to our base camp with a porter and his two sons.

We began climbing our fixed ropes very early and ended the day by sleeping on pitch five

Carlos Garcia Ayala hooking delicately on the 13th pitch of Yawira Batú, with Cecilia Buil on a watchful belay. More than two-thirds of the pitches have hook moves. Chris Giles

Cecilia Buil hooking out to some free moves on the way to the 15th belay on Yawira Batú. Chris Giles

under the shelter of an overhang. At daybreak we heard a great thundering and not far from us watched a huge block fall to earth, shattering at the base of the wall.

We decided to climb in capsule style and set up bivouacs under overhangs. We adhered to Yosemite-style ethics, respecting the rock and establishing our route from the bottom up. For belay anchors we used natural pieces, but we also drilled 16 bolts and 64 rivets altogether, counting both aid placements and anchors. Our route, Simuchi, was 1,025 meters long, and we rated it VI 5.11b A4; it took 16 days.

The rock on the Giant is hard and offers few crack systems but abundant hook placements. It yields a type of climbing different from that demanded by granite; it is a different style, sustained and of high difficulty, and requiring greater care in choosing and placing hardware.

We set up seven bivouacs over sixteen days on the wall, and when our food and water ran out, we notified Don Fernando. When we least expected it rescuers appeared before us, having rappelled in order to (in their eyes) save us. We did not want to leave the wall and merely requested that they stand by. They informed us, however, that we were 300 meters from the top, so we understood that we had no choice but to get off the wall. All of this created a modest scandal and was the source of alarmist reports by the media, which served only to worry our families. Later, we observed sadly that we had been only four pitches away from topping out, or some 150 meters.

The rescuers left their rappel ropes in place, so the next day we went back down to finish our route by climbing and to retrieve our gear, a bit disappointed at the way it all ended.

We left Chihuahua feeling grateful for the support of all those who motivated and allowed this adventure, and we vowed to return some day to tackle another big wall.

Return to Candameña

In 1999 we again found ourselves in Chihuahua with the aim of exploring Sinforosa Canyon in the district of Guachochi, on the hunt for a new rock formation. This time Cecilia and I brought with us a friend from the U.S., Chris Giles. As a professional photographer, he wanted to document our ascent.

Once in Guachochi we began by verifying the information we had received from Carlos Lazcano; then we contacted all those who might prove helpful in a reconnaissance of the area. We chartered a light airplane and, in our flight over the deep canyon, were able to see that the wall in question didn't reach even half the height of El Gigante. We therefore abandoned the area and proceeded again to Candameña, with the intent of putting up another big-wall route.

We organized our porters and other support personnel for our descent into the beautiful canyon. This time we chose a different spot for our base camp, once again situated next to a spring and abundant tree cover. Next, we studied a potential route on El Gigante that followed a beautiful yellow spur via a good crack system. We also planned Chris' role, making clear to him where on the wall our route was to take us. We fixed a couple of pitches and got our haul bags packed. In the meantime, Chris headed out of the canyon and toward the top of our cliff in order to set up a series of rappels that would allow him to intercept us during our climb.

We began our route on the left side of the Giant. The first pitch was a mix of horizontal cracks and blocks. The second was a beautiful horizontal traverse with 250 meters of exposure. We christened it El Paso del Águila, or Eagle's Step.

The third and then the fourth pitch were climbed, and then it was time to bivouac. The next day, as Cecilia worked with the drill, it malfunctioned (we used the drill only for belay anchor bolts and for placing occasional rivets). We decided to go back down and we let Chris know as much. Very early the next morning we were on our way to Rancho San Lorenzo, which we reached in eight hours.

After a five-day rest we returned to the wall. We found the pitches on this route to be sustained, well defined, and enjoyable. The bivouacs, in particular the last one, were very exposed. We had a couple of scares on pitch 13: a rivet hanger anchoring our bivouac broke, causing us to fall five meters but without incident. The next day, after making three placements, Cecilia placed a pin that shattered the rock and sent down a rather large block.

In all, we placed around 50 rivets and 10 bolts, having climbed a total of 750 meters over 10 days on the wall, which we rated VI 5.10d A4+. The route is called Yawira Batú, or "budding corn" in the language of the Tarahumara.

SPORT CLIMBING

We again returned to Chihuahua in 1999 to give the official report of our climb and to present our new project: to put up sport routes in the area of Rancho San Lorenzo. We received the needed support, so we began working our routes. Our chosen style was to work from the bottom up, free climbing on the lead and hanging from skyhook placements in the excellent huecos and flakes in order to place bolts. This style was very helpful in accessing certain areas of the rock and establishing further routes.

The rock is a bit porous, with abundant huecos, and the wall is overhanging for the most part. In two and a half months we put up 50 routes in 8 separate sections. Their difficulty ranges from 5.8 to 5.13b, with 5.10s and 5.11s predominating. There are also many bouldering opportunities in the numerous rocks scattered in the lush woods. The camping area lies nearby.

BASASEACHIC FALLS

After pulling out a block that sent her tumbling, Cecilia Buil nervously finished the 14th pitch of Yawira Batú. Chris Giles

One year later we were back at Rancho San Lorenzo. This time we wanted to climb the waterfall solo, meaning that Cecilia was to put up her route and I my own, separately. We made the necessary preparations and descended the waterfall, putting our base camp on its left bank.

Both routes begin from the same slope, some 300 meters from the waterfall. La Danza del Sol, or "Dance of the Sun," traverses left to a niche and follows a crack system to the top, while Lluvia de Plata, or "Silver Rain," takes a straight line over beautiful over-hanging slabs, presenting a high degree of difficulty.

After fixing three pitches, we began our respective climbs. It took me three days and two nights to complete seven very beautiful pitches of free and aid climbing. I rated La Danza del Sol, V 5.9 A3+.

Cecilia ran into problems and I had go down to her position. I brought batteries for her drill and placed a couple of bolts, which she subsequently used as a belay anchor. Cecilia's route, Lluvia de Plata (V 5.9 A4) took her six days and five nights on the wall and thus became the second route to be established on the waterfall.

CONCLUSION

The state of Chihuahua is the largest in the Republic of Mexico. Its varied geography offers great contrasts between a tropical zone, desert areas, and mountains. It is rich in indigenous cultures, among which the Tarahumara are most prevalent in the highland areas.

Many more canyons await exploration and the search for climbing areas goes on. The potential for the development of rock climbing in all its forms is great, be it in the form of bouldering, sport climbing, multi-pitch sport climbs, or big-wall aid routes. The rock in the state of Chihuahua includes the volcanic variety, limestone, and others.

The stretch of the canyon of Candameña between the village of Basaseachic and the municipality of Ocampo boasts rock walls ranging between 300 and 900 meters in height. Along with these, it is notable for its three striking natural features, namely the Basaseachic Waterfall, Piedra Volada, and the big wall of El Gigante.

This beautiful place has now, thanks to the vision of a few, come to be a matter of public knowledge. The climber's charge now becomes that of respecting the land as well as the work and the ethics that guided its development. For this reason we have taken care to adhere to the ethics practiced in other areas that have set current standards for climbing style, such as Yosemite, Peru, Patagonia, and Europe. We have made ascents that were clean, imaginative, and carried out in a style that adhered to world standards.

Mexico and other Latin American countries, in their desire to contribute toward the evolution of the rock climbing lifestyle, deserve to be respected. The classic style in climbing is to go from bottom to top, such as is done on the great rock formations of our planet. This presents the greatest challenge.

It with all of this in mind that I extend an invitation to climbers to come and contribute to the development of this area with respect and with consideration for the ethical concerns voiced here, and to enjoy the magic to be found in Chihuahua. We eagerly await your visit.

Translated by Oriol Solé-Costa

SUMMARY OF STATISTICS:

AREA: Parque Nacional Cascada de Basaseachic, Chihuahua, Mexico

FIRST ASCENTS: El Gigante (first ascent of the wall), via Simuchi (1,025m, VI 5.11b A4, 16 days, Buil-Garcia, 1998. (AAJ 1999)
Yawira Batú, 750m, VI 5.10d A4+, 10 days on the wall, Buil-Garcia, 1999. (*AAJ* 2000)

Fifty sport and gear climbs near Rancho San Lorenzo, 5.8-5.13b, Buil-Garcia, 1999.

Basaseachic Waterfall, La Danza del Sol (V 5.9 A3+), Carlos Garcia Ayala, solo, 2000.

Basaseachic Waterfall, Lluvia de Plata (V 5.9 A4), Cecilia Buil, solo, 2000. (*AAJ* 2001)

A NOTE ABOUT THE AUTHOR

Born in Mexico City in 1967, Luis Carlos Garcia Ayala now lives in the little town of San Luis Ayucan, outside the city. Single, he works as a carpenter and climbs as much as he can. In addition to his exploration of remote walls throughout Mexico, he has opened roughly 200 sport routes, "more or less from the ground." He loves nature, the sea, the desert, the forest, but his "wonder is to work in a team for opening big walls." His favorite route is Yawira Batú, with the best bivy he has ever done, one pitch below the summit.

FADED GLORY

Two weeks of committed aid climbing on El Gigante's fractured andesite.

BRENT EDELEN

El Gigante dominates the view as one travels down the beautiful Candemeña Canyon. Alard Hüfner

It took me a year to find Mexico's El Gigante. Carlos Garcia and Cecilia Buil, the first-ascent team, made a point of keeping its whereabouts a secret. Fueled by the mystery, I searched maps and interrogated people until I discovered its location. When I finally set eyes on El Gigante, I couldn't blame Carlos and Cecilia for keeping it a secret.

El Gigante is not your typical monolith; it's for the adventurer. It demands a certain respect, a grudging admiration. Jungle-like vegetation blankets its walls. Flora armed with spikes and blade-like fronds stand ready to strike. Flocks of stink beetles hide in every crevice, and make a distinct crunching sound when you bury your fingers in cracks. And the rock is loose. Not rotten, like some desert sandstone, or flaky like the gneiss of the Black Canyon, but fractured and

A big wall is a big wall when it comes to hiking in the gear and rations. Alard Hüfner

loose. Razor-sharp edges of andesite stand poised, ready to pounce on unsuspecting rope. On both trips I've made to the area, lead ropes have fallen victim to rockfall or edges.

We experienced only moderate success on our first trip to El Gigante. Gareth Llewellin (Australia), Jakub Gajda (Czech Republic), and I (U.S.) were hoping to complete the longest route on the mountain, the Nose. Conditions were brutal (see above). Jakub nearly died in a rope-cutting lead fall. Gareth almost succumbed to hypothermia. And I came close to dislodging a quarter of the mountain and burying us all. We were lucky enough to hammer out the first line on the west face, but unfortunately the summit of the route rested on El Gigante's shoulder, far right of the beautiful, spire-like summit. When we ran short of time, we agreed to return one day for another shot at the Nose.

It took two full years to recover from the beating El Gigante unleashed during that trip—if not physically, then mentally. And

Brent Edelen getting a feel for the rock, the plants, and the bugs on the first pitch. Alard Hüfner

A bewildered Brent setting off on his lead. Alard Hüfner

now we were going back. Yippee! "Going back?" asked Jakub warily, with an ear-to-ear smile. "Not sure I'm ready."

"Oh, come on," I pleaded. "It won't be that bad this time...we're wiser." Jakub loves adventure, and it wasn't long before I had him excited about returning to complete our original objective. Gareth, on the other hand, hadn't been heard from since the end of the trip. We reckoned he was spending his days on some Brisbane beach, having given up the silly notion of climbing rocks.

This time our third team member would be an adventurous climber from South Africa, Alard Hüfner. I was excited to have him along. We got along just splendidly, as we should, since he's just like me: pleasant, smart, a great climber... and almost as good-looking. Living in South Africa, he has had the opportunity to do some adventurous first ascents right in his own backyard. He was no stranger to Vega-climbing or loose rocks.

Committing to the wall would be a huge priority, as to siege such a massive feature would be withholding the respect it deserved. We established the following ethics in recognition that this was not some limestone wall on the outskirts of an overcrowded European town. This was a fractured pile of andesite in the mountains of Mexico. Our system would fix only three ropes, leaving the tag line specifically for its duty. The extra lead line would stay in the haul bag unless needed. Bolting would be kept to a minimum. We were here for adventure, not to cater to the masses. If a pitch couldn't be free climbed on-sight, then it would be aided. If a bolt had to be placed, it would be earned by drilling on lead with a hand drill (a reminder that if you don't work with the rock, then the rock will work to destroy your shoulder).

Finally, it was time to start. We decided that I would solo the first pitch while Jakub and Alard hauled loads and carried water. The first few moves quickly reminded me of what we were in for: tree-root pull-up here, grass mantle there...oops, grass failed, lunge to that loose boulder...ahh, finally I made it to the base.

To the left of our route was a string of bolts a half-mile long. They were no more than eight feet apart, snaking up and out of sight. The line reminded me of one of those connect-the-dot children's books. I wanted a giant pencil...or a chisel. It made me stop and think about what this place might become. Was this the future? Was I going to be one of those crotchety old climbers who banter about how wonderful El Gigante was before they built log cabins with hot water at the base? With a route like that, any Tom, Dick, or Harry could pack a couple of ropes and a handful of draws, take a leisurely hike down the canyon and blast right up...probably in a day. It is this kind of convenience that has made El Portero Chico the talk of every sport cragger on the continent. What would it do to this place? Is this where climbing is headed? Perhaps someday everything will be "sport bolted." Perhaps aid climbing will be illegal, like base-jumping. Well, I hope I'm dead by then.

The laborious work of hand drilling the anchor bolts. Alard Hüfner

Well, back to the climb. The first three pitches followed a crack that trended right into a major dihedral system. At the end of the third day we had three ropes hanging and were ready to say goodbye to soil. I had managed to talk Alard and Jakub into hauling the lower pitches while I soloed the fourth. Like on any wall, the first few pitches of hauling were inconceivably hard. This old mountain wasn't helping. Everywhere the haul lines touched the rock a bombing campaign ensued. Throughout the afternoon, deep bass tones echoed and bounced off adjacent walls as massive boulders converted potential energy to kinetic energy.

I finished my pitch and rappelled, smiling as I remembered the warmth of the afternoon sun and enjoying what had proven to be a fun and interesting aid pitch. Two gaunt men with pale faces greeted me. Jakub had abandoned English and was roundly cussing in Czech. Alard was far

This route provided a variety of interesting aid climbing. Alard Hüfner

The magnificent scenery improves as height is gained above the curving canyon floor. Alard ascending. Brent Edelen

below, battling a bush. They had had a rough day—and now it started to rain.

We set up camp and nestled under our rain flies. It was then that Jakub expressed concern about the amount of rockfall and seriously questioned our motives. By bedtime he had convinced himself that we were doomed. In the morning, despite attempts to persuade him otherwise, Jakub quit. We tied the ropes together and sent him down along with his haul bag and the extra portaledge.

His departure put Alard and me in an awkward predicament. Not only did Jakub have the good camera that was to capture our devilishly good looks; but also a three-person team is vital in hauling such heavy loads. Of greater concern was that in the event of an injury, two rescuers are six times better than one. We debated about whether to continue, but eventually decided to press on. However, before he left, we asked Jakub to wait below for a few days. That way, if we found we couldn't manage without him, we could at least hike out together, albeit with our heads held low.

But manage we did, as we methodically picked our way, pitch by pitch. At night, we could see a lone fire at base camp. We knew it was little comfort for poor Kuby, now alone with his demons. We cracked a beer, shouted him a toast, and stuffed our faces with the food he had left behind (including some gourmet cookies his girlfriend had made).

Day seven found us at the bottom of a giant inset that we dubbed "the Eye." Jakub was long gone, and the isolation of El Gigante had settled around us. The Eye was our middle mark for the wall. Until now, the crack systems we had scoped had connected quite nicely. But the Eye was blank. The few edges we could see looked loose, so I advised Alard to bat-hook when necessary. He acquired the skill quickly. After every eight holes or so, he would drill a 2"x 1/4" hole and slam in a solid steel rivet. Steel rivets had been a source of disagreement on our trip two years earlier. In leading a pitch near the summit, I had placed five rivets that I felt were strong enough to hold a fairly sizable fall. Gareth and Jakub disagreed. The debate continued throughout that trip, and now Alard was about to put the debate to rest. As he neared the end of his pitch, a small seam opened into a crack under a small roof. His last rivet was some distance below, and the one before that was far left toward the dihedral. As he slid a blue Alien under the roof, his mind made brief reference to a warning I had given him earlier about the nature of andesite: "It's very hard and very slick, and sometimes cams don't like to grab."

Alard bounce-tested the Alien and eased on to the piece. Then, like Wile E. Coyote, he hung suspended in mid-air for what seemed forever, then plunged, squealing like a pig. But I was right: the rivet held. If I'd been wrong, we would never have finished the climb.

Fourteen days after we had strung the first rope, Alard clambered up a loose chimney to the summit. Late afternoon found us lying on the haul bags, sharing shots of homemade Czech brandy and polishing off the beers we had saved for the occasion. As the sun fell into the west, Alard gave a toast. "To Jakub," he said. "May he cope with his decision bravely."

"Hear, hear," I replied.

SUMMARY OF STATISTICS:

AREA: El Gigante, in Parque Nacional Cascada de Basaseachic, Mexico

ASCENT: Faded Glory, VI 5.9 A3, Alard Hüfner and Brent Edelen, November, 2002.

NOTE ABOUT THE AUTHOR:

Brent Edelen is a professional bee-keeper in Colorado.

A solid clean corner system three pitches from the summit was a welcome change from the questionable rock below. Alard Hüfner

Alard Hüfner, Brent Edelen, and Jakub Gadja. Alard Hüfner

CONSPIRACY OF FOOLS

The second ascent of La Conjura de Los Necios reveals plenty of adventure between the bolts on El Gigante.

ANDREJ GRMOVSEK

Stefan Glowacz on the 18th pitch during the first ascent of La Conjura de los Necios.

In the spring of 2002 my fiancé Tanja Rojs and I drove from Colorado to Chihuahua's Cañon de Candamena. Our plan was to establish a new traditionally climbed free route on El Gigante.

We spent the first few days in the national park researching how to reach the base of El Gigante. This was really hard because the area is hilly and it's difficult to see the canyon. After a few days of exploration we descended into the canyon with three porters and a lot of equipment. Then we finally had a closer look that the wall. We discovered it to be full of vegetation, very loose, and rotten. Because of this we decided not to climb a new route (we would spend more time cleaning than climbing), and our adjusted goal was to repeat the German free route, La Conjura de los Necios.

We climbed the route in four days, and found the climbing to be very serious and interesting—a lot of vegetation, poor rock quality, and long runouts. The first two days we rappelled to the base on fixed ropes. After 2 p.m. the sun came onto the wall. Then it became very hot, and hard free climbing was almost impossible. So we climbed mostly early in the day.

I climbed the entire route free, on sight. I think the hardest pitch of the route, graded 5.13a by the Germans, is really around 5.12c. Still, the whole route is really serious and hard. The middle part has especially rotten rock, and the climbing here is extremely dangerous. On the last day of climbing we witnessed a huge rockfall from the right portion of the wall. We were very happy to reach the top without hurting ourselves.

The first ascent party did a very good job establishing this route! We found run outs of 7-10 meters, with no decent protection between. The climbing is pretty slow because it's very technical. If you are a strong party you could repeat this route in two days, or maybe in one if you are really fast. You could sleep in small but not ideal ledges above pitches 8 and 15 (the bigger ledge is called Rancho San Lorenzo). By sleeping on those ledges you won't need a portaledge.

We want climbers to know about the bad rock and the dangers of the wall and this route.

Editor's note: Please read the short but delightfully written story by Stefan Glowacz about the first ascent of La Conjura de Los Necios, published in the Climbs & Expeditions section of AAJ *2002, ppg. 288-289.*

Summary of Statistics

Area: El Gigante, in Parque Nacional Cascada de Basaseachic, Mexico

Ascent: Second ascent of La Conjura de los Necios (Conspiracy of Fools) (900m, 26 pitches, 5.12c), Andrej Grmovsek and Tanja Rojs, 2002. Note that these numbers differ from the 22 pitches and 5.13a described in the Germans' topo at Rancho San Lorenzo.

A Note About the Author

Andrej Grmovsek lives in Slovenia, where he was born in 1973, and where he is currently working on his Ph. D. in geography. He has climbed many long free or mostly free routes in the Slovenian Alps, Dolomites, Western Alps, Norway, U.S., and Mexico. His best climbingadventures were on a trip to Madagascar in 1998 (a new free route on the virgin wall of Dondy) and to Peru in 2002 (new free route on La Esfinge).

Andrej Grmovsek taking the sharp end during the second ascent of La Conjura de los Necios. Tanja Rojs Grmovsek

LOGICAL PROGRESSION

Sometimes the best rock and traditional bolting ethics follow different lines.
What's an enterprising climber to do? Going down on El Gigante.

LUKE LAESER

Pete Baumeister scopes the giant from the other side. Luke Laeser

The original intention of Peter Baumeister, Dierk Sittner, and myself on our 2001 trip was to establish a new free climb on El Gigante. But due to the difficulty of getting to the wall we chose a much closer objective, and established Subiendo el Arcoiris, a 10-pitch, rappel-bolted sport climb up a prominent buttress on Cascada Wall; it was the first multi-pitch free climb in the canyon. Rap-bolting was simply the easiest way to put up a free route here, and it yielded clean, safe, and excellent climbing.

In February 2002, Pete, Bert van Lint, and I traveled to Basaseachic with one goal: to establish a bolt-protected free climb on the northwest face of El Gigante. The idea of a downward-bound mission made us a bit uncomfortable, but it seemed the most efficient way to establish a quality route. There are many advantages to the top-to-bottom approach, such as: no hauling, no belayers (which meant we could all work at the same time), no bat-hook holes, and the ability to preview all the moves before placing a single bolt. Since this was probably the biggest route ever attempted in this style, we knew we might be vilified. But when the road ends at the top of the wall, as it does on El Gigante, you simply come in from the top.

Van Lint, from Belgium, met us at Hueco Tanks, and we all traveled to Basaseachic together. Bert had been touring Mexico for several months, sharpening his Spanish and multi-pitch sport-climbing skills. Once in Mexico, we proceeded to get our visas for an extended stay, but both Pete and Bert had passport complications. "Border Horror" is what we nicknamed the expense of having to pay off the customs official to "adjust" the paperwork.

Wallets thinner, we continued south from Juárez to Ciudad Chihuahua, where we stopped for tacos and gas. The people of this city are great and always curious about what you're up to. The year before, with Dierk, we were lost and needed to find a big grocery. A policeman, impressed that we had traveled to climb and vacation in the state, gave us a flashing-light escort, with the traffic parting around us, straight to the market.

From the capital of Mexico's biggest state we headed west through Cuauhtemoc and into the mountains, where the welded-tuff formations begin to appear. We were equipped for a two-month stay in Basaseachic, having learned the previous year what to expect. My truck, packed to the max with food and supplies, sagged from the weight.

Basaseachic, a village of about 1,000, has a few small markets, a pricey phone service, and limited electricity due to the difficulty of running lines to such rural areas. This made it hard to charge our battery packs. Pete, however, had engineered a portable solar-

Holger Heuber climbs the stunning last pitch of Subiendo el Arcoiris. Klaus Fengler

Bert van Lint drilling high on the wall.
Luke Laeser

power station for charging the batteries for our hammer drills, lights, and CD player. The system was perfect in that it was fairly lightweight and portable. However, every system has its weaknesses. El Gigante is a northwest-facing wall, and the sun doesn't provide enough light in the depths of Candameña Canyon. As a solution, Bert had borrowed a Ryobi gas drill from the Flemish Mountaineering Federation to use on the dark territory of the lower face.

On our first few days in the park we established Contessa Inessa (two pitches, 5.10), the first route on the super-pocketed, west-facing formation above the cul-de-sac at the north entrance of the park. The volcanic rock in Basaseachic is like that in all the areas around my home in New Mexico: Cochiti Mesa's clean faces dotted with pockets, Enchanted Tower's fairytale formations, White Rock's dark basaltic textures, and the Dungeon's blocky roofs can all be found there.

After warming up a bit we decided it was time to go to work. Fernando Dominguez—the boss of the area—owns Rancho San Lorenzo, which borders the east side of the park. He has helped the sponsored "expeditions" get their equipment to the wall and deal with the logistics of getting around this rugged, desperate country. Since we were on a tight budget, we couldn't afford such support, so we decided to move our gear around ourselves. Fernando introduced us to a great guide, Don Rafael, who knows the canyons of Basaseachic better than anyone. For a small fee Don Rafael showed us how to find the rugged 4x4 logging roads that end near the summit of El Gigante. This was the method the first descentionists had used to approach the formation and, in similar style to the original rappelling team, we began our adventure from the top.

We shuttled the first loads out a narrow, twisting trail through pine and scrub oak across the "Devil's Backbone," a narrow ridge that drops steeply on both sides. The summit, which ironically served as our "base camp," is an island in the sky, with a 360-degree view of the canyon country. Its bushy oaks and junipers provide relief from the sun and wind, making it quite comfortable. After almost a week of preparations, we were eager to finally get on the wall, with all our systems and equipment ready.

The goal was to create the most continuous and sustained free route on El Gigante. Grade VI, going down. Anti-alpine. It's not fast, it's not light—and by most climbers' standards it's the most unethical thing one could do: the creation of a fully bolt-protected, site-specific "art installation." So, with that in mind, we began rappelling the wall and soon found ourselves on a steep, super-pocketed welded-tuff buttress.

In the beginning we were cautious and placed very few bolts because we were uncertain where the route would go. We used removable bolts, which require only a small hole and thus conserves battery power. We referenced photos of the wall Pete had collected from other teams, guiding ourselves onto the steepest, longest, cleanest faces away from the other routes.

We fixed about four ropes down the wall before we actually began bolting any pitches.

Our system was to have all three of us working on something at all times. To do this, the lowest climber would always be searching for where to climb and set belays. The next climber would be a couple of pitches higher, or wherever he could safely maneuver without dropping anything on the worker below, trying moves on jumars, marking bolt placements, cleaning rock, and eventually bolting the pitch. The last climber would either go back across the "Devil's Backbone," shuttling loads of water and supplies back to camp, or finalizing pitches by brushing and cleaning. Before finally bolting each pitch, all three of us had inspected it several times.

Over the next few weeks we began to piece together the upper section of the route at less than one pitch per day. It went so slowly because the person pushing the low point was confronted with so many options. Some days we made no progress; on other days we inspected a dozen different paths. But poor rock quality, no good stance, and other factors forced us to abandon most paths. The fractured rhyolite and andesite could be hollow and rotten, which made it difficult to locate solid continuous sections. It's amazing that we managed not to hurt each other or cut a fixed rope in almost two months on the loose face.

Since we began from the top, we used "pitch one" for what would be the last number from

Luke Laeser looking gripped on pitch 11. Peter Baumeister

Pete Baumeister contemplates the salami at the critter bivy. Bert van Lint

the bottom. Pitch six, also known as "the Diarrhea Pitch" because of all the brown streaks (there was loose shit almost everywhere), took more time than any other section. The vertical face was covered with razorblade flakes and almost no features. For three days Pete, Bert, and I swung to the left and right before deciding to go directly through the middle, where we originally thought it would go. Diarrhea turned out to be a terrific pitch, one of the hardest on the route; we had taken great care to figure out a way through the sustained crimper sequences.

After about a month we had equipped what seemed like half the route (the top half), reaching a long, sloping ledge that would serve as the midpoint bivy. We called it the "Critter Bivy" because there was a raccoon (or ringtail?) skeleton on the ledge, along with a family of mice. Before leaving on this trip Pete and I had constructed a one-person wooden portaledge to use as a scaffold ,or big bosun's chair. Our theory was that since we would never haul the portaledges, it wouldn't matter how heavy they were; however, I thought I was going to pass out when Bert and I carried that thing to the top of the wall. Fortunately, it lowered just fine.

On a rest day we took a trip to the other side of the canyon to photograph and scope El Gigante. When we observed the portaledge camp only two-fifths of the way down the wall, we were dumbfounded. At this rate we were going to run out of time. With as much rope as we had fixed (about 1,200 feet), we could go no lower. Our next step was to move onto the wall, capsule style, and sever our connection with the top.

With enough supplies for five days, the three of us rappelled with the haul bags, pulling the ropes as we went. We made good progress on this downward push, but we had only one charge on our drill batteries. We began to empty the gas drill, which worked like a charm. We cleaned, bolted, moved ropes lower, and inspected farther down and found good climbing on what seemed to be another crux pitch. A steep, flaky, pocketed, chocolaty, frosted-with-yellow-lichen bulge guarded the gray slabs below. Bert spent almost a whole day before finally finding the "passage" through this beautiful section. On the fifth day we spotted anchors on the German route, Conspiracy of Fools, and swung onto their gear. We were exhausted and tired of bad rock, so we rapped their route for seven pitches to reach an oasis on the canyon floor.

We had almost no food left and also no ideas about how to get back to the top, where our truck was parked. Hungry and tired, we bushwhacked up gullies and steep talus for several hours straight back to the truck, discovering a great new connection. Now we had a way to get to the bottom easily.

Conspiracy was fully but poorly bolted, a bit run-out, and loose; however, it was climbable. If we chose to use it to access our route, we would be done. After several rest days we returned to the canyon floor to finish the job. But for fear of wrecking what we had worked so hard for, we established seven clean and safe pitches about 50 feet to the left. The route shares only the first two pitches of Conspiracy, which are pretty good. Finally, the project was established after six-and-a-half weeks of work. We estimated that we had placed 380 bolts and jumared the wall five times each.

Pete's girlfriend from Germany, Ines, arrived with her friend Michaela to support us for our last week. They helped carry the last round of supplies, clean out the base camps, and keep our psyche up. After several rest days we returned to the bottom of the canyon to begin climbing out. Sieging the lower section, we rapped to the ground every night on our fixed ropes. Pete, Bert, and I climbed the first eight 5.10+ and 5.11 lower pitches on clean slabs, (a terrific warm-up for what was to come). At pitch 9 (5.12c) and the 10th ("Bert's Passage," guarding the upper wall, 5.12d), the angle steepened. I managed a redpoint of the 9th pitch, but the 10th kept spitting us off.

With only days remaining till we had to leave, we packed the haul bags and ascended the fixed ropes for the last time to our high point. Bert tried the 10th pitch one last time. He almost sent it, but a hold broke after he had passed the crux. We continued up the wall but, with only three days left, could try the harder pitches only once or twice. Despite being exhausted, we all managed to do some terrific flashes. The climbing was awesome! Diarrhea a 12d, another short and brown 12c, and two 12a's long and thin, we fell on, and didn't redpoint because we had to keep going. However, we were still really proud of the route we'd made. We had done all the moves free and placed all the draws on the route, proving to ourselves that we could climb it. We knew someone strong could on-sight the entire route.

We decided to call it Logical Progression because our method seemed like the best way to establish a high-quality free climb on a loose and vegetated cliff. The bolts are of stainless steel, which should last forever. This 28-pitch route, the longest sport climb in the world, provides a unique free-climbing experience. For Pete, Bert, and me it was a difficult project, but the rappel-bolting technique produced a wonderful route. Beautiful setting, dependable climate, challenging pitches, gut-wrenching exposure, and solid protection—the criteria for a one-of-a-kind world classic.

SUMMARY OF STATISTICS

AREA: Parque Nacional Cascada de Basaseachic, Chihuahua, Mexico

ASCENTS: Cascada Wall, Subiendo el Arcoiris (10 pitches, IV 5.12d A0), Peter Baumeister, Luke Laeser, Dierk Sittner, 2001. (See *AAJ* 2001, ppg 268-269)

El Gigante, Logical Progression (28 pitches, VI 5.12d), Peter Baumeister, Luke Laeser, Bert van Lint, 2002.

A NOTE ON THE AUTHOR

Luke Laeser, 29, works as a graphic designer at *Climbing* magazine in Carbondale, Colorado. A lifelong artist and native New Mexican, Laeser has been climbing for 15 years. When not out at the rocks, or dominating in the rollerball arena, Laeser chills with his wife, Melissa, their dog, Priscilla, and cat, Portia.

The Logical Progression Team on the final days before climbing out: Bert van Lint, Pete Baumeister, Luke Laeser.

A LOGICAL DILEMMA

*When "logic" is seen as an ethical failure, one climber's "progress" becomes
another's "regression"—or worse, a theft from the future of adventure.
Herewith, another installment in the eternal argument
on bolts and how they're placed.*

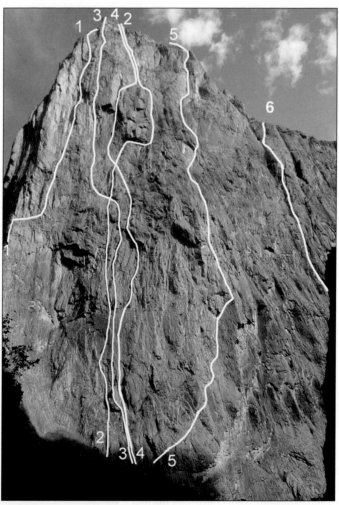

The 2,900-foot face of El Gigante: 1. Yawira Batú (Buil-Garcia, 1999). 2. Simuchi (Buil-Garcia, 1998). 3. Logical
Progression (Baumeister-Laeser-van Lint, 2002). 4. La Conjura de los Necios (Albert-Fengler-Glowacz-Heuber,
2001). 5. Faded Glory (Edelen-Hüfner, 2002). 6. Blade, Scars, and Stars (Edelen-Gajda-Llewellin, 2000).
Andrej Grmovsek *Uncredited small photos by Peter Baumeister*

This year's lead articles on El Gigante had already made it to my editor's desk when an electronic bomb went off on my monitor. The following email arrived on March 7, 2003:

> **Subject:** *elimination of a rap-bolted route on Mexico's El Gigante*
> *Hello John!*
> *Maybe you have heard already something about El Gigante. It is an 800m wall. Onto it has been installed a 400-bolt sport-climbing route named Logical Progression. It is a desecration of that face. Worse, the German magazine Klettern printed an article implying support, calling the manner of ascent a "new style."*
> *With Nicholas Mailänder I am organizing the erasure of the bolts and would like international support. I would like opinion leaders to give moral support, while I myself will give financial support.*
> *Please let me know whether you would take part and whom else I could contact.*
>
> *Best regards,*
> *Alexander Huber*

It seemed that action might take place even before the *AAJ* went to press, before the controversy could be widely discussed. So I quickly wrote to a number of climbers familiar with Mexican climbing, with big walls around the world, and with the ethical issues involved in bolting. The following pages offer a sampling of the responses, all edited for clarity and brevity, but not intended to affect the ideas of the authors. I have tried to be unbiased in my editing and in the selection of climbers involved, though I must disclose that my personal ideology stresses tolerance over other issues in the debate, as explained in the Preface to this Journal. The following discussion seems particularly relevant coming as it does on the heels of the Tyrol Declaration, also published in this Journal.

JOHN HARLIN III, Editor

In general I'm against routes such as Logical Progression going up so early in an area's climbing history. But I'm also no fan of erasure. In the Black Canyon we have a strict no-rap-bolting tradition, but a history of routefinding and cleaning on rappel. Air Voyage, Stratosfear, and the Nose—three of the most adventurous free climbs in the canyon—used top-down tactics. Dangerous blocks and flakes were pried off and secret passages discovered. A multiday, heavily armed, stay-on-the-wall ground-up approach (such as has been used on "traditional" El Gigante climbs) also might have worked, but would not have added to the first-ascent adventure—both Air Voyage and Stratosfear were first climbed in a day, in committing, lightweight style. The recon of the Nose spent a long time discovering how best to connect two major weaknesses; the wall was eventually climbed employing a minimum number of bolts. I feel that a pure ground-up ascent would have resulted in more bolting, and an inferior and more difficult line.

How do you determine what constitutes the best style? Is ground-up always superior? In the Verdon Gorge it makes the best "mountaineering" sense—it's the most efficient, straightforward tactic—to approach

many objectives via rappel. You arrive at the top of the cliff, and there's no logical way up to many sectors from the Gorge bottom, save pointless bolt ladders, since many sectors are undercut by poor rock. Most Verdon routes were bolted on rappel, but many are highly adventurous. The local guidebooks have an "overbolted" symbol for routes with bolts spaced more closely than three meters. Thirty-foot runouts are common. The original style of rap-bolting made it a point to maximize the adventure of climbing in the Verdon. And given the approach to these routes from above, it seems to me that they were done in the best possible style—for Verdon. Unfortunately, rap-bolting seems to have deteriorated stylistically into "making routes safe," which I think is both false and misguided.

JEFF ACHEY, *March 19, 2003*

Jeff Achey is a widely traveled American climber who made the first ascents of the Free Nose on North Chasm View (AAJ 1997) and the Serpent, a free variation to the Dragon Route on the Painted Wall (AAJ 2000), both in the Black Canyon of the Gunnison.

I recently came back from Kenya, where we tried a ground-up first ascent on the 600-meter wall of Mt. Poi. We stopped after five pitches because the rock was too fragile for a ground-up first ascent. We instead climbed the rap-bolted Slovenian Route, which is just to the right of the American Route, also rap-bolted. It is a brilliant free climb, and we said, "Thank you very much," for the work and cleaning the Slovenians did. Rap-bolted first ascents on big walls are not what I am looking for, but we really enjoyed repeating such a route. Without the Slovenians' and Americans' efforts the only routes would be bushy corners climbed by British far to the right of the main wall. The rock of the main wall is just too fragile. In my opinion it would be sad if arrogant climbing police chopped these routes. Their creators invested a lot of energy and gave us something enjoyable to climb.

Kurt Albert on La Conjura de los Necios. Stefan Glowacz

When we did our ground-up first ascent on El Gigante, La Conjura de los Necios, we were fighting bad rock and vegetation, and did not enjoy the climbing so much—but it was a great adventure. After we fought our climb to the top, we repeated Subiendo el Arcoiris, a 300m wall to the left of the Cascada de Basaseachic, which was set up by rap-bolting. It is one the best climbs I have done, and we said, "Thank you very much, Peter and friends."

Variety in climbing is a good thing, and I enjoy everything: adventurous ground-up ascents, soloing, repeating rap-bolted routes. I dislike missionaries who want to tell me how to climb. I have ethics and dogmas, but only for myself. There are still new routes to do in the Candameña Cañon, possibilities for hair-raising ground-up first ascents. I think it would be better if those who arrogantly want to chop invested their energies in new routes, in that way leaving their vision of what they want climbing to be. It would be sad if great routes get chopped.

KURT ALBERT, *March 25, 2003*

Kurt Albert has been a leading German free-climber for over two decades, with major first ascents on five continents. His team made the first ascent of La Conjura de los Necios, the first free route on El Gigante (AAJ 2002, pp. 288-289).

If these ethical violations had been done in a U.S. national park, this climb would not be reported as a triumph. It is a common Mexican perception that many U.S. climbers (and tourists and spring-breakers) come here to do what they don't dare do in their home country.

RODULFO ARAUJO, *March 20, 2003*

Rodulfo Araujo is Director at Large of the Mexican Federation of Mountain Sports and Climbing.

Chopping bolts as a unilateral act leads to more resentment and more conflict. The way to deal with the bolt issue is through talk and education. I don't think you can say, "All bolts are bad," but I do believe that using natural protection gives a much better experience. The climber is attuned to the rock and its natural features, accepting them for what they are, rather than imposing his will upon them. On crags which have natural lines I believe blank spaces between those lines are best left blank until, you never know, someone is bold or good enough to climb them with whatever is there. There are crags, however, which either have a long tradition of bolted climbing or

Drilling anchors on Faded Glory.
Brent Edelen

have no natural protection, and I believe sport/pleasure climbers should be able to enjoy their version of the sport on these crags. What is needed is a dialogue between all users of the crags and mountains to understand each other's point of view, and to thrash out agreements that enable all of us to enjoy the mountains without damaging the environment or spoiling them for others.

SIR CHRISTIAN BONINGTON CBE, *April 1, 2003*

Chris Bonington was one of the leading British Alpinists of the 1960s and Himalayan climbers of the 1970s and '80s. At the age of 69 he continues to make at least an expedition each year. He was the closing speaker and a style-and-ethics working-group member at the 2002 Tyrol Declaration.

I feel that Logical Progression is a crime done to a beautiful wall. Carlos and I opened the first two routes on El Gigante, in 1998 and 1999. We also bolted 58 sport routes in the Rancho San Lorenzo, putting in hundreds of bolts—which appears to be the excuse for Logical Progression on El Gigante. However, our sport routes are 10 minutes from the road, are outside the park, and are 50 meters high, maximum. Even so, we bolted around 20 of them ground up, using hooks, because the rock is perfect for that.

I think there is a huge difference between our short routes and El Gigante. It isn't fair to shrink such a difficult wall by bolting it. Logical Progression is close to the wall's first route and eliminates the wall's adventure. El Gigante is not like El Capitan. The cracks are small, discontinuous, and difficult to protect. Loose blocks and dirt are part of the wall. We should change the nature of big walls as little as possible, even if most climbers will never be able to free the route. For me this discussion about how to climb new routes on big walls is like discussing the rules of an established game, such as football. It doesn't matter where you play; the rules are the same. That El Gigante is the biggest wall in Mexico, with world significance, should earn it respect as a ground for adventure.

Carlos Garcia and Cecilia Buil after Yawira Batú. Chris Giles

I favor erasing the bolts and will help if it happens. I have a special love for El Gigante as the place where I learned what a real wall is. To promote the Logical Progression type of route is to kill the spirit of adventure and to forget that strength of mind is the main tool for improvements in climbing. I think safe, bolted climbing is the base for becoming a good climber, but it has its place. As a lover of all types of climbing, I hope this place is clear in the climbing community.

CECILIA BUIL, *March 17, 2003*

Cecilia Buil, from Spain, is putting up new routes in Kyrgyzstan and elsewhere. Her climbs in the Basaseachic are documented in Carlos Garcia Ayala's lead story earlier in this Journal, in AAJ 1999 pp. 60–66, and in AAJ 2000 pp. 247–249.

Most Mexican big-wall climbers begin in Yosemite. There, everyone knows the "rule": no drilling unless there are no natural placements. If you drill bolts where others didn't, you are not prepared for that climb. Rock climbing is growing fast, and we must take care in which direction it moves. If there is a sport route on El Gigante, people are going to climb it, because it is safer and easier: no cams, hooks, pins—just quickdraws. Where is the challenge and charm of the big wall? It is important to respect the ethics and values of other countries, communities, and climbers. I am against this route, though not sure if it is a good idea to remove the bolts.

ARMANDO DATTOLI, *March 24, 2003*

Armando Dattoli , 34, is the rock-climbing commissioner of the Mexican Federation of Mountain Sports and Climbing. He has climbed El Cap three times, and also in the Alps, the Andes, and the Karakoram twice, including an ascent of the Trango Tower.

Basaseachic is a long way to travel just to chop some bolts. I bet Logical Progression is the best route there. My new route in the canyon, Soy Caliente, was ground-up power drilling and trad gear, a grungy adventure. The best thing that could happen is for someone to retro rap-bolt it and make it worthwhile. The climbing is similar to limestone: the worst rock is in the cracks where the pro is; the good climbing and rock has no pro. Soy Caliente went 90% free at 511+, with some A1. It could be straightened out with bolts to make a fun sport route—which would be a lot of work, though.

I like ground-up adventures and have never put up a true sport route, but I have nothing against a well-designed multipitch clip-up. Why does a rap-bolted sport route degrade the rock more than a ground-up route? If someone wants to put up a low-commitment, secure bolted route, I think that is great; there is room. Whoever gets onto the rock first can determine the style of the first ascent. Just don't go messing with established routes.

Would someone erase the dream, hard work, and fruition of Lucas et al's efforts? And deny climbers interested in repeating this route? Anyone can put up the remaining lines in trad style; then they won't become sport routes. Future generations will still have a vast reserve of unexplored rock. No need to ban bolts yet. If rap-bolters

Drilling down on Logical Progression. Luke Laeser

want to come to the Rockies, we have potential for HUGE top-down alpine sport routes for those willing to invest the time and money. I would love to repeat a sport route on some of the huge limestone or quartzite faces here, but there is no way I would put in the effort to create one.

SEAN EASTON, *May 2, 2003*

Sean Easton is a climbing guide from the Canadian Rockies who has established big, bold new routes in Baffin Island, Patagonia, Peru, Canada, Alaska, and Mexico. Soy Caliente is described in AAJ 2002, pp. 289–90.

Logical Progression is negative evolution. The challenge is to preserve the ethics of climbing big walls. The canyon offers the world a chance to enjoy and preserve it. Early ascents were made in good style. Other activities in the canyon, like the 50 sport routes and the two solo ascents alongside the Basaseachic Waterfall, were hard, because we had a strong background in climbing ethics. All routes were done from the ground-up; we hung from hooks when necessary for placing bolts. I demand respect for the principles of climbing. Respect for other climbers. I have a question about Logical Progression: Where is the challenge of climbing a big wall? Where is the opportunity for the next generation? Where is the progression? Stronger climbers need to push for better ascents

LUIS CARLOS GARCIA AYALA, *March 18, 2003*

Carlos Garcia, from Mexico City, with Cecelia Buil, discovered the climbing potential of the Parque Nacional de Basaseachic and made the first ascents of El Gigante. His lead article "El Gigante" appears earlier in this Journal. Garcia is perhaps the leading activist on Mexico's many newly discovered big walls.

El Gigante is unique. I have climbed many walls around the world, including walls in exotic places like Madagascar, vegetated walls like Norway's Kjerag, and very loose walls in the Slovenian Alps. But El Gigante is much more vegetated than anything else I climbed and extremely loose and rotten. I can understand the climbers who rappeled, cleaned the wall, and bolted what is probably a nice sport route.

I live in central Europe, where many Alpine walls have traditional routes, ground-up bolted routes, and rap-bolted routes. Walls are part of nature, and everybody has access to them, the

Andrej Grmovsek and Tanja Rojs celebrating their ascent of El Gigante. Andrej Grmovsek

same as rivers and lakes, which are used by fishermen, kayakers, and others. I don't like rap-bolting, because it gives me no adventure and no satisfaction. But I'm against chopping bolts, especially on Logical Progression. I think nobody has the right to destroy another's work, and rap-bolting was not prohibited when the route was made. Maybe the trick is to develop worldwide ethical regulations, which would tell young climbers that rap-bolting exotic and alpine walls is bad style.

I hope most climbers know the difference between ground-up free ascents, ground-up aid ascents, and rap-bolted ascents. The climbing media should report rap-bolted ascents critically, because they are a step back and not acceptable. It's a pity that some young climbers speak about their rap-bolted routes as the hardest free routes in the world. Such routes can't be compared with ground-up ascents. Rap-bolting is fitting the wall to your abilities, instead of fitting your abilities to the wall!

Finally, I must give my opinion about aid climbing on El Gigante. El Gigante's rhyolite is more featured than granite, where aid is sometimes the only way to climb thin cracks. Because of El Gigante's featured rock, aid climbing isn't the best style. La Conjura de los Necios and Simuchi share some pitches. The climbers on Simuchi drilled many bat-hook holes where relatively easy free climbing (5.11) is possible a few meters above good pro. Such aid climbing has to give way to free ascents.

ANDREJ GRMOVSEK, *April 13, 2003*

Andrej Grmovsek, a widely traveled young climber from Slovenia, made the second ascent of El Gigante's La Conjura de los Necios. See "Conspiracy of Fools" earlier in this Journal.

El Gigante has the features of an alpine face: size, remoteness, quality of rock. In the Alps, as in all mountain ranges, a ground-up ascent is considered the only acceptable way to establish a climb. This point of view is backed by paragraph 3 of the article on first ascents in the Tyrol Declaration: "In alpine regions, first ascents should be done exclusively on lead (no prefixing from above)."

The establishment of Logical Progression clearly challenges this international consensus and implicitly advocates a laissez-faire approach.

If the example set by Baumeister & Co. and publicized in *Klettern* is unopposed, there is a good chance it will lead to innumerable routes put up in the same style. This would rapidly diminish the potential for first ascents on all alpine faces and big walls. For instance, a team of 20 "route-setters" could reduce the time to put up—and equip—all climbs on the classic south face of the Schüsselkarspitze from nine decades to a month.

This would be in conflict with point 3 of Article 8 of the Tyrol Declaration: "Rock and mountains are a limited resource for adventure that must be shared by climbers with many interests and over many generations to come. We realize that future generations will need to find their own NEW adventures within this limited resource. We try to develop crags or mountains in a way that doesn't steal opportunity from the future." It is clear that people like Baumeister and his friends—under the guise of "tolerance"—are stealing projects from parties who are willing to stick to the slow and honest ground-up approach.

For this reason we are in favor of erasing Logical Progression. But the decision should lie with local Mexican climbers and their national climbing association. It would be a mistake if foreign climbers chopped the route.

The situation gives the international climbing community an excellent opportunity to thoroughly discuss the issue of legitimate styles of first ascents on alpine faces and big walls. This discussion could be organized by the UIAA and include leading rock climbers from the whole spectrum of the

El Gigante looming large. Brent Edelen

game. A decision in the case of Logical Progression vs. The Tradition of Climbing should be made only after all aspects of the problem have been discussed.

NICHOLAS MAILÄNDER & ALEXANDER HUBER, *April 17, 2003*

Nicholas Mailänder was one of the architects of the Tyrol Declaration and is a leading activist in access issues for climbing in Germany. Alexander Huber is one of today's top big-wall free climbers, with groundbreaking new routes in America and Europe. Both are German.

Alard Hüfner on Faded Glory. Brent Edelen

For that crag—El Gigante—I strongly disagree with the style in which Logical Progression was bolted. Four other routes had been opened ground-up. Why could Logical Progression not have been opened ground-up? It took about six weeks to bolt top-down. I think that in six weeks the team could have climbed it bottom-up. The route might not have been as perfect, but it could have been done. I think of Yosemite. If people abseiled down with power drills, there would be millions of bolts on El Cap.

To chop the route or not? That is the question. Yes, Logical Progression will see many more ascents than our route, Faded Glory, because it is bolted. But it was opened in a style that does not suit El Gigante. So I think the bolts should go. If we don't take a stand now, a hundred more routes could be bolted top-down on El Gigante. Where is the challenge? I believe we go to places like El Gigante to push our limits. I have pondered this decision for many months since my visit to El Gigante.

ALARD HÜFNER, *April 11, 2003*

Alard Hüfner, from South Africa, is a leading new-route activist throughout southern Africa, and specializes in big-wall climbing. He made the first ascent of Faded Glory on El Gigante, described earlier in this Journal.

Does it really matter how a sport climb is established? Our project was about making a path that will challenge all who attempt it. Bolting free climbs on lead requires making poor choices. For example, drilling bat-hook holes scars the rock, and placing a bolt in a certain place because it was all you could reach and being unable to know in advance if a section is the best choice for free climbing results in a weird, indecisive line. It's hard labor to bolt a big route, and when the wall is steep, you're hanging off gear or a rope either way, so going ground-up or top-down is a silly dispute; only the final product is important.

Luke Laeser (left) and Pete Baumeister. Bert van Lint

In 2001, before establishing Subiendo, we explored the canyons for other lines. We saw many potential great sport routes. The andesite, rhyolite, and welded tuff walls offer discontinuous, blocky, fractured systems—typically filled with bushes, grass, and cactus—but with clean faces to either side. Artificial climbing, where the rock must support only body weight, can force through any crap. A free climb, where you're grabbing the rock, requires a higher quality. The future of free climbing in this area lies on the faces, where the rock is featured and covered with pockets. By forcing a line into a natural weakness, one displaces plants with pitons. Placing a bolt on a face, so as to not disturb the flora and fauna that live in the cracks, is a more respectful gesture. Ponder this: Once a route has been bolted, it doesn't change. It's the same for every climber. Scars aren't growing, eroding, or being re-excavated by pins.

LUKE LAESER, *February 23, 2003*

Luke Laeser, from New Mexico, is a graphic designer at Climbing. *He established Subiendo el Arcoiris in 2001 (a 10-pitch rappel-bolted route on the Cascada Wall), and Logical Progression in 2002. See "Logical Progression," earlier in this Journal.*

Climbers are killing the sacred word Adventure, even on small cliffs close to Mexico City. There are climbers who, to improve the difficulty of a route, rappel from the top and install bolts or, worse, glue a piece of rock or chop holds. They believe they are the ultimate climbers, and have the right to "improve" the rock. They think that they can cheat because no one could climb the route another way. In Mexico it seems to be acceptable to climb this way. However, I also I think that our sport represents the last chances for Free Will and Free Living; these are the essence of climbing. So I do believe that the bolts installed on Logical Progression should be left in place. And that route will allow Mexican climbers to move from small sport cliffs to real adventure environments. It is a pity that Mexican climbers are now playing the sport in gyms and sport routes.

I read about the Dawn Wall on El Capitan, which Warren Harding climbed with many bolts. Royal Robbins chopped some of the bolts, but then decided to respect the line. I agree: I do not think that anyone has the right to remove bolts that other climbers have fixed. That is the way our sport has developed.

MARIO ANDRÉS OÑATE, *March 15, 2003*

Mario Andrés Oñate, of Mexico City, has been climbing for 35 years. He made his first trip to Yosemite in 1984 and has climbed El Cap three times. He mostly climbs cracks, and works as a guide on the Mexican volcanoes.

A rap-bolted route on El Gigante could have its place in the future, when most lines have been climbed on aid, from the ground up. But this is not the time for a rap-bolted route. There are so few lines on the cliff now, and Carlos Garcia and others have made such good efforts. They have climbed fairly and exposed themselves to the risks that ground-up and aid climbing involve.

Still, I don't see the point in chopping the route now that it is there. I do support a discussion between climbers interested in doing new routes in this area. If they decide the place should be for ground-up climbing only, that should absolutely be respected. If, after this kind of agreement has been reached, someone decides to put up a rap-bolted route, I do think the route should be chopped.

HÉCTOR PONCE DE LEÒN, *March 27, 2003*

Héctor Ponce de Leòn is a Mexican mountaineer with considerable experience in the Himalaya, Andes, and Alps. He says he is neither a sport climber nor a big-wall climber.

The name Logical Progression is brilliant—the climb was a logical next step by "modernists" in the attack on the classical mountaineering approach. The next logical progression would be to do the same thing on El Capitan, but why not add the "logical" step of chipping holds by quarrying the granite with hammer and chisel? One of the things we most love about climbing is the sense of freedom it gives. I believe anyone has the right to put up a route in any fashion he or she pleases. It follows that anyone else has the right to remove any route he or she pleases. I notice that those bold and visionary climbers who created Logical Progression didn't ask permission. Why do we need an international consensus to erase the route? If it is up to consensus, nothing will happen. One of the things I admired about Warren Harding, who was on the opposite side of the style debate from myself, is that it never occurred to him to suggest that I didn't have a perfect right to remove any bolts he had a perfect right to place. If the route is allowed to stand and we say politely that we don't like it and there shouldn't be more like it, more such routes will be established, if for no other reason than the pleasure of thumbing noses. I vote for erasing the route in question, but I believe that it won't be done. So I prefer to ignore what I have no control over, and concentrate on what I admire and respect: ground-up adventure climbing!

ROYAL ROBBINS, *May 2, 2003*

Royal Robbins was the leading Yosemite climber during its big-wall explosion of the 1960s, and was known for his strong stance on climbing style. In 1971 he began erasing Warren Harding's heavily bolted Dawn Wall route on El Capitan, but he stopped chopping after the first of five days on the route.

THE TREE OF LIFE

Los Tepuyeros and the Jungle Messiah at the birthplace of humanity.
A first ascent on Tepui Autana, deep into Venezuela.

TIM O'NEILL

Bongo riding with Hernando, Crispin, and José, on the Rio Autana, with The Tree of Life rising in the background. Henry Gonzales

The southeast aspect of Autana Tepui. Henry Gonzales

José Luis Pereyra, bearded, wearing a coarse poncho, stands beside the Merced River. Equal parts prophetic shaman and mathematician, extreme athlete and major slacker, he pushes his bare feet into the granular beach, takes a breath, and begins to read aloud. What follows is his description of his epic attempt on Autana Tepui, which took place several months before.

He speaks of plagues of insects, days of torrential rains, and an aborted effort due to snooping park guards, imminent starvation, and prolonged suffering. A small group of Camp IV vagabonds surrounds him. They hang on his words, hanging on them, as if clinging to a monstrous flank of granite. The narrative ends with José's words, "To be continued…," and a lingering pause seems to suggest an invitation for fresh recruits. My mind nervously begins to calculate the insect bites and the days of waterlogged existence trapped within the overwhelming jungle. I scan the others for any hint of enthusiasm towards the return expedition and I discern mainly stony countenances. Although the invite intrigues me, my flight instinct is stronger, and I decide, "Thanks but no thanks." As José said, "Out of the infinite possibilities some are offered, some are taken."

Did I take the offer or was I Jedi mind-tricked? It is mid-March 2002—five months after José's discourse alongside the Merced—nine of us are bound for the depths of the Orinocan jungle. The roster includes six all-star Venezuelan jungle-rats, Britain's unassuming gnarl couple, John and Anne Arran, and one skinny jokester from Philly (that would be me). We are cruising upriver in Lucho's bongo, a massive dugout canoe with a roaring 50-horsepower motor strapped to its rear. The left riverbank forms Colombia's border and Hernando jokes that a healthy Yank like me can fetch a few hundred bucks from the rebel army or, at the minimum, a carton of smokes. A mixture of exhaust, "monte" fumes, and Coca-Cola produces an intoxicating sense of wonderment.

Not only the pulsating jungle, but also my decision to become a member of José's Autana Tepui continuum amazes me. A week ago, I was in Henry's Caracas apartment, the headquarters of "Los Tepuyeros," stating that I was content with the last three months' adventures in South America, and I intended to fly home early. They knew, although I did not mention it, that hideous bug attacks and unrelenting rainstorms flooded my mind, due in large part to José's harrowing firsthand accounts. My vision of unabated suffering went like this: mix equal parts wasps, horse flies, and mosquitoes, slowly blend in an ocean of rain, then combine with a hyperactive imagination. Yield: two dozen nightmares.

Henry, laughing, offered me a brownie and opened a coffee-table book to a two-page spread of Autana. He reassured me with, "Tranquilo pana, es super impresionante." Impressive is right. It is Devil's Tower jacked on steroids meets Jurassic Park. José considered the 2,000-foot southwest face to be Venezuela's "greatest remaining challenge," and he once thought it impossible to climb in his lifetime. Even though I was afraid of the experience, insecure of the unknown, I was captivated, slowly drawn into their Tepuyero vortex. José sealed the deal when he poignantly told me, "Timmy we have a million wild horses inside, sometimes barely contained …there is no better outlet than climbing." Sometimes I feel José knows me better than I do. After 10 days in Venezuela's chaotic capital city, gathering food and equipment and assembling the remainder of our team, we left civilization in our wake. The improbable had occurred.

Ivan at the bow, ascending the crux rapid on the Rio Orinoco.

Lucho guns the engine, and the bongo goes into spawning mode. Employing a mixture of bravado and skill, he motors up the crux rapid, a series of boulders hungry for a bite of the hull or prop. Above the drop, we reload our portaged supplies and as I push the boat from the shore, one of my two-dollar flip-flops blows out. The fluted limestone I am standing on deeply gouges my sole and the blood flows as I belly flop over the gunwale. The grotesque flapper resembles a thick scoop of gouda cheese covered in raspberry sauce. Visions of jungle gangrene spreading up my leg—necessitating amputation—cause a wave of nausea to swamp me. A pertinent phrase from José's story echoes in my brain, "The jungle is ruthless with the weak."

Andre, the un-official expedition medic, finishes squeezing out "nigua" larvae from beneath the skin on the back of his hand, unwelcome guests he picked up a few weeks ago on Angel Falls. He wipes his fingers on his shorts, grabs my foot, and performs minor surgery using nail clippers and alcohol. A skilled physician is indispensable on these journeys. Swaying in a hammock beneath the bongo's thatched roof, my injury and heartbeat throb in unison, emulating the ancient rhythms between man and his environment. I watch the water slip by, wondering if my trip is over.

After two days in the bongo piloting the Rio Orinoco, the Sipapo tributary, and finishing on the Rio Autana, we disembark at Coño Manteco Seguera. The village's children, wild-eyed and barefoot, rush to meet our group. Strangers are a spectacle, especially white ones, and the two Brits are particularly pasty. The adults also descend to extend a warm welcome to those returning from last year. For Henry and José, this is their fourth visit to Seguera, and they recognize the village chieftain. They give him gifts of food, batteries, and clothing. We hang our hammocks, complete with bug netting, under a massive open-sided churuata and set up the dinner kitchen. Andre notes the low level of the river, and Crispin adds that the local Piaroas are experiencing drought conditions. Due to the lack of rainfall, the clouds of bugs experienced last season are, by comparison, nonexistent. Nonetheless, I am clothed head to toe, complete with a bit of bug juice, while the locals relax in shorts and tank tops. The childhood game "Which one doesn't belong" comes to mind.

In the morning, the team ferries across the river to the trailhead. I have decided to remain in Seguera a couple of days to allow my foot more time to heal. The others begin the arduous tasks of humping loads, establishing base camp and ultimately ABC at the base of the wall. They curse my absence as I lounge in my hammock, reading an elementary school book titled, El Rey de Katoran. At nine o'clock every evening the village's generator goes silent, the locals go back to their huts, and complete darkness descends. I close my bug net and fall asleep listening to the musical vibrations of the jungle and the river.

My foot has healed surprisingly fast, and I pack my things as my Piaroran guide Juan Pablo readies a small canoe. He is a cheerful boy of 15 and can speak enough Spanish to enable simple conversation, which mainly consists of him repeating whatever I say. "Asi es," or "It is what it is," becomes his instant favorite. We paddle across the river in the early morning mist and pull into the mouth of a narrow creek. I feel like an intrepid anthropologist in search of a lost race more than a climbing bum from Philly. Although it is important not to forget your roots, it is as vital to allow them to keep searching for deeper meaning.

Each of us hoists a heavy pack, and Juan Pablo leads the way with an occasional swing of his machete. The jungle is not as thick and impenetrable as I had imagined. It is more open, filled with light and continual jungle harmonies. José had told the story of the 11 days it had taken them to reach the base of the wall during last year's attempt. They even named each camp along the way in honor of the day's most voracious insect.

Andre Vancampenhoud relaxes on Double Decker Ledge. Henry Gonzales

Lucho, who runs a guide service in this area, thankfully established a new direct trail to the wall. Instead of multiple days hacking and thrashing through the jungle, it is now a mere five-hour hike. I cannot help but feel that I am drinking from the Lite-beer variety of the jungle experience, as it is far less grueling. Juan Pablo loses the faint trail at times but quickly regains it after locating a freshly chopped branch. The trees overhead obscure the wall, and a powerful desire to join the campaign draws me closer. I am three days behind and wonder what progress the team has accomplished.

Base camp is deserted. The only sounds are bird chatter and Juan Pablo picking through a pile of cans and small packets. The Piaroa diet is simple, mostly fish and ground palm nuts, with the occasional wild bird or turtle thrown in for variety. He shoots me a smile and snatches an apple-flavored breakfast bar. Blue tarps stretched tight shelter the hammocks from the daily afternoon deluges. Blue barrels protect the food from the humidity and furtive marauders. Every other color is a shade of green or brown, except for Autana. The white soaring walls are

like a canvas containing bold brushstrokes of salmon pink, purple, and orange. In Piaroa and Guahibo mythology, Autana is the remains of the tree of life, which connected the earth with the sky and fed the entire universe with its fruits. They believe this tree to be the birthplace of humanity.

Eventually Henry and several others come walking into base camp. They have just delivered the remainder of the wall food and stockpiled 50 liters of water at the base. They inform me that José and Crispin have jumared the fixed lines to the top of pitch nine, last year's highpoint, and have already added two new pitches. The Arrans are below them, in the midst of their audacious plan to free climb the wall. Andre goes into an animated account of John's ballsy, gritstone–style lead of the first pitch, "No pro, dude, it was amazing, and if he fell, broken legs for sure." Andre would know, as he is the Tepuyero authority on broken legs and heinous evacuations.

During a 1998 attempt of Acopan Tepui with José, Scott Lazar fell 60 feet and fractured both legs, including a horrible compound of his right tib-fib. Andre carried him out, on his back, for five hours. He then ran 30 kilometers, returned in a helicopter, and essentially ensured that Lazar would not lose his badly infected leg.

Perhaps he was returning an act of   John Arran cruising 5.11 on pitch 18. Tim O'Neill

José Pereyra getting primitive on pitch 17. Tim O'Neill

kindness granted to him in 1994. It was on Kukenam Tepui, in the midst of a first ascent, that Andre fell 50 feet after dislodging a boulder. He destroyed his knee and compound fractured his ankle. His partner, Sebastian, piggybacked him to safety for three hours, marathoned 40 kilometers, and returned with a helicopter. Both Scott and Andre have permanent hardware in their legs. José's words flash through my head, "The jungle teaches with blood and steel."

That night Henry radios the upper team and discovers that Crispin is ill. Over the last two days he has been getting progressively weaker and is now unable to eat. Henry thinks it may be hepatitis. The frogs are indifferent and serenade us to sleep. In the morning I jumar up to replace Crispin, as his illness has become too debilitating. As he descends, I think about the possibility of contracting his sickness. When I see his fatigued yellow eyes and down-turned mouth, I reach out for his daisy chain and clip him into our shared anchor. We exchange goodbyes and a handshake and I watch him slowly disappear into the jungle canopy. That same day Lucho and Crispin hike out to the bongo and motor downriver as quickly as possible to Puerto Ayacucho. The following morning Crispin takes a flight back to Caracas, where a hospital visit confirms hep. A. He spends three days in treatment and the next year recovering. Lucho's trip also ends prematurely, due to his selfless decision to transport his ill friend back to civilization.

Before continuing up the fixed lines, I vigorously rub my hands on the abrasive wall to "sterilize" them, as water weighs a precious eight pounds per gallon, and anyway, who brings soap on a big wall? Hernando and Andre are busy below hauling water and food in order to re-supply the Arrans and stock up Autana Spire. I tow a haul bag, with enough rations and water for two for the next five days. The rock looks ideal, and the climbing connects various sizes of cracks with well-featured face. John has freed eight pitches so far, all on-sight, and seems to be unstoppable. As I approach the anchor, I hear a few subtle grunts above and look up as John, "la Maquina" ("the machine"), proudly completes his first required red-point, a 5.13 with a 100-foot fall potential.

The distinct British tendency to risk life and limb in pursuit of a pure ascent intrigues me. For example, their grading system incorporates not only a route's technical and strength requirements, but also the likelihood of a hospital/morgue visit. It must be something about living on an island with such a finite amount of climbing. Whatever the reasons, they generally have nerves of steel, and they perform well under extreme duress. In fact, John is so tranquil I offer to check for a pulse as I jug past.

José is peacefully napping when I reach him. I finish the haul and insert myself in one of two small caves that are like eyes peering out into the void. Two hammocks hang in front of them, like eyelids. On the floor of the cave, enormous prehistoric cockroaches scurry my way, freaking me out. They have lived here for millennia without encountering humans, and my guess is they will be around long after humankind disappears entirely. Our vantage point provides incredible views of the Orinocan jungle stretching out to the horizon, a vast carpet of green life that some describe as the earths' verdant lungs.

We are about half way up the formation. A fixed line snakes above, suspended about 10 feet from the wall. Amazingly clean rock that overhangs at least 50 feet in the last 500 protects us from the daily thunderstorms. José prepares the rack as I slip into my climbing shoes before launching onto my first lead into the untouched, the unknown. The team has been making slow but steady progress using siege-style tactics. On lead, I fully experience the texture and hardness of the sandstone. In places, calcium precipitate covers the wall, and quartz crystals emerge. The vegetation also takes on new meaning. At the end of the pitch, I drill a two-bolt anchor, and as I adjust my position, I inadvertently poke a spike from a "wall cabbage" into my ear. Luckily, it miss my eardrum.

The plants' shallow roots grip well on the dry, steep wall, but only a few meters away things are wet and about to get funky. John jumars up from below and swings into the lead. He tension traverses to the left, then face climbs across soaking rock, placing natural pro in excavated cracks and pockets. This is the end of the steep primo rock and the beginning of the lower angle "Welcome to the Jungle" fun and games. John places a natural anchor and brings me over. The next 50 feet is running with water and as I maneuver up, I peel off layers of vegetation to reveal horizontal cracks. I free and aid slowly, placing marginal cams. Thunderclaps rip the clouds open, releasing torrential rain. We rappel back to the dry Cave Bivy, where José and Anne are having a transcendental discussion about quantum mechanics and the afterlife.

The following morning, the Arrans descend to redpoint the crux 5.13b pitch, 40 feet of super-technical stemming and laybacking with a potential ledge fall. José and I jumar to the high point, and as I prepare for round two on my lead, John's yell from below signals his success. The sun does not reach us until late in the day, and the waterfall dripping on my head chills me. I am sketched out, and as I weight a flared Alien it pops and I daisy-whip onto a lower piece. My finger smashes and my groin feels like I just ripped out most of pubic hair. At the end of the pitch, I peel large sections of plants and dirt off the wall like a sardine tin lid. They soar through the air, acting as Orinocan flying carpets.

At the end of my lead, I attempt in vain to gain a slimy, garden-filled ledge. José, a veteran of many tepui first ascents, yells up and tells me to take off my boots and socks in order to negotiate the traverse. Bugs wriggle between my toes and I know that by tooth or toenail, we are going to the top. I slam in a couple of bolts as José comes up. He grabs the rack and traverses to the left barefoot, aping his best jungle messiah. The setting is surreal, over 1,000 feet up on the side of an island in the sky, and there's "Pepe" out there getting primitive. John joins us for

José Pereyra, the Jungle Messiah, stylin' his final pitch. Tim O'Neill

another of his exemplary leads, and we complete five new pitches, a banner tepui day. Henry, Hernando, and Andre have committed to the wall as we only have a few pitches left to gain the top.

The rain is pouring so hard it feels like we are going to drown standing up. José and I huddle together under a tiny tarp a few feet below the remarkable summit mantle. Fortunately, I completed the final 5.4 slab and slammed in two bolts just before thunder tore open the sky and turned the place into water world. Lightening flashes around us, so close I wonder if it hit anyone below. Andre appears unscathed, followed in kind by the rest. John made the final move as the storm unleashed, completing 21 free pitches, in an impressively deter-mined effort. Somehow, Henry and Anne brew up a pot of celebratory hot Nescafe. We cluster together, sharing body heat, drinking from a communal mug and from the experience of a lifetime.

The summit is level save for a small hill, which we bypass on our way to the East Face descent. The ground is spongy and covered with thousands of funnel shaped bromeliads and several types of carnivorous plants. It is dark; we are all soaked to the bone and the descent proves too elusive. We return to the flat, rock slabs near our top-out point and hastily erect a huge, semicircular stone windbreak. The clouds open, unveiling a brilliant full moon, and as José powers up the Manu Chao disc, Hernando begins to dance. We all follow his lead.

The next day we rappel the opposite side of the formation and fix five ropes to gain a broad, wooded ledge that leads to a setting so sublime it captures you. An ancient river has carved a series of colossal columns and channels that actually pierce the entire formation. Day-light permeates through several 100-foot tall, gaping mouths. Sun shines on the cave's solitary tree, whose single-sided branches bend toward its touch. Henry regards it as Autana Tree, the tree within the Tree of Life.

We spend two days and nights within the cavern simply being. I sense that the wisdom and beauty discovered on this trip will resonate within me for the remainder of my life. After a meager breakfast on the second day, José and I recline on top of a flat angular boulder gazing up. The massive ceiling of the main chamber has astonishingly perfect, concentric circles that descend to a principal point, and to José's words, "Tepuis are where it all began, this humanity chapter, the thirst for beauty, for intensity." Serenity and sweat exude from every pore.

In January of 2003, José Luis Pereyra died from injuries sustained in a fall while climbing in Mexico. He was 40 years old. He enlightened us with his expressive hands and expansive mind. He was a funny, compassionate, philosopher who always lived in the moment. His spirit continues to climb tepuis and his words live on, "The fire rages, knowledge wins again."

The giant cave, where it's good to simply be. Tim O'Neill

SUMMARY OF STATISTICS

AREA: Venezuela, 400 miles south of Caracas.

ASCENT: Autana Tepui, 2,400', 25 pitches. Aided and freed (511+A2) by Hernando Arnal, Anne Arran, Ivan Calderon, Henry Gonzales, Tim O'Neill, José Pereyra, Xavier Potronco (2001), and Andre Vancampenhoud. Freed by John Arran (one pitch of 5.13b, two of 5.13a, two of mid-5.12, most of the rest at 5.11). March, 2002.

A NOTE ABOUT THE AUTHOR

Tim O'Neill, percussionist and comedian, climbs because it provides an engaging outlet for his attention-deficit affected mind and body. The focus, commitment, and athleticism required to ascend big walls, from Patagonia's Torre Egger, to record-setting speed ascents of Yosemite's walls, to jungle tepuis, nourish his soul. He dedicates the above story to José, "El Maestro."

THE SABER

A pitch a day and bone-numbing cold define the first two routes on the north face of Gora Sablya, the biggest wall in the northern Urals, Russia.

BY KONSTANTIN BEKETOV

Base camp under the east flank of the Saber. Konstantin Beketov

Nowhere is the frontier of Europe more clearly expressed than in the east, where the Ural mountain range separates Europe from the Siberian expanses. The narrow range stretches south to north across 2,400 kilometers, extending from the steppes to the shores of the Arctic Ocean.

In general the Urals are low, gently sloping mountains, and only near the Arctic Circle does the range become interesting for alpinists. This is where the highest part of the entire mountain system is located, including its highest elevation, Gora Narodnaya (the People's Peak), at 1,894 meters (6,214'). Regardless of their moderate altitudes, the mountains have a stern appearance because they are subject to polar weather. The valley bottoms certainly are low, but the peaks themselves rise more than a kilometer.

Several peaks of the far-northern Urals end abruptly with real walls, sharply contrasting with the general appearance of these ancient, eroded mountains. For the

The team leader Kirill Korabel'nikov on belay low on the wall.
Tatyana Parfishina

climber, the most interesting target of these peaks is Gora Sablya (The Saber), located on the European side of the range. At 1,497 meters, its eastern side is characterized by steep walls. Precisely because of its terrifying appearance, this mountain has earned its name (for indeed, Sablya has the look of sharp, cold steel).

The far-northern Urals began to attract the attention of travelers and sportsmen in the 1960s. Now each year several dozen groups and individual adventure-seekers undertake journeys on skis, on foot, or by traveling along the rivers. One can get to these mountains from the cities and villages that are strung out along the railway line connecting Vorkuta with the cities of central Russia. Pechora, which has an airport, is the most convenient place to begin one's travels. From Pechora to the mountains there still lie about 70 kilometers of taiga and swamps, which can be avoided by helicopter, in the winter on snowmobiles, or by going under one's own steam.

The Ekaterinburg team with Blinov, Kofanov, and their tent platform in the upper part of the wall.
Kirill Korabel'nikov

The climate of the far-northern Urals is severe: protracted, snowy winters and hot summers with an abundance of mosquitoes. The weather is unstable; snow may fall in the mountains during any summer month, and in the winter occasional warm winds increase the danger of avalanches. The coldest month is January, when frosts can reach –55°C (–67°F). And in July the temperature can climb to 35°C (95°F).

The sub-range in which Sablya is located stretches south to north some 25 kilometers (15 mi.). The western slopes of the range rise above a swampy plain and foothills covered with larches. From this side the approach to Sablya is relatively uncomplicated and can be accomplished without special equipment, especially during the summer. The eastern escarpment is the precise opposite, however; along its entire length

The Saber's routes from the east, from left to right: east buttress (Beketov-Shamalo, 2000); Ladoga, leader Korabel'nikov, 2002 (center of the northeast wall); leader V. Puchnin, 2002. *Tatyana Parfishina*

it is sliced by glacial cirques with sheer walls, small emerald lakes, and a chaos of moraines. Below and northeast of the peak sprawls the Hoffman Glacier. On its eastern side Sablya has two interesting walls, a southeastern face and a northeastern face; both rise more than 800 meters.

The history of taming Sablya's walls is short but fascinating. It is not known for certain who was the first to reach the summit, but many ascents, including winter ascents, have been successfully completed over the last 40 years. Until recently, however, no one had attempted an ascent from the eastern side.

On August 7-8, 1992, alpinists from Perm climbed the southeastern wall via its central chimney, estimating the difficulty at 5A-5B on the Russian scale. Eight years later, Valery Shamalo, famous in Russia for his extreme routes, and I tried to solve the problem of the northeastern wall. Not wanting (and not having the financial means) to use an airplane, we adhered to the style of real exploratory expeditions. But ahead of us lay a long approach on foot through rough terrain with a massive amount of equipment. It would be a complicated ascent without any support whatsoever; and then we would have to float back on a river to the railway. We had to conserve our funds in every way possible, and on the wall we felt the lack of equipment. Consequently we had to abandon the northeastern wall and switch over to an eastern buttress.

Vladimir Baranov jugging above the first tent platform. Konstantin Beketov

On July 9, 2000, we climbed the buttress and rated it as 4B. But the most challenging wall of the Urals remained unconquered.

In April 2002, alpinists from St. Petersburg, Ekaterinburg, and Perm decided to pool their resources in order to definitively solve the "northeast problem." This time we availed ourselves of a helicopter, especially because the winter conditions demanded a great deal of equipment.

Our two teams (St. Petersburg and Ekaterinburg had joined forces) established base camp on the shore of a lake below the tongue of the Hoffman Glacier. We had to surround our tents with snow walls because of the frequent strong winds. In the background, Sablya rose like a terrifying black obelisk (one of the Perm alpinists confessed that when he first saw the wall, he wanted to leap back into the helicopter). We decided that both expeditions would work from the same common base camp: the Petersburg team would attempt the center of the wall, while the Perm group would go to the right.

The first five pitches of our route ascended a steep slope with outcroppings of rock, and then

After the climb came the snowmobiles. But the temperature rose, the snow turned to mush, and the machines frequently failed. Tatyana Parfishina

the line went straight upward, without compromise. Our progress wasn't great—about one pitch a day—because of the continuous aid climbing. There was very little definition in the middle part of the wall; the cracks were filled with ice or frozen soil. The snow sticking to the underside of overhangs took its toll on our nerves—such conditions apparently occur when the wind blows upward. Sections of shattered rock in the middle part of the wall posed a great danger, and although we were trying to climb carefully, now and then rocks fell. Clearly showing the steepness of the wall, the rocks did not touch the cliff face before hitting the glacier. One other problem was routefinding. From a distance the route had been obvious, especially when viewed through binoculars, but once we were on the climb, we lost our orientation. Therefore we adopted the tactic of constant communication via walkie-talkie. But even this

The game warden of Grigory Batula National Park, who helped considerably in the climbers' escape from the rapidly melting snowpack. *Tatyana Parfishina*

did not save us from several mistakes.

It usually took about an hour to reach the wall from base camp, so we placed an advanced camp closer, on a snowslope right below the wall. There, in a tent, we kept much of our gear for the first section of our climb.

Working on the wall had little romantic appeal. This was especially clear in the evenings at base, when, after the standard radio message—"We are coming home; hope dinner is ready"— the climbers arrived in camp the same way as factory workers returning from their shift. Only foul weather and visits to neighboring tents brought diversity to the dull routine.

When we had fixed about a dozen ropes, we felt it was time to "take off." Wonderful weather had set in, rather astonishing for the northern region, but in the shadows the temperature hovered around the freezing point. Yet the sun was glaring brightly. The upper part of the wall, which during the winter is usually covered with a layer of hoarfrost, thawed out, and the speed of the team abruptly increased. Free climbing became possible.

On April 18, during our usual radio session, we estimated that there were but five rope-lengths to go. It was now clear that our St. Petersburg team would reach the summit the next day, about the same time as the Perm team would.

On April 19, we met on the summit of the Saber after having climbed the two most complex routes in the Urals. But from here we again split off in different directions: our group began to descend our ascent route, while the Perm climbers decided to head back by an easier route on the other side of the range.

After our descent we had to hurry: we were supposed to head back to civilization on snowmobiles by April 19, by agreement with the national park rangers. Spring had arrived, and on the plains the rain began falling. The snow quickly soaked up the moisture, and the snow-mobiles lost traction. The ice on the rivers began to break up and we had difficulty getting across them. That 70-kilometer route—which just a week before our snowmobiles, fully loaded with all our equipment, could have traveled in three hours—took us three days to negotiate.

Translation by Henry Pickford, with additions by Otto Chketiani

SUMMARY OF STATISTICS:

AREA: Russia, northern Urals

ASCENTS: The Ladoga route on Sablya (The Saber) (820m, Russian grade VI). 10 days for the climb. Kirill Korabel'nikov (team leader), Gennady Blinov (died in the Caucasus, summer 2002), Sergey Kofanov, Vladimir Baranov, Alexey Gorbatenkov, Konstantin Beketov. Auxiliary group: Tatyana Parfishina (photographer), Julia Terpugova (radio communication).

Structure of the Perm command: Vyacheslav Puchnin (leader), Vladimir Malofeev, Juryi Zaitsev

The joint Petersburg-Ekaterinburg "command" took second place in the Russian 2002 mountain climbing championship for this climb, while the Perm team took third place.

A NOTE ON THE AUTHOR

Born in 1971 in Saint Petersburg, Konstantin Beketov has a degree in geography from Saint Petersburg University. He has been traveling since 1983, and made his first trip to the mountains in 1986. He feels his greatest achievements were as a leader and organizer of several difficult ski expeditions: Sayany (Siberia), Russian-Mongolian Altay (reported in this year's Climbs And Expeditions), Touva-Eastern Altay. He is the Russian ski-mountaineering champion (2003). Single, he works as a web editor.

ARWA TOWER, SPIRE, AND CREST

When the weather gods smiled: two perfect weeks in the Indian Garhwal with the French High Mountain Military Group.

BY ANTOINE DE CHOUDENS

The Arwa Tower's northwest buttress, showing the French Route (left) from 2002, and the Fowler-Sustad, 1999.

Last spring, eight of us from the French High Mountain Military Group (GMHM), inspired by Mick Fowler's pictures of Arwa Tower, went on an expedition to the Indian Garhwal. Our team—Thomas Faucheur, Philippe Renard, Laurent Miston, François Savary, Grégory Muffat Joly, Emmanuel Pellissier, Dimitry Munoz, and I—was blessed with the best weather any of us had ever seen in the Himalaya. We could climb as much as we wanted—and we did! We successfully climbed a new route on the Arwa Crest, and made two ascents each of Arwa Tower and Arwa Spire, including a new route on the Tower.

We left France near the end of April. After flying to Delhi, we took a bus to Joshimath, a small town in the mountains, where we had an exasperating struggle getting government authorization to continue. Because Arwa Tower and Arwa Spire are in a restricted area near the Chinese border, we had to overcome a lot of red tape just to reach base camp.

A little further on, just before the village of Badrinath (famous for its hot springs), the road was still

Snow climbing on the north face of Arwa Crest.
Antoine de Choudens

buried under the snow from winter avalanches. At that point, we put the porters to work and started walking. We ended up spending the night in a deserted bus station, but not before taking a delightful bath in the hot springs, with snow gently falling on our heads, which helped us relax and forget about our hassles with the authorities.

The next day, we obtained our final authorization to continue from the military camp at Mana. Then we began a long trek through fog and through snow that was unusually deep for that time of year. At 3,700 meters, the hard snow was still almost a meter deep (three years ago, at Shivling base camp, there was absolutely no snow, even at 4,300 meters).

Before long, most of the porters became frightened of avalanches and deserted us. The few who remained had to make many trips back and forth, and it took eight days for some of our loads to get to our base camp at 4,350 meters (it should have taken just two days). But looking at the bright side, this gave us plenty of time to acclimatize. Finally, on May 6, the last of the loads made it to base camp.

During the first few days of sunny weather we put in an advanced camp on the glacier, near Arwa Tower, at 5,100 meters. Then we spent a few days doing some warm-up climbing:

François and Manu ascended a gully near camp, while some of us skied to the bottom of Arwa Spire and climbed a summit that sat out in front of it.

On May 10, a party of four—Philippe, Gregory, Laurent and myself—did a wonderful mixed route to 6,196 meters on the Arwa Crest, left of the Tower (TD, 1,100m). We were helped by technology that day. At the bottom of the face it was very dark and we couldn't find the beginning of the route. Fortunately, we had a digital video camera with us and only had to look at the film to find the good way!

The very same day, François and Manu climbed a couloir on the same side of the Tower, then reached 6,100 meters (the needle-like tower) on the east ridge. But when they encountered some enormous gendarmes up there, they decided to rappel back to the foot of the south face for the night. The next day, they climbed a pleasant gully up the south face, reaching the summit of Arwa Tower.

During that time, Thomas and Dimitry attempted the west ridge of the Tower, reaching 6,100 meters.

On May 14, two parties of two—Manu and François, plus Thomas and Philippe—began a climb of the east ridge of Arwa Spire (the English Route, taken by the first Arwa Spire ascent party in 2000). The first pair reached the top the next day, while the second team made it on the 16th.

Meanwhile, our four-man team—Dimitry, Gregory, Laurent, and myself—were on the northwest buttress of the Tower. Though we had brought our portaledges along, we abandoned them on a ledge after the first two pitches. We began with two "climbers" and two "porters" (carrying the loads), with plans to switch roles on the second day, but then decided to go for the summit in one push. After climbing 600 meters up a perfect granite pyramid in 14 pitches (6b), we reached the summit of Arwa Tower, and named the route Pilier Guilhem Chaffiol, after our friend who had died during the 2002 Mountain Guide Stage. During the climb we found exceptionally good and dry rock. It was a succession of slabs and cracks, and we only had to use pitons for the belays. We bivied on a very small ledge, where three of us sat slipping on a slab with no pads. The morning was so cold that we had to wait for the sun before putting on our rock shoes (free climbing was very important for us!). The most difficult pitch was a superb parallel hand crack on a smooth shield, encountered on the second day. In the middle of the afternoon we reached the top of Arwa tower. What a great satisfaction it was for us to have freed the entire route! We stayed a long time to savor our pleasure.

While we were making all of these ascents, there was not a cloud in the sky. In the resulting snowmelt, rocks fell from the moraine above base camp, night and day. Some of our tents were drowned by the swelling river. Our gear became soaked, but fortunately nothing was lost.

With 15 days of sunny weather, our expedition went so perfectly that it seemed like it was a dream. This area is perfect for alpine-style first ascents and for ski touring, with magnificent scenery, including awesome views of huge neighboring mountains like Kamet, Nilkanth, and Chaukamba.

THE FRENCH HIGH MOUNTAIN MILITARY GROUP (GMHM)—A BRIEF HISTORY

("Who are those guys?"—Butch Cassidy)

As far as we know, only the French Army maintains a cadre like ours. Though other armies sometimes make similar expeditions, they usually do so by forming special groups, which are disbanded afterward.

The elegant, endless east ridge of the Arwa Spire. Antoine de Choudens

Based in Chamonix, the GMHM (Group Militaire de Hautes Montagnes) was founded in 1976 by Jean Claude Marmier, a famous French climber. Our primary mission is to develop and maintain a mastery of extreme alpine conditions—high altitudes and low temperatures—and to promote the French Army. We conduct exercises in mountains and ice deserts throughout the world, while performing medical, nutritional, and equipment experiments in order to assure that the French Army maintains a special, permanent group of elite alpinists. The GMHM has strong ties with the high mountain military school, and each year we provide instructors for its top levels. The French army maintains a few high level athletes from various disciplines in its ranks, including skiers, paragliders, and triathletes. The GMHM is a good organization to help some French alpinists.

In the beginning, the GMHM made many first winter ascents in the Alps. Our first expedition outside of France took place in the Ketil region of Greenland, in 1978. Three years later, we made an unsuccessful attempt on Mt. Everest, from the Tibetan side, and helped show the world that Everest's north ridge was not the easiest way to reach the top.

For the next 12 years, we made many expeditions to Peru, Alaska, and the Himalaya. We had our greatest successes on Gyachungkang, Lhotse Shar, and Kamet. In 1993, we went back to Everest, and climbed it from Nepal. The next year, Alain Estève (our chief), decided to change our emphasis, and we began a five-year exploration of the polar deserts. We developed

California dreaming? Finding wired bliss on Arwa Tower's north-west buttress. Antoine de Choudens

our knowledge and experience for this type of trip by going to the Canadian North, first to Ellesmere Island, to walk on the ice pack, and then to Baffin Island in the winter. We found out how to live when the temperature drops to -40°C. Our next test was to cross Greenland, unsupported. In 1995, our 1,000-kilometer trek from Ammassalik to Upernavik was excellent preparation for what would be our biggest project: the North and South Poles.

The trip to the North Pole, in 1996, was the hardest of the two. For 55 days, we walked across the ice pack, covering 1,000 kilometers. We spent day after day climbing up and down compression ridges, and crossing open arms of frigid water. At first, we pulled a 130-kilogram sledge. The last 15 days, we walked more than 10 hours each day—when we finally arrived at the pole, we were out of food, but had completed the journey on our own, without any support. Going to the South Pole wasn't as difficult, but it was longer—we took 50 days to cover 1,300 kilometers. For three of us (François Bernard, Antoine Cayrol, and myself), it wound up as a "Three Poles Challenge" (Everest and the two Poles).

In 1999, the GMHM went to India and did the third ascent of Shivling's east ridge. Then, in the Indian Mountaineer, we saw that incredible Mick Fowler photo of Arwa Tower, and we were gone—we felt we had no choice but to go for that awesome mountain.

To train for big wall climbing, we first went to Yosemite, in the fall of 2000. Six months later, we flew to Baffin Island's Eastern Fjords, where we put up a new route on a wonderful peak that we called "Alain Estève Peak," in memory of our late chief (who had died in a fall, ice climbing in Norway). Our new route was 1,000 meters high, and all the pitches were freed, up to 7c.

Then, we were ready for the Indian Garhwal.

SUMMARY OF STATISTICS:

AREA: Indian Garhwal, Arwa Valley

ASCENTS:

Arwa Crest: north face, first ascent of the French Route (1,100m,TD M5). Philippe Renard, Grégory Muffat Joly, Laurent Miston, and Antoine de Choudens. May 10, 2002.

Arwa Tower: south face, first ascent of the French Route (500m, 4c M5 80°). May 11, 2002. This is the south face gully, approached from the north face of the needle tower on the east shoulder of Arwa Tower. Emmanuel Pellissier and François Savary.

Needle Tower: first ascent of the French Route (900m, 5a M4 80°). Emmanuel Pellissier and François Savary. May 10, 2002.

Arwa Spire: east ridge, third ascent of the English Route (600m,TD), Emmanuel Pellissier and François Savary. May 15, 2002.

East ridge, fourth ascent of the English Route, Philippe Renard and Thomas Faucheur. May 16, 2002.

Arwa Tower: northwest buttress, first ascent of Pilier Guilhem Chaffiol (550m, 14 pitches, 6b). Dimitry Munoz, Grégory Muffat Joly, Laurent Miston, and Antoine de Choudens. May 16, 2002.

Born in France in 1969, Antoine de Choudens lives in Gieres near Grenoble, France. He is married with no children. He has an engineering diploma, is a mountain guide and ski instructor, and has been with the GMHM since 1994. His first climbs were in the Alps in the 1980s, and some of his highlights in cold places include: Korjenevskaia Peak (7,105m) in the Pamir (1992), the North Pole unsupported from Siberia in 55 days (1996), Everest without supplemental oxygen (1997), new routes on virgin peaks in Antarctica (1997), the South Pole unsupported in 50 days (1998/99), Shivling's east ridge (1999), big walls in Baffin Island's eastern fjords (2001), and Minya Konka (2002).

The GMHM team at the South Pole in 1999. Antoine de Choudens is standing in the upper right (before the American flag).

ARWA SPIRE

Spicy granite on pointed peaks—two amazing routes on the stunning north faces of Arwa Spire's main and west peaks, in India's Garhwal Himalaya.

BY STEPHAN HARVEY

The stunning north faces of Arwa Spire, showing the central and west summits from the north. The English Route (2000) follows the east (left) ridge, while the two Swiss routes are shown, with Fior di Vite heading toward the main summit and Capsico leading to the west summit. Bruno Hasler

The graceful, sky-scraping granite monoliths known as Arwa Tower and Arwa Spire have excited every climber who has seen their photographs, like the one on the cover of the *American Alpine Journal* (2000). That picture was taken during the 1999 first ascent of Arwa Tower, by Mick Fowler and Steve Sustad. The same year, another team tried to climb Arwa Spire, and the next year, British climbers Andy and Pete Benson climbed the slightly lower east peak, following two attempts on the north face.

The beauty of these peaks and the unclimbed north face of Arwa Spire lured Bruno Hasler, Roger Schäli, and me to the Garhwal Himalaya in May, 2002. We began with a three-day bus trip from Delhi to Badrinath. We finally reached base camp, at 4,660 meters, after two more days on foot. But problems with the porters—only half of them showed up, then they went on strike, and loads were lost along the way—cost us some time and energy. Then, after a hard last day of trekking, Roger seemed to be suffering from pulmonary edema. So we went back to Joshimath for four days of rest. Bruno stayed at base camp with our cook, Suraj, hoping we would show up soon, because the weather stayed sunny and warm the whole time.

Stephan Harvey in the couloir on Fior di Vite. The couloir divides the east from the central pillars on Arwa Spire. Bruno Hasler

One week later, Roger had recovered, and we returned to make another approach to Arwa Spire. Thus far, we hadn't even seen it yet.

Finally, after 16 days, Arwa Spire appeared: the granite monolith seemed to rise up out of a moraine as we walked closer, revealing more of its huge size with each advancing step through the rubble. The three pillars on the north face looked impressive, to put it mildly. After another

The bivouac on Fior di Vite. Two people slept in the portaledge, while one person used a hidden snow cave.
Bruno Harvey

three hours of dragging loads, we reached a perfect place for advanced base camp (ABC), at 5,400 meters, on a rock island opposite the north face of the Spire. The rest of the day we just ogled the wall, looking for the best line. We settled on the central pillar, where a potential line followed a snow and ice gully, then went to the right across a rock shield, to reach a snowfield. From the snowfield, it looked like it would be easy to reach the pillar, where 250 meters of hard rock climbing awaited us. But first, we had to return to base camp for more loads. It only took us a fun 30-minutes to ski back down the glacier that it had taken six hours to climb. After all the loads had been brought up to ABC, we started climbing the snow and ice gully. We had intended to drop gear at the top of the gully, but of course the sunny weather began to deteriorate just as we began to climb (Murphy's Law?). So we returned to base and waited for three days, enjoying Suraj's delicious meals.

Finally, the weather improved and we walked back up to ABC. The next day, we climbed the snow and ice gully, again, to our first real challenge: the rock shield. The rock was so wet that we had to climb it on aid (A2). Then we reached the snowfield, and found a safe place for our bivouac. While Bruno and Roger fixed ropes for the following day, I prepared our "suite" for the night. The next day, we followed the fixed ropes and began climbing the central pillar. The cracks were often filled with snow, and we had to clean them out before they were any good for jamming or placing pro. The climbing on the pillar was exposed, and mostly aid. After four pitches of hard work, we reached a snow ledge. Then we made an easy traverse to the right, and at 6 p.m. became the first to stand on the summit of the main peak of Arwa Spire. One after another, we mounted the summit needle—there was only room on top for one at a time. After

Reporting for the morning shift. Roger Schäli jumaring past a granite flake on Capsico, on Arwa's west summit.
Bruno Harvey

Dinner time. Roger Schäli headed back to camp on Capsico. Bruno Harvey

enjoying the twilight, we rappelled down to our bivouac. Back at base camp, we celebrated our success with some Italian grappa, "Fior di vite," and somehow, that became the name of our new route.

Three days of rest and fantastic meals stoked us for yet another climb: the west peak of Arwa Spire. We spied some fine looking cracks that we thought might be a workable line. But since it looked much more difficult than our previous route, we concocted a new plan: two of us would climb and fix ropes, while the third man would enjoy a rest day at ABC and be responsible for providing a hot meal each evening for the returning "workers." It turned out that two days of climbing to one of rest was perfect. And climbing the fixed ropes was much less strenuous than hauling gear and sleeping on portaledges, under all sorts of weather conditions. But getting up in the cold morning was sometimes a little hard, especially when it was snowing. Luckily, it never snowed for the whole day, and we managed to stay motivated to keep going back up onto the wall.

On the last pitch of the second day, I was squeezed into a tight groove, clearing out snow and hoping to find some good placements. But I couldn't find anything useful; up above, it looked just as bad. Then I recalled seeing a chimney to the left, so I backed down to the belay, climbed a little nose to a spot where I could look around a corner, and peered into the chimney. It looked overhanging, and huge, and I thought that our cams would probably be too small. Disappointed, I placed a sling and rappelled back to the belay. Bruno and I returned to camp, with no idea how we'd carry on the next day.

But in the morning, after thinking about the problem all night, Roger and I started out with renewed enthusiasm. For some reason, I thought the first way I had tried might yet go. Powered by newfound energy, I managed to get up the first difficult bit, which gave us even more incentive to push on.

The next day, it was Bruno and Roger's turn again. They managed to ascend some fine cracks in a steep rock face, reaching a ledge, while I followed their progress from ABC through binoculars. Suddenly, I heard shouting from the wall—Roger had fallen. Fortunately, a well-placed hook held, and the fall was not serious. The two came back at sunset, just as snow began falling again.

After six days of climbing and rappelling, we were ready for the final push. We clipped jumars onto the ropes for the last time. After three hours of jugging, we were warmed up for the last four pitches of the route. At 2 p.m., we reached the unclimbed west summit of Arwa Spire.

In honor of the spicy meals we enjoyed back at base camp, we named our route Capsico (like Indian Tabasco).

SUMMARY OF STATISTICS

AREA: India, Uttaranchal, Garhwal Himalaya.

ASCENTS: Fior di Vite (780m, 6+ A2 80°), summit reached on May 24, 2002
Capsico (850m, M6+ A3), summit reached on June 5, 2002. Both climbs were made by Stephan Harvey, Bruno Hasler, and Roger Schäli.

A NOTE ON THE AUTHOR

Stephan Harvey, 34 years old, was born and brought up in Switzerland, though his last name comes from an English father. He has a degree in geography from the University of Zurich, and has been a mountain guide since 1998 when he is not working as an avalanche forecaster for the Swiss Avalanche Warning Service in Davos. A climber since the age of 16, he participates in many mountain sports. Most of his climbing takes place in the Alps, though a few expeditions have taken him to Alaska, Yosemite, Nepal, Pakistan, and India. His favorite climbs are long steep walls with fantastic lines.

Bruno Hasler, Roger Schäli, and Stephan Harvey enjoying the after-glow from Fior di Vite.

THE FLAME

Before 9-11, this 500-foot granite spike sitting on top of a 2,000-foot face had been the talk of the Trango Valley. Now there was no one to talk with, but when the rain finally stopped, the Flame got fired. Pakistan.

BRIAN McMAHON

The Flame, as seen from advanced basecamp. Under Fire follows the tongue of snow just right of center, up cracks and chimneys to the ridge and from there climbs the backside of the top spire. Brian McMahon

The crux of our trip to Pakistan was convincing the rest of the world that we weren't insane. Josh Wharton, 23, of Boulder, had approached me with the plan shortly after the World Trade Towers were hit. His original partner, Phil Gruber, was married, and with his first child on the way, had opted out. Josh and I had climbed together in Pakistan in the summer of 2000, and he knew that I could be talked into almost anything. I made an earnest effort to convince him that we should go on a mellow, safe, and sane trip to Peru. He pointed out that not a single one of those adjectives describes why he and I climb, and then pulled out his trump card: a photo of the Flame that we had snapped in 2000. The argument was over.

Of course, I still had to tell my mother.

Josh's father (an exceptional climber of the 1950s) was all for it, even to the point of floating me a small loan for the bit of airfare not covered by grants. I, however, was terrified to tell my parents and avoided doing so until well after the trip was nearly irrevocable. Josh and I both became news junkies, putting a good spin on almost any political event. We also had the benefit of past experience in Pakistan and a good sense of how open and friendly almost all Pakistanis are. My daily litany to incredulous friends revolved around the theme of "I'm sure I'll be safer wandering around Pakistan than I would be in the wrong part of Denver at night." I stand by that idea. Not once did I feel threatened or endangered by other people during my time in Pakistan. Of course, the climbing was a different story.

Tensions between India and Pakistan reached a crucial stage right before we left on August 14, but we opted to go anyway. Little did we expect that our first major stumbling block would occur at Denver International Airport, where officials pointed out that my brand new Pakistani visa had already expired. I finally convinced an official from American Airlines to let me fly as far as London, where we had an airline change. Then I promptly smeared my visa into illegibility in a bathroom sink. The visa caused a few more problems here and there, but we weren't about to let a little piece of paper keep us from the Flame.

With the help of our guide, Muzaffar, Josh and I cruised through the red tape in Islamabad—letting countless officials go to town with their little stamps (in triplicate) on umpteen irrelevant forms. We then picked up a suitcase full of rupees at the bank and began the seven-day journey to Shipton Base Camp.

As many climbers are aware, there are two choices regarding travel to the village of Skardu, where the pavement ends and the real journey begins. The first choice is a two-hour flight on Pakistan International Air (PIA—fondly known to the locals as "Perhaps It Arrives"), with breathtaking views of Nanga Parbat and the Hindu Kush. Unfortunately, due to a distinct lack of technology (including radar) at the destination airstrip, the scheduling of these flights is completely weather dependent, and somewhat iffy in general. You never know if a scheduled flight will actually depart until the wheels leave the tarmac.

The second option is two days on a bus traveling along the jaw-droppingly beautiful Karakoram Highway. This road was carved through the highest mountain range in the world over a period of 15 years under Chinese supervision. It was built to connect the two countries for trade. Even two years ago, I considered this ride to be one of the most dangerous parts of the trip, as the road is often only one lane wide, with enormous cliffs sucking at the outside wheels of the bus. On blind corners, drivers who trust completely to Inshallah (God's Will) simply approach the curves with a prayer and a honk. On top of that, the highway traverses through regions where the western media and U. S. State Department widely proclaimed Taliban occupation.

The Flame, Hainabrakk Glacier, and the oft repeated approach. Brian McMahon

I promised my mother and girlfriend that we would wait as long as necessary for a flight. That's not the only promise I've broken.

The bus ride turned out to be uneventful. We were met with great courtesy, friendliness, and an endless supply of nearly undrinkable rancid goat-milk tea (Josh loved it). After the first stop we dropped our cover of being Canadian college students when I failed to come up with the name of the university in Ontario I was purportedly attending. Mostly, though, a cover seemed wholly unnecessary and downright insulting in the face of the kindnesses we received.

We spent a few busy days buying supplies in Skardu, then hired porters and headed out on Jeeps for the village of Askole, where one begins the trek to base camp. We left town feeling guilty that we needed only 20 porters; I wish we could have hired more. Portering is the best-paying job in rural Pakistan and many families count on it for their livelihood. With the huge decline in tourism, many porters are unable to find work. A normal summer in Pakistan caters to nearly 150 expeditions, many of which hire hundreds of porters. In 2002 we were one of only a handful of expeditions, and the result upon the Pakistani economy was obvious. Not only were porters out of work, the hotels were empty. Many shops—from cloth weavers to jewelry stores to butchers—were mostly closed. Even the road workers were slowing down.

The Jeep ride passed relatively uneventfully, and, as we began walking, Josh and I both experienced a strong sense of déja vu from our trek to base camp in 2000 (except that neither of us became violently ill this time around!).

We at last reached the Shipton Base Camp. The Flame had been central in our minds for the previous six months, and now there it was—a mere six miles, two icefalls, and 4,000 vertical feet away. Oh, and one very active avalanche slope.

Two years before, the base camp had been a regular climbing jamboree, hosting six Americans and a group of Italians. Half an hour away, two more Americans, Timmy O'Neill and

Miles Smart, were at Trango Base, along with a contingent of Japanese and a group of Mexicans. This year, it was just me and Josh, Muzaffar, and our new English student/cook, Gaffoor.

In 2000 the Flame had been the talk of our base camp. Its sheer beauty and physical improbability are almost indescribable, and it surely would have been climbed already had it been closer. The Flame earned its name through its unique shape: a 2,000-foot wall with an exquisite 500-foot tower perched on top. We like to think of it as the face of Half Dome with Moses sitting on top. At 20,700 feet, it is the tallest feature in the Trango Valley.

In 2001 a team of three Austrians attempted to climb the Flame (Norbett Reizelsdorfer, Herbert Kobler, and Tony Neudorfer). According to Muzaffar, who had been present in 2001, they attempted a line slightly left of center on the lower wall. They likely followed a system of thin, left-trending cracks to the base of the spire—where they turned around. The Austrians had attempted a mix of alpine and classic wall-style climbing, ferrying gear up to a 17,000-foot camp at the base of the Flame and attempting the route over several days.

Josh and I were convinced, however, that light and fast was the only option for a reasonable chance of success. In 2000 Mike Pennings and Jonathan Copp had proven what was possible with their lightning-fast first ascents of the Cat's Ear Spire and Hainabrakk East Tower, as well as a three-day repeat of Inshallah on Shipton Spire. To us, the next logical step was to apply this light-and-fast, go-for-broke style on a route that lacked a well-supplied base camp an hour away.

So, after waiting out a few days of light rain we made our initial approach. We left after an alpine-start breakfast whipped up by our new friend and cook, Gaffoor, with Muzaffar carrying a few pieces of gear and coming along for companionship. He turned around when the glacier steepened, and Josh and I donned our crampons and immediately realized our first mistake. Earlier that morning, after lathering on some sunscreen, I had left the bottle next to Josh's pack for him to use. He hadn't noticed it—and so our only bottle of sunscreen was back catching rays all by itself. We pressed on, thinking that if we were light and fast enough, maybe we could outrun the sun.

We climbed through the first icefall uneventfully, without a rope. Apparently, each time the Austrians had approached they took anywhere from two to four days, depending on conditions. We didn't have time for that and figured a great timesaver would be to eschew "safe" glacier-travel techniques altogether, and just walk real fast. Hopefully, neither of us would

fall into any of those big holes that glaciers always seem to have.

Our second mistake came when I talked Josh into a short-cut straight up a hillside to the ridge that protects the Hainabrakk Glacier, on which the Flame sits. The hill, unsurprisingly, cliffed out after about 1,000 vertical feet—but still well below the ridge we needed to gain. So we found another little hill that might connect us to a traverse, that just might go

Left to right: Muzafaar, Brian, Josh, and Gaffoor, waiting out the rain. Brian McMahon

The crew at base camp. Brian McMahon

somewhere useful. But when that hill started a small avalanche as soon as we stepped on it (and set off a resounding OOOOOMMPH sound on the first hill we had climbed), we realized that we had likely erred. We decided that it was suicide (and inefficient) to go back down the first hill, and so being the wise and skilled mountain travelers that we are, decided to rappel straight off the side of the cliff next to us. The hill at the bottom (which differed in no way from those threatening to avalanche all around us) must be perfectly safe. Right?

I rapped first and upon disconnecting from the rope promptly sunk in well over my head. This didn't bode well for our plan to sprint down the hill toward the safety of the glacier. By the time Josh was off rappel I had managed to thrash my way to the surface, with only one major crampon gash in my leg (in order to leave behind lots of well-marked red snow in case we had to find our way back). Josh was unable to come up with a good answer for why we weren't cragging in the Sport Park in Boulder Canyon.

Our first good choice of the day came in deciding that the next hill attempt would best be tackled in the early morning, when the snow was hard and relatively safe. So we set up our single-wall tent in the safest place we could find, busted out a delicious energy bar each, and settled down for the evening. We had some wonderful lightweight gear—our favorites were incredibly light and small zipperless down sleeping bags, rated to 30°F. Combined, they weighed less than one summer-weight synthetic bag and stuffed to the size of a liter bottle. In the interest of weight, however, we had opted against taking sleeping pads—so I probably don't need to describe how we slept.

The next morning, after quaffing some hot water from our homemade hanging stove, and another gourmet energy bar, we continued our walk. But this time the snow crust was beautiful—better than any sidewalk in Boulder. One more lesson learned.

The weather remained crystal clear and beautiful for the entire walk, and we arrived at our planned advanced base camp uneventfully. Except for the sun blisters covering Josh's face.

It began snowing soon after we set up our tent. It kept snowing all night while Josh tried to find a way to sleep on a glacier, at 17,000 feet, in a 30-degree sleeping bag, without a pad—all without letting his blistered and pus-covered face touch anything. It continued to snow all the next morning, and as we had brought food for only four days at ABC, we left behind a gear cache and retreated to base camp.

When we arrived at base camp, it was raining. The next two days dawned clear, but we were stuck in camp while Josh's face healed. On the third day it was raining when I awoke. And it continued to rain, every day, for the next 36 days.

On three different occasions we became so frustrated by being stuck in base camp with all of our climbing gear waiting for us a mere six miles away, that we just did the approach through the storm. And an exciting approach it was. We never got around to naming it, but it probably goes at about V, 5.5X WI4. Luckily, it didn't entail any aid pitches. Neither of us ever went for the big ride through a crevasse, but we both fell in to our shoulders on each approach, and unwisely became adept at jumping some wide abysses.

None of these optimistic approaches to the Flame panned out, although on one attempt we managed to establish the general course of our route and actually reached the top of the main wall, climbing almost entirely in a

Josh Wharton jugging pitch one on The Flame. This was the only pitch fixed on either route. Brian McMahon

Josh Wharton leading the first pitch up The Flame's spire. Brian McMahon

whiteout. Our route up the lower wall followed a wet crack and chimney system that exits onto the shoulder just right of the final spire. It went at mostly 5.9 and 5.10, with many exciting bits stemming around huge, loose icicles and precarious swords of rock. The few bits of aid on the first half of the route will certainly go free at difficult 5.11, if conditions permit.

The mood back in camp was getting grim. Ten days remained before we had to leave the valley to catch our plane. Our first clear sunrise, with nine days left, saw us pounding up the approach. By this time the previous avalanche slope had melted off, and in its place was an amusement park of enormous, precariously perched rocks. But we had the approach wired and got to our trusty tent uneventfully.

And then a miracle occurred: dawn came without rain once again. By the time it was light, Josh and I were already atop the single fixed line we had left on our failed first attempt and were moving quickly up the wet 5.10 terrain, a veritable waterfall from the first pair of good-weather days in many weeks.

The crux M5 pitch that I had lead on our first attempt was falling apart by the time we got to it, and Josh initiated a long traverse to the right in hope of finding another way to the ridge. He found it, but it turned out to be even worse than my detached M5 and involved a long and virtually unprotected pitch up a detached waterfall—with occasional mini-avalanches trying to rip him off. From the top of this pitch we easily reached our previous highpoint via a 500-foot pitch up steep but loose snow.

Brian McMahon jumping a crevasse on the approach to The Flame. Josh Wharton

This put us about 50 feet up the backside of the final spire, where a blank wall led up to what we hoped would be a decent Beak seam. I drilled the first hole of the route and placed a removable bolt (which we left in place) to get started on the crux aid pitch of the route. A few hook moves, and a few falls, led to some decent Birdbeak placements and easier aid territory.

It was a rope-stretcher pitch to a hanging belay somewhere near the summit. We had a handful of incredibly lightweight titanium pitons that were a lifesaver on that pitch (I used the smallest ice piton, "The Sphincter," as an admirable alternative to standard Birdbeaks).

That hanging belay was the scene of my luckiest decision of our climb. Because Josh had masterminded the trip—and it was obvious to both of us that the summit was a mere 25 or 30 feet away on easy 5.10 ground—it seemed to me that offering him the last lead would be the courteous thing to do. I was also sure he would let me keep

Josh Wharton snuggling in for the night on Shipton Spire. Brian McMahon

Josh Wharton enjoying fine weather for a change on The Flame. Brian McMahon

the final lead, since we had brought only one pair of rock shoes, and changing shoes at the hanging belay just wouldn't be worth the time. So I confidently made the offer, knowing I risked nothing and that he would not accept. But he jumped at the chance to be the first on top and quickly demanded the rack and shoes. It figures.

My disappointment, though, faded after he had climbed 30 feet. From there he could see the summit another 160 feet away, protected by a completely blank and difficult-looking slab. He yelled down to me for advice, and because I certainly didn't want to lead it, but I really wanted to get to the top, I made the obvious choice. I pretended I couldn't hear him.

Standing on a pair of dime edges, above a poorly placed knifeblade, next to an Alien with only two lobes cammed, Josh cast off onto the most impressive lead I have ever seen. The opening moves were 5.10+, and the occasional broken hold that careened past my head attested to the rock's quality. After 30 or 40 feet the climbing eased back to a 5.9 slab with the occasional 5.10 move–but without a single piece of gear. By the time I had 10 feet of rope left to pay out, I was getting really nervous that it would turn into the most horrifying simul-climb imaginable. But no, 190 feet above my belay Josh reached the summit, thus avoiding the very real potential of a 350-footer.

There wasn't a single crack near the top, so Josh tossed a long sling around the summit of the Flame and yelled "off belay." Even jugging the pitch was exciting, because every time the slab pushed me too far left, Josh would yell down that ìswinging back right would be a good idea, since the summit is a bit too round for the anchor to hold on that side.î

By the time I got to him he had the second (and last) hole of the route almost drilled, and it was time for a few snapshots and a quick overnight retreat. Under Fire had gone at V+, 5.10+X A3 M5 AI4.

We arrived in base camp two days later in time for lunch and congratulations from our Pakistani friends. By dinnertime, Josh had a gleam in his eyes. The weather was still good, and we had a whole six days left before we had to leave for the airport. What better time than now for a new route up Shipton Spire? After all, the previous fastest first ascent had taken a mere 17 days, right?

So, after one day of rest we went for it. The result was two days up, a day and a half down; and a great deal of spectacular, Yosemite-like climbing. We named our route the Kanadahn Buttress (Family Buttress in Urdu), after our supportive family and friends who had chosen to stand behind our trip. It came out at VI, 5.11+ X, C1.

We made the flight.

SUMMARY OF STATISTICS:

AREA: Trango Valley, Baltoro, Pakistan

ASCENTS: Under Fire (V+, 5.10+X A3 M5 AI4) on The Flame. Brian McMahon and Josh Wharton.

Drilling a rap anchor on the summit of The Flame. Brian McMahon

Kanadahn Buttress (VI, 5.11+X C1) on Shipton Spire. (More details on Kanadahn Buttress in Climbs and Expeditions.) Brian McMahon and Josh Wharton.

Josh and Brian would like to thank The American Alpine Club for the Lyman-Spitzer Grant, the Mountaineering Fellowship Grant, and the Robert H. Bates Youth Climbing Award.

AN OPTIMISTIC PLAN

*A series of new routes in Tibet, in preparation for climbing
Gyachung Kang, ends when Mike Bearzi slips during the descent
from the north face of Ngozumpa Kang II.*

BRUCE MILLER

The north faces of Ngozumpa Kang III and II. The route starts up the icefield between the two peaks, then doglegs up and right to the summit of Ngozumpa Kang II. Bruce Miller

"Not a good place to be a yak," said Mike, accurately summing up the scene. Mike Bearzi and I were adding three more tents to the hundred-plus already set up at Everest's North Face base camp. It was mid-April and half of those sat empty, since many of the North Ridge hopefuls had already moved up-valley to their advanced base camp. Dozens more were on their way, filtering out of camp with yaks in tow, while trucks unloaded heaps of gear for yet another group of North Ridgers. Mike wasn't too surprised that our diminutive expedition was distinct from the others, and it wasn't because our yaks would be any less burdened (they would be the only ones carrying bouldering slippers and chalkbags). What set us apart, indeed our only significant weight savings, was the smaller amount of mental baggage we were carrying.

Mike and I had the optimistic plan of making a first ascent on a peak 22 kilometers northwest of Everest: The northeast face of Gyachung Kang. Mike had spotted this ignored facet of the prominent 7,952-meter peak on an earlier Everest trip and had filed away a photo of it for a few years until we started talking. From our first discussions, the assumption was always that this was something we could pull off alpine-style. While that sort of thing isn't common, I'd seen enough Himalayan alpine-style success stories since Messner and Habeler flashed the northwest face of Hidden Peak in 1975 to demystify it. Success depended more often on patient pre-route acclimatization, blue-collar alpine skills, and minimizing weight, than on mutant, high-altitude physiology, M-climbing specialization, or a willingness to lose toes. Unlike me, Mike had come to these same conclusions at 8,000 meters, not over coffee at Dot's Diner, which made him an ideal partner. I brought some good experience to

Mike Bearzi headed up during the first day on Ngozumpa Kang II. Bruce Miller

the table (all sub-6,200 meters) that complemented Mike's, but neither one of us were part of alpine climbing's killer elite. We didn't think that's what it would take.

We had planned on approaching up the Rongto Glacier, which flows directly from the northeast face of Gyachung Kang and ends above Everest's North Face base camp to the west. A couple of days after we arrived we went on an ankle-twisting reconnaissance of the Rongto and dismissed it as yak-impassable. The following day we happily shifted down-valley and committed to the longer option outlined by the omnipresent Marko Prezelj (member: killer elite) back in Kathmandu. Marko had been part of a strong Slovene expedition that climbed the north face in 1999. Their ascent represented the complete history of climbing on the Tibetan side of the mountain.

We spent the next couple weeks of dodgy weather eating our sirdar Namgyol's excellent greasy cooking, shuffling gear, stumbling over the talus-strewn glacier, and wrestling with Mike's and my respective sinus and stomach troubles. We finally arrived at the base of Gyachung Kang to scope our proposed route on May 2. Mike's oblique telephoto of the northeast face (the photo we'd planned our trip on) left some room for doubt as to the possible quality of our route, but standing below the face our doubts were erased. Despite the face being spanned by vertical bands of Canadian Rockies-style horizontal strata, we were able to piece together a continuous, albeit difficult-looking, ice line.

With advanced base camp (6,300 meters) established we made the long stumble back to our base camp (5,700 meters), but not before making the first ascents of Jiuda Ri (6,711 meters) and Peak 6600 by an east-west traverse. Also, I earlier soloed the probable first ascent of Peak 6190 by a north-south traverse and made the first ascent of the west ridge of Peak 6271, each roundtrip

Mike Bearzi rest stepping on day two of Ngozumpa Kang II.
Bruce Miller

from BC. All of this activity fell into the moderate snow and ice/5.4 category.

The next objective was certainly more than we needed to further acclimatize, but the dogleg couloir on Peak 7646 (Schnieder map) was absolutely *the* line on the serrated ridge between Gyachung Kang and Cho Oyu. I'd lost the guidebook, and we didn't know we were looking at Ngozumpa Kang II or that a more accurate survey puts it at 7,743 meters. We didn't even know if the peak had been climbed (it had been—first ascent by Pemba Tenzing and Naomi Uemura from Nepal in 1965). I thought it might be too steep for us to really move quickly on, but Mike convinced me otherwise and he was right.

At about noon on May 8, after a day and a half approach, we climbed one steep ice pitch over the bergschrund at 6,400 meters. The rest of the day we climbed single and simul-pitches of consistent 55° ice. Not exactly easy, as we neared 7,000 meters wearing packs weighed down with bivy gear, but certainly not extreme. We were actually enjoying ourselves. Even that night wasn't too bad in our summer bags and bivy sacks; no sleep, but no headaches either, just hours of massaging our toes.

Constant spindrift the next morning kept us struggling with the stove until the sun was well up. All we managed to coax out was a meager couple of quarts of water for the day. When we finally got going, we left all of our bivouac gear and one of our ropes. We never even tied into the rope we did bring. As the couloir necked down above, the angle eased off a few degrees, and the ice turned to snow. The main difficulties were simply in maintaining our pace as steps collapsed.

That sort of oxygen-deprived, quad-burning snow climbing isn't my forte. We were both moving slowly, even when following in the other's tracks. I told Mike, "We can always turn around at the final headwall if it gets too late." But I wasn't really talking to Mike. I was talking to the skeptic in me, playing a practiced con that keeps the part of me that's pointing down, going up. I had no intention of turning around, whatever the hour, as long as the weather held.

When the final headwall, a black triangle of rock, at last appeared to be getting closer, I pushed hard for 200 meters to its base. The faint diagonal weakness I'd been shooting for thankfully turned out to be a 60° ice gully. I kicked out a stance and got my camera out to take a photo of Mike coming up. Somehow, as I pulled my glove off, I managed to yank the sewn-in liner inside out from the shell, while it remained attached at the wrist. I spent the next 15 frantic minutes dealing with a topology problem too complex for my altitude-addled brain. I finally had to rip a couple fingers off the liner with my teeth to get my frozen digits back in the shell.

When Mike arrived I grabbed my down jacket out of our one otherwise empty pack. While I restored a modicum of finger function, I realized Mike was suffering, but not from any serious altitude symptoms. It occurred to me later, looking at my summit self-portraits, that Mike was probably thinking the same thing about me. Anyway, we were each convincing enough that with three hours of daylight left I started into the crux snow and ice of the day.

The gully opened up into a small bowl overhung with cornices. Sneaking through this last obstacle involved shaft planting up snow that approached vertical, followed by a few rock moves, and then I was on the summit ridge. Ambition had taken me that far, but as I approached the summit I didn't care about what we'd done or that our optimistic plan was now a realistic next step. I was too cold, tired, and anxious for ambition. A more essential drive was at work. I stopped a few meters short of the summit cornice and was dimly appreciative of the sun setting on the roof of the world. I was, however, acutely aware that the top of Ngozumpa Kang II wouldn't be a good place to actually watch the sun set.

I fumbled with taking photos of Gyachung Kang and Everest to the east and Cho Oyu to the west. My middle finger still hadn't come back. Where was Mike? I'd hoped to stand on the summit with him, but it was definitely time to go down. I descended to above the steep bowl and started setting up a rap anchor in some chossy rock. I was struck with the fragility of our position as I watched Mike coming up the last part of that bowl. I told Mike we'd made it but he didn't take the "out," and continued to the summit. Twenty minutes later he was back and I was more than ready.

We alternately rapped and down-climbed to the base of the headwall. Extremely relieved to be back on the snowslopes that had so exhausted us on coming up, I was imagining us in our sleeping bags before dark. After less than an hour of rapid down-climbing, with tools plowing parallel tracks through the snow as I descended, I was within 100 meters of our bivouac. Mike was about that same distance above me, possibly facing out as I had,

Bruce Miller on the summit, considering the sun setting on the west face of Nuptse, over his shoulder. Bruce Miller

in the lowest-angled (40°) section of the entire route, when I heard his shout. I looked up in time to see him spinning over my head. He covered the next couple of hundred meters in a few bounces and disappeared over the vertical rock and ice we'd avoided on the way up. In those few seconds I went from total disbelief to almost equal certainty that Mike was dead.

I downclimbed below our bivouac on the one-in-a-million chance Mike had hung up down there, out of sight. But I was wasted, groveling in the dark on ice again, and I finally had to give up. I climbed back to the bivouac, crawled into my now-frozen lump of a bag, and made a cup of tea.

"You found that he was dead; you made a cup of tea?" said Frietag. Frietag? It was Frietag, from The Eiger Sanction. He was the first of a few visitors I had that night. They kept the more serious craziness of losing my friend at bay. I still had a lot to do right to get down okay.

At last the sun hit and I started rapping the remainder of the face on V-threads. I kept looking across at Mike's fall line for some sign of him. It wasn't until I was nearly down that I could see that, of course, he'd gone all the way to the glacier. In an accident as unlikely as my ridiculous glove episode, Mike had somehow pulled our expedition inside out. One of us dying was always a possibility we'd kept neatly tucked away. But there it was, yanked out, just one of the possibilities that was exposed to me on Ngozumpa Kang II.

SUMMARY OF STATISTICS:

AREA: Tibet

ASCENTS: First ascent of the north face of Ngozumpa Kang II (7,743m). Mike Bearzi and Bruce Miller.

Also: First ascents of Jiuda Ri (6,711m) and Peak 6600 by an east-west traverse. Probable first ascent (solo) of Peak 6190 by a north-south traverse and first ascent (solo) of the west ridge of Peak 6271, each roundtrip from BC. All were moderate snow and ice with 5.4 rock.

A NOTE ON THE AUTHOR

Bruce Miller, 39, lives a couple of miles down the road from Colorado's Eldorado Canyon with his soon-to-be wife, Michelle, and stepson, Satchel. Working as a carpenter the last several years has allowed him to put significant energy into climbing in Alaska, Patagonia, and the Himalaya. However, he most enjoys cragging with his friends on the Diamond or in his backyard, where he learned to climb 20 years ago.

MICHAEL ANTHONY BEARZI

Profile of a climber. 1953–2002

DIETER KLOSE

Mike Bearzi during his last expedition, with Ngozumpa Kang II (right), and Gyachung Kang (left). Bruce Miller

Mike died in the mountains and is buried by the snows. It seems so sadly appropriate, doing what he loved, ending there. The odd thing is that he had stood on a glorious summit shortly beforehand, something he hadn't done for 22 years.

A couple of months before he left on his last Himalayan trip, I asked Mike if I could write a profile on him. The take would be about a world-class alpinist who just doesn't get to summits. Being a writer, he appreciated the unique angle and agreed. I was too late in getting the article out; now it's an obituary. Yet, somehow that same take fairly describes my closest friend.

Mike and I mentored each other in the late 1970s, suffering on Colorado winter climbs mostly. We soon took our faith northward, opening routes in the Arrigetch region of the Brooks Range. Later we climbed new routes on Devil's Thumb and Mt. Burkett in the Coast Range of Alaska. Mike continued his annual pilgrimages to the great ranges of the world with a passion. Yet, although he virtually devoted his life to climbing, it was there in Alaska, in 1980, that he would stand on his last major summit until the day of his death. It surely wasn't a lack of ability or commitment on his part. Fate simply didn't have summits in Mike's book, which is what makes him an anomaly among the world's best climbers: a true "great," but not one you'd see in the headlines. He would even joke about it, which to me underlined his complete acceptance of how life dishes it out on its own terms.

Most folks, after hearing Mike's climbing vitae, would say he had bad luck. Not so: he had no luck at all—it simply didn't exist. Describing his youth, he told me, "If there were a dog turd on a crowded sidewalk, I'd be the one to step in it." At a young age he learned to take what fate dealt him, without chagrin, yet with a vast sense of humor and great integrity. This applied to his alpinism acutely.

Climbing wasn't everything for Mike, but his continual pursuit of the perfect climb dictated how he would live his life. He kept things simple, not buying anything he didn't absolutely need, living a Spartan life. Almost every expedition he undertook would squeeze the last bills from his wallet. Afterward he'd work just long enough to pay for the next one, and come back penniless again. I'm not talking about a youth searching; Mike was 49 and knew exactly what he wanted.

A big part of his summitless thing was that his goals were so high and his ethics so pure. He'd never choose the easy way up, claiming, "That's like kissing your sister." In 1980, while perusing his photos of Devils Thumb, Mike spied a wild direttissima on its heinous 6,500-foot northwest wall. Recognizing it as a futuristic route, he threw himself at it on four expeditions, virtually possessed. I shared one of those trips with him, and watching him comfortably free-solo hard technical terrain 3,000 feet up convinced me he was a master with great promise. Yet the weather or conditions on that fickle face eluded him every time. Although nine other parties have tried as well, it remains unclimbed.

In 1985 Mike almost pulled a summit from fate's grasp. Darkness and an ailing partner stopped them two pitches shy of the top on what would have been the first alpine-style ascent of the Desmaison Route on the south face of Chacaraju, in Peru.

On Cerro Torre, Mike and Eric Winkelman made the first free ascent by its remote west face. While belaying on the final pitch, Mike made the decision to retreat in the stormy tempest just as Eric was pulling onto the top; again, Mike got no summit. Two years later they went back, in the Patagonian winter, to try a new route on the west side, but vicious storms hammered them. Numerous climbs before and afterward simply would not see him on a summit; it eventually became weird.

During those first dozen expeditions his purist standards dictated having no radio, no support—just him and his partner, going boldly. He figured having a radio would give a false sense of security, and wanted instead to rely simply on his own chops. As an intellectual he would scrutinize every aspect of the task at hand and dissect it scientifically, then launch at the thing with a calm confidence.

In the 1980s and early 1990s, he and Bill Meyers developed several bold and boltless, from-the-ground-up, mixed climbs in Rocky Mountain National Park, Mike's favorite winter playground. To join Mike on those wintry forays, Eric Winkelman warned, "You better bring your goggles. He doesn't let the weather spoil the day." His fascination with mixed climbing as a pursuit in itself had him inventing the M-rating system, saying jokingly that the "M" stood for Mike.

On his three trips to the north face of Everest he went with just a tiny group, going alpine style and without oxygen. Mike wanted it by fair means, or not at all. He spent many days and nights at great altitudes. Finding that he performed quite well at such extremes, he described feeling a profound sense of peace and contentment there. But bad weather followed him on all his Himalayan endeavors of the 1990s: Shisha Pangma, Gyachung Kang, K2, Everest. He climbed for the love of it, or more specifically, it was his calling and he answered it with quiet devotion, eschewing the often arrogant dogma of the modern-day commercial alpinist. He lived for the love of pure ascent, of being there, summit or not.

So too was his carpentry, going about it as a mathematician in alpine style: with a scant set of tools he would create masterpieces relying simply on his own finesse and intellect. Colorado is graced with hundreds, if not thousands, of wooden testimonies to this man of superb talent. All of his creations, be they in hidden alpine valleys or tucked away in private homes, are quiet and enduring legacies that speak for themselves.

But it isn't his climbing or career that make the remarkable man I remember. He was a success as a purists' purist, with a life-focus like no one I've ever known. Mike knew what mattered and was true to himself. After dropping out of high school and studying in an ashram in India, he would read no further philosophy, being firm within his own. And yet he had the intellect of a scholar, and could muse on any subject. He always seemed to know what to say, no matter the dilemma, having an uncanny savvy of the core of things.

His purity extended into his kind of friendship: when I wrecked my back working in Alaska, he just happened to be getting out from another expedition. He eventually escorted me to a hospital in Denver, and drove two hours every day after work for three weeks just to visit and offer solace. Then he nursed me at his home for the next two months, asking nothing in return. He was so hilarious, it seems we laughed about everything under the sun. My pain notwithstanding, those were the funniest months of my life, having Mike and his great sense of humor all to myself.

On May 9, 2002, Mike actually summited a mountain for a change: 25,061-foot Ngozumpa Kang II in the Tibetan Himalaya. On a micro-expedition, he and Bruce Miller had quickly dispatched a new route in alpine style and without oxygen, on a peak above 7,600 meters, a first for Americans. Strangely, while descending on the kind of moderate terrain he was most comfortable on, Mike apparently slipped and fell to his death. This was just a warm-up climb for a new line on Gyachung Kang, the world's fifteenth highest peak according to Mike's detailed studies. Mike was doing what he loved, true to himself as usual: going simply, boldly, and by fair means. But now I often wonder: if he hadn't summited, might he still be around?

SEPU KANGRI

*Completing a dream, two climbers finally reach the summit
of the "secret mountain" of East Tibet.*

CARLOS BUHLER

The then-virgin 6,956-meter summit of Sepu Kangri, as viewed from Sepu lake. Carlos Buhler

To begin with it was a dream: a season, a place, a mountain, and a team. We were lucky climbers: those whose privilege it would be to attempt to scale this peak lost in the vastness of the Eastern Tibet highlands. The Nyainqentanglha Mountains, a range I couldn't even pronounce, lay somewhere north of the main Himalaya, somewhere very few Tibetans had been to, to say nothing of foreigners. This was an area so cut off from Lhasa that no one in the capital even knew if the roads to reach it were passable. The mountain itself had likely been seen by less than 20 climbers in all history. To our knowledge, only Christian Bonington and Charlie Clarke's 1996, 1997, and 1998 teams had ever attempted to climb the mysterious peak named Sepu Kangri.

 We chose the season: autumn, 2002—four years since Bonington's last attempt. Obviously, this was not a very popular place. Not even for Tibetans. Only seven families live permanently on the exquisitely beautiful shores of Sam Tso Taring, the lake beneath the mountain's daunting north face. Seven families and a hermit, Sam Ten Tsokpu. High above Sam Tso Taring, perched on the crest of an ancient terminal moraine with a magnificent view of Sepu's lake-filled valley and the stunning peaks to the west and north, this Tibetan monk lives in physical isolation from the world. As far as we know, he never comes down, not even to the shores of the lake.

TO LHASA

What a change since I first experienced the calm and spiritual city of Lhasa in 1983! Then I had been part of the American team on the Kangshung Face of Everest. Now it's 2002, and before me is a modern city. I am overwhelmed by bustling streets full of business people in suits, phone booths packed with families in traditional Tibetan costume, cars careening through tight passageways not intended for automobiles, and fancy cosmetics sold by pretty girls in modern department stores to Chinese newcomers trying to save their pale skin from the high-altitude sun's intense rays. It is too much for me at first; I can't accept these cataclysmic changes. The Potala Palace has become to Lhasa what Disneyland is to San Diego, or the Eiffel Tower is to Paris: a tourist attraction engulfed in a modern city. It is a tribute to the Tibetans that any semblance of a once powerful and graceful religion known as Tibetan Buddhism can still be seen in Lhasa.

Still, such a modern city enables us to assemble an expedition kitchen not so different from one in Alaska. Though there are some unfamiliar squirmy, slimy things in the covered

Skiing above the fixed ropes toward Sepu Kangri. Carlos Buhler

food markets of Lhasa, generally speaking, the assortment of tempting products is enormous and fresh. How sadly simple it is under the modern Chinese mandate.

TO SAM TSO TARING BASE CAMP

On September 9, we (Mark Newcomb, expedition leader, from Jackson Hole, Wyoming; Carina Ostberg, Mark's wife; Jordan Campbell, from Moab, Utah; Ace Kvale and Kate Clayton, both from Ophir, Colorado; and myself from Bozeman, Montana) climb into two modern Toyota SUV's and a large Chinese truck for three days of transport across continuously worsening roads into the heart of Eastern Tibet. This grinding, bumpy, bone-bruising drive defines our entry into an almost lost Tibetan culture; it's a time machine of distance from Chinese influence that takes us back through the tragic events of the last 50 years. We pass through the wild west towns of Nakchu, Diru, and Khinda, then endure a 20-kilometer "4-wheel-drive only" track into the heart of the Nyainqentanglha range to the village of Samda, about 14,000 feet above sea level.

An enjoyable seven-hour hike brings us to the spot, at about 15,500 feet, where Clarke and Bonington's team based their two serious attempts on Sepu Kangri, in 1997 and 1998. We are within shouting distance from four family homes we recognize from photographs in Bonington and Clarke's book, *Tibet's Secret Mountain: The Triumph of Sepu Kangri*. Somewhat shy at first, the inhabitants turn out to be warm-hearted and friendly. It's been four years since they've seen a Westerner here (the British groups were likely the only Westerners they'd encountered unless on pilgrimage to Lhasa), and not much appears to have changed. Within a few days of our arrival we are invited for tea, chapattis, and a most delicious cup of thick, fresh yogurt with sugar. At first we are wary of this completely raw food served out of hand-hewn wooden buckets with yak hairs pasted on the rim. But soon our defenses relax, and we set up a good bartering system that supplies us with daily deliveries of creamy yogurt.

ONTO THE MOUNTAIN

We see immediately how humid post monsoon weather behaves in our area—and why the glaciers are so large. The mountain is uncovered from cloud on very few complete days. With full winter cold expected near the middle of October, I find myself constantly calculating the time we have remaining, knowing that a storm could easily take a week out of our climbing schedule.

On Sept 18, we establish a camp at about 17,700 feet on the ridge where the British have obviously toiled to build tent platforms. We bring up ski touring boots, skis and skins, and the gear we'll need above. For now, the snow conditions above seem reasonable. After ascending 1,000 feet of snow slopes, Mark, Carina, and I manage to fix 200 feet of rope up a steep corner formed between the glacier serac on the left and rock on the right. This tricky access past the serac solves the problem of how to reach the upper Thong Wuk Glacier. The next day, all seven of us climb back to this point with skis on our rucksacks. From here, we don our skis and for 40 minutes cut across some unnerving side slopes above ice cliffs until we reach the 19,200-foot crest of this ridge, just before it drops 300 feet and joins the upper Thong Wuk Glacier.

By mid day, nasty storm clouds are closing in on us from the south. We bury our gear in the snow and descend to BC. For the next six days we wait for this storm cycle to end, spending many enjoyable hours interacting with our Tibetan friends and reading.

TO HIGH CAMP

On the 29th of September, five of us make the climb back up to Camp One. Mark and Carina, anxious to climb, have gone up two days before. The deep, fresh snow slows us significantly. The idea that is gathering in popularity is to

Three kilometers of skiing on the upper Thong Wuk Glacier leads to Camp 3. Carlos Buhler

attempt to summit on this, our second reconnaissance. On September 30, we carry more gear and food to the little cache we have buried on the ridge crest. Skiing down to where our ridge links with the upper Thong Wuk, we place our tents at about 19,000 feet, below a 40-foot serac in a sheltered snow bowl out of the wind.

During the afternoon, while others are organizing the camp, Mark and I ski up into the ice fall. Aware that this obstacle is difficult to calculate from below, we test its defenses repeatedly but are always stopped by crevasses. In the late afternoon we make an end run completely around the right of the icefall and find a way through to 20,100 feet. We are rewarded with our first view of Sepu's final slopes. Fantastic! We eagerly study the mountain's final defenses. Great walls of ice seracs and dreadfully prone avalanche slopes meet our eyes. When I return to our camp I am wary of the days ahead. Both tired and hungry, I must replenish my reserves. In camp, however, our morale is high. Our first glimpse of the final route is energizing. Though the last 2,000 feet is clearly dangerous, we agree that it is surmountable.

Unfortunately, Carina becomes sick the following night, and by morning of Oct 1, she is dehydrated and depleted. Mark would like to take her all the way to BC, but we need him for the summit attempt. Finally, he decides to accompany her down as far as the fixed rope and will remain in contact with her via walkie talkie. He'll then catch up as we ski the three kilometers to our top camp, at almost 21,000 feet. What a blessing the skis are! We quickly cover terrain that without skis would consume exhausting hours in knee-deep snow. True to the weather patterns, however, threatening clouds fill the skies to the west. With unwelcome thoughts of the frustration of the two Brits who turned back in a storm, we pray to have 24 hours before another blizzard rolls in.

By late afternoon Mark has rejoined us and we six reach the snowy walls of the final cirque. Huge piles of avalanche debris lie scattered across the glacier beneath the steep summit mass of

Mark Newcomb watching the sunrise and the clouds move in during the dash for the summit. Carlos Buhler

snow and ice. Staying in the right side of the cwm and as near to the ridge on our right as we dare, we pitch our two small tents at 20,700 feet. Ace is feeling the altitude and crawls into his bag.

Summit Day

At 2 a.m. we are already lighting the stove. I'm groggy and lethargic, having been anxious all night. I'm preoccupied with weighing alternatives for the climb. In the night we learn from the other tent that, while Ace is feeling slightly better, Kate's feet are not warming up. And with me, I see that Frank cannot finish his hot chocolate this morning, a bad sign. By 5:30 a.m. Mark, Jordan, and I set off up the avalanche-prone slopes toward the ridge on our right. We ascend the debris of huge slides, relieved that the slopes above us have already released. Still, I feel anxious climbing around two-foot crown-fractures revealed by the light of our headlamps.

We kick steps up easy slopes for about 600 feet until the wind pummels us, unobstructed from the south side of the ridge. Jordan is nervous about what lies above. Knowing that a third person will slow us down if we have to belay, he turns around. Before his retreat, he kindly lends me his insulated Marmot overpants, something of a life-savior in this teeth-rattling cold. Mark and I continue up in the dark, third-classing an exposed, 55-degree slope that hangs over the west face. Rays of morning light gently caress the mountain summits to our north.

We crampon up the steep bed of another huge slide path. Crossing the entire slope above us, a crown fracture looms eight or ten feet tall. We front point up the 35-degree slope beneath this behemoth of a crown, "knowing" that it could not slide again until the next significant snowfall. Mark bravely mantles onto the first level and traverses leftward to where he can just pull over the second, steeply inclined crown. I ask for the rope as clouds engulf Sepu's summit.

By 9 a.m., as we reach a steeply guarded ridge, a blizzard has engulfed the Sepu Kangri massif. Again, I sense the frustration that Bonington's teammates must have felt when they were turned back just 500 feet shy of their objective in 1998. Mark and I are not yet ready to call it off. We climb another steep snow slope and I belay Mark up a 20-foot near-vertical wall of unconsolidated, wind-packed snow feathers many inches thick. There is little purchase on this tense terrain, but Mark climbs confidently. I haul myself up the rope suspended from nothing more than Mark's harness. Wind and snow sweep across the mountain, cutting visibility to 60 feet, but we've reached the ridge crest and the route is obvious.

We follow the narrow ridge upward about 150 feet to where it merges with open snow fields. The terrain scares us in these white-out conditions. Our rapidly filling tracks and the compass on my Suunto wrist computer will be our only guides for the return to the ridge. The wind whips snow at our faces, stinging and blinding us. After another 300 feet of lightly ascending slope, Mark stops and waits for me. There is no more up. Are we on the summit? We brace ourselves in the wind and try to look around. The plateau appears to fall away in front of us, but we are hesitant to go poking around. A few clouds blow by, leaving a slight clearing. We glimpse shadowy drop-offs all around us. It is 10 a.m. when Mark takes out the radio and calls to Carina down in Camp One. Yes, we are on the summit; no, we can't see a thing. Yes, we'll be down by evening; with any luck, all the way to Camp One.

With haste, we're retracing our steps to the ridge and descending the steep wall. Burying a small padded stove sack jammed with snow for an anchor, we rappel the steep step. Cautiously front pointing and down climbing, we strain to retrace our nearly-filled-in tracks.

The rope comes out as I front point down the exposed 55-degree slope and nearly step off an ice cliff in the whiteout. At one point we are separated and I leave my ice axe to rappel another step. It takes us four hours to reach the high camp. When we arrive at the tents, the four others are immediately ready to descend. But I need a half hour's respite from the wind and snow before packing up.

We ski down the three-kilometer, wanded glacier, barely able see from one fluttering orange tape to the next. Yet we are eternally grateful for the skis on our feet. In an hour we glide around the giant crevasses of the ice fall. In two hours we are back in Camp 2, where we've left a tent and supplies. We drink hot fluids and set off toward the top of the fixed ropes. My mind is fixed on "downwards."

By nightfall we reach our sturdy Marmot tents at Camp One. My body craves a rest, and I flop down in our tent, exhausted and dehydrated. Jordan throws a pot of snow on the stove, and a sense of happiness begins to glide over me. I'll sleep soundly this night.

The vast Nyainqentanglha mountains stretch out for miles, both east and west of us. We have only visited the summit of one in a sea of peaks. With Sepu unclimbed, it was hard to focus much energy in the direction of the stunning adjacent peaks that just beg to be explored. But now the true gems of the range lure me toward their aura. I know we will return to this immensely beautiful landscape of endless vertical opportunities.

SUMMARY OF STATISTICS

AREA: Nyainqentanglha Range (also spelled Nyanchen Tangla), East Tibet

ASCENT: The first ascent of Sepu Kangri, 6,956m, October 2, 2002. Summit team: Carlos Buhler and Mark Newcomb. Other team members: Jordan Campbell, Kate Clayton, Ace Kvale, and Carina Ostberg.

A NOTE ABOUT THE AUTHOR

Carlos Buhler's climbing career spans 30 years, with major ascents on five continents, including summits of Mt. Everest via a new route on the Kangshung (east) face, K2 via the north ridge, Nanga Parbat, and a new big-wall route on the north face of Changabang. Buhler works with a number of partners in the outdoor industry, especially Marmot, Outdoor Research, Tecnica, and Tubbs.

EAST OF THE HIMALAYA

*From the "Alps of Tibet" to the eastern fringes of the Hengduan Mountains,
this mysterious land holds countless unclimbed summits. Incredibly complex,
the region can be explained, but it will long remain an enigma.*

TAMOTSU NAKAMURA

*Photographs by the author
Maps by Martin Gamache*

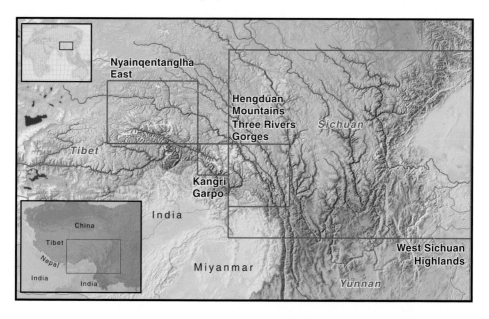

*Today the map has no more secrets. Idle minds repeat that parrot phrase.
But who knows all Tibet, or its far-away frontier on western China? Even its
own prayer-muttering tribes know only their own bleak, wind-swept valleys.*

—*Joseph Rock,* National Geographic *magazine, February 1930*

East of the Himalaya there is a vast mountain region that spreads from the Qinghai-Tibetan
Plateau to the western rim of the Sichuan Basin. The upper streams of East Asia's five great
rivers flow north to south through here, carving fantastically deep valleys between giant mountain folds. In one place the five rivers are squeezed into a span of merely 150 kilometers before
fanning out on their journeys to independent seas from the Pacific near Shanghai to the Bay of
Bengal in the Indian Ocean.

For climbers, the great region of East and Southeast Tibet, West Sichuan, Northwest

Yunnan, West Qinghai, and North Myanmar (Burma), offers ranges upon ranges of stunning 5,000- and 6,000-meter peaks. Very few of these have been explored by mountaineers, fewer still have felt crampons on their summits. Below them lie equally untrodden glaciers, hidden gorges, lush forests, verdant pastures, exotic flora and fauna, historic monasteries, and friendly villagers, most of Tibetan heritage. The Tibetan ethnic group embraces this entire region, extending far beyond the high plateau or even the Tibet Autonomous Region most of us imagine when we hear the name "Tibet."

The open-door policy carried out since 1980 by China's former premier, Deng Xiao-ping, has enabled foreigners to reach ranges previously unknown to climbers. Today access is opening even further under the West China Development Plan, which is reaching the most isolated frontiers. Even the least-frequented rural areas are experiencing rapid changes. Unfortunately, access for mountaineers is still not a simple matter, involving many permits and sometimes considerable cost, especially within Tibet proper.

In this article, which stems from my 25 exploratory journeys to the border country since 1990, I have divided this huge "East of the Himalayas" region into three broad sections, each with its own collection of mountain ranges. These are East Tibet, The Three Rivers Gorges of the Hengduan Mountains, and the West Sichuan Highland in the Yangtze River Basin. Within these sections are many named mountain ranges. And within the ranges themselves, I have defined further subdivisions for convenience in describing the peaks.

This area is becoming increasingly known to climbers, and I hope that my survey will prove helpful in understanding its complexity and its opportunities. I wish to express my heartfelt gratitude to Mr. Nicholas B. Clinch, Dr. Michael Ward, Mr. Harish Kapadia, Mr. Ed Douglas, Mr. Christian Beckwith, Mr. John Harlin, Mr. Bernard Domenech, and many friends overseas and in Japan as well for their continued support and encouragement.

SPECIAL NOTES:

Pronunciation: The letter "q" is used for something between a "ch" and "je" sound. Thus, "Nyainqentanglha" is most easily pronounced "Nyainchentanglha," and the same principle applies for Jieqinnalagabu, etc.

Names: The names we see in print result from a complicated process. After deciding which name to use when there are several local choices, we must interpret the sound through our foreign ears, and then approximate it with a phonetic English spelling. Sometimes the process involves four languages, each with its own alphabet: Tibetan, Chinese, Japanese, and English. Therefore, don't be surprised when you find several spellings or even names for the same mountain. The names in this article are the ones that I judge to be the most commonly used. For many of these peaks, I have personally translated the oral Tibetan into English spelling. Often the altitude can be used to confirm a peak, but even this is complicated by the existence of several maps with conflicting altitudes. I use the 1:50,000 and/or 1:100,000 scale China People's Liberation Army (PLA) maps as the final arbiter whenever these are open to me (the maps are restricted and not commercially available). For areas where I have not seen PLA maps, the 1:100,000 or 1:200,000 scale Russian topographical maps we have applied.

Climbing seasons: In general, good timing for climbing is before or after the rainy season that runs from the end of June to the end of September. That is, most climbers will want to visit from May to mid June, or from the end of September to November. However, the climate here is complex and not necessarily uniform. I discuss many variations within the different sections.

EAST OF THE HIMALAYA

Part 1

EAST TIBET

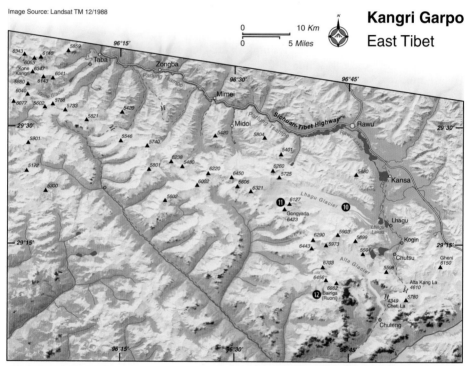

Image Source: Landsat TM 12/1988

Kangri Garpo
East Tibet

THE NUMBERS INSIDE CIRCLES ON THE MAPS CORRESPOND WITH PHOTOGRAPHS. ALL PEAKS ARE VIRGIN UNLESS OTHERWISE NOTED.

East Tibet holds two principle mountain ranges, the Nyainqentanglha and the Kangri Garpo. Nyainqentanglha is a huge range: 750 kilometers long, it extends west-east between latitude 30°N and 31°N. The westernmost end is a massif of four 7,000-meter peaks south of the Tibetan sacred lake, Nam Tso, while the easternmost end extends to Rawu, east of the Great Bend of the Tsangpo River. Over this tremendous distance there are two primary natural divisions; they split east versus west near the town of Lhari. Kangri Garpo is a sizeable mountain range stretching 280 kilometers from northwest to southeast in N:28°30'-29°60' and E:95°30'-97°30'. It exists between Tsangpo Great Bend, the eastern end of Himalaya, and Baxoila Ling, the western end of the Hengduan Mountains.

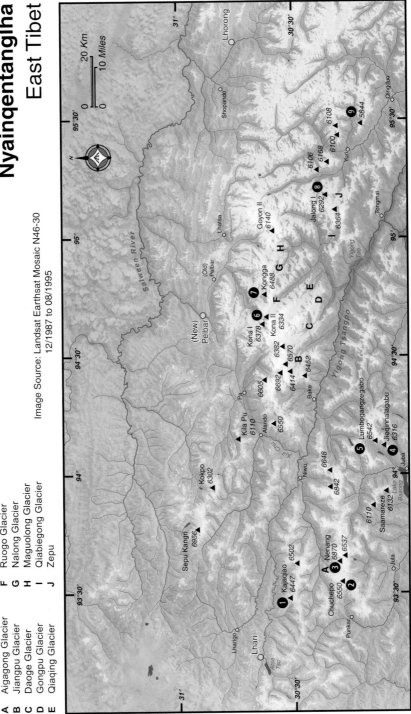

Nyainqentanglha
East Tibet

Image Source: Landsat Earthsat Mosaic N46-30
12/1987 to 08/1995

A   Aigagong Glacier   F   Ruogo Glacier
B   Jiangpu Glacier   G   Nalong Glacier
C   Daoge Glacier   H   Maguolong Glacier
D   Gongpu Glacier   I   Qiabiegong Glacier
E   Qiaqing Glacier   J   Zepu

No.1: The Matterhorn of Nyainqentanglha, Kajaqiao (or Jajacho) (6,447m), in a view from west.

No.4-5: Lake Basong and the west face of Jieqinnalagabu (6,316m) (right) and Lumbogangzegabo (6,542m) (left).

NYAINQENTANGLHA WEST

Nyainqentanglha West forms a part of the high altitude Qinghai-Tibetan Plateau. Climbers from the Tohoku University of Japan made the first ascent of the highest peak here, Nyainqentanglha (7,162m) in 1986. All of the other 7,000-meter peaks have already been climbed. Glacier development is concentrated only in the vicinity of the mountaintops. Snow lines are as high as 5,700 meters. (See *AAJ* 2002, ppg 427-429, Jon Otto.)

NYAINQENTANGLHA EAST

Nyainqentanglha East is located on the southeastern rim of Qinghai-Tibetan Plateau. The upper tributaries of Yalung Tsangpo erode the plateau into deep valleys like creases in wrinkled cloth, sewing seams. The topography becomes complicated. The climate is humid and brings much snowfall, which buries the summits, fosters glaciers below, and grows beautiful conifer forests below the permanent snowline. The highest peak of the main range is Sepu Kangri (6,956m), which was first climbed in 2002 following repeated attempts in the late 1990s. All the other stunning 6,000-meter peaks in the range remain unclimbed.

The main range of Nyainqentanglha East forms the watershed between Yalung Tsangpo and the Salween River (a.k.a., the Nu Jiang). The upper Salween flows in the north, and two tributaries of the Yalung Tsangpo—Yigong Tsangpo and Parlung Tsangpo—flow in the south. Countless peaks exceeding 6,000 meters still exist, veiled and unvisited, while unexplored glaciers reach up to 35 kilometers (22 mi.) in length (the Qiaqing Glacier). Few of these peaks are even known to climbers; Sepu Kangri is the only significant peak to have been summited. One branch of the Nyainqentanglha East separates from the main range near Lhari to the east in the south of Yigong Tsangpo. Here are many fascinating snow peaks. At Lake Basong (Bassom Tso), mountains and valleys surround a scenic and historic spot with an island lamasery. Turquoise blue Lake Basong, with neighboring peaks that rise 3,000 meters higher, brings to mind the European Alps; I call this region the "Alps of Tibet." The highest peak, Nenang (6,870m) is guarded with a precipitous snow face and a treacherous ridge. The breathtaking pyramid, Jajacho (or Kajaqiao, 6,447m) soars into the sky in an impressive Matterhorn-like tower.

Within the main Nyenqentanglha East, we can think of four geographic groupings. The following is a brief chronicle of the explorations, scientific researches and climbings in these areas:

Northwest Region: north of Yigong Tsangpo to Sepu Kangri massif
Sepu Kangri (6,956m) was challenged by the British parties lead by Chris Bonington and Charles Clarke in 1996, '97, and '98 successively. They came within 500 feet of the summit in 1998 (*Tibet's Secret Mountain: The Triumph of Sepu Kangri*, 1999). On October 2 , 2002, Americans Carlos Buhler and Mark Newcomb reached the summit (see "Sepu Kangri", later in this Journal). No other peaks have been attempted.

Lhari to Lake Basong region south of Yigong Tsangpo (1-5)
Japanese parties from Nagano Prefecture visited in 1994 and 2000. They explored the northern

Top: No.2: The beautiful west face of Chuchepo (6,550m), east of Punkar. No.3: Middle: The south face of Nenang (6,870m). No.7: Bottom: The north face of Kongga (6,488m).

side of Kajaqiao in 1994 and entered the valley north of Lake Basong in 2000. In October 1999 a New Zealand party led by John Nankervis attempted a 6,250-meter peak to the east of Basong Lake and reached nearly 6,000 meters on Jieqinnalagabu (Namla Karpo, 6,316m). In 2001, T. Nakamura's Japanese party tried to go down Yigong Tsangpo from Lhari, but frequent and dangerous landslides blocked them soon after they left Lhari. In 2001 John Town and colleague visited the valley north of Lake Basong. In March-April 2002 Nicola Hart and John Town (U.K.) entered Yigong Tsangpo from Lhari and made a reconnaissance of the northwestern side of Nenang (6,870m, currently the highest unclimbed peak in Nyainqentanglha) and other peaks that surround Niwu Qu. In April 2002 John Harlin and Mark Jenkins (USA) reached 5,250 meters on Jieqinnalagabu but retreated due to avalanche danger (they plan to return in 2003); they then trekked north of Lake Basong and looped over a 5,000-meter pass to southwest of Basong. In October-November 2002 T. Nakamura's party made a reconnaissance of the southern slope of Nenang from Jula and ascended to a high pass, Laqin La (5,300m), on the watershed to Niwu Chu.

Central Region: north of Yigong Tsangpo to Tsangpo-Salween Divide (6, 7)

In 2000 Charles Clarke (U.K.) approached from the north to unvisited glaciers south of Shargung La. In April and May 2002 T. Nakamura's party (Japan) searched for peaks and glaciers in the north central part of the range south of Pelbar (Pemba) on the Tsangpo-Salween Divide.

East Region: Botoi Tsangpo basin north of Parlung Tsangpo (8, 9)

In 1989 a joint Chinese and Japanese party of science institutions carried out a field survey and research of Zepu Glacier and its vicinity of Botoi Tsangpo north of Parlung Tsangpo. In October-November 2002 T. Nakamura's party explored unknown peaks surrounding Zepu Glacier and Jalong Glacier in Botoi Tsangpo basin, a tributary of Parlung Tsangpo. Here remain many magnificent untouched 6,000-meter peaks.

KANGRI GARPO

In this almost unknown mountain range lies the lowest-altitude Tibetan glacier (Ata Glacier South, 2,440m) and Tibet's largest glacier by surface area (Lhagu Glacier, 30 kilometers long by 2 to 5 kilometers wide). The range is encircled by three tributaries of the Tsangpo-Brahmaputra River. The northern side is deeply eroded where the Parlung Tsangpo, a tributary of the main Tsangpo, forms a narrow and precipitous gorge. To the south and east of the range, the Lohit River (Chinese name Zayul Qu) plays an important role. The river separates into two tributaries, Kangrigarpo Qu (qu and chu mean river) to the northwest and the Sang Qu to the northeast. The confluence is in a small point at Samai, in Zayul County not far from the border with Arnachal Pradesh, India.

Top: No. 6: The east face of Kona I (6,378m) (right) & Kona II (6,334) (left), Puyu valley. No.8: Middle: The stunning east face of Jalong I (6,292m), west of Zepu Qu, Botoi Tsangpo. No.9: Bottom: The west face of a spiky peak (5,844m), east of Yuri village, Botoi Tsangpo.

In the south of the range, the Dihang River (a tributary of the Brahmaputra) flows at 2,000-3,000 meters, while the mountain ridges only reach 4,000 meters, which is too low to provide a climatic barrier effect. Therefore, Kangri Garpo on the southernmost rim of the Qinghai-Tibet Plateau receives a humid southwest seasonal wind direct from the Indian Ocean, resulting in considerable precipitation during the monsoon season and heavy snowfall in winter and spring. North of the watershed the topography is complicated. The eastern end is a high plateau, while to the west the valley of Parlung Tsangpo becomes a deep forested gorge. In the south the valleys are extremely eroded. For at least three months a year villages are isolated from the outside world because of heavy snow. All the 6,000-meter peaks in Kangri Garpo remain unclimbed. The New Zealand party climbed only one minor and nameless 5,000-meter peak along the Lhagu Glacier.

Kangri Garpo East: Mountains surrounding Lhagu Glacier and Ata Glacier (10-12)
In May 1999 T. Nakamura's party entered Lhagu Valley and first explored Ata Glacier North to make a reconnaissance for a climbing route to the highest peak Ruoni (or Bairiga, 6,882m). In October to November 2000, the Silver Turtle Party (Japan) explored the Lhagu Glacier to 5200 meters near the ridge dividing Lhagu and Ata Glaciers. In October-November 2001 the Silver Turtle Party again visited Lhagu Glacier and then went to Ata Kang La and descended the Zayul side to the north for a complete view of the eastern side of Ruoni. In October to November 2001 a New Zealand party headed by John Nankervis: Lhagu Glacier investigated the glacier extensively, but were unsuccessful at climbing due to bad weather. In October 2002 the Kobe University Alpine Club (Japan) made a reconnaissance of Ruoni; they have a permit to climb it in fall 2003.

No. 10: The Lhagu Glacier and the east face of Hamokongga (6,260m) west of Lhagu village.

No.11: The east face of Gongyada (6,423m) (left) & Zeh (6,127m) (right), Lhagu Glacier.

No.12: The northeast face of Ruoni (or Bairiga) (6,882m), the highest peak of the range, southwest of Kogin, Lhagu valley.

Kangri Garpo West: Mountains west of Lhagu Glacier extending to Kone Kangri

In September to October 1999 the Gakushuin University team (Japan) searched for what was expected to be the second highest massif, Kangrigarpola Feng (6,602m). They entered the Gone valley from Taba village (3000m) on the left bank of Parlung Tsangpo. However, no peak of that altitude was found; they concluded it must be Peak 6,347m according to the 1:50,000 China People's Liberation Army (PLA) map. They named it Kone Kangri.

EAST OF THE HIMALAYA

Part II:

THREE RIVERS GORGES OF THE HENGDUAN MOUNTAINS

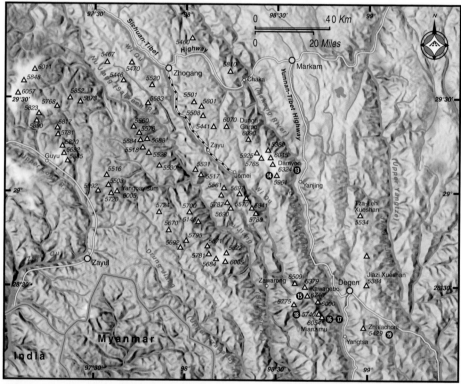

Hengduan Mountains- Three Rivers Gorges
Sichuan/ Yunnan

The Chinese name for this complex region is "Hengduan Shan," which means "traverse cutting mountains." Early Chinese geographers understood that most of Asia's mountain chains trend west-east, whereas the Hengduan Mountains slice north-south. These mountains form a considerable communication barrier between the people of the Tibetan Plateau and those of the Sichuan Basin. The barrier effect was especially prominent before the 1950s, when travel depended entirely on tortuous mountain trails and rope bridges or iron suspension bridges.

Of all the subranges within the Hengduan Mountains, the most geographically distinctive is the "Three River Gorges Country" on the frontier between Tibet, Sichuan, and Yunnan, with its tremendous bow-shaped geomorphologic structure. Unique in the world, these parallel ridges separate three mighty rivers: the Salween (Nujiang), the Mekong (Lancangjiang), and the River of Golden Sand (Jinshajiang). Between them, they constitute the headwaters of the Yangtze (Changjiang). The vertical relief between river and ridgecrests reaches 1,000 meters in the north and 2,500 meters in the south.

The Hengduan region is climatologically a transition zone between the lowland subtropical climate of Southeast Asia and the highland climate of the Tibetan Plateau. The Hengduan region correspondingly displays a wide variety of microclimates, but all are dominated by the southwest Asian monsoon rhythm, characterized by a seasonal change of wind systems. A recent study suggests that the Tibetan Plateau has its own permanent pressure system, which is also marked by changes in the prevailing wind direction between winter and summeróan independent plateau monsoon system. This system dominates the weather and climate of the Plateau, and may cause some deviation from average Asiatic monsoon conditions in the adjacent areas, including the Hengduang Mountains. In general, the snowline is between 4,800 and 5,200 meters.

ROHIT-IRRAWADDY DIVIDE

The Rohit River is the easternmost tributary of the Brahmaputra River, which forms a watershed called the Dandalika Shan range with the upper Irrawaddy River in north Myanmar and southeast Tibet.

Hkakabo Razi

The Irrawaddy and its tributaries have their sources in the Dandalika Shan that spreads over 200 kilometers along the border of China, Myanmar (Burma), and India. There are two peaks higher than 5,800 meters, which includes Hkakabo Razi (5,881m), the highest mountain in Myanmar. There are many small glaciers and snowfields. Hkakabo Razi was first discovered and its height measured by an Indian surveyor in 1923. In 1931 Kingdon-Ward tried an access to the mountain from the Burmese side and in 1937 he reached the upper Adung valley searching for possible climbing routes. In September 1996 Takashi Ozaki made the first ascent of Khakabo Razi. The route taken is on the northeastern side of the mountain along the upper Adung valley. They cut a footpath which has not been maintained. No one has entered the region for climbing after the Ozaki's attempt.

BAXOILA-GAOLIGONG RANGES: LOHIT/IRRAWADDY-SALWEEN DIVIDE

In the northwest of the Dandalika Shan range, the Rohit River separates into two tributaries, the Kangri Garpo Qu to the northwest and the Zayul Qu to the northeast. The Kangri Garpo range lies in between the two tributaries, while the Zayul Qu (the upper Rohit), the Drung Jiang (the upper Irrawaddy), and the Salween River form a watershed called the Baxoila Ling Range. Baxoila Ling changes its name to Gaoligong Range in the south.

Baxoila Ling Range-Lohit / Irrawaddy (north)-Salween divide

The western divide of the Salween River is topographically complicated. The two rivers Irrawaddy and Lohit have their source in the divide of the Salween. The Baxoila Ling range has many unknown 6,000-meter peaks and no climbing attempt has yet been made. The outstanding 6,000-meter peaks from south to north are Peak 6,005m, Peak 6,146m, and Yangbayisum (6,005m). Pk 6,005m and Pk 6,146m can be seen from a pilgrimage route around Meili Xueshan (Kang Karpo). The area from Baxoila Ling to the Salween-Mekong divide is called Tsawarong, the Heart of the Deep Gorge Country, which has long had a small isolated human population. No one has visited the range for climbing.

Gaoligong Shan range-Irrawaddy (south)-Salween divide

The 250-kilometer-long Gaoligong Shan range starts near the Yunnan-Tibet border and extends southward along the Yunnan-Myanmar border. These 4,000-meter mountains have no value for mountaineering except one glaciated unclimbed 5,123-meter peak that the local people call Kawakabu, north of Gongshan.

TANIANTAWENG SHAN/NU SHAN

The Salween-Mekong divide in the Hengduan Mountains region stretches over 700 kilometers from the Tibetan Plateau to the south.

Damyon and Dungri Garpo (13, 14)

The Sichuan-Tibet Highway passes through the southern rim of the Tibetan Plateau, crossing the southern part of the Taniantaweng range at Tungda La (5,008m). To the north of the high pass there are no prominent mountains that exceed 6,000 meters, while to the south soars Damyon, a sizeable massif with two 6,000-meter peaks. Kingdon-Ward first called this mountain "Ta-miu" during his journey in 1911. Kingdon-Ward tried to climb one of the southernmost peaks from Yanjing (Yakalo) and reached a point of 5,170 meters in 1922, where he found a number of dead glaciers.

Damyon is a sacred mountain for local Tibetan people. A whole panorama of the eastern side can be seen at the point where the Yunnan-Tibet Highway passes over the Mekong-Yangtze divide. The mountain massif has many high rock peaks, but the glaciers are small and retreating. The Chinese map indicates two 6,000-meter peaks: Dungri Garpo (6,090m) and Damyon (6,324m), the highest in the massif. All the peaks remain untouched.

Meili Xueshan (15-18)

Meili Xueshan (also known as Ka-Kar-Po, Kang Karpo, and Moirigkawagarbo) is located at 98.6°E and 28.4°N and is engulfed by over 20 peaks with permanent snowcover, six of which exceed 6,000 meters. Meili Xueshan is topographically higher in the north and lower in the

No.13: The east face of Damyon (main peak) (6,324m), west of Mekong.

No.14: The east face of the 5,900m peak of Damyon Massif, south of Damyon near Yangjing.

Top:No.16: The east face of Mianzimu (6,054m), the most beautiful mountain of Meili Xueshan. No.17: Middle: The north face of Mianzimu (6,054m). No.18: Bottom:The east face of Jiariren-an (5,470m) (Five Crown Peaks) of Meili Xheshan.

south. Its river valley is so wide in the south that an air current travels easily up the valley. As a result, the Meili Xueshan area is strongly affected by the monsoon, and there is a marked difference between the dry and humid seasons. In addition, the high and steep mountains help to produce vertical climatic belts with utterly different features. Above the snowline of 4,000 meters, the tall snow peaks shine white; in the valley, the glaciers extend dozens of kilometers. The glaciers around the highest peak were first explored by Kingdon-Ward in 1913. Below snowline, dense alpine shrubs and coniferous forests blanket the mountain slopes.

Melili Xueshan has received significant attention from mountaineers, thanks to Japanese and American attempts. The first to have attempted the highest peak, Kawagebo (6,740m) was a Japanese party, the Joetsu Alpine Club, in 1987, followed by the Academic Alpine Club of Kyoto University (AACK). In winter 1990-91they attempted the peak from the eastern side in a joint expedition with China. In January a snow avalanche struck the mountaineering team at night. The campsite vanished and all 17 mountaineers were killed. AACK again challenged the peak from November to December 1996, but in spite of good weather conditions they were not successful. Meanwhile, American parties led by

No.15: The east face of sacred Kawagebo (6,740m), the highest peak of Meili Xueshan, west of Mekong.

Nicholas B. Clinch visited the mountains four times in 1988, '89, '92, and '93. They attempted Peak 6,379m but gave up due to dangerous snow conditions, and then focused on Peak 6,509m, the second highest in the massif. In 1992 and '93 the Americans made attempts on Peak 6,509m from the northwestern side, but were unsuccessful due to bad snow conditions, then heavy precipitation in 1992, and dangers of avalanches and overhanging cornices in 1993. All the peaks including incredibly beautiful Mianzimu (6,054m) remain unclimbed.

Baimang Shan: Mekong-Yangtse Divide (19)
The Mekong-Yangtze (River of Golden Sand) divide contains three sections, from north to south they are the Markam Shan, Ninching Shan, and the Yunling. Markam Shan and Ninching Shan have no particular snow peaks. Yunling is divided to two sections.

To the north of Baimang Shan (Paima Shan) pass (4,292m) near Deqen, the topography is much complicated where there are two groups of Jiazi snow mountains and Tza-Leh snow mountains. Both groups have a number of 5,000-meter peaks. The mountain ridges are composed of thousands of rock pillars and pinnacles. An Australian climbed a minor peak of 5,200 meters, but no other climbs are recorded.

No.19: The north face of Zharachoni (5,429m), the highest peak of Baimang Xueshan.

To the south of the pass is the well-known Baimang Shan, which appeared frequently in explorers' journals. The highest peak, Zhalachoni Feng (5,429m), snow-clad and glaciated, remains unclimbed.

Yulong Xueshan and Haba Xueshan: across Yangtze Great Bend (20,21)

The river of Golden Sand is the main stream of the Yangtze (Chinese name: Jinsha Jiang), dropping southward from the Tibet Plateau along the border of Sichuan and Yunnan Provinces. It turns abruptly 110 degrees to northeast at Changjiang (Yangtze). It then flows into the world famous Tiger Leaping Gorge, where tremendous waters rage through a 30-60-meter passage. Huge mountain walls and ridges drop precipitously on both sides of the gorge. The main mountains are Yulong Xueshan to the east and Haba Xueshan to the west.

Yulong Xueshan (5,596m), also known as "Jade Dragon Mountain," is at the southern end of Yulong Xueshan range in the Lijiang district of Yunnan Province. Running north-south, Yulong Xueshan is some 34 kilometers long by 13 kilometers wide. There are 18 towering peaks over 5,000 meters. The main peak Shanzidou (5,596m), lies at 100.1°E and 27.0°N. In 1987 Americans made the first ascent of the main peak from the eastern side. No second ascent has been made.

To the west of the Tiger Leaping Gorge, Haba Xueshan (5,396m) rises 3,500 meters directly above the riverbed. Further to the northwest several small groups of distinctive 4,700-meter rock peaks surround the Zhongdian plateau. Haba Xueshan was first climbed by a Chinese party in 1995.

No.20: The rock peaks of the west Ridge of Yulong Xueshan soaring above the Tiger Leaping Gorge of the Upper Yangtze, Yunnan.

No.21: The east face of Yulong Xueshan, north of Lijiang, Yunnan. Climbed.

EAST OF THE HIMALAYA

Part III

WEST SICHUAN HIGHLAND–YANGTZE RIVER BASIN

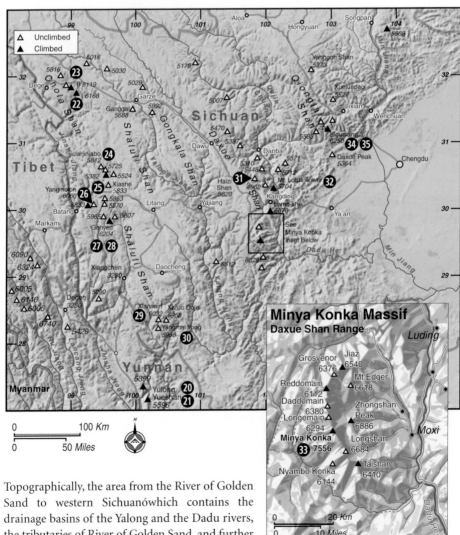

Topographically, the area from the River of Golden Sand to western Sichuan—which contains the drainage basins of the Yalong and the Dadu rivers, the tributaries of River of Golden Sand, and further east the Min River—is usually described together as a geomorphological region called the "West Sichuan Highland." This area shares the same land-scape characteristics as the Three River Gorge country, but it possesses a little different geological history and structure.

Western Sichuan and the adjacent areas of Yunnan to the south are characterized by much more varied topography. The extensive plateau-type landforms stretch north to unite with the Tibetan Plateau proper. Many of the highest peaks of this area exceed 6,000 meters, the most conspicuous massif being Minya Konka, otherwise known as Gongga Shan (7,556m) (see *AAJ* 2002, ppg. 22-23, for the story of the 1932 first ascent).

Unlike southeast Tibet, where almost all 6,000-meter peaks remain unclimbed, in Sichuan there are only a couple of virgin 6,000ers. Nevertheless, countless alluring unclimbed rock and snow peaks lower than 6,000 meters await their first ascents. (See Rock Peaks of the Siguniang Region, by Tamotsu Nakamura, *AAJ* 2000, ppg. 127-134, for a comprehensive survey and a regional map.)

The first part of this section outlines the major mountain ranges and massifs in the eastern Hengduan Mountains between Jingsha Jiang (River of Golden Sand) and Min Jiang of the Upper Yangtze River. These are described from west to east. Unless otherwise mentioned, all these peaks are unclimbed.

CHOLA SHAN (22, 23)

Towering at the southern fringe of Qinghai-Tibet Plateau, Chola Shan stretches northwest-southeast in the northern part of the Hengduan Mountains. It is linked up with Mola Shan in the north and joins Shaluli Shan in the south. Within its large and complex terrain of rock and snow peaks, Chola Shan's main peak is lofty and magnificent at 6,168 meters (99.1°E and

No.22: The north face of Chola Shan I (6,168m), south of Lake Xinluhai. Climbed.

No.23: The west face of 5,000m rock peaks of Chola Shan massif, west of Lake Xinluhai.

31.8°N). The second highest peak is 6,119 meters, three kilometers away; there are several dozen snowy peaks above 5,000 meters. In September 1988, the main summit was first ascended by the joint expedition team of Kobe University and the Geological University of China, taking their route up to an eastern glacier from the base camp of Lake Xingluhhai. Some 5,000-meter peaks were climbed by a UIAA team in September, 1997. Chola II (6,119 meters) was first climbed by the American Charlie Fowler, solo in 1997.

SHALULI SHAN

This mountain range covers a vast area and there is no clear boundary between it and the other mountain ranges. Each massif is introduced in succession from north to south.

Gangga Massif
This massif stretches to the southeast from the end of Chola Shan, south of Yalong Jiang. The main peak, Gangga (5,688m), and other 5,000-meter peaks have small glaciers. No one has attempted climbing here.

Jarjinjabo Massif (24)
The highest peak is 5,812 meters and the second highest is 5,725 meters. Both are unclimbed. The most impressive peak is a brilliant granite rock tower (5,382m) soaring like a small Fitzroy in Patagonia. These mountains are located along the northern rim of the wide Zhopu Pasture north of Xiashe (5,833m). To the west there are several 5,500-meter peaks, and to the east the challenging fortress of Hati (5,524m) rises proudly. The granite rock tower (5,382m) was first climbed by a Japanese party in July, 2001. An American party climbed various rock peaks in August, 2002. (See Jarjinjabo, by Peter Athans, in this Journal.)

No.24: The southeast face of Jarjinjabo (5,812m), northwest of Zhopu pasture.

No.25: The north face of Xiaxhe (5,833m), a view from Zhopu Monastery.

Xiashe Massif (25)

Xiashe (5,833m), the highest peak, has beautiful lakes on its southern side, while the north face attracts climbers. The massif also has 5,500- to 5,600-meter peaks adjacent to the Sichuan-Tibet Highway. Everything is unclimbed, including Xiashe.

Top: No.26 The south face of Yangmolong (6,060m), east of Batang.

No.27 The west face of Genyen (6,204m) (right, climbed), and 5,965m peak (left, unclimbed).

Yangmolong and Dangchezhengla Massif (26)

This massif is situated 15-20 kilometers from Batang to the east. Access to basecamp is short and easy. Four principal peaks of 6,060 meters (Yangmolong), 6033 meters, 5833 meters (Dangchezhengla), and 5,850 meters dominate. A Japanese party attempted the highest peak from the northern side in 1991, but they were stopped by avalanche danger. The two 6,000-meter peaks remain unclimbed. On the southern side of the massif, a heavenly lake called Yamochouken lies at 4,800 meters. Dangchezhengla was first climbed by Japanese party on June 17, 2002. (See Climbs and Expeditions in this Journal.)

Genyen Massif and neighboring mountains to the north and northwest (27-28)
To the south of the Sichuan-Tibet Highway, between Litang Plateau and Batang, lies a vast mountain area. The highest peak, Genyen (6,204m), is a divine mountain situated at 99.6°E and 29.8°N. It was first climbed by a Japanese party in 1988. However, more than 10 untouched rock and snow peaks of over 5,800 meters await climbers. In particular, a 5,965-meter peak towering like a sharp beak looks magnificent, and the scenery surrounding the 600-year-old Rengo Monastery amid spiky rock pinnacles is truly enchanting. In 1877, William Gill had a glorious view of the highest peak. He wrote in his narrative ("The River of Golden Sand") that "No word can describe the majestic grandeur of that mighty peak.... The traveler can appreciate the feelings of the Tibetans that have led them to call it Nen-Da, or The Sacred Mountain."

Gongga Xueshan (Kongkaling) Massif (29-30)
These mountains with three snow peaks are located in the boundary of Muli county and Daocheng County, the southern end of Shaluli Shan. They are well-known among the Tibetan people as the Heavenly Charms in the Snow World. The highest north peak, Xiannairi (6,032m, 100.3°E and 28.4°N) means Buddha's Mother. Yangmaiyong, the south peak (5,958m) means

Manjuist Buddha. Xiaruoduoji (5,958m) means "the Buddha with warriors' hands." J.F. Rock visited this mountain in 1928 and took a beautiful photograph of Yangmaiyong (he called it "Jambeyang"), which appeared in *National Geographic* (Vol. 191. No. January 1997). In 1989, the Himalayan Association of Japan sent a climbing expedition. Bad weather defeated them. In 2001, an American party attempted Xiaruoduoji but was not successful. All the peaks remain unclimbed. Now the Daocheng County government strictly controls climbing permits. (See Gildea in this Journal.)

GONGKALA SHAN

This is a small mountain range located 30 kilometers from Garze. In 1998 a Japanese party made a reconnaissance from the south of the highest peak, Kawarani (5,992m), and the second highest

Top: No.28: The 600-year-old Rengo Monastery, near Genyen. Bottom: No.29 The north face of Xiannairi (6,032m) of Gongga Xueshan.

No.30: The east face of Yangmaiyong (5,958m) of Kongga Xueshan.

one, Peak 5,928m. According to the topographical map of the China People's Liberation Army (1:100,000), there seem to be well-developed glaciers on the northern side. No other records are known.

DAXUE SHAN

This range has the most famous mountains, including Minya Konka (Gongga Shan, 7,556m). The Tibet-Qinghai Plateau ends at Daxue Shan. The scope of the range is rather ambiguous. Each Sub-Range is described from north to south.

Haizi Shan "Ja-ra" (31)
Tibetans called Haizi Shan (5,820m) 'Ja-ra' to signify "King of Mountains," and many explorers have noticed this outstanding peak. A good close-up view of the southwest side can be had from the Sichuan-Tibet Highway. The north face would provide a possible climbing route. An American attempted the peak in 2001 but failed.

Mountains of Dadu River basin
Along the deep valley of Dadu He, one of the large tributaries of the Yangtze River, there are many 5,000-meter peaks. The highest is a 5,712-meter peak on the left bank of the river. The eastern end shares a boundary with the Jiaojin Shan, a minor range, and the Qionglai Shan ranges. There is no record of climbing.

Lotus Flower Mountains (32)
Although no glaciers have developed, eminent rock peaks can be seen north of Kangding, the capital of the Garze Tibetan Autonomous Prefecture. A Japanese party climbed the highest peak (5,704m) in 1998. The other 5,000-meter rock peaks remain untouched.

Lamo-she Massif
This massif, east of Kangding, has been called the Mountains of Tachienlu. In 1993 its highest peak, Lamo-she (a.k.a. Tianhaizi Shan, 6070m) was scaled by Americans, and the fourth highest (Shehaizi Shan, 5,878m) was climbed by an American-Canadian-New Zealand team. Two virgin peaks, 5,924 meters (Baihaizi Shan) and 5,880 meters, are guarded by rocks and hanging glaciers.

Minya Konka (Gongga Shan, 7,556m) and its satellite peaks (33)
Minya Konka, or Gongga Shan in Chinese, is the highlight of the Hengduan Mountains. Minya Konka, which means "Highest Snowy Mountain" in Tibetan, is located in the middle section of Daxue Shan to the north of Lamo-she. Some 60 kilometers from south to north and 30 kilometers

No.31: The north face of Haizi Shan (or Ja-ra) (5,820m).

No.32: The west face of 5,000m rock peaks of the Lotus Flower Mountains, north of Kangding.

Top: No.33: The west face of glorious Minya Konka (7,556m) from Zimei Pass. Northwest ridge climbed.
Bottom: No.34: The south face of Mt. Siguniang (6,250m), the highest peak in Qonglai Mountains. Climbed.

from east to west, its main peak (7,556m) lies at 101.8°E and 29.6°N. It has only been climbed eight times, and by just two routes (the northwest and northeast ridges). Remaining problems are the difficult south ridge and south-west ridge. (See Choudens in this Journal.)

Frequent geological movement in the Minya Konka area has brought about a lot of folds and fractures. As the mountain rises, valleys are formed with a height difference of 5,000 meters on the east and west slopes. Teamed with more than 20 neighboring high peaks over 6,000 meters, it has a total area of 290 square kilometers, with 45 glaciers. Five glaciers have lengths of about 10 kilometers each, the longest being Hailuogou (Conck Ditch) Glacier, with a 1,000-meter-long icefall and a glacial tongue that dips to 2,600 meters. The climate undergoes great changes, with the rainy season extending from June to October and the dry season from November to May.

There still remain unclimbed satellite peaks over 6,000 meters. The following list shows the most important peaks still to be attempted: Northern part: Grosvenor (6,376m) and Mt. Edger (E-Gongga, 6,618m). Central part: Daddomain (6,380m) and Longemain (6,294m). Southern part: Longshan (6,684m) and Nyambo Konka (6,144m).

6,079-meter Massif

This is an independent massif with an unclimbed 6,000-meter peak to the south of Minya Konka. No one has made a reconnaissance of the highest peak at 6,079 meters. Farther to the south, a 5,584-meter mountain is shown on the Chinese map, but no specific information is available.

Qionglai Shan Range

To the east of the deep canyon of the Dadu river lies Jiaojing Mountain, which is famous as the historical "Crossing of the Daxue Shan," where the Red Army soldiers overcame great difficulties during Long March in 1935. There are several snow peaks over 5,000 meters, but there is no detailed information. Further to the northeast of Jiajing mountain, Qionglai Shan runs south to north. In the middle section of Qionglai Shan, where it joins the western fringe of Sichuan Basin, lie the highest peaks, Siguniang Shan. Further north are a number of untrodden 5,000-meter snow and rock peaks.

Mt. Siguniang (34)

Siguniang Shan (also known as Four Girls Mountain) is considered a holy mountain by Tibetans.. The legend says that four warm-hearted girls fought bravely with a ferocious leopard to save their treasured giant pandas, thereby becoming the four graceful peaks. Rising at 6,250, 5,614, 5,454, and 5,355 meters respectively, the four peaks stand at the boundary between Xiaojing County and Wenchuan County. The main peak, Yaomei Feng (peak of the youngest girl), is 6250 meters, and lies at 102.9°E and 31.1°N. Its extremely steep walls and ridges feature hanging glaciers on the south slopes and vertical rock walls hundreds of meters high on the west and north slopes.

The main Siguniang peak (6,250m) has been climbed three times from the south and once from the north. The first ascent was in 1981 by a Japanese team via the east ridge; they took 16 days and used 2,000 meters of fixed rope. The second ascent in 1992 took 23 days via the south face using 600 meters of fixed rope; also by Japanese. The third ascent was made by an American, Charlie Fowler, who soloed a line between the two Japanese routes in three days.

The north face sports extremely steep and smooth granite walls with intermittent ice streaks. It was first attempted on the right hand side in 1981 by Jack Tackle, Jim Donini, Kim Schmitz, and Jim Kantzler (USA). They reached 5,000 meters after 11 days above high camp, six of which were spent on the final push. The first ascent of the north face was made by Mick Fowler and Paul Ramsden over 6 days in April, 2002. They descended the unclimbed north ridge in two days. (See Siguniang, inthis Journal.)

Rock Peaks north of Siguniang (35)

Mt. Siguniang has become so famous and popular within China that the southern side of the mountain, which can easily be reached from Chengdu, is now congested with hundreds of tourists and trekkers, domestic as well as foreign. However, to the north are many towering granite 5,300- to 5,900-meter peaks encircling two beautiful valleys as if to form a grand coliseum. Many of these are unclimbed.

No.35: The east face of a 5,466m granite rock peak, Qonglai Mountains.

A brief climbing history follows. 1983: Celestial Peak (5,413m) (Tibetan name: Punyu; Chinese name: Mountain of Gods). First ascent by American party led by Ted Vaill. 1985: Celestial Peak. Second ascent, via a new route of the southeast ridge, by Keith Brown, solo. 1994: Nameless 5,383-meter peak west of Celestial Peak. First ascent by Charlie Fowler, solo. 1994: Nameless 5,484-meter peak and adjacent peak north of the main summit of Siguniang. First ascent by Charlie Fowler, solo. 1997: Nameless 5,666-meter peak north of the main summit of Siguniang. First ascent by Charlie Fowler, solo. 1997: Rock tower southwest of Celestial Peak, first ascent by John Mesler.

MIN SHAN RANGE–EASTERN END OF HENGDUAN MOUNTAINS

To the east of the upper Min river lies the Min Shan range in Songpan County; it defines the eastern end of the Hengduan Mountains. Xuebao Ding (5,588m, 103.8°and 32.7°N), in the middle section of the range, is listed as the highest peak of Min Shan. The main summit has many surrounding peaks such as Yuzhan Feng (5,119m, "the peak of jade hairpin") to the southwest, Sigenxiang Feng (5,359m, "the peak of four incenses"), and the lesser Xuebao Ding (5,440m), towering to the southeast. On the northern side sits the world famous Huanglong (Yellow Dragon) Scenic Spot.

The main peak was first climbed by a Himalayan Association of Japan party in August, 1986, and the second and the third ascents were made by the Japanese in 1991 and 1992.

BEYOND THE HENGDUAN MOUNTAINS-SICHUAN BASIN

No snow and rock peaks with glaciers that attract climbers exist beyond the eastern fringe of the Hengduan Mountains where they meet the fertile Sichuan Basin.

REFERENCES

For more information on mountaineering East of the Himalaya, please refer to the *Japanese Alpine News* (*JAN*) Vol. 4 "Special Submission on East of the Himalayas—To the Alps of Tibet" (published in May 2003) that contains 40 pages text, 40 pages with 75 color photos, and 32 pages with 27 maps to cover the entire region. The *JAN* Vol. 4 may be purchased from Chessler Books, Chesslerbk@aol.com, (800) 654-8502 or (303) 670-0093, fax (303) 670-9727. For more information you may write to Tamotsu Nakamura, Editor, Japanese Alpine News, The Japanese Alpine Club, 6-3-21 Matsubara, Setagaya-ku, Tokyo 156-0043, Japan, Tel & Fax: 813-3325-3612, email: t-naka@est.hi-ho.ne.jp

BIBLIOGRAPHY

The Alpine Journal 1983, 84, 85, 88/89, 90 and 91/92, 2000, 01, 02.

Alpinist 1 (Winter 2002-2003).

The American Alpine Journal 1982, 83, 84, 86, 87, 88, 89, 90, 2000, 01,02.

Bonington, C. & Clarke, C. *Tibet's Secret Mountain: The Triumph of Sepu Kanri* (1999).

Brackenbuury, W., *Yak Butter & Black Tea* (1997).

Burdshall, R.E., *Men against the clouds*. London (Bodley Head) 1935.

Chinese Academy of Sciences (Chinese version).

An introduction to the Glaciers in China, China (Science Press Beijing) 1988.

Physical Geography of Hengduan Mountains, China (Science Press Beijing) 1997.

Glaciers in Hengduan Mountains, China (Science Press Beijing) 1996.

Glacier of Xizang (Tibet). China (Science Press Beijing) 1986.

China Tourism 1993, *The Conquest of Snowy Haba Mountain,* (Hong Kong) 1996.

China Mountaineering Association, *A Guide to Mountaineering in China,* (Chengdu Maps Publishers) 1993.

China Mountaineering Association, *Immortal Mountains in the Snow Region,* Tibet (Tibet People's Publishing House) 1995.

Hiroshima Mountaineering Club, *Siguniang* (south face), Hiroshima, Japan 1994.

Heim, A, *Minya Gongkar*, Berlin (Verlag Hans Huber) 1933.

The Himalayan Journal, 1997, 99, 2000, 01, 02.

Iwato Yuki, *First Ascent of Yulong Xzueshan*, Tokyo *(YAMA-KEI)* 1988.

Kobe University, *The First Ascent of Chola Shan,* Kobe *(Kobe University)* 1989.

Kyoto University, *Report on Meili Xueshan Expedition*, Kyoto *(AACK)* 1992.

Nakamura, T, *East of Himalaya*, Tokyo *(YAMA-KEI Publishers)* 1996.

Nakamura, T, *Deep Gorge Country*, Tokyo *(YAMA-KEI Publishers)* 2000.

Ozaki, T, *Ascent of Hkakabo Razi*, Tokyo *(YAMA-KEI Publishers)* 1997.

Rowell, G, *Mountains of the Middle Kingdom*. San Francisco *(Sierra Club Books)* 1983.

MAPS

Operational Navigation Chart 1:1,000,000 (ONC) and Tactical Pilotage Chart 1:500,000 (TPC) of Aerospace Center, Defense Mapping Agency, St. Louis Air Force Station, Missouri.

Russian Topographic Maps, 1:100,000, 1:200,000, 1:500,000, and 1:1,000,000 (color) covering all the area. (Available in libraries at major universities.)

Map of Mountain Peaks on the Qinghai-Xizang Plateau 1:2,500,000 compiled by the Chinese Research Institute of Surveying and Mapping, China Mountaineering Association. (Can be purchased from China Mountaineering Association.)

Survey Department of China People's Liberation Army (PLA), China, Topographical Maps, 1:50,000 and 1:100,000. (This map is strictly confidential. It is impossible to purchase.)

Map 1 inch: 2 miles and 1 inch: 4 miles of North Burma, surveyed by the British Government in 1942.

SIGUNIANG

Behold one of the great ice lines of all time: the distressingly steep, thin, and long basalt dike on the northwest face of Siguniang, Sichuan Province.

BY MICK FOWLER

Siguniang's north face, where the line is the climb. Mick Fowler

Sometimes a scene remains indelibly imprinted on one's mind. On April 5, 2002 I came across such a scene. I was in central China, cresting a 4,500-meter col (in a bus!) when a range of spiky mountains became visible. They were impressive enough for me to rouse my climbing partner, Paul Ramsden, from his slumbers.

Paul awoke with a start. "Hell! What's that?"

The skyline was dominated by an outrageously spectacular snow-covered peak that towered a good 500 meters over everything else that was visible. It dawned on us that this was it—Siguniang, the mountain we had come to climb. That first view remains etched in my memory.

Siguniang (6,250m), the highest point of the Qionglai Range, is about 250 kilometers from Chengdu, the capital of Sichuan Province. After a six-hour bus ride to the village of Rilong (soon to become a tourist resort), we ferried our gear upward, first using horses, then our backs.

On April 14 we stood, feeling very small, below the towering, unclimbed northwest face, the feature we had come halfway round the world to try. An American team had tried it in 1981 and a Japanese team in 2001. Jack Tackle, one of the Americans, had been kind enough to provide a mouthwatering photograph. Back in England Paul and I had been bold enough to think that we were in with a chance. Now we were not quite so sure. Emotions had rollercoasted since that first sighting from the bus. From directly below, the face had appeared as a 6,000-foot blank granite wall with no obvious lines of weakness. Closer inspection, though, revealed the secret exposed in the Tackle photograph: a hidden basalt dike facing north and cutting clean through the most impressive part of the face. It was choked with ice and just called out to be climbed—in fact it was without doubt the most enticing line that either of us had ever seen. But were we up to it?

It took a day to reach an uncomfortable bivouac at the point where the serious ice climbing began. Already we were having trouble. What Jack's photo had shown as a straight-forward snowslope back in 1981 was now ice punctuated by smooth, featureless granite slabs. Adrenaline flowed freely, and looking up we could see that the ice streak that would form the meat of the route was frequently vertical and intermittently thin. It all looked very distressing.

Day two started badly with me putting in an unconvincing performance on the first ice-streak pitch.

"Do you think it will go?" Paul obviously sensed the adrenaline flow and noted my disturbingly slow progress.

Progress was slow and hesitant, but by dusk our problem was a different one. We were over the first steep section and could see nowhere at all to spend the night. We had brought a small tent with us, but pitching it was out of the question. Fresh snow was pouring mercilessly down the face and we couldn't even find anywhere to cut out a bum ledge.

"Tent over the head?"

It took me a moment to register what Paul was saying. I had been optimistically waiting for a lull that would enable us to use the tent as a double bivouac sack. I had never before used it as a bag over the head although I had read about Joe Tasker and Dick Renshaw spending a night like this on the north face of the Dent Blanche back in the 1970s. It all sounded very unpleasant and I was keen not to emulate their experience. But it had to be admitted that the weather was particularly grim, and any attempt to get into the tent fabric from the top was inevitably destined to end with the tent and everything else full of spindrift.

"As unpleasant as your Taweche bivouac?"

Paul Ramsden appreciating the protection on the third pitch of the second day. Mick Fowler

It was nice of Paul to remind me of the most uncomfortable night of my life. Pat Littlejohn and I had squeezed claustrophobically into a narrow, icy, wind tunnel at 6,000 meters on the northeast buttress of Taweche, in Nepal. Spindrift had poured into the tunnel all night, and we never managed to get inside our sleeping bags. The "one on top of the other" position was not exactly comfortable. Surely this couldn't be that bad? Perhaps it could.

I stood there miserably, making negative noises about the difficulties of belaying securely with a bag over one's head. But I knew that I was tired and cooling down rapidly. We had to do something quickly, and in the conditions I was bleakly aware that I couldn't offer a better suggestion.

Wrapping a large nut in the tent fabric, Paul larksfooted it into our solitary belay and clipped himself into the sling on the inside of the tent.

"Different world in here," he announced cheerfully.

I stared dubiously through the gloom at the tent fabric and wondered why I apparently enjoy mountaineering so much. The tent was well used, and I feared that any serious strain on the worn fabric could have unfortunate results.

"Are you getting in or what?" came from deep in the fabric.

It was dark outside now and the urgency in Paul's voice brought home to me the fact that I was moving lethargically. It was time to doublecheck the safety of the arrangement and make a move.

He was right. It was a different world inside. A world where we hung like a bunch of

Paul Ramsden belaying the start of pitch four, day two. Mick Fowler

Just hanging around having fun. Paul Ramsden belaying pitch three, day three. Mick Fowler

bananas from a single sling while the fabric flapped against our faces and the entrance zipper flailed disconcertingly around our ankles. Extreme care was required, as anything dropped would disappear straight out the bottom of the tent. As if to prove the point, my sleeping mat had miraculously disappeared by the time I came to look for it.

Cooking, or even melting snow, was out of the question. Conversation drifted intermittently as we dozed. We had been unable to get into our sleeping bags and so had opted for standing/hanging in our climbing clothes supplemented by down jackets. Nevertheless, despite minus 20 degrees or so outside, we did not feel worryingly cold. What I mean, of course, is that it was bloody freezing—but, remarkably, frostbite was not a major concern. Good stuff, this modern gear.

The next day we didn't feel very perky and decided to move up just to the first decent bivouac spot and call it a day. The ice was thicker now but with long vertical sections that made climbing with a rucksack ridiculously exhausting. We persevered, with the leader frequently climbing without a sack and then hauling it up after him. This was effective but bad for blisters. We never did find the longed-for decent ledge, but the weather improved and we made much better progress than expected. Our bivouac, another sitting/hanging effort, was slightly better than the previous one in that we at least managed to get into our sleeping bags and melt a small quantity of snow to relieve our parched throats. We passed the long hours listening to the incessant hiss of spindrift and searching endlessly for the much dreamt of, but unachievable, positions of comfort.

Usually I enjoy ice climbing, but after three days laboring in the deep, sun-less freeze of the fault line it was getting a bit wearing. Although the climbing had only a few technically desperate pitches, it was continually steep and we were frequently blasted by cold, enervating waves of spindrift. The altitude and relentless angle made it utterly exhausting. But there was no reason to go down. We were safe, relatively warm, and still had plenty of gas and food. Also we were steadily, if slowly, gaining height. With each pitch climbed the horizon broadened, and the expectant glow of success grew just a little bit stronger.

After three days in the confines of the fault we were just one pitch short of the end of the ice streak and were able to pull out onto what initially promised to be a reasonable bivouac spot. For the first time we were able to get the tent the right way up and put the poles in. Unfortunately

Starting the fourth cold day on the same unrelenting ice hose—Paul Ramsden on the sharp end. Mick Fowler

Paul Ramsden taking the hardware before heading up the fourth pitch of the fourth day. Mick Fowler

though, Paul's end of the "ledge" then collapsed and he ended up spending the night with his head two feet or so lower than his feet. We were desperate for something to drink and eat, but the unconventional pitching arrangement meant that the stove hung awkwardly against the fabric of the side wall. Holding it in a safe position was out of the question; we were far too tired to stay alert for the time it would take to get a decent volume of water from the fine, powdery snow. Instead I wedged my plastic mug between the windshield and the side wall. This was not a good solution. Soon clouds of acrid smoke filled the tent and red plastic globules dripped into Paul's sleeping bag. From his inverted position he was most voluble in voicing his dissatisfaction and insisted in taking over for the culinary highlight of the evening—noodles. Our inability to understand a word of written Chinese was to prompt some surprise on the food front. Much as Paul applied himself magnificently, vindaloo curry noodles are not to be recommended as high-altitude bivouac food.

But mountaineering is full of ups and downs. In the morning the sun was shining and the Ramsden face smiling. Only one more pitch of ice streak remained, a fact that I felt grateful for as I struggled to overcome ring sting and early morning lethargy. Above us now was the line of ice cliffs marking the lower edge of the summit icefields. Back down in base camp, using our binoculars, we had seen an easy-looking line of weakness; but now, as so often happens, things didn't look quite so straightforward. Firstly, the line of apparent weakness turned out to be a slanting vertical section on a series of overhanging ice walls; and, secondly, the serac ice itself was truly awful, dinner-plating in large, uncontrollable sections. Paul set off with gusto but soon ground to a halt.

"Nightmare! You going to have a look?"

I wasn't. I had great faith in his ability and the problems were all too readily apparent. We quickly agreed that outflanking the ice cliffs on the right was the best option. But all this was taking time. After abseiling out of the seracs and traversing laboriously rightward, it was dark by the time we were struggling on easier-angled, but iron-hard, serac ice bounding the right edge of the cliffs.

We ground to a halt and endured yet another sitting/hanging bivouac just 50 meters short of the summit snowslopes. This was the fifth bivouac in a row where we had failed to properly pitch the tent—a new and unwelcome record for both of us! The snowfall, always variable, was particularly grim in the night, building up behind us and forcing our bums off our already inadequate bum ledge. I hung uncomfortably, half in my harness and half in the tent fabric. Paul was just above me in a position whereby the tension in the tent fabric crushed his head to the extent that his helmet was even more useful than usual.

Paul Ramsden (left) and Mick Fowler on the summit at last. Mick Fowler

Good weather on the summit day would be critical for routefinding and pleasant for views. And, as luck would have it, the next morning the angle eased and the skies cleared to reveal an unbroken panorama. The hardships suddenly began to feel worthwhile. We plodded slowly up snowslopes and a corniced ridge to the summit…and felt on top of the world.

The plan now was to descend the unclimbed north ridge. Thankfully, the good weather allowed us to easily locate the top of it. If it had been misty I fear that much summit snowfield wandering would have occurred. As it was, we were soon engrossed in abseiling down a very steep ridge decorated with Peruvian-style snow formations. This had been our reserve objective if the ice streak had gone all wrong, but it would have been a nightmare to ascend.

Beyond this it was endless abseils off Abalakov threads and then we were down, a combined 30 kilograms lighter. Paul also managed 12 days without a crap, a personal best.

It had been a very fine holiday indeed.

SUMMARY OF STATISTICS:

AREA: Qionglai Range, Sichuan Province.

ASCENTS: North face of Siguniang (6,250m). 1,500m, ED(sup). Climbers: Mick Fowler, Paul Ramsden. Also Mike Morrison, Roger Gibbs.

A NOTE ON THE AUTHOR

Born in 1956, Briton Mick Fowler is married with two children, Tessa (11) and Alec (8). "Assistant Director of Capital Taxes" by day, he started climbing seriously in 1976. He was the first climber to do a grade V1 in Scotland (Shield Direct, 1979), and with the ascent of Linden he became one of the first rockclimbers to establish the E6 grade in Britain. He has climbed a string of EDsup routes in Asia and South America, most recently the north face of Changabang (1997) and Arwa Tower (1999). Siguniang's northwest face route won the 2002 Piolet D'Or award for the finest climb of the year (France).

JARJINJABO

New routes, old worlds, and other epiphanies from the Tibetan borderlands.

EDITED BY PETER ATHANS

The unclimbed Todju Puba Spire in the Jarjinjabo Mountains. Robert Mackinlay

It felt like jumping off the edge of the world. Where China's Sichuan Province and Tibet meet in the Tibetan Borderlands, the ranges appear wavelike, one rising behind the other, and exploring such realms has been a passion of mine for years. Having stood atop Everest seven times, and having witnessed countless celebrations and desecrations of that colossal mountain, I was ready to immerse myself in a lesser-known region.

In the summer of 2002, Kasha Rigby, Hilaree Nelson, Jared Ogden, Mark Synnott, Robert MacKinlay, and I joined together on an expedition that did not follow the linear path of most endeavors. Rather, it was cyclical, beginning with a cultural introduction to Tibet. Afterward, our temporary home was the spectacular Jarjinjabo massif of alpine peaks, granite spires, and a monastery with 800 years of history. The expedition's dreamlike quality allowed us to dwell in a place of unlimited possibilities. We established a dozen new routes over the course of our weeks there. Each climber had stories to tell, and the diary excerpts below present varied images of this transcendent and now-accessible place.

MARK SYNNOTT: Here in this valley, surrounded by green-rolling hills, we've spent the last few days at the Litang Horse Festival, an amazing event. There are about 1,000 tents set up here, and we have been mingling with the Tibetans, gaining insights into their culture. The Tibetan Border-lands region is a swath of land that runs north to south, maybe 200 miles wide and 1,000 miles long. On the east are hills with farmlands; on the west is the high Tibetan plateau, basically a desert. Until four years ago, outsiders had rarely visited—there was no road. But after a silver mine was discovered, a new road gave access to an incredible mountain valley with, among other features, one of the few monasteries in Tibet that wasn't destroyed by the Chinese.

JARED OGDEN: We spent the first two days traveling by Jeep over the harshest roads you can imagine. We arrived at a beautiful pass around 14,000 feet, with a rock shrine that formed the gateway onto the plateau. It was an amazing landscape of light, green valleys, and forests. We finally arrived in the village of Litang, where we will be spending two days. This is where the Horse Festi-val is held, and many people are doing traditional songs and dances. Everyone feels good and the weather has been fantastic. We're traveling to the Jarjinjabo Range shortly, where our base camp

Mark Synnott on the second pitch of the southeast face route of Janmo Spire. Robert Mackinlay

Synnott on or near the fourth pitch of the southeast face of Janmo Spire. Jared Ogden

will be for three weeks. There is a monastery and a hot spring there at 12,500 feet, and everyone is excited to start climbing and skiing. It's been great to see and interact with the Tibetans. Their dress is unbelievable! On our first night we went out for dinner and saw a disco next door, so we went over and partied to rave music with Tibetan horsemen—incredible equestrians and rowdy dancers.

PETER ATHANS: As Mark, Jared, and I loaded gear for the approach to a camp beneath slender Janmo Spire, we passed through fragrant cedars with only fluttering prayer flags and the occasional grazing yak to disturb our thoughts. Everywhere, symbols of an ancient culture spoke of ardent faith: carved mantra rock art, paintings, and prayer flags. Although the Red Guard desecrated this area 40 years ago, their shameless work is only a distant nightmare, and now the beauty of this place is miraculous.

We arrived in camp by mid-morning, erected the tent, and then labored uphill to the bottom of the spire. The burning questions for me before the expedition were, "Is the rock sound," and "Are the climbs well protected?" Both answers, as we soon discovered, were a resounding "Yes!"

Pete Athans launching onto Janmo Spire. Robert Mackinlay

Mark Synnott belaying Pete Athans on the southwest buttress of Jarjinjabo. Jared Ogden

Jared won the toss for the first pitch and stepped from snow onto rock. Corners and finger cracks began steeply but were of good size, and he moved up smoothly into a pod before the crack opened to fist and off-width size. These cracks were remarkably clean, and Jared flowed through them confidently with an array of off-width moves. A hundred feet up, on a tiny ledge beneath an overhang, he stopped and constructed a belay.

Mark followed, climbing swiftly through the crux. Then he attacked an overhanging corner, throwing finger-locks into the crack that relented with a perfect hand jam where the angle eased. Pulling through sustained moves like this at nearly 17,000 feet was a challenge aerobically, so Mark took a short break before continuing up an elegant corner.

Routefinding is an acquired skill that borders on art, where one's imagination perceives a line in the absence of weaknesses. On Janmo Spire climbable options were everywhere, and pitch after pitch unfolded, with some of the cleanest and most enjoyable rock climbing I have ever experienced. All of us drew excellent pitches, mostly pure crack climbing with occasional face moves to add variety. The climb went free at a challenging standard.

As we reached the top of the seventh pitch, it appeared that we had it made. But my memory told me otherwise: from photos I had unearthed earlier, I recalled the summit block as an impregnable obelisk, devoid of features. I was hopeful that the photos weren't showing everything—that a hidden line existed. I was wrong. Incipient crack systems on all sides ended at half height on the summit block, and to complete the route we would need to place at least eight bolts. In the supernatural orange twilight we debated our next move. We hadn't yet drilled, our intention being to leave the tower unchanged. The idea of not imposing ourselves on the landscape seemed attractive, and so, in harmony with the style of our ascent and with the local Buddhist attitudes, we chose to descend, leaving the summit block untouched.

KASHA RIGBY: It's another 4:15 wake up, with rain pouring against our tent. How many days has it been now? The routine: wake up with goals of a summit, then go back to sleep with the sound of rain. Yesterday there was a giant hailstorm, today a small earthquake. I think it's been only four days, but somehow it feels like more. When returning home after being on an expedition, I find people thinking the trip had been "glamorous." Shoulder to shoulder with Hilaree in our little cocoon, she asks me if I am aware of the rat's nest in my hair. What glamour! I wonder if other women in the developed world get the luxury of feeling competent and glamorous irrespective of how they look. I don't want to go back to the "real" world.

SYNNOTT: Today we climbed what may well be the best route of the trip: the eye-catching southwest buttress of Jarjinjabo. We wanted to tackle the south face head on, but when we arrived at the base we found that the rock was wet and the crack systems discontinuous. There's a good line tackling the bottom half of the face and the same goes for the top, but the problem is that they don't link up. The southwest buttress, on the other hand, was a dream climb, except for one overhanging crack filled with mud and green slime. I knew it was free climbable, but it was so nasty that I found myself pulling on a couple of pieces to get through.

Jared, Pete, and I swapped leads all the way, traversing back and forth, negotiating tricky detours around gendarmes. It was a long day because it just isn't fast to climb with three. The route was around 13 pitches, and we were pretty tired when we pulled up over the top. Jarjinjabo, at 17,200 feet, is the biggest peak in this massif. Climbing this peak had been one of the main objectives of the expedition, so it was great to stroll the last few yards to the summit.

On some of my previous "first ascents" I'd arrived on top only to find an old piece of gear, a bolt, or some other item. We were nervous about this happening, but there was nothing. We sat silently for a few minutes, absorbing the magnificent surroundings. The setting sun sent a million shafts of light through the purple, blue, and gray clouds, illuminating the valley below in that magical light we had seen many times on the Tibetan plateau. I took a few photos but realized that no image could ever do it justice. Better to sit still and let it burn into my memory. Days like this are what climbing is all about.

ATHANS: During the course of our expedition, MacKinlay and I made two first ascents that I count among my best in 30 years of

Jared Ogden, Mark Synnott, and Pete Athans on the southwest buttress of Jarjinjabo. Robert Mackinlay

The northern Jarjinjabo Massif, showing Janmo Spire in the upper right and Jarjinjabo itself is on far upper right. Note that this is slightly north and slightly less high than the Jarjinjabo (5,812') in Tamotsu Nakamura's East of the Himalaya story, in this issue. Robert Mackinlay

climbing. One of these was on Janmo Spire, which paralleled the trip's first route. I had been eyeing a crack system that disappeared up into overhangs. An initial short chimney and face gave access to the bottom of the system, and I could see that this pitch was going to be excellent in its steepness, cleanness, and sweeping elegance. Janmo continued its reputation as being created solely for climbers, as the crack above was ideal jamming size for an unbroken 200 feet. I slung a perfectly placed flake for protection, then launched myself upward. The dreamlike pitch seemed endless. I could feel the tension in my abdomen from having to breathe excessively because of the altitude. Yet my mind, relaxed and focused, allowed me to be in the moment. For me, pitches like that are true gratification—simply to live with no past or future consider- ations, savoring the moment, losing identity. It's this "action without I" that gives me such an intense feeling of liberation. Climbing is about liberation of the spirit—away from ego, desire, and sometimes even the sensation of body.

SYNNOTT: Just got back from high camp last night, having managed three new routes in three days. Yesterday, Jared and I made the first ascent of a beautiful tower we're calling Jarjinjabo's Son. It was about 1,300 feet high, and we did it all free, with the crux being a 5.10+ finger crack leading out a small roof. I was able to get in two bomber cams below the roof and then punched through a holdless section for five feet to another good hand jam. 5.10 feels a lot harder at 17,000 feet than it does at home. Shortly after that, Jared and I were sitting on the summit, a flat granite block about as big as a picnic table.

We rappelled, downclimbed, and then hiked back to advanced base camp. We packed everything and headed down because we had a plan for today: to climb the huge ridge rising above the nunnery. "Nunnery Ridge" was what we proposed calling it, even before we set foot on it. We were a little presumptuous.

We got up at about 6 a.m. I was tired but the weather was beautiful and we weren't about to waste the day. Our plan was to follow the ridge, and from base to top we estimated it to involve 4,000 feet of gain. We'd carry only one quart of water each, energy gels, and raingear. To save weight we decided not to carry sneakers, instead hiking up in our Sportivas.

It turned out we had misinterpreted the topography. What appeared from a distance to be a continuous ridge turned out to be a bunch of disjointed gendarmes. The outcome was apparent, and Jared was first to say, "This route is a piece of junk." We bailed.

HILAREE NELSON: Kasha and I came along to fill in the skiing/mountaineering side of the group. Both of us were a bit skeptical of trying to ski in the northern hemisphere in August, even if the objectives soared to 17,000 feet; nonetheless, we were game to give it a try. For three weeks we had been utterly denied. We had set foot on snow once, but our skis hadn't left their bags. Our frustration was now palpable, especially given the fact that the "boys" have been so successful with their climbing. Their excitement was killing us.

We had two days left to turn our fortunes around, and it wasn't going to happen on snow; we had to transform ourselves into rock climbers.

Morning dawned and we felt like today might be the day for success. I had a lot more climbing experience than Kasha, so I led a route while she suffered through long belays. We simul-climbed, got lost, got stuck, got cuts and bruises, but we made the summit! Eight hours after we started, we stood on top of Jarjinjabo. For all our excitement, it might as well have been Everest. We finally got the view we had been dreaming about. It was all air below and our previous frustrations blew away with the wind.

ATHANS: Late August arrived unwelcome; it was time to bid Jarjinjabo farewell. The monastery, with its surrounding forests and clustered huts, had become our temporary home, but it was time to relinquish it. Our expedition was a temporal experience in an environment that seemed to defy time until recently, with the advent of local mining. It might have been easy for us to criticize the development of the area's wealth; however, we certainly wouldn't have learned of the region's existence without the new access roads. We came away with one wish: that this remarkable and spiritual place will remain cherished by those in Tibet, China, and, indeed, all nations.

SUMMARY OF STATISTICS:

AREA: Kham Region of West Sichuan on the Tibetan Plateau

Mark Synnott, Jared Ogden, and Pete Athans racking up at the Zhoupu Monastery. Robert Mackinlay

ALONE

After three ascents with a rope, it was time to cast the lifeline asunder.
Witness what may be the most technically difficult free-solo climb
in the Alps, on the Cima Grande, Dolomites.

ALEXANDER HUBER

Alexander Huber hanging out on the upper 7a+ crux pitch. Heinz Zak

Negotiating the lower crux move—an insecure lieback hold—on the fifth pitch. Heinz Zak

Beforehand, there was a feeling of fear, fear that I could make a mistake. If a hold broke, if I fell backward into the tremendous space, what would I think about? Would I be angry? What would happen when my body smashed onto the talus? Would I feel anything?

I also knew that I was familiar with every single meter of the Hasse-Brandler Direttissima on the north face of the Cima Grande di Lavaredo, having done the route four times recently. I was capable of controlling all the moves of the route, which had one pitch of 5.12a and four of 5.11. Yet during the day and the night before my climb, I was attacked again and again by ever-changing feelings. If I were to continue after reaching the "Point of No Return" 60 meters above the ground, then there was just one exit—finish the 500 meters of the face.

The hour-long hike to the base passed without my noticing the real world. A wild fight between my feelings of fear and confidence ensued, and every minute these feelings changed. I knew that once I began climbing, my positive feelings could control my actions. Yet I also felt that I would have only one chance—if I could not do it this day, then the overwhelming dimension of the 560-meter face would have knocked me away.

Restless, I hiked along the base of the wall, forward and backward, again and again. I sat down once again where the route began. I knew that my feelings, completely caught up by the idea, wouldn't let me go before I would give it a try, yet I wished I had never thought of climbing the Direttissima free solo. But now I had no other choice; I was totally possessed, caught by the pressure that I had always wanted to avoid. My brain was stressed.

Having put on my climbing shoes, a chalk bag, and my helmet (this was all the gear I took with me), I left the ground. But I couldn't feel what I was doing and was totally numb.

Alexander Huber during his on-camera repeat free solo ascent of the Direttissima route on the Cima Grande.
Heinz Zak

This was no way to free solo a big face! I retreated to the ground. This was a moment of relief, however, since I knew that for the first 60 meters I had the chance to get my feelings under control, to change from fear-mode into super-high concentration.

Much more relaxed, I started again. The difficulties appeared to be easy, and I didn't feel even a little bit of fear—I was 100 percent focused on the next move. When I reached the "Point of No Return," I realized that the

The Tre Cime di Lavaredo, showing the Direttissima route on the Cime Grande. Heinz Zak

crux had been at the base: leaving the ground had been the greatest barrier. Under full control I climbed meters and meters of steep dolomite, move by move. I well remembered all the difficult sections from my previous climbs, and everything went well and smoothly, almost as if I were a machine.

After 50 minutes and 200 meters of climbing I reached a ledge just below the most difficult 100 meters. I felt tired—not my muscles but my brain. I had just done 50 minutes of the highest concentration climbing without a single second of rest. Needing a break, I lay on the ledge and looked straight up to the overhangs above, the most difficult and impressive part of the Direttissima.

After a 20-minute break I went on, completely focused on the next moves. Climbing the remaining 300 meters, move by move in an ever-constant rhythm, I found my emotions getting more intense. More and more I noticed the world around me—the clouds, the fog. The higher I went, the more relaxed I became, like a river whose rapids die in its delta.

Editor's note: Huber was completely alone on this remarkable solo climb—the photographs shown here were taken several weeks later. Huber says that his route was "mentally, the hardest thing I have done in mountaineering. Regarding the danger, when I began the route I had my emotions well balanced and the knowledge that my mental strength was stable. Of course, this route is valid only for myself and any other free-solo climber with similar mental strengths." To prepare for this climb, Huber spent six days training on the route with partners and alone. He also free-soloed a number of shorter climbs up to 5.13c.

SUMMARY OF STATISTICS:

AREA: Tre Cime di Lavaredo, Dolomites, Italy

ASCENT: Free solo of the Direttissima, a.k.a. "Hasse-Brandler," on the Cima Grande (500m, 20 "pitches," 1 of 5.12a, 4 of 5.11, 4 of 5.10). August 1, 2002. The first 350m are continuously overhanging.

A Code to Climb By

Leading climbers gather in Tyrolia to shape the ethical foundation of their sport.

Eliza Moran

Costumed actors in Austria represent periods from climbing history. Gerold Benedikter

In September, 2002, more than 100 representatives of mountaineering federations and elite climbers from around the world arrived in Innsbruck, Austria, to craft the final version of "The Mountain Code," a document that had grown out of a five-year initiative begun within the UIAA. (UIAA is the French-based acronym for the International Mountaineering and Climbing Federation).

The opening festivities were entertainment on a grand scale, courtesy of hosts that included the Austrian government and the city of Innsbruck, in addition to the Austrian and German alpine clubs. The mayor of Innsbruck and other dignitaries addressed the gathering, followed by a concert by the European Philharmonic Orchestra to the slides of climbing photographer Heinz Zak. Sir Christian Bonington, Tom Frost, Alexander Huber, Reinhold Messner, and Doug Scott were among the speakers who set the inspirational tone at the podium for the heart of the weekend, which was two days of intense discussions within diverse working groups. Each of these groups consisted of 10 to 20 climbers, and was responsible for refining its own set of "Articles" that would become the "Tyrol Declaration." The resulting text is presented verbatim on the following 10 pages of this Journal.

The goal was to define a set of principles that would stand as a foundation for generations of climbers, imparting a sense of personal responsibility to guide the freedom and risks in the sport. To close the gathering, a passionate Bonington distilled the message into "Stretch your limits, lift your spirits, and aim for the top," which became the motto for the final paper.

Eliza Moran is Vice President of the UIAA Mountaineering Commission

FREEDOM, WITH BOUNDARIES

*The following is condensed from an opening address
to the delegates of the Innsbruck Congress.*

TOM FROST

During the golden age of Yosemite big wall climbing in the 1960s, we loved the movement, the beauty of the creation, and the depth of our companionship. Those El Cap climbs changed my life. They changed who I was.

The golden age was all about style. We did not have any concerns about regulations, over-use, worn out routes, topos, or public opinion. We were very mindful of the example of our pioneer predecessors, but we felt free to do as we saw fit.

El Cap in the 1960s was a blank page waiting to be written upon. But life always has two opposing views—and so it was in the beginning of the golden age. One view emerged which supported style and preservation. The motto was, "leave no trace." These proponents believed, "It isn't getting to the top that counts, it's the way you do it." This mentality shaped character. Climbing became an internal game. It was based on responsibility.

The opposing view was not about style or responsibility. Its foundation was entitlement. These climbers were not concerned about how they climbed, nor about the environment, or about future climbers. Getting to the top was the goal. Theirs was an external game.

The clean climbing revolution of the 1970s replaced the use of pitons with nuts, runners, and spring-loaded cams. This switch to clean climbing saved our cracks.

In the 1980s, the arrival of sport climbing opened climbing on previously unprotectable walls with the use of artificial protection. This type of climbing inflamed the existing conflict among climbers between "leave no trace" and "do what you want."

The rise of gym climbing in the 1970s popularized the sport. Climbing no longer is an obscure sport done by a few, with makeshift equipment, in remote places. In 2002 climbing is big business, highly visible, extremely popular, diversified, unmanaged, and highly scrutinized. We are here today to address these issues.

We now live in a mobile, ravenous information age. This has afforded many with much, and greatly shrunk the world. It has created a subculture of wanna-bes, seeking instant gratification with little or no accountability. This group has invaded climbing. They act like unmanaged youth: I want it, I take it, I walk away from it, and there are no consequences.

To increase awareness we must become conversant with: The Problem, The Cause, The Solution, and The Implementation. The skills we need for this task, both during this conference and after the "Tyrol Declaration" is completed, are: Identification, Listening, Communication, Understanding, Education, Negotiation, and Respect. The groups we need to reach are these: All climbers of every type, land managers, governments, outdoor organizations, adventure-sport businesses, and environmentalists.

Crafting a document that outlines freedom governed by boundaries has always been a challenge. Yet, I believe this convention will find its way through the issues and present a set of guidelines that will stand as a firm foundation and ensure the continuation of climbing for generations.

Illustration by Mike Clelland

THE TYROL DECLARATION ON BEST PRACTICE IN MOUNTAIN SPORTS

"Stretch your limits, lift your spirits and aim for the top"

ADOPTED BY THE FUTURE OF MOUNTAIN SPORTS CONFERENCE, INNSBRUCK, SEPTEMBER 6–8, 2002

All over the world, millions of people practice mountaineering, hiking, trekking and rock climbing. In many countries mountain sports have become a significant factor of everyday life.

Hardly any other activity encompasses such a broad motivational spectrum as does mountain sports. It gives people the opportunity to realize personal goals and pursue meaningful lifelong activity. Motives for being active in the mountains and on the rocks range from health benefits, pleasure of movement, contact with nature and social incentives, to the thrill of exploration and adventure.

The Tyrol Declaration on Best Practice in Mountain Sports passed by the conference on the Future of Mountain Sports in Innsbruck on September 8, 2002, contains a set of values and maxims to provide guidance on best practice in mountain sports. These are not rules or detailed instructions, rather they:

1. Define today's fundamental values in mountain sports
2. Contain principles and standards of conduct
3. Formulate the ethical criteria for decision-making in uncertain situations
4. Present the ethical principles by which the public can judge mountain sports
5. Introduce beginners to the values and moral principles of their sport.

It is the aim of the Tyrol Declaration to help realize the innate potential of mountain sports for recreation and personal growth as well as for promoting social development, cultural understanding and environmental awareness. To this end, the Tyrol Declaration picks up on the traditional unwritten values and codes of conduct inherent in the sport and expands on them to meet the demands of our times. The fundamental values on which the Tyrol Declaration is based, hold true for all individuals engaged in mountain sports worldwide – whether they be hikers and trekkers, sport climbers, or mountaineers seeking to push their limits at high altitudes. Even if some of the guidelines for conduct are of relevance for only a small elite, a lot of the proposals formulated in the Tyrol Declaration are addressed to the mountain sports community as a whole. With these suggestions we especially hope to reach our youth, for they are the future of mountain sports.

THE TYROL DECLARATION IS AN APPEAL TO:

- Accept the risks and assume responsibility
- Balance your goals with your skills and equipment
- Play by fair means and report honestly
- Strive for best practice and never stop learning
- Be tolerant, considerate and help each other
- Protect the wild and natural character of mountains and cliffs
- Support local communities and their sustainable development.

THE TYROL DECLARATION IS BASED ON THE FOLLOWING HIERARCHY OF VALUES:

- **Human dignity** – the premise that human beings are born free and equal in dignity and rights and should treat one another in the spirit of brotherhood. Particular attention should be given to equal rights of men and women.
- **Life, liberty and happiness** – as inalienable human rights and with a special responsibility in mountains sports to help protect the rights of communities in mountain areas.
- **Intactness of nature** – as a commitment to secure the ecological value and natural characteristics of mountains and cliffs worldwide. This includes the protection of endangered species of flora and fauna, their ecosystems and the landscape.
- **Solidarity** – as an opportunity through participation in mountain sports to promote teamwork, cooperation and understanding and overcome barriers due to gender, age, nationality, level of ability, social or ethnic origin, religion or belief.
- **Self-actualization** – as a chance through participation in mountain sports to make meaningful progress towards important goals and achieve personal fulfillment.
- **Truth** – as recognition that in mountain sports honesty is essential to evaluate accomplishments. If arbitrariness replaces truth, it becomes impossible to assess performance in climbing.
- **Excellence** – as an opportunity through participation in mountain sports to strive for previously unattained goals and to set higher standards.
- **Adventure** – as recognition that in mountain sports the management of risk through judgment, skills and personal responsibility is an essential factor. The diversity of mountain sports allows everyone to chose their own adventure, where skills and dangers are in balance.

THE ARTICLES OF THE TYROL DECLARATION

Article 1 – Individual Responsibility
MAXIM
Mountaineers and climbers practice their sport in situations where there is risk of accidents and outside help may not be available. With this in mind, they pursue this activity at their own responsibility and are accountable for their own safety. The individual's actions should not endanger those around them nor the environment.

Article 2 – Team Spirit
MAXIM

Members of the team should be prepared to make compromises in order to balance the interests and abilities of all the group.

Article 3 – Climbing & Mountaineering Community
MAXIM

We owe every person we meet in the mountains or on the rocks an equal measure of respect. Even in isolated conditions and stressful situations, we should not forget to treat others as we want to be treated ourselves.

Article 4 – Visiting Foreign Countries
MAXIM

As guests in foreign cultures, we should always conduct ourselves politely and with restraint towards the people there – our hosts. We will respect holy mountains and other sacred places while seeking to benefit and assist local economy and people. Understanding of foreign cultures is part of a complete climbing experience.

Article 5 – Responsibilities of Mountain Guides and other Leaders
MAXIM

Professional mountain guides, other leaders and group members should each understand their respective roles and respect the freedoms and rights of other groups and individuals. In order to be prepared guides, leaders and group members should understand the demands, hazards and risks of the objective, have the necessary skills, experience and correct equipment, and check the weather and conditions.

Article 6 – Emergencies, Dying and Death
MAXIM

To be prepared for emergencies and situations involving serious accidents and death all participants in mountain sports should clearly understand the risks and hazards and the need to have appropriate skills, knowledge and equipment. All participants need to be ready to help others in the event of an emergency or accident and also be ready to face the consequences of a tragedy.

Article 7 – Access and Conservation
MAXIM

We believe that freedom of access to mountains and cliffs in a responsible manner is a fundamental right. We should always practice our activities in an environmentally sensitive way and be proactive in preserving nature. We respect access restrictions and regulations agreed by climbers with nature conservation organizations and authorities.

Article 8 – Style
MAXIM

The quality of the experience and how we solve a problem is more important than whether we solve it. We strive to leave no trace.

Article 9 – First Ascents
MAXIM

The first ascent of a route or a mountain is a creative act. It should be done in at least as good a style as the traditions of the region and show responsibility toward the local climbing community and the needs of future climbers.

Article 10 – Sponsorship, Advertising and Public Relations
MAXIM

The cooperation between sponsors and athletes must be a professional relationship that serves the best interests of mountain sports. It is the responsibility of the mountain sports community in all its aspects to educate and inform both media and public in a proactive manner.

THE MAXIMS AND GUIDELINES OF THE TYROL DECLARATION

Article 1 – Individual Responsibility
MAXIM

Mountaineers and climbers practice their sport in situations where there is risk of accidents and outside help may not be available. With this in mind, they pursue this activity at their own responsibility and are accountable for their own safety. The individual's actions should not endanger those around them nor the environment.

> **1.** We choose our goals according to our own actual skills or those of the team and according to the conditions on the mountains. Refraining from doing the climb should be a valid option.
> **2.** We make sure that we have the proper training for our goal, that we have planned the climb or trip carefully and have gone through the necessary preparations.
> **3.** We make sure we're properly equipped on every trip and know how to use the equipment.

Article 2 – Team Spirit
MAXIM

Members of the team should be prepared to make compromises in order to balance the interests and abilities of all the group.

> **1.** Each member of the team should have regard and take responsibility for the safety of their team members.
> **2.** No team member should be left alone if this risks his/her well-being.

Article 3 – Climbing & Mountaineering Community
MAXIM

We owe every person we meet in the mountains or on the rocks an equal measure of respect. Even in isolated conditions and stressful situations, we should not forget to treat others as we want to be treated ourselves.

1. We do everything we can, not to endanger others and we warn others of potential dangers.

2. We ensure that no one is discriminated against.

3. As visitors, we respect the local rules.

4. We do not hinder or disturb others more than necessary. We let faster parties pass. We don't occupy routes others are waiting to do.

5. Our reports on climbs truthfully reflect the actual events in detail.

Article 4 – Visiting Foreign Countries
MAXIM

As guests in foreign cultures, we should always conduct ourselves politely and with restraint towards the people there – our hosts. We will respect holy mountains and other sacred places while seeking to benefit and assist local economy and people. Understanding of foreign cultures is part of a complete climbing experience.

1. Always treat the people in your host country with kindness, tolerance and respect.

2. Strictly adhere to any climbing regulations implemented by your host country.

3. It is advisable to read up on the history, society, political structure, art and religion of the country visited before embarking on the trip to enhance our understanding of its people and their environment. In case of political uncertainty, seek official advice.

4. It's wise to develop some basic skills in the language of our host country: forms of greeting, please and thank you, days of the week, time, numbers, etc. It is always astounding to see how much this little investment improves the quality of communication. By this we contribute to the understanding between cultures.

5. Never pass up an opportunity to share your climbing skills with interested locals. Joint expeditions with climbers from the host country are the best setting for an exchange of experience.

6. At all costs we avoid offending the religious feelings of our hosts. For example, we should not display naked skin in places, where it is unacceptable for religious or social reasons. If some expressions of other religions are beyond our comprehension, we are tolerant and refrain from passing judgment.

7. We give all possible assistance to local inhabitants in need. An expedition doctor is often in a position to make a decisive difference in the life of an acutely ill person.

8. To benefit the mountain communities economically, we buy regional products, if feasible, and take advantage of local services.

9. We are encouraged to assist local mountain communities by initiating and supporting facilities favoring sustainable development, for example training and educational services or ecologically compatible economic enterprises.

Article 5 – Responsibilities of Mountain Guides and other Leaders
MAXIM

Professional mountain guides, other leaders and group members should each understand their respective roles and respect the freedoms and rights of other groups and individuals. In order to be prepared guides, leaders and group members should understand the demands, hazards and risks of the objective, have the necessary skills, experience and correct equipment, and check the weather and conditions.

1. The guide or leader informs the client or group about the risk inherent in a climb and the current danger level and if they are suitably experienced involves them in the decision-making process.
2. The selected route should relate to the skill and experience of the client or group in order to ensure it is an enjoyable and developmental experience.
3. If necessary the guide or leader points out the limits of his or her own ability and where appropriate refers clients or groups to more capable colleagues. It is the responsibility of clients and group members to point out if they believe a risk or hazard is too great and that retreat or alternative options should be followed.
4. In circumstances such as extreme climbs and high altitude ascents guides and leaders should carefully brief their clients and groups to ensure everyone is fully aware of the limits of support that guides and leaders can provide.
5. Local guides inform visiting colleagues about the distinctive features of their area and the current conditions.

Article 6 – Emergencies, Dying and Death
MAXIM
To be prepared for emergencies and situations involving serious accidents and death all participants in mountain sports should clearly understand the risks and hazards and the need to have appropriate skills, knowledge and equipment. All participants need to be ready to help others in the event of an emergency or accident and also be ready to face the consequences of a tragedy.

1. Helping someone in trouble has absolute priority over reaching goals we set for ourselves in the mountains. Saving a life or reducing damage to an injured person's health is far more valuable than the hardest of first ascents.
2. In an emergency if outside assistance is not available and we are in a position to help, we should be prepared to give all the support we can to persons in trouble as far as is feasible without endangering ourselves.
3. Someone who is seriously injured or dying should be made as comfortable as possible and offered life preserving support.
4. In a remote area if it is not possible to recover the body, the location should be recorded as accurately as possible with any indications as to the identity of the deceased.
5. Personal possessions, such as camera, diary, notebook, photographs, letters and other personal artifacts should be safeguarded for and delivered to the bereaved.
6. Under no circumstances may pictures of the deceased be published without prior consent of the family.

Article 7 – Access and Conservation

MAXIM

We believe that freedom of access to mountains and cliffs in a responsible manner is a fundamental right. We should always practice our activities in an environmentally sensitive way and be proactive in preserving nature. We respect access restrictions and regulations agreed by climbers with nature conservation organizations and authorities.

1. We respect the measures to preserve cliff and mountain environments and the wildlife they support and we encourage our fellow climbers to do likewise. By avoiding noise, we strive to reduce disturbing wildlife to a minimum.

2. If possible, we approach our destination using public transportation or car pools in order to minimize traffic on the roads.

3. In order to avoid erosion and not to disturb wildlife, we stay on trails during approaches and descents and, in the wilderness, pick out the most eco-compatible route.

4. During the breeding and nesting periods of cliff dwelling species we respect seasonal access restrictions. As soon as we learn about any breeding activity, we should pass on this knowledge to fellow climbers and ensure that they stay away from the nesting area.

5. During first ascents, we are careful not to endanger the biotopes of rare species of plants and animals. In equipping and redeveloping routes, we should take all precautions to minimize their environmental impact.

6. The broad implications of popularizing areas through retro-bolting should be carefully considered. Increased numbers may cause access problems.

7. We minimize rock damage by using the least detrimental protection technique.

8. Not only do we carry our own garbage back to civilization, but we also pick up any rubbish left by others.

9. In the absence of sanitary installations, we keep an adequate distance from homes, camp sites, creeks, rivers or lakes while defecating and take all the necessary measures to avoid damage to the ecosystem. We refrain from offending other people's aesthetic feelings. In highly frequented areas with a low level of biological activity, climbers take the trouble to pack out their feces.

10. We keep the campsite clean, avoiding waste as much as possible or dispose our rubbish adequately. All climbing material – fixed ropes, tents and oxygen bottles – must be removed from the mountain.

11. We keep energy consumption to a minimum. Especially in countries with a wood shortage, we refrain from action that could contribute to the further decline of forests. In countries with endangered forests, we need to carry adequate fuel to prepare food for all participants in an expedition.

12. Helicopter tourism should be minimized where it is detrimental to nature or culture.

13. In conflicts over access issues, landowners, authorities and associations should negotiate to find solutions satisfactory to all parties.

14. We take an active part in the implementation of these regulations, especially by publicizing them and establishing the necessary infrastructure.

15. Together with the mountaineering associations and other conservation groups we are proactive on the political level in protecting natural habitats and the environment.

Article 8 – Style
MAXIM
The quality of the experience and how we solve a problem is more important than whether we solve it. We strive to leave no trace.

1. We aim to preserve the original character of all climbs, most especially those with historical significance. This means that climbers should not increase fixed protection on existing routes. The exception is when there is a local consensus – including agreement from the first ascensionists – to change the level of fixed protection by placing new gear or removing existing gear.

2. We respect the diversity of regional traditions and will not try to impose our point of view upon other climbing cultures – nor will we accept their ways imposed upon ours.

3. Rock and mountains are a limited resource for adventure that must be shared by climbers with many interests and over many generations to come. We realize that future generations will need to find their own NEW adventures within this limited resource. We try to develop crags or mountains in a way that doesn't steal opportunity from the future.

4. Within a region where bolts are accepted, it is desirable to keep routes, sections of cliffs, or entire cliffs free of bolts in order to preserve a refuge for adventure and to show respect for diverse climbing interests.

5. Naturally protected routes can be just as fun and safe for recreational climbers as bolted routes. Most climbers can learn to place safe natural protection and should be educated to the fact that this provides additional adventure and a rich and natural experience with comparable safety, once the techniques have been learned.

6. In cases of conflicting interest groups, climbers should resolve their differences through dialogue and negotiation to avoid access being threatened.

7. Commercial pressures should never influence the climbing ethics of a person or a region.

8. Good style on big mountains implies not using fixed ropes, performance-enhancing drugs, or bottled oxygen.

Article 9 – First Ascents
MAXIM
The first ascent of a route or a mountain is a creative act. It should be done in at least as good a style as the traditions of the region and show responsibility toward the local climbing community and the needs of future climbers.

1. First ascents should be environmentally sound and compatible with local regulations, the wishes of landowners, and the spiritual values of the local population.

2. We will not deface the rock by chopping or adding holds.

3. In alpine regions, first ascents should be done exclusively on lead (no prefixing from above).

4. After giving full respect to local traditions, it is up to the first ascentionist to determine the level of fixed protection on their route (taking into account the suggestions in Article 8).

5. In areas designated as wilderness or natural reserves by land managers or the local access committee, bolts should be limited to an absolute minimum to preserve access.

6. Drilling holes and placing fixed gear during the first ascent of aid climbs should be kept to a bare minimum (bolts should be avoided even on belay anchors unless absolutely necessary).

7. Adventure routes should be left as natural as possible, relying on removable protection whenever it is available and using bolts only when necessary and always subject to local traditions.

8. The independent character of adjacent routes must not be compromised.

9. When reporting first ascents, it is important to report the details as accurately as possible. A climber's honesty and integrity will be assumed unless there is compromising evidence.

10. High-altitude mountains are a limited resource. We especially encourage climbers to use the best style.

Article 10 – Sponsorship, Advertising and Public Relations
MAXIM

The cooperation between sponsors and athletes must be a professional relationship that serves the best interests of mountain sports. It is the responsibility of the mountain sports community in all its aspects to educate and inform both media and public in a proactive manner.

1. Mutual understanding between sponsor and athlete is necessary to define common goals. The many facets of mountain sports require clear identification of the specific expertise of both athlete and sponsor to maximize opportunities.

2. To maintain and improve their level of performance, climbers are dependent on continuous support from their sponsors. For this reason it is important that the sponsors keep backing their partners even after a series of failures. Under no circumstances may the sponsor pressure the climber into performing.

3. To establish a permanent presence in all media, clear channels of communication must be organized and maintained.

4. Climbers should take pains to report their activities realistically. An accurate account enhances not only the credibility of the climber, but also the public reputation of his sport.

5. The athlete is ultimately responsible for representing to sponsor and media the ethics, style, social and environmental responsibility stated in the Tyrol Declaration.

Climbs and Expeditions

2003

Accounts from the various climbs and expeditions of the world are listed geographically from north to south and from west to east within the noted countries. We begin our coverage with the Contiguous United States and move to Alaska in order for the climbs in the Alaska's Wrangell Mountains to segue into the St. Elias climbs in Canada.

We encourage all climbers to submit accounts of notable activity, especially long new routes (generally defined as U.S. commitment Grade IV—full-day climbs—or longer). Please submit reports as early as possible (see Submissions Guidelines at the back of this Journal).

For conversions of meters to feet, multiply by 3.28; for feet to meters, multiply by 0.30.

Unless otherwise noted, all reports are from the 2002 calendar year.

NORTH AMERICA
CONTIGUOUS UNITED STATES

Washington

Washington climbing, trends and new routes. In recent years alpine climbing in the Washington Cascades has become less exploratory. First ascents are still being made but less frequently. However, speed ascents and enchainments have become more popular. Many climbs traditionally done over two to three days are now often climbed in under 12 hours. Speed ascents, as well as other activities, have focused on well-documented classics with easy access. "Select" and "Classic" guidebooks have concentrated crowds on certain routes, while other routes are ignored. Also, the amount of "beta," including route conditions and gear suggestions, that is available for classic climbs has increased dramatically, partially due to the popular website www.Cascadeclimbers.com.

Other trends have resulted from increased Forest Service and Park Service control of access, for instance by permit requirements for areas such as Boston Basin, The Enchantments, Mt. Baker, Mt. Rainier, Mt. St. Helens, and Mt. Adams. Furthermore, Mt. Rainier National Park doubled its climbing permit fee to $30 per person, though the permit is now valid for the calendar year. The Fee Demonstration Program has been increasingly enforced by the Forest Service within Wenatchee, Mt. Baker, and Snoqualmie national forests.

In addition to the individual new-route reports below, the following shorter new routes have been recently established.

On July 19–20 Jens Klubberud and Loren Campbell established a route (12 pitches, III+ 5.6, glacier travel) on the northeast face of Mt. Formidable. The route leaves the Formidable Glacier at the lowest point where the face meets the glacier, on the right side of the face. It goes up for two dirty pitches before traversing left and up on ledge systems, into a delightful, hidden, firn couloir. The couloir, steeper than 50° at the top, leads up and farther left, to a point more or less directly below the summit. In six more pitches the route joins the North Ridge, just short of the summit. While the technical crux is on the ninth pitch, the first two pitches offer challenging climbing on dirty, loose rock, with few protection opportunities.

During summer 2001 a new II+ 5.9 route was climbed on the west face of Lichtenberg Mountain by James Nakagami, Dan Cappellini, and Ray Borbon. The climb began below a headwall shaped like Idaho, just left of a gully. After five 5th class pitches that link cracks systems, the route joined the Northwest Ridge, which was scrambled to the summit. Descent was made by a gully to the south.

Also in 2001 Larry Goldie and Scott Johnston established a route on Goat Wall above Mazama. It is a bolted route, established in full siege style. The eight-pitch route begins 500' left of Bryan Burdo's classic Promised Land, near the base of a prominent buttress.

On September 26, 2000 Tim Kelley and Gordy Skoog approached the toe of the north face rib of McAlester Mountain via the northwest talus fields. They made a new route (II, class 5) that starts left of the North Face Rib route on class 4 slabs and permanent snow, then goes up a loose gully and right on a slanting ramp to the North.Face Rib. From there they climbed arrow-straight to the summit on good rock.

GORDY SKOOG, *AAC, and* COLIN HALEY, *AAC*

Silver Star Mountain, Gato Negro. On June 21, 2001 Larry Goldie and Scott Johnston, both of Mazama, WA, established a probable new route on the west face of Silver Star Mountain near Washington Pass in the North Cascades. The climb follows the line of weakness on a spire, named "Whine Spire" by the pair, that is separated from, and lower than, the true west summit of Silver Star, and south of, but adjacent to, the Wine Spires. Using the climbers' trail that leads from Highway 20 to Burgundy Col, the pair left the road at 5 a.m. and returned at 10 p.m. Of the 11 pitches climbed, five or six are outstanding 5.7–5.9 hand cracks. The crux fourth pitch involves a wonderful, but poorly protected, 5.8 chimney, a hard 5.9 offwidth, and is topped by a vicious overhanging 5.10+ double corner. A few other 5.10 pitches should entertain most parties. The route was climbed onsight and clean. Descent was by rappel and downclimbing in the gully between Whine Spire and the west summit of Silver Star. In the spirit of the Wine Spires the climb was called Gato Negro, rated IV 5.10+.

SCOTT JOHNSTON

Sloan Peak, Northwest Buttress. In late September 2000 Mike Preiss and I completed what we suspect is a new route on Sloan Peak. The Northwest Buttress (IV 5.8 A0) starts at the lowest rock on the far left side of the broad west face and ascends the dark buttress to one-third of its height. We found rap slings to the top of the seventh pitch, but no other human sign until we met the north ridge. The first pitch climbs just right of the sharp crest, then crosses the crest past a dead tree. Pitches two to four climb through trees to a gully topped with large chockstones and finish at a detached pillar. Climb behind the pillar to a tree ledge and traverse right (unpleasant) until you can climb broken rock to the top of the lower buttress, a good bivy site. Climb a short rotten step and head slightly left onto the northern face. Two pitches of easy rock and heather lead to a nice chimney (5.8). Above the chimney, traverse to the right skyline on a narrow heather bench with an inspiring view down the vertical to overhanging section of the west wall. Climb left past a roof and blocks, then up a clean crack to a mantle onto a small, sandy shelf (5.8 and French free) to easier ground (fixed pin just above clean crack). From here we made a rising right traverse to more mid-5th class rock, with a 5.8 exit. Follow gullies and ribs to the north ridge, 200 vertical feet from the summit. We rapped and downclimbed the southwest ridge. A fast party that had the descent dialed could probably complete the route car-to-car in a very long day (we bivied once on the route). On the enjoyable 1,000m buttress we belayed 17 pitches on mostly good rock, with lots of running belays. Our rack included 8–10 wires and cams to 3.5"; pins are not needed.

MARK BUNKER, *AAC*

Mount Index, North Norwegian Buttress, Voodoo Proj. Over five days in mid-July Blair Williams, with William Tharpe, Todd Karner, and me, added a steep new route to the North Norwegian Buttress. Voodoo Proj starts 100 yards to the right of the Doorish Route and joins it at the top of the buttress, after eight new pitches. After having difficulties with the moat, we began the first pitch with a green Alien and continued with beaks and RURPs for 100' to the left side of a large, sloping ledge. This pitch combined aid with free climbing up to 5.8. The following day Blair traversed the sloping ledge for 30' before climbing a 10' head-and-beak seam. He then followed a left-leaning expanding crack, requiring blades, arrows, and beaks, before finishing the rope-stretching pitch with an A1 roof. While cleaning this, the crux, pitch, the second removed every piece before the A1 roof with one or two moderate yanks. The third pitch started with runout 5.10 on bad gear, before gaining a 120' dirty seam requiring multiple heads, hooks, and the occasional tied-off baby angle. It ended at a two-bolt belay below a large roof. Determined to minimize drilling, and acting against my recommendation, Blair started up the fourth pitch using a combination of offsets, blades, and arrows. An offset blew 10 feet up, and Blair fell 20' before stopping, upside-down, below the portaledge. Having gained his senses in the fall, he drilled three rivets to bypass loose blocks in the roof and continued for another 100' of moderate nailing. At this point, because of time constraints, Bill, Todd, and I had to rappel, but left Blair a luxurious portaledge camp two pitches below. Over the next three days Blair climbed the remaining four pitches solo, encountering moderate to difficult nailing. The eighth and last pitch, on which he placed two rivets, followed a 20' discontinuous crack to a large brow, and then traversed downward 100' to where he established a bolted belay parallel to the anchors on pitch seven. With threatening skies, Blair opted to airmail all but the portaledge and hardware to the snowfield above Lake Serene. He made four 60m rappels and reached the bergschrund in time to begin the long journey back to the car in a typical Northwest rainstorm. Blair and I feel that Voodoo Proj (VI 5.10R A4) provided some of the most challenging and interesting big-wall climbing we have found in the Cascades.

ROGER STRONG

California

YOSEMITE VALLEY

Yosemite Valley, various activity. While it has not been on the free-climbing cutting edge for decades, Yosemite still ranks as the world's premier big-wall arena. With new lines a rarity, this lately has meant hard free-climbing on the massive walls of El Capitan and other formations, while Hans Florine and others keep the speed-climbing flame alive as well.

Tommy Caldwell returned to the Salathé Wall this year, perhaps to prove to himself that his loss of an index finger is no drawback to his aspirations. Caldwell, who free-climbed the Free Salathé Lite* in 1999, returned to tick the first one-day free ascent. Climbing with wife Beth Rodden, Caldwell scaled the wall in only 19 hours. In 1998 Alexander Huber climbed Free Rider (another variation to the Free Salathé Lite, it avoids the 5.13 headwall pitches) in a day. These two ascents, and Lynn Hill's 1994 ascent of the Nose, were the only one-day free-climbs of a major El Cap route. (The West Face and East Buttress routes don't count as major.) That soon changed.

Dean Potter continues to redefine what's possible in a day. He, with Timmy O'Neill, had linked Half Dome, Mt. Watkins, and El Capitan in a day. The speed demon has now turned to free-climbing walls, but with his characteristic endurance twist. Not content to merely be one of the "El Cap Free In A Day" crowd, Potter freed the Regular Northwest Face of Half Dome (23 pitches, 5.12a), apparently via a variation (whether a new variation, the Higbee Hedral variation, or the Huber Hedral variation is unclear) and followed it with a free lead of Free Rider (34 pitches, 5.13a), all in 23 hours, 23 minutes. He freed the crux pitch of Free Rider at night, wearing five headlamps in order to see the holds. After this ascent he said his immediate goal was to "concentrate on becoming a better free climber."

While Potter was busy with 24-hour free-climbs, Hans Florine continued to focus on speed. He welcomed the competition from Potter and O'Neill, who climbed the 34-pitch Nose in a blistering 3:24 in October 2001. The 38-year-old Florine devised a new strategy. In the past, speed records had been set by leading the route in four or more blocks. Florine now set off to do the route as one continuous pitch, and he partnered with Japanese speed demon Yuji Hirayama. Hirayama led the route as one pitch, pulling up gear on a 40-foot, 5mm cord. Of the 3000' of climbing, all but 400' were simul-climbed, the 400' being short-fixed. The pair regrouped once, after the King Swing. Remarkably, the route was devoid of other parties, and the pair turned in the jaw-dropping time of 2:48. Florine says this record might last another ten years; his 4:22 record set with Peter Croft in 1993 stood for nine years before broken by Potter and O'Neill.

Hirayama's visit to Yosemite enhanced his reputation as the best crack climber in the world. Prior to his Nose record, Yuji climbed the Free Salathé Lite in 13 hours. Showing a mastery of the route and no apparent tendency to get pumped, Hirayama turned five pitches into two. He said his goal was to climb from ledge to ledge, without hanging belays; he considers this the purest style for free ascents. First, he linked Sous le Toit ledge to the stance over the Salathé Roof, a section normally done as three pitches (5.11b, 5.12b, and 5.12a). Hirayama then climbed in one pitch the 70m headwall, normally two 5.13b pitches and originally done as three by Skinner and Piana.

The Salathé and Nose records are now so fast that 5.13 free-climbing skills are required to even get close. Hirayama and Jim Herson, the only persons to redpoint every pitch on the Free Salathé (as opposed to the Free Salathé Lite) and the holder of the Salathé and Half Dome records, lead the Salathé and the Nose sans aiders, since they can French-free the most difficult sections, even Harding's overhanging bolt ladder.

Ammon McNeely solidified his position as one of the Valley's elite speed climbers with three records, each with different partners. With Chris Van Luevan and Eric Walden he did the first one-day ascent of Born Under a Bad Sign (VI 5.10 A5). They completed the sixth ascent in 22:22. With Flyin' Brian McCray, McNeely blasted up New Jersey Turnpike (VI 5.8 A5) in 14 hours. Finally, with Cedar Wright he climbed the Tangerine Trip (VI 5.8 A2+) in 10:24.

Nick Martino capped an excellent season of speed ascents with a new record on the South Face of Washington Column: he and Matt Wilder climbed the 12-pitch route in 1:19. This Column record, like the Nose and the Salathé records, can be attributed to free-climbing. Wilder had recently pulled off the first free ascent of the South Face, a popular route frequently done as a climber's first wall. The route is moderate free-climbing, save for the three pitches above Dinner Ledge. Wilder's crux was the Kor Roof, which he rated as a boulder problem. His rating of V10/V11 translates to the first pitch rated 5.14 on a Yosemite wall route, though the two crux pitches on the Nose could well be 5.14.

Wilder broke the next, long, left-angling aid pitch into two, using a no-hands stance for the belay. These went at 5.12c and 5.12a. The Stopper Pitch, which sucks up stoppers when being aided, went at 5.12b. Because he had waited at the Kor Roof for an ideal temperature, Wilder led the Stopper Pitch in the dark with a headlamp. His next project was to try to free the West Buttress of El Capitan. He has not yet pulled it off, but he believes the great traverse pitch will be 5.14a when free.

Washington Column was also the site of two new free routes. The outstanding new route put up in 2002 was Rob Miller's all-free Quantum Mechanic. This traditionally protected crack climb is just right of Astroman and perhaps a new-wave alternative for top crack climbers. The crux pitch is 5.13a, but the route sports a handful of 5.12 pitches as well. In October Hirayama nabbed the second ascent, onsighting it.

Alexander Huber pieced together Crosstown Traffic (5.13a) on Washington Column. This route connects parts of the Prow, Electric Ladyland, Afroman, and Astroman. After an earlier aid ascent Huber,

Jacek Czyz on the fifth pitch of Quo Vadis, El Capitan. Szczepan Glogowski with Ben van der Klooster, redpointed every pitch on May 24. With Scott Franklin, Huber freed Half Dome, via a new variation to the Regular Northwest Face route that he calls the Huber Hedral. This a one-pitch variation to the Ericson–Higbee free variation is said to provide cleaner climbing.

Speed climbing aficionado Cedar Wright also directed his talents at free climbing new and existing routes. With Jake Whittaker, Wright freed the Psychedelic Wall on the north face of Sentinel Rock at 5.12c. The route sports three 5.12 pitches. Also on Sentinel, Wright teamed with Jose Pereyra for the first ascent of the Uncertainly Principle (V 5.13a). Wright also freed a new route on Higher Cathedral Rock's north face. The 1,000' route's most striking feature is the 50' Gravity Ceiling (5.13a), believed to be the biggest roof free climbed in Yosemite.

Jacqueline Florine, Hans' wife, became the first woman to solo the Nose, with her June 17–21 ascent. Bev Johnson was the first woman to solo El Capitan, via the Dihedral Wall route, in 1978.

On September 14 Hans Florine teamed with Steve Gerberding to climb the Dihedral Wall, hammerless, in a record time of 14:06. This was the 100th ascent of El Capitan for each but the first time the two had climbed together.

Jim Beyer put up a new aid route that is a candidate for the "hardest route on El Cap." Dubbed Martyr's Brigade (5.11 a5cR—his own twist on the rating system), the line was put up over 20+ days of stormy weather. The line is located near the North American Wall, between Reticent Wall and Space. One of the radical aid moves involved using an ice axe, taped to a long stick-clip, to blindly hook a block 20 feet away. In *Alpinist* magazine (Issue 1) Beyer wrote, "I drilled a lot of bolts, but chopped about an equal number on surrounding routes. Creating hard pitches, destroying pathetic bolt ladders (Early Morning Light)—it seemed to balance out in the end."

We also lack details on a new free route called Gates of Delirium, a 19-pitch 5.12c route on the right side of Ribbon Falls. After the opening 5.12c pitch the route is mostly 5.10 and 5.11 cracks and is supposedly of Astroman quality. The first 10 pitches are in one spectacular dihedral, and the route is equipped so that it can be rappelled from the top of this corner.

On Yosemite Falls Wall, Eric Kohl soloed a new route, called Reign in Blood, over five days in late August. The route follows the Falls' fall line and tops out in the Falls' notch. Needless to say, the climb is only possible when the Falls are dry, preferably when no rain is expected. Continuing the trend of meaningless ratings, Kohl rated the route PDK: Pretty Damn Klaus (Kohl's nickname is Klaus).

Finally Jacek Czyz finished Quo Vadis (VI 5.9 A4/A4+) during the night of November 20. The 22-pitch route, located near the Muir Wall and the Dorn Direct, has 16 new pitches.

Please note: "Free climbing" the Salathé Wall is more complex that it first seems. As with many of the big-wall routes on El Cap, significant variations are used to free-climb the route, and not every climber takes the same path. The different variations are explained at www.wwwright. com/climbing/?report=news/FreeingBigWalls. htm.

BILL WRIGHT, *Satan's Minions Scrambling Club, AAC*

El Capitan, Quo Vadis. During the night of November 20–21 Jacek Czyz, solo, finished Quo Vadis (VI 5.9 A4/A4+), a new route near the Muir Wall and the Dorn Direct, with which it shares a couple of pitches, and left of the Nose. Of the 22 pitches, 16 entered new terrain. Four pitches are rated A4/A4+. The sixth pitch is the crux, involving about 30' on skyhooks and a 15' pendulum to a crack climbed with RURPs and copperheads. A further 13 or 14 pitches are A3. The climb took 25 days, and Czyz's return to the base of the wall took two additional days of rappelling. He left 40 bolts, 30 as belay anchors, and used 40 rivets. Jacek Czyz is a Polish climber residing in Chicago and an AAC member. He has climbed El Cap 16 times, including solo ascents of the Reticent Wall and Zanyatta Mondatta.

WLADYSLAW JANOWSKI

Salathé, one-day free ascents. In December 2001 I was in a hospital bed after severing my left index finger in a home-remodeling accident. The digit had been reattached but wasn't looking good. There were stitches and pins protruding through the skin here and there, and the surgery point was swollen to the size of a golf ball. There had been a constant drip of blood from the end of my finger for two weeks, causing me to lose over half of my blood.

During my time in the hospital I did a lot of thinking. Some of the time my mind was full of doubt about whether I would ever again be able to climb near my previous potential. But as the days went on, something else grew inside me. I realized how much climbing meant to me and how I wanted to be as much a part of it as possible. I felt driven as I had never felt before. I decided not to let this injury slow me down.

In March my fiancée Beth Rodden and I headed to Yosemite. I had decided that the Salathé, free in a day, would be the first big test of my recovery. On May 15, after a few warm-up climbs, we started up the Salathé. The lower part of the route went fast, and at 3 p.m. we were approaching the headwall and the hardest pitch.

The first headwall pitch is one of the most beautiful I have seen. It is 180' long, over-hanging, and shockingly exposed. As I climbed my forearms swelled. Fifteen feet from the top I stopped and tried to recover, placed my one remaining piece and furiously shook one arm at a time, trying to relieve my pump. If I fell here, that would be the end of my energy, and I would have to accept defeat. I jammed my fingertips as hard as I could and pulled the last few moves to the anchor. A few hours later we were on top. We arrived just as the sun set. It was a huge victory for me. I knew I had overcome my injury.

A few weeks later Yuji Hirayama arrived in the Valley, also to free-climb the Salathé in a day. During one week he tried the route twice. Although he came close, a complete free ascent eluded him. In September he returned with a bigger goal: to combine some of the crux pitches, thereby eliminating all hanging belays except one at the lip of the headwall roof. He succeeded on his second try, in 13 hours and 20 gigantic pitches. Yuji's style bumped the grade of the hardest pitch from 5.13b to 5.13d. It was a truly proud ascent.

TOMMY CALDWELL, *AAC*

El Capitan, The Nose, speed record. Events leading up to the record speed ascent of the Nose in 2 hours and 48 minutes: September 2001, Hans Florine and Tommy Caldwell climb the Nose in 4:31. They miss the nine-year-old record of 4:22 by only nine minutes. Mid-October 2001, Timmy O'Neill and Dean Potter climb the Nose in 3:59, breaking the record. Later in October 2001, Jim Herson and Florine climb it in 3:57. November 1, 2001, O'Neill and Potter set a blazing time of 3:24.

In June 2002 Yuji Hirayama came to Yosemite to work on hard, long free-climbing routes. With his partner Tamotsu he twice ran up the Nose for training, once in nine hours, once in seven hours and change. Yuji and Florine tried to hook up for an attempt at the Nose record, but Yuji's focus on free-climbing the Salathé in a day had priority. Hans and Yuji had climbed the Nose twice together in 1997, to explore the free climbing possibilities; they did it with a bivy both times.

In September 2002 Yuji returned to Yosemite with plans for more long free climbs and to give the Nose speed record a go with Hans. On September 23 they ran up the route in 3:27, passing seven parties. Having missed the record by only three minutes, plus having to pass all those parties, the two thought it would be well worth their time to give it another whirl. Time allowed on September 29, and the two raced up the route in 2 hours, 48 minutes, and 30 seconds. No other parties were on the route. On both of these ascents, Yuji led the entire route. It was thought this method was best, as trading leaders mid-route would cause a lull. On their first go they made it to Sickle Ledge, four pitches up, in 19 minutes. On their second go they made Sickle Ledge in 16 minutes. On their first go they made Camp 4 in 1:52, on their second go in 1:28.

HANS FLORINE, *AAC*

Free climbing. Yosemite 2002 was the setting for what I can only call a dream season. In the spring Jake Whittaker and I freed the Psychedelic Wall on Sentinel Rock—solid 5.12. This route was first ascended by Boche and Hennek in 1966. Memorable sections include a 5.12c sloper crack traverse, a 12c slab boulder problem, and a 12' roof that goes from squeeze to offwidth to fists to hands to fingers.

In the summer José Pereyra and I freed The Medicine Wall (a.k.a. The Uncertainty Principle), also on Sentinel. This entailed five completely new pitches, but also freed existing aid pitches of several routes, including the first three pitches of a line first attempted by Steve Roadie and Ben "Wa" Zartman, and four pitches of Early Times (FA by Bryan "Coiler" Kay and Josh Thompson). The route joins with the North Face (FA Frost and Robbins, 1962; FFA Thaw and Wainwright, 1995) for one pitch in the middle, and for the two summiting pitches.

We rated the Medicine Wall 5.13a, or really hard 5.12. The crux pitch was bolted on the lead and provided 80' of brilliant, slightly overhanging face climbing. But perhaps the finest pitch is the second, which starts with 100' of 45° overhanging hands, leading to a short, hard offwidth section, to tight fingers, and finally to an overhanging, run-out boltless face. Both the Medicine Wall and Psychedelic Wall were redpointed, no falls, in a day, after being freed from the ground up over weeks of effort, using fixed lines. On both routes I swapped pitches with my partner and had the pleasure of leading the respective cruxes.

As fall gave way to winter, I managed a three-pitch variation to the Northeast Buttress of Higher Cathedral Rock. I redpointed pitches one and three, but managed only a pinkpoint of the prize pitch, a 50' roof 800' off the ground. This pitch, the "Gravity Ceiling" (5.13a), and the preceding one were first aid climbed by Brian Kay, Mark "TBag" Garbarinni, and Johnny "B" Blair. The Gravity Ceiling is, hands down, the single most impressive pitch of freeclimbing I have ever had the pleasure of playing on, and seems destined to become a megaclassic.

As winter rolled around, I found my world crushed by the news that José Pereyra had passed away. José was not only one of the best finger-crack climbers the world has known, but he was the most realized, spiritually in-tune person I have known. I am very thankful that he

The west face of Castle Rock Spire, showing, left to right: Cinco de Mayo (V 5.10+ A3—Bindner-Thau, 2002—only the upper half is shown). West Face (IV 5.9 A4, Beckey-Borson-Hempel-Rowell, 1969). Spike Hairdo (IV 5.10 A3, Bindner-Coomer, 1996). Brandon Thau

and I shared the experience of freeing the Medicine Wall, before he moved on to bigger and better things. I dedicate all of these climbs to José; may his soulful, honest, penetrating spirit inspire climbers for centuries to come.

CEDAR WRIGHT, *AAC*

SIERRA NEVADA

West Fuller Butte, The Twisted Bit. Doniel Drazin and Brandon Thau completed an eight pitch route (IV 5.12b) on the blank 1,000' face of West Fuller Butte on November 9, 2001. Aside from one splitter-crack pitch, the route is mainly consistent 5.10/5.11 face climbing, with one crux 5.12 pitch. A semiremote Sierra environment adds to the quality of the route.

BRANDON THAU, *AAC*

Third Recess Peak, Serving Detention. The northeast side of Third Recess Peak features two striking arêtes that merge near the summit. In July Micha Miller and I climbed a new route (IV 5.10) that followed the left-hand arête for ten pitches. Starting left of the prow we worked up steep cracks and corners for a few hundred feet before Micha found a traverse down and right, onto the arête. This put us right on the beautiful edge, which we climbed to the top, racing a thunderstorm. We lost the race, but tagged the seldom-visited summit pinnacle as the rain and hail tapered off to the north.

DAVID HARDEN, *AAC*

Castle Rock Spire, Cinco de Mayo. Bruce Bindner and I completed a 12-pitch route (V 5.10+ A3) on Castle Rock Spire, slightly to the right of the north arête, over May 3–4. The route parallels the north arête, 150' away. It features excellent, mostly moderate climbing up steep features, with less than 200' of aid. The quickest descent is off the south arête, down Spike Hairdo.

BRANDON THAU, *AAC*

Nikolay Petkov low on the Comanche Ridge. The route follows the arête above. John Harlin III

Arizona

Grand Canyon National Park, Comanche Point, Comanche Ridge. In November 2000, while hiking the Escalante Route, I couldn't take my eyes off the long skinny arête ascending from Tanner Rapids on the Colorado River all the way to the Grand Canyon's South Rim on Comanche Point (7,073'). As the river lies at 2,700' at the rapids, the full ridge is about 4,400' tall and spans over 1.5 horizontal miles. Alas, the lower buttresses can easily be bypassed, and only 2,500 vertical feet require technical climbing—in about half a horizontal mile. On inquiry, a local desert rat (who had paraglided from Comanche Point to the Colorado) told me that no one had climbed from the inner canyon to the rim anywhere in the entire multimile-long Palisades of the Desert. A prominent 200' spire near the top had been climbed (Comanche Point Pinnacle, A1 or 5.12) by rappelling in from the rim. He said that on my proposed route

The Comanche Ridge route leading to Comanche Point, as viewed from the Colorado River. John Harlin III

I should expect "a lot of rotten rock, and a really good adventure."

As it turned out, the rock is often solid sandstone and limestone, with a liberal sprinkling of decomposing layers. Comanche Ridge came in at about 17 belayed or simul-climbed pitches, plus considerable 3rd and 4th class scrambling. On October 6, immediately following the UIAA General Assembly meetings in Flagstaff, Anne Arrans (U.K.), Roger Payne (U.K.), Nikolay Petkov (Bulgaria), and I (U.S.) hiked the Tanner Trail to Tanner Rapids and spent the night. The next morning we gained the wall at about 4,600', at the back of the scooped wall just above a rockslide. The entrance overhang had a 5.10 move, followed by scrambling, a 5.8 corner, then easy 5th class along the ridgecrest. The knife-edge part of the ridge (Annie's Arête) was broken by short buttresses (50' to 250' each) offering 5.7 to 5.9 climbing. We bivied on a huge ledge in the middle of the red band after about nine pitches. At the top of the red band we bypassed a couple of beautiful 5.11-looking cracks on the buttress via a 5.7 corner to the left, then scrambled to the left side of the huge greenish buttress, which we climbed in three full pitches of 5.9 to 5.10 (we bypassed the dangerous sofa-sized Monster Pillar via a thin crack on the left). We then moved left to steep scrambling, crossed the ridge at Comanche Point Pinnacle, and continued to the summit via 5.7 to 5.8 cracks, with a couple of sections of scrambling. We arrived on top just as the sun went down on the second day of climbing, thus avoiding a waterless night out. Six or so miles of cross-country and dirt road in the dark led back to Desert View. I think the route is well worth repeating by anyone with a taste for big alpine-style ridges in a spectacular desert environment, provided they don't mind some portable handholds.

JOHN HARLIN III, *Hood River Crag Rats, AAC*

Lost Horizon, first free ascent. On January 29 Ty Mack and I made the first free ascent of the stunning Lost Horizon route, located in Lost Canyon in Sedona, AZ. Lost Horizon follows an impeccable corner system for four long pitches. The climbing is both strenuous and technical. We added three protection bolts where natural gear was not possible. The four pitches are rated 5.12c, 5.13a, 5.12c/d, and 5.11. Lost Canyon, also the location of the ultraclassic five-pitch 5.12, Shangri-La, now features a stellar concentration of hard long free climbs.

MATT CHILDERS

Utah

The Desert, various activity. Significant new routes were established on the Navajo Sandstone of the Colorado Plateau in 2002. Paul Ross, age 65, has been extremely active on the long slabs of the imposing reef at the eastern edge of the San Rafael Swell, known as the San Rafael Reef. Ross writes of his activity, "Just too much unclimbed rock in the desert; it's enough to tire an old guy out. My climbing mate, Layne Potter, added up the footage of the slabs we have climbed in the Swell area since March 2002, and it came to over 23,000'. No wonder I'm wearing out my Tricouni-nailed boots." Some of his longer and better routes, established with a variety of partners, are Reefer Madness (1,780', 9 pitches, III 5.9R), Surfing the Swell (1,400', 7 pitches, III 5.9R), Slipnot Slab (1,400', 7 pitches, III 5.7R/X), Tsunami (1,200', 7 pitches, III 5.9R), Sinister Slab (1,200', 6 pitches, III 5.7R), Slab Happy (1,360', 5 pitches, III 5.8 R), Sunshine Slab (1,520', III 5.6R) the North Ridge route (2,000', III 5.6) on North Peak, and Hot Tin Slab (1,390', 6 pitches,

The Triple Slab Buttress in the San Rafael Swell, showing (left to right): The Giraffe (1,130', 5.9R, four stars), Jack Russell Buttress (980', 5.6R), Mellow Yellow (1,060', 5.9R, four stars). Paul Ross

The Eastern Reef Slabs (the climbing area is about six miles long), showing (A) Triple Slab Buttress area, (B) Surfing The Swell formation (1,800', 5.9), (C) Reefer Madness Slab (1,700', 5.9R), (D) North Peak and North Ridge route (2,000', 5.6R). Paul Ross

III 5.8R). "The route was climbed in extreme heat, hence the name. The temperature in the shade at 2 p.m. was 105°."

In the northern San Rafael Swell, Ross and Paul Marshall (U.K.) established Brits in the Belfry (310', III 5.9 C1) on Belfry Spire.

In April, in the Lost World Butte section (covered in the new *Desert Rock IV*, by Bjornstad) of the Island in the Sky area west of Moab, Paul Ross and Paul Marshall established The Gift

(360', III 5.8 C2) on The Tombstone. The route ascends an open book 100' left of Keswick Lads' Day Out.

In the Fisher Towers in May, Stevie Haston made the first free ascent of Sundevil Chimney (previously VI 5.9 A3) on The Titan. Haston's impressive ascent included five pitches of 5.12 or 5.12+ and a crux 5.13-. As with his free ascents of Echo Tower, The Hindu, and The Mongoose, Haston climbed clean, with a basic free rack—no pins or hammer.

In the west desert, on the north face of Notch Peak, Jim Howe and Dave Shewell established an intimidating 20-pitch line which Paul Ross calls "The best effort in the Southwest in 2002." The route was established ground-up and reportedly goes at run-out, loose 5.11+.

Two major new routes were established in Texas and Arch canyons of southern Utah. Cameron Burns describes the area as "a wildly remote area of spires, buttes, and mesas. It is easily one of the most beautiful areas in the desert southwest. The rock climbs are true wilderness experiences that require hard driving, long approaches, and difficult, sometimes scary, climbing." In June Paul Ross and Jeff Pheasant put up a route on the east face of Texas Tower, the most popular of the dozen-plus towers in these remote canyons. In Arch Canyon, a new route was established on Dream Speaker via its north face (280', III 5.9 C2) by Paul Ross, Andy Ross, and Paul Marshall in October.

Compiled primarily by ERIC BJORNSTAD

San Rafael Swell, Mudstrosity. In March Strappo Hughes and I climbed the Mudstrosity (350', V- A3+). This tower is in the southern San Rafael Swell, located 10 miles northwest of Factory Butte (the summit of which provides a wild view of the whole area). It is approached by a confusing series of washes and old roads (high clearance required). USGS maps refer to the area as Salt Wash, just south of the Moroni Slopes. From a distance the Mudstrosity looks like a pint-sized Titan. Our route starts on the left side of the southeast face, at a relatively prominent crack. No free climbing here; this is some of the rottenest stuff I've ever climbed on. Every non-vertical surface is deeply rotted. Luckily, vertical faces hold some higher quality rock. Sustained aid, using everything from birdbeaks to lost arrows and specters, nuts used as "stopperheads," and various cams, led to a two-bolt hanging belay just below the south shoulder. This excellent 200' pitch evolved as a two-day joint effort. A short nasty pitch across the shoulder led to a small ledge below the

Mudstrosity, living up to its name. Steve Crusher Bartlett

headwall. Several bolts and thin nailing gained a mud-choked offwidth-size crack, which splits the summit. The summit is the size and shape of a pair of motorcycle seats, end to end, with a 300' drop-off on each side. The summit vibrated like an old motorcycle as I cleaned pitons 40 feet below. We left three mediocre bolts and a register for the hordes who will flock to repeat this route.

STEVE CRUSHER BARTLETT, *AAC*

Potash Road/Wall Street, Desert Spindrift. In the middle of September Nathan Martin and I climbed a new route that went to the rim overlooking Potash. Our route began with an existing route called Pinhead (5.10). We then continued up the prominent crack system above for five very sandy pitches to create Desert Spindrift (200m, IV 5.10 C2).

JOSH GROSS, *AAC*

Fisher Towers, The Titan, Sundevil Chimney, first free ascent. The Fisher Towers represent a Daliesque dream barely metamorphosed into rock. The highest tower, the Titan, is the highest free-standing tower in the U.S. and, in my opinion, is unique in the world for its haunting majesty. Because of the soft nature of the Cutler Sandstone and the dangerous nature of the climbing, artificial techniques have predominated. Many of these aid routes are dangerous and technically taxing, but the continual piton use is eroding the cracks. This is beneficial in only one way: it has led to the possibility of free climbing some of these magnificent routes! Over the last 12 years Laurence Gouault and I have visited these towers, sometimes to just stand and stare, and sometimes to slip and slide on their sandy skin.

In the spring we spent an extended period of time on Sundevil Chimney, using wire brushes and toothbrushes to clean cracks and ledges. We experienced many falls on sometimes run-out pitches of bad or sandy rock—it cannot be described as simple climbing. The climb had previously been aided clean by Andy Donson, who free-climbed the penultimate pitch and who gave me the nod. The Sundevil was originally done at A3+ by H.T. Carter and friends in 1971, when it was primarily a mud climb, but is now clean enough to be free-climbed by people who enjoy the challenge of fearful odds. The first pitch is a brilliant combination of crack and face climbing on yellowish rock. Be careful to belay at two bolts where you can balance with your hands off the rock and not at the original belay higher. The next pitch is long and one of the best crack pitches in the desert; it ends just short of the Mud Chimney. These first two pitches can be looked at as the cream of the route. They are clean and well-protected, except for one section of the first pitch where you could take a big one (I took three). The climbing may be easy 5.13, but it is hard to tell when you are not relaxed. The next section, in the chimney, provides perhaps three pitches of 5.12, but again it is hard to tell, as the hard bits are either insecure, wide, or both—good luck. You then arrive at the first place to sit. (I took a nap.) The next pitch is dirty and wide, with a nasty twisting fall before you get to the wide section. The last pitch is a 5.7 chimney, but if you are lucky, you will top out at sunset, as we did, and have to rappel at night without a head torch. Clean-aid or free-climbing these routes represents a less destructive method of climbing, which seems in keeping with the times. For people with more ability than us, the Sundevil might just be a brilliant climb. For us it was much more.

STEVIE HASTON, *France*

Jason Keith freeing the fifth pitch (5.12-) of Appetite for Destruction. Jim Howe

Under the 2,000' north face of Notch Peak. Jason Keith

Westwater Canyon, Arch Tower, Dry Heaves. In June Bill Duncan and John Burnham made the first ascent of Arch Tower, naming their route Dry Heaves (400', 6 pitches, III 5.10 A1). To reach this remote spire, float the Colorado River from Loma to Mee Canyon. Hike three miles up canyon and the tower will be obvious. Another wilderness experience!

ERIC BJORNSTAD

House Range, Notch Peak, Appetite for Destruction, La Fin du Monde, and Empty Sky. Notch Peak is located approximately 45 miles west of Delta on U.S. 6/50. Directions to it are given in James Garrett's Ibex and Selected Climbs of Utah's West Desert. Dave Shewell and I climbed Appetite for Destruction (IV 5.11 A0 or 5.12-) on Notch Peak over six or seven days, finishing in May 2001. We did this 300m route in ground-up style, hanging from hooks when necessary for bolt placements. A set of cams (TCUs to 3.5") is mandatory, to supplement the 50 protection bolts. All belays are bolted. Appetite for Destruction ascends the lower north face and tops out on the large band leading across the north face and around the northwest ridge. The route has four pitches that are 5.10 or harder. Jason Keith eked out the FFA of pitch five with the draws hanging. Mortals can aid that pitch or avoid it with a 5.11- variation. The route is approached as Book of Saturday is, but is reached after only 50 minutes of hiking up the drainage. It is marked by a cairn in the drainage. The wall remains hidden until the last 10 minutes of hiking before the cairn. Bolts are visible 20' up. The first two pitches ascend the left side of the lower band. The route crosses a large, low-angle band to the center of the face and is marked by a threaded red sling. Climbing is sustained through the first six pitches. The final two pitches are moderate and allow you to walk off or exit to the upper north face. Beware of the final moderate pitch, originally going in and around the chimney that splits the final wall. It

The north and west faces of Notch Peak (9,725', House Range, Utah) as seen from the top of Appetite for Destruction (IV 5.11 A0 or 5.12- ; a route on the lower north face). Note that in this foreshortened angle, routes 1 and 2 appear to finish atop a buttress, but they traverse to finish on the left, as indicated. See p. 177, 2001 AAJ for another perspective. 1. Empty Sky (III 5.8, Howe-Keith, 1998). 2. La Fin du Monde (400m, III/IV 5.10, Howe-Shewell, 2002). 3. Road to Perdition (3-pitch variant finish, 5.10+, Howe-Howe, 2002). 4. Book of Saturday (IV 5.11-, Lyde-Price, 1999). Not shown: Swiss Route (V 5.10+ A3, Deinen-Koch, 1986). The exactly location of the Swiss Route on the north face route is unknown, beyond, "...right of center to a prominent chimney, mostly on poor rock." (1987 AAJ, p. 178). Jim Howe

is loose, even by Notch Peak standards. A safer alternative is a left-facing corner system 60m to the right (5.7). By combining this route with one on the upper headwall, a limestone route of 18–20 pitches can be climbed! In June Dave and I climbed Appetite and La Fin in one push of 11 hours.

In April 2002, also from the ground up, Dave and I established La Fin du Monde (a.k.a. Northwest Ridge Direct, 400m, 9 pitches, III/IV 5.10), visible as the right skyline in the photo in the 2001 *AAJ*, p. 177. This beautiful route, on the extreme right side of the north face, nearly follows the crest of the northwest ridge. It gets more sun and has an airier feel than the north face routes. There are 17 protection bolts, placed on lead. Most of the belays are fixed. The route is accessed as Book of Saturday is, but head right along the base of the north face instead of left. La Fin starts right at the base of the northwest ridge; a bolt is visible about 30' up. La Fin joins Empty Sky (which begins to the right, or west, of the northwest ridge) three pitches from the summit, where both routes traverse to an exit chimney/gully over the north face. Descent is best done by abseiling from the top of Book of Saturday, which is not easy to locate unless you have been on that route.

In September Tommie Howe and I hiked up the back side of Notch Peak and abseiled 130m to the base of La Fin's final headwall. We led this, placing ten protection bolts and pins. This variation (Road to Perdition, 3 pitches, 5.10+) gives another two pitches of 5.10 climbing and is a worthwhile alternative to La Fin's exit chimney. Its start is marked by fixed anchors 40m from the crest of the northwest ridge. The belays are fixed, but the variation includes a sporty, 30' runout on 5.10- terrain. Tommie and I summited in deteriorating weather and raced down the backside, only to spend a rainy bivouac huddled in a shallow overhang. We remain happily married.

The original route, Empty Sky, was established in February 1998 by Jason Keith and me, after we searched for a nonexistent ice route on the north face. In a 23-hour round trip from Salt Lake City, we climbed this route, made about a dozen abseils to get off the peak, and were stopped by the highway patrol in their quest to stem the flow of drugs through the Utah corridor. The route begins a few hundred yards right of the northwest ridge, in a notch between a large pinnacle and the west face. It follows the line of least resistance toward the north face. Expect moderate climbing and plenty of simul-climbing, with only a few short 5.7 and 5.8 bits. The crux is in the exit gully over the north face. We found a few pins, probably marking the descent route of the Swiss after their ascent of the north face in 1986 (1987 *AAJ*, p. 178).

Notch Peak provides high adventure. The rock quality is generally poorer than the classic limestone of the Dolomites and Yamnuska, but for those unfortunate souls attracted to this type of rock, these routes are entertaining. Do not take them lightly; though the pitches are often moderate in difficulty, they require competence in this type of terrain. Notch Peak has its loose rock, unappealing strata, and rockfall (particularly during and after rain and melt-freeze cycles). Divots and craters along the approach bands inspire you to contemplate the value of a helmet. A rescue here, if it ever came, would be long and arduous. That said, Notch Peak is a rare, remote place in the heart of the west desert offering beautiful position, grand vistas, a true summit, and good adventure value.

JAMES HOWE

Texas Tower, East Face. Texas Tower has a big reputation, as it is one of the tallest pure sandstone towers in the desert southwest. The only existing route, first climbed in 1987 by Tim Toula and Kathy Zaiser on the west face, still seems to see as many failures as ascents. It was originally 5.10+ A1, but was free climbed in 1990 by Derek Hersey and Steve Bartlett at 5.11cR.

The east face was just as formidable looking and was an obvious desert project. As Ross (AARP, ex-pat Brit) was now in his 66th year, and seeing how the young lads of today did not seem too keen to leave their single-pitch routes, he recruited a not-quite-as-old friend from his New Hampshire days, Jeff Pheasant, now retired in Hawaii. The pair spent a delightful two days on the spectacular east face.

The seven-pitch route went smoothly at 5.10 C2. It may go free at a higher grade. Nobody fell off, died, etc. The worst pain was hangovers at our campsite.

PAUL ROSS

ZION NATIONAL PARK

Kolob Canyon, Nagunt Mesa, Cos the Boss. In late October and early November 2001 I did a new wall route in Kolob Canyon with Steve Gerberding and Scott Cosgrove. The formation is called Nagunt Mesa, and we made the first ascent of the east-northeast face, following an obvious big corner system in the center of the face. The route involved nine pitches on the wall, plus a 5.9

pitch on the approach. The approach is serious, with loads of 3rd and 4th class slabs. The previous year Cosgrove had climbed 2.5 pitches of the wall solo, before bailing. We re-climbed those pitches, then continued. The climbing followed obvious systems and required minimal drilling. Most pitches involved aid on high-quality sandstone—good for Gerberding and me, the sandstone rookies. The climbing was never desperate, with most pitches logging in at A2 or so. We didn't bivy on the wall, but had fixed five pitches before we finished the route in a long day. We rappelled more or less the line of ascent. We've had a hard time coming up with a name, but it's probably gonna end up Cos the Boss (V 5.9R A2+).

ODD-ROAR WIIK, *Norway*

IdiOdyssey. In April James Garrett and I climbed a new route (V 5.10 A2+) via a crack system on the 1,000' wall left of Swoop Gimp. This route, which I began with Brian Cabe, climbs the first two and a half pitches of Swoop Gimp, then branches left via a bolt ladder (placed during a previous party's attempt) to a narrow ledge. One more pitch took us to another ledge, below a steep, improbable-looking corner; from there we descended.

Returning with James, I found the spectacular corner much easier than it looked and continued to a sling belay. The next two pitches, mostly free, followed an ever-widening face crack to a large, brushy ledge. Luckily, a 1.5" crack ran parallel to an offwidth section of the main crack, allowing us to avoid the offwidth. From the brushy ledge we traversed 40' left to another face crack, which we followed, mostly with aid, for two and a half pitches to the top.

BRIAN SMOOT

Big Bend Gendarme, Mean High Tide. This route climbs the obvious crack system on the southwest face, facing the Big Bend shuttle stop. It can be recognized by the rubble stack in the fifth-pitch chimney. It reaches the top of the spirelike formation in six pitches, with lots of wide climbing. The fourth, Banana Pitch, is reportedly a "go for it" pitch. Begin descending using two sets of rap anchors left of the route, then continue by rapping the route. First ascent by Joe French and Brody Greere, Spring 2001; FFA Joe French, Nate Brown, and Dan Carson, fall 2001 (IV 5.10+).

ERIC DRAPER

Angel's Landing, Mostly American Route. It's getting harder to find a new route on Angel's Landing. This face inspired some of the first big routes in the park and contains the park's greatest concentration of wall routes. We had eyed a route on the north face for years. We debated whether certain features would go, and how many features would have to go for the route to be worthy. Eventually we (Bryan Bird, Nate Brown, Eric Draper, Jon Sedon) climbed the route (V 5.9 A3+) in May 2001. Some of the features were climbable; some were too thin and delicate, and we drilled. We consoled ourselves by noting that our route had less than half the holes of the popular Prodigal Sun and by comparing it with Valley standards. And the route turned out to be good, climbing a steep, beautiful section of wall that was previously unexplored.

After climbing the first two pitches of the Swiss-American route, we went left and up into a pink corner. We followed the crack until it disappeared. We climbed rivets until a new crack appeared, then hooked out left to a belay. We climbed the Cyclop's Eye to a right-leaning beak and RURP crack. The last pitch, out a roof, makes it all worth it! Our route then rejoins the Swiss-American route.

ERIC DRAPER

Mt. Moroni, Voice from the Dust. In November Garrett Kemper, Tommy Chandler, and I climbed a new route (IV 5.11c) on the far south end of the southeast face of Mt. Moroni. A 200' splitter hand-and-finger crack, starting 60' above the ground, had caught my eye. In the winter of 2000 Garrett and I tried to get to that crack from below, but a cam hook that I was standing on pried off a block, causing a short fall. Not wanting to use aid, we discovered a secret passage of a chimney 30' to the right. A ledge, hidden among huecos, led me to the start of the crack. Garrett led the steep one- to two-inch crack above, at 5.11. Two more 5.11 pitches took us to the top of a prominent pedestal, a great ledge. The climbing was so excellent that we decided to call it good, and descended.

As time passed, the lure of getting to the top of the wall proved strong, and we found ourselves back for another attempt. From the pedestal we followed the prominent crack and V-slot above for two 5.10a pitches. The next, loose section led to a steep, clean corner sporting a long offwidth. We avoided this by climbing a beautiful left-facing corner to the south. The last pitch followed an easy diagonal ramp up and right. On the summit we found a cairn, possibly left by the climbers doing the Southwest Face route in 1971. We descended by rappelling our route in fading light.

BRIAN SMOOT

The Sentinel, Farmer Brown. This route (V 5.10+ A3+), by Nate Brown and Joe French, climbs a thin crack system on the pink buttress right of the Streaked Wall waterfall. Approach as for the Streaked Wall. Climb seven pitches of mixed free and aid, with the upper half of the route being steep, thin aid. Rap the route. The first ascent party does not recommend this route, suggesting it is better just to look at it.

ERIC DRAPER

Bridge Mountain, Estrogen Enterprise. This route climbs the finlike buttress on Bridge Mountain's southwest face, below the saddle on the right side of the mountain. The route reaches a ledge in two pitches. It then heads up and right toward an obvious splitter. After eight pitches of climbing it reaches the saddle and finishes with 1,200' of 5th class to the top. Rap the route. The first attempt was made by Joe French and Brody Greere; the first ascent, by French and Kevin Riechle, was made in fall 2001 (V 5.10 A2).

ERIC DRAPER

Left Mary, The Insider. The Insider (IV+ 5.10 A1), established by Bryan Bird and me in 2001, entails nine pitches on the southeast face, in a prominent crack system running parallel to and left of the Gentleman's Agreement. The upper half of the route ascends the obvious gaping chimney. The chimney pitches inspired the name of the route. No bolts were placed. Rap off pine trees to the east into a notch. A few more raps down a gully get you to the ground. We recommend the route, but with a warning of a few "dodgy" pitches.

ERIC DRAPER

Colorado

ROCKY MOUNTAIN NATIONAL PARK

The Cathedral Wall in Rocky Mountain National Park, showing Sublime Buttress. Ryan Jennings

Notchtop area, Special K; and Forbidden Peak, Garmar. On June 24 Krista Javoronok and I climbed a new route on the smaller spire to the right of Notchtop. Special K (600', III 5.10b) climbs this spire in six pitches. The route starts in the middle of a buttress, climbs a 5.10 wide crack, goes through a steep, somewhat loose, 5.10 roof, and aims for the prominent right-facing corner below the summit. Though this spire had no recorded ascents, we found an old sling around a chockstone in the prominent corner and another old sling around a block lower down. We found nothing on the summit and suspect that a previous party may have taken a different line, farther right, joined our route-to-be for the corner pitch, and rappelled before the summit. After summiting, we rigged four rappels between Notchtop and this smaller spire to the ground.

On June 6 Zack Martin and I put up an amazing route in the Andrew's Glacier cirque. We climbed the Garmar in nine pitches, establishing the second route on Forbidden Peak. This unique alpine route begins on the central east face with a splitter crack passing through a roof, and continues up for five long pitches of 5.9 and 5.10 to a false summit, which we called the Gargoyle (a beautiful orange plaque of rock). After a 30' rappel from the Gargoyle, the Garmar follows a 5th class ridge for two pitches, then climbs a steep 5.9 corner and reaches the summit via an airy ridge. It's a great mix of steep face, thin cracks, and beautiful ridge climbing. The route does have a few spicy sections, but this aesthetic line is highly recommended. This was my last climb with Zack, and his spirit has been with me since. His unbounded energy and glowing spirit touched the lives of so many. Thanks, Zack, for sharing your motivation and sharing one of my most memorable climbs in the Park. We will all miss you dearly.

KEITH GARVEY

Cathedral Wall, Sublime Buttress. In May Ryan Jennings and I completed the first free ascent of an unreported route we had established five years earlier on the Cathedral Wall. Climbing the tallest, cleanest piece of Cathedral Wall, this should prove to be a modern classic—seven loooong pitches of wildness, ending in a steep hand crack that takes you to the summit. The second pitch presents the technical crux (5.11+), going over a roof. This pitch was the only one not originally freed onsight. The route has four bolts, all at belays. The first three were placed while we were retreating from a nasty ice storm on a winter attempt; they now serve as cairns to let you know you are on route. The fourth bolt was placed on rappel after the original ascent, to improve pitch six's marginal anchor, as Ryan inspected a direct finish. The direct finish, which we climbed on our free ascent, pulls a 5.10 roof and is steep and exposed. (Our original finish ducks around the corner, hard left, for two pitches.) No pitch is a gimme; all require route finding and proficiency with natural protection. In Boulder Canyon all the pitches would be R/X, but really, it's just a good day in the mountains.

BRENT ARMSTRONG

McHenry's Peak, The Kidnapper Van. In the Glacier Gorge cirque, Justin Dubois and I climbed a new free route on an unclimbed tower on the North Ridge of McHenry's Peak. Our route followed a fairly direct line of discontinuous cracks and corners on the east face of this "Shameless Tower" (the lower, or eastern, of two obvious pillars on the north ridge). The best way to find the start is to locate a large worm-shaped pillar at the start of pitch two. Start below and right of this pillar on a ledge 20' below a right-facing corner with a left-angling splitter on its right wall. A bit of 5th class gets you to this ledge, angling in from the right. The second pitch climbs the left side of the worm pillar and the splitter hand crack above it. The final, crux, pitch climbs an obvious dark, right-facing dihedral to the tower's summit. This pitch is 190' long and features sustained jamming and stemming. The Kidnapper Van (730', III 5.11+) was climbed on August 4, in four long pitches: 5.9, 5.10, 5.10+/11-, 5.11+.

JASON SEAVER

BLACK CANYON OF THE GUNNISON NATIONAL PARK

North Chasm View Wall, Fuzzy Dice. Fuzzy Dice (IV 5.10d/11a) climbs a crack system up the far left side of the North Chasm View Wall (left of the Plunge Pillar, right of the North Pillar). FA: Mike Pennings and myself in one day in the fall.

JONATHAN COPP

Hair in My Cheeseburger, CrystalVision. In April Paul Emrick and I headed down the S.O.F.B. Gully on the South Rim of the Black Canyon to try a new route, The route, which shares the start of 2001's Stay Puft Buttress, was done in a day with no bolts. The route was awesome until it became a total bummer. Eight pitches of fine, clean cracks, and then a wrong turn led to bushy, discontinuous choss. The route, Hair in My Cheeseburger, is rated 1,800', IV+ 5.10.

After further research an alternate finish was discovered just right of the Shining Buttress (Ingalls–Kor). In early May Paul Emrick and Brent Mitchell rapped from the rim to establish this four-pitch variation. Paul led a beautiful crystal-covered slab with just three hooks and a hand drill, establishing what would be one of the route's cruxes. He placed three bolts.

On May 30 Paul and I returned to link Hair in My Cheeseburger's lower eight pitches with the four new upper pitches. The second pitch, which had originally been led with no bolts, was deemed really dangerous—a 50' runout on a 5.8 slab with ground-fall potential—so we added a bolt. The runout is now only 25 feet and not as serious. The result is one of the best routes I've done in the Black, easily on par with the Cruise, only a little more serious. We named it CrystalVision (1,800', IV+ 5.11-).

JOSH BOROF

Great White Wall, Super Wuss and Gouldy Variant. In October Kevin Cochran and I climbed a new route on the eastern side of Fisherman's Gully. Super Wuss (IV 5.11-) tackles the giant red arête just left of the Great White Wall route; it can be seen from Balanced Rock Overlook. The route was climbed clean, without pins or bolts (apart from rappel anchors on the first three pitches left by a previous party). First ascensionists are biased, but I believe Super Wuss to be the best route in the gully. Look for a topo at the North Rim ranger station. In Fall 2000 Chris Basset and I climbed a new, direct finish to the Great White Wall route. The Gouldy Variant, taking the obvious wide system at the top of the cliff where the Great White Wall route traverses off left; consists of two long pitches with difficulties up to 5.10+R.

JOSH WHARTON, *AAC*

Great White Wall, Death Camas Dihedrals. "Back in the saddle," I mused, as Andy Donson and I took aim at a line across from Balanced Rock Overlook. Yet saddle sores remained several months later. Blackened and battered, I harbored the memory with utter ambivalence—grateful for the ongoing recovery but pained by the cause. Having been thrown and kicked, I was anxious and excited about the day's launch, nearly from water-to-rim. I wanted to reacquaint myself with all that is the Black, with living.

The distinct upper dihedral pitches were striking, adjacent to the arête. Less clear was the lower half. We approached via Fisherman's Gully on May 11, almost as far down as the turbulent flow and cooler air. The features we hoped for, while engaging, unfolded with relative moderation. After four pitches we ate from the varied greenery of the halfway terrace, where Andy introduced me to a flower I couldn't identify. I reached to bend the slender stem and have a whiff when he suggested I not touch the death camas (toxicoscordion venenosums). Agreed.

The next pitch looked to be a groaner; two obese cracks with an appetite Andy's rack could not satisfy. Rather than grapple and groan he simply stemmed. A traverse left to a solid face up which we wandered was especially pleasurable. The prominent corner and arête remained. The final length of the dihedral, overhanging in places, had us toeing our way up a pinnacle on the arête. Position and climbing were equally exhilarating. Fortune had found us today. Death Camas Dihedrals (IV+ 5.10R/X).

TERRY MURPHY, *AAC*

South Chasm Wall, Burlgirl. In March Mike Shepherd and I had a vision of free climbing Bull Girl (5.11 A4). We thought we'd need a lot of time to clean and find a way to free the aid, so we spent two nights on the 2,000' climb. Three pitches up we face-climbed to the left for one pitch and gained a steep dihedral system, which gave us three variant pitches to the original A2+ section of Bull Girl. Mike led a steep, overhanging fist and offwidth corner to a ledge (5.11+). The next pitch was an arrow-straight corner with an RP seam that took just enough gear and provided just enough edges to go free at 5.12a. A steep face with incut crimps led us back onto Bull Girl. Following Bull Girl till the next A4, we found exciting steep corners, roofs, and face-climbing.

On our third day we were faced with finding a way past this hard A4 pitch. I traversed 50 feet out of the corner, hammered in two shady pins, climbed into a technical face section (5.11), and stopped at a stance where I could drill. Past this bolt I climbed more technical face, with 40' runouts on 5.11 and 5.10 climbing, finding just enough funky gear placements till I found a solid crack for a belay. Four more pitches, and we arrived at the summit. We had cleaned several sections of the climb but didn't complete the route all free.

In October Topher Donahue and I returned to the Black and completed the route, all free with no falls, in a day. Mike was unavailable but will return soon to try his own free ascent. Seven pitches are 5.11 and one 5.12, with several 5.10s and 5.9s. It's a fun route, but you have to be ready for serious runouts. We added three bolts: on the first traverse pitch, on the crux traverse, and on the 5.11X pitch. We climbed four new pitches and freed the pitches of Bull Girl we climbed to come up with Burlgirl (V 5.12-X).

JARED OGDEN, *AAC*

Wyoming

Enclosure, Prospect of an End. Sune Tamm-Buckle ("The Young Swede") and I departed late for a bivy in the moraine, where we proceeded to "get dizzy." Sune, bringing only a bivy sack, shivered the night away while I slept, warm and cozy in my down bag.

We woke at 3 a.m. on September 1, made our way to the Lower Saddle, crossed the Valhalla Traverse, and arrived at the Enclosure Couloir at 6 a.m. to find it, despite popular opinion, full of ice. We climbed three 60m pitches up the couloir, with some simul-climbing, and arrived at the start of our proposed route.

Four pitches of high-quality, chunky golden granite led to a mixed pitch that exited onto the ice apron of the High Route. We recommend a standard free rack; we left three pins and two heads in place. We proceeded to the top of the Enclosure via the standard High Route finish, topping out in the dark (IV 5.10X M4- AI3).

JOHN KELLEY

Montana

Glacier National Park, Mt. Jackson, Shades of Gray and Alpenglow. Visiting, with limited time, Anna Jansen sought to climb a mountain over the weekend. Excited by high pressure, we made for Glacier. The following day our friends Jeff Shapiro and Gray Thompson arrived, adding to our confidence. Good company, thoughtful conversation, and a restful evening led to a unanimous decision to scale Mt. Jackson (10,052').

The next morning we charged the striking northwest couloir (3,400' from base to ridge), for the possible first ascent. Jeff and Gray advanced left while Anna and I veered right. We climbed casual snow that steepened into a headwall. AI3 climbing led Anna and me into off-vertical snow flutings of near-styrofoam consistency. Protection became slim as I led easy, yet exposed, ground. A ropelength later I hammered a ringer blade: "Thank God." Another rope-length found us additional protection, an anchor, and a break. Anna followed remarking, "The climbing didn't look hard, but you were moving slow. I knew you had shitty protection, so I climbed like I was soloing." Right on! With a carefree smile she took the next section. Twenty-five feet led through a smear of ice in a rock corner, with 500' of exposure. Now to relaxed snow climbing, right? Wrong! After pulling the anchor and simul-climbing onto a huge snowfield, I looked up at Anna running out 600' of snow pack without pro. Dear God, if she slips, spare her and kill me. The recurring nightmare seizes my consciousness like a Post-Traumatic Stress Dis-

Anna Jansen taking Glen Deal out for a romantic stroll on Mt. Jackson, Glacier National Park. Jeff Shapiro

Anna Jansen dreaming of what will be on Mt. Jackson. The two routes take the shady left couloir to the middle summit region (left of the prominent spur, left of the wide gully on the right). Glen Deal

order flashback. Alpine climbing with your girlfriend is twisted! My only comfort is the easy climbing. Back in the couloir proper we greet the other team. Jeff and Gray are having a blast. "Got some awesome pics of you guys. Get any of us?"

"Sorry, we were too gripped to think of snapping any."

The rest of the route involved uncomplicated snow climbing with good protection. When we were 500' below the west ridge, the sun threatened to set. Pursuing the same terrain as the other team was out of the question. Our comrades continued up the couloir, while Anna and I headed left. Terrain remained easy, with ample protection on straightforward rock (5.7) and snow. Alpenglow provided soft colors as I topped the ridge. By the time Anna joined me, we were blanketed in deep magenta. Downclimbing by moonlight, Anna and I reached Gunsight Pass and stumbled four miles back to camp. The other team suffered a wet bivy on the summit ridge. The time spent on Mt. Jackson in March was one of a good route, jolly spirits, and merry making among close friends.

GLEN DEAL

Bitterroot Mountains, Spirolina Tower and Corner With a View. Trapper Creek's Spirolina Tower was named after its first ascent in 1977, by Craig Kenyon and Tom Cosgriff via the southwest corner (5–6 pitches, 5.8). The tower was notable to Kenyon because of his near-death experience on the east face descent. In 1992 Rod Sutherland and I, on a lark, put up the direct south face route, Whimsey (7 pitches, IV 5.10c) (1993 *AAJ*, p. 155), while also experiencing trials on the east face descent.

In 2002 James Pinjuv prophesized that a thin line on a blank gray wall high up Spirolina was a perfect hand crack. With confidence Jimmy led the first pitch, a left-facing corner system

(5.9) 50' east of the start of Whimsey. I led the second pitch (5.8), up clean cracks to a small stance under a little tree. Jimmy led the foretold third pitch, the Jelly Jam (60', 5.9+)—one of the finest hand cracks in the Bitterroots, and named for its exquisite sweetness. I led the fourth pitch, the Orange Corner, a slightly seedy flaring crack, at 5.10b. Three pitches followed, with several options available. One can cut right, out onto the south face, following obvious cracks to the top (5.8–5.10, Whimsey finish) or angle northeast, toward easier terrain (Jelly Jam finish). During the east face descent we followed obvious ramps, placing several fixed pins and stoppers, and made five rappels.

During our descent Jimmy spotted a corner system, one and a half gullies to our east, that appeared to have a perfect crack in it. After two scrambling, roped approach pitches, I started up the third pitch, a clean, near-perfect corner (5.9+). Jimmy led the fourth pitch, a spectacular, vertical continuation of the corner (5.9+). Two more serpentine pitches (5.8) angling northeast led us to the top of the formation and a pleasant northwest walk-off into the descent gully (Corner With a View, III 5.9+).

STEVE PORCELLA

The south face of Spirolina tower in the Bitterroot Mountains. Left to right: Kenyon-Cosgriff (1977), Whimsey (Porcella-Sutherland, 1992), The Jelly Jam (Pinjuv-Porcella, 2002). Steve Porcella

Alaska

BROOKS RANGE

Alaska

Arrigetch Peaks, various activity. After a season of work for the Alaska Outward Bound Center, seven O.B. staff and three others spent 18 days, from August 18 to September 5, in the Arrigetch peaks. Our group was Nettie Pardue, Tina Woolston, Robert MacKinnon, Jared Coburn, Mike Morley, Mike Zawaski, Jeff Brislawn, Mark Sundeen, Erik Bluhm, and I, Jeff Pflueger. We divided into climbing pairs who were off for days at a time from two established base camps, up Arrigetch Creek and Aiyagomahala Creek. Pairs kept in contact via radio. Each of us brought two or three plastic bear containers for food caches.

Winter was coming to the Arrigetch. Frosty conditions had eliminated mosquitoes, but kept northern aspects encrusted with enough snow and ice to limit our climbing to thawed southern aspects. We watched the brilliant reds, golds, and yellows of the tundra deepen and saw the days dramatically shorten as winter came. One-third of the days were crisp, blue, and beautiful; one-third overcast; and one-third produced some rain and snow. The combination of good weather and stunning topography did not grant respite from either climbing or planning the next climb.

The Badille, showing the MacKinnon-Pflueger route.

Jared and Mike M. climbed six pitches of the northwest ridge of an unnamed peak they dubbed "Notchtop" in the upper Aquarius Valley (represented on the Survey Pass B-3 quad as a long ridge between two glaciers at the head of the valley). The approximate GPS is N67.40149 W154.14952. The route covers excellent rock and has interesting moderate climbing (5.7/8). They were stopped a pitch from the summit by difficult climbing and cold temperatures. The two also attempted the unclimbed east ridge of Ariel but retreated because of extremely rotten rock.

Jeff P. and Robert climbed a new route on the south face of the

Caliban, showing Caliban East Summit, (gullies-slabs, 3rd or 4th class). first ascent possibly by Lorna Corson and Norm Larson, 1993; South Face route, attempted by Corson-Larson, 1993 (triangular orange face with loose flakes); route by Pflueger et al 2002. Jeff Pflueger

Badille (III 5.8). The route traverses from the talus on the southeast side of the peak, follows the obvious left-trending crack system/gully to the summit ridge, and continues along the ridge to the summit. This is an excellent and varied route to a stunning central summit in the Arrigetch peaks.

Jeff P. and Nettie climbed six pitches of moderate slabs and cracks (5.8) leading directly to the southeast ridge of the west summit of Caliban (7,181').

Mike Z. and Jeff B. climbed the south face of Elephant's Tooth (5.7) to the summit. They later attempted the northeast buttress of the Parabola, starting from a notch visible from north of the buttress. They climbed six pitches (5.9) before turning back beneath a chimney full of large loose blocks. This was probably the Bitenieks–Reichert route reported in the 1998 AAJ (pp. 205–6). Later, Mike Z. and Jeff B. climbed a route on the south face of the East Maiden and reported about five pitches of good climbing (5.8). The route starts up flakes below a left-facing dihedral in the center of the south face, exits the dihedral to slabs on the right, and continues straight up to the summit. This route may be a direct variation of a route previously described in the 1977 AAJ (pp. 165–6).

Two teams (Jeff P., Robert, and Nettie, and later Jared and Mike M.) climbed the spectacular north-northwest ridge of the Parabola (III 5.7). The ridge is southeast of the largest lake in Aquarius Valley. The teams ascended from the east, via 700 vertical feet of easy 5th class, to the flat ridge top. Six pitches of moderate climbing (5.7) followed the ridge south to a false summit. Neither team climbed the final few pitches of icy slab to the central summit of the

Parabola showing NNW ridge, FA possibly by Stuart Parks-Joan Unger, 1993; NE Buttress route, Joe Reichert-Bitenieks. West Summit (5,900′) Arthur Bacon, George Ripley, David Roberts, Robert Waldorp, 1969. Jeff Pflueger

Parabola. The descent involved one rappel west from the ridge to the slab gully and four rappels down the slabs north of the ridge. A stopper inscribed "R.W. Freed" and bail slings were found along the route.

As a fantastic end to our trip, three teams (Jared and Mike M., Mike Z. and Jeff B., and Jeff P. and Robert) on three consecutive days climbed the west ridge of Shot Tower (IV 5.8 C2). Stunning! Robert aided the final headwall with the help of two fixed pins and a handful of small offsets and TCUs, but he paid the price for a skimpy aid rack and some back cleaning when he fell 20' during the final mantle at the top! To descend it is best to rappel the route and remain on the ridge, including tensioning around the "Mushroom."

Robert MacKinnon on the west ridge of Shot Tower at dawn. Jeff Pflueger

JEFF PFLUEGER

HAYES RANGE

Mt. McGinnis, east face, Cutthroat Couloir. In early March Jed Brown and I skied in to attempt the unclimbed direct east face of McGinnis. The left-hand serac, and constant spew showering down the lower gully of the face, had us choose to repeat Cutthroat Couloir instead. We found thin, overhanging ice (Grade V/VI) and easy mixed in the 3,000' slot. Rockfall, even in the cold of March, was a major issue (wear a titanium sombrero). We descended the corniced northeast ridge after summiting from our only bivy spot (a snow cave at the top of the Cutthroat). It was the second ascent of the classic 1986 Comstock–Dial route and took seven days road-to-road. I strongly recommend only attempting the line in extreme cold, due to rockfall considerations. It was my third summiting of McGinnis, via a different route each time.

JEFF BENOWITZ

DELTA RANGE

Item Peak, North Face. In February, Jed Brown (18 years old) and I (33) ascended a direct line on the north face of Item Peak, to the left of the route I did in 2000. Jed and I found snow up to 65° and avoided all rock bands by stepping left around them. We only roped up for the summit cornice.

JEFF BENOWITZ

ALASKA RANGE

Denali National Park and Preserve, summary. Life is still fragile in the range—our human vulnerability became painfully evident again this year when three brothers perished on Mt. Foraker in an apparent avalanche, and one soloist fell to his death from Denali Pass on Mt. McKinley.

National Park Service mountaineering patrols were kept busy with numerous search-and-rescue incidents. As always, the patrol volunteers and the military pararescuemen were an important asset, working with the rangers in assisting other climbers in distress and providing resource protection.

On a preseason patrol in March, all nine Denali mountaineering rangers climbed Mt. Silverthrone and skied over Anderson Pass and out the West Fork Glacier. This past season also marked the first ranger patrol since 1932 to successfully climb Denali from the north side of the Alaska Range. A foursome ascended via the Muldrow Glacier route, traversing over and down to the 14,200' ranger camp on the West Buttress route. In other patrol firsts, one ranger patrol spent over two weeks at the 17,200' high camp at the end of the season, setting a new standard for high-altitude camping.

Clean Mountain Cans (CMCs) were used extensively above the 14,200' ranger camp to deal with solid human waste. Also in the resource-management realm, preprinted tags were used for the first time to uniformly identify all caches in terms of expedition names, dates, and permit numbers.

The weather was unseasonably warm, with early May temperatures approaching overnight lows of 34°F, causing crevasses to open in early June on the 7,200' Kahiltna Glacier.

Of 1,232 climbers attempting Mt. McKinley (1,093 via the West Buttress), 645 (52%) reached the summit. Of 36 attempting Mt. Foraker, 7 (19%) reached the top. The average trip length for an expedition on Mt. McKinley was 17.7 days, and the average age of a Denali climber was 36. The total of 110 women represented 9% of the climbers.

Guided clients accounted for 20% of climbers on Mt. McKinley. Guided expeditions as a whole (including clients and guides) accounted for 31%.

Also on Denali, two Russian paraplegic climbers, Grigoriy Tsarkov and Igor Ushakov, reached the summit in June via the West Buttress, making direct variations up the rescue gully and from 17,200' to 18,800'. The route was prepared with fixed line by the other nine team members, and then Tsarkov and Ushakov used their mechanical ascending ski sleds to ascend with their arms.

A total of 224 summitings were made during May, 391 in June, and 30 in July. The busiest days on the summit of Denali were June 13th (56 climbers) and June 16th (49). There were only five days in June when climbers did not reach the top.

Climbers came from 38 nations, with the most coming from the United States (754), Japan (56), United Kingdom (47), Canada (43), France (39), Germany (38), and Korea (36).

Denali National Park

Mt. McKinley, Denali Diamond, second ascent. Kenton Cool and I arrived in the Alaska Range at the beginning of May, hoping to steal a march on other potential suitors to a new line on Foraker. After failing to climb the standard West Butt route for acclimatization, with Kenton turned back by dizzy spells around 20,000' and myself not even able to get out of the tent at 17,000', we returned for a peep at Foraker. After a day and night spent staring at the face, I'd about convinced myself that my optimistic guess at "only" three or four hours beneath the myriad death seracs overhanging the lower third of the route was an acceptable risk for the prize. Luckily, Kenton was still thinking straight and vetoed the plan, an example of our partnership kicking in to make sensible decisions.

As a fine consolation we managed the second ascent of the Denali Diamond in five days. It surprised us that this route, first climbed in 1983, hadn't seen a repeat, but perhaps the epic 17 days spent on the first ascent and talk of a 25' A3 roof had put people off. Unbeknown to us, as soon as we left base camp the forecast changed—typical. Having opted for a lightweight approach with one-season bags and a one-person tent to share, and plans to snooze in the afternoon sun, we were shocked to encounter snow for the final four days and no sun at all. Other events of interest were the tent poles breaking beyond repair, a dropped axe just before the crux pitches, and a malfunctioning stove. Our solace was that at least we opted out of our original single-push plan.

The climbing itself was superb, with sustained mixed climbing, several pitches of vertical ice, and a trio of crux pitches that gave me my best day's climbing yet in the mountains. The first of these proved the hardest—a cracked wall with overhanging sections that bypassed the aid roof. I was able to dry tool this with one rest point and a tension point. All free, it would rate Grade VIII, 8 in Scotland. The personal crux for me, however, occurred the following day when I had one of my worst days in the mountains. Plodding on the upper reaches of the Cassin

Ridge, I eventually burst into tears on 40° snow after almost passing out twice. Again the partnership kicked in, and Kenton pulled me through with words of support and a momentous session of single-handed trailbreaking.

We topped the Cassin, ticked the summit, and descended a combination of the Orient Express and West Rib, all in zero visibility. We were surprised to find our arrival at the 14k camp, at 11:30 p.m., met by a welcoming party of climbers and rangers (supposedly the alert was out for us due to the conditions). The support and hospitality offered by our fellow climbers was a heart-warming highlight of the trip.

IAN PARNELL, *United Kingdom*

Mt. Hunter, north buttress, second ascent of Deprivation. Stephen Farrand and I arrived at Kahiltna base camp on June 3 and stayed through June 17. In that time we managed to make the second ascent of Deprivation. The ascent took three days, with bivies on the first and third ice bands. We left our gear at our high bivy and blasted for the summit, returning to the bivy and beginning our descent rappelling down the Moonflower Buttress. On the descent we made a third bivy, then finished the descent and returned to base camp the next day.

JOHN KELLEY

Editor's Note: This is the second ascent of Deprivation that followed the complete original route. In 2000 (2001 AAJ, p 204), Jeff Hollenbaugh and Bruce Miller started on Deprivation, but joined the Moonflower at the third ice band and did not continue above the top of the buttress.

Mt. Hunter, Wall of Shadows, free to third ice band; and Mt. Huntington, West Face Couloir. "It's the best day of the season," our pilot commented as Russ Mitrovich and I flew into the Alaska Range. It was May 12, and we were headed for the Tokositna Glacier and the West Face Couloir (a.k.a. Nettle–Quirk) on Mt. Huntington. We awoke the next morning to a still, clear sky, got our kit together, and left camp at noon. We climbed the initial slopes, before roping up at the base of the couloir. The couloir was perfect 70° ice with an occasional vertical step. We rounded the corner and stopped for a brew in the Alcove. The brew turned into a nap, and four hours later we were off again, summiting in the early morning. A bunch of V threads later we were back in camp in time for lunch. By noon the next day we were off again, flying under perfect blue skies toward Kahiltna International.

Our primary plan was to climb Denali, but the north buttress of Mt. Hunter was undeniably drawing us in. With the weather still perfect, we figured we might as well be climbing instead of towing sleds and acclimatizing on the Big One. We skied up the next morning with packs ready to go, aiming for the Moonflower route. The lower section was totally out of shape, in part because of a huge rockfall and also because of a very warm and dry spring. Our eyes were continually diverted to the Wall of Shadows, which had considerably more ice and looked to be in awesome shape. So off we went. We took the same variant start as Kevin Mahoney and Ben Gilmore, who had made a very fast and mostly free second ascent of the Wall of Shadows the season before. The climbing was perfect, and we were moving fast. We made it to the base of the Crystal Highway, chopped the ice off a sloping rock ledge, and called it home. The next morning I headed up what I thought was the Crystal Highway. Our only topo was a bad picture of the north buttress, and it wasn't helping. Three pitches later the Somewhere Else Wall, which I had hoped to be standing at the base of, was indeed somewhere else. So with tails between our legs we rapped off. Luckily, Kevin Mahoney had just arrived in base camp and provided the missing details, telling us about an awesome bivy at the top of the Crystal Highway.

So, off again for another try. The climbing was comfortably familiar, and we were perched inside the wildest snow mushroom at the top of the Crystal Highway by early evening. We had easily freed a couple of the aid sections lower on the wall, and now the Somewhere Else Wall was the last crux section. The next morning the weather finally turned for the worse, and a thick fog set in. I headed down from the bivy and began traversing left (I traversed in higher than the original start) on a system of ledges linked by blank-looking rock sections. I got solid rock gear in and started teetering across the solid granite on edges only big enough for half of the first tooth of my picks. I kept waiting for the big swing that only came at the end of the pitch, when I finally got my first stick in solid ice. Yee Ha! Another short challenging mixed pitch, and we were on our way to the third ice band. The skies began to dump, and spindrift was building fast. While we were climbing the third ice band toward the last pitches of the Moonflower route, we looked back down at total whiteout. We were a little gripped about finding our way down, and the storm was growing. We decided to bail, and a combination of endless stoppers and V threads deposited us safely back in the horizontal world. A few hours after arriving in base camp we were laughing as the skies unloaded and a four-day storm moved in.

JIMMY HADEN

Peak 11,520', north face to summit ridge; and Mt. Huntington. Around 10 p.m. on May 17 Patricia Deavoll, Anna Keeling, Scott Simper, and I flew onto the Tokositna Glacier. By 3 p.m. May 18, all four of us had reached the summit of Huntington via the West Face Couloir route. The round trip took 22 hours. Three days later Patricia and I climbed the Colton–Leach route on Huntington in 27 hours.

By May 25 the ridge of high pressure was still hanging around, so the four of us skied down valley and established a camp at the base of Peak 11,520'. The following morning around 10:00, after the sun left the north face, our party split into two. Anna and I went to the western side of the north face of Peak 11,520', while Patricia and Scotty headed to the center of the face.

We reached the base of the 'shrund after half an hour, then took an hour to cross it. Our route, on the western side of the north face, fol-

Peak 11,520'. The Keeling-McNeill route follows ice runnels just right of the obvious serac. *Anna Keeling*

lows ice runnels just west of a major serac about halfway up the face. Anna and I climbed 15 pitches to the summit ridge. The climb is primarily ice up to WI4, with mixed pitches of 5.5 and snow higher up. By the time we reached the summit ridge snow had begun to fall, and we retreated, foregoing the summit. The round trip took 15 hours. After getting high on their route, Patricia and Scotty were forced to retreat by unconsolidated snow.

KAREN MCNEILL, *Canada*

Mt. Huntington. The west side of Mount Huntington was in better condition than other terrain at that elevation and as a result saw numerous ascents. The most notable was a 17-hour solo effort by Chris Turiano. He climbed the West Face Couloir to the summit on May 22, finding plastic ice and stable snow conditions.

DENALI NATIONAL PARK

Scott Simper enjoying the thrills of camera tilt on Mt. Huntington's West Face Couloir route. Karen McNeill

Bear's Tooth, You Can't Fly. A six-man Polish Alaska 2002 expedition operated as two independent teams. Two younger climbers repeated routes in the Ruth Gorge, while the four more experienced ones were interested in climbing a big new route on one of the east faces of the Moose's Tooth massif. The latter team, probably the strongest Polish alpine climbers at present, consisted of Jacek Fluder, Janusz Golab, Stanislaw Piecuch, and Grzegorz Skorek. They departed from Talkeetna and landed on the Buckskin Glacier on the afternoon of June 4. They could not identify the exact line of the 2001 Beast route, or the other attempted lines, on the 800m-high monolith of the Moose's Tooth left pillar, but saw fixed ropes hanging on the pillar. So they chose the Bear's Tooth's left-hand pillar, which is less monolithic but offered a totally new line up the full height of the wall.

On June 5 they crossed the small bergschrund and fixed 300m of rope on rock terrain (UIAA VII A1) dominated by wet and lichen-coated slabs and cracks filled with moss. Next day they installed their first portaledge camp above the sixth pitch. On June 8 they started a continuous push but retreated the next evening in a snowstorm. After six days of snow, the weather was sunny on the 14th, and they pushed again, though both portaledges had holes made by stones. First Skorek led and next Piecuch, in mixed but mostly rock terrain up to UIAA VII A0-A1. The day ended at about 2 a.m. with Piecuch leading a section of A3 on pitch 16, just above the second portaledge bivouac. The next day Golab and Fluder fixed 300 ms of rope above the second bivy (up to pitch 23), first finding orange rock—the best of the route—followed by totally wet corners and slabs. At the end of a giant, 100m long, deep groove they made their only tension traverse. On June 16 again Piecuch mostly led, meeting much rotten rock. They established their third bivouac on pitch 32, just above a significant outcrop that culminates the main prow of the pillar. The terrain then became gentler, with steep steps and snowy ledges, and Fluder led in plastic boots.

The Bear's Tooth and the Moose's Tooth, showing: 1. Southeast (left) pillar, You Can't Fly (1,400m, 41 pitches, UIAA-VII A3, Fluder-Golab-Piecuch-Skorek, 2002). 2. East face (right) pillar. Useless Emotion (ca 4,700', VII 5.9 A4 WI4, Bridwell-Christensen-Dunmire-Jonas-McCray, 1999). 3. Southeast face via east couloir (5.8 A3 WI4, House-Gilmore-Mahoney, 2000). 4. East Pillar Direct (approximate 1,600' attempts by Bill-Bonington-Frost-McCarthy, 1971, and Bill-Chouinard-McCarthy-Rowell, 1972). 5. East pillar direct via monolith, The Beast, (Bridwell-Pfingsten, 2001). 6. Northeast face, The Dance of the Woo Li Masters (1,500m, M6 WI 4+ Bridwell-Stump, 1981). Photo: Grzegorz Skorek. Text and topo compiled by GrzegorzGlazek with help from J.Golab and G.Skorek

At night on the 17th the leader of the leading pair fixed the rope on the highest rock, five or ten meters below the top, where he found the highest piton from the 1999 Bridwell route, then rappelled to bivy. The top consisted of a corniced, snowy arête, and the Poles made probably the first ascent to the true top from this side of the mountain. (According to Bridwell's report, his team found the final cornice too unstable; see *AAJ* 2000, p. 45.) On the 18th at 1 p.m. the whole team reached the top in clouds and worsening weather. After a short stay they started to rappel, clearing the fixed ropes. They bivouaced, then continued rappelling through wet snowfall, reaching the base on the night of the 19th.

They spent 10 days on the wall. The climbing itself took six days, plus two days waiting in portaledges during storms and two days to descend. The height of the route is nearly 1,400m, 41 pitches with 60m ropes. They climbed mostly free, at overall US grade VI and UIAA rating VII A0-A1 with one A2 section (on pitch 35) and one serious A3 section (on pitch 16, with sky-hook and a few bird beak equivalentsæ"figure-of-one pitons," known in the Tatra Mountains since 1955). This hardest section started directly above the second portaledge camp but seemed possible to avoid by slightly easier terrain. The one tension traverse was on pitch 23. Rock was generally poor and crumbly, but not as bad as reports of other routes led the climbers to expect. The rock was quite sound on pitches 17-23 but really rotten on pitches 27-29.

The rappel line is well to the right of pitches 1-6 and to the left of pitches 17-20 and 26-29. The team used 350m of fixed ropes, which they removed during the descent.

On the lower third of the route they found rappel stations from an unknown attempt that joined their route from the left (probably via a big chimney), at a snowfield on the 9th pitch, and continued to the 13th pitch. The anchors had slings that looked no older than three years and pitons made in Austria.

After descent by rappel, the team had only a dozen pitons remaining, so they abandoned plans for other climbs and left the mountains earlier than originally planned. They left for Talkeetna on June 23. The name of the route, You Can't Fly, reflects the words they heard too often as they tried to depart from Europe, from Talkeetna, and returning home.

You Can't Fly is the first big-wall route established by climbers from Poland in North America (though later in the year Poles established slightly harder routes on Mt. Thor on Baffin Island and on El Capitan.) (These are covered elsewhere in this journal – Ed.) *(Based on written reports by team members and talks with G.Skorek and J.Golab)*

GRZEGORZ GLAZEK, *CDW PZA*

Ruth Gorge, ascents and attempts. The popularity of the Ruth Gorge continued, with many routes seeing ascents. The oft-attempted Cobra Pillar (VI 5.10+ A3, Donini–Tackle, 1991) on Mt. Barrill finally was repeated in June, by two parties. Canadians Jean-Pierre Ouellet and Stefane Perron made the second ascent, after fixing four ropes, in a 37-hour tent-to-tent push. Poles Maciej Ciesielski and Jakub Radziejowski, with American Zack Martin, made the third ascent soon after. Their ascent took exactly 36 hours (including a short break to rest and eat), and they reported mostly free climbing up to UIAA VII/VII+ and two pitches of aid, up to C2.

The Polish pair also repeated Game Boy (400m, UIAA VII+, Neswadba– Orgler–Wutscher, 1995) on the Stump Pillar (left pillar of the Wisdom Wall) and the Orgler–Jochler route on Hut Tower (800m, VI+/VII- RP1987) ("RP" means redpoint style). Radziejowski writes of the Orgler–Jochler, "The best rock of the routes we climbed in the Ruth, but still far from perfect."

The Poles were also one of several parties to repeat The Dream in the Spirit of Mugs (V 5.10, Bonapace-Haas-Orgler, 1994) on the Eye Tooth. They report that Zack Martin climbing with a partner ahead of the Poles, led a new pitch just before the headwall, the direct lower corner (about UIAA VII). The Poles report this pitch to be the hardest of the route. *(Ed. note: Zack Martin, a young, ambitious climber, died in a car accident on Thanksgiving.)*

On the immense walls of Mt. Dickey, Mark Synnott and Kevin Thaw made an impressive attempt at a new route between the Roberts-Rowell-Ward route (5,250', VI 5.9 A3, 1974) and the Italian route (5,250', VI 5.11 A4, Bagattoli-Borgonovo-Defrancesco-De Dona-Leoni-Manica-Zampiccoli, 1991). They climbed about 25 pitches, all free, up to 5.11-, in 11 hours, before bailing in bad weather. Synnott estimates their high point to be four or five pitches from the shale band, and reports that their attempted line contains "600-800' of the worst choss I've ever encountered."

Ruth Gorge, Moose's Tooth, correction. The 2000 AAJ (pp. 212-3) reported that, in attempting the second ascent of the now classic and frequently climbed Ham and Eggs, Brian Teale and Carl Tobin retreated short of the couloir top. In fact Teale climbed the upper half of the couloir alone (Tobin was having difficulty because of a previous injury) but retreated from the summit ridge.

Ruth Gorge, The Eye Tooth, West Face, The Dream in the Spirit of Mugs, new variation. After trying to do ice and mixed climbing on Denali and Mt. Hunter, Julian Neumayer and I changed our plans because of Alaska's tropical temperatures, flying to the Ruth Gorge to climb rock. On June 16 we made the sixth ascent of The Dream in the Spirit of Mugs, in 10 hours to the summit ridge, by a new variation. Perhaps because we were happy to climb again, after sitting too long in the tent, we missed the route after the third pitch and climbed a new variation to the right, up to the bivy spot at pitch 13. Right of the big 120m corner, we climbed seven long (up to 80m) pitches on slabs, directly through a small roof system. The climbing went at easy 5.10 on very good rock.

ALEXANDER FIDI, *Austria*

Ruth Gorge, Mt. Dickey, Blood from the Stone. In March, Sean Easton (Canada) and Ueli Steck (Switzerland) established a remarkable mixed route on the 5,000' east face of Mt. Dickey. The route, which they named Blood from the Stone, includes difficulties of M7+ and AI6+X. An article on this climb appears earlier in this Journal.

Ruth Gorge, Mt. Dickey, south pillar, Crime of the Century; and Mt. Bradley, northeast spur, Welcome to Alaska. Our group flew to Ruth Gorge on May 4 with Doug Geeting Aviation (they were impressed by the amount of food we took!). We were nine members of the national youth group of Fédération Française de la Montagne et de l'Escalade*. Our expedition lasted from May 4 to May 25. Before departure we all studied photos and imagined the most awesome new routes.

It was funny then to see our faces after the last plane vanished, leaving us alone on this cold and windy glacier! Our two objectives, Mt. Bradley and Mt. Dickey, were in front of us, like dark giant ships, covered with snow. The awesome new routes did not seem so realistic any more.

We first experienced a week of storm and snow. But morale remained high, thanks to the big dome tent and palatable food. The weather then became totally clear and warm for 15 days. However, avalanche risk remained high, and we always met rotten snow in the mixed sections. Five of us climbed Mt. Dickey, while the four others climbed Mt. Bradley. Both routes had been attempted previously (we found gear on each), but not, to our knowledge, completed.

On the south pillar of Mt. Dickey (2,909m), the climbers were Guillaume Avrisani, Yann Bonneville, Cédric Cruaud, Paul Robach, and Romain Wagner.

Mt. Bradley, showing: Welcome to Alaska (1,400m, 31 pitches, VI 6b A3+ M6-, Charon-Faure-Moulin-Ponson, 2002). The left skyline is the East Ridge route (1,400m, UIAA-VI 70°, Jöchler-Orgler, 1987). Paul Robach

The route we opened (Crime of the Century, 1,550m, 27 pitches, VI 6c A4) was located in the middle of Dickey's huge south face. We think this line may be the only safe one on the face, much of which is threatened by a high snow and rock avalanche risk, due to rotten schist slopes above.

The route consisted of a 1,050m big wall, followed by 500m of mixed climbing with loose schist. We fixed ropes for three days (May 12–14), spending nights at base camp, then ascended in capsule-style from May 15 to May 20. The rock varied from excellent to awful. Some aid pitches were on very poor "sugar" rock, from which bolts could be removed by hand. The aid climbing was often hard. However, we also free climbed several pleasant sections on excellent granite. A wonderful terrace is located one-third of the way up the route, but bivouac sites are virtually nonexistent above. Above the wall we spent unpleasant hours digging into rotten snow and climbing on moving schist. After an afternoon rest we reached the summit on May 20, at 9:00 p.m., then went down by the easy Dickey Pass route.

The giant south face of Mt. Dickey (2,909m), revealing Crime of the Century (1,550m, 27 pitches, VI 6c A4, Avrisani-Benneville-Cruaud-Robach-Wagner, 2002). Paul Robach

The climbers on the northeast spur of Mt. Bradley (2,775m) were Victor Charon, Alban Faure, Christophe Moulin, and Jérémie Ponson. They called their route Welcome to Alaska (1,400m, 31 pitches, snow/rock/mixed, VI 6b A3+ M6-). After three days (May 11–13) of preparing 300m of fixed rope, the group ascended May 14–19. The conditions (a lot of snow) made this ascent a hard trip. The route corresponded to what climbers from the Alps might expect in Alaska: incredible snow formations, such as huge mushrooms and cornices, and a 350m wall of good rock on the ridge. Since bivouac sites were lacking on the 350m wall, the team made a 35-hour nonstop push to reach its top. From there they were obliged to rappel to gain the following ridge, which involved hard aid and mixed climbing, before joining the east ridge (the final part of the Orgler route). They reached the summit at 4:00 p.m. on May 19. The team spent a full day descending to the pass between Mt. Bradley and Mt. Wake, then rappelling to the glacier and base camp. Although this route is safe to climb, we believe that a retreat from it would be quite hazardous.

PAUL ROBACH, *Fédération Française de la Montagne et de l'Escalade, France.*

* This expedition was part of the program of the national young climber team of the Fédération Française de la Montagne et de l'Escalade. The coaches were Christophe Moulin (expedition leader,

Mt. Wake, showing: 1. Pilier de la Tolerance (1,500m, 5c A1 90°, Desprat-Lestienne-Salles, 1996) (this is the left-hand ridge coming down to the glacier). 2. Lowney-Teale (1,500m, M4 WI5, Lowney-Teale, 2002). 3. Northeast Buttress, Screaming Blue Messiah (1,500m, 5.7 A2 70°, Atkinson-Kay, 1990). 4. Wake Up. (900m, IV WI5, Desprat-Lestienne-Salles, 1996). 5. Mt. Johnson, Elevator Shaft. (3,000', 5.7 A3 AI5+, Chabot-Tackle, 1995). Kelly Cordes

FFME) and Paul Robach (ENSA). Each two years, nine young climbers (age 20–25) are selected to compose this group (testing in rock, mixed and ice climbing, endurance, mountain experience) and participate in several courses and an expedition, supported by FFME.

Ruth Gorge, Mt. Wake, east face. The high pressure that centered over Alaska for three months brought clear skies and superb climbing conditions. Two weeks earlier in the Ruth, I attempted to solo Shaken Not Stirred on the Moose's Tooth, while J.J. Brooks and Charlie Sassara climbed Ham and Eggs.

Local crab fisherman Pete Lowney and I head from Valdez back to the Ruth with several objectives in mind. We end up at the base of Mount Wake and spot the obvious center route up the east face. Though the route looks exposed, in early April it's still frigid, and the face looks locked up. We strike out on April 6 and, after surmounting a big crack, are committed. Right up the center of the face, moderate climbing with sparse pro finds us bivied before the gully entry. Second day we enter the gully, and Pete leads a little WI5 pitch. Superb climbing, rock pro, and long runnels of 45° to 55° water ice, with the occasional M4 crux. Second bivy in a great spot to the side, and the isobutane stove goes out. Last time I take one stove up a route this time of year. Third day we bust a move for the top, waterless, super moderate climbing, changing from granite to the summit caprock. The exit that was obvious from the plane isn't from the route, so we just follow the ever-steepening ice to a vertical crux. One pitch from the top, our pilot Paul Roderick flies by, and I feel like I can reach out and touch his wing. We summit and race the clouds to the Wake–Bradley col, but they catch us and we bivy in a crevasse. No stove, low on food, and socked in on the backside of Wake. I tell Pete this is a classic Alaska Range situation, and we could be in this crevasse for days. We discover that our body heat can melt ice chips we place in ziplock bags, which saves us from serious consequences.

The Alaska Range is kind this spring, however, the clouds lift, and we descend uneventfully. The next day it snows in camp and socks the mountain in, but we are safe and vow to return.

BRIAN TEALE

Surprise Glacier peaks. On May 26 Steve Mock and I flew into the upper end of the southern lobe of the Surprise Glacier, a remote and lower-elevation area (Talkeetna C-5 quad map) in the southwest portion of the Alaska Range, located between Mt. Dall and Mt. Russell.

We placed our base camp in the middle of the glacier at about 5,200', and during the brief weather windows we were afforded good views as far as the distant Kichatna Spires, Mt. Dall, and Mt. Russell.

We initially had good weather and bagged a couple of nice peaks via snow couloirs and ridges. (None of the peaks in the area have established names.) Due west of our base camp we climbed a northeast couloir of Peak 6,500' (located at UTM 5 539110E 6948891N). South of base camp, at the very head of the southern lobe of the Surprise Glacier, we climbed the west ridge of Peak 6,000', passing a small rock tower along the way that looked very much like a chortenæhence "Chorten Peak" (UTM 5 539618E 6946748N).

Then the weather took a turn for the worse. Very high winds (inverted tent and broken poles), sleet, rain, and snow plagued us for the balance of our trip. During a brief respite from the bad weather, we attempted Peak 6,302' via its east ridge (from the pass at UTM 5 540827E 6947835N) but were thwarted by horrendously loose rock. This peak is south of the impressive west face of what we were calling the "Little Eiger" (Peak 7,200').

Then we ran out of beer. In 17 days we had five days of fair weather, and, needless to say, our mood was subdued. This area seemed good for solitude, ski touring, and easy peak bagging, with difficult ascent possibilities in colder temperatures. (We found unconsolidated snow and crumbly rock.) In searching *AAJs* and the libraries at AMH and the Talkeetna Ranger Station, and in speaking with several long-time Alaska Range climbers, including Roger Robinson and Brian Okonek, I didn't learn of anyone who'd previously been in this area.

Missing our original pickup date of June 6, we finally flew out on the 11th, in blustery weather, with many thanks to the persistent efforts of McKinley Air.

BRIAN CABE, *AAC*

KICHATNA SPIRES

The Citadel, east buttress. The mythical Cathedral Spires of the remote, rarely frequented Kichatna Mountains were our destination. Pictures of granite spires forcing their way through bellowing cloud had sparked our imagination. Unfortunately, journals also suggested the worst weather in Alaska. Could it be worse than a wet Llanberis winter's day? Not a chance! Worse than Scotland in winter? Surely not! Stu McAleese and I had to go.

The Kichatna Spires spike the horizon as Cerro Torre and the Towers of Paine do in Patagonia. Although less than 9,000' in elevation and encompassing only 20 square miles, they have a reputation beyond their size. Ninety miles from Talkeetna, they were among the last Alaskan mountains to be explored. Aerial photos had been taken by Austin Post and published in Summit magazine by someone perhaps trying to mislead other climbers, as the Reisenstein of British Columbia. Eventually, in 1965, New Yorker Al DeMaria resolved the enigma and visited the area with friends.

Clumping into a Talkeetna cafe, we made for the bar. We sat next to two climbers obviously just back from the hill. Thierry, the tallest, greeted us with a strong French accent. We noted his bandaged hands; most of his fingers were frostbitten. Alaskan climbing obviously had potential for unpleasantness.

We had been advised to take as much as we wanted on the plane, that weight was no problem, but arriving at the Talkeetna airport, we noted that the supercharged Cessna resembled little more than a flying kite. Weight, or lack of it, was crucial to flying at attitude and landing on the glaciers. Our eight boxes of food, bucket, frying pan, four haulbags, three rucksacks, boom box, three camera bags, extra-large family tray of Doritos, cooler full of meat and cheese, did look a little over the top. Our personal allowance was 125 pounds; we had over 1,000 pounds. We repacked, ate and drank as much as possible, stoked up the barbeque grill, and threw an impromptu party for everybody stranded at the airstrip.

Paul Roderick of Talkeetna Air Taxi, or TAT, pulled back on his controls as we hurtled down the runway. Paul seemed as keen as we were to fly into the Kichatnas, for him a change from the frequent flights into Denali. The weather was perfect; Alaska was suffering from a heat wave. We had crystal-clear views as we traveled west, parallel to the main range, over 90 miles of frozen swamp. We saw that walking out was not a possibility. If we didn't drown crossing the rivers, bears and mosquitoes would surely devour us. The scale of the place hit us, mountain after mountain, and we would be the only folk climbing west of the main range.

The Spires grew closer. Paul cranked down the skids to land. I couldn't get all the peaks in my camera's viewfinder. We hooted and pointed at peaks we had seen in books. Paul threw the plane over hard, and we could almost touch the East Pillar of Triple Middle Peak, one of the best lines in the world, first climbed alpine style by Embick and crew. Finally we swept through the col between Gurney and Kichatna Spire, with the biggest face in the range—over 1,000m of pink granite. The long, slender Shadows Glacier, which was to be our home for the next four and a half weeks, opened out in front of us. Paul took a tight spin to check out the landing, Stu and I became quiet, and Paul skillfully dropped onto the snow—a landing so smooth that Stu and I realized we'd put down only when Paul told us. Paul faced the plane back down the glacier and cut the engine. We fell out from the cramped plane; even Paul seemed impressed with the place. The kit was dropped onto the snow, a quick farewell, and Paul was off. Only when the plane was out of sight did our remoteness hit us. Just the two of us in the whole of the Kichatnas. There was nothing to do but turn on the boom box. Nobody was going to tell us to turn it down.

Base quickly took shape. The tent was pitched and snow walls built. Everywhere you looked you were inspired. Once Stu had unpacked his vast wardrobe, we put on snowshoes and set off for a recce. Our initial plan was to climb to the col between Shadows Glacier and Sunshine Glacier, then attempt objectives on various peaks. But lots of snow and unseasonably warm conditions had made the col a risk game. We reckoned that we needed to cross the col at least eight times into the lion's jaws. Seracs threatened the approach, and a steep final snow slope sported crown walls where avalanches regularly peeled off, day and in the Land of Midnight Sun-night. Plus, snow at our low altitude didn't want to freeze at any time. Any gully was suicide, and snow was like wading in porridge, so for us it had to be rock.

We decided to attempt a new line on either the east face of Kichatna Spire or the east face of The Citadel. We first plumped for Kichatna and dragged our equipment to the base. We forayed onto the face, but a band of very loose rock repelled us. We returned to steak and chips at the Hotel Shadows and dug out the binos. The best chunk of rock in the valley lay opposite—the east buttress of The Citadel, which had been climbed in 1976 but sported many fantastic-looking lines. An obvious direct was asking to be climbed.

Early next morning we finished the Danish pastries and loaded the haul bags. Off we plodded and postholed up steep snow to the wall. We came to the steepest slope just as the 4 a.m. sun hit it. We decided to bail and return when things had cooled off. It was too chancy to risk getting avalanched with the prospect of a four-week wait with a broken leg. Leaving our huge loads, we slid down the slope. From the bottom we turned to admire our tracks, only to see an avalanche sweep down, covering our tracks and catapulting one haul bag to the bottom of the slope.

Next day we were back earlier, and, with the snow harder, made the base of the wall in good time. After some faffing around we got to grips with the rock, which was clean granite with the occasional loose block. Negotiating these was terrifying for both leader and belayer. The weather was fine, hot in the sun though instantly a fridge once the shade came around. On our first day we climbed 100m. Each pitch slightly overhung, as did most of the wall. Climbing was mostly aid, with occasional free climbing thrown in for our sanity. The granite was coarse, tearing skin and shredding ropes. On that first day our only lead line was cut to the core in three places. Its sheath was soon more duct tape than nylon, more silver than blue.

For two more days we continued fixing 250m of rope and sliding back to the base. Each evening we waited till the snow in our approach gully had firmed up before we dared descend it. Each day, as the temperature increased, so did the number of avalanches, making the daily journey definitely stressful. We celebrated arriving back at the base with such delights as steak and chips.

We finally moved our kit 160m up the wall to a flat six-foot-square ledge. On one wall we hung the portaledge; on the other hung a 20'-high flake. We could not see how this shield of granite was hanging in there. We contemplated reattaching it to the wall but instead tried to ignore it. As wall bivies go it was not bad, and we hung out listening to our short-wave radio. Our favorite channel was Retro Anchorage, which played music from the '80s. Name That Tune was a popular game; being slightly older, I won a bit more often.

The climbing was still steep but now included bands of loose rock. Some days we climbed only 50m because of the difficulty and the terrifying rock. The leader would climb on an 11mm and trail a zip line. The second jumared. The weather stayed perfect, but we could see change in the distance. We fixed all our rope and decided to go for the top the next day, climbing as fast and for as long as we could.

We woke early to discover that the weather had changed. It started to snow lightly and was obviously going to get worse. We waited but then decided to go for it. Jumaring back up was terrifying, with the ropes' many duct-tape-covered cuts. It was a relief to reach an anchor. Above the fixed ropes the angle eased, and we climbed quickly for a number of pitches. Snow was now falling fast; visibility was poor. Finally we squeezed through a chimney to stand on a precarious pinnacle. We had reached the top of the wall. The ridge dropped sharply beyond and then wandered up to the summit. Things were going to crap out big time, so we called it a day. Pleased to be where we were, we took the compulsory photos and fled down our climb.

The weather turned to pouring rain. We collected our equipment and abseiled to the glacier. After dragging our haul bags and ourselves back to base camp, we slept for many hours. In the morning it was again snowing, and snowed for 14 more days.

On the 15th day Paul flew over at 10 in the evening, as I was reading my book for the third time. In seconds the plane had landed, and we were packing bags. It was great to see another person after four and a half weeks by ourselves. The flight out gave a different view from the flight in: the 90 miles of snow had melted; rivers replaced ice. At 11:45 we touched down at Talkeetna International, by midnight we made the bar, the England match had just started, and the party had just begun.

TWID TURNER, *United Kingdom*

CHUGACH MOUNTAINS

Peak 9,968' (?), west ridge. On May 5, Kelly Bay of Wrangell Mountain Air flew Drew Lovell and me into the Martin River Glacier at the western end of the Bagley Icefield. We landed on the glacier at 4,200', just south of the impressive 7,000' south face of Mt. Tom White. Our objective was a peak I had seen some years ago on another trip. I had tried twice to fly in to attempt the peak, but both times weather prevented us from landing. We were lucky in 2002, as Alaska had been enjoying a run of sunny weather.

Depending on which map you look at, the elevation of the peak we were attempting is 9,968', 9,066', or, on aviation maps, over 10,000'. It doesn't matter, as it rises some 6,000' out of the surrounding glaciers to a beautiful summit pyramid. It sits just outside Wrangell–St. Elias National Park and looks down on the Gulf of Alaska, some 15 miles to the south across the Bering Glacier.

As we flew in, we scouted the two routes I had originally thought possible. One route had considerably less snow than in my photograph and was objectively more hazardous, with hanging seracs, cornices, and crevasses. The other route looked more possible, although rather long. It would require us to traverse a long ridge and ascend a couple of smaller summits.

After setting up camp Drew did a ski ascent and descent of Peak 6,311', across the Martin River Glacier and northeast of camp.

On May 6 we headed up the north ridge of Peak 6,970', but snow and clouds stopped us 2,000' up. On May 7 we ascended this ridge in better weather. The slope varied from 35° to 45° hard-packed snow and ice. On the summit we melted snow to replenish our water and left the stove and Drew's skis behind. We traversed down and along the ridge to 6,700' before picking our way across the bergshrund and ascending moderate slopes up and over Peak 7,700'+. We again descended, before ascending moderate slopes to Peak 8,200'+. More descending and ridge traversing brought us to the base of the west ridge of Peak 9,968'. We took an extended break to rest and look at the final ridge. It was hard to determine how much more climbing was required. I was tired, from heat and intense sun, and less motivated than Drew. He was ready, so he took off along the ridge. I rested for another 30 minutes before taking off. We left the rope and other gear behind to save weight. The final 1,000' was moderately angled; most of it maybe 30°, with a few short steeper sections near the top that required us to climb the 45° ridge crest. The lower-angled sections were exciting, with cornices on one side and 4,000' of exposure on the other. The exposed side began as a 20° slope that was just long enough that you might have been able to self-arrest before going over rocks into oblivion. I reached the summit five minutes behind Drew. We were blessed with continued clear skies and took a few minutes to enjoy the sweeping views from Mt. Bona to Mt. Logan to the Gulf of Alaska and on around to the Copper River to our west. Mt. St. Elias was hidden behind Mt. Steller, just to our east. I shot a string of photos before we headed down. We arrived back in camp just before dark, or in Alaska at that time of year, as dark as it gets. It was a long, 16-hour day that, by the time we climbed back up over all of the subpeaks, included some 6,200' of ascent. We did most of the route unroped, but roped up in sections with crevasse danger. We thought about climbing the south face of Mt. Tom White, but the weather turned on the evening of May 8. We were due to be picked up on the morning of May 10, but Kelly could not get in until the evening of May 12.

I try to keep up on the climbing history in the Wrangell–St. Elias region, and this may have been the first ascent of the peak. But a lot of climbs and adventures in Alaska go unreported.

DANNY KOST, *AAC*

ALASKA ST. ELIAS MOUNTAINS

Goat Glacier, various ascents. U.K. climbers Glenn Wilks, Geoff Hornby, Alistair Duff, and Susie Sammut flew into the upper part of the southwest fork of the Goat Glacier in the Granite Range. This fork had not been explored by climbers from Ultima Thule or A.A.I., who have cleaned up the other forks of the Goat Glacier. We Brits made ascents of the following peaks: Peak 8,110', east face, new route (FA of the peak made previously from the west, by an A.A.I. group), by Wilks, Hornby, and Sammut, June 12; Peak 8,882', first ascent via its southwest ridge, by Hornby and Wilks, June 14; Peak 8,172', first ascent via its west face, by Wilks solo, June 16; Peak 7,791', first ascent via its west face, by Hornby, Sammut, Wilks, and Duff, June 17; Peak 8,351', new route (FA of the peak made previously from the east, by an A.A.I. group) via south-west ridge, Wilks and Sammut, June 19. The only notable occurrence was a visit to base camp by a grizzly, crossing the glacial divide. I guess we smelled too bad, so he kept on going.

GEOFF HORNBY, *Alpine Climbing Group*

St. Elias Mountains, ski traverse. A ski traverse through the St. Elias Mountains that culminated in an ascent of Mt. Logan is reported in Climbs and Expeditions under Canada.

Mt. Miller, Double Exposure—Lady With a Fan. In April Mike Lynch and I headed to Alaska for two months of climbing, skiing, and work at the Claus Ultima Thule Lodge. The northwest face of Mt. Miller in the St. Elias Range was our first objective. The mountain had only been climbed once, in 1996, by Paul Claus, Carlos Buhler, Charlie Sassara, Ruedi Homberger, and Reto Reusch, from the south. I had seen one of Ruedi's photos, which showed only the beautiful top half of the central couloir on the northwest face.

   After five days of scouting and observing the face, we headed out from our base on the Bering Glacier at 2:00 a.m. on April 26. Our primary goal was to climb and ski the central couloir, but two large cliff bands in the lower 3,000' made that unattractive. The line we finally decided on started to the left of the central couloir, heading up another, smaller couloir, then widening to a fan-shaped face. From the top of that fan we would traverse right on Grade 3 ice and mixed rock to the central couloir, then on to the summit. The 30' 'schrund wall took some time, but by 6:00 a.m. we were at 8,000'. Topping out on the fan, we agreed on a high traverse. A near-vertical ice ribbon in the back of a tight gully led to a fairly easy traverse on mixed ground. The central couloir was a beautiful sight: smooth, steep snow led to rime-coated ice blobs on the left, and the couloir continued to the summit on clean ice to the right. By the time we reached the clouds it was around 3:00 p.m. We stashed our packs to the left under rime-crusted ice bulges guarding the summit ridge. Moving on with three screws and two pickets, we ran the rope out, making good time, though the ice was brittle and shattered off in plates. Alternating leads, we took five long pitches to reach the summit ridge. The wind had gone from mild to intense; 60–80 m.p.h. gusts tried to lift us from the ridge, and rime-crusted snow pellets

Mt. Miller, showing the route of its second ascent. Bob Kingsley

blasted any exposed skin. I stepped onto the summit and out of the wind. Mike joined me, and we celebrated the second ascent of Mt. Miller.

We rappelled the five pitches to our packs. It was 7:00 p.m. when Mike cut the first turn on 50° snow. After we had downclimbed and rappelled to the top of the fan, it was dark and we had 4,000' remaining. A full moon lit the far side of the cirque but did us little good. As we descended toward the 55° crux of the ski descent, the snow became crusted and glazed. We passed the crux cautiously in the dark. Back at the 'schrund Mike tried to salvage our bollard while I moved down to see what I could. The bridge was still there, as far as I could tell. Mike was satisfied with the bollard, and we rappelled from it. Still on skis, we belayed till we were past snowbridges and on the flats of the glacier. We arrived back at base camp almost exactly 24 hours after starting.

BOB KINGSLEY

Mt. St. Elias, ascent and paraglider descent. On June 16 Hamish Robertson (Australia) became the first person to paraglide from the summit of Mt. St. Elias. He flew all 18,000 vertical feet of the mountain and 21 miles horizontally to land on the shores of Icy Bay. Nic Bendelli (Austalia) and I were the other expedition members.

We were dropped at 3,500' on the Harvard Route on May 21. Bendelli and I bailed at 10,000' on the 11th. Not to be thwarted, Robertson soloed the last 8,000', including the crux 60° ice slope, then flew from the summit.

CHARLES SMITH

Devil's Thumb and satellites, routes from the south side: (1) West Witches' Tit, southwest face, Belcourt-Rackliff, 1995; (2) West Witches' Tit, south face, Jack Hicks Memorial Route, Edwards-Millar, 2002; (3) Cat's Ears Spire, west face, Elias-McMullen, 1996; (4) Cat's Ears Spire, east face, Culbert-Douglas-Starr, 1972; (5) Cat's Ears Spire, south face, The Least Snowed-up Route, Edwards-Millar, 2002; (6) Cat's Ears Couloir to west buttress, attempt to 200' from summit, Down-Foreman-Haberl, 1990; (7) Bearzi-Klose Couloir to west buttress, attempt to 600' from summit, 1980; (8) south face, Flores-Jones-Lowe, 1973; (9) south pillar, Bebie-Pilling, 1991; (10) attempted line on south pillar-south face to 250' from summit, Elias-McMullen-Selvig, 1996; (11) Becky Route (SE face to E ridge), Becky-Craig-Schmidke, 1946; (12) Krakauer Route, 1997; (13) Bearzi-Klose variation, 1980; (14) east ridge, Culbert-Douglas-Starr, 1970. Photo and route information by Dieter Klose

ALASKA COAST MOUNTAINS

Correction. On page 253 of the 2002 AAJ, the photograph is by Ryszard Pawlowski, and the drawing and photo layout is by Grzegorz Glazek.

Juneau Icefield, ski traverse. As a mechanical engineering undergraduate, I studied glacial mechanics on the southern portion the Juneau Icefield of southeast Alaska and northwest British Columbia with Dr. Maynard M. Miller's Glaciological Institute. I always dreamed of returning, with my father to traverse the entire length of the Icefield, commencing with the northernmost glaciers and, after traversing 120 miles along the spine of the Boundary Range, to disembark from the Icefield at its southernmost terminus and Alaska's capital, Juneau. The lure of exploring vast expanses of wilderness, some of it virtually unexplored, has always captured my imagination.

Standing at sea level in the old gold-rush town of Skagway, looking up thousands of feet into the rugged snowy mountains, I could only think that the toughest part of our expedition would be gaining the "high ice"; we were not to be disappointed. On the morning of May 27, 2001, four of us, including Charles B. Daellenbach, Allen H. Throop, and John P. Parsons, loaded our skis onto our 80lb. + packs and walked out of town past amused townsfolk and cruise ship tourists, up a forest trail and onto our first snows. For three punishing days, our team progressed upward past Upper Dewey Lake and the Devil's Punch Bowl, then in a southerly direction above

John Millar belaying on the south face of the West Witches' Tit. Guy Edwards

headwaters of Kasidaya Creek and finally east onto the locally named "Dog Sled Glacier."

We aspired to make our traverse completely self-contained and unsupported. However, on the fourth day, just as we were about to finish our grueling ascent and access the massive Denver Glacier, we found ourselves stymied by a seemingly impassable mountain face. Avalanche tracks laced the face and, high above, a corniced palisade seemed to protect the interior. We reached the unappealing conclusion that the only way to continue was to use our satellite phone to call a local helicopter charter and be deposited on the other side.

Generally our route ski-traversed the Denver, North Branch Meade, and Meade glaciers, a large unnamed glacier, and Bucher, Llewellyn, Matthes, Taku, Southwest Branch Taku, Norris, Lemon Creek, and Ptarmigan glaciers. We had a couple of days of nearly complete whiteouts during which we relied solely on map, compass, and GPS to follow our course over the huge glaciers. Leaving the accumulation area of the upper Bucher, we crossed the international border between Mt. London and Border Peak 99 and then skied across the Llewellyn's upper névé and over the highest point reached on the tour, a col on the east flank of Mt. Nesselrode at 6,960'. As we started to exit the southern Icefield, we crossed Echo Pass into Death Valley (Norris Glacier), around the east flank of Nugget Mountain past Split Thumb and dropped down onto the Lemon Creek Glacier. With nostalgia we passed Dr. Miller's research station at Camp 17 and then con-

The two Witches' Tits (West and East) and Cat's Ears Spire, with John Millar at the start of the ridge leading up to the south face. Guy Edwards

tinued our descent of the Ptarmigan Glacier and into the steep Lemon Creek drainage. We arrived in Juneau on the 15th day after leaving Skagway.

We are grateful for the financial support provided by The American Alpine Club Research Grant and a Mazama Expedition Grant, as well as the resources of the Foundation for Glacier and Environmental Research.

KEITH K. DAELLENBACH, *AAC*

West Witches' Tit, south face, Jack Hicks Memorial Route; and Cat's Ears Spire, Least Snowed-up Route. From May 16 to June 5 Guy Edwards and I visited the Devil's Thumb region of the Stikine Icecap in southeast Alaska and northwest British Columbia. We had traveled through this region the previous year and were mighty inspired to return for less touring and more climbing. Dieter Klose, the mountaineering authority on the Stikine Icecap, had put us in touch with Jack Hicks, who was more than happy to give us a boat ride across Frederick Sound to Thomas Bay, where we would start our approach to the region. However, his boat was not working, so we spent several days in Petersburg enjoying the hospitality of John Pickens and Liz Cabrerra before the boat was ready.

After two and a half days of perhaps the easiest approach in the entire Coast Range, we were below the awesome northwest face of Devil's Thumb. It didn't take long to realize that we were too late in the season for this face. In very high winds we skied around to the south side of the Devil's Thumb massif. We climbed up the unpleasant icefall below the south face of Devil's Thumb and then spent three days in a deluxe snow cave. On the fourth morning we woke to our first blue-sky, "go-for-it" day. We had a splendid climb up the previously unclimbed south face of the West Witche's Tit. The rock was some of the best I've ever encountered in the mountains—vertical, white, solid granite. The next day was again good weather, so we established the Least Snowed-up Route on Cat's Ears Spire. Throughout the climb I marveled at the 1972 first ascent of the spire by Dick Culbert, Fred Douglas, and Paul Starr, and Culbert's subsequent very modest account of their climb.

These two climbs concluded the climbing component of our trip, due to the weather for the rest of the trip. We were, however, successful in route posturing. First we camped under Burkett Needle for a few days, in hopes of repeating the stunning Cauthorn–Collum–Foweraker route. We also attempted Peak 7,190' across the Burkett Glacier, and skied around to the southeast face of Devil's Thumb in hopes of trying the Beckey route. Eventually we bailed on June 4, after a very enjoyable trip that included much reading, poem memorizing, and some brief but intense and beautiful climbing.

Our first ascents: Jack Hicks Memorial Route (800m, V 5.10+ A1), south face of West Witches' Tit, and The Least Snowed-up Route, Cat's Ears Spire (900m, IV 5.10+). (Sadly, Jack Hicks died in August 2002 while on a solo hunting trip. He was an amazing person with a kind character and loving heart—a big friendly bear.)

JOHN MILLAR, *Canada*

Editor's note: In April 2003, Edwards and Millar perished while attempting the unclimbed northwest face of the Devil's Thumb (see article earlier in this Journal). Their energy and contributions to the world will be missed.

Canada

ST. ELIAS RANGE

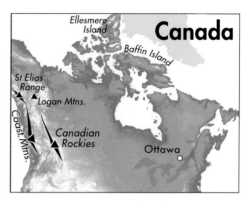

Fairweather and St. Elias mountains traverse.
On April 25 a group of four acquaintances-cum-friends were shuttled across Haines inlet in an outboard motor boat. At Davidson Point, just across the water from Haines, Kari Medig, Merrie-Beth Board, Jacqui Hudson, and I, Lena Rowat, were dropped off and left to our own devices to find our way across the Fairweather and St. Elias Mountains. This was to be the final leg of an effort to connect a route from the group's roots in Vancouver, B.C., to Canada's highest peak, Mt. Logan, climbing its east ridge and skiing down the King Trench on its west side.

If you have ever traversed a range of heavily glaciated mountains, you know generally what happened next. Days stretched into fine long periods of meditation, as we took in the continually changing beauty around us. Of course a few misadventures made our story more interesting.

The weather smiled upon us in the first two weeks, so much so that I began to feel snow blindness coming on. Eye drops only worsened the problem, dilating my pupils for the next week. We entered "The Twilight Zone," traveling only at sunset and sunrise. We would set up and break camp twice a day. After 10 days we had crossed the Fairweather Range and returned to sea level at Alsek Lake, where we stopped at Gary Gray's wilderness lodge. This was the only point along our route where we were off snow and ice, and, with its grassy runway and marine radio, was our closest contact with civilization. We bathed by heating tubs of water that were hauled from the river.

On May 7 Gary boated us across the Alsek River, and our journey took a turn through a milk bottle as clouds descended upon us for the better part of two weeks. We followed a compass that invariably led us in zigzags.

On May 18 we finally approached the much-anticipated Logan massif. I approached with a lopsided gait for three days, as I had lost a pole down a crevasse. The Logan East Ridge base camp was the trip's biggest social event, and Kari was particularly psyched to be meshing with other testosterone. He was learning what many women mountaineers face regularly: it can be fun being the only one of your sex in the group, but it adds emotional challenge.

Climbing Logan begat considerable changes to our routines and group dynamics. Whereas we were all comfortable skiing across mostly flat terrain with relative independence, suddenly we were literally tied to each other, and the differences in our styles of doing things could not be avoided. With the added stress of constant exposure, group dynamics went through some growing pains. Having never climbed all together before, we all worked hard to adapt our methods, and managed to stick it out, supporting each other well through the upper altitudes, where thin air wore badly on Jaqui and me. We all took turns skipping or hurling our meals.

After 15 days of mostly magnificent East Ridge climbing, ferrying loads, and sitting out a few bad-weather days, a beautifully calm and sunny day allowed us to crawl along, skirting the tops of the clouds, to reach the summit col at 18,500'. We camped as low as possible on the west side of the summit plateau, feeling good for having made it "over the middle." From that camp three of us made one failed summit attempt in bad weather, before proceeding toward our descent. We stumbled across a research camp on our way off the plateau, where in good company we rested and fattened up for 24 hours. From here Kari and M.-B. climbed to within meters of the west summit and got some excellent powder turns on the descent.

On June 7, after 18 days on the mountain, in four hours we got 9,000' of good skiing to the King Trench base camp. It was all kudos and boundless energy, as our lungs filled with the intoxicating dense air of the lower elevations.

Here we switched back into flat-terrain mode and sped off across the last 250 km of glacier to our exit point, Cordova, Alaska. The first half of this leg was a straight line across the massive Bagley Icefield. Once across the icefield, we were glad to be back in more exciting terrain, with passes and small icefalls to navigate. On June 14, day 51, this terrain proved to be more exciting than hoped for, when Jacqui miraculously survived a 25' fall on her head, on the rocky bottom of a crevasse.

The last four days continued to serve up unexpected challenges. Glacial recession had taken away much of the ice that we had hoped to travel upon in order to reach Miles Lake and the Million Dollar Bridge. We were especially impressed by Jacqui's continued endurance, especially when later x-rays revealed that she had fractured several vertebrae in her fall.

Finally, on June 18, after 675 kilometers, an elevation range of 19,000', and 55 days in the wilderness, we stood by the first road that we had come across, and waved down a ride into town.

This trip would not have been possible without support from a myriad of sources, both personal and organizational. Mountain Equipment Co-op, The Canadian Himalayan Foundation, and The Jen Higgins' Fund all contributed significantly to reducing the financial burden. We are most thankful.

LENA T. ROWAT, *Canada*

Juneau Icefield, traverse. A ski traverse of the Juneau Icefield, with part of the terrain crossed being in Canada, is reported in Climbs and Expeditions under Alaska.

KLUANE NATIONAL PARK RESERVE

Kluane National Park Reserve, mountaineering summary and statistics. During the 2002 climbing season in Kluane National Park Reserve, a total of 130 persons participated in 35 mountaineering expeditions. This accounted for 2,258 person-days in the Icefields of Kluane. This is somewhat lower use than in previous years.

The weather this year was relatively normal—unpredictable, depending on where and when you were in the Icefields. Snow conditions were a bit unusual. It appears that low winter snowfall and warm conditions made for a shallow, unconsolidated snowpack. Many expeditions reported crevasses being poorly bridged, and in many areas a breakable crust and deep sugar snow prevailed, while on the King Trench route in the early season hard wind pack and huge sastrugi created problems for expeditions.

Most expeditions aimed for Mt. Logan, with 27 teams attempting it—16 on the King Trench, 7 on the East Ridge, and 4 on other routes. Fifteen teams were successful at reaching one of the main summits (Main Peak, East Peak, West Peak). Successful expeditions took from

17 to 26 days to complete their climbs.

Other mountains that saw climbing activity were Kennedy (two expeditions), Hubbard (one), Alverstone (one), King Peak (one), McArthur (one), Gibson (one), Wates (one), Walsh (one), and Augusta (one).

Of note this year was a new route on Mt. Logan, just east of Independence Ridge, climbed by two British Columbia boys. A crew of four from B.C. did a 675km traverse of the St. Elias and Chugach mountains starting in Haines, Alaska, and ending in Cordova, Alaska. En route they climbed the East Ridge route of Mt. Logan, traversed the summit plateau, and descended the King Trench route. An Alaskan used an 18-foot aluminum ladder/harness combination to make a solo climb of Mt. Logan via the King Trench route. A Parks Canada team celebrated the International Year of the Mountain by revisiting the Alpine Club of Canada's camp of 1967 (Canada's Centennial) on the Steele Glacier. Some of the early explorers of this area and First Nation elders who were involved with early expeditions related stories of that era during a visit to the site. Park Warden staff spent a week in the area doing mountaineering and rescue training.

Only one major search-and-rescue operation occurred during 2002. A climber attempting a new route on Mt. Augusta suffered serious injuries from rockfall. His partner descended to their base camp and was able to call out on a satellite phone. However, weather prevented rescue teams from getting to the area immediately. Attempts to get to the climber were made from both the Canadian and Alaskan sides, with a military helicopter and crew from Anchorage, Alaska, and Denali National Park finally reaching the site and performing a very technical heli-hoist. Other public-safety incidents were more minor, with a few crevasse-fall injuries, frostbite, and other medical problems that were dealt with by the climbers' teams and other expeditions.

Researchers were once again active in the Icefields. Three groups—Geological Surveys of Canada (GSC), National Institute of Polar Research of Japan (NIPR), and the Climate Change Research Center of New Hampshire—were involved in a coordinated ice core drilling program both on Mt. Logan and on the Eclipse Icefield. Scientists removed ice cores from both locations and will analyze the cores to better understand the world's climate.

A few incidents occurred this season which concern Park officials. Climbing groups on the East Ridge of Mt. Logan reported that some climbers are leaving garbage, food, gear, and fixed line. Some clean up was done by the reporting groups, and this is appreciated. Climbers must be prepared to pack out what they pack in. Another concern was a team of climbers who entered the Icefields from Alaska without clearing Customs or registering with Kluane National Park. Unfortunately, one member of this team suffered serious frostbite while on the summit plateau of Mt. Logan and had to be assisted off the mountain by other climbers. The team was met at base camp by RCMP and Park Wardens and dealt with accordingly. Climbers coming to Kluane must remember the pack-in, pack-out policy, that registration is mandatory, and that failing to follow the rules is illegal and, more importantly, affects the experience of other mountaineers.

Anyone interested in mountaineering in Kluane National Park Reserve should write Mountaineering Warden, Kluane National Park, Box 5495, Haines Jct., Yukon, Y0B 1LO; call 867-634-7279; fax 867-634-7277; or E-mail kluane_info@pch.gc.ca. Ask for a "Mountaineering package." Also, visit the park's web site at www.parkscanada.gc.ca/kluane.

RICK STALEY, PARK WARDEN, *Kluane National Park Reserve*

Eclipse Glacier, ascents. Glenn Wilks (U.K.) and Geoff Hornby (U.K.) flew into the Eclipse Glacier for 10 days and made ascents of peaks near Mt. Badham. On June 1 they made the first ascent of Peak 3,390m, via its southeast ridge, and climbed a new route, the Northwest Ridge, on Peak 3,330m. On June 3 Wilks made the first ascent, solo, of Peak 3,320m, via its east face.

GEOFF HORNBY, *Alpine Climbing Group*

The northeast side of Mt. Logan with the Orion Spur rising directly above the tent and the Independence Ridge on the righthand side of the photo. Both the West and the True summits are hidden by foreshortening. Jeremy Frimer

Mt. Logan, The Orion Spur. In late May Jeremy Frimer and I climbed a new route on the northeast side of Mt. Logan (5,956m). The Orion Spur drops from Logan's summit plateau into the basin formed by the Catenary Ridge (1967) and the Independence Ridge (1964). From its toe at 2,600m the spur gains the summit plateau at 4,800m in just 2.5 km, making this the shortest route to the plateau yet established. As with most routes on Logan, the plateau itself presents a significant challenge, with another 1,200m over six km remaining to the true (center) summit.

Due to high winds near the mountain, Andy Williams dropped us 20 km out on the Logan Glacier on May 20. We reached the plateau in five days, climbing alpine style, establishing no supplied camps or fixed ropes. We spent two days waiting out weather on our way across to the true summit, which was reached in a blinding whiteout on May 29. One more day was spent traversing across to the King Trench route, which was descended in two days. We flew out from the Trench base camp on June 3.

The climbing was exclusively on snow and ice, with occasional steep pitches (up to 60°) encountered while crossing the many serac bands. Most difficulties could be avoided by traversing off the ridge crest, but onto softer, deeper snow. The upper ridge was more consolidated and knife-edged, which made for easier trailbreaking, but campsites required excavation. At the top of the spur we exited right (west) to avoid a rock band, gaining a snow slope that led to the plateau.

We thank Dave Jones and Andy Williams for their support in the planning and execution of this trip. Partial funding was supplied by the Helly Hansen Mountain Adventure Award (administered through the Alpine Club of Canada).

JAY BURBEE, *Canada*

McArthur Peak, Huge in Europe and Night Shift; Mt. Logan, attempt. In early May, Jesse Thompson, Rich Searle, and I, Joe Josephson, flew with Andy Williams from Kluane Lake, Yukon, to the south face of McArthur Peak, which shares a base camp site with the popular East Ridge route of Mt. Logan. Our first objective was to repeat the 1992 Statham/Kay 6,000' mixed route, AstroFloyd, and then climb anything else that looked good. Due to a light snow year and unseasonably warm weather, we couldn't find ice in the AstroFloyd couloir. To its left, and right of the 1988 Friesen-Scott-Wallator route, was the last major unclimbed buttress on the south face.

An attempt on May 9 ended after six hours in a snowstorm, but we started up again in the early hours of May 11, with a stove, a rope, a small rack, gooey food substitutes, and no bivy gear. We started up an obvious weakness east of the true ridge but on the left side of the buttress. We climbed moderate gullies of ice and snow for several thousand feet to the ridge proper. Another 1,000' led to a short à cheval section on rock at about 10,500'. Several hundred feet higher we came to what proved to be the route-finding crux—a 500' section climbed by an exposed traverse on the east side followed by a tight chimney on a large block. Another steep snow section led back to the ridge. Here we roped for the first time, for an exposed pitch around the west side of a rock horn to a knife-edge snow ridge, then up a gully and a rock wall on the left (5.5). A second pitch, up a gully and snow face, led to a short step into a chimney and a good slab on the left (5.6). To avoid rock towers above, we rappelled into the large gully to the east and climbed to a prominent col and then up to a small rock step at about 11,360', where we brewed and napped for four hours. We continued up a long, glaciated ice ridge we dubbed the "Jessewand." Near the top we traversed left under rocks to a hard-ice gully leading to the summit ridge at about 13,470' (6,100' elevation gain, 14 hours of climbing).

Due to the late hour and a building storm, we passed on the unclimbed ridge leading to the East Summit (14,134', perhaps five hours away). We immediately headed down the East Ridge, which required complicated route finding, especially after dark. After about six hours we stopped for a miserable open bivy in -20° cold and swirling snow. At sunrise we continued more easily down the ridge to an obvious rock tower (great bivy site). We rappelled from a single hex just below the ridge, on the east side of the tower. Lots of down climbing and about eight rappels led to the bottom of the avalanche-prone gully (5,600' of descent in the gully). This was followed by time-consuming route finding through the icefall to the flat glacier. The round trip took 35 hours. This route, which we called Huge in Europe; the1988 route, which is the best-looking line on the face; and several buttresses to the west are excellent: all are long yet relatively moderate and doable in either a multiday or single-push style.

The next day brought a four-day (brief for the St. Elias Range) storm, followed by one good day, during which Rich left with minor frostbite, and another four-day wind storm. Jesse and I then spent two days skiing via Water Pass to the unclimbed south-southeast buttress of Mt. Logan. Off the end of the main buttress are two subridges ending in the Seward Icefield. We ascended the west side of the east subridge. Warm temperatures and hateful isothermal snow made the climbing very slow. After half a day climbing and a bivy, we climbed a subpeak, with classic moderate cornice climbing, followed by a mixed section that exacted routefinding on poor rock to avoid a steep step on the ridge proper.

Moving together, we traversed 400' into a long gully (5.6). We climbed the gully to a more moderate mixed face, which led to a false summit and a comfortable bivy below a large rock. More corniced climbing led to a summit at about 9,600'. The ridge beyond, which leads to the main Logan massif, featured large, rotten rock towers with little snow stuck to them. Since the traveling was slow and we had only one rope with a minimal rock rack, we bailed, down climbing a major gully to the east. We dubbed the peak "Wolf Bird Peak" in deference to the Warbler and Hummingbird ridges to the left. We think this was the second ascent of this peak, and the ridge beyond remains unclimbed, despite several determined efforts over the last few years. We dubbed this the "Raven Ridge"; it is the biggest of the few unclimbed ridges on Mt. Logan.

Andy Williams then flew Jesse and me to the north side of McArthur Peak, where we climbed a major variation to the classic North Ridge route. Starting at 8:00 p.m. on the 24th we climbed on the left side of the northwest face, on a lower-angled mixed face. Climbing together through several short mixed sections (5.5), we reached the north ridge proper after about 10 hours of superb, moderate climbing. A brilliant 45° ice/snow arête led for 600' to a short step littered with fixed gear and ropes from the handful of ascents the route has had. This short section proved to be the crux, with near-vertical snow/ice and an awkward move around a large rock. The pitch ends on a large flat spot that would be a brilliant tent site. Easy glacier walking led to the broad col between the East and West Summits, from which we went to the slightly lower East Summit, making what we think is only the second ascent. We descended the normal North Ridge route and were able to cut back on the lower ridge to slopes leading directly to base camp below the north face (24 hours round trip). We called this variation Night Shift and recommend it as alternative to the snow-slogging North Ridge.

JOE JOSEPHSON, *Calgary Mountain Club*

Mt. Baird, correction. A presumed first ascent of Mt. Baird was reported in the 2001 *AAJ* (p. 232). However, in July 1999, after attempts on the south face of Mt. Logan and the northeast shoulder of Mt. Augusta, Stan Horn and Paul Penno ascended Mt. Baird by a route similar to, or possibly the same as, that reported in the 2001 *AAJ*. Horn reports that Baird may have been climbed previous to 1999, but such a climb has not been documented. Of their 1999 ascent, Horn writes, "On July 12 we arrived at Baird Pass in less than seven hours, with bivy equipment. After three hours of rest, on July 13 we climbed 18 pitches to the summit of Mt. Baird (11,500') in nine hours. The bottom pitches had ice up to 50°; the crux was the next-to-last pitch, where you could see through a hole in ridge. Superb views of Logan and Augusta gave us a lot of joy. We decided to descend farther south, but were faced with hard ice on 15 pitches and belayed on screws for seven hours. Paul slept at Baird Pass again, while I went all the way to the tent. We rested and waited a couple of days for our glacier pilot, Kurt Gloyer, who flew us back to Yakutat on July 18."

ELLESMERE ISLAND

Various ascents, descents, and exploration. Flying to Ellesmere Island on June 17, Blue Eisele, Jonas Cabiles, and I (all U.S.A.) landed at Mt. Barbeau, intent on trekking to Lake Hazen, the largest freshwater lake in the Arctic, some 50 miles away. We set up camp on the ice cap to the west of Barbeau's summit. From this camp I made the first snowboard descent of Barbeau (8,535'), the highest mountain in the Canadian Arctic, while Eisele and Cabiles made ski descents. The next day Eisele and I climbed, skied, and snowboarded Barbeau's nearest neighbor. I believe these split-board descents, at 81° north, to be the northernmost snowboard descents ever.

From Barbeau Camp we moved toward an unnamed valley that leads to the upper reaches of the Henrietta-Nesmith Glacier. Park wardens previously at Lake Hazen had told us that, to their knowledge, no route from Barbeau to Lake Hazen had been completed, and that no parties had ever traveled via the Henrietta-Nesmith Glacier. We set up Camp II at the entrance to the valley, which we dubbed "Deception Valley," because the scale of the landscape was deceptively large. The following day Cabiles nearly fell into an unseen cavernous crevasse, so we fine-tuned our crevasse-rescue system at Camp III, from which the Henrietta-Nesmith Glacier could be seen. We had chosen to travel with no communication device, but park officials issued us a personal-locator beacon before we were dropped at Barbeau.

As we descended to the upper reaches of the Henrietta-Nesmith Glacier, the ice cap turned from a hollow to a solid compact ice sheet running with melt water. We crossed the five-mile-wide glacier encountering many small ice-river crossings. Arriving near the eastern side of the Henrietta-Nesmith Glacier about 11 miles from its terminus, we erected Camp IV among pools of melt water. As we traveled farther across, the following day, we set ice-screw belays to protect large snowbridge crossings over steep drainages and encountered many more small ice-river crossings.

Rest break before crossing the Henrietta-Nesmith Glacier, Ellesmere Island. Pete Dronkers

Just another melt-stream crossing on Ellesmere Island. Pete Dronkers

Camp V was placed on the edge of the glacier about four miles from its terminus near 100' ice cliffs. We lowered our equipment down these cliffs, because the only option was to attempt to cross several massive drainages that we had noticed in satellite images of the area. We touched down on solid ground after free rappelling and double-carried loads beside the remaining stretches of the glacier and one mile past its terminus. We put Camp VI just a few miles from the north shore of Lake Hazen.

When we reloaded our sleds on the deteriorating lake ice of Hazen, we wondered how much open water would separate us from the shore when we approached the air strip and warden station 11 miles to the east. On the last day of June we arrived safely—and eased the minds of the park wardens who had worried about us. This trip received the Helly Hansen adventure grant, and $300 for the REI challenge fund.

PETE DRONKERS

BAFFIN ISLAND

Great Sail Peak, Rubikon. Baffin Land—astonishing land of vertical walls, unearthly landscapes, permanent sun. And erotic dreams. Our gang included Alexander Odintsov (continuous leader of crazy project "The Russian Way—Walls of the World"), Valery Rozov (flight leader of even crazier "Russian Extreme Project," Moscow Batman, Man with Wings), Alexandr Ruchkin (just climber, versatile, moves often, cosmopolite), Alexander Klenov (good climber, singer, doctor, has female fan club), Michael Devi (climber, partner of Klenov), Michael Bakin (kind doctor but jobless during the expedition), Ivan Samoilenko (coordinator), Lev Dorfman (tireless director of video scenery), Dmitry Lifanov (relaxed director of video scenery, singer of Russian folklore, Muscovite), Sergei Porodnov (businessman, porter, sponsor), Vladimir Morozov (Russian-Canadian adventurer and researcher, fisherman and hunter).

Getting to Baffin Land is difficult; it is difficult to get into any fairy tale. Russian emigrants met us at the Toronto airport. Their encounter with us only sharpened their nostalgia for ungrateful but beloved Russia. Nowhere were we greeted with such warmth as in Canada, not even in Russia. Everybody was ready to help.

Iqaluit, capital of the vast Nunavut Province, is at the south end of Baffin Island. Native inhabitants: Inuit. In their struggle for life in polar conditions, where winter lasts for 10 months and night for six, northern people are similar in different countries. They are dumpy, but skillful and good-natured, and find fun even in long winters.

Our last civilized point: Clyde River. Finally we catch winter. Nipping frost and sun. The proximity of the wall surprised us; it can be reached in just seven hours. American team spent nine days, but weather was bad, and they were filming. After our last showers for a month, our caravan started to Stuart Valley and our goal, Great Sail Peak. For each two members of the expedition we had one sledge, ski-doo, and Inuit guide.

Alexandr Ruchkin on Rubikon, Great Sail Peak, Baffin Island.
Dmitry Lifanov

One day was not enough for reaching the Great Sail. Our way was blocked by steep moraine with huge stones—obstacles too difficult for ski-doo's. Alex Lowe's team went the same way, but there was much more snow. According to our map we'd stopped 25-30 km from the wall. It meant at least one, probably two, weeks of hauling stuff to base camp. We decided to find another way. We followed famous Sam Ford Fjord, which was just 12-15 km from Great Sail Peak.

Sam Ford Fjord's landscape is amazing. Perfectly smooth 600m walls rise from the ocean. Numerous walls are unclimbable at present, since there is not the smallest crack in several hundred meters of overhanging stone. Ideal sleek shapes, inflated to huge dimensions, impress the imagination. Silent world of incredibly straight lines creates an illusion of an outer planet. You are the Pathfinder. This is the island of modern and future mountaineering, BASE jumping, and things yet to be invented

Sam Ford Fjord did not let ski-doo's reach the wall either. Fifteen km to go. According to Russian tradition, we treated our guides to vodka, though violating their law. The Inuit left us on the fjord coast, with polar

Alexandr Ruchkin on Rubikon, Great Sail Peak, Baffin Island. Lev Dorfman

bears. We set up camp on the bears' tracks and waited, with a small gun and a few signal flares to frighten the bears. We were lucky. Several days before American backpackers had passed by. The bears followed them and did not return. Either the Americans were fast or the bears were full.

For two days we carried loads to where the wall of Great Sail comes into view. There we set up our base camp. The weather was challenging. North wind tore our tents and blew snow through the smallest holes. Daytime temperatures were -10°C, dropping to -25° at night. No visibility, permanent low clouds, and very windy.

We set up ABC on May 6. The wall floated in mist. We traced a route following a system of ruined cracks, running to the sky. On May 9, too tired with inactivity to wait for good weather, Devi and Klenov started work below a ledge at the base of the main wall. In cold, wind, and snow Devi climbed 30m. The next day the weather worsened, and they came back to ABC. The same day Valery made a BASE jump from a vertical wall we called Pobeda ("Victory" in Russian, and May 9 is Victory Day in WWII). To reinforce the victory, Valery made another jump. The following several days were extremely windy. Even a bear would not leave his refuge. Neither would we.

On May 12 spring arrived, and the sun

Great Sail Peak, showing the Rubikon route. Alexandr Ruchkin

warmed the wall. Hard work started. Taking turns leading, we made one pitch a day. In six 75° to 90° pitches, almost exclusively A1-A2 aid, we reached the ledge below the main wall.

On May 16, together with the brave video operators who did not only their job but helped carry loads, we were ready for the main wall. With our support group so helpful and close, we had an unlimited supply of food, fuel, and gear.

There were five climbers, and everyone led, giving us reliability and recovery time. It was cold, and sometimes the wall threw a few stones. But there were cracks on the wall, meaning an opportunity to climb. All constituents of success were there. Despite our slow advance, two pitches per day maximum, the team finished the absolutely vertical wall in 16 days. Two of those days were spent accommodating our video operators.

The fun of being on a large wall was tempered by the weight of our gear. The wall's steepness deprived us of snow and water. We had to use sun and fuel to melt fallen ice into 60 liters of water in plastic containers. The water froze immediately and was put into haul bags. When the containers were cut, the ice was broken and melted again. Not an intellectual activity, but one does want to drink.

The team used two portaledges. Often after a good meal we sang Russian songs, and the sounds, reflecting from the walls of Stuart Valley, blended into a marvelous chorale. In general we have fun.

During most of the climb thick clouds hung at 500–1,000m, and we were like Santa Claus, covered with frost. But when we were above the cloud blanket, we became Children of the Sun, which caressed us all day long. The stubborn polar sun interfered with our sleep. We slept only when tired from climbing. Sun began shining on the wall at 3 p.m. and left at 3 a.m. We resisted, but our working day ended up fitting with Nature. We started at 3 p.m. and with effort went to sleep at 3 a.m. Unreal landscapes gave birth to unreal dreams. Women were not lacking in these dreams.

Vertical climbing is difficult in itself, but when complicated by corroded granite, it becomes tense and tricky. The climbing was like working in a minefield. Blocks were humming, hanging. Free-standing stones held our weight in some mystic way. Unwitting reminders of our unity with Nature. The wall was mostly A3, A3+, but sometimes A4.

We were just starting to enjoy the climbing when the wall surprisingly ended. In the sunny polar night of May 26-27 we reached the summit of Great Sail Peak. Fantastic view: an ocean of clouds covered everything to the horizon. We were on a huge ship, on the mast of the Great Sail. Ships moved in the ocean, tearing the clouds. New route: Rubikon (1,300m, 6B difficulty A4, 85-90°—note: 6B is the hardest category of the route in the Russian mountaineering classification) on Great Sail Peak (1,615m) in Baffin Land, Canada.

Our Batman, Valery Rozov—tired of waiting and wistful for freedom, Icarus—detached the ropes, spread his wings, and jumped from the wall. Fifty seconds of free flight in the wing suit, unbelievable! Many people do not believe and ask even now, "Does he have a parachute?" Descent from a wall in one minute and be alive—the dream of any climber. I am not an exception. Spread the wings and fly. The only problem is the climbing gear—somebody has to carry it down. But I think that soon this problem will be solved also. Baffin Island, Land of Future, waits for Pathfinders.

ALEXANDR RUCHKIN, *Russia*

Eastern Fjords, ascents, descents, and exploration. From mid-April to mid-May, Brad Barlage and I explored the ski mountaineering potential of Baffin's legendary eastern fjords. It was a highly experimental trip, as we were going into an area that few people have ever visited, let alone skied in. To further the commitment we planned on using lightweight NASA wing kites to move around on the ice. As these kites are capable of high speeds, we also built sleds that could handle our heavy loads, track well at speed, and step over rough sea ice. These sleds also had to break down for shipping and be light enough to carry if necessary. We were going into an area known for its carnivorous polar bears, extreme cold, high winds, and remoteness. We had no idea if the winds would be strong enough to pull us across the vast distances, if the couloirs would be safe to ski, if we would be pinned down by late winter weather, or if other unforeseen calamities might befall us. There were many opportunities for things to go wrong.

But this trip seemed to be charmed. We ended up traveling through five fjords and valleys, covering hundreds of kilometers with our kites and sleds, climbing and skiing 19 new couloirs, with a mix of good and impressively bad weather. The couloir skiing was beyond our wildest dreams. All the couloirs were superb, with the top 10 being in a league by themselves and providing the best skiing I have ever experienced. However, as good as the skiing was, it was perhaps eclipsed by the kiting. With 24 hours of daylight, smooth sea ice, towering rock walls lining vast

Skiing Intestinal Fortitude in Sam Ford Fjord, Baffin Island. *Andrew McLean*

Sledding past the 3,640-foot Polar Star Couloir, Baffin Island. *Brad Barlage*

fjords, seals, and strong, steady winds, Baffin has to be one of the most exotic places on earth to practice the fledgling art of kite skiing. Map and photos can be found at www.pawprince.com /baftemp/home.html.

First ascents and descents (couloir names by Barlage and McLean, heights in vertical feet):

Eglington Fjord: Eileen's and Innushuk couloirs (1,700' each).

Walker Fjord: Broken Dreams (on Walker Citadel), Polar Star (on Mt. Beluga, 3,640', "best chute we've ever skied"), Southern Cross and Iron Cross (both on Great Cross Peak), Crosshairs, Debris, Northwest Passage (4,000') couloirs, and Polar Sun Spire, east face (5,100').

Sam Ford Fjord: AC Cobra, Mustang, Pinto, Escort, Model T, and Bronco couloirs (all on Kiguti Peak); Inquisition (4,100'), Intestinal Fortitude (3,760'), and Polar Disorder couloirs.

ANDREW MCLEAN

Auyuittuq National Park, various activities. Three Australians, Marcel Geelen, Geoff Butcher, and I spent six weeks in Auyuittuq National Park during June and July.

A small prop plane was taken to the township of Pangnirtung, from where a skidoo was taken to the national park, a journey of 30 km over treacherous broken sea ice. Over the next six days the team ferried heavy loads up the valley by foot, bringing about 200 kg of equipment and provisions into high camp at Summit Lake.

For several days it blew a gale, snow fell, and views were obscured by thick clouds. Once the weather cleared Marcel and I spent a day plowing through knee- and waist-deep snow toward Asgard. Without skis the going was very slow. Camp was made in a small col between Friga and Asgard. In a 14-hour push we summited Asgard via the Swiss Route (5.9) and made it back to camp. Problems encountered included snow-covered loose rock, falling rock cutting ropes, and deep snow on the descent—so deep that we had to "swim" down by lying flat and doing freestyle and backstroke. We spent another day getting back to Summit Lake camp.

The next objective was Mt. Thor, via the 5.9 A4 Diagonal Buttress, which hadn't been freed, as far as we knew. We crossed the raging ice-filled torrent of the Owl River to make camp in the huge boulder field directly below the northern end of Mt. Thor's imposing east face. Geoff had left the previous day to explore surrounding valleys and returned home, leaving Marcel and I as the only two humans in the entire national park. The lower part of Thor was horribly loose, with every hold and ledge waiting to send rubble down on the belayer. The route wandered up slabby, angled cracks and slab systems with many options for variations. We climbed 13 60m pitches and simul-climbed easier ground to a large, sloping snowslope. No direct aid was used. The snow was deep, and slippery rock lurking underneath required much vigilance. Two pitches on this mixed ground led to the summit ridge. We did not reach the summit, as treacherous, almost vertical, snow blocked the path. Without ice axes or crampons we decided to retreat 100m below the summit.

The final climbing objective was a new route on Mt. Tirokwa. It was near Windy Hut and seemed to be free of the rockfall of many of the other mountains. More bad weather, however, forced us to rest for close to a week before we could begin the climb. Direct aid was used extensively, as most of the rock was either wet or too blank for ground-up free climbing. After two days of fixing ropes we committed to the wall, spending three nights in rain and storm before running out of bolts and food at 500m, an estimated 200m from the top. One particularly bad day saw us swamped with rain, as our portaledge was perched below a "classic" corner. The climb followed a prominent corner system for 10 pitches, with mostly easy aid (A2+) and hanging portaledge stances. The upper head-wall looked steeper and harder. We abseiled, making it back to camp on the fourth day.

The first hikers of the season arrived during the climb. The ice had cleared from the fjord, letting boats travel from Pangnirtung to the national park trailhead. These hikers were the first people that Marcel and I had seen in over a month. For further info visit www.baffinisland2002.com. A video docu-mentary of this expedition will be finished in late 2003.

NEIL MONTEITH, *Australia*

Mt. Thor, Absolute End. This summer saw the first-ever Polish climbing expedition to the big-wall paradise of Baffin Island; it culminat-ed in an impressive new line on the north-facing flank right of the main west face of Mt. Thor. Thor's west face is one of the tallest

Marcin Tomaszewski cleaning the ninth pitch on Mt. Thor's Absolute End. Michal Bulik

walls in the world (1,250m), and the mountain, located just beyond the Arctic Circle in Auyuittuq National Park, has attracted climbers from all over the world. Four routes existed on the main west face, all highly technical and requiring extreme aid: West Face (American), VII A4 (first big-wall VII in the world); Midgard Serpent (American), VI A5; Aromes de Monoserat (Spanish), VI A4+; and the mind-bending American route, Project Mayhem, VII A5+.

Three of us, Chris Belczynski, Marcin Tomaszewski, and Michal Bulik, came to Baffin Island's Gibbs Fjord in early July. We tried to hire local Inuit to carry our loads (25-30 kg each) for $300 Canadian. At first they were enthusiastic, but things deteriorated. They lacked the stam-ina of Pakistani porters and seemed

Chris Belczynski leading the big roof on Mt. Thor's Absolute End. Michal Bulik

Mt Thor (1675m) W face

Photo: **Michał Bulik**
Topo: Grzegorz Głazek
& Marcin Tomaszewski (2002)

Mt. Thor's west face: (1) Diagonal Buttress, located far off the left hand side (beyond the proper wall and not running to the summit): Steve Ampter, Rick Cronk, Ron Sachs, 1978, 5.8, short section A4, 26 pitches. (2) Japanese route 1984, first on the wall, with long traverse to the north ridge. (3) West face direct: John Bagley, Tom Belper, Eric Brand, Earl Redfern, June 1985 (after 5 attempts), 40 days on the wall, U.S. VII 5.10 A4, the first Grade VII in North America, still no full repeat. Placed 115 rivets. (4) Go Abe solo attempt (Japanese solo attempt), Go Abe 1996 and 1997 (he died when his rope cut on a flake). (5) Project Mayhem: Jim Beyer solo, 2000-2001, VII 5.10 A5c. (6) Midgard Serpent: Brad Jarret and John Rzeczycki, 1995, VII 5.9 A5; solo repetition Jason "Singer" Smith 1998. (7) Aromas de Montserrat: Cristobal Diaz, Juan Espuny, 1997, 10 days of fixing and 21 days in the wall, VI A4+, UIAA V+, 18 pitches 55-70m. (8) Absolute End, Polish route: Krzysztof Belczynski, Marcin Tomaszewski, and Michal Bulik, July 2–August 16 2002 (including 9 days of fixing, summit on Aug 1), descent by the south ridge, VI 5.11 (UIAA: VII+/VIII-) A4, 17 pitches 55-70m to south ridge. Photo diagrams and caption information supplied courtesy of Grzegorz Glazek, CDW PZA

unfit for the task. They forgot to bring extra shoes for river crossings (some even walked without socks!) and required one of us to be constantly finding the trail, adjusting their rucksacks, etc. After a day or so they were blistered, sore, and unable to walk farther. We sent them home with half the agreed-on pay.

It took us over a week and 200 km of walking to shuttle our 400 kg of gear and food to the base of Mt. Thor. Inspection of the west face showed that the most obvious lines had already been climbed. Moreover, recent routes (other than Jim Beyer's Project Mayhem) had required extensive drilling—over 100 holes for Midgard and over 200 for Aromes. The only remaining logical line ascended the north-facing vertical flank just right of the main west face. Over 18 consecutive days we climbed a new line on this flank. We called our route Absolute End.

The route follows a system of seams, cracks, and dihedrals, sporadically broken by roofs and short, vertical, blank sections, which we either hooked or free-climbed. We rated the route VI 5.11 A4; reaching the ridge of Thor required 1,070m of climbing. Another 300m of easy climbing (below 5.6) took us to the top of Mt. Thor, which we reached on August 1. The route was opened in capsule style, with three hanging portaledge camps. The main difficulties included aiding loosely attached pillars and expanding flakes. For the first nine days the wall was hidden in fog and battered by rain, snow, and high winds. Thereafter we experienced good weather.

With luck we survived a couple of rock and ice falls, almost without injury, and none of us took a fall longer than 30'. We dedicate our route to the Japanese climber Go Abe, who died trying to solo a new route on Mt. Thor several years ago.

CHRIS BELCZYNSKI, MARCIN TOMASZEWSKI, & MICHAL BULIK, *Polish Climbing Association*

COAST MOUNTAINS

Coast Mountains, remote areas summary. The year 2002 was one of remarkable activity in the Coast Mountains, both in southwest British Columbia near Vancouver and in remoter areas. Most new-route activity in the "greater" Coast Mountains, as always, took place in the Waddington Range.

April and May were very fine, and a large number of parties enjoyed long stretches of settled weather, allowing several extreme ski descents and some outstanding climbing. Craig McGee and Brad White made two ascents involving significant new climbing, though both climbs took off from existing routes. On the southwest face of Waddington they climbed the initial notch-couloir section of the Wiessner–House route, then from low on the ramp climbed directly up the south buttress toward the summit, following a distinct chimney for many pitches of 5.9 to 5.10a on good rock. An offwidth led to a notch, where they spent a very cold night, which dictated retreat in the morning. But first they climbed steep ice and rock leading diagonally up to the traverse section high on the Wiessner–House. From there, only a few pitches beneath the summit, they rappelled to the triangular snowfield and on down into the lower reaches of Meteor Gully. They climbed eleven or twelve new 70m pitches above the ramp.

Later, McGee and White climbed the South Buttress route on Tiedemann Tower. Where the ramp on the South Face breaks left, the pair continued directly up the crest with 13 new pitches, most in the 5.9-to-easy-5.10 range, to gain the summit.

As well as climbing, McGee and White also made outstanding ski descents. The North Face Couloir on Hickson was the biggest, but they also skied the Gerbolet Couloir on Shand, the previously unclimbed couloir dropping into the Radiant from the Argewicz–Tellot Spire col (the BMC Couloir), and another couloir (Gin and Juice) on the lower left portion of the west face of Argewicz.

Also in May, Johnny Franko, Martina Holan, and Trevor Hunt climbed the glacier and the 350m couloir tucked just east of the rib halfway between the Splendour Glacier and Whymper Dome. They reached the crest of Splendour Spur, then skied the line back to the Tiedemann Glacier. Franko and Hunt also climbed, then skied, the prominent, slanting snow couloir on the right (northeastern) face of Bravo Spur, one km up-glacier from Rainy Knob at the eastern base of Waddington.

Surprisingly, fewer parties enjoyed the Range in summer than in spring. However, in late July Chris Atkinson and Kevin McLane, Jia Condon and Guy Edwards, and Andrew Boyd and Matt Maddaloni had productive stays on Combatant Col and the Upper Tellot Glacier. On Combatant, Skywalk was climbed twice; Condon and Edwards added a two-pitch 5.8 variation to the left at the big roof at one-third height. Skywalk was confirmed as a superb, challenging climb and reckoned to be considerably more demanding than the Beckey-Chouinard route on the South Howser Tower in the Bugaboos, with few ledges, continuous difficulties, and tricky routefinding. Kshatrya was also repeated, and its high quality also confirmed. Atkinson and McLane attempted the Hidden Rib of the Northwest Peak of Combatant, left of the Great Couloir, but bailed from about two-thirds height. Boyd and Maddaloni climbed most of the Incisor (the initial tower on Belligerence) via a line on its south face between Belligerence and Day Trip, but retreated before reaching the top of the tower. They rated what they climbed 5.11 A3.

On Mt. Tiedemann, Condon and Edwards established Southwest Bartizans on the rib left of the initial couloir on the Southwest Face route, finding only moderately difficult climbing (5.9) and considerable loose rock. Above the initial 700m rib, they joined the earlier Collum–Gerson line to reach the summit. They regained base camp in Combatant Col by descending Tiedemann's North Arête and passing back across Combatant via its Northeast Face. Only two days were consumed in the round trip.

On the Upper Tellot, Condon, Edwards, and Maddaloni put up a two-pitch 5.11 direct finish on the southwest face of Stiletto Needle, around the corner right of the west face. The climb started from the traverse on the Spiral Route.

A nine-person Alpine Club of Canada party spent a productive, if low-key, week on Remote Glacier in mid-July. Luca Bellin, Will Silva, Bruce Fairley, Helen Habgood, Jackie Snodgrass, and Harold Redekop rambled up the easy west ridge of the possibly previously unclimbed Peak 2,750m (a.k.a. Teva Ridge), which lies two km north of Mt. Bell. The east ridge of Angina was attempted but found to be unpleasantly loose. Doug Berner and Robert Nugent climbed Broad Peak, varying the Southwest Face route by climbing directly up the center of the south face for the final 200m. Silva and Habgood climbed Peak 2,880m (Toto) next to Dorothy via the easy snow of the West Face. This makes a nice outing when combined with an ascent of Dorothy. Berner and Nugent climbed the fine East Ridge of Trylon (4 pitches, 5.7), making a long approach over the col west of Dorothy to reach a short, easy gully from the glacier south of the peak. Overly warm weather prevented climbs of Bell, but six party members later climbed the Dogleg Couloir on Geddes, the other "big" peak west of Scimitar Glacier.

Conrad Anker, Jimmy Chin, Peter Croft, and Brady Robinson spent a fine week and a half on Combatant Col in mid-August. Skywalk and Kshatrya received several ascents, and again the high quality of both routes was confirmed. Anker and Croft made a variant start on Skywalk, continuing up the approach gully 20m beyond the original chimney to reach and climb a less-icy crack system (2 long pitches, 5.9) which joins the original route at the end of the fourth pitch. Anker and Chin climbed an alternative start to Kshatrya well to the left of the original line (5 pitches, 5.10). Anker and Croft climbed six new pitches (5.10a) on the left side of the toe of the Middle Buttress, right of Hotel of Lost Companions. A new finishing crack (5.12) through a roof led to the top a huge El Cap-style tower, from which they rappelled. Brady Robinson worked solo on an aid line in an area of black water streaks right of Solo Blue, but did not complete the route.

While the Waddington Range attracted the majority of the traffic, several noteworthy climbs were accomplished elsewhere in the Coast Mountains. Fred Beckey and friends made a trip to the Monarch Icefield, 80 km northwest of Waddington. Matt Perkins and Jim Ruch climbed the attractive Northeast Arête on Cerberus. Chris Kettles and Ptor Spricenieks climbed the west face of Mt. Monarch, following more or less the line of the two previous ascents, then skied this impressive face.

In May, Drew Brayshaw, Gord Betenia, and Don Serl visited the easily accessible Niut Range, 50 km northeast of Waddington, camping in the valley southwest of Blackhorn Mountain. The superbly attractive Mt. Nicholson (five km south of Blackhorn) was climbed via a northwest face approach and the previously climbed west ridge. (Nicholson's northeast ridge was later attempted, by Phil Fortier and Gambrelli Layco.) Peak 9,580' (two km south of Blackhorn) was climbed via superb snow on the west face that led to the northwest ridge. Brayshaw soloed the 4th class north ridge of Peak 8,500', three km southwest of camp, descending the east ridge and northeast face. Unsuccessful attempts were made on the east and northeast faces of Quartz Peak, five km west of camp, and on nearby couloirs.

The perennial Fred Beckey visited the Niut Range in August with Ray Borbon, climbing the northeast ridge of the east peak of Rusty.

Simon Richardson made his third trip from Aberdeen to British Columbia, this time visiting Mt. Gilbert, the remotest of the Coast Range's 3,000m peaks, 100 km southeast of Waddington. With Chris Cartwright he climbed the magnificent West Pillar, finding about 20 pitches of fine, steep granite (5.10).

Ade Miller and Forrest Murphy joined Don Serl for a long weekend dash into the Falls River Valley, 120 km east of Waddington, during fine Indian summer weather in late September. The resulting Passport Couloir on the north face of Mt. Winstone (10 pitches, 1.5 of which were as steep 90°) was only made possible by unusually "placid" serac conditions at the top of the route.

DON SERL, *Alpine Club of Canada*

Southwest British Columbia (southern Coast Mountains and Canadian Cascades) summary. The year 2002 was great for alpine climbing in the coastal mountains of British Columbia. Activity was particularly intense in the southwest corner of the province, probably spurred by the publication in 2001 of Kevin McLane's selected climbs guidebook. This area, commonly referred to as "Southwest British Columbia" or "SWBC," includes the southern Coast Mountains and those portions of the Cascades located in, or most easily accessed from, Canada. SWBC is the most developed alpine climbing area in British Columbia, due to its proximity to Vancouver, and the limits of the region are essentially defined by what is within "weekend range" from the city—although some pockets within that range are pure wilderness and difficult to access, and

Mt. Slesse east face photo-topo and route summary: (A) Labour Day Buttress (Culbert-Douglas-Starr, 1974) D- III 5.7/8. (B) Station D North Buttress (Cassels-Dunlop, 2001) D- III 5.8 Note: This route starts a little to the left of what is shown, near the edge of shadow. (C) Flight 810 buttress attempt. Incomplete route, 6 pitches to 5.9 to junction with D1. (D) Southeast Buttress (Nannery-Flavelle 1977) D+ IV 5.7. (D1) Kubik-Soet start to SE Buttress (1978). (D2) normal start to SE buttress. Can also begin up route F and traverse ledge as shown. (E) SE couloir (Neufeld-Isbell 2003), winter route. TD- IV M4 or M5? (F) Navigator Wall (Burdo-Doorish, 1987) ED1 V 5.10d. (G) The Real McKim (Edwards-Franz 2001) ED1 V 5.10+. (H) East Buttress (Stoddard-Mullen, 1977) TD+ V 5.9 C2. (I) East Buttress Direct (Child-Beckham, 1993) ED1 V 5.10c. (J) East Face (Easton-Edgar, 1997) ED2 VI 5.9 A3+. (K) North East Buttress (Beckey-Bjornstad-Marts, 1963) TD V 5.9 (K1) Bypass route (most commonly climbed start). (K2) Original start (if combined with Buttress Crest Direct, bumps grade to TD+ V 5.10a). Not shown on the north face: North Rib (Keisel–Lowe, 1972) TD V 5.9. North Couloir (Serl-Wittmayer-Beckham, 1980), winter route, TD-IV, alpine snow & ice to 65 °/5.8 rock & mixed. Can be climbed in spring/early summer as variant to North Rib (FA this var: McLane-Murrell, 1977). Fraser Ribber (Fraser-Ourom, 1982) TD- IV 5.8 (original grade) or 5.9 (Alpine Select grade). Arctic Wing (de Jong-McGregor-Gibbs, 1989), winter route, TD, IV/V alpine ice and mixed (rating not known, "steep mixed"). (L) Bamboozled Buttress (Duncan-Hughes, 2002) TD IV 5.10+.
Photo, route lines, and information supplied courtesy of Drew Brayshaw.

unclimbed and rarely visited peaks exist within 75 km of the city (as the crow flies).

In the Squamish area 2002 was notable for several new or newly free long routes, in particular the first free ascent of the ten-pitch Black Dyke by Matt Maddaloni at a reported 5.13b. First climbed with aid (V 5.9 A4) in 1970 by Al Givler and Mead Hargis, the route saw a free ascent of its upper two-thirds by Dean Hart and partners. However, the second climber reportedly pulled off several "key holds" from the loose basalt dike and the climb went unrepeated free until Maddaloni attempted a direct line. The 30' first roof went at 5.12b; the second roof proved the crux. Elsewhere on Squamish, a few new multipitch routes as hard as 5.12b/c went up in the Western Dihedral area. At the other end of the scale, local guide Kris Wild cleaned a new line across the gully from the Squamish Buttress. The Ultimate Everything incorporates parts of the forgotten 1970s lines Echelon and Amazon Slabs, but follows clean slabs and dikes where those routes grovel via classic Squamish tree climbing. When combined with an approach route on the Apron, The U.E. gives up to 22 pitches of climbing in the 5.7 to 5.9 range and became instantly crowded. In the Squamish subalpine zone Brian Pegg and friends climbed a new 12-pitch 5.9 on the unnamed wall to the right of the Fluffy Kitten Wall and continued up 400m of alpine scrambling to summit Mt. Habrich.

In the rapidly developing granite area of the Eldred Valley, 100 km north of Vancouver near the mill town of Powell River, it was a quiet year. The big routes, such as Main Wall (VI 5.11 A4) and Funk Soul Brother (VI 5.9+ A4+) went unrepeated. Most activity occurred on the accessible Psyche Slab, where three new 12-pitch routes in the 5.10 range were developed, two of them by local activist Colin Dionne and the third by a Vancouver Island-based party.

Moving from the crags to the alpine world, not much was done in the winter of 2001-2002. Guy Edwards and John Millar kicked things off in the spring with a new mixed route (TD-) on the northeast face of Mt. Joffre. Smell the Roses reportedly had some hard mixed climbing and poorly bonded snow. Parts of this route had previously been climbed in both summer and winter by traversing in from adjacent lines, but the direct route was uncompleted. Also in spring, Drew Brayshaw climbed a new variation (AD) to the Fairley Route on the north face of Mt. Sloan, avoiding the mixed crux of that route in favor of moderate snow and rock farther right, near the northwest ridge.

Summer 2002 was marked by a rare level of activity, in part due to excellent weather. The big existing lines, like Pacemaker (37 pitches, ED1/2 VI 5.10 A1) on Mt. Robie Reid, the East Face of Slesse (20 pitches, ED2 VI 5.9 A3+), and Pillar of Pi (16 pitches, TD V 5.9 A1) went unrepeated though not unattempted. Instead, climbers sought out interesting new ground. Jamie Chong and Conny Amelunxen started the summer by teaming up on the long-anticipated direct west pillar (now called Cheech and Chong) of Mt. Dione in the Tantalus Range. This 16-pitch route went all free at TD V 5.10d, despite its appearance. Fearing blank rock, Amelunxen brought a wall rack, but only a few pins were placed. This was Chong's first alpine climb, though he had previously sent 5.14a and V12. The line had been tried in the 1970s by Paul Starr and Fred Douglas, who retreated after a block Starr was laybacking detached and sent him for a huge whipper. Chong and Amelunxen, with Rob Arthurs, also added the North-Northeast Buttress of Mt. Slalok (AD+ III 5.10b), and Amelunxen put up the West Buttress route (AD+ III 5.7) on Mt. Trorey in the Whistler backcountry with John Young. Also in the Squamish–Whistler corridor, Craig McGee and Brent Phillips visited Mt. Ashlu and established the Southeast Face at a sustained D+ III 5.10b/c. A large quantity of RPs is reportedly helpful for this line's thin cracks. In the volcanic Meager Group, Fred Touche, Ivan Bandic, and Tim Bennett made the first ascent of the eye-catching pinnacle Perkins's Pillar (D- III 5.7 A2), a demented 100m-high, 20m-thick volcanic spire first attempted in the 1930s by pioneering coastal climbers Tom Fyles and Neal Carter.

East of Vancouver, alpine activity also proceeded apace. Karsten Duncan, from Oregon, and Dan Hughes, from Washington, attempted the classic Northeast Buttress of Slesse on a foggy day, got lost on the glacier approach, and made the first ascent of the 700m Bamboozled Buttress (TD IV 5.10+R) on the ridge running north from Slesse to Crossover Peak. Duncan described his lead of the crux, an overhanging grass-filled crack, as a real wake-up call. In the adjacent Rexford–Illusion group Shaun Neufeld was extremely active. He put up five new lines on the Nesakwatch Spires, from four to six pitches, in the D- to D+ range, with grades from 5.10a to 5.11b. His partners, variously, were Dwayne Barg, Jordan Struthers, and Drew Brayshaw. Neufeld also soloed the 1,500m West Buttress of South Illusion Peak while on a recce to that peak, finding mostly scrambling but with five pitches of technical climbing (D III 5.8).

Elsewhere, John Black and Reinhard Fabische visited the Chehalis Range and climbed a new line on the north face of Mt. Ratney, to the right of the Raisin Rib, with difficulty reported at 5.9 and alpine snow (16 pitches, TD-). Drew Brayshaw and Kurt Fickeisen put up the nine-pitch East Buttress of the south peak of the Old Settler on immaculate rock at AD+ III, 5.7, and Darin Berdinka and Josh DeLong put up Backslide Buttress on Gamuza Peak, with a similar grade and length. In a newly discovered area up Kookipi Creek, Mike Layton and Jordan Peters found an excellent new line in Back of Beyond Buttress (D+ III 5.10b) on Peak 6,800', with the crux Endless Slab featuring a 200m splitter crack system.

On the repeat front, routes which were once rarely climbed saw multiple ascents because of their inclusion in the new selected climbs guide. The north side of Bear Mountain, Widowmaker Arête on Crown Mountain, Pup Buttress on Harvey's Pup, north face ice routes on Mt. Weart, and east side buttresses on Slesse all saw multiple ascents during the summer.

Atypically warm and clear weather continued into the fall and early winter of 2002, resulting in ideal alpine ice conditions. Don Serl, Steven Harng, and Drew Brayshaw climbed a trio of new, north-facing, 500m lines in the Cadwallader Range. The narrow Plutocrat Couloir and wide North Glacier on Plutus Peak both went at AD+ III, with snow and ice to 50°. The curving Paymaster Couloir on nearby Crazy Mountain was a bit stiffer at D-, with snow to 65° and lots of rock-hard alpine ice (plus minor mixed) to 50°. Odin's Ice on the north face of Ossa Mountain (D III M4) saw its probable first repeat in early December by Michael Spagnut and a partner. In early January 2003 Drew Brayshaw and Fred Touche made the second ascent of the northwest face of Mt. Cheam (D+ IV, 1000m of snow and mixed to M3). Also in January Shaun Neufeld and Aaron Isbell climbed the Southeast Couloir on Mt. Slesse (TD- M4or 5ish). The couloir's entrance involved snow on rock slabs and the couloir proper 75° "wet cement." Neufeld had previously climbed more than half the route with Guy Edwards, before breaking a tool and retreating.

In-depth information about many of these ascents is available at www.bivouac.com. Look for Serl's Waddington Range guide sometime in 2003.

DREW BRAYSHAW, *Canada*

Mt. Tiedemann, Southwest Bartizans and various ascents. It took three trips, but in late July I finally scored on the weather in the Waddington Range. Guy Edwards and I drove to Bluff Lake, where we met Kevin McLane, Chris Atkinson, Matt Maddaloni, and Andrew Boyd. White Saddle Air flew us to the Mt. Combatant col at 10,000'; after driving from sea level, we felt the altitude. Guy and I climbed the South Ridge of Mt. Hickson for a warm-up. The next morning we made a predawn start on an awesome-looking new mixed line on Waddington, but warm temperatures at sunrise brought on a shower we figured we didn't need, so we rappelled off. We scurried back to base camp and repacked for a warm, sunny climb up Skywalk Buttress on Mt. Combatant. We descended by four rappels off the ridge and a downclimb of Combatant Couloir. This route was outstanding, with sustained climbing, and took us 11.5 hours roundtrip.

We rested a day and repacked for a go at a 1,400m unclimbed ridge on Mt. Tiedemann. We packed light bivy gear, a stove, and a little food and, at about 4:00 a.m., headed down to Tiedemann Glacier. This descent was a crapshoot, given all the hanging seracs. We darted down, looking over our shoulders with a feeling of commitment that I wasn't expecting until halfway up the climb. We made it through the most exposed slopes without mishap, then encountered

Guy Edwards on the first ascent of Southwest Bartizans. Jia Condon

some broken crevasses negotiated by a short rappel, a little jump over blackness, and a few funky ice moves. After more weaving and a steep snow/ice slope we traversed onto loose rock. With our boots, tools, and crampons stuffed away, we stretched out 60m of rope. There was then a long stretch of running belays until the rock steepened. The steep climbing here proved to be 5.10 something or other. We bypassed two prominent towers on the ridge, for the sake of speed and because they looked precarious and unstable. One short rappel beyond the second tower and three easy pitches brought us to a great spot for hunkering down for the evening. At this point we joined an old route that came up a couloir on the right of the ridge. This route is now a maze of crevasses and seracs. Warm temperatures, no wind, and snow to melt allowed us to sleep soundly for five whole hours.

Early the next morning we woke quickly on the first pitch. It was a long pitch, with loose rock, but brought us to better climbing and, by noon, to a snowfield. We soloed this to steeper ground. Four more fun mixed pitches and some scrambling brought us to the summit by 3:00 p.m. We didn't dawdle on the summit and climbed down the north ridge to the Chaos Glacier. The warm temperatures made the decent tedious due to the balling up of our crampons. From the Chaos we negotiated a few holes to gain the north face of Mt. Combatant. The face was 400m of 55° alpine ice and took little time. We descended the 700m Combatant Couloir and arrived at base camp by 11:00 p.m. All in all, one of the best alpine outings I have embarked on—the climbing grand in spots, though scary loose in others. We called the route the Southwest Bartizans (V 5.10+, with four easy mixed pitches).

After a day off, other climbers arrived and we moved camp to Plumber Hut. Matt joined us, and we moved camp again, to the Upper Tellot Glacier. We then went up to the Stiletto–Sara

col and climbed two new 5.11 pitches to the left of the Beckey–Patterson route. The next day Guy and I climbed the Chilton–Must route on Mt. Stiletto (highly recommended). Guy was still amped and soloed the Ice Chimney route on the north face of Stiletto. The weather was changing, so we called in Mike King and flew back to Bluff Lake, after only being in the hills for 10 days.

This was an eye-opening trip for me, as I see how important it is to be able to jump on decent weather when the opportunity presents itself. The challenge now is to create flexibility so I can pursue these windows of opportunity, and find a partner who can do the same.

JIA CONDON, *Canada*

The Southwest Bartizans route (on Mt. Tiedemann) follows the crest of the thin blade of rock between the two steep couloir-glaciers and continues above the right border of photograph. The visible summit is Combatant (3,756m), and its most prominent buttress has been climbed via the Belligerence route (1,200m, VI 5.11 A3+, Child-Collum-Mascioli, 1994). The next buttress left is Perseverance (1,000m, VI 5.10c A2/3, Cusick-Kearney, 2000). Jia Condon

Mt. Winstone, Passport Couloir. Forrest Murphy, Don Serl, and I climbed the Passport Couloir (TD-) on Mt. Winstone in the Tchaikazan Valley, British Columbia (www.bivouac.com/Arx Pg.asp?ArxId=1247) over a long weekend in September. Climbed on the 22nd, this new route takes the obvious couloir left of the National Pillar.

From below the bergschrund, 200m of simul-climbing, followed by three belayed pitches, led to the base of the serac band. This we tackled on the far left, next to the rock. A 50m pitch (WI3) was followed by 20m of WI4-. Another two pitches on which we moved together led to the summit ridge and the end of technical difficulties. The summit itself was another half hour along the ridge.

We took four hours to approach from a BC just above treeline, and eight hours from bergshrund to summit. The lengthy descent, which involves traversing around the peak, took just under seven hours to BC.

ADE MILLER, *Alpine Club, AAC*

Mt. Gilbert, west pillar. Mt. Gilbert (10,225') is an impressive granite peak that lies 90 km southeast of Mt. Waddington, deep in Canada's Coast Mountains. Although it is the closest 10,000-foot peak to Vancouver, it is one of the most difficult mountains to access in the range and is rarely climbed. On August 3 Mike King flew Chris Cartwright and me in his Jet Ranger from Bluff Lake across the Homathko Icefield to the wide glacial bowl below Gilbert's west face. The west pillar rose directly above our tents, looking totally compelling. We just had to climb it.

Unfortunately, the weather had other ideas. It snowed for three days, dropping a couple of feet. When it stopped, we climbed the glacier shelf on the northwest face of Gilbert and made the first ascent of a fine 8,900' rock peak via the east ridge. It was bitterly cold, and the rock on Gilbert showed little sign of drying. The weather turned bad again, but fortunately this time it rained, which cleared the rock of snow. Finally, after we spent two more days in the tent, the sun came out. We packed our sacks with food for three days and set off for the pillar.

Gilbert's west pillar is guarded by a large bergschrund system. Access is further complicated by a hanging serac and an ice couloir that regularly spew rock and ice down the approach slopes. The whole approach would be unjustifiable if it were not for the Little Tower, a steep rocky crest that cuts into the left side of the serac and shields a narrow segment of the approach slopes from ice fall. From a little way up the crest of the tower it is possible to cross the couloir to reach the west pillar. The base of the pillar is undercut by a series of roofs, but these are breached on their right side by the Beak, a prominent prow with a corner running up its left side. The only weakness on the smooth central section of the pillar is the Great Flake, a hanging, left-facing flake system that leads through seemingly blank walls to the exit chimneys and summit snow slope.

Early on August 11 we crossed the bergschrund, climbed the Little Tower, and traversed across the couloir to reach the foot of the face proper. We expected the climbing to get very technical at this point, but the rock was superbly featured and gave brilliant climbing that was never too hard. All those days in the tent, snatching views of the face with the binoculars and working out the

Mt. Gilbert, showing the West Pillar route, which is the only route on the main face. The gendarmed right skyline (west ridge) is The Friendly Giant (Durtler-Fairley-Legg, 1989)—superb rock, 37 pitches, V 5.10. The top section of the left skyline is the finish of the Northwest Face route (Baldwin-Fairley-Driscoll-Heinemann, 1983). Simon Richardson

easiest way to go, had paid off. The line slotted together perfectly, and that evening we found our-selves racing toward the exit chimneys as a big storm approached. Fortunately, this fizzled out before it reached us, but we ran out of time and had an uncomfortable bivy in the chimneys. Next morning half a dozen more pitches took us to the top of a superb climb (700m, V 5.10a)—perfect granite, all free, and far easier than it had any right to be.

SIMON RICHARDSON, *Scotland*

Mt. Dione, Cheech and Chong. On July 21 Jamie Chong and I summited a new route on Mt. Dione in the Tantalus Range. They dubbed it Cheech and Chong (700m, 16 pitches, V 5.10d). The line ascends the central buttress of the west face. Chong and I were prepared for aid pitches but didn't need to bust out the hooks and copperheads: Cheech and Chong is the first free route on Dione's west face.

The route starts at the toe of the west buttress, about 200m up the prominent couloir. After pitch five we unroped for 100m of 4th and easy 5th class, leaving us on a perfect bivouac ledge. The following three pitches, up the central buttress, proved to be the crux. One rivet was placed for protection near the bottom of pitch eight, and one piton was left on a traverse just before the belay station. We deemed pitch nine the most difficult of the route because of an awkward offwidth. The climbing eased a bit until the upper headwall, where protection was somewhat meager.

We spent two nights on the mountain—the first on an excellent ledge halfway up, the second on the summit, which offered spectacular views of the setting sun. Note that this route could probably be done in one long day with the help of a topo. A double rack of cams to three inches and a set of nuts are required; also bring four pitons for belay stations. Descend the standard Southeast Ridge route.

CONNY AMELUNXEN, *Canada*

Mt. Joffre, Smell the Roses. Joffre's northeast face has a nice chimney/gully line, just left of the central pillar. It rimes up well in winter, with just enough snow and ice to be tempting. On my first attempt, with Mike Spagnut and Andrew Port, in early April 2000, we climbed four pitches to where the chimney steepens to vertical.

On the second attempt, in April, John Millar joined me. We were highly motivated: the route had been a skeleton in my closet for two years. The first few pitches were as challenging as before; clearing snow off the rock and searching out cracks for pro kept the mental challenge high. Three rope-stretching leads took us back up to the previous high point. It was getting dark, so we fixed the rope and descended one pitch to a snow cone, where we were hoping to excavate a bivy ledge.

We kicked and hacked through the ice and snow to create a 12-foot-long bench with room for two. Around midnight the spindrift valve was opened. My legs were buried, and our ledge started filling up with snow. The comfort level wasn't high. Finally morning arrived.

We regained our high point and delved upward into the steeper upper chimneys. I surprised myself with Rockies-like mixed moves up an overhang, moves I certainly wouldn't have tried if the gear hadn't been good. The next pitch was even more formidable. John had to resort to aid. He then belayed me from a perfect hip jam in a strange hueco. More good mixed moves and a smidgen of good ice gave way to the upper snow couloirs. A last mixed pitch and then a steep snow arête led directly to the summit.

Whiteout conditions and the onset of dark almost tricked us into spending another night out. But the old ski-touring trick of tossing a bright-colored stuffsack ahead gave us enough definition to make out the snow surface.

This route (Smell the Roses, 500m, V M7-, some aid) has eight mixed pitches, and is certainly another good line on one of British Columbia's most accessible alpine peaks. The protection is natural yet sufficient; and the climbing is of great quality for Coast Range winter alpinism.

GUY EDWARDS, *Unemployed*

Mt. Cheam, northwest face. Mt. Cheam, at the north end of the Cheam Range, rises 2,100m above the Fraser River. Its north face was first climbed in the 1970s as a summer route, and Cheam became semipopular for winter climbing in the 1980s. In 1987 Carlo Zozikyan and Bruce Kay climbed the northwest face. In the 1990s winter mountaineering in southwest British Columbia fell out of fashion, as ice climbing began to dominate winter activity. Only recently has winter climbing begun a Coastal renaissance.

January 2003 saw almost ideal alpine conditions in the mountains of southwest British Columbia. A Christmas snowfall was followed by two weeks of sunny weather, warm at first, then cooling steadily. Fred Touche and I decided to try the northwest face of Cheam, which was, to our knowledge, unrepeated since the first ascent. I had wanted to climb this face ever since moving to nearby Chilliwack, as I see it every day from my apartment.

We left the car at 6:00 a.m. The face begins as 1,000m of steep, forested slopes leading to a bowl. The headwall of the bowl is an 800m wall consisting of 500m of snow-covered rock and 300m of steep snow that end on the ridge crest. We began bushwhacking by headlamp, but when the sun rose, we were on route. At 11:30 a.m. we emerged into the bowl after a long session of jungle and steep bush-climbing. We donned crampons, and progress up the bowl on frozen avalanche debris went quickly. The headwall lacked obvious lines, but we thought we saw a potential route and began climbing. The climbing consisted of steep snow (50°-65°) mixed with short, bouldery rock steps overlain with verglas. About 400m up the headwall we reached a series of higher rock walls and roped up. Two 60m pitches, climbed 4th class due to a lack of opportunity for gear placement, got us through this crux section (M3). We dispatched the remaining snow slopes (to 50°), avoided remnant cornices, and topped out on the ridge at 3:30 p.m. The West Ridge is a popular hiking route that we had both climbed; we decided to forego the summit and began descending immediately. Fifteen km of postholing, hiking, and scrambling down the West Ridge and logging roads below got us back to the car at 9:30 p.m.

I subsequently questioned Bruce Kay about the route he and Carlo climbed in 1987. They began in a narrow 1,600m avalanche gully, bypassing our bushwack approach, then apparently climbed to the right of our line; their route was on steep snow save for one boulder-problem rockband. Thus, it seems that what Fred and I climbed was largely or entirely new terrain. We rate our climb D/D+ IV M3.

DREW BRAYSHAW, *Canada*

Squamish, Black Dyke, free climb. The Black Dyke on Squamish has been a serious test for aid climbers since it was first climbed by Al Givler and Mead Hargis in 1970, but climbers ascending the Grand Wall route have also peered over and dreamed of freeing the route. I aid-climbed the Dyke with Gordon Ross three years ago. It had had few ascents, and information was difficult to obtain, so we were not prepared for the extremely loose roof on the third pitch. Massive death blocks had to be delicately negotiated using RURPs and a crazy maneuver of reaching behind one's head for a stalactite, then dangling from it like a frog on a crocodile's tooth. The second roof, on pitch four, was easier, but on pitch six we discovered a 45m overhanging sport-climbing marathon. Dean Hart and John McCallum had bolted this pitch hoping to free the whole route, but 10 years ago, after pulling off a crucial hold, they packed it in. Gordon and I didn't do too badly and finished the easier 5.10 climbing for a total of 11 pitches.

I came back to the sport pitch a year later with John Ferno and attempted to redpoint it after rappelling in. We came close, with the crux feeling about 5.12a. Intrigued by our effort, Andrew Querner asked if he could photograph our next try. Andrew hung in space from his 15-foot tripod, snapping photos, while I got the redpoint. We then realized that only pitches three and four of the Dyke were left to free.

Friends helped clean the lower six pitches over the summer. Although the pitch three roof intimidated us the most, the real difficulties were on pitch four. After several days of top-roping, I finally freed the campus-board-like pitch and then bolted it. I led it three times the next day, to make sure I really did it. Probably the hardest single free pitch I had ever climbed at the time, nearing 5.13b. I named it The Nubian Queen—beautiful black lady.

The scary 30' roof of pitch three turned out to be an epic to clean but easy to climb. Most of the death blocks had to be removed, and flattened sections of the forest below. Starfish chimneying allowed the pitch to go free at 5.12b, and everything on the Black Dyke had finally been climbed free.

We rate the 11 pitches 5.10, 5.10+, 5.12b, 5.13b, 5.9, 5.12a, 5.9, 5.10a, 5.9, 5.9, and 5.10a. The route has not yet had a continuous one-day ascent. I suggest bringing a helmet, but nothing major is loose enough to fall. Friends who are comfortable up to 5.11+ say they had a great time on the route, pulling past the more difficult moves using bolts. You get an 11-pitch sport route that requires 20 draws for a rack—quite unusual for us Squamish trad climbers.

MATT MADDALONI, *Canada*

PURCELL MOUNTAINS

BUGABOOS

Bugaboo Spire, Symposium. Wyoming climber Alex McAfee took advantage of excellent early August weather to complete a new route, solo, that he'd started the previous year. Symposium (15 pitches, VI 5.8 A2+) ascends Bugaboo Spire's 1,600' east face, beginning with eight new pitches up a slanting crack system near water streaks. Its upper half coincides with the Cooper-Gran. During the seven-day ascent, rockfall was frequent (standard fare for the east face) and included microwave-oven-sized blocks.

COMPILED FROM *Alpinist Magazine*, SEAN ISAAC, MCAFEE, AND MARC PICHE

Howser Towers, Spinstone Gully and Perma Grin. Until recently The Big Hose (1,000', D+ 5.8 WI3, Jon Krakauer, solo, 1978) on the northeast face of South Howser Tower was the only ice route in the Bugaboos—a range renowned for its alpine rock climbing. After climbing this stellar shaft of ice in September 2001 with Guy Edwards, I was convinced that the potential for more ice and mixed climbing existed in the off-season.

When Brian Webster and I climbed the west face of Central Howser Tower in August 1999, we witnessed constant avalanches and rocks spewing from the gash separating Central Howser from South Howser. However, I wondered if this deep gully might hold some secret icy passage during colder months. In September I decided to explore the possibility, and recruited Scott Semple for the five-hour slog from the Kain Hut, over two passes, to the base of the route-to-be.

We climbed "The Ditch" in eight time-consuming pitches, most of which offered scrappy alpine mixed (i.e., trolling for pick placements in snow-caked rock). There were a total of eight large chockstones wedged in the tight gully-cum-chimney system, separated by easier sections of ice. We climbed over six of these and avoided two, by deking right up a groove/crack on the right wall on pitch three, then making a short rappel back into the main gully. Pitches six and seven proved to be the hardest, with roof-like chockstones and sparse gear placements. The technical difficulty was sustained throughout, with two pitches of M6, one of M6+, and two of M7. The second-to-last pitch was the crux and almost sent us rapping back down. Scott fired the runout overhang after I backed off (bad place to break a leg), thus saving us an epic retreat. We named this new mixed line Spinstone Gully (1,200', TD+ M7R), because of the constant in-your-face spindrift and the numerous chockstone cruxes. As far as we know, this is the first route to be established in a day up and over the remote west faces of the Howser Towers. We topped out in the narrow notch between the Central and South Howsers just before dark. Two straightforward rappels landed us on the glacier, thus beginning the epic hike and drive back home. We arrived in Canmore at 8 a.m. the next morning, making for a 28-hour day.

In late October conditions and weather stabilized again. Scott Semple and I returned, joined by

Scott Semple approaching the northeast face of South Howser Tower, showing Perma Grin on the left, and The Big Hose on the right (Krakauer, 1978). Sean Isaac

Brian Webster, to try the often-looked-at ice runnels on the northeast face of South Howser Tower, just left of The Big Hose. Our new line followed a shallow gully system slightly left of the standard rappel route from the top of South Howser. It consisted of six long pitches of thin ice and beautiful granite mixed. The third pitch was the ice crux, up a foamy smear of stubby thickness, while the mixed crux was on pitch five, which involved secure pick locks and bomber protection in a 30' corner linking discontinuous ice gullies. At times the two seconds, who followed together, could be heard giggling like kids because the climbing was so good. Since the three of us smiled all day, we named the route Perma Grin (1,000', TD- M5 WI4). The best part of the experience was having the Bugaboos to ourselves, which would never happen in summer.

SEAN ISAAC, *Canada*

Scott Semple negotiating one of the roof-like chockstones on the sixth pitch of Spinstone Gully, Central Howser Tower. Sean Isaac

South Howser Minaret, Bad Hair Day. Late in August Lizzy Scully and I drove to the Bugaboo trailhead. After porcupine-proofing Lizzy's Volvo with chicken wire, we began the approach. We hiked the first day to the Applebee Campground, a primitive camp surrounded by towering granite spires protruding from the glacier. The next day we hiked through the clouds and rain to East Creek via the Bugaboo–Snowpatch Col and Pigeon–Howser Col. Setting up our tents at the base of the South Howser Minaret, we decided to try to free-climb this wondrous 2,500-foot hunk of granite. After hiking to every vantage point in the rain the following day, I sketched our proposed line.

Waking the next morning to perfect weather, we set off with Friends to #4, doubles on small TCUs, a set and a half of wires, two light ropes, three liters of water, Clif Bars, and a bivy sack, hoping to nab the first free ascent of the Minaret in a day. After two days of climbing and one night of shivering, we found ourselves sucking on icicles and celebrating on the summit. The route, an 18-pitch meandering line up the south face, afforded beautiful free climbing the whole way. Our line, which we named Bad Hair Day, linked short sections of established lines, with some new climbing mixed in here and there. We encountered hand cracks, offwidths, scary face climbing, and groovy flares.

HEIDI WIRTZ

Bugaboos, various ascents. In addition to climbs reported above, several other new routes and variations were made. In July, Jonathan Copp and Jeff "Pouche" Hollenbaugh added a 600' direct start, called Where's Isaac? (5.11d), to the Pretty Vacant route on Bugaboo Spire, stopping at the ledge system where their variation joins the original route. The route climbs bullet granite to hourglass-shaped flakes and can be done as a direct start or as a short route. The first pitch was freed on top rope, after vegetation was cleaned by the leader.

On North Post Spire's previously unclimbed, somewhat remote, 300m south face, Chris Geisler and Kai Hirvonen established two parallel new routes in August: West Comes East (5 pitches, III 5.10 C1)and Free Heeling (5 pitches, III 5.10++).

On Snowpatch Spire, Paul McSorley, and John Walsh climbed the two-pitch Vulgarian Variation (V 5.9 A2) to the South Face Direct. It is notable that this impressive face has only seen a handful of ascents. Marc Piche and Chris Atkinson, coauthors of the new Bugaboo guidebook, climbed a five-pitch new start (The Beach, IV 5.10+ A1) on the south face, joining the classic Southwest Ridge route at Surf's Up Ledge.

Guy Edwards and Sean Isaac made the first ascent of a five-pitch spire located between the East and Southeast Pigeon Feathers (the group of smaller towers south of the Howser Massif), in mid-August. Isaac writes, "We dubbed the diminutive peak Prince Albert Spire after out friend Lars Andrews." Their route, Dingleberry Spam, involved four pitches of 5.10 (including a bulging offwidth crux on pitch three) and one easy pitch.

Compiled from communications with COPP, HOLLENBAUGH, ISAAC, *and* PICHE

CANADIAN ROCKIES

Canadian Rockies, summary. The variable weather of summer 2002 defied forecasting but paved the way for a remarkable fall. July saw some notable ascents in the front range. The northeast aspect of Mt. Rundle is lined with rock buttresses up to 500m high. A few, such as the First Buttress, also known as the East End of Rundle, are crisscrossed with routes, but most remain virtually untouched. Eric Dumerac and Raphael Slawinski were drawn to the unclimbed north face of the thumblike Second Buttress. Due to difficult routefinding and tricky climbing, it took three attempts to establish La Bastille (500m, 5.11-). Later that month Slawinski teamed with Cody Wollen to make the first traverse of the Three Sisters. The three rocky peaks, rising 1,600m above the valley floor, are a prominent Bow Valley landmark. Slawinski and Wollen enchained the technical routes on the north aspects of the three peaks in a long day, in the process making the FFA of the north ridge of the Middle Sister at chossy 5.10.

The summer also saw a controversial project started on Mt. Louis. The upper east face of this beautiful obelisk is formed by an exceptionally clean vertical bedding plane several hundred meters tall. Over the years this "Diamond Face" has been the subject of speculation and been attempted by a number of strong climbers. But the attempts have floundered due to lack of natural lines. Last summer Dumerac and a variety of partners, after rigging a Tyrolean traverse to the top of the giant flake, began the monumental task of rappel-bolting the face. The ongoing project has sparked a lively debate in the Rockies's climbing community, with reactions spanning the spectrum from outrage to disapproval to enthusiastic support.

After early August's snows receded, the alpine summer finally began. In mid-August Will Gadd, in an impressive display of fitness and skill, soloed the South Face (normal) route of

Mt. Robson in 17 hours car-to-car. Although not highly technical (at most easy 5th class), the route entails an elevation gain of 3,000m, ascends a variety of terrain ranging from steep rain forest to exposed loose rock to steep alpine ice, and is exposed to objective hazards. This was likely the first time that Robson was day-tripped from the road. A couple of days later Gadd teamed with Slawinski to climb the Japanese (normal) Route on Mt. Alberta in 13 hours hut-to-hut, thus bagging two of the Rockies's most coveted summits within a week.

In the fall Americans John Catto and Scott Simper spent time new-routing in the Tonquin Valley, west of Jasper. The Tonquin's superb quartzite peaks are guarded by approaches of up to two days and often inclement weather. Catto and Simper made three first ascents on the Amethyst Lakes Rockwall, including Jokers and Fools (V 5.11), an 18-pitch route on a satellite summit of Redoubt Peak. In recent years a small group of Americans, realizing the potential of the Tonquin, have been quietly putting up some impressive new routes. These include two new lines on the north face of Mt. Geikie—the Hesse–Shilling (VI 5.10 A2) by Mark Hesse and Brad Shilling in August 1994 and Honky Tonquin (VI+ 5.10 A3) by Scott Simper and the late Seth Shaw in July 1999. In September 2001 John Catto and Mark Hesse climbed a 23-pitch new route on the northwest buttress of Mt. Postern (VI 5.10+), making what was likely only the second ascent of the peak.

Late September and early October were cold and wet, making for excellent early-season ice conditions. By contrast late fall was exceptionally warm and dry. The warm weather sublimated much of the ice, rendering the remaining ice season merely average. However, the extended high pressure made possible some outstanding alpine ascents. In mid-October Dumerac and visiting French alpinist Philippe Pellet climbed a likely new route on the northwest face of Mt. Kitchener. (There are indications that it may have been climbed previously, but glacier conditions may have changed significantly over the years.) Rights of Passage stands out as one of the hardest pure ice pitches to have been climbed on a Rockies alpine route. But Kitchener was merely a warm-up for the main event. In late October Dumerac and Pellet teamed with Barry Blanchard and in four days completed an oft-attempted line on the far right side of the Emperor Face of Mt. Robson. They named their route Infinite Patience. The third major fall alpine event was an ascent in early December of the east face of Howse Peak by Gadd, Kevin Mahoney, and Scott Semple. Their Howse of Cards shares some common ground with M-16, the first route on the east face of House. Not only did Gadd, Mahoney, and Semple place no bolts, but they used no aid or jumars, all climbers free-climbing the entire route.

Looking for early-season ice before winter snow made backcountry travel difficult, local guide Larry Stanier ventured to the "backside" or western slope of the Columbia Icefields with Grant Statham. The result was Panama (300m, M5 WI5), an excellent new route on a small peak between Mt. Columbia and Mt. King Edward.. Stanier then teamed with Steve Holeczi to explore the backcountry on the north side of the Goodsir Towers. Their objective was a ribbon of ice coming down from the Central–North Tower col. Steep Foam Alabama (foam grade not given) climbed six harder-than-they-looked pitches of serious foam, with correspondingly challenging belay and rappel anchors. Under better conditions the route could be pushed to the col in another eight to ten pitches.

By early October stringers of ice were appearing all over the Bow Valley, precipitating a flurry of first ascents. In late October Kirsten Anderson and Grant Meekins put up Blackbeard (320m, M5 WI5+) on the north face of the Little Sister. The route featured much thin, poorly protected mixed climbing, with the crux being a fragile overhanging pillar. Farther west, an oft-attempted line of ice, easily visible from the bars of Canmore, forms most years on the southeast face of the East End of Rundle between the summer rock routes Balzac and Dropout. In early November Ben Firth and Jeff Honig took advantage of a rare combination of conditions that allowed for bare-handed rock climbing, as well as for ice climbing, to make the first complete ascent of Balzout (475m, 5.9 M5 WI4).

The Kananaskis Valley was also the scene of early-season first-ascent activity, accompanied by fierce competition. Slawinski and Peter Smolik kicked things off with the first ascent of Ulalume (250m, M5 WI5), an aesthetic narrow strip of ice high on the west face of Mt. Blane. This is another early-season route, forming with the first freeze and ablating away later. Slawinski next turned to the spectacular upper valley of North Ribbon Creek. Barely visible from the road and guarded by a three- to four-hour approach, the valley under the northeast walls of Mt. Sparrowhawk has long been known to hide some of the most spectacular unclimbed ice around. Slawinski and Jason Thompson were

Mt. Geikie's 1,500m north face, showing from left to right: Hesse-Shilling, VI 5.10 A2, 1994 (upper part of route is essentially the same as the H-R). Hudson-Robbins, V 5.9 A3, 1967 (the initial part of the route follows a deep snowfield/gully hidden in the photo). Hannibal-Lowe, VI 5.10 A3, 1979. The two known repeat ascents deviated in spots from the line of the FA, but the route basically follows the left side of the central rib, then up the mixed ground of the upper face. Honky Tonquin (Shaw-Simper), VI+ 5.10 A3,1999 (the lower part of the route is not visible in the photo; the upper part climbs the left side of a huge overhanging white shield). Route info from Raphael Slawinski. Mark Hesse

first on the scene in late October with VSOP (400m, M4 WI5+). The route started on moderate mixed ground, continued up thin, snowy ice, and finished on a series of steep pillars. The crux last pitch was climbed by headlamp. The first ascensionists narrowly beat out Blanchard, Gadd, and Steve House, who went into the area a few days later. Finding the most obvious objective already climbed, they went instead for its thin left-hand neighbor. Squid Drinks Courvoisier (350m, M5+ WI5+) was named in reference to the cloak of secrecy under which Slawinski had attempted to hide this exciting area. With Chomo (210m, WI5+) being climbed by Slawinski and Smolik the day after VSOP, this backcountry venue now holds the highest concentration of long ice routes in the front range. Farther south Dave Marra and Jeff Relph climbed a likely new route they named Billy Goats Gruff (1,200m, WI4) on the east face of the south peak of Mt. Kidd. A fun quasi-alpine route, it ascends a succession of aesthetic ice and snow pitches leading to the summit ridge of the mountain.

The season also saw some unusual ice formations in the Ghost/Waiparous area. On the spectacular rock wall to the right of the classic Hydrophobia, Sean Isaac and Shawn Huisman originally put up Cryophobia (150m, M8+) as a bolted mixed route with long stretches of drytooling between occasional ice smears. But last fall the upper hundred meters formed for the first time as a pure ice climb, more reminiscent of the Terminator than of the original Cryophobia. Gadd and Slawinski are thus unsure whether they made the second ascent of Cryophobia in fat conditions, or the first ascent of Cryophilia. They did agree that it was one of the best and most sustained ice routes either had ever climbed.

Between sustained cold spells and a dangerous snowpack, calendar winter was not conducive to big routes. The Greenwood–Locke (summer IV 5.9) on the north face of Mt. Temple continued to attract interest but remained unclimbed in winter. Farther north, along the Icefields Parkway, Dumerac, Sean Easton, and Firth attempted Against All Odds on the northeast face of Epaulette Mountain in January. After a bivouac at treeline they climbed three long pitches of snowy ice (WI6) and a few hundred meters of alpine terrain above, with severe exposure to serac and snow-avalanche hazards. Eventually heavy spindrift forced retreat. While the lower pitches may be considered to constitute a complete waterfall ice route, the team considers the route incomplete without the summit. In February Firth and Slawinski, over two short days, traversed the four peaks of Mt. Lougheed (summer III 5.5), the probable first winter traverse of the four peaks. The crux was snowed-up slabs, likely trivial in summer, leading to the fourth summit.

As winter gave way to spring and temperatures rose, the snowpack finally stabilized and allowed climbers to venture more safely into the alpine. In early April 2003 Slawinski and Pete Takeda made the first ascent of the West Chimney (II M5) of Mt. Athabasca. This obvious, easily accessible line above the snocoach road is similar in character to nearby Sidestreet on Little Snowdome, and is recommended as an enjoyable alpine alternative to the ice climbing routine. Also in April 2003 Rob Owens and Semple climbed an impressive new line to the summit of Mt. Stephen. Great Western (2,000m, M7 WI5) starts up the popular ice route Extra Light and continues up snow, ice, and mixed ground to join the North Ridge route near its top. The first ascentionists climbed the route in 32 hours car-to-car, with a seven-hour bivy one pitch from the top.

RAPHAEL SLAWINSKI, *Canada*

Philippe Pellet leading up "the magic strip of ice" on day two, Infinite Patience. Barry Blanchard

Mt Robson, Infinite Patience. In midmorning on October 23 Eric Dumerac (Canmore, Alberta), Philippe Pellet (Briançon, France), and I (Canmore) stepped from the warm interior of a Jet Ranger helicopter and into the early winter environs of Berg Lake, below the Emperor Face. For an hour we hiked and scrambled up onto the side of the Mist Glacier. We toiled for the next four hours overcoming the first steep band, via an M5,

The Emperor Face of Mt. Robson showing routes, left to right: Fuhrer Ridge (1938), North Face (1963), Cheesmond-Dick (1981), Stump-Logan (1978), Infinite Patience (2002), Emperor Ridge (1961). Barry Blanchard

WI4+ system that could probably be avoided by going farther right. This was by far the hardest pitch of the route. These pitches gave access to the large couloir that is the prominent feature on the right side of the Emperor Face. Moderate snow climbing brought us to a ledge at about 8,500', where we shoveled a bivy site. The night was calm and the Northern Lights phenomenal.

Day two began with five ropelengths of class 4 up the big gully. A traverse and two ropelengths on 5.7ish mixed ground brought us into the upper ice strip. After three more ropelengths of 4th class on ice, we belayed an M4 ice chimney. Above lay another five rope-lengths of 5th class climbing, each containing cruxes in the M3–M5 range. The last of these pitches merged us with the Emperor Ridge–North Face option and its more substantial gully. We bivied in brisk winds and bitter windchills that night on the ridge at about 10,800'. Day three (October 25) started with one ropelength up the substantial gully, then a fine ice strip up a chimney (finest pitch of the route, absolute classic), followed by a half ropelength of dry and fine rock on the ridge proper. Much 4th-classing and bypassing small and sometimes hard (5.9) cruxes brought us to an ice ledge at about

Philippe Pellet and Eric Dumerac exiting "the big gully" on day two, Infinite Patience. Barry Blanchard

12,000', where we chose to avoid the infamous gargoyles of the Emperor Ridge by traversing an ice ledge for a kilometer. A true test of one's frontpointing and calf-muscle endurance! We finished the route via the gully atop the Wishbone Arête in three pitches at midnight. We bivied just east of the summit in a large, bridged crevasse that provided some protection from an awful windchill. The day clocked in at 20 hours. On October 26 we descended the Schwarz Ledges route to the Forster Hut, where at 4 p.m. the good people at Yellowhead Helicopters agreed to come get us and whisk us off to the trailhead.

Overall an absolute classic route on mostly ice and snow, as good as any on the globe, that gains an impressive 7,500'. The mountain was in perfect condition, and it was a grand adventure in the company of good men.

BARRY BLANCHARD, *Canada*

Editor's Note: This line had been attempted twice previously by Blanchard, Steve House, and Joe Josephson. Their high point had been the summit ridge (The Emperor Ridge), and they had not considered their climb to be a complete ascent. This high point was also reached, in about 13 hours on August 16, by Slovenians Matej Mosnik and Jure Prezelj, before they retreated in bad weather.

The Catapult, Jokers and Fools; Marching Men, Tin Drum and Toy Soldier. June found John Catto and me working together in India, trying to film bull sharks in the Ganges river. During an evening of cruising river channels and drinking extra-strong beer, we discovered that we had both made several trips to the seldom-climbed Ramparts group of the Canadian Rockies. A plan was hatched.

In early August we hiked to the Ramparts on the Macarib Pass Trail. Previous trips helped in sussing the logistics of getting our gear the 25 miles back to the wall. Pack horses carried to a fishing camp only three miles from base camp. The weather was perfect. Hiking to a pass to look at our objective, we had an eye problem: we could not see ourselves hiking up and down 4,000' to reach the base of our objective. Retreating to base camp to swat mosquitoes and think, we spotted a beautiful line up a northwest satellite of Redoubt that we took to calling "The Catapult." It's the closest of the satellite peaks, with the steepest rock face, located left of the large (ca 2,000') snow couloir. The line looked quite good as we glassed it with binoculars: directly up the middle of the north face on the lower band, staying right of the roof system and heading for the obvious chimney, then up to the middle of the snow band and the steep face above. The rock of the Ramparts is made of decent quartzite. We let a few days pass with some weather and an unexpected visit from my wife, Anna Keeling, and her climbing partner, Karen McNeill, who climbed the East Buttress of Oubliette. Eventually departing at 4 a.m. for the wall, we were pleased that the closer we got, the cleaner the route looked. The weather loomed with rolling clouds.

A couple of dihedrals gaining a crack system splitting the lower wall got things started. When the crack ran out, we began face climbing to another crack system up and right of a roof (5.9). Jon pulled over the roof to deposit us in a nice dihedral and ramp system that took us to a ledge several pitches above (5.8). From the ledge the climb ascended a steep stemming chimney until it was possible to escape left above a roof (5.10+). A few scary run-out moves gained a system of several horizontal cracks, eventually accessing a right-leaning crack (5.9+). The next pitch ascended a steep straight-in crack up an otherwise blank face (5.11). Two 5.6 pitches up broken rock brought us to a large ledge. The upper portions of the ledge were covered with snow.

Building thunderheads began to growl, and graupel started to fall. We descended to safer ground via a couloir west of the midway ledge.

The weather came right two days later. We climbed 1,500' up the descent gully to our stopping point. After stashing boots, crampons, and ice axes for the descent, we traversed slightly left along the snowfield to gain an easy ramp and dihedral system. We ascended this for two pitches, simul-climbing 5.8, and stopped under a small roof. John pulled over the roof (5.10) to gain a broken block system ending on a ledge. The next pitch was the crux. I climbed a beautiful tight-fingers corner, then stemmed out, leaving the crack to pull over a roof to a broken ledge (5.11). John took the next pitch through a band of rotten rock, up left, then back right for 55m (5.10). John's efforts gained easier climbing—a kicked-back crack system taking us another two pitches up the face. Above the crack a 5.6 scramble took us to a scenic ledge system. Moving left, we finally gained a view of the final pitches to the top. With the weather holding nicely, John led up large blocks and slightly right (5.8), to belay below the steep wall guarding the summit. I ascended a chimney system, winding my way through this mini-canyon over chockstones, stemming up steep walls, and finally topping out (5.9), with ugly frozen blocks for a belay. John made quick work cleaning the pitch, then led off on the last pitch to the top, up frozen mud, rock, and ice, bringing us to the top and an amazing view of the Ramparts. The route, Jokers and Fools, consists of 17 or 18 pitches (V 5.11).

After enjoying the views for an hour and soaking up the last of the sunshine, we rappelled the route for six or seven 60m rappels back to the ledge. Donning boots and ice gear, we traversed west for three pitches across steep frozen gravel and broken shale into a couloir. Downclimbing and rappelling for 1,500' returned us to the valley floor.

John and I also climbed two other excellent new routes, Tin Drum (III 5.11+) and Toy Soldier (III 5.11). Located at the bottom of Drawbridge Pass on the Marching Men formations, the routes are both six pitches of quality climbing up the centers of two of the formations. No bolts or anchors were left in this pristine area.

The Ramparts are seldom visited, other than by hordes of mosquitoes, occasional grizzly bears, and, fishermen. Despite this, I reckon it's well worth the effort!

SCOTT SIMPER, *AAC*

Mt. Postern, northwest buttress. "Sometimes you just gotta go out there," said Gloria, answering our query about the ugly weather. Having no time to sit around Jasper waiting for the weather to improve, Gloria took our bags to the horses for the approach to Mt. Postern.

Fifteen months earlier Mark Hesse and I had gotten our first, brief glimpse of Mt. Postern, plastered in snow and wetter

The northwest buttress of Mt. Postern, showing the Catto-Hesse route. John Catto

Mark Hesse high on Mt. Postern's northwest buttress. John Catto

than a slippery slide. As rain began we turned around and left, but what we saw was a potentially awesome 3,000' arête of unclimbed quartzite that was, Mark assured me from his experience on nearby Mt. Geikie*, good rock.

Snow fell within 30 minutes of our return in September 2001, and by morning a couple of inches smothered the stunning Rampart Range. Not far from Amethyst Lake, but above the bogs, we stashed food and gear at a bivy with a view of the Tonquin Valley. The next day's weather didn't inspire us to carry large loads 1,500' up and over Drawbridge Pass, then 2,500' down to the river that spews from the mouth of the Bennington Glacier, but we got on with it. By late afternoon we'd established ABC and hoisted a food bag out of the reach of griz. We knew the 11-mile bushwhack around the Ramparts would put us back at our base camp bivy around midnight, but we wanted another perspective of Postern's northwest buttress before dusk. Later, the starry sky made the trudge oddly delightful, though fresh bear tracks along Tonquin Creek had me glancing over my shoulder.

By dusk of day four, we sat at ABC with enough supplies, it seemed, to wait out winter. Exhaustion kept us horizontal until midmorning the following day, but by supper we'd fixed the first pitch in a chilly damp wind. Visions of Indian summer shimmered in our heads as we debated which route to follow: the directissima or the path of least resistance (PLR). Considering time constraints and our desire to summit, we opted for the PLR.

The climb appeared to be a series of five buttresses separated by terraces, and the next day we climbed eight pitches to the top of the first buttress. The climbing was not hard (5.5–5.8) since we avoided the steeper part of the first buttress, but hauling and carrying our loads for eight pitches on a low-angle ridge was a royal pain in the neck. Our strategy was to climb the old-fashioned way, slow and heavy, and we had a Bibler tent, lots of gear, and enough food to propagate several generations more of the nocturnal wall rats that chewed through anything left within their grasp.

A light rain settled in and stayed through the next day. No worries, though: we had food and shelter on a mossy terrace, a steady drip of water for liquid, and a view north to Robson National Park. A down day after six days on the move was welcome.

Crack-o-nine and I was sipping my second cup of java, revving up for the second buttress. Three leads and swap, that was our tactic. The second guy would clean and carry a load, while the leader hauled. My leads were fun, moderate 5.7 to 5.9. We scrambled over another terrace to the third buttress, where Mark tied into the sharp end. His leads were even finer: three steep 5.9 pitches up sparkling quartzite cracks and corners. The climb weaved through some large roofs, like a classic Gunks route. We settled into another five-star bivy, inhaled a bowl or two of wall food and watched the sun set.

Again we awoke to perfect weather. No wind. No clouds. No cold. We were shooting for the summit and left the bivy gear. We carried slings, hardware, and light boots. We also carried crampons and an ice tool, since a snowfield of undermined nature separated the fourth and fifth buttresses. Getting to it proved to be simply seven rhythmic pitches of moderate climbing interspersed with rocky ledges. Three more ropelengths of easy mixed put us on the sunny ridge below the final buttress. This was obviously going to be the crux. The steepest cracks and corners yet, for 500'. Mark led the next three pitches—5.10b, 5.10c, and 5.10d. The 23rd and last pitch was as it should be—the hardest. I belayed nervously, watching the sun approach the horizon, but by 6 p.m. we were standing on the summit with a view that I will never forget.

Postern is somewhat like an overgrown desert spire—no easy way off. Retreat would not be straightforward, as snagging a rope was a real threat. We had placed a cairn at one point to help us find our way back. After a dozen rappels and several rope snags, we happily crawled back into our tent at 1 a.m. At the end of the following day, our tenth, we dropped wearily into ABC after only one close call. A rope pull on the 16th rap dislodged a helmet-size bomb, badly scraping Mark's left shoulder. He sucked it up and continued down.

We'd missed our rendezvous with the horse packers, so two days and 30 miles later we arrived back at the trailhead in a blowing drizzle, barely able to walk. But the elation of finishing our quest numbed the pain somewhat, until we learned what had happened six days earlier, on September 11. Then we went completely numb.

JOHN CATTO

*Previously unreported: In August 1994 Mark Hesse and Brad Shilling established a new route (VI 5.10 A2) on Mt. Geikie's 1,500m north face. Hesse writes: "Ascends prominent buttress directly below the summit as viewed from Tonquin Valley and Moat Lake. The route is well left of the Lowe-Hannibal route and left still from the Robbins-Hudson route. The route is primarily 5.8-5.9 until the rock steepens on the upper part of the wall, where the difficult climbing begins (crux was wide cracks that were wet). The descent is not trivial! It's a great route." The descent: "From the summit we walked west a few hundred yards, then descended a major gully (rappels) on the south side of the peak (first rap slings visible from below the summit ridge, but hard to see). From the gully we traversed west to a saddle, then dropped back into Tonquin Valley." – Editor.

Mt. Kitchener, Rights of Passage. Somehow we had appeased the Mountain gods, for they granted us Rights of Passage. No doubt a reward for being patient while still staying keen. Alpine conditions were finally setting up, and the forecast was promising. There was a magic line I had been waiting to try. I thought I had seen it all. Delicate icicle-spangled pitches so thin, so thin. Wobbling, bonging, narrow pillars, strenuous ice roofs. Not! On the far right side of Mt.

Kitchener's north face lies a beautiful gully system that leads to an aquamarine pocket glacier, notched into the constriction of a classic gully. It presents an obvious objective from the road, yet is only another of those devious alpine trickeries. Barry Blanchard and Albi Sole had tried it years ago, and others as well. I can see them now, enjoying a good day out, covering ground fast, climbing ever up in that fantastic couloir, moderate ice steps and pleasant mixed ground. Like driving your sports car up a pleasant winding mountain road. You turn into that blind corner, the car hugging the curve smartly, RPM's screaming as you down shift, and—SHIT!—there is a cement wall in the middle of the road.

Tronc, in French, means "tree trunk," generally oak. In France Philippe Pellet is known as "Tronc." A humble, gentle, smiling father of three, he is also a rip-roaring, raging machine. He got to Canada, onsighted a 5.13, and we hit the road. We returned from our road trip, and it was time to "get amongst."

We settled into our bivouac for the night, our tent sagging as the poles had snapped in the high winds. The glacier protested its hangover by disgorging seracs toward the valley.

When it comes to ice, living in Canmore has advantages. You can climb frozen waterfalls seven or eight months a year. You naturally tend to play the "ticking game," and I had set out to tackle all the hardest ice routes. Of the range's six ice climbs rated WI7 or WI7+, there were only two left for me to do. On Riptide, Isaac had generously let me lead every pitch, yet once we were at the top, and Grandmaster Lacelle's direct finish was at hand (The Continuing Saga), we'd had enough. As for M-16 on Howse, well, you need perfect conditions, an excellent crew, and the brass balls of Mr. House. Still, after my own scary alpine ice ventures, all that upside-down dangling, after the silliest frozen canyon top-rope problems, I thought that ice would never challenge me beyond what I knew. Until I faced "The Marble"!

The surreal constriction glacier is layered and marbled with gray streaks of rock dust. Peeling from its base are steep, stepped roofs, then a glassy, continuously steep curvature. The only features are gently polished ripples. We affectionately called it "The Marble." We understood why this classic was yet undone. Tronc prescribed a technique I had learned on the Real Big Drip (for one screw): one manicures the ice up to a screw and downclimbs to a stance. After resting one does this again for another screw. It creates good placements and a sequence, banks endurance, and brings courage. Tronc manicured only for the first screw, but somehow got another two in and levitated to a stance. I preferred manicuring for two screws, and, my ass hanging out in space, fear evaporated in the moment's intensity and I almost forgot how gripped I was. Tools popping off were a given.

We climbed a narrow chimney between the glacier and the rock wall. There was a low-angle ice rink at the top, a perfect venue for a Slovenian hockey game. We finished in a daze, smiling and silent, as one feels after weathering a severe storm. Making the free rappel off, we were stunned by how distant the ropes were from the base. We both knew that this was by far the most difficult ice we had ever climbed.

WI8: An ice climb that is both physically and mentally taxing. A long, continually sustained ice formation that due to its consistent overhang requires great amounts of strength, endurance, and technical ability. Protection is scarce, as the energy required to place it takes great effort, due to its angle and its dense and/or fracturing and/or thin and/or aerated nature.

ERIC DUMERAC, *Canada*

Howse Peak, Howse of Cards. In December Will Gadd, Kevin Mahoney, and I made the first complete ascent of the east face of Howse Peak. After the excitement over M-16 (Backes-Blanchard-House, 1999) and the gauntlet that was thrown down with "twice as hard as M8," the tantalizing smears of the east face had become even more tempting to M-climbers like Will and me. Our first attempt was educational; our second, successful. Will , in late November, that we "have a look." The face was thinner than usual, but snow conditions were bomber, and Kevin's visit to the Rockies was too good an opportunity to pass up. We left late and had an unforgivable amount of fun—a strategy not conducive to alpine climbing.

The east face of Howse Peak, showing Howse of Cards. *Not shown: M-16 (Backes-Blanchard-House, 1999), Northeast Buttress (Baker-MacKay-Vockeroth, 1967), North Face (Blanchard-Robinson, 1988). For the former, see report and route line in AAJ 2000, pp. 232-233. For the latter two, see Selected Alpine Climbs in the Canadian Rockies, by Sean Dougherty. Will Gadd*

On our second attempt we spent several predawn hours crossing Chephren Lake and pounding up the lower slopes to the first pitch. The ice had deteriorated from bad to horrible. Will intentionally knocked off ice, revealing a perfect torque crack and M7 edges that led through the bottom of the first pitch. Above, several hundred feet of snow led up and right to pitch two. Photos from 1999 showed two smears, but we encountered only one. A week previous, we had kicked off large fragile sections on rappel. A combination of thin ice and dry-tooling led to the middle snow slope.

On our first attempt Will had led the mental cruxes—thin WI6X and M6+X WI6R— through the prominent cliff band. Kevin and I took over the second time, while Will put his nervous energy into building a dee-luxe snow cave. On day two we reclimbed pitches three and four, trailing Tiblocs as self-belays to keep the route all-free. A pitch of snow-covered 5.7, a 100m snow traverse, and the exit gully led to two stellar thin ice pitches, the cornice, and finally the summit. We topped out at 2:00 p.m., rapped back to our cave, brewed up, and continued down. We had left Canmore at 4:00 a.m. on Thursday, December 5, and were back in town at 11:00 p.m. on Friday, December 6.

Between the time of our ascent and the first magazine pushing the "Print" button, the east face grew by 500' and the curtain of the first pitch by 75. Further journalism suggested that ours was a north face, two-pitch variation to M-16. In reality we shared three pitches with M-16 and added 11 new pitches on the face. We called our route Howse of Cards (3,500', VI M7- WI6X), due to dubious ice, a key hold that resembled a deck of cards, and the ongoing mystique of the face. We copped the attitude of the M-16 crew by adding "no bolts!" to the route description, and finishing it off with "no aid, no jumars!"

SCOTT SEMPLE, *Canada*

Greenland

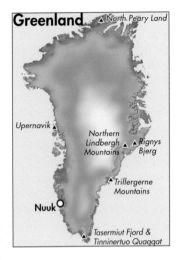

NORTH EAST GREENLAND

Louise Boyd Land, first ascents. We were expecting things to go wrong, but for the first few days of our two months in Greenland, very little seemed to go right. Our Cambridge University expedition comprised Natalie Clegg, Sam Harrison, Madeleine Humphreys, Derek Marshall, and myself. Whilst loading the chartered Twin Otter with our gear, which had gone ahead of us to the desolate airstrip in Mestervig, it soon became apparent that all our tents and some of our food were missing. A quick calculation revealed that we still had just enough food to last for our time in the field but without tents we couldn't go anywhere and the fear of having wasted two years of planning and over $35,000 of hard-earned sponsorship money was overbearing. Fortunately, a stroke of good luck found us stumbling across some unused tents in an airstrip hut. A couple of phone calls later and we were cobbling together poles, inners and flysheets from a number of rather dilapidated specimens and making up our required tent quota.

The southwest face of Pt 2,340m, seen from the vicinity of the Cambridge University Louise Boyd Land Expedition's campsite. This summit was climbed from the southeast via a broad snow ridge, not seen in this photograph. The rock wall is ca 400m high and mainly good granite, although the large rafts of brown metasediments tend to be somewhat looser and consequently there is rockfall danger where the sediments are more dominant.
Madeleine Humphreys

The view south up the glacier from the Cambridge University campsite. The small easy nunatak (2,000m) in the foreground was climbed by the 2002 Cambridge expedition, while those to the left remain unclimbed and rise around 300m above the glacier. The rock is predominantly granite. Moving west through Louise Boyd Land sees granite increasingly the dominant rock. Further east there is still granite, but it tends to occur as thick sheets rather than one big body. West of the area explored by the 2002 Cambridge expedition lie younger sediments of unknown quality. Madeleine Humphreys

Over the next few days things didn't get much better. Our base camp in the northern section of Louise Boyd Land had been carefully chosen with several aims in mind. There were a number of spectacular and accessible climbs that we had identified from aerial photos. In addition, the confluence of two large alpine glaciers was an ideal site for our glaciological research program. Unfortunately, after a long day's trek from our drop off point, the site proved unreachable due to an icefall, which spanned the width of the glacier to steep crumbling walls at each side. We needed to find an alternative and quickly, because we now had only 22 days to complete our scientific and climbing aims. After this we would have to start our long trek to rendezvous with an inflatable boat that was scheduled to pick us up from the fjords 100 miles further south.

There seemed to be one other suitable possibility in the region, but it was at least a day's trek away. However, on arrival we realized that our luck had turned. An idyllic campsite, with a small glacial stream for water and washing needs, provided a spectacular view down to the massive Hamberg Gletscher. What's more, we realized that we had landed an almost perfect central location for numerous climbs, all reachable within a couple of hours on ski.

The routine for completing our climbs involved scientific work in the morning before setting out for a route in the afternoon or evening, hoping to catch better consolidated night-time conditions. We would climb throughout the night, then return for another round of morning glaciological research, the first step in a comparison between Arctic-alpine glaciers and those found in the central European Alps, before taking the afternoon off. The cycle was repeated a number of times and worked well, but took some commitment; not in setting out for the climbs but in getting back down to work the next morning.

In total we completed six separate climbs, which resulted in the ascents of eight previously unclimbed peaks. The most spectacular rock was provided by a ridge backing onto our tents. Two pronounced pinnacles were obvious targets; the first was reached by a steady scramble that helped to get us in the mood (First Granite Pinnacle: 450m, PD, III, July 12). The second, via the west face, was the highlight of our time on rock in the area. The climb required six pitches of delightful granite, becoming steadily more solid as height was gained. The third pitch was a challenging chimney system, consistently IV, while the rest was III+ maximum, and the route completed in a 10-hour round trip (Patience Peak: 350m, IV, July 20). The first of our two significant climbs on snow saw us reaching the summit of two peaks east of base camp after a six-hour ski and climb (Points 2,200m and 2,340m: F, July 19 from the col between the two). The second, which took place on July 27, saw us reach the summits of Points 2,117m and 2,330m from the east. These ascents were completed on ski in a seven-hour round trip from camp. We also climbed the easy Landing Site Nunatak (2000m, F) on July 22 and the west face of The First Granite Pinnacle (The Knobble: 180m, IV) on July 26.

Flying is the only feasible way to reach Louise Boyd Land. Skiing out to Dickson Fjord, as we did, is a tough but very rewarding finish but at least three weeks need to be allowed for this. A good amount of time and a healthy budget need to be found, but the rewards for a climber reaching this area cannot be over emphasized. It is an untouched paradise still waiting to be explored.

CHRIS LOCKYEAR, *Cambridge University*

Gronau Nunatakker Range, first ascents. On July 4 British climbers, Owain Jones, Euan Lawson, Stephen Phillips and John Starbuck, British/American, Will Cross, and myself flew from Reykjavik, Iceland to Constable Point, before continuing on to Gronau Nunatakker (N 69° 28', W 30° 13'), an unmapped and uncharted region, lying 60km north of Gunnbjornsfjeld.

On our first evening, July 7, our group reached the summit of a 2,010m peak. The next evening Owain, John and myself darted up a knife-edge ridge to the summit of a 2,650m beauty. On July 10, after a failed attempt to reach the summit of a peak near to 2,650m on the periphery of Gronau Gletscher, I soloed a 2,800m peak to the west. I climbed the East ridge, zigzagging around bergshrunds and dicey cracks. I reached the summit at 3 a.m., just in time to enjoy the sun's pale orange color spread across the horizon.

Two days later, our team headed north and placed camp on an upper plateau, setting our eyes on new objectives in the Gronau Nunatakker and Gronlands Styrelsens Gletscher expanses. After several days of heavy winds and blinding snow, which left four feet of fresh powder, Will, myself, Owain, and John emerged from our tents and hiked to a summit of a small hump just south of camp. That same evening the four of us reached the summit of a 2,900m peak to the northeast of camp, traversing several icy patches along its west face, then climbing straight up the south ridge. On July 18 our team made its second and last summit as a group, reaching a domed peak in the far northwest corridor of the plateau.

Will and I decided to break off from the group and climb on our own for the remainder of the expedition. We reached the summits of two beautiful virgins (Hhass Peak and Hans Schou Peak) with a gloriously fulfilling 10-hour ski and climb. After another two days stuck in our tent due to blizzard conditions, Will and I surfaced for a 14-hour, five-summit blitz of peaks (rated Alpine PD+), traversing an entire range in the northeast corridor. Back at camp, I decided to make one more solo endeavor and scaled Schou Deux by front pointing up its south ridge

(1,500m, Alpine AD+), before traversing the western face to the summit. On top the wind had died, the air was crisp and I was alone within the vast polar icecap of the Arctic Circle, viewing what no man's eyes had ever seen before, an untouched and unscathed part of our world.

A day later Will and I managed to ski back with our sleds to the British base camp, just before a Twin Otter arrived to fly us out. The exploration had ended as abruptly as it started and, as usual, I wished I could have stayed behind within the natural world.

SEAN BURCH, *AAC*

Niels Holgersen Nunatakker, multiple first ascents. In June and July, the team of Geoff Bonney, James Carnegie, Gordon Downs, David Keaton, John Starbuck, and Paul Walker climbed several peaks in the Niels Holgersen Nunatakker(N 73° 22'). Between us we had a total of more than 50 previous expeditions to Greenland. Upon reflection, one member wistfully quoted a legendary Arctic explorer saying "for old age there is always the Arctic."

Carol Mary Nunatakker NHN, in northeast Greenland. David D. Keaton

Located approximately 30 miles northwest of Petermann's Bjerg (2,933m and considered to be the highest peak in northeast Greenland, a region generally referred to as the High Arctic) and adjacent to the Martin Knudsen Nunatakker, the NHN is one of the most northerly groups of alpine peaks in the world.

On June 17 the team departed from Iceland via a ski-equipped Twin Otter and after a refueling stop at Constable Point landed on an unnamed glacier. The expedition experienced near flawless weather and unexpectedly high temperatures, which necessitated that most ski and climbing tours were accomplished during the cooler hours of night.

As there is no record of any climbing party having visited this extremely remote range, all peaks were previously unnamed and unclimbed. The naming of peaks is not unusual within mountain ranges that have no record of permanent or migratory indigenous populations. True to most of the world's mountains, their appellations are invariably subject to future interpretation.

From a single base camp the following peaks were climbed: June 19, Enlightenment (2,321m); June 20, Domino (2,543m – 73°22.161) and Blackjack (2,505m); June 21, Titania (2,286m), Oberon (2,261m) and Puck (2281m); June 22, Sgurr Alastair (2320m); June 23, Schihallion (2,324m); June 24, Jasan (2,351m – 73°19.885) and Catherine (2,307m – 73°19.925); June 26, Ice Bear (2,413m), Snowstream (2,361m) and Snow Dance (2,300m); June 28, Emma Bjerg (2,209m – 73°20.358); June 30, Carol-Mary Nunattaker (2,061m); July 1, Hercules (2,295m – 73°23.994). The team departed the NHN on July 5 with a spectacular over-flight of Petermann's Bjerg, the Staunings Alps, Liverpool Land, and finally the largest fjord in the world, Scorsby Sund, where the pack ice had recently broken free.

DAVID D. KEATON

EAST GREENLAND

Lemon Mountains, various ascents. During July and August an eight-person British Alpine Club–Alpine Climbing Group team led by Roy Ruddle visited East Greenland. Primary objectives were important new routes in the South Lemons and major first ascents in the previously untrodden North Lemons. Poor glacial conditions forced the party to land some 14km north west of their planned site, but the compensation was that the climbers were now able to look at additional objectives in the western outliers of the Lindbergh range.

Operating in three separate groups, the party was the first to explore the glaciers to the north of the Courtauld Glacier and to make a complete south to north traverse of the Læbæltet Glacier, including the circumscription of the mountains to its northwest. During this exploration Geoff Cohen and Dave Wilkinson managed to penetrate the North Lemons and complete an outstanding first ascent of one of the highest peaks. The Spear (ca 2,500m) was climbed via its North East Face in a continuous 34-hour push (Alpine TD, see below).

Derek Buckle, Andy and Rachel Gallagher, and Martin Scott between them made the first ascents of six peaks in the North and East Lemons. In addition they achieved second and third ascents of Horseshoe Peak East and West via a new route up the central North East couloir. This group also made three first ascents in the western outliers of the Lindbergh Mountains, including the most southerly of the Trillingerne Group and two mountains directly to the north. Second ascents were also made of the Trillingerne Central and Main peaks via new routes up the North Ridge and South Face respectively.

Robert Durran and Roy Ruddle were less successful, failing on their major objectives; the East Face of Mitivagkat East through technical difficulty, Cathedral East through illness and Narren through high avalanche risk. The entire team probably covered more ground than any previous expedition to the Lemons, skiing in total approximately 1,000km. Apart from the routes climbed by Cohen and Wilkinson, covered in a separate report, the expedition made the following ascents (all previously unclimbed peaks except where noted): Cloisters East (2,240m) via the South Ridge; Dinosaur Domes (several summits to 2,178m) climbed on ski from the south; Bantam Point (2,058m) F+; Second ascent of Trillingerne Central (2,176m) via a new route up the North Ridge (PD+); Trillingerne South (2,158m) via North West Ridge (AD); Scimitar (2,735m) via West Ridge (PD+); Tent Peak (2,479m) via East Ridge (PD); Second ascent of Horseshoe Peak East (1,916m) via new route up West Ridge (PD+); Second ascent of Horseshoe Peak West (1,928m) via new route up East Ridge (F+); Snowbunting Point (1,810m) via East Couloir (PD+); Sentinel Peak (1,740m) via West Ridge (PD+); Whaleback (1,964m) via North West Ridge (F); Fin (2100m) via North Ridge (PD-); Goblin (2,175m) via South Ridge (PD); Second ascent of Trillingerne Main (2,295m) via a new route up South Face (AD-).

DEREK BUCKLE *and* ROY RUDDLE, *Alpine Club*

North Lemon Mountains, first ascent of The Spear and others. As our drop-off point was not a suitable base for climbing in the Lemon Mountains, Geoff Cohen and I left for the Frederiksborg Glacier 19 miles away. Two days' of travel were needed to reach an Advanced Base on this glacier. We wanted to explore the North Lemon Mountains, a never previously visited group to the northwest of the main Lemon Mountains and separated from them by the Courtauld Glacier. Four hours and three kilometres further on from Advanced Base we again set up camp on a shallow col and decided to climb the mountain immediately south. This was a long ridge linking a number of peaks running northeast to southwest and marked 2,010m on the Danish Map. Starting at 4 a.m. we climbed snow to a col on this ridge southwest of the first peak. We then turned west and traversed the ridge. This was snowy at first but then became a complex series of rocky pinnacles. We climbed unroped for speed, crossing some towers and turning others, until eventually gaining a snowy summit that appeared to be the top. A long way beyond was yet another summit, which appeared to be roughly the same height. We stopped at this point, uncertain as to whether the distant summit was higher. Further study a few days later from our next summit gave no better indication. We named our mountain Switchback due to the many undulations on its ridge. The route then had to be reversed and we arrived back at our camp 20 hours after leaving. Our climb along the ridge to the central summit, carried out on the 19th July, had been three kilometers in length and Alpine TD—with pitches of III and one of IV. The mountain's southwest summit appears to be about the same height, but is still unclimbed. It appears more easily approachable from the Courtauld Glacier. The far northeast summit (closest to the Frederiksborg glacier) is also unclimbed.

A few days of bad weather gave a welcome rest, after which, on the 24th, we climbed a huge whale-like mountain to the north of our col. The terrain was easy and reminiscent of the Cairngorm plateau in a very snowy winter. We christened our peak Humpback (ca 2,400m) and awarded the 650m route up its southeast flank a grade of PD.

After this we returned to advanced base and on the 26th skied to the glacier on the far side of Humpback, camping at ca 1,100m. Here, we were surrounded by unclimbed peaks but further movement had to be on foot. There were two outstanding peaks in this region. The Shield (our name) had a big snowy north face, and was presumably the one shown as 2,600m on the map. Much closer but more impressive was The Spear (also ca 2,600m). We spent the next two days establishing a camp at the foot of The Spear's North Face. After a rest day we started the route the following evening, climbing the left side of a steep glaciated slope to reach mixed ground. From this point the rest of the route was pitched. The climbing was never hard, but it was sustained with few resting places, so the overall fatigue factor was out of proportion to the difficulty. Most of the belays were on good rock. After 17 pitches of mixed terrain we reached a good ledge on the left-hand ridge and took a 10-minute break. The mountain now became steeper and rockier. Towers barred the ridge ahead, so we traversed back onto the face

After 12 hours on the go, we traversed the forepeak's snowy right face to a col, then turning the corniced crest above, reached the twin summit pinnacles around midday.

Cloudy wreaths threatened a change in the weather, so we began our descent, down-climbing to the ledge where we had made a 10-minute break on the way up. Although we had no bivouac gear (but a stove) we rested here for one-and-a-half hours and melted snow to rehydrate. The cold soon spurred us into renewed action and with rappelling not really feasible, due to lack of suitable anchors for our rappel cord and the constant possibility of rope jam, we down-climbed all the way, staggering into our camp on the glacier 34 hours after setting off. Our 1,300m route on the northeast face, completed on the 29th July, was graded TD.

DAVE WILKINSON, *Alpine Climbing Group*

SCHWEIZERLAND

Tupilak, new route and other first ascents. Previously unreported was a productive expedition to Schweizerland in July–August 2000 by Alexander Fidi, Julian Neumayer, Matthias Leitner, Wolfgang Schöls, Jörg Susnik (all Austrians), and Richard Jewell from the U.K. Neumayer and Susnik skied via the Knud Rasmussen into the 16th September Glacier from the head of the fjord but the rest of us flew by helicopter, taking virtually all the food and gear.

From a base camp on the north bank of the glacier to the south of Tupilak, Leitner, Schöls, Jewell and myself moved our equipment up the lower 700m of glacial ice (60° maximum and a 70m rock wall) to reach the foot of the steep rock wall forming the South face of the mountain's 2,264m West Summit. Directly below the wall we established our Advanced Base. Our plan was to make a capsule style ascent of a route up the middle of the South Face between the 1997 German Route, Nordlicht, which more or less follows the South West Ridge, and the 1999 British Route, Big Air. Our proposed line had been attempted by the Germans in 1997, but they turned back after one pitch.

We set off up this first pitch, astonished to find not only a bolt next to a perfect crack, but also that the difficulty was more like F6b+ (5.10d) rather than the 7b (5.12a) quoted by the Germans. After a slightly easier pitch above, we had to resort to some difficult aid climbing with two pitches up to A3. Over three days we fixed ropes to the top of the seventh pitch and then, deciding that the ground above looked somewhat easier, elected to abandon our plan to use the portaledge and go lightweight to the top. We rested, and on the 31st July set out at 4.00am.

Above our previous high point there was free climbing to 5.10 and a couple of short aid sections at A2+. After 16 pitches we were on the summit, where we found a cairn and a plastic tube containing a message from the four Swiss from Lucerne, who made the first ascent in 1968 via the East Ridge. This contradicts the German report, which stated there was no trace of a previous ascent, and we can only assume the 1997 party did not go to the highest point. With a storm moving in, we located and rappelled Nordlicht, dismayed to find not only two bolts per stance but also many protection bolts next to perfect cracks. High winds made our descent difficult and the occasion was not helped by witnessing one of our tents being blown away (we were later able to rescue it and sleeping bags from a crevasse). We christened our route Pitteraq (650m, 5.10d A3) and placed only three, double-bolt anchors.

We also completed other new routes. War and Peace (170m, 5.10c) by Jewell and Leitner, and Serenity Crack (170m; 5.10a) by myself and Schöls, both climbed on the 29th July, follow cracks in the wall west of our Advanced Base leading up to the lower part of Tupilak's South West Ridge. From the top we moved left a short distance and rappelled the Nordlicht bolts. Prior to this Neumayer and Susnik made a repeat of the 1973 Swiss Route on the Central Pillar of Rodebjerg (1,100m, D+, 5.5) and on the 26th climbed Grün is die Hoffnung on the Wall of Waiting. This is the 500m wall at the end of the long southerly spur descending from Tupilak and the route was graded 510b. The same pair also twice attempted a fine line on the South Face of Pt 1,700m, later christened Schartenspitze, which lies west of the prominent Beacon. This face was already home to the 1999 Italian route, Sedna (F6c and A2). Neumayer and Susnik climbed six pitches up the wall but were forced to retreat on both occasions by bad weather. Later, on the 5th August, Jewell and myself climbed a three-pitch direct start and fixed two ropes. Three days later we returned and climbed a further eight pitches to the top. Holiday on Ice lies wholly to the right of Sedna, is 480m in height and graded 5.11a. It gives perfect crack climbing on excellent rock. We left no gear on the route but there are some bolt anchors between the third and sixth stances originating from the earlier attempts.

On 2nd August Neumayer and Susnik traveled up the glacier east of Tupilak to The Red Wall, a 2070m summit with an immaculate 500-700m south face of red gneiss climbed by three 1999 British routes. The pair added a fourth, Black Nose (ca 500m, 5.10a), to the right side of the wall. Three days later, with Schöls, they climbed the North East Couloir and East ridge of Sonnblick (1,800m), to make what may well be the first ascent of this mountain. The climb, named Der Weg ins Licht, was 900m with a maximum angle of 60° and some short sections of 5.4.

The team then skied out to the Tasilaq Hut, but on the way climbed two new routes. The first ascent of the south pillar of Rytterknaegten (2,020m) was made by myself and Jewell on the 17th August. The pillar was 500m high with difficulties up to 5.10d (no bolts or pitons used), though unfortunately we were not able to pursue a direct line, forced by unclimbable yellow rock onto the left flank. From the top of the pillar we rappelled 60m to reach the south ridge, then followed this to the summit. We then descended the long northwest ridge. We christened our new route Jackpot and estimate from the route book on the summit that Rytterknaegten has received well over 20 ascents. The day after our climb Leitner and Schöls climbed the smallest and most westerly tooth in the Fox Glacier Cirque. Their 350m direct line to the summit of the 1,100m Milk Tooth was christened Gute Zeiten, Schlechte Zeiten, and had eight pitches with maximum difficulties of 5.8.

Alex Fidi, *Austrian Alpine Club*

Tupilak, first ascent of the North face and quasi-winter ascent of Rodebjerg. In 2001, a four-man British team comprising Jon Bracey, Charles "Stan Halstead, Jon Morgan, and Al Powell opted to spend the early part of the year in the Tupilak region in order to attempt what might be the first serious technical winter climbing on the island. On a visit to the region in 1999, where he climbed the new route, Big Air, on the south face, Powell noted that the much larger north face looked steep, damp, somewhat looser, and a prime target for a winter ascent, should suitable ice build-up occur. Wanting to test this theory, he arrived back in the area on April 1.

After spending a few days testing the ski potential of the powder and despite night time temperatures down to -35°C, Bracey and Powell set off for the ca 1,000m high north face. Initially, the pair attempted a line directly up the middle of the wall but finding the terrain buried under deep powder snow, were forced into time-consuming mixed and aid climbing. After a sitting bivouac bombarded by spindrift, the pair continued to a zone of dangerously loose blocks below a roof. Not being able to outflank this, they retreated.

After some rest during a short spell of inclement weather the two returned to the face on the 16th April. This time they decided to exploit the very snowy conditions by taking a line more to the left, ending at a col on the summit ridge between the East and West tops. Following a series of snowy ramps and slabs interspersed with more difficult mixed terrain, Bracey and Powell reached a point two-thirds up the face before bivouacking for the night. The next day more mixed ground led to the final slabs. Here the pair were forced to make a semi-pendulum to reach a poor belay, before setting off over compact rock towards the col. The belay proved to be the last for sometime, as the pair had to resort to moving together with intermediate protection no better than tied-off pegs and skyhooks, After this highly committing section more aid was needed to overcome the final grooves and the col reached in time to construct their second night's bivouac.

At 4:00 the following morning, any hopes of reaching the summit were dashed as the weather closed in. Having prior knowledge of the South face, Powell opted to rappel that side of the mountain to a high glacier basin. Ten rappels later the pair were on the glacier and traversing east to a col on a rocky spur of the South face. Six rappels on the far side of this col led to another glacier, up which the two ascended to a second col at the base of Tupilak's east ridge. Collecting skis cached previously by Halstead and Morgan, Bracey and Powell were able to make a swift descent to Base Camp. Their Silence of the Seracs on the North face was ca 900m high and awarded a grade of Alpine ED2. Maximum technical difficulties, found in a strenuous chimney near the top of the face, were rated at Scottish 7 and A1, but there were several sections of Scottish 6 and more aid in the middle section of the route.

Halstead and Morgan had also been very active during this period with some ski ascents and a new winter line on the South face of 2,140m Rodebjerg. On the 10th April the pair set off up the couloir left of the Central Pillar first climbed in 1973. Higher, they were able to cut back right on snow ramps and mixed ground (Scottish V 6) to reach the Shoulder at 700m, where an easy escape is possible. After a very cold bivouac on the Shoulder followed by deteriorating weather, the pair did indeed escape, returning on the 16th to finish their route via a line of chimneys (Scottish VI 6) and snow bays on the upper west face. These led to an obvious notch in the summit ridge, from where the highest point was reached. The route was felt to warrant an overall grade of TD.

All four climbers then embarked on an impressive series of ski descents, followed by three days of inactivity on the glacier when their scheduled helicopter pick-up failed to materialize. They were eventually flown out late on the 28th. The only excuse given by the air company was that it was overstretched and chose to put the climbers (three of whom were now frost-nipped) on the bottom of their list. This resulted in missed flights home and extra expense. The team strongly advise future parties visiting at that time of year to take extra supplies and a satellite telephone, or consider skiing out to the Tasilaq Mountain Hut (which has a radio), where a pick-up should prove more reliable.

LINDSAY GRIFFIN, *High Mountain INFO*

Viking's Shield Wall, solo first ascent. From August 15 to September 7 Mike Libecki made a solo first ascent of the 4,000-foot Viking's Shield wall, establishing Giving Birth to Reason (VI 5.10b A3+). See his lead story earlier in this Journal for the account.

SOUTH GREENLAND

Tasermiut Fjord, Nalumasortoq, Left-hand pillar British Route, second ascent. John Dickey, Evan Stevens, and myself arrived in Nanortalik in late July. The starting point for our expedition was a lot more hospitable than we imagined, providing groceries (to replace what we threw away to make the baggage limits), beer, ATM, and bad American TV in the hostel. The following day, after a four-hour boat ride into the fjord, we were racking up to get on Pingasut, a prominent pyramid-shaped peak. Sixteen hours later we returned to base camp hungry and thirsty but having repeated an existing line of around 5.10 in standard. On top of that peak we knew why Greenland was a popular climbing destination; the 360° view showed at least 20 big walls rising

3,000 feet out of the sea about 15 miles away. They lay between us and the Polar Ice Cap, The Tasermiut Fjord has an endless supply of granite to rival any place on earth. It was here that we got our first real glimpse of our main goal; Nalumasortoq.

After being turned back on an attempt to establish a new route on an unclimbed peak, we decided to focus our energy on the original goal; a one-day ascent of Nalumasortoq. Several days humping loads were needed before we could establish our second advanced camp in a week. From our new position, we were able to scope most of the lines on the 1800-foot wall. decided to attempt the probable second ascent of the original route on the pillars, the 1995 British Route up the center of the Left-hand Pillar, climbed by Anderson, Dring, Dring, and Tattersall at British E4 and A2. Following Yvon Chouinard's advice from many years ago, we had been using Yosemite's walls as our training ground and felt that the fast and light skills we had gained would help us complete the ascent

With a few liters of water, a handful of energy bars and some warm coats, we started climbing at 8 a.m. on August 3. We fixed no ropes nor did we have any detailed information on the route. However, the line is unmistakable, following a single amazing crack and corner system up the dead vertical wall for 17 pitches. Climbing in blocks and short fixing as much as possible, we were able to free most of the classic crack climbing at 5.10 to 5.11 and never used our hammers (which was good because we only had about four pins). Early in the day, Evan dislodged a rock while leading and it zeroed in on the belay below. The rock tagged my hand and helmet, causing me to black out for a few seconds. After a short but violent release of four letter words I decided my hand might not be broken and I could keep going. Ten hours later I was in the midst of seven-pitch block, climbing through the four-hour night with a headlamp to take us through to the top. All John and Evan had to do was hold the break rope, jumar and watch the most marvellous display of Aurora Borealis that we had ever seen.

After 18 hours of continuous climbing we topped out a little after 4 a.m., catching the first glimpses of sunrise. We treated ourselves to a victory summit nap, ate our last pack of gel and started the 17 raps back to the ground. The next thing we knew we were eating Wasa and Nutella in our base camp cave, enjoying our unbelievable weather and relishing possibly the first one-day ascent of Nalumasortoq. Evan Stevens and I were both recipients of Lyman Spitzer and Fellowship grants for 2002.

MICAH DASH, *AAC*

Tasermiut Fjord, Nalumasortoq new route and other ascents. On July 15 Chris Chitty, Ari Menitove, and I departed for Nanortalik, taking a week to arrive from the States. From there we traveled by boat into the Tasermiut Fjord. The ride proved spectacular as we passed enormous sea cliffs and coastal peaks. At the drop-off site we unloaded gear and food, then got our first taste of the relentless mosquito and fly attacks. The boat would come back for us in 28 days.

Our first climb was a new route on Nalumasortoq, located just right of the Original Left Pillar (1995 British Route), marked incorrectly in AAJ 2001, p.265. Our route started approximately 30' to the right of the 1995 line in an obvious left-leaning crack system. It eventually merged with the 1995 Left Pillar at a sloping ledge that we called Banana Ledge. Our route then shared the final four pitches of the Left Pillar. We named this route Ekstra Lagret (750m, 14 pitches; V 5.11a A2) after the extremely odorous cheese we ate on the route. We guessed that Ekstra Lagret must have meant "extra stinky" in Danish. We fixed the first 800' of the climb on

Nalumasortoq, in the Tasermiut Fjord. Identified routes are (left to right): 1. Jumping Zack Flash (IV 5.10 A2, Chitty-Menitove-Su, 2002). 2. Left Pillar route (E4 A2, 1995)—included to eliminate confusion with Ekstra Lagret route, since they are next to each other. 3. Ekstra Lagret (V 5.11a A2, Chitty-Menitove-Su, 2002). 4. Non C'e Due Senza Tre with variation on the finish (6c A3, 2000).

July 22 but due to rain and snowstorms had to wait another four days before returning to finish the route. We topped out in clear cold moonlit conditions, after being on the face for 16 or so hours. We left no fixed gear on the route and rappelled the British Route. The climbing was straightforward, following excellent cracks on solid rock with one short face section aided with hooks. The route would be a brilliant free climb, with the crack climbing at 5.11d and the face section at around 5.12a.

Our next route took us to the top of the unclimbed spire left of Nalumasortoq. We referred to this formation as Little Nalum. I later named our route Jumpin' Zack Flash (400m, 8 pitches, IV 5.10 A2,) in memory of my friend Zack Martin. He was planning to visit this area in 2003 to climb some of the virgin formations that I had showed him in photographs. Due to the featureless slabs directly below the climb, the approach to our new route involved traversing a long ramp The first pitch was the crux and involved a short section of aid using a beak and some RPs in a shallow left-facing dihedral. We free climbed the rest of the route following crisp hand to offwidth cracks splitting right through the middle of the tower. Close to the summit it looked like we would be shut down. The last pitch was a slab completely covered in black lichen. It would be impossible to climb. Looking closely at the rock, I found that the huge flakes of lichen hid a crack system that led to the top. With each jam my hand completely disappeared into the lichen-covered rock. We finally reached the summit at around 11 p.m. after climbing for about 14 hours. To descend, we rapped the route. No bolts were placed on the climb but two rap stations were drilled to descend the blank slabs below the route.

Our third objective was to make the first free ascent of the French-Italian route, Non C'e Due Senza Tre (850m,19 pitches, VI 6c A3). We came close but no cigar, resting on gear for a few moves near the top. However, the A3 pitch was free climbed at 5.11a with bad gear. We felt that the overall rating of the climb was 5.11c. We climbed the route in a period of two days, fixing three pitches on the first day. The climbing took us into the night on the second day, and high on the route we were fortunate enough to catch a display of the northern lights. It started as a faint green glow and then spread intensely through the sky like wild fire—talk about some major tracers. On the last pitch we could not figure out where the route went and rested on a large ledge until dawn. That morning we found a pin and bolt not far off the ledge. The climbing above the bolt was unprotected and involved face climbing on lichen-covered rock. The route did not seem probable, so I lowered off the bolt, which, coincidently, already had a carabiner. After our ascent another team also backed down from the bolt due to route finding difficulties. To finish the route we made a long traverse to the right, searching for a passage to the top. Finally, I found a way. However, it wasn't pretty—a wet, overhanging offwidth crack. Chris and Ari looked up in disgust, so I guessed I was leading. I aided through the wet section and then groveled up the rest of the 50' offwidth. This put us at the summit ridge, where I made an easy traverse to the top. To my surprise I could not find any anchor left by the first ascent team. I traversed back to the belay and we set up the first numerous rappel anchors leading back to the ground.

In communication with Jérôme Arpin, a member of the first ascent team, he mentioned that he aided past the bolt (where the carabiner was left) until easy ground could be reached. After summiting, he down-climbed due to rope shortage and then rappelled.

STEVE SU, *AAC*

Ari Menitove taking the express line on Ekstra Lagret. Steve Su

Jumpin' Zack Flash ascends the prominent chimney-like feature in the center of the face. Steve Su

Mexico

CHIHUAHUA

PARQUE NACIONAL CASCADA DE BASASEACHIC

El Gigante, Faded Glory. In November Alard Hüfner (South Africa) and Brent Edelen (U.S.) established a 14-pitch wall route on El Gigante's nose (between the northwest and southwest faces). Jakub Gajda (Czech Rep.) began the climb but descended due to rockfall concerns. The route was climbed ground-up with minimal fixing and minimal bolts. The team was on the wall for 14 continuous days, and named their route Faded Glory (VI 5.9 A3). An article on this climb is part of an El Gigante feature earlier in this Journal.

El Gigante, Logical Progression. Over a seven-and-a-half-week period in spring Peter Baumeister (Germany), Luke Laeser (U.S.), and Bert van Lint (Belgium) established an entirely bolt-protected 28-pitch route on El Gigante's northwest face. All of the moves were climbed free, but not every pitch was redpointed. The route, Logical Progression (800m, VI 5.12c A0), has become highly controversial because it was rappel-bolted as a sport climb on a big wall. An article on the climb and a sampling of the ensuing discussion are found in the El Gigante package earlier in this Journal.

El Gigante, La Conjura de los Necios, second ascent. In May Slovenians Tanja Grmovsek (formerly Tanja Rojs) and Andrej Grmovsek took a prehoneymoon trip to El Gigante, where they repeated the 2001 German route, La Conjura de los Necios (The Conspiracy of Fools, 800m, 23 pitches, 5.13a). They report serious and "interesting" climbing, heavily vegetated, with poor rock and very long runouts. Andrej freed the entire route, onsight, reporting the hardest pitch to be actually around 5.12c but emphasizing the danger and overall difficulty of the route. A short article on this ascent is part of the El Gigante package earlier in this Journal.

DURANGO

El Peñón (Cerro) Blanco, El Vedauwoo. In March, on the 800'+ south face of Cerro Blanco, Todd Skinner and I established a new line to the right of the rightmost line pictured on p. 290 of the *AAJ* 2002, joining this existing line at the very top of the wall. El Vedauwoo ascends the huge, obvious crack in five 180' pitches. On pitch three, at the crux unprotected 5.11+ offwidth, vertical plates of shit rock were falling off in our hands, then delicate climbing with no pro for a hundred feet, a tied-off dirt clod for the belay. Yet the first two pitches were gorgeous white granite, 5.9-5.10 crack climbing through giant yucca plants, and the last two pitches on similarly stellar stone—a 5.7 chimney followed by a 5.10 water-groove face pitch which Todd couldn't protect for the first 50'. Bivied on top with no food, no water, no extra clothes. Perfect little adventure for old Vedauwoo craggers.

MARK JENKINS, *AAC*

NUEVO LEÓN

PARQUE NACIONAL CUMBRES DE MONTERREY

Cañón de la Huasteca, Cañón de San Judas, Pico José Pereyra, Peyote Brujo. Paul Vera is a local climber in Monterrey who invited José Pereyra (Venezuela) to climb in the area. Francisco Medina (Mexico) was invited to a meeting at Paul's house, where he met José for the first time. Paul and José discussed different climbing projects in La Huasteca, and José proposed a climb in San Judas canyon based on a picture of this wall. They agreed and invited Francisco to participate in the attempt. Due to the long approach, the idea had only been a dream for Paul and Francisco.

On December 10 they started the approach on horses. One of the horses could not continue and they had to split the extra load. They reached base camp by morning on the 11th, but continued to porter gear until the next day. Paul made some climbing attempts later on the 12th but could not find a route. On December 13, Francisco returned to Monterrey for a night and came back to base camp on the 14th. By then, José and Paul had trad-climbed the first two pitches and fixed a rope to the anchor. A third pitch was accomplished on Sunday the 15th, and a new anchor was bolted by Paul and Francisco, while José and friend Ian Wolf kept portering gear from the distant van.

On December 16 they made an advanced camp, with portaledges, at pitch three, at the base of a wall emerging from this point. For the next two days they attempted a fourth pitch without success, but on the 19th Francisco was able to complete it. This proved to be one of the most difficult of the climb. José continued with a fifth pitch and they all descended to the advanced camp.

The sixth pitch was accomplished by Paul on the 20th. This was a very dusty crack with moving plates and falling rocks. This was very difficult and eventually Paul successfully climbed it with hooks, and installed a rivet hanger and a bolt. They slept again in the advanced camp.On December 21, José and Paul decided on a one push ascent—Francisco had never heard this term before and learned what "one push" meant only when he was asked to lead in the middle of the night, after a full day climbing. The trio climbed to their highest position and continued with a mixture of aid and free. José led the pitch seven, Paul completed pitch eight in the dark, and Francisco climbed the ninth in the middle of the night, finishing at 4 a.m. the next day. José crowned the route with the final 10th pitch. On December 22 they reached the summit and descended to advanced camp. They rested and descended to base camp the next day, then returned to Monterrey on Dec. 24. For route photo and description, see: http://www.aventu-raverde.com/escalada/topos/pereyra1.htm. More information about this climb's location may be found on www.XPMexico.com.

They named the route Peyote Brujo, and the peak was baptized days later in memory of José Pereyra, who died while climbing in Potrero Chico (Mexico) the week after this ascent.

FRANCISCO MEDINA, *Mexico (summarized and translated from Medina by Rodulfo Araujo)*

Cañón de la Huasteca, El Pico Erin, Hunab Ku. Access to this area, located in the municipality of Santa Catarina, is easy: once in the park follow the paved main road for approximately three miles, to where the road turns to gravel. Continue and turn right at the sign "Virikute," found

Tatwarí and Pico Erin, showing Cola de Venado on Tatewarí (left, 2001), Hunab Ku (2002), and Lobsang Dolma (2002). Carlos Garcia

beside the road on the ground. This road leads to the Guitarritas Canyon.

In this area are two quality rock walls: 550m Tatewarí, with two sport routes and, right of Tatewarí, 540m El Pico Erin. El Pico Erin has one traditional route (5.10- A2+), opened by Francisco Medina and Paúl Vera (originally from the city of Monterrey) in the summer of 2002. (Note: A report on this route, Lobsang Dolma, was unavailable at press time. However, a photo and some information can be found at: http://www.aventuraverde.com/escalada/topos/topoframe.html) Medina and Vera provided us with information about El Pico.

Our route, Hunab Ku (which means "life" and "movement" in the Mayan language), was opened in December and is the first sport route on Pico Erin. Mauricio Hernández Sanders, Pablo Iván García Martínez, and I climbed as a team of three, with one porter. We climbed free, but hung from hooks to drill and place bolts. We placed 86 bolts, including belay stations, which were in huecos of excellent rock quality and very clean of vegetation. This project took us five days on the wall; we climbed 11 pitches averaging 40m in length. We descended via our route. The route, which we rate V 5.11+, indicates the wall's potential for multipitch climbs on excellent rock.

LUIS CARLOS GARCÍA AYALA, *Mexico (translated by M. Loomis)*

El Zapatero, Leones y Osos. Beginning March 24, Zack Martin and Sven Krebs established 12 pitches on an unclimbed wall in a remote valley. Traveling on dirt roads slashed across immense mountains south of Monterrey to the Parque Nacional Cumbres de Monterrey, the team found dozens of towering limestone walls up to 600m in height.

With only five days, the team chose a highly accessible wall close to the floor of the canyon. According to the local rancheros, the mountain was named El Zapatero (The Shoemaker) and had seen no ascent via its steep face. The only recorded ascent is thought to have been by Pocha Via, centuries earlier. Local legend claims that while escaping authorities, Pocha Via climbed the steep flanks of the mountain and hid gold in the caves that are precariously perched in the face and only accessible by a dangerous scramble above a 1000-foot drop. The peak bears no resemblance to a shoemaker, and no local seemed to know why the name was chosen. They did, however, join in the climb by cheering and shooting guns as the team pried dangerous rocks from the face while cleaning the route. An Easter weekend feast brought dozens of Mexicans with lawn chairs to the small farms below the route and along the river. The local's encouragement was appreciated during the dry, desert ascent.

The Leones y Osos route on El Zapatero. Richard Durnan

Over five days the team completed 12 steep limestone pitches with difficulties up to 5.11b. The pitches were protected by a mix of bolts placed on lead and natural protection dubiously placed in limestone. Steep faces were negotiated using thin edges and pockets, which connect natural belay stances throughout the wall. Following the path of least resistance the climbers wove a path through cactus, thorns, reptiles, and large green parrots to complete the ascent. On the lower headwall parrots swooped and cawed, reminding the climbers that the face was not for them. High on the route Sven was nearly bitten by a baby rattlesnake while leading, and remained alert for the next potentially fatal encounter with nature.

As if the angry parrots and the threat of sunning rattlesnakes was not enough, the threat of being eaten by a wild animal wore on the minds of the climbers. The team named the route Leones y Osos (Lions and Bears, 12 pitches, IV 5.11b) after an evening discussion with a local landowner who told stories of the bears and mountain lions that live in the valley. He warned the

Zachary "Zack" Tyler Martin, on El Zapatero's Leones y Osos. Richard Durnan

team not to take long walks high on mountains and to never go out alone, for the animals were known to eat those who did. Richard Durnan ascended with the team and shot photographs.

ZACK MARTIN

Peru

CORDILLERA BLANCA

Alpamayo to north ridge, Sensations of History. On August 8 the Catalans Josep Escruela and Tino Tain climbed the gully to the right of the Ferrari Route. From the Alpamayo–Quitaraju pass they reached the start of the Spanish–Chilean Route, subsequently climbing to the left along the base of the bergschrund before crossing it at the start of the French Gully. They climbed 120m leftward across 45°–50° slopes to reach the left-hand gully. Precarious curtains of 90°–95° ice, with poor belays, led to a narrow gully between the Ferrari Route and the French Gully. The gully was climbed, mostly on 60°–75° ice and snow, to the north ridge. They descended the Ferrari Route without continuing to the summit. The team estimated that the route was 400m long, with a UIAA grade of ED, 45°–60°–95°. They called it Sensations of History.

ANTONIO GÓMEZ BOHÓRQUEZ, *Spain (translated by José Luis Bermúdez)*

Taulliraju, east buttress, second ascent. Possibly the most notable event in the Blanca during 2002 was not the creation of a new route but the second ascent of a major line that had remained unrepeated for 20 years. Over eight days from June 26 to July 3 the talented French trio of Stéphane Benoist, Patrice Glairon-Rappaz, and Patrick Pessi made the first complete repeat of Taulliraju's East (Right-Hand) Buttress (Fowler-Watts, 1982) on the southwest face. Although the group has an impressive collective resumé, including the second winter ascent of the Gousseault route, a winter repeat of Rolling Stone, and a solo of No Siesta, all on the north face of the Grandes Jorasses, plus the first ascent of the difficult north face of Chuchubalstering in the Hindu Raj (and Pessi had just led 8b before the trip), they found the route to be the hardest they had climbed in their lives.

    The line is obvious, but even the elite Blanca activist Nicolas Jaeger had decided it was not for him in 1978, and moved well right to climb the shorter south face to the upper south-southeast ridge. Three Japanese, who climbed a hard direct route up the south face in 1976, probably also had the southwest face in mind. It was left to the British pair of Mick Fowler and Chris Watts, on their first expedition to altitude, to complete a test piece that subsequently defeated a number of strong parties. Fowler and Watts, both leading very hard pitches (Fowler took his first fall as a second) and both climbing with packs except on one pitch, spent four-and-a-half days on the route, reaching the 5,830m summit on May 28, 1982. There was superb ice, difficult aid on the generally sound but compact granite, and the usual Peruvian excavating and groveling. One particularly memorable pitch involved an overhanging chimney behind a large, free-hanging icicle. The 800m route was solid ED3 and had difficulties that could probably be rated V A3+ AI6. It was done in perfect, though cold, weather.

Last summer the weather was not obliging for the three French. Apart from the clear and sunny first and last days, it was generally overcast with some snowfall. The trio fixed the first 60m, already aiding where they expected free-climbing, and continued in alpine style with a large haul bag, using bivouac sacks rather than a tent. They reached the top after 30 pitches and six bivouacs, the last just three short pitches below the summit. The icicle seems to have been too fragile to climb, but Pessi managed to aid the wall just to the right, with a long reach at the start that was only possible for someone of his 6'2" height. He then moved carefully over the top ice bulge. The team used a lot of aid (to New Wave A2), free-climbed only one rock section, and confirmed the AI6 rating (sections of 90°–95°). Only one peg was found in place on the entire route. The three descended by rappel. This was another fine French effort in the Cordillera Blanca and was short-listed for the Piolet d'Or. It confirmed, if confirmation was needed, that the first ascent in 1982 set a new benchmark in Peruvian climbing.

LINDSAY GRIFFIN, *High Mountain INFO*

Santa Cruz Chico, east face to within 20m of summit. Scottish-based Jason Currie and Guy Robertson made a new route up the east face of the rarely climbed Santa Cruz Chico (a.k.a. Atuncocha), the 5,800m peak on the ridge between Santa Cruz (6,259m) and Santa Cruz Norte (5,829m). The face is not big and appears largely rocky, but before last year was unclimbed. The only previous recorded line on the mountain seems to be the 1958 American Route (Michael-Ortenburger-Ortenburger).

The Scottish pair reached base camp on July 7 and made their first attempt on the 13th. They tried a single-day push up the center of the face but came to a halt 150m below the summit, being forced to retreat, dehydrated, the following day. On the 17th they tried again, making a very early start and carrying a stove, though no bivouac gear. They first climbed three pitches (75°–80°) up a gully left of the toe of a rock spur in the center of the face, then, after a short rock pitch, followed a 60° gully and snow slopes to a very steep rock band. This was overcome at A1. Above, the pair climbed up right through mushrooms and seracs to a couloir leading to the summit ridge. They climbed the couloir (100m, 55°) to the crest of the ridge and eventually stopped 20m short of the summit due to typical Peruvian unstable cornice formations. A rappel descent was made of the route largely using rock anchors and Abalakov threads. Although there was around 600m of climbing, the height of the face was no more than 400m and the route graded Alpine TD. The pair report that the weather was generally stable throughout their stay in the mountains.

LINDSAY GRIFFIN, *High Mountain INFO*

Abasraju to summit ridge, Moonlighting. On July 7 Tony Barton (U.K.) and I climbed a new route (Moonlighting, 11 pitches, TD) on the west-southwest face of Abasraju (5,550m). There is only one other route on the face, and it goes up to the left of the summit. Our route is an almost vertical line approximately 200m to the right of the summit. At the base of the face, directly below the summit, is a small rock buttress. To the right is another larger rock buttress. Between the two is a snow funnel that leads up to an ice runnel. We followed this into mixed ground and then out into névé runnels which led to a more open face with soft snow. Finally, below the large cornice we traversed right to find a way to the summit ridge. We didn't go to the summit because of the snow conditions.

NICK CARTER, *Glasgow University Mountaineering Club*

La Esfinge, Variante Checa. In June we had the opportunity to attempt to open a big-wall variation on La Esfinge (5,350m). David Font, from Cataluña, Spain, a Mexican friend Emiliano Villanueva, one porter, and I joined as a team. We climbed the first pitch of Papas Rellenas, then traversed left to the route Lobo Estepario. We opened a new pitch to the right of Lobo Estepario. We then climbed the third pitch of Riddle of the Cordillera. Between Via Gringos and Riddle we opened a new pitch that reaches the belay station of Gringos. At this point, after two days of climbing, we fixed ropes and descended.

Two days later we returned to the wall and continued the ascent, climbing the sixth and seventh pitches of Via Gringos. On the eighth pitch we deviated to the right, into a dihedral that forms a chimney and passes through a small roof. We opened the following six pitches, using natural belay stations and rivets, until we found a traverse to the right that ascends directly to the summit. (These last two pitches had been climbed by a previous party.)

The 16-pitch route involved two nights and two and a half days on the wall, with a difficulty of VI 5.10d A2+. During our ascent a fatal accident occurred to a Czech climber on the Cruz del Sur route. For this reason we named our route Variante Checa.

Emiliano Villanueva (Mexico) and Marius Bagnati (Brazil) completed the third ascent of Cruz del Sur a few days after we climbed Variante Checa.

LUIS CARLOS GARCÍA AYALA, *Mexico (translated by Molly Loomis)*

Chacraraju Oeste, Jaeger Route, solo. The 24 year-old French alpinist Didier Jourdain completed a solo ascent of the 700m Jaeger Route (TD+/ED1) on the south face of Chacraraju Oeste (6,001m). This line, first climbed solo on July 5, 1978 by the legendary French mountaineer

Via Traversiade, on the south face of Pisco Oeste. Richard Hidalgo

Nicolas Jaeger follows the broad couloir between two ice ribs/flutes leading directly to the summit. Jourdain, carrying no stove or bivouac equipment, took 15 hours for the ascent and a further seven hours to rappel the route. Confirming once again that the crux of most Peruvian routes is reaching the summit, Jourdain took four hours to overcome the last 100m.

LINDSAY GRIFFIN, *High Mountain INFO*

Pisco Oeste, Via Traversiade. On the south face of Pisco Oeste (5,752m) on August 21 Italians Tarcisio Bello, Ivan Camolini, Michele Grigenti, and Bruno Castegnaro climbed what may be a new route, Via Traversiade (TD+, 90°) in 10 hours from the base of the wall. (Many routes ascend

the south face of this popular mountain but not all are well documented, making new route research difficult.) After climbing nearly to the summit ridge, just below and left of the summit, they were forced to rappel 30m and traverse right to gain the summit on very difficult ice (90°–95°, some aid). The line is thought to be between the 1977 (Bougnaud-Vallençant-Barrand) and 1981 (Bougnaud-Wilson) routes.

RICHARD HIDALGO, *Peru*

Huandoy Sur, Crise del fe. What a crazy idea we had! Five young guys—Yann Bonneville, Benoit Chanal, Francois Dupety, Pierrick Keller, and Theo Dubois—suddenly decided to travel to a mythical destination, not yet knowing exactly where. Finally we chose Peru. Now we needed to decide which mountain to climb. The name Huandoy Sur entered the discussion. "Why? Don't you know of anything steeper?" Benoit asked

Pierrick Keller looking for something cold and steep on Huandoy Sur. *Benoît Chanal*

jokingly. No, I don't. Maybe that's why Huandoy Sur. Anyway, we set to work. We tried to find sponsors, but due to our organizational skills and lack of time, we didn't receive sponsorship. Oh well! We'll go anyway and see what we can do! In the end, some friends helped us gather enough gear to attack this monster.

We began climbing on July 26, and the initial pitches seemed difficult, cold, and committing. For several days the mountain seemed so far above our level that we were hesitant to commit. Each day came down to scratching our way a few meters higher. And then, as I read in a famous passage, "It's necessary to shatter the myths, to go too far too fast, what's important is that you feel ready mentally." There was nothing to do but keep up our morale.

After doubt concerning the conditions came doubt concerning the objective dangers. Getting hit in the head by a falling rock hurts, but when it happens twice, then three times, then

The line of Crise del fe, on Huandoy Sur. Pierrick Keller

becomes routine, you begin to ask what you're doing there. But after evaluating the risks we had already taken, we decided to continue.

The summit, which we gained on August 21 at 5:15 p.m., was a huge relief. The face was definitely a learning experience but not impossible. While climbing we managed to find a little pleasure, but not the rest of the time. You have no desire to jug up the fixed lines again, simply loading your pack is exhausting, your hands are trashed, and women are nowhere to be seenæall good reasons for turning back! However, the attitude of the group was excellent, and the visits and support from women at camp allowed us to keep our spirits up and finally arrive at the summit, exhausted but HAPPY! We called our route Crise del fe (900m, ED+ 6a A4 M5). *(This route ascends the overhanging granite wall left of the Desmaison Route (1972), then continues with the Casarotto–Da Polenza Route (1976), on vertical mixed ground with bad rock, to intersect the southwest ridge, which they followed for the final 100 vertical meters to the summit—Ed.)*

PIERRICK KELLER, *France (translated by Todd Miller)*

Note: Confusion exists regarding the terminology used to describe Nevado Ulta's north and west aspects. The broad face, shown with two route lines in AAJ 2001 (p. 275), was labeled "northwest face," and many climbers refer to it as such. Other climbers, however, call this the "west face," or " west-northwest face." In the interest of consistency, in the reports below we call this the west-northwest face and the adjacent feature (which has been called the north or northwest face or bowl) the northwest bowl—Ed.

Nevado Ulta to summit ridge cornices, northwest bowl. At midnight on July 8 Brits Al Powell and Owen Samuel left a high bivy below the glacier and headed for Ulta's prominent, unclimbed northwest bowl. Their route ascends the couloir to the right of the dividing rib that is prominent in the photo in the *AAJ* 2001 (p. 275) and continues up the headwall. They crossed the glacier, headed up the snow cone for several hundred meters and up an initial, wet icefall. That took them into a snow bowl, followed by steep ramps that led to the main lower couloir. Steep runnels (Scottish 5) then took them to a steep, run-out icefall (Scottish 5) and a big left-trending 50°–60° ice scoop in the middle of the face (Scottish 4). This led to the base of the obvious headwall. They bivied to the right, chopping a site from an ice fin. The first day involved 14–15 pitches and 15 hours of climbing.

On the second day the climbers ascended a shallow corner for 15m, then up and left for another 40m. This proved to be the crux pitch, with some Scottish 7 mixed (but decent protection). A 60m pitch of Scottish 5/6 ice led to a bay. The pair went left, across a ramp, for 60m to a small rock step and gully, then up the gully, then left to a steep rock wall covered with icicles. They continued on scary, dangerous ice and snow-covered rock that involved a few 10m A1 sections. They then trended right, into a scoop, then up and left into a couloir. This they climbed for two pitches (Scottish 4/5, bad pro) to an enormous snow mushroom guarding access to the summit. They'd been climbing for about 14 hours when they found a relatively comfortable bivouac spot below some cornices; here they stayed the night. The next day they rappelled the route, mostly on ice threads. They report considerable rockfall in the lower section when the sun hits the face. The overall grade for the route was about ED2.

OWEN SAMUEL, *U.K. and*
LINDSAY GRIFFIN, *High Mountain INFO*

Nevado Ulta, northwest bowl, attempt. After aborting our plan to climb the southeast face of Jirishanca (6,126m) in the Cordillera Huayhuash, due to storm and illness, Jeremy Frimer (Canada) and I returned to the Cordillera Blanca in July and attempted a new route on the northwest bowl of Nevado Ulta (5,875m). The first day we followed a system of ramps on the left side of the face, to avoid the major rockfall gully in the center of the face. A strenuous pitch up vertical mixed terrain allowed us to leave the ramp system and start up impeccable ice flutings below the first main rock band. We dug an uncomfortable bivy out of a small scoop at ca 5,450m. The next day we climbed toward the rock band two-thirds of the way up the imposing face. We tackled it with a rightward traversing line, connecting ice ramps and broken granite.

Yanik Berube enjoying the combination of steep rock and a big pack during his attempt on the northwest bowl of Nevado Ulta. Jeremy Frimer

The northwest bowl of Nevado Ulta, showing the Berube-Frimer attempt (left) and the Powell-Samuel near-miss.

After climbing numerous ice pitches into the night, we fashioned a bivy platform by hacking a notch in the crest of a fluting at ca 5,700m. We were now about 16 pitches up. A strong snowstorm blew in during the night, forcing us to retreat on the third day, a hard decision since we were within 80m of the northeast ridge, where most difficulties would have ended. Our committing descent, involving multiple traversing rappels, lasted about 10 hours and included one 60m free rappel. Difficulties up to our high point were 5.8 A2 M5 AI4. Thanks to the Mugs Stump Award for supporting our trip.

YANIK BERUBE, *Canada*

Nevado Ulta to summit ridge, west-northwest face, solo. The two days of walking, battling for space in chicken-filled collectivos, and bus transport played hell with my battered body. Al Powell and I had been attempting a new line on the southeast face of Jirishanca in the Huayhuash. Feeling the pressure of time and competition, we had forced the issue a little and paid the price. I had been hit by an avalanche that threw me 200' down the gully nicknamed, aptly, the Death Couloir. Powell joined in the fun for a way but got spit out, becoming my knight in shining armor and digging me from my snowy resting point.

Arriving in Huaraz I was placed on the scrap-heap for broken mountaineers. Powell joined with Owen Samuel to try a line on Ulta's unclimbed northwest bowl. Having sprained ligaments in my knee and shoulder and torn muscles in my groin, back, and ribs, I was faced with an early return to Britain. Listening to the Powell–Samuel battle plan and watching bags being packed was torture. I could take no more, so I doubled the dose of anti-inflamatories and packed my bag, too. In five minutes the job was completed: an ice screw, harness, 50m of 7mm cord, and two axes—I was prepared! I packed extra pills at the expense of food. Keeping my sack light seemed the only way possible for me to complete the approach.

Unsure of my mental state and my ability to climb, I set off with Powell and Samuel the following day, June 7. Eventually, after much grimacing, I joined the pair as they stood beneath the Eigerlike face. Their intended line ran up the height of the face on dripping icicles that were melting rapidly. Having only come for "a look" and maybe to take a photo or two, I wished them well and limped off for a glance around the corner at the west-northwest face.

Watching pin pricks of light move up to the northwest bowl at 11 p.m., I snuggled into my bag feeling no pressure whatever—it was a miracle I had made it up to here. An hour later I set off on my chemically enhanced adventure, moving slowly to reduce the depth of my breathing—an attempt to alleviate the pain from torn intercostal muscles. It didn't work. Harboring secret ambitions that a direct line, climbing the left side of the west-northwest face, might go, I picked my way up the steep ice-slope beneath the face. The mushrooms on the summit ridge had appeared small when I scoped the face on the taxi-drive in, but only time would tell.

Crossing thin bridges over monster crevasses made me glad I had nothing except washing line in my sack. The ice was perfect; my trashed body, in a Voltarol (anti-inflammatory)-induced numbness, appeared to be coping with the demands of the climbing. Steady WI3/4 following deep flutings led to the middle of the face. A left-rising traverse was made to join a series of runnels. In the dark they appeared to be continuous, running up the left side of the face. The climbing became more tenuous and steeper in the runnels, thin ice covering compact rock, until, about six pitches from the mushrooms, things got interesting. Picking my way from one thin, rotten ice patch to another focused my thinking and slowed me. Finally, just beneath the summit, the ice disappeared and was replaced with 90° rock, covered in powder. The climbing was sustained M5, and looking down 1,000' of ice made me realize that the sun was up and working its deadly, destructive powers. The need to get off the face quickly was apparent, but with only a few feet left before reaching the summit slope, I couldn't resist. Crawling between two mushrooms deposited me on the summit plateau. It had taken seven hours to reach this point, sustained climbing at an overall grade of ED1.

The need to start descending immediately, before the sun turned the face into a melting death trap, forced me not to visit the true summit. The original Bullock plan was to downclimb as much of the route as possible, but with the first few steps I discovered that lowering using the knackered left shoulder was as painful as hell. The steep ground would have been impossible to downclimb anyway, so an epic of rappelling on washing-line for 75' at a time began. I found that threading the 7mm cord directly through Abalakov threads worked well. Staring at the melting mushrooms above encouraged me to move quickly, but it still took six hours to reach the base of the face, 13.5 hours from when I started. The following day I hitched a ride in the back of a truck, and one collectivo trip deposited my broken body into Huaraz, land of cake, comfort, and pharmacies.

NICK BULLOCK, *U.K.*

Bullock was unaware of the West-northwest Face route (Earl–Trimble, 2000), and suspects that his solo roughly follows that line. Further investigation indicates that Bullock may have climbed independent ground on the right at the bottom and top, joining the Earl–Trimble line in the middle portion—Ed.

Ocshapalca, south face. Back in Huaraz after the Huayhuash, I rejoined my friend Iñigo Mujica (*Note: Baró Ramon and Mujica had climbed on Chacraraju and Jirishanca Norte. See note in*

Huayhuash section.) A team of four was descending after finishing a new route on the south face of Ocshapalca, which joined the Gato Negro (Black Cat) route two pitches from the summit. Only three of the team members—Ander, Joanfra Farreras, and Olga Torras—had been on the wall. The fourth, Akraitz Yurrita, had been suffering intestinal problems.

I suggested that we join forces on a bid to finish their route to the top. My new companions immediately agreed, so off we went. Things went smoothly, since Akraitz was familiar with the area, and we had no trouble finding traces of our friends' passage, as they had equipped the route for rappelling. We climbed rapidly, reaching our comrades' high point before noon, and forged on for another three exposed pitches on typical Peruvian snow. We reached the ridge soon after 2 p.m. After the first three rappels we reached the existing rappel route, which allowed us to reach base camp before dark. This climb took place on July 30, and I was scheduled to fly back to Spain on August 2, so the rest was a mad rush to make the flight.

ORIOL BARÓ I RAMON, *Spain (translated by Oriol Solé-Costa)*

Milpocraju to summit ridge, Goulotte Gau Txoni. Kepa Escribano from Spain and Cristina Prieto from Chile climbed a new route on the west face of the 5,310m north summit of Milpocraju, located just south of the spectacular, well-known Nevado Cayesh. The ascent took place on August 1, the pair climbing a 330m couloir to finish on the ridge some distance left (north) of the summit. A direct line to the highest point was well-defended by a large and active barrier of seracs. Goulotte Gau Txoni starts with relatively straightforward 45°–60° slopes, which give access to a steep, mixed central section (60°–80° and IV+). The left end of the serac barrier must then be breached (50°) to reach the summit ridge. The pair rappelled from this point. They thought the route warranted an overall grade of around TD.

This is the first route on the west face of the north summit, though the west face of the main summit has been climbed by at least two lines—in June 1985 by the British team of Derwin, Gore, Hinkes, Payne, Peter, and Thorn (TD-, 60°–80°) and in June 1986 by Gigliotti and Marchini, who probably followed the British line to the snowfield and then climbed about 200m left of the upper gully to reach the summit directly.

LINDSAY GRIFFIN, *High Mountain INFO*

Punta Numa, Hasta Luego, Zorro (So Long, Fox). (This report serves as an addendum to p. 303 of the AAJ 2002—Ed.) Our route on Punta Numa (5,179m), located in the Huantsan Group of the Quebrada Rurec, is dedicated to El Zorro, the bashful base camp fox and invited guest at every dinner. Roberto Iannilli and I completed the 1,200m route on August 2, 2001, after seven days of climbing, rating it EX+ (7a free-climbing and A3+ artificial climbing). The first twelve pitches were equipped with fixed ropes, now removed. The rock is good but mossy, especially in the cracks. Belays are equipped with hardware for the descent. The last two pitches are shared with the Spanish route Monttrek.

LUCIANO MASTRACCI, *Italy*

Cordillera Blanca, clarifications and corrections. AAJ *correspondent Antonio Gómez Bohórquez, a noted Cordillera Blanca climbing researcher, sent the following notes regarding reports in the 2002*

AAJ. In writing us with these corrections and clarifications he emphasized, "I would appreciate it if…you keep in mind that it is not my intention to call into question the veracity of the people mentioned in my corrections. Thanks"—Ed.

Santa Cruz Norte, West Face, correction. The June 12, 2001 attempt (*AAJ* 2002, pp. 294-295) of Jay Burbee, Jeremy Frimer, and Michel van der Speck on the "unclimbed" west face of Santa Cruz Norte was a repetition of the first part of the route climbed on July 24, 1967 by Akira Miyashita, Mitsuaki Nishigori, Takehiko Hayashi, and Kazutomo Kobayashi (Nishigori in *Sangaku,* vol. LXIII, 1968). The Japanese expedition climbed this route, gained the west ridge, and continued along it to the summit. It is incorrect to say that the west face had not been climbed and that the west ridge remains unclimbed.

Tuctubamba, Middle Earth, correction. The mountain that Topher and Patience Donahue ascended—also climbed a few days later by Clay Wadman and Christian Beckwith (*AAJ* 2002, p. 296)—is not Tuctubamba. The summit that they reached, closer and immediately to the southeast of Taulliraju Principal, could be considered Taulliraju Sur (South) or Taulliraju Sureste (Southeast). The peak is marked on sheet 0/3a of the 2002 edition of the Austrian Alpine Club map, where it is shown with an altitude of 5,400m (see also sheet 18-h of the Instituto Geográfico Militar del Perú map). It is a characteristically sharp summit of ice and granite, confused in various publications with Nevado Tuctubamba, climbed by the Italians Andrea Farina and Nino Poloni in July 1960. The Donahue climb may be the first ascent of Taulliraju Sur, because it is unknown whether it was ascended since the attempt of Tomaz Strupi and Tone Stern on July 8, 1995. This Slovenian team encountered the remains of climbing gear on the northeast face—to the right of the Donahue route—and descended from the northeast ridge before gaining the summit.

Caraz II, south face variation, correction. The caption for the photo on page 299 of the *AAJ* 2002 says, "Descent is behind left skyline." This phrase contradicts the final paragraph of the note by Matic Jost (p. 300). Jost describes descending Caraz II's original route, the 1955 route of Hermann Huber and Alfred Koch, which is the Northeast Ridge—the right skyline in the photo. From the summit, these Germans descended the ridge until close to the false summit, then the shorter 55°–60° couloir on the southeast face. From a radical point of view, if the climb of Fisher, Warfield, and Sheldrake in 1986 is considered an attempt, because they only reached the northeast ridge, the climb of Mlinar and Jost could be considered a new route, because they gained the summit or, for the purest mentality, a true variation of Huber-Koch route of 1955.

Artesonraju, northeast face, correction. The route climbed in June 2000 by Nemesio Matalobos and Ángel Terrén (*AAJ* 2002, p. 300) indeed seems to be a repeat, with a small variation, of Tim Ammons and Peter Kelemen's route (July 1977) on the left (eastern) side of the northeast face (*AAJ* 1978, pp. 563-4). It is also worth clarifying that the route done in August 1965 by Georg Hartmann, Ernst Reiss, Ruedi Schatz, and Eugen Steiger on the northeast face (*AAJ* 1966, pp. 166-7), joins the North Ridge route climbed by Germans Erwin Hein and Erwin Schneider in August 1932. The Swiss expedition of 1965 climbed 200 steep meters on the north ridge and continued to the summit, and authors such as Ricker (*Yuraq Janka*) consider the 1965 route a variation of the 1932 route. These routes begin to the right of the East Ridge route done in July

1971 by Burton Janis, George Lowe, Mike Lowe, and Leigh Ortenburger, which had been previously climbed by Peter Gessner, Michl Steinbeis, Alfred Koch, and Helmut Schmidt in July 1966. This forgotten and ignored German first ascent, possibly the third to the summit of Artesonraju, was reported in the *AAJ* 1967, p. 388; the final part being climbed by Ammons and Kelemen.

Huandoy Sur, Oro del Inca, correction. The route that Slovenian Pavle Kozjek climbed in August 1995 and reported as new, calling it Oro del Inca (Inca Gold) (*AAJ* 1996, p. 215, and *AAJ* 2002, p. 301), had been ascended unroped by Albi Sole and Greg Spohr in June 1979 and repeated by Mary Ábrego, Javier Muru, and Gerardo Plaza in May 1980. The only new ground covered by Kozjek is a variation that avoids the initial horizontal rock barrier, via climbing at the far right side, and connects with the 1979 Canadian route. Therefore, the phrase in the final paragraph of Kozjek's 2002 note, "my fifth new route on big walls of the Cordillera Blanca" is incorrect. Likewise, it is important to clarify that the route descended by Kozjek (indicated in the photo in the *AAJ* 1996, p. 216) is not that ascended by Yves Astier. The French guide's ascent paralleled the Canadian route and led directly to the ice flute situated just to the left of the summit, that reaches a little further on the west ridge.

Palcaraju Oeste, Tocllaraju Sur, correction. Eduardo Mondragón and Martín Waldhoer did not ascend Palcaraju Oeste (*AAJ* 2002, p. 301) but Tocllaraju Sur, a secondary summit that some publications erroneously call Palcaraju Oeste or "Palcaraju Norte of some 5,750m." The cartography edited in 1939 by the German Alpine Society attributes an elevation of 5,670m to the summit in question, which is situated to the south of Tocllaraju, and shows a 5,550m pass that delimits the northwest ridge of 6,110m Palcaraju Oeste.

Huamashraju, west face, correction. Slovenian Tomaz Zerovnik's name was misspelled as Toma Erovnik (*AAJ* 2002, p. 301).

Churup, 496spa-smos, correction. The route completed in 1972 by North Americans Ronald Fear, William Lahr, and Richard Ridgeway and Dutch climber Michiel Malotoux is to the right (not the left) of the Malinche route climbed by Spanish climbers Juan A. de Lorenzo and Francisco J. Palacios in August 1982. Some publications have indicated the opposite, leading Peruvian guide Ricardo Hidalgo to incorrectly believe that he climbed between the routes and descended by the 1972 route (*AAJ* 2002, p. 302).

ANTONIO GÓMEZ BOHÓRQUEZ, *Spain (translated by Christian Santelices)*

CORDILLERA HUAYHUASH

Jirishanca Chico, southeast face, Sweet Child of Mine. After we returned from the southeast face of Jirishanca Grande, realizing that we wouldn't have a chance to try again, I was nevertheless full of energy. The weather was still sunny, so I proposed to Rok Zalokar that we try the southeast face of Jirishanca Chico, by a direct line seen from base camp. We woke early and spent an hour walking over the moraine and an hour crossing the broken glacier, reaching the face around 6 a.m. The first 250m were easy, and we climbed unroped. At first we thought that we could climb the whole face unroped, but we were surprised. There were ten meters of difficult mixed climbing and steep snow in the lower part. We hadn't expected such steep climbing and didn't take Friends or nuts, only four pitons, some slings, one snow blade, and three ice screws, which we used in the upper part. I led the first mixed pitch, which took us to a snow-and-ice gully. The average angle of the seven pitches we climbed was 65°. We missed the gear lying in base camp, but it didn't help to think about the gear. We didn't even think about the serac that overhung the gully. We took five hours from the base to the summit of this beautiful mountain.

We had planned to descend by the west ridge, then the short part of south face to the glacier. This descent, however, turned out to be impossible, so I decided to descend the north face. We were forced to downclimb the upper part, because we didn't have enough gear and could make only 30m abseils. After 180m the terrain become too difficult, so we made four Abalakovs. We found a rocky ridge on the lower part of the face, which took us to the bottom. We shook hands smiling, said, "Thank you, God," and walked the long way over ridges back to base camp. We spent 14 hours on this unforgettable adventure.

Jirishanca Chico's southeast face. Azman's route ascends the shady couloir leading directly to the summit. Urban Azman

URBAN AZMAN, *Slovenia*

Note: Although Azman reports finding no sign of previous passage on this route, which ascends the middle of three parallel couloirs dropping directly from the summit, it is unclear whether this route is new or the same as the 1984 Italian route on the face. If the route is new, Azman proposes the name Sweet Child of Mine—Ed.

Jirishanca Norte to summit slopes. It is early July, and my climbing partner Iñigo Mujica and I have just gotten off the south face of Chacraraju, after completing the Bouchard Route in 25 hours. On arrival at our base camp at Laguna Jahucocha we saw that the southwest face of Rondoy was impracticable, owing to loose snow and avalanches. Jirishanca, however, looked be in good condition. We knew that the north summit, or in any case this face, remained virgin. Establishing a route on the face motivated us to mount a fast, nonstop assault.

At the same time the distance to the face was a problem. From the lake it appears to be nearby, but the serac barrier at its base forces one to make a huge detour. Faced with these logistics, we ferried loads and established a camp on the pass between the Ogre and Yerupajá Chico. Just before the pass we were faced with overhanging serac eight meters high, which Iñigo climbed in impeccable style. Camp was in a truly impressive place, with the Yerupajá glacier on one side and the one issuing from Jirishanca on the other. We stayed at this camp an entire day, resting

The west and southwest faces of Jirishanca (6,126m), showing:
1. Spanish attempt (Mujica-Ramon, 2002). 2. Polish route (Pawlikowski-Probulski, 1982). 3. Italian route (Airoldi-Cassin-Ferrari-Lafranconi-Lanzetta-Liati-Zucchi, 1969). 4. Slovenian route (unconfirmed location). 5. Austrian route (Bürger-Ponholzer, 1987). 6 American route (Bowlin-Caldwell, 1971). 7. Czech route (Drlík-Stejskal, 1982).
Jeremy Frimer

and preparing for our assault.

On July 19 we left our tent at 1 a.m. and began the descent towards the base of the wall. The first part of the route up the face turned out to be trickier than expected, with difficult pitches among seracs. Daybreak found us 300m up, at the foot of the great slope that makes up the route's middle section. There we encountered relatively easy, though exposed, climbing that took us to the base of the great final dihedral. To reach the dihedral we overcame difficulties involving very hard 70° ice and mixed sections, yet it became clear that the hardest climbing was still to come. We started up the great dihedral with a 70m, grade 5 pitch, followed by another of the same length but of 5+ M5+ difficulty. The following pitch began with difficult aid climbing on rock and ended below the final summit slopes. However, my partner had lost a crampon, and since without it there was no chance of reaching the summit, we retreated about two pitches shy of the top, though it was only 3:30 p.m. So began a long series of rappels, interrupted only by a stop so we could melt snow, followed by what was without a doubt the hardest part of the day—the climb back up to camp.

We reached the tent at 2 a.m., concluding a 25-hour push. The following morning we continued down to our base camp in Jahuacocha, where fried trout awaited our return. From base camp my friend and our gear departed toward Huaraz. I still hankered to see the Huayhuash, so I went for a hike around the base of the massif.

ORIOL BARÓ I RAMON, *Spain (translated by Oriol Solé-Costa)*

Tsacra Grande, West Face. In mid-August Mark Richey and I left our families at our base camp at Laguna Jahuacocha and hiked up the Quebrada Huacrish to above Laguna Saquicocha. We camped that night on a grassy hillside just below the west side of the moraine that drops off steeply on its east side into the lake. Early the next morning we woke to cloudy skies and at first decided to wait another day for better weather. But a few hours later it was clear, and we decided to go. We climbed above our camp and traversed to the east across a steep, loose slope, high above the south end of Laguna Saquicocha. From there we dropped down onto the glacier draining the west side of Tsacra Grande. Once on the glacier we headed up a shallow trough in the middle that avoided icefalls on either side. As we approached the base of the west face, we skirted the large rock wall in the center by following the glacier up and to the right. After climbing up the broken glacier below the face, we angled up and left and got onto the west face where the ice face came down and met the glacier. Several pitches of alpine ice led to mixed climbing topped with a short WI4 pitch. From there we traversed left into a series of classic Peruvian ice runnels that led to the summit ridge. We took turns traversing unconsolidated snow along the summit ridge to the top. We rappelled the route (about 2,500') and reached the glacier after dark. We wandered around the glacier trying to find our way with headlamps in a dense fog. We eventually made it back to our camp around morning. The next day we hiked back to our base camp for lunch and some great trout fishing, as the sun was setting on Jirishanca and Yerupaja. We believe this was the first ascent of the west face.

STEVEN J SWENSON, *AAC*

Siula Grande, Los Rapidos. On July 3 Marjan Kovac and Pavle Kozjek (both from Slovenia) and Aritza Monasterio (Spanish Basque living in Peru) climbed a new route on the northeast face of Siula Grande (Los Rapidos, 1000m, ED, 90° [crux]/55°–70° [average]) in eight hours, with

another seven for the descent. This is the first route in the center of the face. The last ascent of this remote wall was probably made in 1978 on the far right side (ED, Blumenthaler–Gruner– Kaser–Schoisswahl).

The 2002 team started on July 1 from base camp at Lake Carhuacocha and reached the glacier below Yerupaja at 4,800m in variable weather. Next day they found their way across the chaotic glaciers of Yerupaja and Siula to the base of Siula's northeast face at about

The line of Los Rapidos on Siula Grande, and Marjan Kovac caught in a brief slow moment. Pavle Kozjek (2)

5,300m. During the night the weather improved and they started climbing at 5 a.m. Conditions were good, and they could follow the line in the center of the wide face, avoiding the obvious horizontal rock barriers that give a special character to this wall. The hardest climbing was in the last 150m, where they had to find their way through overhanging seracs, following steep gullies with hard ice and powder snow. They reached the top at 1 p.m. and descended their route, downclimbing and rappelling. They descended the last 300m at night and returned to the glacier to find their tent destroyed by wind. They climbed in a rapid, lightweight style, taking only drinks and climbing equipment. Except for the last 150m, they climbed unroped.

PAVLE KOZJEK, *Slovenia*

Siula Grande, west face nearly to summit ridge. Dutch climbers Eva Oomen and Rogier van Rijn made an attempt on the west face of Siula Grande (6,348m), climbing 800m in nine hours on July 31. They climbed (ED 90°+) to the left of the three existing lines on the face. They report: "It is an ice line with sections of rotten vertical ice. We took almost no gear and tried to climb the whole face in a day. We had to descend from a couple of meters below the main summit ridge because of very unstable snow conditions. During the descent we were almost killed by a huge serac avalanche."

LINDSAY GRIFFIN, *High Mountain INFO*

Puscanturpa Norte and Nevado Cuyoc. In June a four-man Italian team climbed a new variant on the most imposing part of the northwest face of Puscanturpa Norte (5,652m), between the 2000 French routes (*AAJ* 2001, pp. 284–6) Pasta Religion and Macanacota. The Italians, Francesco Balzan, Bice Bones, Fabrizio Conforto, and Andrea Zanetti, appear to have climbed not far from Pasta Religion, with difficulties up to VII and A4. After they had covered 600m of new ground, the weather deteriorated, and the four were forced to finish on Pasta Religion.

The Italians also climbed the east spur of Nevado Cuyoc (5,500m), almost a subsidiary summit of the Puscanturpa Group. This may well have been a first ascent.

LINDSAY GRIFFIN, *High Mountain INFO*

CORDILLERA CENTRAL

Cordillera de la Viuda, ascents. In late June 1999 Gerardo Telletxea and I arrived at the village of Culluhuay, in the northwest part of this cordillera. From the Leóncocha lake shore, where we camped, we explored the valleys draining west. On July 1 we climbed Nevado de la Viuda (5,200m/17,061'), a second ascent—two Peruvians had been on top in 1959. Ours may have been a new route up the south face, on rock and ice. From base camp we had noticed a bold, massive, rock tower (ca 4,750m/15,885'), which we climbed by a technical route on its west face, on excellent rock. We named it Torre del Curco, after a local hunchback duck. Three days later, we attempted another equally fine rock tower, but bad weather forced us to abandon the climb.

JORGE MALLES, *Spain*

Cordillera Jatún Chácua, clarification, and Cerro Janpari, ascent. The Cordillera Jatún Chácua is located south of the Cordillera Raura and north of the Cordillera de la Viuda. The only access is through the mining town of Oyón and up the Pucayacu valley. This range was first explored by a 1971 Polish expedition (*AAJ* 1972, p. 167), which climbed several peaks in the southern end of the range, including the highest, Nevado Chácua Grande (5,350m). In mid-2001, a German Alpine Club party repeated that climb and made several others in the same area, but the Germans mistakenly stated that they had been in the Cordillera Raura, which is some 40 km to the north (*AAJ* 2001, p. 283). In July I entered the range and reached as far south as Pistag Pass, the only access to the eastern side and its attractive ice peaks. Bad weather forced me to retreat from the misty eastern side of the range to the western slopes. On July 3 I climbed the serrated P5,000m above Cochapata Pass, by its west face on good rock. But its true elevation was probably only 4,900m, and it had a cairn on top. I named it Cerro Janpari (Quechua for "Many Points"). After exploring the Jancapata Valley in bad weather, I retreated to Oyón.

EVELIO ECHEVARRIA, *AAC*

Nevado Llongote, Los Pecados se Rien!, I-Célines, and Longue, Haute, et Magnifico. Two teams of young French climbers sponsored by the FFME visited the unfrequented Nevado Llongote massif in August. A group of four young men was joined toward the end of their stay by a team of five women. From a base camp at 4,400m, approached via the village of Yauyos (2,800m), Fréderic Auvet, Aymeric Clouet, Arnaud Drouet, and Thomas Villecourt on August 5 climbed the elegant left-hand pillar on the south face of Nevado Llongote (5,781m) to create a 550m route christened Los Pecados se Rien! This gave predominantly fine climbing on sound rock at D (4+ M4, 60°–70°). This ascent led to an exit onto the west ridge, which they descended.

On the 9th Auvet and Villecourt climbed Nevado Llongote's splendid east ridge, which they christened I-Célines. This 700m route had general snow-and-ice difficulties, rock steps of 4+, and was felt to warrant an overall grade of AD+/D. At the same time, climbing for two days on the 8th and 9th, Clouet and Drouet tackled the prominent pillar in the center of the south face, finishing just left of the summit. This gave an excellent climb at TD+/ED1, with technical difficulties of 6b+ on sound rock and ice/mixed up to 85° and M5. The committing route was christened Longue, Haute, et Magnifico. The two teams arrived on the summit at the same time and descended the east ridge together.

The women now arrived, to find most of the good lines already climbed. After setting up a high camp at 4,800m, they attempted one route, only to have one of their group, Fanny Delachaux, take a short fall, break her wrist, and damage her knee. Unable to descend, Delachaux was left while help was summoned. The men, who were packing up their base camp, quickly came, and the injured climber was brought off the mountain and eventually evacuated by mule. Aude Aznavour, Marie Rousselot, and Helen Claudel then managed the second ascent of I-Célines before leaving the region.

Llongote is the highest of a five-peak massif in the southern Cordillera Central and was virtually unknown before a visit by a Spanish expedition in 1963. The highest point, connected to its satellite peaks by delicate knife-edges and unstable corniced arêtes, proved a difficult challenge, and the first-ascent party was forced into an unplanned bivouac just below the summit. There were no reports of climbers visiting these mountains between the 1960s and the 1997 arrival of a British expedition to the highest peak, Ticlla (5,897m), in the northern part of the region (see *INFO* 189). Two members of this team moved south and attempted Llongote but retreated due to poor snow conditions. The French ascent may have been only the second of this enigmatic mountain.

LINDSAY GRIFFIN, *High Mountain INFO*

CORDILLERA APOLOBAMBA

Ananea Group, various ascents. John Biggar led an expedition to the seldom-visited Peruvian section of the Cordillera Apolobamba. Traveling via Puno and Juliaca the team, which comprised Biggar, M. Aurelio, J. Cargill, J. Lewis, R. Nuttall, and J. Starbuck, arrived in August at the small gold-mining village of Ananea, set at a remarkable altitude of 4,700m. This is a very remote part of Peru, rarely visited by climbers, so it is not surprising that the team saw no other western travelers during their two weeks in this area. Snow conditions were poor, due to unusually unsettled weather, but the team made four ascents.

On August 9 Biggar, Cargill, and Starbuck climbed Nocaria (5,412m) via its easy south ridge. The whole team then walked from Ananea to a base camp at beautiful Laguna Callumachayo, from which on the 11th all the climbers made an ascent of Asnococha (ca 5,300m). From the 12th to the 14th the whole team made what they believe to be the first ascent of the southeast ridge of Ananea (5,853m). This peakæwhich, together with the equally high Callijon (a.k.a. Poderosa) a little to the east, is one of the two highest in the immediate areaæis one of the few with much climbing history. It was first ascended, probably from the south, in 1958 by the Italian team of Frigieri, Magni, Mellano, Merendi, Oggioni, Sterna, and Zamboni. (As the first mountaineering expedition to visit the Peruvian section of the Apolobamba, this group was responsible for nearly all the first ascents in this region.) Ananea was climbed again in 1960, and in 1973 a French team made a difficult ice route up the southwest face. In 1983 another French team climbed the relatively straightforward north face. The southeast ridge, climbed by the 2002 British party, was an excellent, narrow, but straightforward ascent.

Moving to the border peaks, the whole team made a probable first ascent on August 17 of the southeast ridge of Chocñacota Este (5,350m, first climbed by the Italians in 1958), which gave a pleasant rock scramble. Three days later Biggar, Nuttall, and Starbuck attempted Palomani Norte (5,629m, also first climbed by the Italians) but were forced back just 50m below the top due to avalanche risk on a short headwall.

LINDSAY GRIFFIN, *High Mountain INFO*

Venezuela

Autana Tepui, first ascent of southern aspect. This tepui, 400 miles south of Caracas in the Orinocan jungle, was climbed in March by a team of aid climbers and another of free climbers. The route up the southeast face was 2,400', 25 pitches. It was aided by Hernando Arnal, Anne Arran, Ivan Calderon, Henry Gonzales, Tim O'Neill, José Pereyra, and Xavier Potronco (2001). Freed by John Arran (one pitch of 5.13b, two of 5.13a, two of mid-5.12, most of the rest at 5.11). See "The Tree of Life" earlier in this Journal for an account.

Brazil

Recent new routes. As of a few years ago the 1970 Leste Route on Pico Maior in Rio de Janeiro was the longest (700m, 5.8R) established. Harder routes were established, like Terra de Gigantes (550m, A4+) on Pedra do Sino, also in Rio, but the big faces were still untouched. After 2000, when sport climbing was increasingly in the news, big-wallers established such new routes as the North Face of Morro dos Cabritos (840m, A1 5.11b) in Teresópolis (Rio de Janeiro), by André Ilha, Flavio Wasniewki, Guilherme

The West Face from Pedra Riscada, Brazil, showing (left to right): Diedro Peladeira, Vai Mais Nao Cai, and Esmurgeitor. Eduardo Viana

Conde, and Paulo Chaves; the West Face of Pedra Riscada (850m, A2+ 5.11R) in São José do Divino (Minas Gerais), by Eduardo Viana, Emerson Lampião, Edgardo Kaca and André Coutinho; Abuso (950m, 5.11b) on Morro dos Cabritos, Teresópolis (Rio de Janeiro), by Antonio Paulo Faria and Daniel Guimarães; Maria Nebulosa (1,040m, 5.8 A3) on Maria Comprida Peak at Petrópolis (Rio de Janeiro); Vai Mais Não Cai (Go But Don't Fall) (1,260m, 5.11R) on Pedra Riscada, in São José do Divino (Minas Gerais), by Marcio Bortolusso, Chander Silva, Breno, Leandro, and Oscar. Nevertheless, at Aymore's Sierra, on the border of Espirito Santo and Minas Gerais states, walls less than 300m high are still unnamed, since there are so many of them, and most of them still await first ascents. This information was gathered from Mountain Voices and Universo Vertical, Brazilian climbing newsletters/magazines.

MARIUS BAGNATI, *Brazil*

Enjoying the good ledges on Pedra Riscada. Eduardo Viana

Bolivia

Pico Gotico, Via del Arco. Erik Monasterio, with the French climber Marie France Ducret, added a second route to the rock peak of Pico Gotico, marked 5,750m on the DAV map. This peak, a subsidiary summit west of the Ancohuma and Illampu massifs, received its name from the shape of its north and south ridges, which resemble the incomplete arches of Gothic cathedrals.

In July Ducret and Monasterio reached the Laguna Glacier Base Camp on the northwest side of Ancohuma and continued, placing a camp on the moraine directly below the west face of Pico Gotico at 5,250m. Starting up the left side of the face late in the day on the 30th, the pair fixed the first and crux pitch (6c and A2). On the following day they ascended the rope and continued for two more pitches (5/5+) to the northwest ridge. Nine further rope lengths, up to 6a/b, were climbed on the ridge before Monasterio, in deteriorating weather, continued alone for the final 150m to the summit. Conditions on the climb were difficult due to the strong prevailing wind, low temperature and melt water from accumulated snow. Pegs and a full rack were essential for protection. The route, climbed round trip from Sorata in 72 hours, was christened Via del Arco.

LINDSAY GRIFFIN, *High Mountain INFO*

Cabeza de Condor, La Promenade des Braves; Huallomen, Duende del Diablo; and Illampu, La Conjuration des Imbecile. Jerome Mercader and I were in Bolivia for one month. We first acclimatized in the Condoriri Range, with a BC at 4,600m/15,100'. We climbed classics and also did two new gullies, on Cabeza de Condor and on Huallomen. Then we climbed 2,300' of the famous west face of Huyana Potosi (19,970') in only three hours, and were back in La Paz the same day. Soon after, we went to Illampu (6,368m/20,890') which is one of the most complicated and impressive summits of this range, with the hardest normal route in Bolivia.

On May 25, on the south face of Cabeza de Condor (5,648m/18,525'), we established La Promenade des Braves (The Walk of the Braves, 220m/720' in the gully, 570m/1,870' to the top, IV M6 WI4), spending four hours in the gully and another hour and 45 minutes to reach the summit. This gully is located on the right bank of the glacier. Climb directly to the bottom of a mixed pitch (M6), then follow a narrow ice line (55° to 75°, with a snow mushroom). Cross to the right on a snow ledge to a snow shoulder. A last pitch, with a 65° ice section, reaches the snow ridge at 5,300m (17,385'), where the route joins the normal route to the top.

On May 27 we climbed the east face of Huallomen (5,550m) via what we called Duende del Diablo (Spirit of the Devil, 500m/1,640', 570m/1,870' to the top, V M5 WI5), climbing the gully in 6:30 and taking another hour to reach the summit. We are not sure if we did the first ascent. The ice line is in the middle of the face—a narrow line with steep ice and dry-tooling sections. The start is the same as for the 2001 Bon Anniversaire Annick route. In the lower part of the gully were two pitches with ice sections of 70° to 85°. The line reaches the bottom of the headwall and turns left onto a snow ramp (55°, with some dry). Then the line ascends a steep, narrow gully (90°). The first crux, "Cross on your Feet," is a 90° M5 pitch with small icicles. The next pitch and second crux, "The Belly," is a 90° wall which leads toward a breach in a snow gully. However, just before reaching this breach, follow a snow ledge (50/55°) to the right for almost two pitches. A 70° M4 pitch to the right gives access to the central gully, which cuts into a second breach (60° to 75°). Escape right just before it. You are at the bottom of the rocky foresummit. A horizontal ledge takes you right for two easy pitches to the summit snow ridge and the normal route. Follow it to the top via snow and a rocky step. Descend by downclimbing the northeast ridge, always on the right side of the ridge.

Illampu is located in the Cordillera Real, close to the village of Sorata. It's a remote summit, with a three-day approach to base camp (17,400'). La Conjuration des Imbeciles (The Confederacy of Dunces, 870m/2,860', VI M4 WI5) is a great, aesthetic line that we established on June 9. It follows the impressive central gully of the north face. One-push style being the fastest and the safest way to climb this route, we reduced our gear to four ice screws, four pitons, four Friends, some nuts, one 200' 7.7mm rope, a little water, and two goose gilets. Such a way of climbing allows you to be fast, but only if everything is going okay. The start is the same as that of the 1978 Mesili Route, which heads to the left side of the face and surmounts three seracs to reach the foresummit (6,344m/20,810'). This face is now far drier than in 1978. The first part of the couloir we climbed is now a six-pitch gully with 85° ice steps and M4 dry-tooling sections. The gully reaches the bottom of a 50m-high serac. This, the crux, was a 70m pitch (WI5, with some M4 to start). Above a 150m, 55° snow slope, head right to a second serac. Climb it on the left (70°). Then climb snow below the last serac for one 70° pitch. Climb to the left, on snow with mixed sections, to avoid a rocky headwall. Follow a secondary ridge to the foresummit, which we reached in 7hrs, 30min from the start. From the foresummit we reached the main summit in two hours via a corniced ridge with no protection. We had 30 minutes of daylight left when we summited, and began down climbing the normal, Southwest Ridge route (III 65°). It wasn't easy finding our way through the icefall, avoiding ghostly crevasses, with a lamp that only gave 15 minutes of light, but without bivy gear we couldn't afford a night out. The only solution was to find the tent, which we did around 10 p.m.

We had an exceptional journey, an adventure that brought us to wild places without a soul around. We pushed our dream to the end, to be sure that life was worth being lived. The spirit of your climb is still more important than the climb itself. As long as there are climbers willing to escape from trails, adventure will exist.

SEBASTIEN CONSTANT, *France*

CORDILLERA QUIMSA CRUZ

The Big Wall, The AA Crack. After all the usual hassles of overweight and oversized baggage, and of making connections on the long trip from Yosemite, Donny Alexander and I arrived in the Cordillera Quimsa Cruz in June, just as the wet season was ending and winter was beginning.

When we got everything to our Laguna Blanca base camp, I spent the next couple of days eating ciproflaxen-like candy, trying to counteract the effects of something I ate in La Paz. After living no longer seemed such a bad idea, we humped a load into Mocoya Valley, which is at about 15,700 feet. There is no water where we bivied, so we only brought up enough supplies for about a week. However, that was enough time to do what we are pretty sure is a first ascent (The AA Crack, IV 5.8 C2) on The Big Wall. When we got to the base of the most-obvious line, we saw slings 150 feet up. But it was such a beautiful line, we decided to climb it anyway. After following low angle slabs, I got to an old anchor consisting of a pin and a tied-off horn. Donny led the next pitch, about 30 feet up coming to three old tied-off Austrian pins, apparently a bail point. (Above, we saw no further evidence of the route having been climbed). A 20-foot section of rock on that pitch is poor quality, and both Donny and I took 30-foot whippers. The third pitch follows a gorgeous left-facing, left-leaning orange/gold corner system for 160 feet. The fourth pitch starts in the same corner, which turns into a three-foot-deep, shoulder-width-wide water groove. Fortunately, the crack we had been following continues up the back of the groove. The fourth pitch ends on a ledge after 170 feet. The top is then another 185 feet of broken climbing, with occasional 5.8ish moves. Because the crack we followed was somewhat dirty, and rotten in a few places, the going was slow. Climbing at 16,000 feet was also probably a factor. Each lead took about five hours, most of which involved cleaning placements, then trying to cry the dirt out of our eyes and sneeze it out of our noses. Because of the slow going we debated going back to Laguna Blanca for the portaledge, but decided not to because the wall is only 800 feet high. So every night we rapped down and in the morning jugged back up to our high point.

After finishing the route we walked back down to Laguna Blanca. After a couple of rest days, we hiked back to Mocoya Valley for another week, hoping for more climbing there, then on Cuernos de Diablo in the next valley east. But my climbing trip soon ended when a hold broke and I fell, injuring my ankle, on Penis Pinnacle. A few days later I played belay slave for Donny on short crack climbs above our bivy. Then we hiked (I gimped) back to Laguna Blanca.

Mocoya Valley has lots of potential, though I recommend going in Bolivian spring rather than winter. We did not get to check out the next valley north, which supposedly has had no development. Directly north of The Big Wall are several formations up to 500 feet high, with beautiful splitter cracks. The problem, beside my ankle, was that it would be 80° in the sun, 25 in the shade. Since it was winter, the north side of the valley only saw the sun for about an hour every morning. Therefore, snow from the wet season was not melting, and cracks and ledges had snow and ice. Winters are dry, though, so I imagine that when those formations get spring sun, they become very climbable.

I give many thanks to the American Alpine Club, not only for the grant they were so kind to give, but also for their support through my pretrip changes. Although our trip did not work out exactly as planned, we had a great time and say thank you very much for helping make it happen!

Lynnea Anderson, *AAC*

The northeast tower of Nordostl Turm, showing the original German route of 1987 (the ridge on the cliff's upper right), and the Bach-Burns route in 2002 (rising from the lower left). Cameron Burns

Araca Group, various ascents. Mike Walker, Cameron Burns (Basalt Bigfoot Coalition), and I spent June 29–July 10 in the Mocoya and Teacota valleys of the northern Araca Group of the Quimsa Cruz. While there, we spent most of our time bivouacked under a large boulder, avoiding high winds, cold, and driving snow. We did manage three ascents, two of which were firsts.

In La Paz we hired a 4x4 Jeep to drive us eight hours to the depressed mining village of Viloco, on the western slopes of the Quimsa Cruz. Once in Viloco we solicited the locals for directions north to the Mocoya Valley, where we established the first in a series of unseasonably wet camps. From the Mocoya Valley we employed a passing miner, Juan Maydana Choque, his sons, and their two mules to assist us over two passes to the Teacota Valley and the eastern slopes of this jaw-dropping range.

On July 7, the weather began clearing, and so did our minds. Cam and I climbed a direct route (2,800', IV 5.9) up Point 5,304m, referred to as the Northeast Tower (Nordostl Turm) by the 1987 German Bolivia expedition. The descent was straight back down via sand-filled gullies and rappels. On July 9, with clear skies and warmer temperatures, Cam and I climbed Hamburguesa Daydreams (1,200', III 5.7) on a huge slab of rock just west of the Northeast Tower and part of the same complex of rock. The descent was a walk off to the west. During our stay we also climbed a nice, small, Bugaboos-like tower (that may have been previously climbed)—mostly scrambling, one pitch of moderate rock—just north of the Pico Penis, in a blizzard, via the east (Amazon) side.

On July 10 the snow returned and so did Juan, his sons, and the mules for our trip back to Viloco. We returned to La Paz on July 11th via the local bus system, which is a story in itself.

BENNY BACH, *Team Rio de Caca*

Various ascents and descents. Wade McKoy, Porter Fox, Hal Thomson, Ptor Spriceneiks, and I found ourselves in the Cordillera Quimsa Cruz last June. A bit of ski mountaineering the main goal. A few peaks bagged. No signs of any other climbers or skiers. Bissell and Ptor on the southeast face of Korichuma (18,200'), rated at 60° but more like between 50° and 55°. Perfectly beautiful, exposed face. An enjoyable solo climb. A bit of ice. Semibreakable crust on the face, but good enough for a ski descent. No falls allowed. Super fun. Chamonix-like spires, emerald-green high alpine lakes, first descents, receding glaciers (like my hairline), and five great friends. Summits with swirling clouds. Laughing uncontrollably with Porter. A four-foot tall, friendly farmer selling us a lamb and potatoes, and us devouring it in an afternoon. Stomach ache. Llama poo fires at night, with Wade shooting star trails. Beautiful. Pretty easy. A paradise indeed.

Also climbed and skied Bitch's Brew (17,600'), Porter Fox and Bissell Hazen on a mellow, rolling glacier route. Ptor Spriceneiks on Cerro Yaypuri. An exposed, perfect first ski descent. Wade McKoy, Hal Thomson, and Ptor on a nameless peak on the far right of the valley.

BISSELL HAZEN

The sunny southeast face of Korichuma (18,200'), with its amazing ski slopes. Wade McKoy

Argentina and Chile

CENTRAL ANDES, ARGENTINA

Bonete Region, correction. The *AAJ* 2002, p. 328, erroneously lists the Bonete Region as belonging to Chile. The mountains Bonete, Veladero, "Veladero Northeast," and Reclus are in Argentine territory, in the Province of la Rioja, far from the Chilean border. The mountain called "Veladero Northeast" (6,070m) is named Cerro del Baboso (ca 6,050m on Argentine maps). The name (Baboso) was given to me by a local hill man and guide. Cerro del Baboso had been ascended previously, but by motorcycle (*AAJ* 1997, p. 243). Therefore, the ascent mentioned in the *AAJ* 2002 must be credited as the first made by fair means. For other details, see the *AAJ* 1994, p.173. Also, this region must be entered from Argentina; otherwise there can be problems with the Gendarmeria Nacional (Border Police).

MARCELO SCANU, *Argentina*

San Juan Province, Agua Negra and Valle del Cura regions. The Valle del Cura is an interesting glacial valley, with many summits along the Chile border. I went there in February with Argentine Santiago Rocha and Pole Parys Liesicki, a resident of Spain. Liesicki acclimatized in the Agua Negra Region, where he reached many summits, including Cerro de la Fortuna (4,376m) by new route from the south. From a base camp by an ancient mine at Rincón del Río (S 30° 02′49.9" W 69° 47′45.6") Parys made the first ascent to the fine mountain west of camp. He named it Cerro Rincón del Río (4,822m, roughly S 30° 04′ W 69° 50′45"). On the 14th we all climbed Cerro Cabeceras del Carmen (4,821m, S 30° 04′12.5" W 69° 51′02.4") by its east ridge. On the summit we found a prospector's wooden pole. On the 15th Parys and I went north and ascended a mountain from its west col. We christened it Cerro Promontorio (ca. 4,200m, 4,235m by GPS, S 30° 00′36.5" W 69° 47′22"). The next day I found an Inca hut next to a well, and nearby an exquisite Inca stone figurine representing a pregnant llama, surely a sacred offering to their gods. On the 17th Parys trekked south toward the Arroyo de la Lagunita and climbed the virgin summit of the Nevado de Mondaca (ca 5,200m, S 30° 07′08.7" W 69° 48′42"). The Gendarmeria Nacional (Border Police) came the next day and took Parys and me to the Arroyo de las Máquinas, and Santiago descended. On the 24th we attempted the international summit of Volcán Vacas Heladas (ca. 5300m), but a big camp of penitentes aborted the ascent just above 5,000m, so we changed our objective to a minor summit on the international border. We ascended it by its northwest ridge, making its first ascent and calling it Cerro del Paso de las Tórtolas (ca. 5,100m, 5,145m by GPS, S 29°53′35.7" W 69°53′32.5").

MARCELO SCANU, *Argentina*

Aconcagua, 2002-2003 season overview. Aconcagua Park saw a record 5,519 people enter for trekking or climbing, 20 percent more than last year. This increase can be explained by the devaluation of the Argentine peso and by a series of improvements in the park. Two million pesos collected as fees had been reinvested in the park, a considerable amount, though the Gendarmeria Nacional (Border Police) helicopter had more work. There were 208 evacuations (153 the previous season) and, unfortunately, three deaths are a reminder that, while the normal route is easy technically, the altitude, climate, and other factors make the ascent dangerous. In one day in January there were 11 evacuations. On the other hand, there are seven additional rangers, and 180-kg barrels have been installed in the bathrooms to collect organic waste. Despite this ecological improvement, there are no such facilities in Nido de Condores and Berlin camps, and human waste there is a real problem.

The traditional wine feast, Fiesta de la Vendimia, attended in Mendoza, also took place in Plaza de Mulas this year. Also, there was a reality show! It was produced by TV3 from Cataluna, Spain. These people threw a big party in the Geotrek pub in Plaza de Mulas. Other climbers couldn't sleep until 4 a.m.! The pub was banned.

A 74-year-old woman reached 6,000m, and a 14-year-old reached the summit, the youngest girl to do so. On some days there was a line of climbers in the Canaleta, waiting their turn to summit. On January 27, 40 climbers reached the top. Even as late as the end days of March, out of the regular season, climbers, including a well-known Argentine actor and his guides, summited Aconcagua.

A remarkable ascent was achieved by Frenchman Bruno Sourzac. He climbed the French Route, Messner Variation, on the south face. He was alone in base camp beginning December 1, but bad weather and snow prevented him from attacking the route. Finally, on December 12 he climbed the route nonstop, without assistance, from base camp in Plaza Francia to the end of the difficulties at the Filo del Guanaco, between the summits, in only 22 hours. He reported that the face, due to the middle seracs, was very exposed and dangerous, and recommends getting information from rangers or local guides before deciding to try the route. (*In spite of poor conditions and continuous avalanches in the upper part, which forced him to stop for several hours in the Messner exit before continuing, Sourzac's ascent was likely the second fastest of Aconcagua's south face, and his time includes the approach. Although Austrian Thomas Bubendorfer climbed the face in 15 hours in 1991, he received considerable support from other climbers, who carried gear and broke trail for him on the first half of the route—Ed.*)

MARCELO SCANU, *Argentina*

CENTRAL ANDES AND NORTHERN PATAGONIA, CHILE AND ARGENTINA

Various ascents and ski descents. A dry winter in several areas James Bracken and I were interested in required us to adopt a "go where there's snow" approach. Unfortunately, where there's snow in the Andes, there's often prodigious wind. Bariloche, Argentina proved to have the right stuff in terms of terrain, but a warm, dry late winter left the snowlines high on the peaks. Off we went north, to ski volcanoes in the central cordillera en route to a reconnaissance of the South American ski mecca, Las Leñas. First the great volcano Lanin spit us out like watermelon seeds, then the spectacular Valley of the Volcanoes, home to over 20 3,000m-to-4,000m ski peaks and no skiers to be found. We found fabulous objectives but winds as a savage and cruel as those in the notorious south of these countries.

Ah, finally a refuge at the international destination of Las Leñas, where we attempted to find our ski legs amid the swirling confusion of this social and environmental maelstrom. While poaching lines from ski-movie hotshots, international swanksters, and rug rats in pink one-piece suits, we also found time to grind out late nights at the disco and kite-ski in the barren valley below Las Leñas.

Ten days of this cycle of madness prompted us to head yet farther north, to the high desert mountains of the central cordillera of Argentina. We traveled to the Rio Colorado valley, 100km north of Aconcagua, and made the first ascent and first ski descent of the spectacular 5,000' Alma Fuerte Couloir on the striking Alma Fuerte Peak (5,700m). Next we skied the east face of La Mesa (6,200m) from just below the summit. Regretfully, the wind caught up with us again and blew our emaciated asses out of the peaks and back into the disco. Retreat complete, with condor escort and loads too big for shattered skeletons. After gorging on prime Argentine beef, pig, goat, chicken, and guanaco, the team decided to split into two strong, experienced teams of one. I went to Chile and skied the four peaks of Chillan in a single day, as well as making possibly the first complete ski descent (7,000') of the stunning "jewel of the central Andes of Chile," Cerro Viuda (3,900m), via the west face couloir. In seven days I skied 11 major volcanoes between the cities of Concepcion and Osorno, including a 14,000' roundtrip (half up and half down) of the beautiful Volcano Llaima (3,500m) in six hours. Then the fabled El Niño swept me again into the thumping, bumping discos for my swan song. It was kill or be killed and, remarkably, I came up breathing. Alas, it was time to leave Chile and catch up on poaching stateside. As for James, I can't tell you what became of the lad, other than that he has taken up residence in Bariloche.

OK, so the wind got the best of us and maybe the DJs and Buenos Aires girls too, but we sure did cover some ground and lay down some tracks in those fantastic and lonely, windswept expanses of the great Andes chain.

James Bracken and I wish to thank the AAC and Helly Hansen for their support of our September and October ski-mountaineering trip to the central Andes of Chile and Argentina.

DOUG BYERLY

CENTRAL PATAGONIA, CHILE

Volcán Melimoyu. This ice volcano, exactly 2,400m (7,874') high, is located by the sources of the Palena river in Chilean Patagonia. *(Editor's note: more specifically, Volcán Melimoyu [44.08 S, 72.88 W] is in the northern part of Chile's XI's region, near the towns of Villa Melimoyu, Raúl Marín Balmaceda, and La Junta, along the Carretera Austral [Southern Road], 150 miles north of Coyhaique.)* Its name is Mapuche and means "Four Peaks."

Our group of six university students from Santiago left the mouth of the Moraleda Fjord on December 21, 1999, and marched up the Palena and Correntoso valleys. It took until January 11, 2000, to reach the Melimoyu Glacier. It rained constantly. We launched two attempts on Volcán Melimoyu, succeeding on the second. The final climb above the ice cap, on January 12, was made over walls and towers of poor volcanic rock, ice, and frozen conglomerate. It was a well-earned first ascent. On the summit were Matías Aurtenechea, Manuel Bugeño and Camilo

The southeast face of Chile's Cerro Castillo, as seen from Villa Cerro Castillo, the nearest town. The route follows the prominent snow slopes and gully to the notch, then right to the summit. Rodrigo Fica

Rada. The whole trip took 26 days, of which only two were without rain. Other members of the expedition were Oliver Flores, Juan Villarroel, and I.

EUGENIO GUZMAN, *Chile*

Cerro Castillo, Southeast Face. Eduardo Mondragón (España), Pablo Crovetto (Chile) and I, Rodrigo Fica (Chile), climbed the Southeast Face (650m, D+/TD-, 55° average, with a few 70° –80° sections) of Cerro Castillo (2,675m). The route had been unrepeated since the first ascent, in December 1982, by Golnar, Hansel, Kyan, and Wangh. (Cerro Castillo is located in Chile's XI region, about 100 miles south of Coyhaique.) On February 15, 2003, we arrived at the base of the mountain in good weather. The next day we started at 3:30 a.m., and two hours later, because of excellent snow and ice conditions, we unroped. At the end of the first ramp we roped for two short pitches, then again unroped for the second icy ramp. At midday we were at the bottom of the final ten-meter headwall, which was hard to climb free at 5.8, but bad rock covered with verglas. After two falls and four hours of attempts, we summited at 4:00 p.m. We down-climbed the normal route, thus making the first traverse of the mountain, and arrived at base camp at 10:00 p.m.

RODRIGO FICA, *Chile*

CENTRAL PATAGONIA, ARGENTINA

San Lorenzo Group, Cerro Hermoso, southwest summit. From a base camp in Rio Oro Valley, Italians Luca Maspes and Diego Fregona made what they believe to be the first ascent of Cerro Hermoso's southwest summit, calling it "Cumbre Silvia." They climbed a new route up the 1,000m west face on November 1 in ten hours, alpine style, with difficulties of 5.8 rock and 70° ice and mixed. On November 4 they attempted the first ascent of San Lorenzo's northeast face but climbed only 100m (ice and mixed) before retreating amid rock and ice fall.

Compiled from communications with LUCA MASPES, *Italy*

SOUTHERN PATAGONIA, ARGENTINA

CHALTEN MASSIF

Cerro Azara and Cerro Bravo. These two summits are located just north of Paso del Viento, and are linked by a shallow ridge. Cerro Azara (1,950m) was first climbed in March 1916 by Alfredo Kolliker and Lutz Witte. On December 6 Spaniards José Fernández Arrieta and Raúl Lora made the second ascent via a new route on the east face. They climbed a line leading to the col between the two summits, involving 200m of mixed terrain to 60°–65°, with short steeper sections, and 5.4 rock climbing. From the summit of Azara they moved north along the ridge and climbed previously unclimbed Cerro Bravo (2,040m). This involved an easy traverse along a ridge and 5.4 rock climbing in very rotten rock.

ROLANDO GARIBOTTI, *Club Andino Bariloche*

Adela Group, Cerro Grande. In the Fitz Roy Range, in November, Italian Luca Maspes made two solo attempts on Techado Negro (located at the southern end of the Fitz Roy group) climbing 300m of mixed ground and bad rock. On December 5, Maspes and Marcello Cominetti, also from Italy, climbed a new route on the south face of Cerro Grande (2,751m), joining the East Ridge route, from which they retreated, some 200m below the

View of the southeast face of Cerro Grande from the Cominetti-Maspes new route, which ascends outside the right edge of this view. Luca Maspes

summit. They climbed in alpine style, starting from Paso del Viento; their line ascends the south-southeast face, to the right of Ferrari route, with ice and mixed up to 75°.

Compiled from communications with
LUCA MASPES, *Italy*

Cerro Torre; Saint Exupery, Chiaro di Luna; and Aguja Rafael, Artebelleza. The weather in Patagonia this year dished out its usual tricks. Between December 15 and February 15 there were five climbable days—windows of good weather more than 16 hours long—with a couple of these windows after significant weather events that created quite snowy and icy conditions.

Dave Nettle and I welcomed the New Year on Cerro Torre's Compressor Route's Bridwell Pitch, pushing on by headlamp in the dark. To our pleasant surprise we encountered the notorious

On the southeast face of Cerro Grande.
Luca Maspes

mushroom in more benign conditions than normal; it involved ramping ice to a short vertical section of rime ice/snow, which led to the very top. Route conditions were mixed, requiring free climbing in boots and, usually, cleaning with one ice tool. We found the route to be quite a classic.

On January 5 it looked like the weather might break again. Having had enough icy rock, we set our sights on Chiaro di Luna, an 800m route on the west buttress of Saint Exupery, across the valley from the Torres. The morning of the 6th dawned windy and rainy. We waited out the weather in the Polish camp and on the morning of the 7th awoke to clear, calm conditions. As we approached the rock, we eyed a crack system well to the right of the original route. After an 80m approach pitch up the obvious, angling dike at the base of the wall, we followed an obvious crack and corner system for four 60m pitches. This section sported a 5.10+ corner and splitter system and a 5.11- offwidth. At the top of these four pitches we joined Chiaro di Luna for 300m. We then veered from the original line up high and went for the splitters in the top headwall, with two 60m pitches of 5.10+ corner and crack climbing. We called this variation Supertrek (V 5.11a), dedicating it to the glacier guides who kept us laughing in camp through the bad weather.

On February 17 I raced up to the base of Aguja Rafael's north face with Argentines Juan "Piraña" Canale and Esteban Arellano. We free climbed the route Artebelleza, a route put up earlier in the season by the Swiss couple Carsten Von Birckhahn and Anke Clauss. We freed all the pitches originally aided, giving the route a rating of V 5.11b, but we could not finish the last 5.8 pitch due to rapidly deteriorating weather, descending just shy of the summit.

BEAN BOWERS

Aguja Mermoz, Vol de Nuit, first winter ascent. In early August Ian Parnell and I arrived in a cold and snowy Chalten, bound for Fitz Roy. Within three days we had dug a meter-deep trench all the way to the Paso Superior, spending two of those days swimming up from Rio Blanco against waves of spindrift and avalanche, under rucksacks that even Sherpas would refuse to carry. Morale was low, and I feared that Ian thought that I'd tricked him into believing it was summer in Patagonia, not winter. (We didn't spot any slack lines or Americans.) Luckily for me, two of Ian's expensive cameras broke due to cold-related illness, which took his mind off the weather.

After a few days of snow-hole fun, we set off to try the Devil's Dihedral on Fitz Roy, a.k.a. the "Flushing Slovenian Death Couloir." Looking back it seems overoptimistic for us to have thought we could climb the 1,300m route alpine style, in winter, sans portaledges or camera crew, especially with the non-Slovenian bodies we were using. When Ian (the U.K.'s very own alpine Evel Knievel) said he was scared, it made me question the sanity of our mission. One-thousand feet up the route and with thankfully nowhere to sleep, we had a sudden urge to spend the night in our wet sleeping bags, in our enchanted, urine-coated snow cave, so we bailed.

Looking for something else to occupy ourselves, we decided to try the Parkin route (Vol de Nuit) on the east face of Mermoz. I'd tried this route two winters previously and been washed off it by a storm, so I knew there was a good chance we would fail, then go home. Luckily, cold pressure sat over the mountain for three days. We both like the cold, but even we found this cold tough to cope with and, despite wearing every piece of clothing we had (including synthetic belay parkas), froze our asses off. The climbing was primarily mixed free (hard Scottish VI/VII) up corners, with one A1 pitch. There was also a lot of steep powder. Highlights included moving together up a 70m pitch of paper-thin 80° ice, me taking a 40' fall, and spending the night in a frozen sleeping bag with the same insulating properties as the string hammock I was hanging in. At around midnight on the third day we reached the end of the route at the summit ridge (200m horizontally from the summit) and, after spending several frozen seconds there, rapped the route in four hours (fourteen 60m raps). We agreed that this had been one of the toughest routes we had climbed, due to the extreme conditions encountered. That night the weather broke.

Andy Parkin soloed the route in a day, and the route is a testament to his skill and mental imbalance. So is winter climbing in Patagonia worth the pain? Well, with the whole massif to yourself, who cares?

ANDY KIRKPATRICK, *U.K.*

Fitz Roy, Tehuelche and Supercanaleta, attempts. I spent a month with Chris Turiano, a very good and strong guy from Colorado. We were in Piedra del Fraile with the intention of attempting Tehuelche (1,200m, VI 5.11 A2) on the north face of Fitz Roy. The plan was to do it in one day. The plan seemed crazy to me, but I trusted Chris. We spent a night in Paso del Cuadrado. We set out from Paso at 2 a.m. and arrived at the base of the route at 7 a.m. We traveled superlight but superdangerous—no boots, no stove, no extra clothes. Also no food; only a small pack with water. We climbed very fast. Chris freed the third pitch (originally A2), grading it 5.10R. We simul-climbed almost all the time, only exchanging the gear and the pack. We reached the Grand Hotel, 600m up, in just four hours. We hoped to be on top by late night, but trouble had just started. We tried to continue climbing fast, but the first pitch above the Grand Hotel, a notoriously difficult offwidth, was hard to free and slowed us considerably. After three and one-half hours Chris reached the belay. It would be easy to aid the pitch with another #6 Friend. I led another long pitch, linking two of our topo's pitches, and then we decided to go down. That pitch had exhausted us, and we didn't carry bivy gear, just Gore-Tex jackets. Late at night we returned to the start of the wall. During the night the weather became really bad. I think it is possible to do Tehuelche in one day but with a different approach. Next time!

We also tried Supercanaleta. We started directly from Piedra del Fraile and began climbing the couloir 10 p.m. When we came to the Bloque Empotrado (The jammed block, about 1,000m up, at the end of the initial couloir.), the weather collapsed again, so we rappelled off. On the way down we were almost killed by rockfall but came back safe to Piedra del Fraile the next day.

You know how it goes in Patagonia. I hope we have better luck next year.

KLEMEN MALI, *Slovenia*

Chalten Massif, summary of activity. During the austral winter (July-August 2002), French Canadians Martin Bointeau and Claude Gagnon made the first winter ascent of Tomahawk (450m, TD+ 5.9 WI6) on Aguja Standhardt. Dry conditions (little ice) forced them to retreat as they attempted to push on to the summit via the upper portion of Exocet. They also made an attempt on Cerro Torre's Southeast Ridge (Compressor Route), but were driven back by bad weather five pitches above the Col of Patience. Exocet (800m, ED- 5.9 WI6) was repeated in November by German Alex Huber and Swiss Stephan Siegrist, Roger Schaeli, and Ralph Weber after an unsuccessful attempt on the east face of Cerro Torre.

The Franco-Argentine Route (500m, ED- 5.11) on Fitz Roy saw a half dozen ascents, including ascents by Argentines Luciano y Gabriel Fiorenza in December 2002, Japanese Masahiro Takiyama and Hidenobu Hata in early January 2003, and Austrians Raimund Moser and Gunter Gapp in February 2003. The Supercanaleta route (1500m, TD+ 5.10 AI4) on Cerro Fitz Roy was climbed by Swiss David Fasel and Mike Schuwey on New Year's Day. In November 2002 Frenchmen Nicolas Fabbri and Silvain Rivoire attempted the same route but retreated upon reaching the summit slopes, 150m from the summit.

On December 16 Swiss Carsten Von Birckhahn and Anke Clauss climbed a new route on the north face of Aguja Innominata. Their line, which they christened Artebelleza (400m, TD- 5.10 A2) climbs six new pitches on the north face, then joins the Piola-Anker route for its last three pitches along the east side of the tower. On February 17, 2003 Argentines Esteban Arellano and Juan Canale, with American Bean Bowers, freeclimbed most of this line (5.11b), but were forced to give up one pitch short of the summit due to deteriorating weather. On January 10, 2003 Von Birckhahn and Clauss repeated the Kearney-Harrington route (580m, TD- 5.10c) on the north face of Aguja Saint Exupery; it joins the upper portion of the Italian East Face route. This route (700m, TD, 5.11+) was repeated by Argentines Agustin Inchausti and Alejandro Lucena on January 8, 2003.

ROLANDO GARIBOTTI, *Club Andino Bariloche*

SOUTHERN PATAGONIA, CHILE

Southern Continental Icecap, exploration and ascents. Chilean climber Camilo Rada, interested in classical andinism, asked me in 2001 for details of the 1986 and 1999 exploration and climbing visits I made to the Riso Patrón Range and Dos Hermanos Range, which lies west of the Riso Patrón Range. Specifically he asked about the unclimbed Cerro 3,018m (as is named in the Chilean maps), which rises above the Falcon Fjord at the western border of the Southern Continental Icecap (49°33'10"S, 73°34'30"W). An icy fortress a few miles northeast of Cerro Riso Patrón, it was believed to be one of the last unclimbed Patagonian 3,000m mountains. The late Casimiro Ferrari once told me that when he summited Riso Patrón Central (3,019m on available maps), Cerro 3,018m appeared higher. His comments and the report of Rada's expedition, giving Cerro 3,018m an elevation of about 2,800m, raise questions about the accuracy of measurements in these remote cordilleras. As for climbing Cerro 3,018, my advice to the Chileans was to tackle it from the Pacific Ocean, via the Exmouth Fjord, thereby accessing the Icecap by a known route, then going south. I suggested trying the north side of the mountain, since I had noted on my visits that the south face looked steep and exposed to objective dangers.

Rada, the leader, and the other four members—three young women, Maria Paz Ibarra, Fiorenza Marinkovic, and Viviana Callaham, and Sebastian Varela, all from the Universidad Catolica de Chile and in their early 20s—first tried to reach Cerro 3,018m in January 2002. They decided, because of their limited budget, to approach from the east, crossing the Icecap from Paso del Viento in Argentina, thus avoiding the expensive sea approach. Some weeks and several storms later, they were at the foot of the east summit of Cerro 3,018m East, a lower summit but an attractive pyramid of rock and ice. From there they had to retreat due to weather, which happened to be worse than at the same latitude on the eastern side of the Icecap.

The team made a second attempt on Cerro 3,018m, with a similar approach because of icy channels, in the last austral winter. They left Santiago on July 11, reached El Chalten on July 15, and installed a camp at Paso Marconi on July 18. Despite bad weather they continued and established successive camps, the fourth at Nunatak Witte. They progressed to the south, between Nunatak Viedma and the Mariano Moreno Range. Some days later, at the southern end of this massif, they turned west. In poor weather but with the help of a GPS, they climbed to the Rokko Pass and set up Camp 8. From here they continued toward Cerro 3,018m, having fantastic views of Cerros Riso Patrón Central and Gaviota. On July 29, after climbing to a lower pass and abseiling 90 difficult meters to a plateau not far from Cerro 3,018m, they set up Camp 10 and converted it into a sort of base camp.

On July 31 Camilo and Maria Paz (Pachi) decided, instead of exploring the presumed easier north side of the mountain, to try the south face, deciding that with the intense cold and permanent shade it looked safe. They installed 60m of fixed rope on the wall, while Sebastian, Fiorenza and Viviana climbed a nearby, unnamed mushroom summit which they called Mirador Callaham. On August 3, after several days of storm spent at camp 10, Camilo and Pachi —observing no traces of avalanches on the face—began an alpine-style push, jumaring the fixed ropes and then climbing another 200m to their first bivouac at an altitude (GPS) of 2343m. The next day, Camilo and Pachi climbed another 300 difficult meters, over ice up to 90°, and placed the second bivouac on the face at around 2649m. On August 5, after climbing more pitches, and at 2750m and only a few meters from the top, Camilo took a 10m fall. Caught by another sudden storm and with the final mushroom still to climb, they decided to descend. On the south wall, they had climbed 600m (12 pitches, 5.6 AI4+ 70-90°). After abseiling for the rest of the day, they arrived very late that night at base camp, which had been collapsed by the wind, forcing them to dig a cave. Also on August 5, Sebastian, Fiorenza and Viviana made a second virgin mushroom summit which they called Mirador Marinkovic.

The entire group then rested for some days, waiting for the storm to stop, then began their return to Argentina. They successfully managed their way back up the difficult 90m step on their way to Rokko Pass. At this time they decided to leave the Icecap thru Paso del Viento instead of Paso Marconi, and were back to El Chalten on August 15. They officially proposed the name of Cerro Buracchio for Cerro 3,018m. (Christian Buracchio, who died in a plane crash in 2001, was one of the most active Chilean climbers and a member of the successful 1992 Everest Kangshung Face Chilean Expedition).

CARLOS E. COMESAÑA, *Brazil*

(Mr. Comesaña, Patagonia climbing pioneer, writes: "I consider this area—due to its extreme weather conditions, isolation, and the combination of a difficult approach with severe technical difficulties—a mecca for this and future generations of classical mountain climbers. Here, most of the ranges and summits not only remain unclimbed and unnamed but are very much unknown and poorly located in the official cartography.")

TORRES DEL PAINE NATIONAL PARK

North Tower of Paine, Los Esclavos del Barometro and other ascents. On December 31 Tina DiBatista and I (Slovenians) climbed a new route to the North Summit of the North Tower of Paine. We climbed a beautiful crack line to the right of the route Armas y Rozas. I had tried the line with my friend Nejc Bevk two days before, but we had to retreat because of a sudden snowstorm. We climbed around 250m that day. It was cold, but the rock was dry, and we were mostly free climbing. We did not leave fixed ropes.

Two days later cracks were full of snow and ice, so Tina and I were forced to aid most of the hard pitches. We were angry about the conditions, but our time was running out, and we had to take what was offered. At 6 p.m. we reached the summit and rappelled the route. The roundtrip from base camp took 19 hours. The name of our 500m route is Los Esclavos del Barometro (Barometer Slaves), and we graded it V 5.10 A2. We believe it would be possible to free climb the route, with

On the fourth pitch of Barometer Slaves.
Tomaz Jakofcic

Los Esclavos del Barometro (Barometer Slaves) on the west face of the North Tower of Paine. Tomaz Jakofcic

difficulties around 5.11. On the first two pitches we found pieces of old fixed ropes.

On December 16 we climbed the Piola–Sprungli 1992 route, La Ultima Esperanza (500m, 5.11 A1). Our friends Janez Peterlin and Nejc Brescak repeated Taller del Sol (500m, 5.10+).

TOMAZ JAKOFCIC, *Slovenia*

Torre Central, Riders on the Storm, second ascent. David Stastny and I, both Czech, repeated the route Riders on the Storm on the east face of Torre Central in February 2002. The climb took 12 days (1/31–2/10), with four days spent in a portaledge in bad weather. We climbed alpine style, without fixing and without contact with base camp. During the first ascent German climbers Albert, Arnold, Batz, Gullich, and Dietrich used aid on pitches 7,10,15, and 20. We too used aid on these pitches, as well as on pitches 14 (5.12c on the first ascent) and 25 (5.12b). However, above the big roof on pitch 25 we managed to climb free (5.11) because of good conditions; during the first ascent this upper section was iced and was climbed with aid. After nine days and 38 pitches we reached the summit of Torre Central. The descent took three days (two days in the portaledge in bad weather). Ours was the second ascent of the route, 12 years after the first ascent.

JAN KREISINGER, *Czech Republic*

Torre Central, Riders on the Storm, attempt and third ascent. In November Frenchmen Jerome Arpin and Sylvain Empereur attempted to climb Riders on the Storm in alpine style. They climbed 18 pitches in four days, but the weather changed, bringing very cold temperatures, and they retreated. From the French report it appears that the Czechs who made the second ascent (see report above) may have added a number of bolts, both at belays and in the middle of pitches. In early December Frenchmen Arnaud Boudet, Martial Dumas, Jean Yves Fredericksen, and Yann Mimet made the third ascent of this route. Over 14 days, eight of which they spent climbing, they fixed 500m of rope on the lower portion. On December 4 they started up on their final attempt, taking portaledges and food for five days. They set up a camp at the top of the fixed ropes and for four days fixed 400m of rope above, using the rope they had used in the lower section. On December 8 they started up the ropes, climbed the last difficult section, a big 50m overhanging dihedral, and continued up easy ground to the summit, which they reached around noon. That same day they retrieved all their ropes, dismantled their camp, and descended all the way to base-camp, reaching it around 11 p.m. Not counting belay bolts, the route apparently has around 46 bolts and drilled holes. The Frenchmen added one drilled hook on pitch 16, where a flake had broken. They climbed free the three main off-width pitches (17, 18, 19), for which the route is notorious, not using the many drilled hooks (whether from the first ascent or drilled by the Czechs is unknown). The French note that their 4.5 and 5 Camalots were not enough, and suggest taking a 6 Camalot or a bigger Big Bro. They also note that many of the bolts do not have hangers, so they recommend taking 8mm Petzl self-drive bolts and hangers.

ROLANDO GARIBOTTI, *Club Andino Bariloche*

SOUTH OF PAINE

Cerro Balmaceda, west face, possible new route. In February 2002 Spaniards Iñaki San Vicente and Carlos Garcia de Cortazar made what appears to be the second, or perhaps third, ascent of this beautiful 2,035m peak, which lies at the northern end of Fiordo Ultima Esperanza. They approached the peak from the Torres del Paine National Park, using kayaks to descend 70km of the Rio Serrano to the fjord, which they crossed to its western end to reach Laguna Azul. They made their ascent via the west face, starting early in the morning from a bivy at around 700m, and reached the south summit eight hours later. The most difficult section involved a steep 80m face with ice up to 85°. The central summit appears to be a few meters lower than the south summit, but they were not able to reach it because a big crevasse barred passage along an otherwise straight-forward ridge. The first ascent of Balmaceda was done from the north by Argentines Meiling, Arnsek, and Botazzi, and Chilean Saavedra in 1957.

ROLANDO GARIBOTTI, *Club Andino Bariloche*

TIERRA DEL FUEGO, CORDILLERA DARWIN, CHILE

Monte Shipton–Monte Darwin, naming and reconnaissance. In 1962 my father, Eric Shipton, made the first ascent of the highest peak of the Cordillera Darwin in Tierra del Fuego with three Chilean companions, Cedomir Marangunic, Eduardo Garcia, and Francisco Vivanco (*Alpine Journal*, November 1962). It was the first attempt to get near this peak, guarded from the Beagle Channel to the fjords to the north by ice cap. Because their then-unnamed peak is the high point of the range, they called it Monte Darwin. However, they left cartographers with a problem, as the second-highest peak (2,438m), farther south, was already Monte Darwin. This peak was first climbed by a 1970 New Zealand expedition, who neatly resolved the confusion by referring to their peak as Monte Darwin, while referring to my father's Monte Darwin as Monte Shipton.

In February I engaged a fishing boat for the three-day voyage from Punta Arenas to the head of the Cuevas Arm of Bahia Parry with three New Zealand climbers, Paddy Freaney, Rochelle Rafferty, and Bill King. We intended to approach both Monte Darwin and Monte Shipton. As far as I know neither of the mountains has been climbed since 1962 and 1970, so we wanted to at least have a look at them. We were unable to get onto the ice cap, due to the Cuevas Glacier being too crevassed, but we did gain excellent perspectives of the eastern sides of the two very different mountains. We then made a traverse to the Beagle Channel via the alpine Paso Nuevo Ano, the Vedova Glacier, and the Lapataia Valley. At Yendegaia we gained passage back to Punta Arenas. I have since gone some way with Chilean authorities to confirm the naming of Monte Shipton.

JOHN SHIPTON, *U.K.*

Antarctica

SENTINEL RANGE

Ronge &
Wiencke Islands
Forbidden
Plateau

Sentinel
Range

Antarctica

Summary of activities. A total of 68 climbers attempted 4,897m Vinson Massif, including seven women. Unusually poor weather was experienced in the second half of the season, one reason that only 55 climbers reached the summit, to give a success rate of barely 81%.

In addition to this regular activity, several teams this season had other, more interesting objectives. Undoubtedly the most ambitious of these was the Chilean team, led by Rodrigo Jordan, who planned a length-wise traverse of the range from north to south, including ascents of some high peaks—two of them virgin, plus a new route on Vinson. This was the first time such a traverse had been attempted, although much of the terrain, such as the Embree, Patton, and Dater Glaciers, had been visited by climbing expeditions in recent years.

However, the Chileans encountered not only poor weather, but difficult sledging terrain, being forced to cross numerous east-west ridges and lower their sledges down technically difficult passes. The team only attempted one of its main unclimbed objectives, Mt. Giovinetto, but retreated due to the cold and high winds on November 29th. They did, however, make the first ascent of a smaller peak, Mt. Segers (2460m), on December 6th. Segers is a rocky peak to the northeast of Vinson, situated above the head of the Crosswell Glacier. After descending the Thomas Glacier, the Chileans made fast time once out of the Sentinels, and after a 368km journey of 53 days reached ANI's Patriot Hills base camp on January 2nd, from where they were flown out on January 4th.

Mt. Epperly (left) and Mt. Tyree (right) from the summit of Mt. Shinn. Damien Gildea

The Omega Foundation again sent a team to obtain an accurate height for Mt. Shinn, long considered Antarctica's third highest mountain. Damien Gildea, 33, of Australia, and Rodrigo Fica, 35, of Chile, flew in to Vinson base camp on November 19th and on November 28th occupied Vinson Camp 3, which is situated on the col between Vinson and Shinn and is the normal last camp for ascents of both peaks. Even after the range was resurveyed in 1979, resulting in a revised USGS map, no height was given for Shinn. USGS publications merely defined it as "…a mountain over 4800m." Gildea had long thought that Shinn was probably lower than this, an idea reinforced by his first attempt to measure the mountain in November 2001 (see *AAJ* 2002 ppg. 339–342).

Rodrigo Fica traversing the upper slopes of Mt. Shinn, Sentinel Range, Antarctica. Damien Gildea

The pair left camp at 5pm on November 30th, deliberately late so as to run the GPS unit wholly within one UTC Day, for best data collection. The lower part of the route is low-angled and passed very quickly, but the upper slope steepened, with sections of 55° on poor ice and snow. The upper section was climbed unroped and no avalanche hazard was encountered, save for a large, partially detached shield of hard, hollow ice perched at the top of the slope, immediately beneath the summit seracs. The channel through the seracs was around 60°, but brought the climbers right on to the summit itself, which gives stunning views of the nearby peaks such as Tyree and Epperly.

Once anchored, the pair set up the GPS unit and began logging data, then set up a Marmot summit tent around 5m below the summit on the only flat place available, which was right on top of one of the summit seracs. A handline was rigged back up to the summit, which Gildea used to periodically check the functioning of the GPS unit. The weather on the day was perfect, probably the best of the season, making the job much easier and safer. After logging data for six hours, most of which was spent dozing in the tent, the pair packed up and down-climbed the route, again unroped, until Fica encountered a deep crevasse on the middle slopes of Shinn, cutting across the route.

After returning to camp 3, two days were spent in poor weather, after which the pair quickly returned to Vinson base camp, only to wait several days to fly out, due to more bad weather. Unlike the previous year, conditions on the Branscombe Glacier were relatively soft and snowy, enabling the pair to enjoy a leisurely ski all the way from camp 2 back to base camp.

However, at base camp the pair undertook the second part of their objective, which was to submit the GPS data to the Australian government AUSPOS website, via Iridium satellite phone, and have the results of their work automatically emailed back to them. This process worked flawlessly and the Omega team obtained the new height of 4660.508m for Mt. Shinn. This is around 140m lower than previously thought and therefore a significant contribution to Antarctic science and mapping. A full report of this expedition can be found at www.theomegafoundation.org.

It should be noted that not only had the route up the "headwall" changed considerably from the previous year—much more to the right, to avoid the seracs and crevassing in the center at the top—but that the old camp 2 site, nestled in next to a stable serac just above the corner of the upper Branscombe, had avalanche debris to within 20m of it, this having fallen from the lower cliffs on the south west face of Shinn and crossed the cwm.

In early January, Robert Anderson guided four clients on a new route from the south-west. Anderson had visited this side of Vinson previously, when in November and December of 1992 he climbed two new routes up Vinson, one on the southwest face and another on the west-southwest ridge. The 2003 route was the first time that commercially guided clients had either attempted or completed a new route on any of the highest Sentinel peaks. (See report below.)

Around the same time, regular Sentinels visitor Conrad Anker was attempting another new route on the east side of the mountain, also with clients. Anker, with Chileans Misael Alvial, Andronico Luksic and Maximo Pacheco, was landed on the Dater Glacier. Though the team established a first camp, bad weather prevented any further progress and they were flown out in late January.

DAMIEN GILDEA, *AAC, Australia*

Mt. Vinson, southwest face, first ascent of Double003. In 1992 I'd completed the first solo ascent of a new route on a prominent ridge bordering the southwest face (The Rolex Ridge) and looked across at the huge unclimbed expanse of the mountain to the west of it. It took 10 years to organize the return and have a chance to climb it.

We departed Punta Arenas on 27 December, 2002, flying on Adventure Networks Ilushin 76 to Patriot Hills, and then continued another hour in the air in a Single Otter over to Vinson the following day. We landed five miles away from our hoped for drop off point due to deteriorating

The southwest face of Mt. Vinson. Robert Anderson

weather. We had skis, so spent that night and the following four days skiing though mixed weather up to the base of the peak. From this side of Vinson, four long ridges lead out, separated by five glaciers, only two of which have been explored.

At the head of the glacier along the base of the mountain (8,300') we reached a spectacular camp set on the col of a ridge suspended between two immense glaciers. In honor of the man who originally inspired our journey, Jim Clash, we named this the Clash Col.

At 9,500' on Vinson's southwest face just before midnight, Bob Guthrie, Peggy Foster, Intesar Haider, and Chris Heintz are climbing out of the ice fog lens en-route to the summit. *Robert Anderson*

The 7,000' face leading to the summit plateau didn't appear to have any camp sites, so we made our first attempt on the peak in a single non-stop effort, that attained the top of the face, but left us still a good distance from the summit. We retreated for an 18-hour nap in the eternal sunshine, ate the rest of our food, and then on the evening of four January we set out again, utilizing a small ice nubbin to place a tent and rest at a high camp for four hours before continuing on the next morning.

We reached the plateau in eight hours, and another seven hours of wandering across the immense expanse of the plateau and up the summit ridge led to the top at 1:30 a.m. on January 6.

The face itself offers a mix of snow, ice and the occasional rock band to climb through, at a gradient of 35° to 60°-plus degrees. With a rapid elevation gain, views south toward the Pole open up over the ice rapidly and the final stroll across the summit plateau, all at over 15,000', makes for a memorable experience, to put it mildly.

Amongst our team, Peggy Foster became the first Canadian woman to complete a new route on Vinson, Intesar Haider became the first person from Bangladesh to ascend Vinson, Chris Heintz became the youngest person to complete a new route to the top of Antarctica, Bob Guthrie ascended two years after recovery from a potentially life threatening case of cancer, and Robert Anderson completed his third new route to the summit.

ROBERT ANDERSON, *AAC*

ANTARCTIC PENINSULA

Summary of activities. Livingston Island is a rugged mountain massif, home to the highest point of the South Shetland Islands, off the northwestern tip of the Peninsula. It is also the location of a number of scientific research stations from different nations. On January 5th, Alex Simon i Casanovas, Jordi Sorribas i Cervantes, David Hita i Sanchez and Vicente Castro Sotos, personnel from the Spanish Juan Carlos I base, made the first ascent of Mt. Bowles, a rounded peak on eastern part of the island. Argentine sources put the altitude of Mt. Bowles at 914m, but the Spanish team's GPS recorded only 839m. Though the route was only of moderate difficulty, it is one of the few summits ever reached on the island. Vicente Castro Sotos had climbed on the Peninsula in March 2001, when he made the first ascent of Mt. Tennant (690m) on Rongé Island (*AAJ* 2001), as well as an ascent of Mt. Shackleton (1,465m) and other smaller peaks.

The recent high levels of climbing activity by Antipodean groups in the Peninsula area continued, with the Spirit of Sydney, skippered by Roger Wallis, being chartered by a group of experienced Australian and New Zealand guides and clients—Jon Chapman, John Fitzgibbon, Karl Hillary, Theodore Kossart, Jon Morgan, Chuck Olbery, Stuart Morris, and Rob Rymill. The latter is the great-nephew of the legendary polar explorer John Rymill, who led the audacious British Graham Land Expedition of 1934-37. That expedition explored a large area of the southern Antarctic Peninsula, including many of the high inland mountains and discovered King George VI Sound.

The first summit for this year's expedition, on January 8th, was the probable fourth ascent of Harris Peak (1,005m) on the Reclus Peninsula. The whole team summited via a route from the north, which they then skied to descend. Harris Peak had been climbed in late December 2001 by three members of a British military expedition. Two days later Chapman, Fitzgibbon, Kossart, Morris, and Rymill made the third ascent of Mt. Johnston (2,304m). Ascents of the higher inland peaks are relatively rare and Johnston had only received its second ascent last year, by the same British military group that climbed Harris Peak.

The team sailed further south and on January 15th Hillary, Morgan and Olbery climbed and skied the north face of Mt. Demaria (635m), a picturesque small peak that has been climbed many times and skied by American teams in both February 2000 (see *AAJ* 2000 p.294) and March 2001, both trips involving the late Hans Saari.

On January 16th, some of the team climbed the northern peak of the popular Mt. Scott, from the easy-angled south side. Hillary, Kossart, Morgan, Olbery, and Rymill made the ascent, then descended the route on skis. While that group was on North Mt. Scott, Chapman and Morris simul-climbed about eight pitches worth of rock and mixed terrain to the summit of nearby Duseberg Buttress (500m) via its west face. This buttress is the obvious dark rocky cone on the south-west side of Mt. Scott, just above the shoreline. In many distant photos of Scott from the west this feature is often indistinguishable against the larger bulk of Scott, but in fact the normal approach to Scott goes between Duseberg Buttress and the south-western slopes of Mt. Scott itself.

Saving the best until last, the highest peak in the area, Mt. Francais (2,822m) on Anvers Island, received its sixth ascent, via the eastern Bull Ridge. This long ridge was named after John Bull, a member of the British Antarctic Survey team that made the 1955 first ascent of the stunning nearby peak Mt. William. It was climbed in February 1999 by the Australians David Adams and Duncan Thomas. This year, Kossart, Morgan, Morris and Olbery ascended Green Spur, climbed to Copper Col (305m) between Billie Peak (725m) and Copper Peak (1,125m), then gained the western side of Bull Ridge, which they followed to the summit. Morgan and Olbery made a ski descent, the second time that Francais has been skied, the first being Greg Landreth's 1987 expedition aboard *Northanger*, which made the fourth ascent of Francais.

A ski descent of Francais was also the objective of Americans Andrew Maclean and Doug Stoup, who arrived in the area in early February aboard the yacht *Pelagic*. Starting from a base slightly further west than the Australian/NZ group, Stoup and Maclean made an ascent of a minor peak known as The Minaret (ca 1,050m), which is part of a small group running east to west from Mt. William. The pair skinned up the first 900m then removed their skis and donned crampons to ascend more broken terrain to the summit. On the descent, they skied from the point where they had left their skis, enjoying their turns all the way back to their base camp. Poor weather prevented any significant attempt on Francais.

The yacht *Northanger* made a return to Antarctic waters, again skippered by Canadian residents Greg Landreth and Keri Pashuk. On board were Eduard Birnbacher of Germany, Niel Fox and Roger Robinson of the UK and Jonathan Selby of New Zealand. The team experienced a very rough crossing of the Drake Passage in mid-February and *Northanger* arrived at the Port Lockroy area on Wiencke Island requiring a significant amount of repair work. This was undertaken by Landreth and Pashuk, thus removing them from any climbing activity.

Around the end of February Birnbacher and Fox climbed to the southernmost of the rocky points on the ridge between Jabet Peak (545m) and Noble Peak (720m) on Wiencke Island. They climbed from the eastern side, up a 50°-60° couloir for 400m before climbing two and a half pitches along the loose, rocky ridge to a point they reported as being 700m. This ridge was first traversed on November 16th, 1948 by the British climbers Pawson and Blyth, who had made the first ascent of Noble Peak the previous week. Numerous routes on this massif, and on Wiencke Island in general, have been climbed since the first ascent of Jabet in May, 1948. The Wiencke Island area is now probably the most-visited Peninsula destination for yacht-based climbers, due in part to the good anchorage at Port Lockroy. Though other parties have traversed off this ridge, on this occasion Birnbacher and Fox saw fit to rappel their route of ascent, leaving behind pitons and slings for anchors.

The same pair later climbed to a 650m ridge-point on the north ridge of Wandel Peak (980m). Wandel is the highest point of Booth Island and is unclimbed (see photo in *AAJ* 2001). Its north ridge was attempted in February 1997 by Greg Landreth, Jia Condon and Rich Prohaska while Keri Pashuk minded *Northanger*. Booth Island forms the eastern side of the spectacular and popular Lemaire Channel, so Wandel Peak is seen, at least in good weather, by over 10,000 ship-bound tourists a year. Though relatively accessible, it remains one of the most challenging unclimbed objectives on the Antarctic Peninsula.

Though Birnbacher and Fox climbed a significant amount of technical terrain, with ice to 75° and poor quality rock to UIAA V, they were halted by the heavily corniced ridge between their high-point and the summit of Wandel Peak. The pair rappelled and downclimbed their route of ascent and returned to *Northanger* for a seven-day voyage back to Ushuaia, arriving on March 18th.

DAMIEN GILDEA, *AAC, Australia*

DRONNING MAUD LAND

Summary of activities. In late January an experienced team of Russian mountaineers flew in to Dronning Maud Land, aiming to make a number of ascents among the spectacular spires for which this area is now famous. The group flew from Cape Town, South Africa in an Ilyushin-76, landing at the Russian base Novolazarevskaya ('Novo') on January 25th.

A reconnaissance party had already been in during December, traveling in two six-wheeled diesel-powered buggies, the same type used for a journey to the South Pole in the 1999-2000 season. The buggies arrived via the Russian ship Akademic Federov and were unloaded on to the ice shelf on December 18th. In early January a crew of three drove the buggies on a 450km return trip in to the Orvin Mountains, to scout a suitable landing area for the Antonov-2 plane that was planning to deliver the climbing team.

Instead, the team eventually used the buggies to travel from Novo base around 150km into the Wohlthat Mountains. The peaks visited are over 100km to the east and slightly north of the better-known massifs containing peaks like Ulvetanna and Rakekniven. One of the buggies became inoperable and the remaining buggy was used to reconnoiter the area for climbing objectives. The first ascent was an unnamed peak at 71°36.375S 12°38.12E, climbed by Yevgeniy Vinogradsky, Valeriy Pershin and Alexandr Foigt on January 30th and given the unofficial name "Georgi Zhukov."

On February 1st Vinogradsky and Pershin, with Yuriy Baikovsky and Georgi Gatagov climbed another peak, supposedly 2,255m, 15km to the north-west of the previous peak. This second peak they named "Holy Boris and Gleb." The climbers reportedly placed a cross of the Russian Orthodox Church on its summit. (*Though unconfirmed, if true, this move is to be condemned, as it sets an undesirable precedent and violates the regulations of the "Protocol on Environmental Protection to the Antarctic Treaty" that deal with removal of all introduced material by expeditions. Generally, Antarctic mountaineers neither take nor leave anything from a summit.—DG*)

Two days later Foigt, Pershin, and Vinogradsky climbed a 2,239m peak around 5km from their base camp. Then, on February 5th, Baikovsky, Gatagov, Vinogradsky, Maxim Volkov, and the leader, Valeri Kuzin, climbed another peak close to their base camp, which they named "Geser Peak."

While these ascents were taking place, Khvostenko, Kuznetsov, Sokolov, and Zakharov were climbing a difficult new wall route on one of the Svarthorna Peaks, in this case a 2,585m spire that the team named "Peak Valery Chkalov." These Svarthorna Peaks have sometimes been known as "Mount Schwarze" or "Shvartse," another name that the Russians used on this occasion. This new route involved two days of fixing ropes to start, then another six days of climbing, plus a day to descend on February 6th. The team reported excellent crack climbing, much of it freed up to 6b, on sound rock that took both natural and bolt protection. Nights were spent in portaledges, though luckily the weather was excellent for the duration of the climb.

The expedition then began plans to return north to Novo, proposing three round trips in the one remaining buggy. However, shortly in to the first trip, not far from their base camp, the buggy went in to a crevasse and was damaged beyond repair. The team was then rescued by an Antonov-2 plane from the Russian Antarctic program and left Antarctica for Cape Town on February 10th.

DAMIEN GILDEA, *AAC, Australia*

South Georgia, various activity. Bad weather thwarted attempts by a team off the 15m ketch Gambo to make three first ascents on South Georgia, and a new route up the island's highest peak, Mt. Paget. During the team's month-long stay, mass balance and radar data of the Nordenskjold Glacier and a bathymetric survey of its front were also gathered in support of a scientific research program to quantify the impact of climate change and water-quality on the southern high-latitudes. We called ours the Antarctic Convergence Zone Expedition: South Georgia '03.

The international team of seven, led by myself, a Welsh glaciologist and mountaineer, set out from Cape Horn for South Georgia in mid-February on the second year of this adventure-research program. After a challenging voyage made interesting by an above-average density of large (up to 120km) tabular burgs surrounding the island, and compounded by the complete loss of the yacht's auxiliary diesel when an unmarked line became entangled in its prop, *Gambo* arrived at Grytviken on March 3. From here, two attempts were made on three unclimbed mountains: Paulsen Peak (1,877m), Quad Five (1,693m), and Marakoppa (1,840m), that lie above the Lyell Glacier in Cumberland West Bay; whilst a second party focused its attention on the unclimbed east ridge of 2,993m Mt. Paget, the island's highest peak. A third party explored smaller peaks on the overland route to St. Andrews Bay

Hamish Millar at the start of the 4 km E Ridge of Mt Paget showing the sub-peak in the foreground with Paget's (2,996m) summit behind. *Alun Hubbard*

and cleared discarded jerry cans and other detritus.

Stuart Holmes, Grant Redvers, and Davie Robinson made two attempts on Paulsen Peak, Quad Five, and Marakoppa. They first aimed for the col between Paulsen peak and Quad Five, from where access to both summits appeared to be relatively easy. However, after climbing up the Lyell Glacier, their progress was blocked by an icefall at around the 600m level. Their second attempt a week later and focused on ascending the Geikie Glacier to the col between Marakoppa and Quad Five. Seracs and an intimidating icefall were encountered, and in failing conditions, with significant avalanche risks, they turned back.

The second team led by myself (who had pulled, split, and attempted repairs on the diesel) focused on Mt. Paget. Tim Hall, Hamish Millar, and I skied up the eastern margin of the Nordenskjold glacier towards the col between Paget and Roots at ca 1,800m. After five days dug into a crevasse in atrocious weather, we eventually hit the col on March 25. With a cloudless dawn, Millar and I set off for the final four km's to Paget's summit along an airy and corniced but straightforward ridge, in conditions varying between soft sugary snow and excellent water ice. Below Paget's sub-peak, we climbed through seracs and up a small south face that ended with a steep ice pitch. We then skirted south of the sub-peak on 40° snow slopes, up another steep ice pitch to regain the ridge, leaving easy ground to the summit. At ca 2,550m, with an ominously rapid deterioration in weather we retreated. A prudent decision given the total whiteout and phenomenal winds of the next fraught five hours. With little food and fuel we eventually made it back to Cumberland Bay East on 28 March. *Gambo* left Grytviken a few days later enjoying a brief spell with a fully functioning diesel which sadly, was not to last and spelt a frustrating three-week voyage back to Mar del Plata, where we made landfall on Easter Sunday.

ALUN HUBBARD, *U.K.*

Africa

SUDAN

Kassala area, various new routes. Lost in the Sudanese East, only a few kilometers from the border with Eritrea, a small island of a dozen granitic monoliths dominate the town of Kassala. Baboons and vultures live there. French climbers Matthieu Noury and I returned from this incredible area enchanted by the country and by the local African tribes we met (Rashaiba, Haddendowah, and Beni Amir), and the routes we opened. Only two known routes existed before our arrival. The first, opened in 1939 by L.W. Brown and R.A. Hodgkin, was described by its first ascenders as the most beautiful climbing in Africa. It allowed them to gain Jebel Taka, the highest point of the granite domes (approximately 1,500m). Two pitons are still in place in a splendid 5+ (5.9) dihedral. The first repetitions took place in November 1981 by a Czech team, and in December 1983 by Tony Howard (U.K.). The second route is near the village of Totil, on one of the additional Turns of Jebel Totil, and was probably climbed by the Czech team in 1981. It offers constant athletic crack climbing at ED-, 6c.

In addition to the free repetitions of these two routes, Matthieu and I opened three new routes during our stay: Mohammed et Mustapha au Pays des Enfants (120m, TD, 6b), with aesthetic crack climbing located above village huts. Chaud Crâne (250m, TD+, 6b) is a broad system

Domes of Jebel Kassala. The lower 300m line is Khawadja on north Taka. The upper line is the 200m Brown-Hodgkin route on Taka summit. The obvious 250m dihedral on the big dome (west Taka) has not been climbed, probably because there are no cracks leading to it. According to Jonglez, it should be a "fantastic hand crack." David Jonglez

of cracks leading to the southern shoulder of Jebel Taka. Khawadja (means "white man") (300m, TD+, 6b+) climbs a rectilinear crack between two immense smooth and compact flagstones. This crack offers exceptional climbing on carved rock. It is a beautiful route that leads near the top of Jebel Taka.

The climbing area and its neighbors seem to conceal great potential for climbing. The immediate border of Kassala (from north to south, Mucram, Totil, and Taka) consist of 12 principal towers ranging from 100m to 450m, and many other domes from 50m to 100m. Nevertheless, the compactness of the rock offers only rare lines for natural protection. Some faces seem to await generations of climbers to come, as they are stiff and smooth.

DAVID JONGLEZ, *France*

Editor's note: A comprehensive article on desert climbing in "North Africa and the Middle East," including the Kassala area (above) and Oman and Sinai (below), can be found in the AAJ 1999.

MIDDLE EAST

OMAN

Western Hajar mountains report. There has been another bout of new route activity since my last report in *AAJ* 2001. In November, possibly the best line in the range was climbed on Jabal Misht by resident guide Jacob Oberhause (Austria) and Brian Davison (U.K.). The direct line up the crest of the south pillar had been much talked about. The guys stormed the 1,200m route in a day at ED3 (5.11+) and named their line "The English Arête." An interesting and possibly frightening development during the winter of 2001-02 was the arrival of the highly prolific Austrian team of Albert Precht and Sigi Brachmayer. This pair have dominated new route developments in Jordan's Wadi Rum over recent years and have now turned their attentions to the cream of Arabian limestone, all at the invitation of Oswald Oelz.

Oswald and Albert were part of a team attempting Makalu 25 years ago. Since then Albert has declined high altitude mountaineering in favor of his exploratory alpine and subalpine rock climbing. Oswald, though, went on to climb many Himalayan peaks, sometimes with Reinhold Messner. This invitation was designed to be a reunion as well as to ensure that this pair of mountaineering gentlemen summited a big piece of rock together after all this time. A nice touch.

The eastern wall of Jabal Misht, known as the Al Jil wall, had received an ascent courtesy of this author and David Barlow in 2000, but our route avoided the obvious difficulties of the central pillar. After an exploratory ascent of a line called Half Moon Corner with Gerhard Hafner, the Precht, Brachmayer, and Oelz team climbed the central pillar and named it in Oswald's honor as the Doc.Bulle pillar (500m, TD).

The Precht-Brachmayer team then took to the southwest face of Misht to climb the left edge of the wall. Watergate (500m, TD), takes the obvious corner system with the difficulties predominantly in the lower half. Not satisfied with this new route, the Austrians swung around the back and climbed a 200m new route on the north face of the First Tower at TD, just to fill in the rest of the afternoon!

In March 2003, Geoff Hornby with Mark Turnbull and Susie Sammut climbed the face right of Watergate to finish up the front face on the upper pillar. Sorely Misht is 600m, D sup.

The south pillar and southeast faces of Jabal Misht, showing: 1. French Pillar (1,500m, ED with 1 pitch of ED3, Renauld et. al., 1979). 2. The English Arête (1,200m, ED3 [5.11+], 2001). 3. Icarrus (1,100m, 5.11, Littlejohn-Sustad, 2001). 4. The Empty Quarter (1,000m, ED2 [5.10R], Chaudhry-Eastwood-Ramsden, 2000). 5. Eastern Promise (1,000m, TD+/ED1 [5.10], Nonis-Ramsden, 1999). 6. Intifada (1,000m, TD+ [5.10], Hornby-Wallis, 2001). 7. Southern Groove (TD/TD+, Colleague-Hadwin). 8. Riddle in the Sands (850m, TD inf, Bishop-Barlow-Chaudhry, 2001). 9. Tony Howard route. Geoff Hornby

The Austrians added another independent line up the central section of the south face of Misht at TD, with 800m of climbing. Yet again, they were up and down with a fair amount of the day remaining, and Oswald, who watched them through bino's, described them as mutant dwarfs. Way of the Dwarves, or Wichtlmannchen, looks like a good outing. The British team of Peter Bishop, Aqil Chaudhry, and David Barlow attempted the right-hand pillar on the southeast face. Riddle in the Sands (850m, TD inf) traverses into Intifada for three pitches at half-height, and so loses some of its attractiveness, but was an excellent voyage up an obvious feature.

From Misht, the view southward is dominated by the mass of Jabal Kawr. This so-called "mountain of waterfalls" is surrounded on all sides by walls of between 400m and 900m in height. On the northeast side a system of towers become visible with the changing light of the late afternoon. The Austrians invited me to join them in exploring the potential of these towers, and I couldn't refuse. Our first venture was the striking north ridge of Jabal Asait. This beautiful towered ridge rises for 600m above the small village and provided us with steady climbing: a few pitches of 5.9 and a steep 5.10c. "Internationale" is one of the finest routes I have ever done, and deserves repeat ascents.

The north pillar of Jabal Asala gave 500m of TD rock and a further 500m of scrambling, which is a good day in its own right, but not enough for Precht. So he soloed a 500m line on Asait's north rib as he passed it on the way down! Solo Climb (D sup) now has a pair of parallel lines, courtesy of myself and Susie Sammut, named Two's Company and Three's a Crowd both 500m and D sup. Brian Davison soloed the wall left of Three's a Crowd to give Alone in Space (500m, TD) and two shorter and easier lines further to the south end of the face.

An attractive tower to the West of Asala's summit has become known as the Asala Tower. First out the full Austrian contingent climbed the Luadabuam pillar at TD and 250m. Whilst the others wound their way down the back, Albert soloed down another line before soloing back up a third line. These two lines are Down Hill and Straight Up; both contain climbing to 5.9!

Whilst this fiesta of solo climbing was going on, Peter Bishop and myself were beavering away on Asait's West face. This 600m wall is brilliant. Our route, Snake Charmer climbed the pillar separating the NW and SW aspects and went straight to the summit. Face climbing, cracks, and grooves, never harder than 5.10a—it is truly superb. Our ascent was made during the Islamic festival of Ramadan and we descended from the hill and into the village at sunset feeling totally trolleyed. We had been watched by the shepherds all day and they then invited us to break the fast with them. Sitting around the camp fire with the whole village, sharing dates and drinking cardoman coffee, whilst the children did imitations of bouldering moves, was very, very special.

Aqil Chaudhry and David Barlow cranked away at a steeper line to the left of Snake Charmer. After six pitches, including E2 offwidths, the boys hit a patch of soft rock and were forced to rap down. Left as a climb in its own right, they named it Muscat Rap, and graded it TD sup.

The next day, Albert and Sigi left their last mark on the range for the year with a second line up the North face of Asala. Rock Fascination weighs in at TD and has 600m of climbing and 500m of scrambling. The British posse then took off to investigate the potential of Jabal Misfah at the head of Wadi Ghul. The only existing rock climb on Misfah was the excellent looking Sisi pillar up the south buttress. We took to the southeast face and added a pair of fairly moderate 400m climbs called Sunburst and Shadowlands.

Our last route of the trip was a second line on the beautiful Mistal Tower. This gorgeous-looking feature did not provide us with the quality climbing we were expecting, and The Way of the Goat is an apt name (450m, TD-).

Oswald Oelz was not finished though; back he came in January of 2002 with Robi Boesch to add a third line to the west face of Asait. Close to the top of this sustained TD (5.9) route the pair found a bizarre man-made bridge between two towers of rock. Unable to conclude how and why this feature had appeared, they named their route Mystery. I presume that the shepherds had found a spot that their goats occasionally escape to and had climbed over the summit to build the bridge.

The Brachmeyer- Oelz-Precht team returned in November of 2002 to continue their explorations. They climbed another pair of lines on the Mystery Wall of Asait, Annas Tango (400m, 6+) and Meshmeshkela (400m, 8-). On the west face of Asala they added Jabalistas (400m, 6+) whilst on the north face of the same peak they added Ramadan for Bolts (450m, 6+).

When this teamed left the mountains, Brian Davison, Susie Sammut, and I arrived from the UK. Davison completed an extensive program of soloed first ascents on Jabals Asait, Asala, and Khormilla, whilst the three of us added two important first ascents on previously untouched mountain features. Jabal Manzoob is a subsidiary peak of Jabal Kawr; it provides a handsome 600m north face. Our line climbs a 400m arête on the left side of the face; Gully Arête weighs in at ED2 (5.11).

On the other side of the range, Jabal Ghul has an extensive ridge line with north facing buttresses on it. From the highest point drops a pair of 650m high pillars and we climbed the eastern one via a series of walls, ramps, and corners to give Original route (5.11).

GEOFF HORNBY, *The Alpine Club*

EGYPT

Sinai, Jebel Safsafa (Willow Mountain), Holey Moses. Sinai, the land of the Bedouin, conjures a rich and evocative image of lyrical, shifting sands, flowing robes, and the long, loping strides of camels. It also offers many opportunities to open new climbs from two to 14 pitches on superb granite around St. Catherine's Monastery. John Arran's and my line needed an early start; four direct pitches up to E3 standard flew us a good way up the solid gray granite. At 10 a.m. we were poised beneath the huge impending wind-sculpted face, ready for adventure. The first steep pitch ended with a beehive-like pillar of crumbly rock perched between me and the belay. It had the consistency of petrified mud, staying in place purely by virtue of its flat base. John

Jebel Safsafa, showing Holey Moses. The dotted line is a scramble with two rappels. Anne Arran

saw me eyeing both it and the belay nervously, and reassuringly explained that the rock was better than it looks! Sure enough, a fist-width under the surface the rock seemed much more reliable, and the belay actually looked like it might hold us. Above, however, looked demanding and perhaps impossible for us without a siege.

A choice of paths presented itself: insecure barn-dooring weirdness with a long runout, or a stout fingertip crack over a blank and powder-dusted bulge. John opted first for the former, hoping that difficulties would be short. He was looking unstable and I found concerned belayer-mutterings just seemed to slip out of me. "You can always come down you know," was met with a withering look from above. How could I have been so stupid? The crack proved our best hope after all, going at hard E6 or easy E7 and finishing with some wonderful contorting and curious egyptioning against the sidewall, also veiled with a thin layer of talc. The sound and beautifully sculpted red rock above offered a selection of charismatic features, including a huge folded earlobe which was great fun crawling beneath at E5, emerging to an assortment of Hueco Tanks–style holes. We were now only a pitch or so from the top, but still weren't certain of finding an exit. Moving from one hole to another was like a Swiss-cheese puzzle; if there wasn't a hold or hole within reach you could find yourself completely stuck. Much 3D ingenuity and lateral thinking was required, but this left me feeling satisfied and privileged to be surfing this ocean of petrified waves. Fortuitously, Holey Moses came into being just before sunset. Holey Moses: 250m, E6/7 6b, on the northwest face of Jebel Safsafa (Willow Mountain). St. Catherine's is about 145km northeast of Sharm El Sheikh, a popular diving resort. You can get the local bus there for £4.50, or pay about £50 in a taxi.

ANNE ARRAN, *U.K.*

Russia

URAL RANGE

Northern Urals, Peak Sablya, two new routes in winter. These ascents took 10 days for the climbs (820m, Russian grade VI) and were done simultaneously by two teams. The joint Peterburg-Ekaterinburg team earned second place in the "first-ascent class" of the Russia-2002 mountain climbing championship. See "The Sabre" earlier in this Journal.

Sat Peak and its ridgeline traverse. Alexander Novik

PAMIR RANGE

Zaalaisky Range, Sat Peak traverse. In July 2002, I led a team of Moscow climbers on several climbs in the western Zaalaisky Range (the Pamir), and the first full traverse of the Sat Peak massif. Because the western Zaalaisky Range is separated from Lenin Peak (7,135m) by Ters-Agar pass, it is actually a separate range, with steep ice-falls and many rock faces and ice walls. The highest point, Sat Peak (5,900m), is located in the long southern branch of the Zaalaisky Range. The second highest summit, Surkhangoy Peak (5,627m), is also situated in the southern branch. The Sat Peak massif consists of Sat Main (5,900m) and, from east to west, 5,781m, 5,820m, 5,840m (Sat Middle), and 5,740m high summits. Sat Peak plateau is within the triangle formed between Sat Middle, Sat Main, and the 5,740m summit.

Though exploration began in the 1930s, the western Zaalaisky is rarely visited today because nearby Lenin Peak attracts most of the attention. Several teams made ascents of Sat

The Sat Peak ridgeline.
Alexander Novik

Peak in 1985, 1996, and 1998 by a variety of routes, all from South Kyzilsy Glacier, and all leading across Sat Peak plateau (5,700m). We began our traverse from the southwest tributary of South Kyzilsy Glacier, on a 30° to 45° crevassed snow and ice slope. An easy rock and ice ridge led to the traverse of the 5,781m and 5,820m summits, then Sat Peak was climbed from Sat Peak plateau. Afterward, we continued west on an eroded rock ridge via summit 5,740m. Then it took two days to descend to Surkhangoy Glacier because bad weather made it necessary to fix ropes all the way down.

We also made a first ascent of two beautiful summits (about 5,200m) several kilometers east of Sat Peak. These summits were named Kyzilkul East and Kyzilkul West. The Western Zaalay still holds great potential for first ascents on 4,800m to 5,500m peaks, with routes of varying levels of difficulty.

ALEXANDER NOVIK, *Russia*

KAMCHATKA PENINSULA

Kamchatka exploration. Our self-sufficient, four-person team—Melis Coady, Aubrey Knapp, Keri Meagher, and myself—made the first ski-mountaineering expedition to the Pinechevo Pass area on Russia's Kamchatka Peninsula. With support from the American Alpine Club's Mountaineering Fellowship, we departed from Yelsova in April, 2002. From Pinechevo Valley, we set up base camp on the southwest side of Pinechevo Pass, and made many forays into the surrounding valleys to climb and ski.

We made a number of first ascents on small unnamed peaks near Pinechevo Pass (up to 8,000'), including a route up the south ridge of Volcano Aag's southwestern sub-summit. We

Kamchatka view. Molly Loomis

Melis Coady heading up the Pinechevo Valley, Kamchatka. Molly Loomis

also made many ski descents on slopes up to 40° and as long as 4,000 vertical feet. The snow varied from exceptional to "survival." Our initial objective had been to climb and ski some of the larger volcanoes in this area, but horrible weather, wet snow, and problems with stove fuel (Russian diesel) thwarted us.

This area offers tremendous potential for alpine mountaineering routes. Steep narrow couloirs, jagged rock, and clean ridgelines abound with potential routes ranging from moderate to long and challenging. It is a ski-mountaineering paradise with the added bonus of smoking volcanoes and natural hot springs. Planning an expedition to Kamchatka requires time and patience. Only recently opened by the Soviet government, the logistical challenges include tourist invitations, travel to the peninsula, the Russian bureaucracy, and a scarcity of accurate maps. The payoff is an unexplored area with unlimited possibilities.

MOLLY LOOMIS, *Wyoming*

Kyrgyzstan

TIEN SHAN

INYLCHEK REGION

Tien Shan Mountains, mapping expedition. In August and September, 13 of us, mostly students from Dresden University of Technology, conducted a mapping expedition to the central Tien Shan Mountains. The objective of this university project (the Institute of Cartography) was to create a new 1:100,000 scale map of central Tien Shan in the style and quality of European mountaineering maps. This new map will probably be available in two or three years. We received support from, and worked with, Tien Shan Travel—the biggest Travel Agency in Kyrgyzstan—and from The Geodetic and Cartographic Service of the Kyrgyz Republic.

Useful maps at a large scale are not currently available—a universal problem in Russia and its former member states. The best available maps are of 1:200,000 scale, which are not very useful for mountaineering. There is also a map of central Tien Shan at 1:150,000, but this map only shows the major mountains and ridges, and is not a topographic map.

We worked in three teams: two in non-glacier areas and one on the glaciers or at higher altitudes. During this mapping, the "glacier team" probably did two first ascents, one on a previously unclimbed mountain. But it is difficult to know for sure if they were in fact first ascents—the best information about this still comes from local guides.

Khan Tengri (6,995m) from base camp on the southern Inylchek Glacier. Sebastian Wolf

Two of us reached the top of Khan Tengri at the end of August. Along with two Russian climbers, we removed about 20kg of garbage from the upper camps (except Camp 4) on the south side. We were shocked to see how much trash had been left behind, mostly by Americans.

Surveyors from Kyrgyzstan made a new survey of Khan Tengri this summer, showing that the summit is 6,995m—definitely below the magical 7,000m mark. Consequently, Pik Pobeda (7,439m), several kilometers to the south, is still the northernmost 7,000m peak in the world.

The weather was good in August, and we collected more data than we had planned. The expedition was very successful, and revealed a lot of potential for mountaineers in Tien Shan. However, most people seem to want to climb Khan Tengri or Pik Pobeda, and are not interested in the surrounding, less famous, peaks.

Further details about the expedition, including the first ascents and photos are available in the expedition report, which is online in a PDF-file at www.inf.tu-dresden.de/~sw760654/Tienschan (in English and German).

SEBASTIAN WOLF, *Deutche Alpenverein*

KUILU RANGE

Peak Milo (pik 4,800) and Peak Misha (pik 4,750), ski descents. Martin Strasser and I went to the Kuilu range, travelling to the site of Pat Littlejohn's base camp (ca 3,300m) in a surplus Soviet military vehicle (2001 AAJ, Pat Littlejohn, p. 341–2). But shortly after our arrival, I came down with strep throat. While I recovered, Martin made a solo ascent and descent of Pik 4,375, just southwest of our camp. Then we followed the Karator River east to the next drainage, which we followed south to the base of a large glacier, and set up Advanced Base Camp I (AB-I) at ca 3,800m.

From AB-I we climbed and skied two peaks—both first ascents, we believe. We climbed the first of these, located on the west side of the glacier and due south of AB-I, on June 16. Starting at 4:30 a.m., we skied up the glacier to the base of a 40° slope leading to the south ridge, then cramponed up firm snow that, unfortunately, gave way to post-holing. But conditions improved when we gained the top of the ridge, where a series of steps (up to 50°) with alternating ice and deep snow lead us to the summit (ca 4,800m) by noon.

We skied down the ridge that we had climbed up. Initially we enjoyed cold, dry snow, but half-way down the ridge we dropped onto the east face and threaded through seracs, where the snow became atrocious. Although each turn on the east face triggered a wet avalanche, we made it to the base without mishap.

On June 17, we climbed the peak on the east side of the glacier.

Peak Milo, showing the line of the complete descent, and Martin Strasser's second shorter descent. Kyle Amstadter

Martin Strasser carving on Peak Milo. Kyle Amstadter

Martin left an hour early, while the snow was still firm, to climb and ski a new line on the 50° face of Peak Milo (pik 4,800). Then we met on the glacier, and skied up Peak Misha (pik 4,750) from the south col, on its western slopes. Our ski descent took us down the northwest face, including a 50° chute, on snow that stayed dry and firm until late in the day.

We believe these were first ascents, and are suggesting the names Peak Milo and Peak Misha to the Russian Mountaineering Federation, and to our outfitter in Bishkek.

We reached Advanced Base Camp II (AB-II) by following the Kuilu River west (on an animal trail) to the first river valley west of the Karator Valley. Then we hiked south along the river for about 10 km until we came to the glacier. We established AB-II at 3,750m, close to the spot where we could begin skiing.

After one rest day, we skied to the base of pik 4,750, at 3:30 a.m. We skied up a ramp that led from the low angled glacier to the base of the northwest face. There were crevasses on the ramp, so we roped up and climbed 40° slopes to the steeper part of the face, where crusty snow offered poor protection (the rock was worse). So we soloed together up 50 to 55° chutes, reaching the rocky summit of Pik 4,750 after three pitches. Because of the crusty snow and rock cliffs, we set up an anchor on the summit and skied down the steep part of the northwest face on belay. When we got back down to the 40° slopes, we unroped and skied down our route of ascent. All of our descents were made on telemark skis.

This area has a lot of potential for technical routes during the cold part of the year. With lower temperatures, much of the unstable snow we encountered could be avoided. The rock we encountered was generally poor.

KYLE AMSTADTER, *AAC*

WESTERN KOKSHAAL-TOO

Kizil Asker, new route attempt. In July and August, Guy Robertson and I made two attempts on the most compelling alpine ice route either of us has ever seen: the 1300m virgin southeast face of Kizil Asker, the highest peak in the Western Kokshaal-Too area of the Tien Shan. The wall was steep and split by the dream line: a snaking couloir of ice, overhanging in several places, vertical elsewhere, ran nearly the entire length of the face. It petered out directly below the summit, leaving the crux where it should be: at the top! But both attempts were thwarted by rapid thawing when the sun hit the face. The first attempt ended at around 300m, before any of the real climbing had begun. We hid for most of the day under a small overhang from ice falling off the most wild ice smear imaginable. Then we abseiled off through the icy torrent that had formed down the middle of the couloir.

On the second attempt, we climbed the initial easy section in the dark, arriving at the foot of the first really steep section at dawn. Three superb pitches of mostly perfect ice, up to 95°, led to ominous hanging icicles. Here we skirted left, climbing overhanging, fluted, and thawing ice just as the sun hit. This led to a "non-belay" in a small bay and a very bold pitch of thin ice to reach a small hanging ice field. After rehydrating from the stream that was beginning to flow from the ice, we tried to carry on. But we were rebuffed at every option by sodden, thawing névé

that wouldn't hold a pick. Four hours earlier, what would have been a pleasant pitch of 80° Scottish V (WI4, I guess?), the easiest pitch encountered since breakfast—but now it was impossible. We abseiled off from just below the obvious snow ledge on the left, about 500m – 600m up.

This last attempt was at the very end of the trip, and we had to be back at base camp in three days. Too much time had been wasted sitting in advanced base, getting snowed on, and unable to see the face, but we usually were aware of its presence from the sound of avalanches sloughing off all around. We intend to go back in 2004 to finish the job.

ESMOND TRESIDDER, *Edinburgh University Mountaineering Club*

Komarova Glacier, Pic Babushka and Pt 4,850m ("Pic Sabor"), new routes. As half of the Scottish Kizil Asker expedition, Blair Fyffe and I climbed two alpine style routes. The expedition visited the Kokshaal-Too region with the aim of climbing the northwest face of Kizil Asker. However due to poor weather

Scoping the incredible ice line on the main buttress leading to the summit of Kizil Asker. Esmond Tresidder

and the distance from base camp this turned out to be unfeasible. Instead the base camp was established beneath the Komarova glaciers and a number of routes were climbed from there.

First as a warm up was the north face of Pik Babushka (5,282m), a beautiful alpine snow/ice face with about 700m of climbing up to Scottish V, climbed in a long day from the Central Komarova Glacier. The route took the prominent central groove and upper snow arête of the snowy north face, clearly visible from the base camp at the glacier snout. Descent was made down the west ridge and then the south face, followed by a walk back to the central glacier via the window col separating Pik Jerry Garcia and Pik Unmarked Soldier. This route was first climbed in 1998 by Christian Beckwith and Mark Price.

We then moved to the glacier below Kizil Asker and climbed the north ridge of the mountain marked as Pt 4,850m on the map, making the first ascent of what we christened Peak Sabor (Cathedral Peak), cathedral being one of the few words in our phrase book that could describe a mountain. The route ascended the left hand side of the icefall before gaining the ridge proper. We climbed the long low-angled section easily until the brèche (notch). A few tricky pitches and an abseil overcame the brèche and the steeper, blunt ridge above was gained. The ridge gave good climbing in icy runnels and rock steps, although relatively warm temperatures, being a general feature of the trip, led to some poor snow and ice conditions. After a bivi at one-third height we reached the summit by mid afternoon of the second day. The descent was made by abseiling the route until the breche and then abseiling the broad gully on the east side of the breche. The route gave some technical climbing and is perhaps worthy of an alpine grade of TD+. We think Pic Sabor has been climbed by a Russian expedition from the south side, although we think our route is a first ascent. (Editor's note: this peak was first climbed via the west-southwest rib in 1985 by Kasbek Valiev's team during the competition era.)

During the descent the weather deteriorated and the descent to the Kizil Glacier was hazardous due to avalanches from either side. The snow persisted for another three days, leaving waist-deep snow for the walk back to base camp at the snout of the neighboring Komarova glaciers.

NEAL CRAMPTON, *U.K.*

Ak Saitan. After a difficult journey through Kyrgyzstan in August, Iñaki Cabo, Elena de Castro, Ferran Latorre, and I finally arrive at base camp on the Komarova Glacier. The potential of the area is immense. One formation in particular draws our attention: a rock pillar reaching between Carnovski and Zukerman peak. But we have come to climb and make a movie of Kizil Asker, located in nearby China north of the "Great Walls of China." We file away the image as one of many first ascent possibilities in the area.

The line of Ak Saitan, on the Ochre Walls. Cecilia Buil

After five days on the Komarova, we head to China to see Kizil Asker. It is immense. We dream of the route possibilities: lines of ice, rock, and mixed sections on a wall almost two km. wide. While we examine our objective, a storm moves in and soon snow is blowing horizontally around us. We begin the return trek to Komarova.

Upon arriving at base camp we debate if we have the time needed for a successful ascent. With many doubts concerning relinquishing our dream, we decide instead to attempt a first ascent on the rock pillar above base camp, and afterward to attempt the Chinese Wall, a four-hour hike from base camp. We make the first carry to the base of the pillar and begin climbing the obvious line.

On the fourth pitch there is an eight-meter blank section and we place six of the route's eight bolts. For four days we are busy on the lower pitches—up and down the ropes, back and forth the hour between basecamp and the pillar, jumaring, rappelling, frustration,

Topping out on the spectacular Ak Saitan, Punta Aragon. Cecilia Buil

and cursing the continuous blasts of snow. It does not stop. A meter of snow covers camp. Each flake that falls convinces us it is best to focus on where we are and forget the Chinese Wall.

"As a distinguished one said, Hell is white, no?" jokes Ferran, "and the Devil too, at least in China. That's what we could name the route. Ruslan, how would you say that in Kyrgyz?"

"Ak Saitan," our liaison officer Ruslan responds.

As a courtesy to us for dedicating the route to him, the Devil gives us three days in a row of good weather. We can't believe it.

On the fifth pitch my fingertips split and after four hours when I arrive at the belay I am shaking. The flaring crack is dirty and I move slow and blind. The same happens in the dihedral pitch that Elena begins and Iñaki finishes, and also in the beginning of the ninth pitch that Ferran opens. The granite is similar to Corsica: very eroded, large granules, and flaky in places.

Then the tenth pitch and three more pitches that Elena and Iñaki free climb. After 15 days we have fixed lines all the way to the top of the tower. This is the moment to launch for the summit. We worry that the stable weather won't last long. Early the next morning we jumar up the fixed lines and Inaki begins the final four pitches that separate us from the summit, which we reach late in the day.

The granite on the wall is a bright orange color and is very solid and abrasive. Most cracks are rounded and flaring, requiring much work in engineering placements. The Ak-Saitan route is 600m in height, VI, 5.10+ A3+ 85°. It begins with a 450m rock tower and continues via an airy ridge where we encountered steps of UIAA grade IV rock, snow, and 65° ice with occasional short sections of 80°.

CECILIA BUIL, *Spain (translated by M. Loomis and Oriol Solé-Costa)*

Editor's note: The summit of the point that Ak Saitan reaches was first crossed by Guy Edwards during his solo traverse of the Ochre Walls in 1998, and then reached again in 2001 by Scott de Capio and Sean Isaac via their ascent of Beef Cake (see AAJ 2002).

Pik Unmarked Soldier, China View. In the summer of 2001, we put up a previously unreported route on Pik Unmarked Soldier (5,322m). "China View" ascends the east face on snow and ice to the right of the main gully (560m, 50° to 70°).

IRENA MRAK, *Slovenia,* AND GARTH WILLIS

The final steps of the west ridge of Ak-bai-tal, above the Ak-bai-tal Glacier in the West Kokshaal-too. Pat Littlejohn

At-Bashy Range and West Kokshaal-too, first ascents. In early September an International School of Mountaineering expedition comprising Pat Littlejohn, Adrian Nelhams, Vladimir Komissarov (guides), Julian Duxfield, Peter Kemble, Nigel Kettle, Ursula Mulcahy, Mark Pontin, John Porter, and Dr Jane Whitmore reached the West Kokshaal-too range on the Kyrgyzstan-China border.

This was the fifth visit to this area by an ISM team. Recent snowfall and waterlogged ground stopped the expedition approaching its intended base camp beside the Aytaly Glacier, so they decided to acclimatize by exploring the At-Bashy (Horse's Head) Range— limestone peaks immediately north of the Kizil Asker group in the West Kokshaal-too. Having no peaks above 5,000m, there are no records of anyone having climbed in the At-Bashy range before.

Base camp was established at 3,800m in the valley of Aksu-lu-tor above a wrecked ex-Soviet military base. After acclimatizing on a couple of easy peaks, advanced bases were established at 4,054m and 4,200m. Peaks ascended included

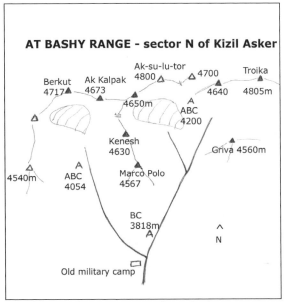

Map of the At Bashy Range courtesy of Pat Littlejohn

the snow dome of Ak-Kalpak (4,673m; PD), the long west ridge of Pik Troika (AD), a traverse of the impressive Berkut (beak) (4,717m; AD+) and the icy dome of Kenesh (4,630m; PD+).

More settled weather prompted a move across the valley to the Kokshaal range and after an exciting 25km off-road drive up a river bed, the Ak-bai-tal valley was reached. This is the third valley to the West of Kizil Asker and had probably never been visited by mountaineers. Advanced base was established on the edge of the Ak-bai-tal glacier at 4,200m, from where attention focused on the twin-summited snow peak (4,981m), which dominates the glacier. The easiest routes to each summit involved arduous trail breaking (PD+), then the steep and rocky West Ridge was ascended to give a mixed climb at AD+.

A big team traversed the elegant snow fan (Pik Belyi Veer, 4,757m), which bounds the left side of the glacier and is a prominent landmark for the area. After this, with the weather again ominous, the expedition struck camp and drove for a day to a series of limestone rock domes which Littlejohn had spotted on earlier trips. These were christened Nomad Domes (being surrounded by people living in yurts) and a number of routes were climbed, mostly three pitches and up to British E2. Very little rock climbing has so far been developed in Kyrgyzstan and this area will be of interest to anyone climbing in the West Kokshaal-too, either for acclimatization purposes on the approach or a fun stop-off on the way out.

PAT LITTLEJOHN, *Alpine Climbing Group*

Borkoldoy Khrebet, Pik Alexander, Father's Peak, and Pik Ibex ascents. A British team comprising Sharon Abbott, Wayne Gladwin, Mike Rosser and Stephen Saddler were the first climbers to visit the southwestern sector of the Borkoldoy range. This is an extensive group of low altitude peaks to the north of the Kokshaal-too. The more substantial peaks of the northeast had previously been explored in 1994 by a British expedition. In 2002 the mountains more or less north of Kizil Asker were approached from the same six-wheel-drive track used to reach the western end of the Kokshaal-too, a relatively short walk required to reach a suitable base camp in a north-facing cwm. The peaks of this cwm gave pleasant rocky scrambles with a bit of snow on the north flanks. The south faces were completely bare. Illness dogged the expedition but Pik Alexander (4,655m), Father's Peak (4,850m), and Pik Ibex (4,655m) were climbed.

LINDSAY GRIFFIN, *High Mountain INFO*

Part of the Khrebet Kyokkiar. These walls are ones Gerrard's group didn't get around to doing anything on. About 1,200m vertical from the valley floor to the summit opposite, and the rock was top quality with lots of naturally protectable lines. David Gerrard

Khrebet Kyokkiar and Gory Sarybeles, seven first ascents. After visiting this interesting and unexplored range in 2001, I organized another expedition in August, 2002. Karl Baker, John Cuthbert, Graham Sutton, and I (David Gerrard, as leader) made eight ascents, including seven first ascents. These mountains—only visited twice by mountaineers—offer classic mixed alpine ascents on peaks below 5,000m, plus many hard mixed lines on faces up to 1,000m high. Also, good quality limestone walls, from 500 to 1,000m high, offer an immense amount of rock climbing on cracks, corners, and towers, where snow can usually be avoided on the descent.

As before, we camped near the foothills of the Khrebet Kyokkiar—a small but perfect group of snowy peaks and limestone walls. The approach to the Khrebet Kyokkiar, which is on the Kyrgyz-Chinese border at the end of the Kokshaal Too Range, was easy. We hired a truck and driver from ITMC, a Bishkek based travel company (who also helped with the permits and paperwork). First we went to Naryn, then over the hills through Ak-Muz, skirting the At-Bashy range before a long downhill track took us to the border region. In the lush open valleys, we saw farmers living in yurts for the summer, and an occasional military border post. Everyone we met was friendly and welcoming.

Wet weather had caused dangerously high river levels, so while we waited for them to subside we crossed another pass to the Gory Sarybeles: a smaller range of snowcapped 4,500m mountains with fine alpine ridges and rock walls. After surviving a night of local hospitality, Karl and I climbed a 4,300m peak (PD) for acclimatization, then moved to a higher camp, where we traversed two other unclimbed peaks (AD), getting chased off by an electrical storm that had been brewing all day. Meanwhile, John and Graham attempted a prominent unclimbed peak (to the right of another peak that had been climbed the previous year), but retreated after reaching the main ridge.

Returning to the Kyokkiar, we rode horses for one day, then carried loads for two more days to reach a base camp surrounded by 1,000m unclimbed limestone walls. The next day, Karl and I continued up the valley to a glacial basin, near most of the alpine-type summits, while John and Graham went into a different cwm to attempt a stunning face on another unclimbed peak.

With two days of good weather, Karl and I made three more first ascents. First, we climbed a 4,600m peak by a couloir and rock ridge (AD). The following day, we traversed from the highest peak in the range (4,760m) to its neighbor (AD) on a fine mixed ridge, down-climbing a steep face of snow and ice to the glacier. The next day, we went to another high cwm, then climbed through seracs to a steep snow slope which led to the main ridge of the range. From there we made an easy traverse to a 4,600m (PD) summit, with fine views of some impressive mixed faces.

Then, although the weather turned bad, we still managed to climb a 400m rock route, and fit in a day of load carrying before John and Graham joined us again. They had made a spirited attempt on a stunning ice line on one of the large faces before being turned back by difficulties. Then they had done some exploring and reached the upper glacier before the weather turned bad, forcing them down again.

Since the Khrebet Kyokkiar and Gory Sarybeles Ranges are lower in altitude than the surrounding higher ranges, we probably had better weather than other expeditions in the area. The next day, temperatures fell as we carried loads to meet the horses. We had a beautiful ride out of the range in six inches of new snow.

Our expedition was generously supported by the Mount Everest Foundation and British Mountaineering Council.

DAVID GERRARD, *U.K.*

Pamir Alai

KARAVSHIN

Kara-Su Valley, north face of a ridge east of Piramidalny summit. The Karavshin Valley in southern Kyrgyzstan was eerily deserted in the fall. There were no large groups of climbers on the towering granite faces (as in the Soviet era), and no fighting between Islamic rebels and Kyrgyz troops. Even the local farmers and families that used to live in stone huts were gone. In the whole area, there were only two climbers, a cook at base camp, and one hunter who sometimes stopped by.

We (Irena Mrak and Garth Willis) arrived in Karavshin on October 1 after a three-day drive from Bishkek and a two-day stay in Batken (where we gathered the necessary documents and signatures). At the end of the last dirt road along the Karavshin River, we met soldiers at a small group of dirt buildings they'd made into a fort. We paid eight soldiers $5 each to help us carry a month of food and gear to our camp at the base of the Yellow Wall.

Our first climb was a diagonal route on the Yellow Wall (mostly 5.8, with an overhang that went, for me, at A0—although it has been reported as 5.10c). This 500m route had every-thing you really don't want in a climb: a wet start, long sloping pitches, an awkward overhang, and a grassy finish. But the panorama from the top gave us a great feeling for the region, with views of Asan-Usen, Piramidalny, and Pik 4,810.

After sitting out some bad weather, we headed for the dramatic Peak Piramidalny (5,506m). This peak's north face has been climbed by soviet teams and by a solo Italian climber in 1991 (Ed note: also by French and partially by British). We did not climb the peak itself—our goal was a route on the north face of a ridge east of the summit. We started from our advanced base camp, at 4,100m. The route went up an ice gully (50°–60°) for 250 meters. It was a bowling alley of falling snow and ice, so we climbed out over a rock wall to the right. In a time consuming battle, we climbed over 150m of 5.8 loose rock covered with snow, then continued up a snowfield to a bivy at 4,600m. The second morning was clear, cold, and windy. The first pitch was a snow-filled rock couloir, followed by a 120m ice gully of 70° to 85° black ice that broke into plates with each swing. The wind blew stinging pellets of snow into our faces all day. Wind-blown snow built up on the route above, pouring down on us constantly. More snow and ice pitches followed, until we finally reached the ridge (5,200m) at 7:00 p.m. We began our descent as the sun set.

Returning to our bivy, we decided to continue the rappel in the dark. With a clear sky and cold temperatures, we hoped the avalanche danger would be minimal. We kept our eye on the

The north face of Peak Piramidalny, showing Russian Roulette. Garth Willis

ridge as the wind-blown snow flowed down over our feet like a river. Twice avalanches hit us as we rappelled, but they roared on by in the steep gully, leaving us behind. At 9:00 a.m., 50 hours after we had started the climb, we reached the base. We named the route Russian Roulette, because we doubted we'd survive it a second time. We rated it 1100m, V+, M3-M5 WI4 50–85°. The dramatic Italian line (*AAJ* 1992, p. 35) seemed to have much less ice than before. The ice visible in the picture only extends halfway down the face now. Either the climate has changed, or we were much later in the season than when the picture was taken.

IRENA MRAK, *Slovenia,* *and* GARTH WILLIS

Pik 4810m showing, left to right: Zlaté Písky, Otíkovy Mokré Sny, Krizok. Jan Kreisinger.

Kara-Su Valley, Pik 4810 m, various new routes. In July 2002, our group of 11 Czechs who drink and climb everything, went to the Karavshin, where we split into four climbing teams. Three teams decided to climb the 1,200m northwest face of Pik 4,810m by three different routes. The fourth team climbed the Yellow Wall.

The first team—Jan Kreisinger, Jirka Srutek, Petr Balcar, and Mirek Turek—climbed a new route to the left of Sacharov 94. After 24 pitches, they joined with the Sacharov Route (Russian) on the north summit ridge. We called our new route "Zlate písky" (Golden Sands); it was 1,000m, 8 (OS)/A2—the first 350m were fixed, followed by 10 days capsule style.

The second team—Vazek Satava, Pavel Jonak and Marek Holecek—climbed a new line to the right of Sacharov 94. After 15 pitches they joined the Sacharov Route, then continued free to the top. We named this new route "Otikovy mokre sny" (Otik's Wet Dream); it was 1,100m, 23 pitches, 9-/9 AF—the first 350m were fixed, followed by 9 days capsule style. The third team—couple Jan Doudlebsky and Dusan Janak—climbed the Russian route Krizok (6b, Russian scale), with a 200m variation on the central part of the NW face. We named the variation "Fifteen to the Chimney," because Jan fell off on 20th pitch. Its difficulty was 1100m to the summit ridge, 26 pitches total, 8+(PP)/A4- (with an A4 pitch on the variation)—the first two pitches were fixed, then nine days on the wall.

Tomas Zákora and Pavel Kopázek started a new route on the 500m east face of Yellow Wall (American climbers were kidnapped from this face in 2000). After about 200m, they retreated and returned to basecamp in the Karasu Valley. After a period of bad weather, Tomas went back to the line and soloed it in 6 days. He called it Meresjev. It was 14 pitches, 9-/9 A3— the first 200m were fixed, then Tomas made his 6 day solo.

DUSAN JANAK *and* JAN KREISINGER, *Czech Republic*

Pakistan

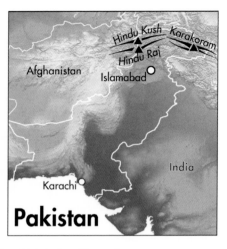

Change in peak and trekking fees. It is with great relief and pleasure that I announce the formal acceptance by the government of our longstanding demand to waive mountain royalties on all peaks up to 6,500m. Thus anything below 6,500m will be considered a trekking peak. This was decided at a high level meeting at the Ministry of Tourism. The decision comes into effect immediately and will apply for several years. It will be a great boon for individuals and smaller teams as now they will be able to climb many of world's most exciting peaks without a fee. Only in restricted areas they will bear a trekking fee of $50 per person per month, which is the old practice.

This gesture has been made to attract climbers who are not hunting for 8,000m peaks but instead want to climb in unexplored areas. We also hope this will send a positive message to the mountaineering community at large about the normalization of security in Pakistan after the peaceful elections and rehabilitation of democracy. Tourism in Pakistan including climbing has been seriously hurt since September 11, 2001, but this is undeserved because the climbing regions are relatively safe. Another motive is to offer incentives when we celebrate the Golden Jubilees of the first ascents of Nanga Parbat and K2, in 2003 and 2004 respectively. It is hoped that the mountaineering community will draw the utmost benefit from this unique opportunity and join us in 2003 and 2004 in celebrating the two greatest mountains on Earth. Other incentives like simplifying trekking and climbing procedures and easy availability of visas are also being worked out by a special committee.

NAZIR SABIR, *Pakistan*

Expeditions to Pakistan in 2002. In 2001 around 70 expeditions came to the Karakoram. However, with the change in political climate following the events of September 11 and reprisals in neighboring Afghanistan, plus the subsequent threat of an Indo-Pakistan nuclear war, a little less than 40 were due to turn up at the start of the 2002 season. Then, a dozen or so cancelled at short notice, leaving no more than 28 permits being taken up by visiting expeditions. As several expeditions operating on the high Baltoro mountains had more than one peak booked, the actually number of climbing teams on the ground was somewhat less than 28.

Many of the last minute cancellations came from commercially organised enterprises, which because of the prevailing political situation either did not get enough clients or felt it unwise to visit Pakistan at the time. However, as many suspected, those who did decide to continue with their plans generally experienced no real problem traveling through the country and found almost everyone they met extremely pleasant. From the point of view of the local economy a far greater effect was felt by the drop in number of trekking parties, which was, proportionally, considerably greater than the drop in mountaineering expeditions

LINDSAY GRIFFIN, *High Mountain INFO*

Gasherbrum IV, attempt of Bonatti-Mauri route. It appears from our records and those of the Ministry of Tourism that no completely new routes were attempted in 2002 on any of the major mountains, but an old route on G-IV (7,980m), the Bonatti-Mauri route, was attempted again after a very long time by a Swiss/Italian seven-member expedition led by documentary producer Mario Casella. The expedition reached camp III at 7,400m *(Editor's note: other information has them reaching a little over camp 2 at around 6,100m).* They were in the process of establishing this camp when a spell of bad weather forced them down. The expedition had to abandon the climb after that as the weather turned nasty and avalanches were feared.

This route was first climbed by a strong Italian expedition led by Ricardo Cassin in 1958, who scaled the peak via the north-east ridge after a hard climb. Walter Bonatti and Carlo Mauri reached the summit. They spent a night at camp 6 on the descent before continuing down to camp 5 via a very technical and dangerous route. Another member, Giuseppi de Francesch, miraculously stopped himself from falling to his death.

NAZIR SABIR, *Pakistan*

Broad Peak, winter attempt. A Spanish team led by Juanito Oiarzabal attempted Broad Peak (8,048m) this winter. They came in January 2003 and left in middle of March. They climbed up to 6,500m and had to abandon the climb owing to strong winds that destroyed their high camp at 6,400m, fortunately while no one was in it.

NAZIR SABIR, *Pakistan*

K2, snowboarding attempt. Spanish extreme skier and snowboarder Jordi Tosas failed to climb K2 on account of bad weather. He reached 6,300m on the Cesen route (a.k.a. the south southeast spur or the Basque Route) before jumping on the board to come down.

NAZIR SABIR, *Pakistan*

K2, discovery of Dudley Wolfe's body. Most of the expeditions gave up toward the end of July and headed for home, but Araceli Segarra's team, which included the Mexican, Hector Ponce de Léon, and American cameraman, Jeff Rhoades, remained and were, to their surprise, rewarded in August with more than a week of fine weather. Unfortunately, this brought different problems. The temperatures soared, avalanches poured from the mountain, and subsequently the Abruzzi was subjected to severe stonefall, cutting some of the fixed ropes and making climbing extremely dangerous. The Spanish also had to admit defeat at 7,100m and return home empty handed. However, one day during the expedition Rhoades and fellow film maker Jennifer Jordan were exploring the Godwin-Austen Glacier when they discovered the remains of human bones, alongside which were the remnants of an old canvas tent, clearly marked with the tag, Made in India. Later, some tattered clothing, labeled Cambridge (Massachusetts) came to light pointing toward the owner being a member of the ill-fated 1939 American-German expedition led by Fritz Wiessner. Then finally a glove was uncovered with the name Wolfe clearly written on it. It is presumed that the bones formed the remains of Dudley Wolfe, a rich American climbing novice, who had been invited on the expedition largely to help finance its execution. Wolfe ended up spending a long time at around 7,000m, and after Wiessner's summit attempt, remained at Camp 7 (some have argued he was abandoned by Wiessner). A week later three Sherpas set out to try to rescue Wolfe but none of the four was ever seen alive again. These were the first four fatalities on the mountain, whereas Rehman and Iqbal were the 51st and 52nd respectively, both in 2002.

Wolfe's was not the only body to be discovered in the area during 2002. In 1997 eight members of a 17-strong Japanese team made the second ascent of nearby Skilbrum (7,360m) but three days later their base camp on the Savoia Glacier was hit by a gigantic avalanche falling from the flanks of Angel Peak. Expedition leader, Mitsuo Hiroshima (second ascent of K2 in 1977), and five companions were buried in their sleep and killed. Last year the bodies appeared from the glacier and two of the surviving members traveled from Japan to arrange a proper burial.

LINDSAY GRIFFIN, *High Mountain INFO*

Trango Valley, first ascent of The Flame, new route on Shipton Spire. In August Josh Wharton and I, hailing from Colorado, put up two new routes in the Trango Valley of Pakistan. Following a 40-day stint of rain, broken up by two clear days to relieve the monotony, splitter weather arrived. We climbed the Flame in blocks. Once we gained the ridge, a 600-foot pitch up straight-forward but avalanche-prone snow and ice brought us to the base of the pillar for which The Flame is named. Wharton led the summit pitch with a 160-foot runout of 5.10 slab climbing. With no cracks on top, Wharton slung its rounded summit and drilled the second hole of the route while I jugged to the top of Under Fire (VI 5.10+X A3 M5 AI4). The route took 18 hours tent to tent, and brought us to an untouched summit 20,700' above sea level. (See "The Flame," in this Journal, for a more complete story.) (Note: three Austrians attempted the Flame in 2001. We have no details of their attempt other than their names: Herbert Kobler, Tony Neudorfer, and Norbett Reizelsdorfer.)

After a rest day at Shipton base the weather was still good and we made the jaunt to Shipton Spire in the hope of finding a new line left of the skyline visible from base camp. Three hours later, we were heading up block style. The second jugged with a pack with two sleeping bags, some water, a handful of energy bars, and two cans of sardines, topped off by a pair of down jackets and waterproof tops. The first day ended on a large ledge, The Hotel California, more than halfway up the wall.

After an energy bar each for breakfast we continued up, with only one major routefinding mistake, which necessitated the only bolt hole of the climb—for a retreat off the middle of a blank face. Following a great deal of excellent free climbing, with only one section of aid to free a wet roof, we reached the summit at about 8 p.m., and began the rappels—which we finished the next morning after a second night spent at The Hotel California.

We named the route The Kanadahn Buttress (VI, 5.11X A1, steep snow) which means "The Family Buttress" after our families who supported our decision to travel to a post-9/11 Pakistan in the midst of the nuclear crisis.

BRIAN MCMAHON

Shimshal Valley, exploration and survey. In 2001, when the Yokohama Alpine Club went to the Shimshal Pass area to climb Mungarig-Sar (Lupjoi-Sar), we found the whole area to be almost completely unsurveyed. We had so much trouble identifying the surrounding peaks that we decided to go back there in 2002, to explore the unknown peaks and produce more information about this remote, rarely visited spot. A complete report of this expedition can be found in *Japan Alpine News #3*, April 2003.

First, here is a brief history of the only previous explorations that we know of:

1889: F. E. Younghusband discovered the Shimshal Pass.

1892: G.K. Cockerill surveyed the Virjerab Glacier and observed the south side of the Chot-Pert Group (he did not see its inaccessible north side).

1913: An Indo-Russian survey was made at each frontier area, but surveys of remote areas, such as Chot-Pert and Shuijerab, were not made.

1925: C. & J. Visser surveyed the upper part of Virjerab Glacier, and roughly located three peaksin the Chot-Pert Group on their map: Gim-Gim (18,270', 5,568m), Chot-Pert (19,670',5,995m), and a peak at the eastern edge of the group (20,810', 6343m).

1934: R.C.F. Schomberg entered the Shuijerab Valley and saw the valley from above, looking down from a small side valley branching left of the main valley. But no detailed record of his observations exists.

1937: E. Shipton led a party which surveyed the north side of the Karakoram Range. Their map shows Shimshal Pass (4,735m), an unnamed peak which is probably Mungarig-Sar (6,050m), and a 5,930m peak at the east edge of the Chot-Pert Group (up to the east side of the Shuwert Glacier, and the east part of Chot-Pert).

The Ganj-i-Tang Valley, Shuijerab Valley, Shuwert Glacier, and the Chot-Pert Group were still unsurveyed.

The Yokohama Alpine Club left Pasu on July 6 following the Shimshal River and Pamir-i-Tang. We reached Shimshal Pass, where we set up our base camp, on July 12. From there, we followed the East Joi-Dur Glacier seven kilometers up from its snout. We had intended to climb a 5,930m peak located south of the head of the glacier, but abandoned that climb because of hidden crevasses. We also followed the West Joi-Dur Glacier for 7 kilometers—coming close to its intersection with the Phurzin Glacier—and ascended Mungarig-Sar (6,034m) and Kuz-Sar (5,500m).

On July 19, we spent a few days moving our base camp to Shuijerab Village, then went up the Shuijerab Glacier, where we had some more bad luck. We had planned to climb a 6,200m peak at the northern head of the glacier, but were forced back by bad weather and perilous glacier conditions. So we aimed for Halshamas-Sar (5,836m) instead, but had to retreat 15 meters below the summit after escaping from an avalanche. Next, we entered an east branching valley and went to the snout of the East Shuijerab Glacier, but couldn't see the surrounding peaks because of poor visibility.

On July 23, we split into two parties, then spent the next two weeks exploring Shuijerab Village, Arbab-Phurien, S-Mai-Dur, Shipodin-Pir, Shipodin, Boesam-Pir (the watershed pass to the Chujerab Valley), Shipodin, Zard-i-Gar-Dur, Shimshal Village, Ziarat, Karimabad, Yazgil Glacier (up to its snout), Past-Helga, Shiririn, Sekrwar, and Khurdopin Glacier (high camp at 4,467m).

We found the mountains on the south side of the Shimshal River to be precipitous, like those in the main Karakoram Range. The pass leads to gently curved peaks on the north, like those seen in the Pamir. These mountains are characterized by snow-covered slopes above glacier filled valleys, separated by scree zones.

At the western extremity of the Chot-Pert Group, we saw a group of needle-like peaks. In the Chot-Pert-Nala, a deep gorge splits, higher up, into two valleys, surrounded by the rock walls of Chot-Pert-Sar (5,950m) and Phurzin-Pert-Sar (5,900m). Even the villagers don't go into this valley. Joi-Dur was not named on any map, but Shimshalis refers to a valley of that name. It divides into two parallel glaciers 4 kilometers from the main valley, both flowing northward. Both glaciers were much larger than we had imagined. The East Joi-Dur Glacier is about 8 kilometers long, extending from the south icefall, below a 5,930m peak (the peak surveyed by M. Spender of Shipton's party). The West Joi-Dur Glacier is about 5 km long, joined by the overflow from the middle of the east glacier of Phurzin-i-Dur. Although it had been reported that there are seven peaks over 6,000m in the Chot-Pert Group, based on our observations from Mungarig-Sar and Kuz-Sar, only a few peaks in the central part of Phurzin-i-Dur are that high. The topography of this group is complicated, and a revision of the existing maps is needed.

Based on the view from three peaks we ascended in the Shuijerab Glacier area (Mungarig-Sar, Kuz-Sar, and Halshamas-Sar), there are six peaks over 6,000m. Most are unnamed, but one was named Halshamas-Sar, after our porter.

Although existing maps show 6,400m peaks in the Shuwert Glacier area, we found none that high. We only saw some ca 6,150m peaks on the ridge dividing the East Shuijerab and Shuwert Glaciers. Though we had intended to look at the south side of the Chot-Pert Group from Khurdopin Pass, we ran out of time. Also, the north side of the Shujerab Group is still unknown, and will stay that way until the southwest part of the Oprang River is opened up.

TADASHI KAMEI, *Yokohama Alpine Club (translated by Kei Kurachi)*

Correction: The uncredited map on page 369 of AAJ *2002 was excerpted from a 1990 Swiss Foundation for Alpine Research map prepared by Jerzy Wala, of Poland.*

Batura II, attempt at its first ascent. A six-man team from the Saxon Alpine Club of Germany made a spirited attempt on the unclimbed Batura II (7,762m), one of the highest unclimbed points remaining in the Karakoram. Tilo Dittrich, Günter Jung, Jan Lettke, Tom Niederlein, Christian and Markus Walter set up base camp on the Baltar Glacier in June and followed the route of the first ascensionists of 7,786m Batura I. In 1976 a German Alpine Club expedition penetrated the Eastern Baltar Glacier to the south of the peak and climbed up to the Batokshi Pass (ca 5,900m) on the ridge running north from Hachindar Chish. In the process they climbed the 6,050m Batokshi or Saddle Peak. Above the col the ridge fades into the steep upper slopes of the high Batura Group and the team set out across the south face of the main peak. After establishing five camps above Base, Hubert Bleicher and Herbert Oberhofer, who just two years previously had made the first ascent of neighboring Shispare, climbed the final 40°–45° snow slopes and reached the summit on June 30. Batokshi Peak was climbed again in July 1996 by a small international group that made the largely alpine-style fourth ascent of Batura I via the German Route.

The 2002 Saxon expedition crossed the rubble-covered Baltar Glacier to an advanced base at 4,250m and established Camp 1 towards the end of June at 5,240m. To reach the site of Camp 2 they had to climb through a narrow and dangerous couloir, dubbed the Gunbarrel by the 1976 German team, which squeezed through a small gap between a rock wall and large serac barrier. Camp 2 was placed at ca 5,800m on July 2 and shortly after, camp 3 above the Batokshi Pass. The team took around 250m of fixed rope and placed most of it on this section. On July 15 several team members were situated at camp 4 (6,560m) on the south face of Batura II, somewhat left of the German line, preparing for a summit assault the following day.

Generally the weather had been very mixed with frequent snow fall but on the 16th the day dawned gloriously and Jung with the two Walter brothers set off at 3:30 a.m. The snow conditions seemed reasonably acceptable to about 7,000m but above they realized the névé field they were climbing was loosely bonded over ice and would undoubtedly slide when hit by the rays of the sun. The three progressed to 7,100m before deciding it was too dangerous. The route was subsequently abandoned but not before four members had climbed Batokshi Peak.

Back at Base Camp the group split, half going for an exploratory walk up the Toltar Glacier, while the rest climbed a 150m rock tower above camp. This gave three bold pitches (IV, VI and VII or 5.10c) on excellent granite and was christened Phalwan Chish (ca 4,200m).

LINDSAY GRIFFIN, *High Mountain INFO*

The east face of Buni Zom Main peak (6,551m) and North peak (6,338m). Nikolas Kroupis

Gordoghan Zom attempt. Our goal was to climb Buni Zom mountain (6,551m) in the Hindukush range of northwest Pakistan. The nearest access is from the village of Harchin, located about 120 km from Chitral, on the Gilgit road. Our expedition consisted of two Greek persons, Nikolas Kroupis and George Zardalidis. We spent 10 days in the mountains in July. Our two days trekking (14 km) started at Harchin (2,900m) and ended at the base camp (3,900m) in Kulakmali, a big plateau on the way to Phargam An pass. We used four porters to transport our equipment to the base camp. The path goes through Rahman and Phargam villages. We had an intermediate camp at 3,700m, where we found drinkable water at the beginning of the huge rocky slopes. We crossed the stream from Gordoghan glacier the next day early in the morning, because the stream flux increases due to ice melting during the day. We spent the next three days in base camp attempting some ascents for acclimatization. The weather was rainy during the day and was snowing at night. There was a rocky wall about 100m high on the route to Buni Zom, in order to reach Khora Bohrt glacier. Pitons are necessary to climb this rocky wall; since we didn't have pitons, we decided to climb another peak in the Buni Zom range, named Gordoghan Zom (6,240m). The peak is located east of the main Buni Zom peak, and so we approached it from the Gordoghan glacier. On July 12 we settled camp 1 (4,000m) near the stream which comes from Gordoghan glacier. Next day we reached Gordoghan glacier and settled our camp 2 (4,800m) near a lake. The peak was located northeast from the camp and was out of our sight. July 14 was the summit day. To reach Gordoghan Zom we recommend walking along the right side of the glacier. On the right there is an icy, thin and narrow gully that leads to the big slope that continues to the peak. Without the use of any ropes, we climbed the 40°–60° narrow gully on stiff ice. At about 5,300m there is an ideal place for an advanced camp, which we didn't use, because the ascent of nearly 1,500m to the peak from camp 2 is exhausting. Climbing the snow-capped slope (40°–50°) we reached 6,100m at 15:00. There we had really wonderful glimpses of Buni Zom Main peak. The temperature there was about -10°C and the weather was getting worse, so we decided to turn back just a few meters below the summit. Late in the afternoon we arrived in our camp and passed there a very cold night. Next day, after five hours of walk we arrived to camp 1. On the last day of the expedition, we made the long trek from camp 1 to Harchin village. To our knowledge fewer than 10 expeditions have visited the Buni Zom area in the last 50 years, and the only record we can find of climbing on Gordoghan Zom concerns the first ascent in 1965 (*AAJ* 1966). We do not know if we followed the original route or a new line.

NIKOLAS KROUPIS *and* GEORGE ZARDALIDIS, *Greece*

Note on record keeping for trekking peaks. The Pakistan Ministry of Tourism doesn't keep any records on trekking peaks. The Gordoghan Zom I (6,240m) was climbed in 1965 by Munich section of German Alpine Club. There is no other record of further climbs. Only the climbers would know.

NAZIR SABIR, *Pakistan*

Deaths in 2002. Japanese Saito Kenji died from AMS on Spantik while returning after scaling the 7,027m peak. He was brought down to camp III in critical condition but soon died. Captain Mohammad Iqbal, member of Pak-China K2 Expedition had a fatal fall when a fixed rope broke during the descent from camp II at about 6,000m on July 22. He was loved and respected by fellow climbers as a gentleman. Twice he abandoned his summit bids to bring down sick climbers. High altitude porter Sher Rehman died in an avalanche on K2 near camp II. He was with the Spanish K2 Expedition led by Senator Luis Fraga. The noted Hungarian rock climber and mountaineer, Attila Ozsváth, disappeared in the Charakusa region of Hushe on July 24. He had gone to the area with a partner, Peter Tibor, although they do not appear to have been climbing together at the time. According to a spokesperson from North Pakistan Treks and Tours, who believe Ozsváth was swept away by an avalanche, a search was conducted but no trace was found.

NAZIR SABIR, *Pakistan, and* LINSAY GRIFFIN, *High Mountain INFO*

India

SIKKIM

Nepal Peak, ascent via the southeast and south ridges. A 12-member expedition from the DAV Summit Club (German Alpine Club) led by Herbert Streibel went to the very rarely visited region of North Sikkim to attempt Nepal peak (7,153m). The team travelled from Gangtok via Lachen, Yakthang, and Yabuk to a base camp at 3,900m on the glacier leading up to Nepal Gap. Camp 3 was established at 6,620m on the south east ridge of Nepal peak. On October 21 the leader with Claudia Carl and Johann Paul Hinterimmer climbed the final section of the south ridge to the summit.

HARISH KAPADIA, *Honorary Editor, The Himalayan Journal*

KUMAON

Adi Kailash Range, first ascents and an attempt on Adi Kailash. A joint Indo-British expedition led by Martin Moran explored the Adi Kailash mountain range of Eastern Kumaon in Sept–Oct. No previous climbing had been recorded in this area, which lies between the Darma Ganga and Kuthi Yankti valleys east of Panch Chuli, and within the Inner Line security zone adjacent to the Tibetan border. The range was found to possess six 20,000' peaks and dozens of challenging 5,000m summits. The main objective was Adi Kailash (6,191m: a.k.a Little Kailash), a peak with distinct resemblance to Holy Mount Kailash some 110km to the north in Tibet.

The team obtained Inner Line permits and a climbing permit for Little Kailash and its surrounding tops. Since Adi Kailash is itself regarded as a holy peak, the team undertook not to tread the final 10m of the mountain. Approaching via the Darma valley, the party reconnoitred the western approaches to the range and found that access to Little Kailash is blocked by a higher peak of ca 6,300m. They therefore crossed to Jolingkong in the Kuthi Yankti via the Shin La (5,500m), which is advertised as a trekkers' pass but has a tricky and potentially dangerous western wall of PD+ standard. Adi Kailash rises directly above Jolingkong, where there is a sacred lake and small temple.

An attractive 5,950m snow peak north of the Shin La was ascended at PD+ by a team of six (Richard Ausden, Martin Moran, Tom Rankin, Mangal Singh, Steve Ward and Andrew Williams). They wish to christen this The Maiden. Two smaller 5,000m peaks were climbed close to Jolingkong lake at grades F and AD respectively. Mike Freeman, James Gibb, Pat Harborow and Moran then attempted the north face of Adi Kailash, following the left-hand of three prominent glacier tongues. Having found a way through the crux rock band at Scottish III/IV, they were stopped by a combination of 55° powder snow lying over loose shale 200m from the summit. On the return journey John Allott, Freeman, Moran and Hari Singh crossed the 5,200m Nama Pass (PD), which links the two valleys between Kuthi and Sela. Long-known as a traditional route for local people, this glacier pass is now rarely traversed but gives access to several of the other peaks in the range.

The nomenclature and altitudes of many peaks could not be accurately ascertained. The team was not allowed to take a GPS device nor given sight of any recent military maps. Instead they had to rely on a dated 1:200,000 Survey of India extract. The Army and Indo-Tibetan Border Police personnel were otherwise helpful and co-operative throughout the visit.

This remarkable area was entirely unspoilt save for Border Police check posts. Many highly challenging peaks were discovered, most particularly 5,950m Yungtangto, the five-toothed ridge of Pandav Parvat, and 6,321m Nikurch Rama, which has an nightmarish north east face.

In recent years a gradual relaxation of restrictions to joint and foreign expeditions has enabled climbers to penetrate many exciting border ranges in India for the first time in 40 years. Official Climbing and Inner Line permits must be obtained and fees are currently $4,900 for all border peaks.

MARTIN MORAN, *U.K.*

Suj Tilla West (earlier known as Suitilla), first and second ascents. Two of the finest ascents of the season were on Suj Tilla West (6,373m). These were made by two separate teams in different styles. The peak rises steeply near Ralam village in eastern Kumaon and had been attempted previously. The recorded height was 6,373m, but on recent maps the true height has been given as 6,394m. First a team from the Indian Mountaineering Foundation attempted the peak, fixing ropes to the ridge. However one of the members slipped and was injured. Other team members helped in the rescue and the attempt was given up.

Then came an alpine-style climb of the peak—a wonderful first ascent by two British climbers, Graham Little and Jim Lowther. They reached the summit on September 28. This is what Jim Lowther had to write about the climb: "Graham and I climbed the peak in pure alpine style in a 22-hour long continuous push. By the time we got to the western summit at 6,373m (which we thought was going to be the highest point on the ridge but turned out not to be) we were totally spent and didn't have any reserves left to traverse the ridge to the other, eastern point, which we now believe to be 21m higher. We had to get down fast because we had no bivi gear. This we did, and when we met up with the Navy a day later, we told their leader about the height differences of the two summits. The western summit we climbed is the one that you'd naturally assume is the highest point, as it is the dominant snow peak visible from Ralam. The eastern summit is set back along the ridge."

Within a few days they were followed by a team from the Indian Navy, who fixed 1,100m of rope and followed almost the same route to reach the same point. This was a worthwhile second ascent of the peak. (See report below by Satyabrata Dam.)

HARISH KAPADIA, *Honorary Editor, The Himalayan Journal*

Suj Tilla West, second ascent. The Ralam valley lies between the more famous Milam valley to its west and the little-known Lassar Yankti to its east. It harbors the breathtakingly beautiful village of Ralam and a system of three glaciers, namely; Kalabaland, Sankalp, and Yankchari Dhurra. The area has several unclimbed peaks and many that have been climbed only once. It also has many stupendous routes that are yet to be attempted. None of the peaks rise more than 6,600m, but in terms of technical ice and rock challenges the summits are extremely inviting, especially to small teams of alpine climbers looking for some hard, technical climbs. Due to Inner Line regulations, these glaciers had never seen a western climber and very few Indian climbers till the year 2002, when the area was opened to foreigners. Some of the majestic peaks of this area are: Chiring We (one

Suj Tilla West, showing the line of the British and the Indian ascents. *Satyabrata Dam*

ascent); Chiring We I and II (virgin); Suli Top (one ascent); Burphu Dhurra (one ascent); Suj Tilla East (virgin); Chaudhara (one ascent). The roadhead for this valley is Munsyari, which can be reached via Almora either from Delhi, Kathgodam or Haldwani.

Resembling the shape of a needle towering high above the Yankchari Dhurra Glacier, and located deep into the lush Ralam Valley of the Kumaon hills, Suj Tilla is one of the finest pieces of mountain architecture in the Indian Himalaya. It had remained unclimbed even after four previous attempts by some of the finest mountaineers. The Indian Navy team that I led was comprised of nine members. Only my deputy leader, Lt. Amit Pande, was a seasoned mountaineer with several ascents to his credit. We reached Munsyari on September 16 and on the 19th commenced our trek along the Gori Ganga river. We used campsites at Paton, Liungrani, Kiltam, and Ralam, finally establishing base camp on the 23rd at 4,260m on a snow-covered meadow that overlooked the confluence of the Sankalp and Kalabaland glaciers. We started ferrying loads to advanced base on the 25th. This involved first climbing the 4,828m Yankchari Dhurra pass and then descending onto the Yankchari Dhurra glacier. We established advanced base on the 28th at 4,670m. The route ahead lay through a severely broken and serrated icefall. A pair of British climbers (Jim Lowther and Graham Little; see above) had preceded us on the mountain and made the first ascent of Suj Tilla West on the 29th, using a similar route to that we had planned through the southwest face. We established Camp 1 on the 30th at 5,350m, just above a line of huge crevasses. The entire face was prone to rock and ice falls and we had to do most of the climb before the sun hit it. The face had no let-up anywhere for even a tiny bivouac site, as it rose in a sheer wall of ice all the way to the summit. We would have to climb the one kilometer face in one go from Camp 1.

After five days of route opening and rope fixing, we made our first summit attempt on October 6. Starting from C1 at midnight, three members summited the peak after a continuous climb of 15.5 hours. They descended to C1 through a severe blizzard that raged all night and the next day. On the 8th, as the first team returned to advanced base, the southwest face remained plastered with a heavy and dangerous layer of loose snow, making it extremely hazardous for any immediate further attempt. None of the fixed ropes were visible and all traces of our route were buried. A second team of six members summited Suj Tilla West on October 11.

LT CDR. SATYABRATA DAM, *India*

Changabang, west face; Purbi Dunagiri, south pillar and east ridge; three attempts. After three years of training and organization, the DAV-Expeditionskader '02 left Germany for India in mid September. Our goals were the first repetition of Changabang (6,866m) west face (Boardman-Tasker, 1975) and the first ascent of Purbi Dunagiri (6,523m) east ridge. We had no information on the latter other than indistinct photographs. Both mountains are located in the quite famous Nanda Devi Sanctuary. Purbi Dunagiri was our alternative for Dunagiri, since Indian authorities wouldn't give permission for the Rishi Gorge, the normal access to Dunagiri. In any case to get to Changabang's west face we had decided to approach via the Bagini Glacier.

From the village of Juma on the Dhauliganga river, we trekked for two days via Dunagiri village (3,600m) to our base camp, a dreamlike meadow surrounded by impressive mountain scenery. The following days were considerably less romantic. Piles of equipment had to be transported to advanced base by all 11 members of our team along a chaotic sea of loose rock. The "path" led to our proposed camp site at the end of Bagini Glacier, right between Changabang and Purbi Dunagiri.

Four members tried to climb the steep ice slope to Bagini Col, the starting point of the west face, but on this north facing slope there was nothing but meters of deep powder. The climbers were forced to retreat in spite of some stubborn attempts to reach the face.

After this defeat three of them decided to try an alternative line on Purbi Dunagiri, the marvelous south pillar. In super-light alpine style they solo-climbed 60°–80° ice slopes to the beginning of the difficulties. Ten pitches of excellent and severe mixed ground led to a rock barrier, where overhanging loose terrain at ca 6,300m stopped their big effort and forced a retreat.

In the meantime the rest of our group fought up Purbi Dunagiri's east ridge meter by meter. The extremely high rock difficulties and problems with the altitude by most of the members forced us to operate with fixed ropes. The ridge turned out to be much more difficult and severe than we expected. After 100m of hard rock climbing, fixing, hauling, and jumaring, we stood in front of the "chandelle," as we called the key passage of the ridge at 6,200m. We couldn't find a way over this compact, overhanging, and fragile rock pillar, so once again had to retreat with the summit in sight. In addition, increased snowfall and icy storms heralded the beginning of winter (it was mid October).

So, after four weeks, we turned our backs on base camp and the huge mountains. We reached no summit but returned to civilization healthy, full of new experiences, and as friends.

MAX BOLLAND *and* JAN MERSCH, *German Alpine Club (DAV)*

David Goettler on the south pillar of Purbi. Hans Mitterer

The route on the south pillar of Purbi.
Max Bolland

Trisul II, attempt. An 11-member expedition from Calcutta, led by Amitava Roy, attempted Trisul II, a 6,690m peak situated above the Bidalgwar Glacier. This peak was first climbed by a former Yugoslavian expedition in 1960 (by the Japanese in 1978 and for a third time by former Yugoslavs in 1987) and has probably not been attempted for 15 years. From the glacier the team established two camps (almost certainly on the south ridge, the route of the first ascensionists and probably not attempted again since that date) and were in position for a summit attempt, when an avalanche destroyed the site of Camp 2 at 5,600m (their high point) and buried lots of equipment.

HARISH KAPADIA, *Honorary Editor,*
The Himalayan Journal

CENTRAL GARHWAL

Devban, second ascent? An Indo-Tibet Border Police Expedition led by Y.S. Sandhu made what was probably the first ascent of this 6,852m peak south east of Kamet since Frank Smythe climbed it in 1937, although in the meantime several false claims have been made. The strong ITBP team reached the top on September 19. The summiters were Mohammed Ali, Tashi Motop, Jyot Singh and Vijender Singh. Approaching from the east, they climbed the south ridge.

HARISH KAPADIA, *Honorary Editor, The Himalayan Journal*

Editor's note: Peter Oliver and Frank Smythe climbed Devban (formally Deoban) from the Bank Plateau to the south. Unconfirmed repeat ascents via this route were reported in 1980 and 1997, both by Indian Military expeditions.

Arwa Tower and Arwa Spires, various new routes. A French expedition led by Antoine de Choudens (with 11 members) climbed the recently discovered Arwa Tower (6,352m) by two different routes. First they established base camp on May 4 at the foot of this peak, and climbed the south face. Then another team climbed the northwest face. The East Summit of the Arwa Spires (6,132m) was also climbed in a three-day push via the original British route. (See "Arwa Tower, Spire, and Crest," earlier in this Journal for a more complete report.)

HARISH KAPADIA, *Honorary Editor, The Himalayan Journal*

Arwa Spires, first ascents of north face and the central and west summits. The 6,193m-high granite top of the Arwa Spires was first climbed in 2000 by two Scotsmen, Andy and Pete Benson. They reached the East Summit via the east ridge, but three attempts to ascend the north face of the Spires failed. In 2002 three Swiss mountain guides, Bruno Hasler, Stephan Harvey, and Roger Schäli, climbed the north face of the Arwa Spires by two independent routes to the central and west summits. They were the first to reach either of these summits and were nominated for the "Piolet d'Or 2002." for their two first ascents. See "Arwa Spire" lead story earlier in this Journal for a more complete account.

HARISH KAPADIA, *Honorary Editor, The Himalayan Journal*

Arwa Tower, new route. A Swiss expedition led by Frederic Roux climbed the north face and the east ridge of Arwa Tower in 17 hours on October 7. The summit was reached by the leader with Gabriel Basson and Benoit Jean-Paul Darbellay. They had excellent weather and climbed in the best style.

HARISH KAPADIA, *Honorary Editor, The Himalayan Journal*

Peak 6,175m, first ascent, medical research, map errors, and documentary. The aims of our expedition were threefold: to complete a first assent; to carry out medical research into the prediction of altitude sickness; and to make a documentary of the climb with a local Northern Irish media company. Information and photographs of the Bhagirath Kharak valley were scarce. The valley lies immediately south of the Arwa valley, made famous by Mick Fowler's ascent of the Arwa Tower (*AAJ* 2000). Our reference sources were Shipton's 1934 expedition and Harish Kapadia's 1997 crossing of the Shrak La (pass).

After setting up base camp and overcoming the usual logistical problems, we established an advance camp on the glacier and attempted to identify our peak. It became clear that there was an error in one of the accounts, in particular the published location of the Shrak La. Harish Kapadia identifies the Shrak La as lying between Pk 6,044m and Pk 6,175m. His published photograph (*Himalayan Journal* Vol.54) does not match this pass in any way. In fact, high vertical cliffs and a hanging glacier defend the col. It

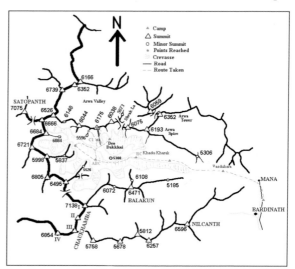

A preliminary map of the Bhagirath Kharak valley and region. Roger McMorrow

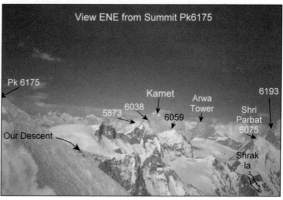

The view from near the summit of Peak 6,175. Roger McMorrow

would be extremely difficult and foolish to cross here, especially as a much easier pass lies a short distance to the east, between Pk 6,038m and Pk 6,075m.

Shipton in 1934 used the Shrak La to cross into the Arwa valley. While there he ascended a peak from the pass, describing it as an "interesting ridge climb" that allowed him to get a "hang of the geography of the Arwa glaciers on to which we were about to descend." It is not possible to definitively identify this peak, as his altimeter was not working correctly. It is likely he climbed either Pk 6,075m or Pk 6,038m, which border the col. Suffice to say that Pk 6,038m has what appears to be an interesting ridge and would provide excellent views of the Arwa glaciers. The col's location is important, as the mountain to the right of it is called Shri Parvat. This means Pk 6,075m is Shri Parvat, and not Pk 6,175 as labeled in Kapadia's texts.

Our own expedition established a camp at the foot of Pk 6,175m on April 11, and on the morning of the 13th used the southeast ridge to ascend over easy mixed ground and gain the right-hand side of its upper face. This was sustained Scottish III all the way. At 4 p.m. on April 13 Michael McCann, Gustau Catalan, Alan Manning, Sara Spencer, and I reached the summit. We set about a difficult abseil descent taking 14 hours (throughout the night), following a gully on the south face of the east ridge.

Data was gathered from all participants in relation to the medical research study. The film crew, Connor Kane, Alan Manning, and Angus Mitchel, also had a successful expedition achieving all their objectives. The Bhagirath Kharak glacier is a remote valley that has not seen much activity. It has many beautiful unclimbed and unnamed peaks. These are quite accessible and have many potential routes with a vast range of difficulties.

ROGER McMORROW, *Ireland*

CENTRAL GARHWAL—GANGOTRI

Chaukhamba II, first ascent of the southwest face. One summer day in 2002 my friends and I decided on the Garhwal as our fall expedition destination. Researching it, we chose Chaukhamba II, the most remote summit of the region. With the help of a small photo of the pillar we intended to climb, more preparations followed until at the end of August, Patrick Wagnon, Christian Tromsdorff, Greg Sauget, and I packed up and were off. After a long guiding season we were all eager to go on an adventure to discover a new region and perhaps an unclimbed route in the particularly fascinating area of the Garhwal, a cultural and spiritual sanctuary at the source of the Ganges.

We got off to a slow start. Ten days of bad weather at the beginning of September dumped more than one meter of snow at 4,300m. Luckily the Indian agency had prepared our voyage so well that the patience of our staff and the creativity of the cooks made the waiting bearable. Tapovan (4,300m), a two-day walk from the road head at Gangotri, is the communal base camp for all climbs in this region. It's also a meditation area. At the foot of Shivling we shared our camp with climbers, pilgrims, and sadhus meditating in the caves.

Although our local porters refused to cross the glacier, our staff from the agency (cook, etc.) offered to take their place. Because of them, three days later we installed our advanced base at 5,300m at the end of the long flat Gangotri glacier.

It was only there that we caught sight of the west pillar of Chaukhamba II. All the information we had for this route had been gathered from a small photo. Now, we could see it. Just to get to this point had already been a complicated logistical affair. After acclimatizing, we decided to climb the west pillar in a style that was half big wall and half alpine.

During our first attempt we realized that we were carrying way too much; 200m up the haul bag broke. An ascent in this style wasn't going to work. We descended and modified our chosen itinerary in order to be able to travel lighter and therefore faster. We needed to adapt the route to alpine style, so we changed our line to the right of the pillar on the south west face. On October 3 we set off from advanced base. The climb, on a 50°–60° snow slope with occasional ice cliffs, wasn't too difficult (approximately alpine grade D). After a bivouac at 6,400m, we continued the second day up a long slope to the summit (7,070m), where we spent the night.

But that was only part one. We still had to descend. Down-climbing 1,600m of 50°–60°+ some rappelling didn't really appeal to us, so we decided we would traverse the ridge to Chaukhamba I and descend its gentler snow slopes. We made this decision from what we could see of the route, realizing we would be venturing a little into the unknown. While traversing the ridge, it started to snow. At around 6,700m, we found a short-cut. It seemed that three or four rappels would take us to a col, from which we could easily descend to advanced base. Late that evening we arrived at the unnamed col and spent our third night above 6,000m. The following morning, lethargic from the previous day, we only left our bivouac at noon. The clouds were already on their way. Half an hour later we were in a storm. To make matters worse, the itinerary down to the glacier wasn't as straightforward as it had seemed. Seracs made it dangerous and bad weather made it difficult to find the correct route. But around 5 p.m., in 30cm of fresh snow, we finally arrived at our camp, where our staff were waiting for us, all ready to go for the 15-hour trek back to Tapovan the following morning.

Now back in Chamonix, I should reiterate how climbing in remote areas like this requires a lot of foresight. Even though the actual ascent wasn't very technical, we wouldn't have succeeded in climbing this summit if we hadn't been flexible. Since we didn't have a lot of prior information, we had to be ready to adapt our plan to the circumstances and be prepared and willing to make changes.

YANNICK GRAZIANI, *France*

Januhut, attempt. The Austrian team of Josef Jochler and Christian Zenz were the first party to attempt this 6,807m peak. Following the usual Gangotri-Tapovan approach, they established base camp on May 19, then reached the head of the long Gangotri Glacier in early June. However, they had plenty of porter problems due too-heavy snow cover on the glacier and, later, bad weather intervened, causing some cold injury to the fingers of one member. No serious attempt was made on the peak

HARISH KAPADIA, *Honorary Editor, The Himalayan Journal*

Swachand, first ascent of west face and second ascent of peak. This year's post-monsoon season in the Gangotri region of the Garhwal was greatly affected by a mid-September dump of three to four feet of snow. Climbing expeditions focusing on east- or north-facing snow or ice routes were unable even to start their routes. Our project, the unclimbed 1,400m west face of Swachand (6,721m), caught the sun in the afternoon, allowing the snow to consolidate.

Swachand is situated in a side valley approximately 25km up the Gangotri Glacier from

Tapovan. It is a few kilometers from the main trekking and approach route, and certainly is a tantalizing view in the distance. Swachand has only been climbed once: in 1938, via the Maiandi Glacier and the snowy southeast side to the south ridge, by the Austrians T. Messner and L. Spannraft. The much steeper west face was first attempted by Malcolm Bass and Julian Clamp (U.K.) in 1998, however they were not successful because of abnormally warm weather and stonefall.

John Millar, Conor Reynolds, and I spent several days watching the face from a few different angles, acclimatizing, watching for avalanches, and planning our route. A few days before we were to attempt the climb, Conor developed a bad boil the size of a ping-pong ball on his back. He had to quit and descend to go seek medical help and antibiotics. Thus, it was just John and myself.

Early in the morning of October 3, John and I started out from ABC ready to climb. Up the first snowfield, and onto the ice-shield at the base of the wall. We hunkered in a bergshrund and roped up for the first rock band. After four good M5 pitches we were on the "dragon" snow patch and just managed to frontpoint to the top of it by dark. It took at least an hour to hack out a sizeable platform for our tent, but the refuge was welcome. The nights and mornings were cold (-15° to -20°C)!

The following morning John found a WI5 chimney to get us up to an ice ramp, which led in the direction of a larger left-diagonal weakness that proved a bit of a funnel for rockfall. In the only significant rockfall that we saw while climbing, I was hit hard in the foot, enough to cause some swelling and to hamper my ability to frontpoint. I grimaced and followed, while John led all the pitches for the next day-and-a-half.

The second pitch of day three was definitely the crux of the whole route. John led a full 60m M6 WI5 pitch. I struggled to follow the pitch carrying the heavy second's pack. We started swapping leads again and reached the upper snow/ice face at sunset.

On the fourth morning, four pitches up ice, snow, and sugar-over-ice brought us to the summit ridge. We were hoping for some easy going at this point, but the traverse to the summit was far from that: big cornices and very windy. We simul-climbed up the ridge on firm corniced snow with one fiddly rock step, at a rate of two breaths per footstep, to arrive on the summit at about 4:00 p.m.

We only spent a couple of minutes on top. It was a sharp summit dropping steeply in all directions, and we were worried about the descent (never underestimate 1938 climbers). The first 300m down the south ridge were sharp and required focused concentration. Finally, we got to safer terrain, did a few rappels, and camped down a little lower for the night.

On the fifth day we were out of food after breakfast. We slogged back up the upper Maiandi Glacier to the col south of Swachand,

John Millar in action on the west face of Swachand.
Guy Edwards

The Edwards-Millar route on the west face of Swachand. Guy Edwards

then dropped down toward the Swachand Glacier. After a few rappels, some down-climbing, and lots of kick-stepping, we reached the base of the face. In the last moments of visibility before some very threatening storm clouds were upon us, we found our tracks from five days before. In a whiteout and with thick and determined snow falling, we managed to follow our old tracks back to the security of fuel, food, and a bigger tent: our advanced base camp. We collapsed relieved and de-stressed.

We were very lucky. Six inches of snow fell that night, plastering every slope. The next morning lots of fresh avalanche debris was visible and new slides and sloughs were coming down everywhere. Patience and good posture are necessary when climbing at altitude. Thus we named the route Mulabhanda, meaning "sphincter clenching," a yoga-Sanskrit term.

GUY EDWARDS, *Canada*

Editor's note: Guy Edwards and John Millar were killed on the Devil's Thumb, Alaska, in late April 2003, presumably by avalanche. See the epilogue to The Fickle Face earlier in this Journal.

Meru Shark's Fin, yet another attempt. British climbers Jon Bracey, Julian Cartwright and Matt Dickinson approached this attractive rock face from the Gangotri Glacier and established base camp on September 16 . The team was quickly reduced to two members, making logistics on the face difficult, so although the weather was good, they were unable to reach the summit.

HARISH KAPADIA, *Honorary Editor, The Himalayan Journal*

Bhilangna Valley, Satling peaks, first ascents. A British team made several first ascents in the Satling group of peaks at the head of the Bhilangna valley in early spring 2002. With rock as good as Chamonix granite, virgin walls up to 600m high, ice couloirs, and dozens of miniature aiguilles, the Satling offers a veritable feast of alpine climbing at altitudes between 5,000m and 5,850m. The "Sat-ling" or "Seven Phalluses" were first spotted by the British team that climbed Thelay Sagar's south face in 1992. Remarkably, no climbing expedition had been up the valley in the intervening 10 years, even though the often-climbed peaks of Shivling and Meru are only 15km distant over the Gangotri watershed.

Having established an advance camp at 4,980m on the Satling Glacier, Mark Davidson, Martin Moran, and John Venier climbed two rock peaks; The Rabbit's Ear (5,530m, D- with one pitch of UIAA V) and The Cathedral (5,360m, D with five pitches of UIAA IV, V, and V+). Meanwhile Keith Milne and Gordon Scott, who were part of the 1992 British team, climbed the north couloir of The Fortress (5,541m). The ascent took 10 hours and featured three pitches at an overall grade of Scottish IV/V (TD-).

The main objective in the range is the triple-headed peak of 5,850m, which was provisionally named Brahmasar (Brahma's Head). Davidson, Moran, and Venier made a bold attempt to climb its west ridge, which featured an ice and mixed approach followed by some immaculate rock climbing on a slender arête. After 15 pitches of climbing, including several of grade V and one of VI (TD overall), they were repulsed 60m under the summit when faced by a series of delicate traverses late in the day.

Meanwhile, Milne and Scott circumnavigated the peak to gain an easier approach from the Dudhganga Glacier on its southeast side. They climbed the South Summit at D- with two pitches of IV, but commented that, viewed from every angle, the final 100m to the highest Central Peak would give difficult climbing. Brahmasar also sports a magnificent 800m north ridge.

Weather conditions in early May were excellent and a good cover of winter snow simplified the approaches. The glaciers and snow peaks of this area have considerable scope for ski-touring at this time of year. Technical difficulties on the granite faces look to be of a high order.

MARTIN MORAN, *U.K.*

WESTERN GARHWAL

Peak 6,075 m, first ascent. In early September a nine-member all women team from the IMF led by Chandraprabha Aitwal approached an unclimbed 6,075m peak in Kakora Gad from Harsil on the Gangotri Road. After acclimatizing at Kana Tal, base camp was established at 3,100m. The team placed two camps on the mountain and reached the summit in one long day on the 19th September. Altogether six members, Sushma Thakur, Kavita Burathoki, Reena Kaushal, Sundri Devi, Babita Gosawi and Ekta) plus three High Altitude Porters and Mr Narerndra Kutyal, reached the top. This team also climbed an unnamed peak of 5,645m north east of their base camp on September 21. The leader with Reena Kaushal, Sushma Thakur, Kavita Burathoki, Mr. Kutyal and a High Altitude Porter reached the top.

HARISH KAPADIA, *Honorary Editor, The Himalayan Journal*

HIMACHAL PRADESH

LAHAUL

Ramjak, first ascent. An Indian Mountaineering Foundation expedition led by Sangay Dorjee Sherpa made the first ascent of Ramjak (6,318m). This peak has attracted many climbers in the past, including attempts by IMF expeditions in 2000 and 2001. At least three other attempts on this peak by different parties had also failed. The 2002 expedition left Delhi on July 22 and established base camp at 4,620m on the 27th, after fording several ice-cold streams on the approach. Camp 1 was established on August 3 after negotiating difficult terrain, crevasses, and exposed slopes. Finally, on August 4 the leader reached the summit along with Mul Dorjay, Nima Dorjay, and HAP Dawa Wanchuk

HARISH KAPADIA, *Honorary Editor, The Himalayan Journal*

East Karakoram

Teram Shehr Ice Plateau traverse. The Indian–Japanese East Karakoram Expedition, consisting of five Indian and five Japanese mountaineers, undertook a long traverse of the Eastern Karakoram valleys between May 8 and July 9. We achieved a lot, covering almost 550km with various repeated load ferries. We carried almost 2,500kg of food, equipment and personal gear, first on 55 mules, later with personal ferries by 11 members and 15 Sherpas and porters. We lived continuously on the snow for almost 35 days, braving rather cold temperatures. There were no injuries, accident or sickness except to one porter.

The team traversed an historic route in the Shyok Valley and returned via the Nubra Valley (the Siachen Glacier). Five passes were reached or crossed, two large glaciers were fully traversed and a vast unknown ice plateau was explored. Above all, the first ascent of virgin and difficult Padmanabh (7,030m) was achieved.

The team traveled the Shyok River valley from Shyok village (Tankse-Darbuk) to the Karakoram Pass, following the ancient winter trade route between India and China and becoming the first expedition to achieve this in the last five decades. It was also the first time in the history of independent India that a team involving foreign mountaineers was permitted to visit the Pass. A lone British photographer had reached the pass in 1997. This was also the first time that Japanese had stood on the pass in the last 93 years.

The team traversed the entire Central Rimo and Teram Shehr glaciers by crossing Col Italia, the high pass between the two glaciers. It was the first time the pass had been traversed since the original crossing in 1929. Most of the Indian members had previously reached the pass in 2000 but had not crossed it.

The high and vast Teram Shehr Ice Plateau was explored and various cols surrounding the Plateau were investigated. The Plateau is a unique feature in the Karakoram, with ice and snow at a height of about 6,200m surrounded by high peaks on all sides. Harish Kapadia and Ryuji Hayashibara were the first people to reach the Plateau, seen so often in photos taken from peaks such as Rimo.

The first ascent of Padmanabh (7,030m) was made on June 25 by two Japanese members, Hiroshi Sakai and Yasushi Tanahashi (see Sakai's report below). Both had previously climbed Nanga Parbat but rated this peak more difficult in some aspects. Padmanabh is the highest peak on the Teram Shehr Plateau and the first major unclimbed peak in the Siachen Glacier to be ascended for many years. The team returned via the Siachen Glacier to the Nubra Valley.

The international team was the first to climb on the war-torn Siachen glacier since 1986 and the Japanese were the first mountaineers from their country to visit the glacier from the Indian side since the conflict began in 1984. Many Japanese teams had climbed on the Siachen Glacier between 1972 and 1983, approaching it from the west.

The Indian portion of the team was Harish Kapadia (Leader), Motup Chewang, Lt. Commander S. Dam, Huzefa Electricwala, and Rushad Nanavatty. The Japanese portion was: Hiroshi Sakai (Deputy & Climbing Leader), Tadashi Fukuwada, Ryuji Hayashibara, Dr. Hirofumi Oe, and Yasushi Tanahashi. A liaison officer from the Indian army, Capt. Madhab Boro, accompanied the team. Our expedition was organized by the Japanese Alpine Club and The Mountaineers Bombay, Mumbai, India. The expedition is grateful to the Indian Army for permission and support to undertake this venture. We are specially thankful to Lt. General R. K. Nanavatty, PVSM, UYSM, AVSM, General Officer in Command, Northern Command,

Indian Army, without whose strong support we would not have been able to climb in this area or complete the expedition under the difficult situation that developed.

HARISH KAPADIA, *Honorary Editor,*
The Himalayan Journal

Padmanabh 7,030m (center) from midway between Col Italia and base camp. Hiroshi Sakai

Padmanabh, first ascent. Almost all the unclimbed 7,000m peaks surrounding the Siachen Glacier were scaled in the 1970s by expeditions entering the region from Pakistan. Padmanabh remained virgin. The period allocated to climbing during our traverse of the Teram Shehr Ice Plateau (see above) was 15 days from a second base camp at 5,650m back to the same camp. On June 14 an advance party went up an easy glacier and reached a col on the south ridge at 6,250m. Their reconnaissance led to the conclusion that an attack camp should be set up near the col. The mostly granite south ridge has an average angle of 45°-50°. We thought this would yield to relatively easy climbing. However, the south ridge comprised small but complicated snow ridges, which appeared one after another. In some places the angle reached 70°–80°. Route preparation up to 6,750m required four working days, and 16 rope lengths were fixed to this point. Two teams consisting of Japanese and Indian mountaineers worked together to open the route.

On June 25, the 12th day after commencing the climb, we attempted the summit. Three members comprising Commander S. Dam, Yasushi Tanahashi and myself departed from our attack camp at 3:50 a.m. Unfortunately S. Dam soon had to drop out as he was unable to keep pace with the other two. We reached our previous high point at 8:30 a.m. Every pitch from there was extremely hard, even though it was less than 300m to the summit. We moved steadily pitch by pitch against a strong wind and the clouds that prevailed on the upper part of the south ridge.

About 11 hours after leaving camp we reached a treacherous snow wall. I led this wall, climbing vertical granulated sugar snow that was very difficult to negotiate. We kicked and stamped down the snow to make it more solid but all our efforts were in vain. We continued our struggle as the wall became even more precipitous. The last 30m ended with a cornice. To overcome it, we first had to dig a trench two meters deep and then excavate a tunnel. If conditions as critical as this had carried on for another five minutes, I would have given up and descended. Tanahashi led the final (26th) pitch, which took us to the foot of an ice tower resembling a cream puff. We stood atop Padmanabh at 3:10 p.m. after over 11 hours of continuous climbing.

A few days later Motup Chewang, Rushad Nanavatty, Dr Oe and Tadashi Fukuwada (each of whom worked hard and climbed quite high while preparing the final route) were poised for another attempt on the summit. However, due to the onset of bad weather, they gave up the attempt.

HIROSHI SAKAI, *Japanese Alpine Club*

Nepal

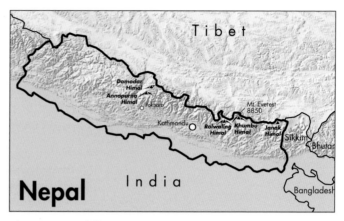

Recent changes in regulations. New regulations coming into force during 2002 were generally very beneficial to the mountaineering community and particularly to those climbers wishing to try lightweight ascents of new routes and virgin peaks. The most significant changes are as follows:

(a) A Liaison Officer is generally no longer required for peaks below 6,500m.
(b) No climber under 16 is permitted
(c) Permits are no longer granted only for a particular season, they can now be obtained for any time of the year.
(d) The outdated letter of approval from the national mountaineering federation of the country of origin of each expedition, or from the embassy of the country, has been waived.
(e) New payment rates have recently been fixed at: sirdar Rs400, high altitude porter Rs300, base camp staff Rs300.

New peaks for the autumn of 2002. To coincide with the start of the post-monsoon season 2002 the Ministry of Culture, Tourism and Civil Aviation announced that the following 13 mountains were being added to the existing list of peaks permitted for foreign expeditions. The new peaks are a strange mixture, comprising not only high, serious, technical, and remote peaks, but also lower altitude mountains that eminently fit the category of "trekking peaks." A number of these have already been climbed—some, like Mera South (an easier, subsidiary snow dome of the popular Khumbu trekking peak) on many occasions—while the formidable Nemjung has already been attempted by more than a half-dozen foreign teams over the last 15 years. The new peaks, progressing roughly from east to west, are listed below. Notes as to their location are given in parenthesis.

KHUMBU
Mahalangur Himal South
    Naulekh 6,240m
    "Mera South" (Mera East) 6,064m

Mahalangur Himal North
    Changri Shar 6,811m
    Changri West 6,773m
    Lungsampa 6,100m

LANGTANG
Langtang Himal
    Ghenye Liru 6,571m

MANASLU
Peri Himal
    Nemjung 7,139m (7,140m)

MANANG
Purkhung Himal
    Khatung Kang 6,484m

DHAULAGIRI
Mukut Himal
    Tsartse 6,398m
    Tashi Kang 6,386m

DOLPO
Palchung Hamga Himal
    Danfe Sail 6,103m
    Kangfu Gaton (Kanta Gaton) 5,916m
    Kanjiroba Himal
    Norbu Kang 6,005m

At the same time the Nepal Mountaineering Association was given 15 new mountains to add to its list of Trekking Peaks, bringing the total to 33. The fees associated with these 15 new peaks are: one $500 permit for expeditions with up to seven members; an extra $100 per person for teams with over seven members up to a maximum of 12 members, above which a second permit will apply; a $250 deposit will be required for all 33 peaks as a garbage/environmental bond, which should be refunded on the basis of satisfactory report, jointly signed by the team leader, sirdar, and climber. Fees for the original 18 peaks remain unchanged. Many of the new peaks, such as the technical Cholatse, have been demoted from full expedition status and are indicated by a *. Yala Peak and Chhukung Ri, although new to any official list, have been climbed by many people over the years.

The new peaks, listed roughly from east to west, are:

KANGCHENJUNGA
Khumbhakarna Himal
    Bokta Peak* 6,143m

KHUMBU
Mahalangur North
    Chhukung Ri 5,550m
    Lobuche West* 6,145m
    Cholatse* 6,440m
    Nirekha Peak* 6,159m
    Kyazo (Kyajo) Ri* 6,186m
    Machermo 6,273m
    Phari Lapcha 6,017m
Mahalangur South
    Abi* 6,097m
    Ombigaichen* 6,340m

ROWALING
Rowaling Himal
    Chekigo* 6,257m

LANGTANG
Jugal Himal
    Langshisha Ri* 6,427m
Langtang Himal
    Yubra 6,035m
    Yala Peak 5,732m

MANASLU
Manaslu Himal
    Larkya Peak* 6,010m

Rowaling Himal

Tengi Ragi Tau, first ascent of newly opened peak. In the spring of 2000 I saw Tengi Ragi Tau (6943m) for the first time while we climbed Parchamo (6,279m). It strongly attracted my attention, but it was a forbidden peak according to our guide. In 2002 the Nepali government released 103 mountains, including Tengi Ragi Tau. Since the Hokkaido Mountaineering Association celebrated its jubilee in the same year, we organized a celebration expedition to Tengi Ragi Tau. From Parchamo the southeast face had looked unclimbable and it seemed wiser to search for an easier route on its west side. Our conclusion based on maps and information then available was that one of the two rock ribs on the 1,600m wall might be feasible, and our plan was prepared based on that assumption. On November 26 the five members with five Sherpas and four kitchen-staff. established BC at 4,800m at the snout of Thyagb Glacier. On reconnaissance, those rock ribs drawn on maps were an illusion. What to do? To make sure we climbed something, we all ascended Parchamo and returned to BC on November 11. During this time I began reconsidering the seemingly unclimbable southeast face of Tengi Ragi Tau. Looking closer, we discovered a sharp ridge stretching up from around the middle height at the center of the wall. At least it should be safe to follow it.

After an earlier reconnaissance, on October 15, Onda, two Sherpas, and I extended the route through the steepening snow slope and we finally reached the rock ridge. Luckily snow conditions were not bad and the weather was fine. On the 17th we pitched C1 at 6050m. Takahashi and two Sherpas continued to fix the route up the ridge to 6400m, spending two full days, then we all retreated to BC for a rest. On the 23rd, the summit team consisting of Takahashi, two Sherpas, and myself left BC. We left C1 at 3 a.m. the next day and climbed up through a fluted ice wall, but the face was so complicated that we were forced into an impossible passage at about 6750m, still 200 meters below the summit. We rappelled down 200 meters and then tackled a left-leaning gully. After climbing it part way, we decided to follow the gully on our next attempt. We left the gear in place and descended to BC.

Strong winds blew during the following three days, and on the 28th we returned to C1. The next day Onda, Morishita, and two Sherpas departed C1 at 3 a.m. Huge mushroom-shaped cornices hung from the main ridge down to the wall. The gully led beneath the cornices but it was not easy to get through the mushroom to reach the main ridge. Fortunately a narrow slit between cornices allowed them to break out onto the ridge. It was such a thin ridge that they looked down Drolambau Glacier below their feet to the opposite side. The summit was just 250 meters ahead, but there was only enough time to descend to C1.

Again strong winds continued to blow during the following few days until at last the summit day came. On December 4, Takahashi, two Sherpas, and I left C1 at 3 a.m. Hard wind from the west howled on the main ridge. We could not stop shivering even in down-filled jackets and anoraks. We were afraid of being blown off, but this might be our last chance. Determined to reach the top, we attacked one cornice after another until two hours, 30 minutes later we reached the summit. Looking back over the ridge, Parchamo seemed such a small hill! And of course we enjoyed an enormous panoramic view of Gaurishankar, Tibetan frontier ranges, Everest, Makalu, etc.

We climbed down the 1,600m wall to BC that day, and on the following day (Dec. 5), Onoda, Morishita, and a Sherpa made the second ascent from C1 and returned to BC on the

6th. It must have been the last chance for the season, as desperate winter gales began to blow.

KOICHI EZAKI, *Hokkaido Mountaineering Association (translation by Kei Kurachi)*

Teng Kang Poche, pre-monsoon attempts. Taking advantage of the recent addition to the permitted list of peaks of this splendid 6,500m mountain on the ridge west of Kwangde, the French Alpine Club chose Teng Kang Poche as the venue for an expedition comprising several well-known guides and 14 young alpinists from the CAF's "Excellence Group." The expedition divided into two groups; one attempting the mountain from the difficult north side above the Thame Valley, while the second would try the easier but more remote southern flanks. Both hoped to make the first official ascent.

In recent years a number of parties have attempted to get permission to climb the magnificent granite north pillar of Teng Kang Poche or the more icy northeast face, both well-known and clearly visible Khumbu objectives, but it wasn't until 2001 that the peak was brought on to the official permitted list. It is not certain who were the first ascensionists of Teng Kang Poche, though the mountain was certainly climbed in 1984 via the east ridge from the Lumding Valley by the late Trevor Pilling and Andy Zimet.

The southern slopes of Teng Kang Poche lie toward the head of the remotely situated and largely uninhabited Lumding Valley, reached via a high pass from the main valley of the Dudh Kosi. The French arrived at their 5,100m base camp by a lake below Kwangde in early April. However, considerable snow fall and warm temperatures did not allow much progress and after reaching around 5,900m on both the south ridge and east ridge during the middle of the month, the climbers decided all possible routes were too dangerous and gave up.

On the north side the second group started up the easier lower section of the impressive north pillar, then moved left on to the northeast face. Again, poor weather prevented success and a high point of 6,100m was achieved.

LINDSAY GRIFFIN, *High Mountain INFO*

Teng Kang Poche, northeast Pillar attempt, and Tengi Ragi Tau South, south ridge. Our expedition lasted from October 1 to November 8. We went to the Khumbu at this time because during our autumn visit there the previous year we had enjoyed very good weather. However, 2002 was rather different. ' and looked at the north side of Teng Kang Poche (6,500m), the face was covered by

The still unclimbed northeast pillar of Teng Kang Poche (6,500m), from Thengpo. Phil Wickens

The north face of Teng Kang Poche from the northwest. Phil Wickens

snow with very little rock showing. We split into two teams. Jaro Dutka and Martin Heuger from Slovakia started immediately on a direct line up the northeast pillar. This is a magic line on very steep rock, but now it was all covered in snow. Alexadr Toloch and I decided to wait and attempt a line up the left side of the pillar, which was not so steep and therefore offered a better chance of an all free ascent. However, each day a few more centimeters of snow fell. In the end both teams failed after 500-700m of climbing at an altitude of 5,450m. Unstable snow covered steep rock slabs and made progress dangerous. Jaro and Martin climbed difficulties from III to V+ and gave up on the October 20, we from III to V and finished two days earlier. We also found equipment abandoned by the French team earlier in the year.

After a couple of days rest in base camp, Alexadr and I went to try a beautiful rocky ridge on Tengi Ragi Tau. This led up toward the 6,180m South Summit, the smallest in the Tengi Ragi Tau massif. The ridge faced south and we began our ascent in the afternoon of the 21st and took two days to reach the summit. During the climb the weather was very sunny but a strong wind blew from the northwest. The latter wasn't a problem in the lower section, as we were protected, but after the second bivouac it hit us directly. Fortunately, the climbing from this point was easier with more snow and ice. We joined the southeast ridge and continued up this to the top, reaching it at 2:00 p.m. on the 23rd. The view was beautiful but we were concerned about our descent of the southeast ridge. The snow was not as good as it had been on our south ridge but we managed to descend quite quickly. A couple of rappels put us on the small glacier at the bottom and continued on down to bivouac in grassy meadows, reaching them at dark. We named our 1,700m route Like a Dhal Bhat, because it was a very beautiful route, and graded it ED (VII- and 75°). The ascent took 20 hours climbing time and the descent (grade D+) six hours.

After this we only had time to climb the Normal Route on Parcharmo before returning home, but maybe we will come back, as Teng Kang Poche is a fantastic granite monument.

RADEK LIENERTH, *Czech Republic*

The north face of Kwangde Lho (6,187m), showing, left to right: Extra Blue Sky (Beaugey-Profit-Rhem-Ruby, 1996), Nakagawa (2002), Breashears-Lowe (1982), Mandala (Lorenzo-Munoz, 1985). Hiroyuki Nakagawa

Kwangde Lho (6,187m), new north face route. Koji Ito and I made the seventh ascent of the north face of Kwangde Lho, by a new route (ED+ M5 WI6). After spending six days climbing 37 pitches, we reached the summit of the 1,150m face on December 13. The north (Hungo) face of Kwangde Lho was first climbed by Americans David Breashears and Jeff Lowe in 1982, and repeated by a British party in 2001. The route Extra Blue Sky of Kwangde Shar (6,100m) was climbed by the French in 1996, by the Czechs and British in 2000 and again by British in 2001. In addition, a Spanish team succeeded in 1985, while in 2001 a Czech team put a new direct finish on the 1989 American route of the north buttress of Kwangde Nup (6,035m)—see *AAJ* 2002.

We began climbing from an advanced base camp, near 4,900m on December 8. Despite frequent snow showers and poor ice conditions (we only got screws in on one pitch), we competed nine pitches before digging out a bivy in a snow wall. The next day we did six pitches, beginning with two VS WI6 pitches on 70° to 80° very thin ice where protection was almost impossible. Our third day on the face we did seven more pitches, ending with a bivouac at a dihedral. We enjoyed good ice on just one pitch—the fourth—but suffered with the usual bad conditions for the other six.

Day four began with a S WI5, 70°-80° pitch (plus a little at 90°) where protection was difficult, followed by a S M5 WI6 with dry-tooling on thin and discontinuous ice. After five pitches, we found a comfortable bivy under a rock roof. The next day we climbed toward the right on bad 50°-70° fluted snow and ice, trying to follow a ridge leading to the summit ridge. But we ran into an unclimbable slab, then descended a rock band (M5) to a 70° hammock bivy, after a total of six pitches that day.

On our sixth and final day, we began by traversing left to get back onto ice, then went up and right on discontinuous ice that was M5 in two places. The snow conditions were even worse below the summit ridge, where we topped out at 6,050m.

We began our descent with three diagonal rappels down the south face, followed by a downclimb to the glacier on the south side of Shar, where we bivied. The next day, we walked southeast on the glacier to a point near the lowest col between Shar and a nameless peak, then descended to the Namche side. We reached the moraine after seven raps and more down-climbing, then bivied again on the east side of the northeast ridge. The next day, December 15, we finally descended to our advanced base camp by detouring around the northeast ridge.

HIROYUKI NAKAGAWA, *North Japan Climbing Team (translated by Tamotsu Nakamura)*

ANNAPURNA HIMAL

Annapurna I traverse. Unquestionably the best climb of the season was the Annapurna I traverse by Jean-Christophe Lafaille and Alberto Inurrategi. They were members of a six-man expedition jointly led by Inurrategi and Ed Viesturs. They had no Sherpa climbers with them at all, so the members did the work together to make the route, pitch the camps and stock them with supplies as far as their third high-altitude camp at 7,100m, nearly 100m below the summit of their eastern-most peak, Glacier Dome (now officially known as Tarkekang). They had no bottled oxygen with them.

Viesturs climbed beyond camp 3 westwards along the ridge until 7,300m, but went no farther. He judged the avalanche risk unacceptable and was worried about the problem of returning from Annapurna's summit by the same long ridge. He descended to base camp and remained there for the remainder of the climbing period.

Lafaille and Inurrategi remained to continue alone. On May 14, they left camp 3 at 6 a.m. and moved along the sawtooth ridge. It had a steep and technically difficult section up to the summit of the 7,485m (24,557') peak known as Roc Noir (Khangsar Kang). They took three hours to surmount the last 250m-300m to the top; here the incline was 55° – 60° with a rock band running across it and bad powder snow. From here, they had only two alternatives, according to Lafaille: to retreat from the top of Roc Noir back the way they had come, or to con-tinue west. It was not possible for them to descend the north or south faces, both of which were very steep; the distance down the north face was too great, while on the south face there were numerous unacceptably dangerous seracs and cornices.

They elected to continue west from Roc Noir by traversing on the north face between 20m and 100m below the ridge depending on the snow conditions. Sometimes they could walk along it with a pole, sometimes it became a very steep (65° –70°) snow face which involved very technical climbing and some rappeling. At 4 p.m. they bivouacked at about 7,500m, the aver-age altitude of this part of their traverse. They had climbed more than four km. from camp 3.

On the 15th they went back onto the ridge for about a kilometer and then, at about 7,700m, they crossed again down onto the north face, where all the snow was very good and firm whereas the ridge had become only bare rock. However, they did have some technical ice and snow climbing to do. They now were actually on the huge expanse of Annapurna I, and they bivouacked at 7,950m at the top of a couloir below its east summit. They stopped their traverse at about 3 p.m. because they knew it would take them hours to chop out enough space to stay for the night. That afternoon Lafaille also spent some time fixing 100m of rope above their bivouac site for the next day's climb.

On May 16 they completed their east-west traverse. The route now lay along a steep rock face that was technically very difficult. They had trouble finding a route here. About 40m below the east summit (8,026m), they moved westward along the north face. They crossed the middle summit area on the face and joined the normal north face route at a couloir at about 7,800m, climbed up the couloir, and at 10 a.m. were at last on the main 8,091m summit (26,545'). Half of their grand traverse had been done.

Now to get down safely. After half an hour on the top, they started out on their west-east return traverse. They took a different line on the face from the one they had just been using because they were very tired and the snow conditions were not good. In the middle of the afternoon they returned to their bivouac tent, stayed there an hour, then moved to a lower altitude to make a new bivouac on a small plateau at 7,400m. They were very weary, and there was no food and little cooking gas; their supper consisted of some biscuits with milk tea.

On the 17th they continued their return climb. They were still very tired, but at their bivouac of the 14th found their cache of food and gas; they spent two hours to have some food. Then back to Roc Noir and camp 3, which they reached at 4 p.m. Here there was a proper camp with a tent and more food, and they could be more relaxed. The next day, they descended all the way to base camp at 4,000m, where they arrived at the end of that morning.

Throughout their remarkable climb, they had used no bottled oxygen and experienced no accident or frostbite. "I was very happy," Lafaille said about his success on Annapurna after three previous attempts and his "bad experience" on its south face 10 years ago. (In October 1992, he and the noted French alpinist Pierre Beghin had been attempting an alpine-style ascent of the south face when Beghin fell to his death. Lafaille's difficult solo descent developed into a growing nightmare when a falling rock shattered his right arm.)

ELIZABETH HAWLEY, *Nepal*

DAMODAR HIMAL

Gaugiri, first ascent. Jim Frush (then-president of the AAC) and I went exploring for an obscure 6,110m (20,046') peak called Gaugiri, which is in the Upper Mustang district northeast of the Annapurna massif on the Tibetan border.

We had an idea of roughly where the peak was from a trip to Mustang in the fall of 2001, but no one had ever attempted to climb the peak and there were no photos or description of it or its exact location. This was the first permit issued for a peak under the new regulations, and the first ever in Upper Mustang. It was one out of the list of 103 newly opened mountains, many of them unknown to mountaineers, ranging in altitude from 5,407m (17,740') to 7,349m (24,111'). Eighty-three of them are between 6,000m and 7,000m high. As we set out for Gaugiri from Kathmandu in mid-May, we didn't know whether we would be tackling something that was technically difficult or an easy walk uphill. But first we had to find it. We had the latest 1:50,000 maps, produced in 2000, from a detailed Finnish Meteorological Institute survey, but even these maps proved to have put some significant lakes in totally the wrong place, which caused us some problems. However, we found Gaugiri and were pleased to discover a southwest ridge that would definitely not be just a trek to the top and decided to climb it.

From our base camp at about 5,400m (17,700'), we set out at 7:30 a.m. on 28 May in relatively good weather after some days of snowfall, and quickly reached and ascended the ridge. Most of it was covered by good snow, with some loose rock in places. Some sections were quite steep (45° – 55°). Unaccompanied by any Sherpas, we were on the summit at 1:20 p.m., stayed an hour enjoying the view, and were back at base late the same afternoon . It is a fun, classic route with no great difficulties. Our total time out from Jomosom was 20 days.

The mountain dominates its area as the high peak on a long southeast ridge. Its summit, on the border with Tibet, has dramatic views of the giant 8,167m Dhaulagiri I to the southwest, a wide panorama of Tibet to the north and east, and a range of glaciated 6,000m–7,000m peaks to the south.

PETER ACKROYD, AAC

Pokharkan, first ascent. Sherpa Panima Lama (51) and I (61) made the first ascent of Pokharkan (6,346m) on October 31. We climbed the north ridge via a route that is not highly technical. I selected this route because the south face is a difficult rock wall. Sherpas Pemba Cherin (58) and Suba Maju (55) were also part of our team. Pokharkan is northeast of Annapurna near the Tibetan border at latitude N24°48', longitude E84°13'. It is one of 103 new peaks that the government of Nepal opened to climbing in 2002.

We left Kathmandu on October 10, via Besidsal and Naru Khola, and set up base camp at 4,850m, north of Nagoru (4,500m), on October 19. From BC, we followed a moraine up a gentle ridge, and set up C1 at 5,360m, two days later. One week later, we set up C2 on a ridge at 5,700m, with the summit hidden from view. On October 30, we established C3 above a steep snow face, at 6,050m. The next day, Panima Lama and I reached the main summit, at 6,346m. The summit is really two peaks 100m apart, which are about the same height. So we climbed up a steep gully to the top of the left peak first, and then climbed the right peak too. We departed from base camp on November 3, and returned to Kathmandu via Thorang La and Pokhara, arriving on November 11.

KOICHI KATO, *Japan* (*translated by Tamotsu Nakamura*)

Pokharkan, first ascent of the south face. The Alpine Club Damodar expedition was led by Steve Town with Dick Isherwood as deputy. Other members were David Baldock, John Fairley, Toto Gronlund, Martin Scott, Pete and Sara Spillet, Bill Thurston, and myself. Our Sirdar and climbing Sherpa was Kaji, the fastest man up Everest. We approached along the Annapurna Circuit as far as Koto, from where we struck off north toward the Tibetan border and into the spectacular Naur gorge of the Phu Khola. Three days later we reached the village of Phugaon and began a reconnaissance of Pokharkan, which proved to be a far more complex mountain than the maps suggested.

A very long ridge running southwest from the summit to a pass west of Phugaon (which Tilman crossed in 1950) turned out to have several difficult rock steps. The southeast ridge, though shorter, also looked rugged, with a deep saddle between what we came to call Pokharkan Southeast (5,700m) and what was, in effect, the southeast ridge of Pokharkan II (6250m). The east face of Pokharkan II appeared to have a straightforward snow/ice route winding up around serac barriers, so we established base camp at 4,800m below this face. By then illness and the bitter cold had persuaded David and Steve to leave, so Dick took over the leadership. A close encounter with a snow leopard had nothing to do with their decision.

Advanced base was established in a deep saddle at 5,300m, with a view to out-flanking the southeast ridge and gaining the east face. From this point Toto and I climbed Pokharkan Southeast. Vestigial tracks indicated that one of the French or Belgian expeditions, unsuccessful with their attempts at the main summit earlier in the season, had made the first ascent. From the summit we could see that the east face was feasible, but had doubts that the top we could see was the true summit. However, from the saddle it was possible to access a huge high glacier bay below the south face, and our Sherpa team, inspecting this approach, came back full of enthusiasm. We therefore placed another camp at 5,600m in the glacier bay. At this point the Spillets became ill, leaving only six of us to attempt the summit.

We set off from our high camp on November 17 but very soon Dick succumbed to the chest infection that had troubled him for some time and was forced to descend. A glacier ramp led to serac barriers at 5,900m, where I was lucky to be able to lead a 10m pitch of steep ice, about Scottish 3. This proved to be the crux of the route. Above a second ice cliff another glacier ramp led easily to the southeast ridge at about midpoint. Buffeted by strong winds, we climbed the ridge to the summit of Pokharkan II. Here, John, Bill, and Toto descended, while Kaji, Martin, and myself continued across a saddle towards the main summit approximately one km. distant. We reached the 6,350m top and a fantastic viewpoint at 2 p.m. There appeared to be no tracks or other conclusive evidence of the mountain having been climbed previously, although we had understood in Koto that a lone Japanese with a Sherpa team believed he had climbed it just two weeks earlier from the north. A Sherpa's description of waist deep powder snow had influenced our decision to make the ascent from the south. In two hours we regained our tents and the following day descended to base camp. The consensus was that the route equated to Alpine AD+.

DAVE WYNNE-JONES, *The Alpine Club*

MUSTANG HIMAL

Arniko Chuli, first ascent and survey. In the summer of 2001, I began topographical research of the mountains west of Lo Manthang and Chharang, and made the first ascent of Arniko Chuli (6,034m). Arniko Chuli is at the northern edge of the range between Lo and Dolpo, on the border between Nepal and Tibet. I was attracted to this mysterious peak for its height, its strange name, and because no foreigner had ever seen it. The Indian surveyors gave the peak a Nepalese—not a Tibetan—name. Aruniko (or Araniko) is the name of a famous artist from Nepal who, in the latter half of the 13th century, went to Tibet to design statues for Buddhist monasteries.

I planned, along with two Nepalese friends—Ang Purba and his wife Pasang Diki (Thame)—to approach Aruniko Chuli from the Dolpo side. On July 3, we left Jomsom at Kaligandaki with five pack animals, and walked to Sangda village along the historical route taken by Sharmana Ekai Kawaguchi—a Japanese priest, the first foreigner to reach Lhasa from Nepal, 102 years ago.

After crossing Geba La, we followed another trail north along Lhanhimar Khola to a nameless pass. Then we descended along a northwestern stream, Sano Kiraphuk Khola. On July 8, we set up our base camp very close to Chanagor Bhanjyang (5,665m), on the northern border. The next morning, we climbed the pass on the border, and were rewarded with a good view of the Tibetan side.

West and northwest of us, there were four other passes in the northeastern Dolpo: Daknak Bhanjyang (Sena La 5,465m), Jyanche Bhanjyang (5,534m), Kang Kung Bhanjyang (5,564m), and Pindu Bhanjyang (5,600m). The trails from Dolpo to Tibet cross these five passes and converge at the Raka Nadi River. We also saw one of the tributaries of Yalung Tsampo, flowing north. On the eastern two passes, there was no sign of activity nor cattle; blue poppies and other alpine plants were abundant. Presumably, these passes have been abandoned as roads have been built. Old markets have been disappearing too.

On July 10, we left base camp in fine weather. From a small pokari (pond) just below the pass, we walked east and northeast along the border ridge, and after an hour of climbing a gentle ridge of rock and snow, we were on top of Araniko Chuli, surrounded by other 6,000m peaks.

From the highest point, a vast ice field extended east. I confirmed various bearings and elevations of nearby peaks on the Nepalese New Topographical Map (1:50,000), using surveying instruments. But to the northeast, the peaks of the Man Shail group were hidden by clouds. We returned to base camp by another route: straight down a scree slope on the south face of Araniko Chuli, where, unlike on the Tibetan side, there was no snow. Then we finished our research and climbing around Aruniko Chuli in three days, by following an old path directly to Mustang from Chharka, via Ghami Bhanjyang (5,740m), to Ghami.

The second stage of our activity in Damodar Himal started at Ghami. We set up a base camp at the northern foot of Saribung (Selibung or Soribung, 6,327m) following a route via Chharang, Dhi, Yara, and Nakkali Damodar Kund (a sacred place for Hindus). Another party had already pitched a high camp, at 5,720m, on the northwest glacier of Kumlung North Peak (6,378m). In the central part of this huge glacier are the two highest peaks of Damodar Himal: Khumjungar Himal (6,759m) and Chhiv Himal (6,591m). They were both climbed by The Himalayan Association of Japan in 1983. Although the other party had attempted Saribung, they were unsuccessful because of sudden bad weather.

We continued the topographical research in this area—the east glaciers of Bhrikuti Sail (6,361m), and north of a nameless high peak (6,899m) in the east—then we returned to Pokhara, via Jomsom.

TAMOTSU OHNISHI, *Japan (translated by Tamotsu Nakamura)*

MAHALANGUR HIMAL (KHUMBU)

Nuptse, south pillar attempt. The Nuptse International South Face Expedition (a.k.a. the Slo/Can/Am—emphasis on Slo) was concluded at the end of May, 2002. Team members were Marko Prezelj (Slovenia), Barry Blanchard (Canada), Stephen Koch (USA), and myself (also USA) as leader. In support was Barry's wife Catherine Mulvihill and our wonderful cook, known to us as Prakash.

We arrived in B.C. on April 15. Basecamp was on the western side of the Lhotse Nup Glacier, about a two-hour walk from the small village of Chukung. We spent about two weeks acclimating and all members climbed to 6,800m on the 1961 British route—the route of first ascent. On the last trip up that ridge Stephen Koch had a small mishap with a snow cornice which dropped on him from a height of 50cm (really) and tore his medial-collateral ligament on his right knee. Stephen left for Thailand four days after this incident.

The three remaining members stayed healthy long enough to see the season's good weather spell. Barry, Marko, and I started up an untried route in the center of the face between the '61 route and the often-attempted-not-yet-completed south pillar route. We left B.C. early the morning of May 15. We soloed to about 5,400m, and then belayed the ensuing 400m-450m to establish a bivy site at approximately 5,800m. That first day offered excellent mixed climbing on fine granite up a very natural and objectively safe line. For all of us this day was the best of the trip—the quality of the climbing combined with the joy of discovery made for an exceptional day in the mountains. The second day on the route saw five more belayed pitches of moderate mixed terrain that led to easier climbing. We then unroped and climbed to 6,600m. The third day we climbed to 7,200m and bivied in the bergshrund at the top of the south face névé.

Marko and I continued with the ropes and rack a bit higher on the ice face to 7,300m. This eventually proved to be our highpoint. On the fourth day we woke up to windy and much

colder weather with a lot of black clouds down valley. We spent the day in the tent and woke to the same weather on the fifth day at which point we elected to descend. We downclimbed to 6,500m where we joined the '61 route and continued down now-familiar terrain to reach B.C. at 9:30 that night. Nuptse East, 7,804m, is still unclimbed.

We are happy to report that Stephen didn't require surgery and his MCL is apparently healing up nicely. We saw no Maoist insurgents, though we heard many rumors and the steets of Thamel were strangely quiet without normal tourist volumes.

We had originally proposed to attempt the route in a single-push variation of alpine-style. Upon climbing on the lower '61 route and trekking two days to the west to get a view of the summit rockband, we collectively decided that there appeared to be too much hard climbing up high (between 7,300m and 7,600m) to make that approach feasible. We switched to "classic" alpine style, carrying a bivy tent and

Top: Routes and attempts on Nuptse's south face. Left to right: the British route, the Slo-Can-Am attempt (2002), and the line of most previous attempts (originally by Lowe-Twight). Left: Acclimatizing on Nuptse's British route. Right: A good day on the Nuptse south pillar attempt, with Makalu behind. Marko Prezelj (3)

two sleeping bags in addition to our food/stove/fuel/clothing. Having climbed to 7,300m on the face I would elect to use the same "classic" approach if I were to attempt the route again.

Steve House, *AAC*

Everest, summary of the spring season, questions on the use of bottled oxygen and sedan chairs. Altogether 46 teams sent 155 people to Everest's summit this spring. Seventy-seven of them reached the summit on May 16—61 from the southern side in Nepal and 16 from Tibet. But the spring of 2001 still holds the record with 50 teams, 182 summiters, and 88 on top on a single day (May 23). Of the 155 summiters in 2002, 66 men and one woman had made ascents in previous years, so the total of first-time summiters was 88.

The high number of summiters on the Nepalese side of Everest on May 16 forced one of them to wait 56 minutes at the top of the fixed ropes on the Hillary Step before he could resume his descent—it took that long for ascending climbers to get off the ropes.

Among the various firsts in 2002 were the first Armenian summiter, the first Hungarian, the first Basques living in France, and an American who believes he was the first cancer survivor on Everest's summit. There was also the first person to scale the mountain 12 times: 40-year-old Apa Sherpa. And there were the oldest man and the oldest woman.

One would think that the question of who is the oldest person to reach the summit would be quite simple. Until this year, that distinction belonged to an American, Sherman Bull, who was 64 years old last spring. On May 17, 2002 the title passed to Tomiyasu Ishikawa, a 65-year-old Japanese. Or did it? Another climber who was also on the Tibetan side of the mountain, Mario Curnis of Italy—only 26 days younger than Ishikawa—has put forward his claim to the title on the grounds that he is the oldest to have climbed to the top, which he achieved on May 24. No one doubts that Ishikawa did arrive at the summit, but his Sherpas, according to Curnis's fellow summiter, Simone Moro, carried him up the final 50 meters to the top. Furthermore, Curnis returned from top to bottom on his own two feet. An Austrian who also was on Everest, Wilfried Studer, said that he saw Ishikawa being carried down the mountain on the back of one Sherpa while breathing oxygen through a tube from a bottle on the back of another. This reputedly took place from Ishikawa's first high-altitude camp at 7,000m (23,000') all the way down to base camp at 5,200m (17,000'). Ishikawa needed other help during the ascent as well. Another climber on the mountain, New Zealander Russell Brice, reported that on the Second Step ladder Ishikawa had the help of three Sherpas: two were immediately behind him and placed his feet on each rung while a Sherpa in front pulled him by a short rope.

Ishikawa had made extensive use of artificial oxygen. By his own account, he started using it on his push for the summit at about 7,500m (24,600'), and continued using it sleeping and climbing above there. And not all of it came from his own supply. A different Japanese expedition had to abandon their own summit bid on the 18th and descend from 8,500m because they were told that Ishikawa "was in big trouble" 200 meters above their summit party, and their Sherpas had to carry more oxygen up to him.

Is this use of Sherpas to pull or carry a climber, and this use of considerable amounts of artificial oxygen, really mountaineering? Four climbers on the Tibet side said they used absolutely no bottled oxygen throughout their time on Everest. A few commentators take the view that only four people, rather than 155, should be credited with ascents this spring. They believe that after Reinhold Messner and Peter Habler proved in May 1978 that summiting

Everest and safe and sane returns do not require oxygen, only climbs without bottled oxygen should actually be counted as successful.

No problem exists about who is the oldest woman atop Everest. That record was set in May 2000 by a 50-year-old Pole, Anna Czerwinska. This spring a Japanese woman 13 years older than she, Tamae Watanabe, went to the summit from Nepal's southern side on the busiest day, May 16. Her use of bottled oxygen was confined to climbing from her camp 3 at 7,300m (23,950') to the top and back to 7,300m plus sleeping two nights in camp 4 on her ascent and descent.

ELIZABETH HAWLEY, *Nepal*

Cholatse north face new route attempt. The Corean Alpine Club Cholatse Expedition led by Kang, Sung-woo departed from Seoul August 24. Team members were as follows: Shin, Dong-seok, Cho, Yu-dong, Ji, Jeong-deuk, Hong, Sung-woo, Hwang, In-sun, Kim, Chae-ho, and Lee, Young-joon, and myself.

We fixed ropes to 5,200m but were plagued by the weather during the entire expedition. The most paralyzing conditions occurred from September 21 until September 29, when we were inundated by heavy fog conditions, tent-bound by a deluge of rain, and left to ponder the thunderous sound of avalanches as the heavy wet snow blanketed base camp. Clear weather finally allotted us only time enough to clean the fixed lines, pack up ABC, and head down to Lukla.

Future climbers should note that the Shangri-la Trekking Map of the Khumbu region confuses the locations of Arakamtse (6,423m), Cholatse (6,440m), and Tawoche (6,542m). Aramkatse has been labeled as the mountain that should be Cholatse.

PETER JENSEN-CHOI, *Korea*

Nagpai Gosum, Chinese military encounter. My partner Jeff Lamoureux and I traveled to Kathmandu on September 5 to attempt a new route on 7,350m Nagpai Gosum. We discovered three different names for the mountain: Nagpai Gosum I, Cho Aui, and Pasang Lhamu Chuli. The third of these names was given after the death in 1993 of Pasang Lhamu Sherpa on her descent from the summit of Mt. Everest. The peak is now usually referred to by that name. The peak had three previously recorded ascents. One team ascended in 1986 from the north gaining the prominent north west ridge to the summit. The second and third teams followed the entire northwest ridge from its base near the Tibet-Nepal border in 1996.

On September 11 we flew to Lukla to begin our trekking route via Namche Bazaar, Tham, and Arye before arriving at basecamp. This is the standard trade route eventually crossing the Nangpa La on the border between Nepal and Tibet. On the 16th we arrived at our planned basecamp on the Sumna Glacier at approximately 5,100m.

Early on September 20 we left our basecamp to trek up toward the Nangpa La and have a better look at the planned descent route. After an hour or so of walking we had almost arrived at the yak herder's post of Lunag (approximately 13 km. south of the Tibet border) when we encountered someone in a military uniform carrying an A.K.-style firearm. He seemed startled by our presence and told us to sit down on the ground. He spoke a few words of English. Through motioning and broken words he told us he was Chinese military and repeatedly pointed at his uniform's emblems. He asked for food and water, which we gave him. Despite the strange encounter we continued up the valley.

After another hour I saw a different individual 100m in front of us dressed the same as the first. He jumped behind a large boulder when he saw us. We tried unsuccessfully to make verbal contact with him, but he did not come out from behind the rock. We were uncomfortable with the situation, so we turned around and headed back down the valley to the south. As we returned to Lunag we encountered the first individual again where we'd left him, and again we gave him food and water. We kept walking down valley for 10 minutes until we heard a shot. A little while later another bullet passed within feet of our heads. The two men were together, shooting at us from about 100m behind. We began to run but soon realized we couldn't continue with our packs on. After ducking behind a large boulder we ditched our packs and continued on. The two men continued to follow us firing shots at us. We ran for 45 minutes until we were able to hide for three hours in a side valley before returning to basecamp.

When we reached basecamp, our sirdar and local cook felt we must return to Namche Bazaar that night, so we packed up and hid our basecamp equipment. We traveled through the night and reached Namche the next afternoon, where we reported the incident to the military and to the police.

Two days later we returned to the site of the incident with the Namche police chief. En route we met a Tibetan refugee who had crossed the pass the evening before our shooting incident took place. He told us he crossed the pass with a group of approximately 20 other Tibetans but had been left behind because he was too slow. He also indicated that he was in our vicinity when the shots were fired because he could hear them and knew there were two foreigners in the area. He had been left near the 5,700m pass for three days without food or water and was making his way down toward Namche Bazaar. At the incident site we recovered shell casings that the police chief took back with him. We were able to recover all of the items from our base camp, however we were not able to recover our backpacks or their contents. Our liaison officer then requested we return to Kathmandu to report the incident to the Ministry and request a credit for our royalty to be used at another time. We also met with the U.S. Embassy and discussed the incident with the Consular General. We give a great thanks to the AAC Helly Hansen Grant for the support of the grant. We have yet to decide whether we will attempt this expedition again.

David Morton, AAC

Khumbu, Nagpai Gosum I, background on the encounter with Chinese soldiers. David Morton's experience was the first incident of this kind ever to befall any mountaineers within Nepalese territory. On the other side of the border not far from the Nangpa La were the tents of Cho Oyu expeditions' advance base camps. One of the leaders who was there at the time, Russell Brice, a New Zealander, explained some background to the incident. Three soldiers of the Chinese military—the People's Liberation Army (PLA)—were searching for a group of about 20 Amdos, Tibetans from northwest Tibet. Since the Nangpa La is an important escape route for Tibetans fleeing their country (usually to pass through Nepal to join the Dalai Lama in northern India), a unit of the PLA is permanently posted close to the Cho Oyu base camp on a highway.

The three soldiers found a woman lying down near the pass; she probably was a decoy, for when they went to look at her closely, they were unexpectedly attacked by Amdos, who hit them on their heads with rocks and stole two of their guns before escaping across the pass into Nepal. The three soldiers, two of whom were Tibetans themselves while only one was Han Chinese, chased after them the next day. The night after that the two Tibetan soldiers came back across the Nangpa La and slept in one of Brice's advance base camp tents. They had no sleeping bags, warm clothing, or food.

On the third day, 15 to 20 more soldiers arrived at advance base camp looking for the same group of Amdos. Some searched the moraine, some went to the Nangpa La and returned to advance base. Three of them spent the night in Brice's tent and the rest slept in tents of a joint Japanese-Chinese/Tibetan women's Cho Oyu expedition. Next day the soldiers went back to their encampment near the road.

Later that morning shots were heard at advance base camp. They were fired by the Han Chinese soldier from the original trio who was now crawling, dragging himself through the snow and firing to attract attention. Brice, his Sherpas, and some Tibetans employed as Sherpas by the women's expedition went to investigate and brought the unfortunate soldier into camp. Brice speculates that the two Americans had been shot at by Amdos in crossfire with the PLA men.

ELIZABETH HAWLEY, *Nepal*

Better conditions finally arrive high on Peak 41. Urban Golob

Khumbu, Peak 41, first ascent. In the middle of October a Slovenian expedition of six climbers made the first ascent of Peak 41 (6,654m). After an acclimatization on Mera peak, Ales Kovac and Bostjan Jezovsek found a reasonably good approach to the great plateau below the west face of Peak 41, and climbed the rock slabs and a snow gully left of hard broken icefall. Next morning they started to climb the west face but after 150m they went back all the way to base camp due to the bad weather. After a week-long period of bad weather the party of three climbers—Matic Jost (the leader of expedition), Uros Samec, and I—set out from base camp and reached the great plateau. Next morning (October 15), we started to climb at 3 a.m. and found quite bad snow conditions on the wall because of very soft snow. The bad conditions forced us to climb near rocks, so we could make better belays. Because of the bad conditions and more steep terrain in the upper part of the wall (60°–80°), and the windy and cold weather, we needed 19 hours of continuous climbing to reach a small col left (north) of the summit, where we bivouacked at

Peak 41 (6,654m), showing the route of its first ascent. The lower left is a snow gully, behind the ridge is a plateau, and looming above is the west face. Urban Golob

6,500m. Next morning, still in cold wind and terrible snow conditions, we needed another hour and a half to climb the exposed ridge (50°–65°) above the west face and reach the summit of Peak 41 (6,654m). After several abseils and downclimbing, we reached our tents on the plateau below the face that evening.

The same day (October 16) the other party (Ales Kovac, Matej Kovacic, and Bostjan Jezovsek) reached only 6,000m on the north ridge due to very soft snow. They rested the next day on the plateau and on October 18 they went on the face and climbed a new route to the right of our party's line. When they reached the same col left of the summit (6,500m) at 4 p.m., they were caught by a strong snow storm, so they went down immediately. After some problems with avalanches on their descent, they successfully reached the tents on the plateau late in the night and the next day came down to the base camp.

After four previous unsuccessful expeditions to Peak 41 (Japanese, Finnish-American, New Zealand, and Finnish), the Slovenian expedition managed to climb two new routes on the west face of Peak 41 and reached the summit of the virgin mountain. Both of the routes are 1,000m high (from the plateau) and rated at V, 4 or TD+ (55°–80°) with a climbing approach to the plateau (500m, 40°–70°), so all together 1,500m of climbing. For more information, visit: http://41.ice-climbing.net.

URBAN GOLOB, *Slovenia*

Kyajo Ri, first recorded ascent of newly opened peak. Sitting at home in front of the computer for a week with a broken leg can be a wonderful source of inspiration. So it was for me in January 2002. The Nepalese government had just opened 103 new peaks for climbing. My wife, Véronique Marché-Wilson, and I chose Kyajo Ri (6,186m), only three long days' walk from Lukla. Kyajo Ri is the highest point in the massif that rises to the north of Namche Bazaar, only 20 miles west of

Everest. Talking about our plans among friends soon had Julien Ferrera, Laurent Beurel, and Véronique's brother Vincent Marché joining in (all French).

We set up base camp a little above Machhermo village. After the puja ceremony we set off up the steep rocky slopes at the end of the cwm to establish camp 1 at the foot of the east face, 5,200m. The next day we gained access to the glacier lying at the foot of the east face via a 40m mixed step, climbed the glacier to the rimaye, and overcame a 100m mixed step to reach the southeast col and camp 2.

October 20, 1 a.m., -20°C, full moon. We set off, only to return four hours later, unable to find a way through the south face to the south-west ridge. A quick tea, and Vincent and I headed off again, this time losing altitude to reach the Kyajo Glacier, south of Kyajo Ri. By 8 a.m. we'd reached the southwest col at 5,700m. Roping up for the first time, we could see a glistening 50° ridge of snow and ice leading to the summit. A few steeper sections (60°–65°) promised sport along

The unclimbed northeast aspect of Kyajo Ri. The 2002 route on the south flank is left of this rocky face. Duncan Wilson

High on Kyajo Ri, where the glacier gives way to rock. Duncan Wilson

the way, especially where a rock buttress appears near the top.

The going was delicate in places, the ice thin and porous. Climbing together with two tools each, occasionally placing the deadman for protection, we took the rock buttress at 6,050m in order to avoid the rotten snow-ice as it steepened to over 70° above. We traversed east across the buttress then followed its right edge up a steep snow field to reach the summit in three pitches. From the sharp snow arête on the summit an impressive view extends in all directions, from Everest to Thamserku and Cho Oyu. After an hour on the summit, we began our descent at 3 p.m, leaving a string of prayer flags fluttering in the slight breeze.

Night soon fell and the temperature plummeted to -25°C. Our toes suffered a little frost nip but the full moon and the sight of bobbing headtorches coming to greet us soon warmed our spirits. We were back in camp 2 by 9 p.m., happily reunited with our friends just as a violent wind storm began. The next day's 1,200m descent to base camp would be long. Route Information: southwest ridge, named En Tente Cordiale. Location: Latitude: 27° 58' 03", Longitude: 86° 40' 58". Altitude: 6,186m (according to Schneider Map 'Khumbu Himal 1:50,000').

DUNCAN WILSON, *U.K.*

Nuptse East 1, south face pillar attempt. Snow conditions made climbing very difficult for a noted Russian mountaineer, Valeri Babanov (37), in his unsuccessful attempt at a solo ascent of a pillar on the south face of Nuptse, the lengthy mountain that stands immediately south of Everest. His aim was to make the first ascent of one of its eastern summits, which presents such difficulties that it was described as "only for Babanov" by Vladislav Terzyul, a highly successful Ukrainian climber who has summited 12 of the world's fourteen 8,000-meter peaks, including Dhaulagiri I last autumn.

Babanov arrived at his base camp on the Lhotse Nup Glacier at 5,200m on September 19, but new snowfall and avalanches prevented him from starting up the mountain until the 29th. His original plan was to fix 500m of rope on the lower part of the pillar, then go to acclimatize on the 1961 British south face route to an altitude of 6,900m before making his push for the top of the pillar in three or four days. He said before leaving Kathmandu for this climb that he expected it to be "the most challenging climb I have ever done." He would have to scale a vertical distance of 2,500m (8,000') from base camp to his goal, the summit known as Nuptse East I, which is 7,804m high on Nuptse's east ridge and only 57m lower than the main summit. Approximately 600m to 700m of Babanov's route would be highly technical, and then big snow mushrooms presented themselves above that.

Babanov had no official permit to climb the 1961 South Face route in addition to his pillar, so he devoted himself entirely to the pillar. He spent days moving up and down the pillar fixing 1,000m of rope until his supply was exhausted. He calculated that he would need to fix 200m more to overcome the steepest section, known as "le Diable" (the Devil), before attempting to go for the summit. Babanov reached an altitude of 6,300m at the bottom of the Diable on October 26, four weeks after he had begun his attack on the pillar. He now had no more rope and "was very, very tired," strong winds had started blowing, and he had other commitments elsewhere. So he abandoned the climb. He wants to return next autumn but not solo. He would like one friend to come with him, partly so he would not have to carry all the rope and other gear needed for this very technical route.

ELIZABETH HAWLEY, *Nepal*

Numri first ascent. Numri is south of Cho Polu and east of Chukung village. The 6,677m mountain was first climbed by a German team led by Olaf Rieck in November. The seven-member expedition established their base camp at 5,140m on the Imja Glacier south of Island Peak. They made two camps above that. From camp 2 in a snow cave at 6,185m, three climbers (Rieck, Carsten Schmidt, and Lydia Schubert) ascended the west face to the summit on November 7. Their team had no Sherpas climbing with them, but they did fix a total of 800m of rope in sections above 6,000m. There was considerable danger from avalanches on the face, and one member's backpack was struck by a chunk of falling ice when he was at about 5,900m, but he was unharmed. Slightly higher up, a large part of a glacier broke away with a loud crash, but again no one was hurt. The climbers had problems with deep snow in several places along their route and a lack of good anchors; the average steepness was 30°.

ELIZABETH HAWLEY, *Nepal*

Ombigaichen, first recorded ascent of newly opened peak and first winter ascent. Ombigaichen (6,340m) is one of the new trekking peaks authorized by the Nepal Mountaineering Association in 2002. Our expedition consisted of Charles Burr (U.K.), Jo Cleere (U.K.), Marlies Sanders (The Netherlands), and myself as guide, with the assistance of Nepalese, Gyenye Lama, Ekka Rai, Syrendra Tamang, and Sonam Yeltsin.

We arrived in Kathmandu from Europe on November 12, flew to Lukla and trekked to Ama Dablam base camp, arriving on the 19th. Here, we spent two days in acclimatization and reconnaissance before moving up with yaks to camp at ca 5,000m. Half a day of load carrying by all the team across the debris of the Nare Glacier saw us established at our 5,200m base camp near an icy stream. Ama Dablam's south face was to our northwest, while Ombigaichen lay to the north-east. The shortest and most logical route to the summit was the south ridge from the Mingbo La. This was because access to the La was relatively straightforward (a 200m snow/ice slope at 50°) and it would enable us to place a tent at ca 5,800m, leaving just under 550m of climbing to the top of the mountain.

We made our first attempt on November 30. Above the La a delightful snow arête led to the "first gendarme." This was turned on its rocky right flank to reach a second snow arête leading to the "Snow Saddle." Above, a steep snow/ice slope rose to a series of gendarmes, all turned on their extremely loose, rocky, right flanks. A final steep 20m wall led to the "first notch." We left this section fixed.

Our second attempt took place on December 3, when Charles Burr, Sonam Yeltsin, and I were successful. On reaching the La we found that our tent had been destroyed by strong winds over the previous two days. Fortunately, we were able to locate the inner tent about a kilometer away across the glacier, and piecing together a couple of poles, managed a tolerable if short night.

Above our previous high point a short vertical rock arête led to more mixed ground and the second notch below the summit block. The last three pitches were spectacular and included a long (45m) steep pitch on completely rotten, loose shale interspersed with extremely unstable snow/ice mushrooms and an overhanging mushroom to finish. Several car-size blocks of ice fell during the climb, crashing noisily down the southeast face. The route was Alpine AD/D in standard and in common with nearby Ama Dablam, summiteers were rewarded with superb views of Everest, Lhotse, and Makalu. Extensive research, using all the normal sources, failed to reveal any previous recorded ascent of Ombigaichen

We noted that the southwest face would give a superb 800m snow/ice climb at around 55°. The Hunku (southeast) side looks loose and complex in the lower half, though the upper face is mainly snow/ice at 50°. The east ridge is the logical finish of the southeast face, while the west (Ama Dablam) ridge looks unattractive, with a number of overhanging snow obstacles. We were unable to properly observe the north (Chukung) face of the mountain.

Late autumn/early winter is normally an excellent period for climbing the lower peaks of Nepal. The main problem for us was the two days of high winds, which completely destroyed the tent on the Mingbo La, and the cold, which produced overnight temperatures of -20°C at the La. To conclude, there is huge potential in Nepal for new routes and new peaks between 6,000m and 7,000m but many of the new trekking peaks will be technically harder than the expedition peaks. For more information and photographs of this expedition see www.basecamp .co.uk/climb.html

VICTOR SAUNDERS, *U.K.*

JANAK HIMAL

Tinjung attempt, Pandra and Danga first ascents. The Danish Janak Himal Expedition comprised Allan Christensen, Bo Belvedere Christensen, Jan Mathorne, and myself as leader. All had made several expeditions to the Himalaya previously, most recently in spring 2000 to the Polish Route on the south pillar of Everest. We planned to fly to Ghunsa by helicopter to save time and avoid both monsoon and terrorist problems, but at the last moment permission was refused by the Nepalese Government because the police station at Ghunsa had been bombed earlier in the year. Instead we used the usual approach from Suketar, arriving at our 4,785m Lhonak base camp on October 1. Our journey had been hampered only by the monsoon and rumors of Maoists.

We decided first to attempt the peak generally considered to be Danga I (6,355m). This had been attempted by Chris Bonington's expedition in 2000. But at the col between the main summit and a subsidiary peak christened Danga II (6,194m), this team turned right and followed the southwest ridge to the latter summit. However, it quickly became clear to us that the new Nepalese map calls the higher summit Tinjung and the real Danga lies more to the southwest.

On October 4 and 5 we established a camp just below the glacier at 5,450m and inspected the glacier to 5,900m. On the 6th we left camp early and followed Bonington's route to the col. From here we ascended the Southeast ridge of Tinjung to a foresummit (GPS reading 6,137m: N 29° 49.803', E 87° 59.473'). So far the climb had been on steep, unstable monsoon snow at a standard of Alpine D-. The real summit lay to the north, appeared to be 100m – 200m higher and required crossing a long mushroomed ridge with loose snow and rock. It looked dangerous, so we retreated to base camp, where the weather also took a turn for the worse (the weather was generally poor for the first half of the month but improved considerably after).

On October 9 we established a camp at 5,250m on the moraine where the Lhonak Glacier splits. At this point I turned back due to a fever and throat infection. The other three continued up a side glacier southeast of Pandra (eventual GPS reading 6,673m: N 27° 51.897', E 87° 59.547') to see whether the attractive south face of this unclimbed mountain was feasible. After a bivouac at 5,500m it started to snow, so they returned to base camp. On the 14th Alan, Bo, and Jan returned to the bivouac and continued next day to a second at 5,700m, above which

Pandra (GPS 6,673m) from the south, showing the line of the first ascent. Bo Belvedere Christensen

they saw a couloir leading out of the glacier basin towards Pandra. Starting at 4.a.m. on the 16th the three climbed the 500m couloir (55° max) and the ridge above to the upper part of Pandra's south face. They continued up steep and partially loose snow (some dry-tooling in parts) and at 6,500m reached a plateau above some seracs and below the final pyramid. The latter gave straightforward snow climbing and the well-defined summit was reached at 1 p.m. After down-climbing the summit pyramid, they began a series of rappels to above the couloir, then descended the latter to arrive at the bivouac site after sunset. The climb was rated TD- and was felt to be good apart from the lack of belays.

With only a few days remaining it was decided to attempt the peak we are now sure is the real Danga. It is a well-defined but complex snow and ice pyramid standing at the head of a side valley that leaves the main trekking route between Ramtang and Lhonak. On the 19th we spent a long day walking down toward Ramtang, then up the stony side valley and onto a complex glacier, where we bivouacked at 5,200m. On the 20th all four of us started up the glacier rising north to Danga but at 5,450m I was again forced to turn back due to continued illness. The others continued over increasingly complex terrain to a snowy ramp, which gave access to the upper part of the mountain. Good alpine snow climbing led to the summit, which was reached at mid-day (GPS reading 6,238m: N 27° 49. 023', E 87° 58. 598'). The route was about D in standard and the same night we were all re-united in base camp. The mountains north of Lhonak still hold many possibilities for first ascents and new routes but future parties should be prepared for long and stony approaches.

HENRIK JESSEN HANSEN, *Denmark*

Danga, showing the line of the first ascent. Bo Belvedere Christensen

Maoist encounters spring season commentary. Insecurity for people throughout Nepal due to an armed rebellion by Maoists, who have become especially active in the more remote areas of the country, was encountered separately by two teams, one Swiss and the other Spanish and Italian, on their treks in April to Makalu base camp. It is not certain whether the teams met genuine Maoists or Nepalis posing as rebels. In any case they were stopped by armed men who demanded money and cameras. No one was injured in these incidents, but they were certainly not pleasant experiences.

The six-member Spanish-Italian expedition, led by Edurne Pasaban from Spain, had their encounter before they had reached Tashigaon, the last village on the trail to Makalu. Here six young men or boys armed with rifles, pistols and grenades, took Rs.5,000 (worth about $64) and a camera from each member.

The Swiss were just two men led by Norbert Joos, and they were stopped at Tashigaon itself. The Nepalis carried rifles but were not in Maoist uniforms; they demanded from each person Rs.10,000 plus one camera. They produced handwritten receipts, but the Kathmandu trekking agency helping this team told Joos that real Maoist receipts are issued on printed forms and rubber-stamped, and that they had probably been robbed by some other people.

Trekking groups in remote areas of Nepal, notably in the far western hilly regions, have occasionally also been forced to surrender money and cameras to armed men claiming to be Maoist insurgents. As a result, the number of trekkers has dropped in recent seasons, especially this spring. Could climbers, too, go elsewhere in the future? Could the number of people dreaming of standing on the top of Everest decide to make their bids from Tibet, despite the fact that many prefer to climb from Nepal?

ELIZABETH HAWLEY, *Nepal*

Maoist encounters fall season commentary. There were encounters by two expeditions, one in the Kangchenjunga area in far eastern Nepal and the other in the west on their way to Putha Hiunchuli, which is sometimes called Dhaulagiri VII. These teams were stopped by armed Nepalis who may have been Maoist rebels fighting against the constitutional monarchy with the aim of replacing it with a "people's republic," or they may have been just bandits taking advantage of the well-known presence of Maoists in those areas.

The Putha Hiunchuli team of ten Austrians led by Gunther Mussnig were stopped when they were approaching their mountain from the north in late September at a village named Kakkot by about 25 local people whom Mussnig called "Maoist-friendly." They refused to let the expedition enter their Kaya Khola (valley), where base camp would be established, unless they were paid Rs.100,000 (equal to about $1,280); when the Austrians refused, they were kept at Kakkot for a day and a half. They were not freed until Rs.67,000 were handed over.

In eastern Nepal, a predominantly Slovenian expedition for Ramtang Chang (called Chang Himal in the new list) (formerly known as Wedge Peak) and Kiratchuli (Tent Peak) near Kangchenjunga were similarly held up. Their leader, Gregor Kresal, and another member flew by helicopter to their base camp with the team's funds while the other 10 members trekked toward the mountains from the Taplejung airfield. One day's trek north of the airport at Chhiruwa village, they were stopped by four armed men who villagers thought probably were Maoists. The men said they knew the team had paid the Nepalese government $3,000 for their climbing permits, and demanded a payment of this sum plus their own "tax" on each member. The climbers explained that they had no money since all the funds had gone ahead by helicopter.

After being locked up in a small lodge for a short time, their captors reduced their demand to a total of only Rs. 8,000 ($103), but the team could not meet even this price. They were allowed to proceed on their way to base camp but were told they would have to pay on their return trek to Taplejung. This expense was avoided by the entire expedition's chartering a helicopter out of the region from a village well north of the airfield. The cost of avoiding Taplejung by hiring a helicopter to Kathmandu was $6,500, whereas they would have had to spend only about $2,000-$2,500 to trek to the local airfield and fly by a scheduled fixed-wing flight from there.

These expeditions' encounters were not the first by mountaineers in Nepal. The earlier ones occurred in the autumn of 2000 to a Spanish Manaslu team, and in the spring of this year to two Makalu expeditions, one Swiss and the other a joint Spanish-Italian party. No doubt they will not be the last, but it is most unlikely that any teams in the immediate Everest region will be affected, at least in the next few years.

ELIZABETH HAWLEY, *Nepal*

China

KARAKORAM

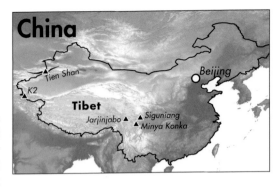

K2, winter attempt on the north ridge.
The Winter Netia K2 Expedition (Netia
is the biggest Polish TV company and
during the expedition there were daily
prime-time television reports) included
four experienced alpinists from CIS. It
departed from Warsaw on December 16, 2002 and arrived at Bishkek, the capital of Krygyzstan,
where we were joined by four climbers from Kazakhstan, Uzbekistan, and Georgia. We all continued to Kashgar (Chinese Sinkiang) and then onward via Mazar by vehicle.

The expedition consisted of Krzysztof Wielicki as a leader, Jacek Berbeka, Marcin Kaczkan,
Piotr Morawski, Jerzy Natkanski, Maciej Pawlikowski, Dariusz Zaluski, and the four-man team
of experienced alpinists from CIS; Gia Tortladze (Georgia), Ilias Thukvatulin (Uzbekistan),
Vasiliy Pivtsov, and Denis Urubko (both from Kazakhstan). There was also a support team for
work on the glacier but a few of these became real high altitude climbers. These were Bartosz
Duda, Jacek Jawien, Piotr Kubicki, Jacek Teler, Zbigniew Terlikowski, and Michal Zielinski (as a
climbing cameraman). In total there were more than 30 people on the expedition.

The north pillar of K2, showing the line of the Polish winter attempt. Photo: Piotr Morawski. Diagram: Grzegorz Glazek

Our aim was to climb the 1982 Japanese route via the north ridge and the prominent hanging glacier, well seen from a distance and lying left of the crest of the upper ridge below the summit. The route was well-known to Krzysztof Wielicki since his 1996 climb. On December 22 our caravan started from the Chinese border police station of Ylik near Bazar Dara. We took six tons of gear and food, and used 70 camels. Over five days we crossed the Aghil Pass (4,850m) to the Shaksgam River and then turned up the Qogir Valley. On December 26 we stopped in a place referred to as the Chinese Base Camp (3,900m) about three kilometers before the terminus of the Qogir Glacier (ca 4,100m). Two days later we reached Middle Base Camp (aka Pakistani BC, 4,650m) midway to the main Base Camp (5,100m), at which we arrived next day. This camp lies five km from the foot of the mountain. The days were sunny but cold, while at night in base camp the temperature fell below -30°C.

On New Year's Day Gia Tortladze and Illias Thukvatulin fixed the first 250m of rope and by January 5 Denis Urubko and Vasiliy Pivtsov had established Camp 1—one tent inside a big snow cave—at ca 6,000m. One kilometer of rope had now been fixed. Over the next few days the wind was very strong and working on the mountain was difficult. There were steep fields of hard black ice and almost no place to rest. On January 16 we reached the big "Rock Barrier," above which were long but easier ice slopes leading to Camp 2. On the 18th Krzysztof Wielicki and Jacek Berbeka fixed 200 meters of rope through the barrier. Unfortunately Krzysztof injured a calf muscle during the descent and this weakened his ability to climb over the next few weeks. On the 20th Denis and Vasiliy established a provisional camp 2 at ca 6,750m. Several days later Maciej Pawlikowski and Dariusz Zaluski were sleeping at this camp, when strong winds completely destroyed their tent, forcing them to descend at sunrise. The weather now got so bad that everyone returned to base.

After a few days of very bad weather Gia and Ilias decided they wanted to leave and the following day Vasiliy also decided to join them. Only Denis said that he had arrived with expedition and he would leave the mountain with the same expedition. It was a blow for us. We knew that the expedition would be much weaker without them and our chances of reaching the summit would decrease. On the other hand our team now consolidated and a few members of the support team (including a climber-film operator) decided to help in transportating the gear up to camp 2 and, in one case (Jacek Jawien), to camp 3.

Denis, Marcin, and I repaired camp 2 and started to put new fixed ropes above it. People were working very hard, carrying food and equipment. On February 4 Wielicki and Berbeka established camp 3 at 7,200m on a little snowfield. On February 12 Denis and I established camp 4 at 7,650m. We put up the tent on little rock ridge near the lower tip of the hanging glacier, which lies left of the crest of the pillar and leads to the summit. We hoped that the next team, Maciej and Darek, would improve this camp. However, the wind became so strong that they had to retreat. On the 15th we were incorrectly informed that the weather in our region was the worst for four years. A few days later we found out the real figure was 40 and not four.

With everyone down at base camp and most either frostbiten, ill, or not properly acclimatized, there were only really four climbers that were in a position to go above camp 3. These were Urubko, Wielicki, Kaczkan and Morawski. Our doctor told me that my frostbite was bad and if I wanted to save my feet, let alone my toes, I should not climb anymore. So I stopped and fortunately in the end lost only one toe.

The expedition took 14 bottles of oxygen, a few of which were carried up to camp 1. Thereafter the summit team decided not to not use them.

On the 21st the wind died and Wielicki decided to go up for the final attempt. It was the only chance. Jurek Natkanski and Jacek Jawien went first. Their task was to check camps and supply them. Next day Kaczkan and Urubko, both without oxygen, began the ascent. They planned to put 200m of fixed rope above camp 4, then maybe attempt the summit. The same day Natkanski and Jawien turned back from the rock barrier, due to considerable stone and ice fall.

On 25th it started to snow and the wind increased. However, Marcin and Denis reached camp 4 still hoping they would fix some ropes above. However, they found the tent destroyed, so they were forced to use a small bivouac tent, which they had carried for the summit push. They both spent a terrible night in one sleeping bag, lying on coiled ropes as they had no insulated mats.

Kaczkan was totally exhausted by the effort over the last few days and during the night began to deteriorate. In the morning after a radio call to the doctor, Urubko recognized that Kaczkan had cerebral oedema. He was unable to wake and the situation seemed serious. Camp 4 was an altitude record for Kaczkan (his previous record was achieved on a solo ascent of 7,439m Pik Pobeda during the past summer). A rescue operation was begun. Everybody who was still able to go above Base Camp did so, and a bottle of oxygen was taken to Camp 2. Fortunately, after a few hours of effort by Denis, Kaczkan was able to move and get dressed. Both climbers started to descend and Kaczkan became stronger with every meter of height loss. When ca 200m above camp 3 they both met Wielicki and all three carried on down. By the afternoon they had reached camp 2, where Kaczkan used the oxygen carried up by by Teler and Duda. All five descended to camp 1 where they met Zielinski and Natkanski. These last two and Kaczkan spent the night at this camp and after a good sleep on oxygen, Kaczkan was able to descend unaided the following day.

On the 27th Wielicki called off the expedition. The next day the wind was so strong that it destroyed our mess tent at base camp. Over the subsequent days, while most members were descending to the Chinese base camp, all the other tents were destroyed by the wind. The expedition returned to Warsaw on March 18. Although K2 has once more held out in winter, this expedition showed that a successful ascent is possible..

PIOTR MORAWSK *and* GRZEGORZ GLAZEK, *Klub Wysokogorski Warszawa, PZA*

Chinese Tien-Shan Range, reconnaissance. Four of us—Anatoly Dzhulie (leader), David Lekhtman, Vladimir Leonenko, and myself, Otto Chkhetiani—explored the remote Tien-Shan mountains of China, on the other side of the Kok-Shaal-Too Range. We covered a total of 270km and traversed seven high passes during a 36-day trek in July and August, 2002.

Beginning with very little information—just old Soviet maps (1:100,000) and satellite photos—we crossed into Irkeshtam on July 12, struggled with the red tape, and traveled across Kashgar to Aksu. Then we drove across a rocky plain toward the Kirghiz village of Talak, where we registered with the military authorities and met our Kirghiz guide. Accompanied by a caravan of four horses, we crossed a low pass at Kok-Yar-Davan into Chon-Teren-su, a deep forested valley. There, we found traces of Chinese expeditions from the late 1970s, the remains of a road, and a large wood hut at the mouth of Sajlyn-su.

We left our caravan and guides at the convergence of the western and eastern branches of the Chon-Teren glacier (3,462m), and headed into a completely deserted area. Since there was almost no vegetation, there were no local shepherds—nor any hunters, since hunting is

The 2,000m southwestern wall of unclimbed Peak Voennykh Topografov. Otto Chkhetiani

forbidden in China.

Originally, we had planned to travel west to visit the Tomur Glacier, which lay beyond a range of rugged mountains. But heavy snowfall and avalanche danger slowed us down, so we diverted to the tributaries of the west fork of the Chon-Teren Glacier. We crossed three technical ice passes to bypass icefalls, then crossed a plateau (5,600m) south of massive Peak 6,435 (cf. Koxkar Feng, attempt, AAJ 1990, p. 347), and north of Peak 6,050. From the plateau, a wide ridge with several rocky peaks led to the highest point. This area is dominated by the impressive southern wall of Tomur 7439 (Peak Pobeda). To

Peak 6747 in the Chinese Tien Shan. Otto Chkhetiani

the east we could see a lot of alpine terrain and Peak 6,571, an impressive unclimbed mountain.

After completing Western Chon-Teren circuit, we climbed the eastern branch of Chon-Teren. We had no information about this part of the glacier, since it was not explored during the 1970s. From the right moraine, we saw grassy meadows and small lakes. The 2,000m southwestern wall of unclimbed Peak Voennykh Topografov towered over the glacier. Combined with Peak 6,747, this wall makes the Southern Inyl'chek Glacier inaccessible from the north.

We encountered high winds and waist-deep snow on the pass Chon-Teren (5,488m), which is well known to climbers approaching from the north—the side of the Zvezdochka Glacier. But we had no information at all about its southern slopes, where we found large cornices overhanging a 55°, 300m ice slope with protruding rocks. To the left loomed Vostochnaya Pobeda, which frequently avalanches, covering the glacier with snow dust and ice debris.

From the upper reaches of Southern Inyl'chek, we continued across a pass (5,300m) between Peak Druzhba and Peak Richarda Zorge. We decided to name the pass after the outstanding Russian and Kazak alpinist Valerii Khrishchaty, who in 1990 made an unprecedented traverse from Peak Vazha Pshavela—crossing Peak Pobeda, Peak Voennykh Topografov, and the Meridional Ridge—to the Vostochnyi (Eastern) Schater.

A huge cornice overhung east of the col, so we decided to descend the north end of the ridge, where an 800m long, 40° to 55° ice slope led to a small plateau that ended at an ice-fall. We finished the descent by sidestepping the ice-fall by going through a 700-meter ice couloir, then onto the Tugabed'chi Glacier. As far as we know, we were the first people to visit this glacier, which is very different from the Inyl'chek area and the Chon-Teren. The air was much drier, and the glaciers were covered with seracs.

To the northeast, we saw an unknown, yellowish 6,000m peak, which was part of the eastern extension of the Tengri-Tag range. We headed onto the first southern tributary, under the southern slope of Peak 6,342. The satellite photos had not been able to foretell the difficulties we encountered there: and very complex ice-fall, which took two very tense days to get through. Then we spent the next 24 hours in a blizzard!

At our final pass, Tugabel'chi (5,200m), we had to descend 350 meters of vertical granite to get out of the cirque (the map showed only ice slopes, and the satellite photographs were no help). At the same time, we had to deal with avalanches from Peak 6,342.

Finally, on our long march out on the Kichi-Teren glacier, then through woods at 3,200m, we encountered a group of surprised Kirghiz locals, who had never seen Europeans before.

OTTO CHKHETIANI, RUSSIA (*translated by Henry Pickford*)

SICHUAN

Minya Konka, eighth ascent and new route on nearby Eva Shan. If you love sunny places, Sichuan isn't the area of your dreams. The climbers of French High Mountain Military Group went there last autumn to climb Minya Konka (or Gongga Shan 7,556m). They spent one month at base camp (4,400m) as there were only 4 days of good weather during which reach the summit. We didn't acclimatize well and there was really a lot of fresh snow. Only two days after arriving at base camp, most of the climbers had already climbed one of the two acclimatisation peaks: Gomba (5,605m) or Nochma (5,575m). Laurent did a paragliding flight from the summit of Nochma. But the day after this, came the snow. They stayed above us for 10 days. We could only walk around base camp. Our main activities were to dig a path into the snow, eating, sleeping, reading, and playing cards, all significant expeditionary skills. Nevertheless, Greg and Manu climbed a gully on Eva Shan 5,705m (Eva is Greg's daughter) Plate-forme (800m, D+).

We gave up our first project, which had been to climb a new route on the southwest ridge of Minya Konka. On October 6th, six climbers returned to and slept at the high point reached earlier, 5,700m. The day after, they climbed into deep snow to 6,300m and put camp 3 behind the "hump." From the top of the "hump," at 6,400m, we rappelled. The third day, at 3:00 a.m., Philippe, Thomas, the two Laurents, François, and Antoine left camp. Four of us had to stop around 7,000m because we were poorly acclimatized. Laurent M. climbed up to 7,400m carrying his paraglider, but he couldn't fly. Antoine reached the top at 10 a.m. Two days later, the snow came back. Nobody could try again. On October 15th, we were trekking back to the monastery. Only eight expeditions have reached that summit from two ridges (northwest and northeast), for a total of 20 climbers since 1932. The main difficulties are situated after 7,100m with 45°/50° slopes.

Team members were: Jérôme Blaise (Doctor), Laurent Carrier, Antoine De Choudens, Thomas Faucheur, Laurent Miston, Grégory Muffat-Joly, Emmanuel Pellissier, Philippe Renard, François Savary. (See "Minya Konka" in *AAJ* 2002 for the story of the first ascent—*Ed.*)

ANTOINE DE CHOUDENS, *French High Mountain Military Group (GMHM)*

Siguniang, first ascent of north face. Taking 6 days, Mick Fowler and Paul Ramsden made the first ascent of the north face of Siguniang, in April, 2002. Then, they made a two-day descent of the unclimbed north ridge. Most of days they endured snow, but they were rewarded with a glorious, clear summit day. Difficulties ranged from grade VI rock to poor quality, nearly vertical ice (Scottish VI). The ice choked dike was 750m long, with several long vertical pitches and two overhanging sections. The climb was made using only natural protection; bolts were not carried. See the "Siguniang" lead article earlier in this Journal.

Jarjinjabo Mountains, Kham Region, various first ascents. In October Peter Athans, Robert Mackinlay, Hilaree Nelson, Jared Ogden, Kasha Rigby, and Mark Synnott made various first ascents on the Zhopu Spires and the first ascent of the northern Jarjinjabo Massif. See the "Jarjinjabo" lead article earlier in this Journal for an account.

Dangchezhengla (5,833m), first ascent. Two climbers from the Hengduan Mountains Club (HMC)—Kiyoaki Miyagawa and Junta Murayama—made the first ascent of this beautiful, hidden snow peak, reaching a foggy summit at noon on June 17. Dangchezhengla is in the Shaluli Shan Range, about 12km northeast of Batang, near the Tibetan border.

Our team—myself, Kimikazu Sakamoto (leader, 62), Kiyoaki Miyagawa (61), Shojiro Tanaka (61), and Junta Murayama (35)—originally applied to the Mountaineering Association of Sichuan (MAS) for permission to climb three peaks: Dangchezhengla (6,060m), Central Peak (6,033m), and West Peak (5,833m). But the MAS named our expedition the "2002 Japan Yangmolong Expedition," and we received a permit for Mt. Yangmolong (not Dangchezhengla). Our "Letter of Invitation" from the China Mountain Association (CMA) also said Yangmolong, so to avoid confusion we decided to call the 6,060m peak Yangmolong.

But after we entered the area, we talked to 30 villagers in Zhongba who go up to the high pastures with their yaks and gather caterpillar fungus for Chinese traditional medicine. They told us that the 5,833m peak, which is visible from their village along the Ichu River, is called Dangchezhengla—and they call the 6,033m peak Makara, and the 6,060m peak is Bongonzhong. They said that Yangmolong is not the name of a mountain, but is the name of a pasture about 2km south of Bongonzhong. In the end, the MAS gave Miyagawa and Murayama climbing certificates for Dangchezhengla.

Our team departed from Chengdu on May 28, arriving in two cars at Batang on May 30 (via Kangding and Yajiang). The village chief of Dongba arranged for 16 horses and yaks, and 6 horsemen from Zhongba. We went to Zhongba (3,835m) and stayed for three nights to acclimatize, and visited an exquisite Tibetan temple called Sandens, where we prayed for success and drank butter tea and ate yak cheese with the lama.

From Zhongba, it was a day's hike to our base camp (4,500m) below a rocky cliff of Peak 5,148m, in a beautiful green meadow that looked just like a valley in the Alps, the Sierra, or the Rockies. On June 5, with three horses and three horsemen, we ferried 160 kg loads of food and equipment to a meadow at 4,900m, just below the southeast ridge of West Peak, which would became C1. At the eastern end of frozen Yamou Lake, we could see our three peaks.

Yangmolong looked almost impossible to climb from the south, with a rock cliff at the bottom, a hanging glacier in the middle, and a large cornice on the summit ridge. But it looked like West Glacier would allow us to reach a col between West Peak and Central Peak.

On June 7, after two nights of rest at BC, we set up C1. That same afternoon, we made a reconnaissance and found that West Glacier does not lead to the col between West Peak and Central Peak, because it falls directly from the south snow face of West Peak and is blocked by the rocky southeast ridge. But we found that Central Glacier does lead to a col between the two peaks, so we spent three days climbing the left side of its lower icefall. We fixed four pitches on the lower icefall, and reached the site of C2 (5,335m) on a plateau below the upper icefall. While Tanaka and I ferried the loads to C2, Miyagawa and Murayama fixed three ropes through the upper icefall, to a col (5,565m) between West Peak and Central Peak. The next day (June 11), we went down to BC for two days of rest. We decided to forget about Yangmolong, which seemed too risky for our elderly party, and to concentrate on West Peak—Dangchezhengla.

We ferried additional loads to C2, then started our final attack on the virgin peak at 4 a.m., June 17. Miyagawa and Murayama climbed at a fast pace, while Tanaka and I followed along behind. When Miyagawa and Murayama reached the col (5,565m) at 7 a.m., Tanaka and I had become exhausted climbing the ice cliff in the upper icefall. Three pitches behind, we decided to give up the summit. Miyagawa and Murayama continued up, and traversed right at a big crevasse resembling a shark's mouth on the shoulder of the ridge. The right side of the ridge was a 500-meter-high steep ice face, which they climbed using double ice axes. The knife-edge ridge was an unstable mixture of hard ice and soft snow, with a treacherous cornice. They proceeded along this tricky ridge cautiously, and reached the summit of West Peak at 12:10. They had climbed 11 pitches between the col and the summit. On top, they found themselves in a dense mist, so for evidence they photographed their wristwatch and GPS together, showing an altitude of 5,870m. They returned to C2 at 5 p.m. We spent three days carrying all of our equipment and garbage down to C1, and then down to BC on June 21.

Although we were unable to climb Yangmolong and Central Peak, we were very satisfied with our expedition. We are proud of our clean mountaineering and safe climbing, and hope that the beauty of this mountain area will be preserved forever.

KIMIKAZU SAKAMOTO, *Hengduan Mountains Club (translated by Tamotsu Nakamura)*

NORTHWEST YUNNAN PROVINCE

Yunnan Province, Hengduan Shan, ascent of Peak 4,750, attempt on Baimang Shan, and reconnaissance of Meilixueshan and Habaxueshan areas. During April and May Paul Macleman and I visited the Hengduan mountains of northwestern Yunnan Province. This was my second journey to the area (*AAJ* 1999), which is still not popular with foreign expeditions but is becoming increasingly popular as a destination for domestic Chinese package tours.

Driving from Kunming to Lijiang can now be done in around eight hours by bus on the new highway. A cable car up the eastern slopes of Yulongxueshan (5,596m) was completed in late 1998; it gave us an interesting day out, with nice views, as well as a minor degree of acclimatization, as it stops at just over 4,500m on snowfields above the glacier. From Lijiang we continued north to Zhongdian (3,200m), where we spent a few days acclimatizing, buying food and visiting the beautiful Songzhalin monastery. Then we took a public bus toward Deqen, but we jumped off at the 4100m high pass to the east of the attractive and unclimbed Baimang Shan (5,500m).

Passing evidence of increased human traffic in the area—partially completed stone huts, trash, human feces, road crews—we camped slightly above the road, beneath the hill that I climbed in 1998. Two days later we ascended this

An avalanche sweeps the route that Damien Gildea and Paul Macleman had just vacated on Baimang Shan. Damien Gildea

peak, our altimeters registering around 4750m, significantly lower than I previously thought. On this occasion we climbed the northern ridge in deep snow and over loose rock to arrive on the summit after a couple of hours. The Konkaling peaks were again visible far to the east but we were lucky enough this time to obtain a magical view of Kawa Karpo (6,740m, a.k.a. Meilixushan, Kagebo) rising to the northwest above a sea of cloud.

Upon descending we decided that Baimang Shan held too much fresh snow, so we immediately hitched a ride on a truck to the city of Deqen. There has been a significant increase in the number of tourists traveling across the Mekong River from Degen to visit the Minyong Glacier, for a fee, and the nearby monastery.

Using a local tour operator for jeep and horse hire, we crossed the Mekong 45 minutes north of Deqen and turned left toward Xigong hot springs where we left the jeep and loaded the horses. Around six hours of pleasant walking up and over a forested ridge, past prayer flags and small meadows, brought us down in to the Yibong valley and its uppermost village of Yibong. Whilst descending to the village at around 3200m, we got several glimpses through the mist of the lower reaches of the main range to the west, including not only the 6000m peak directly south of Kawa Karpo that we wished to attempt, but also the approach gully to the north ridge of the spectacular 6,054m Miancimu (Metsemo). The next day we hoped to reach the "Japanese Camp" used by the ill-fated Sino-Japanese expedition that lost 17 members in one avalanche higher up on Kawa Karpo in January 1991. There is now a very basic trekking-style lodge in Yibong that can accommodate small groups.

While spending the night in Yibong we learned that although the villagers were happy for us to explore the area, they had been told by the monks from the monastery at Minyong that they would be "punished" for allowing foreigners to go above the village without a local guide. Spiritual reasons were cited for not allowing foreigners to climb or trek in the mountains above—not just Kawa Karpo, but all the peaks—and this prohibition also extended to other activities like plant collecting. We knew beforehand that such issues may affect climbing here but wanted to see for ourselves. Though disappointed, we left the area the next day, content to abandon any climbing plans there out of respect for local beliefs and the well being of the villagers.

After a few days in Deqen we again took a public bus to the pass near Baimang Shan. After spending a day scoping the east face and waiting out the usual rain and snow, we descended directly down hill through low brush until we hit a path that followed the river north to south along the valley floor. Shortly after, this path forked and we took the route that headed west, over a ridge then straight up the valley beneath the east face of Baimang. Passing several crumbling herders' huts, we arrived after five hours at a clearing in the cirque beneath Baimang, in view of the approach slopes to the face. There was a larger herder's hut here, with a partially dismembered and mummified dog stored in the corner.

After waiting a day here, hoping the sunny weather would help settle the face, we set off at 3 a.m., planning to enter the rightmost broad couloir, then follow it to a point where we could cross a rock rib to access and follow the upper part of the central couloir to where it exited on to the summit ridge, a climb of around 1,400m. By 5 a.m. we were up on the lower snow slopes, about to climb a diagonal gully to access the first couloir. However for the last 30 minutes we had been winding through increasingly large blocks of avalanche debris, invisible from below. The instinct for self-preservation took over and I suggested that the route was too dangerous in its present condition. Paul, exhibiting a lesser talent for flotation than myself, had been sinking up to his waist in the approach snows and readily agreed to descend upon encountering the television-sized blocks around us. We were back in our bags within an hour, disappointed again. Rising at 9 a.m., we spent over an hour admiring the scene of our most recent failure when a massive boom shook the air and the whole upper section of the central couloir cut loose, tons of snow cascading down the face and obliterating our proposed route. After watching several smaller avalanches bombard the slopes on which we had been recently standing, we had a two-second, non-verbal discussion before happily packing up and walking back to the road that led to Zhongdian, Lijiang, beer, pizza, pancakes, and ice cream.

After a few days of such hardship we decided to visit the northern side of Habaxueshan (5,490m), a peak that has been climbed at least three times and is situated on the northern side of the famous Tiger Leaping Gorge. Crossing the Yangtze on the old ferry near Daju, we slogged uphill to the ugly "new village" on the northern bank of the river. Here we shared a tractor ride with a large cow for three hours, winding over the hills to reach the village of Haba, high on a hillside to the northeast of the peak of the same name. Spending the night at an excellent lodge, where the woman who owned the establishment helped us register with the police for a "trekking permit" and also hire her brother and his horse, we set off the next day and made the 1,400m ascent, past grazing cows and the raging river, up through slippery forest to the picturesque lake known locally as "Black Sea," situated at 4,100m to the north of Habaxueshan. The next day, upon hiking up a small hill near camp, we realized that we did not have enough time to negotiate the approach to the actual climbing on Haba, which necessitated some winding through pinnacles and traversing slopes before touching the main slopes of the peak itself. However, we did gain an awesome view of some jagged, unclimbed 5,000m peaks that were close to the southwest of Habaxueshan and could probably be accessed through Tiger Leaping Gorge. The following day, after a savage hailstorm and a hike up another snowy 4,305m hill, we quickly descended to Haba village, from which we left the next day and retraced our steps to Lijiang and eventually Kunming.

DAMIEN GILDEA, *AAC*

Tibet

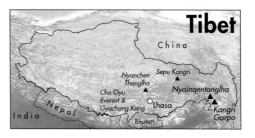

Kangri Garpo, reconnaissance of Ruoni (6,882m). The Alpine Club of Kobe University obtained a permit from the China Mountaineering Association (CMA) to climb the highest peak in Kangri Garpo in the fall of 2003. In October 2002, they sent a reconnaissance party to search for and find a viable climbing route to the summit. Three members arrived at Lhagu village on the 8th, entered the valley to the south and set up the base camp on the bank of Hyuna lake north of Ata Glacier (north). They ascended the glacier and reached 4,650m.

TAMOTSU NAKAMURA, *Japan Alpine News*

NYAINQENTANGLHA RANGE

Sepu Kangri, first ascent. A seven-member team of mountaineers from the U.S. made the first ascent of Sepu Kangri in the Nyainchentanglha Range (previously attempted by Christian Bonington and Charles Clarke—see *AAJ* 1998, 1999). Mark Newcomb and Carlos Buhler reached the 6,956m (22,821') summit on October 2 during a snow storm. See "Sepu Kangri," earlier in this Journal for the story.

Nyanchen Thanglha southeast summit, probable first ascent. From April 12 to June 1 I guided an international expedition to the Nyanchen Thanglha (also spelled Nyainqentanglha) range. Our idea was to acclimatize for 10 days before heading to Mt. Everest. After climbing small peaks up to 5,700m around Yangbajing (the main village in the south of the mountain-range), we moved to the highest part of the area. The base camp was built up in the valley to the south at about 5,050m. It is a five-hour hike from the village near the road from Yangbajing to an area with giant boulders in an alpine lawn.

The mountain rejected us during our first attempt to climb Central Peak in a bad snowstorm (we reached camp 1 at 6,200m), so we took a rest day in base camp. The second try was

The southeast summit of Nyanchen Thanglha. The ascent line was on the left, descent on the right. Stefan Gatt

also in bad weather, with wind, snowfall, and bad visibility all day. The angle is 30° to 45° and very exposed. We did not use any fixed ropes or belays, and we reached the summit in a full snowstorm at about 14:00 Chinese time. Base camp was reached around 21:00.

While our two co-guides led two more groups each consisting of four people to the Central peak, my father (Erich) and I made an attempt to climb the Southeast Peak of Nyanchen Thanglha. Again we climbed the "track" up to the 5,900m col between a small mountain—we called it Mirador— at 6,100m and the slope up to Central Peak. Traversing the avalanche field on the southeast side of the fore summit of the central peak was hard work. The snow was sometimes 80cm deep in this dangerous area. A crevasse-zone at 6,100m brought a small maze for us that we escaped exactly when dusk fell. We stayed the night at 6,200m.

The second day we climbed to the south-ridge of the Southeast summit and traversed it until the flank at about 6,400m. Without belay we climbed the 45° hard firn ice flank until a rock-barrier closed the flank. This barrier consists of 60m of loose rock and is the crux of our route. Difficulties up to UIAA IV-V had to be climbed, partly mixed with ice. From the top of the rock band there came one pitch with 60° ice. After that a 50° later on less steep hard firn ice flank leads to the top. Because we know few people have been in the area of Nyanchen Thanglha and because we have not found any hints of previous parties, we think that this was a first ascent.

We made the descent to the saddle between the Central and the Southeast peaks and then found a track through the maze of crevasses to our tent—twice abseiling 10m over overhanging seracs. From the tent we used the same way back to the basecamp as we came up.

STEFAN GATT, *Austria*

HIMALAYA

Shimokangri, first ascent. The Alpine Club of POSCO (the largest steel mill in Korea) made the first ascent of Shimokangri (7,204m) on September 29. An expedition of eight climbers, led by Li In Oei, put five on top: Nam Yong Mo (climbing leader), Li Ji Ryue, Li Fua Fun, Kim Ze Yong, and Chuen Oir.

Although Shimokangri does not appear on a 1:50,000 topographical map by the Chinese People's Liberation Army (PLA), the map does show the peak climbed by the Korean party (but with a height of 7,202m). Also the PLA map shows a 6,902m peak named Shimori, north of the west peak. Therefore, it can be assumed that "Shimokangri" comes from "Shimori," although the Bhutan people call the mountain Kangphu Kang.

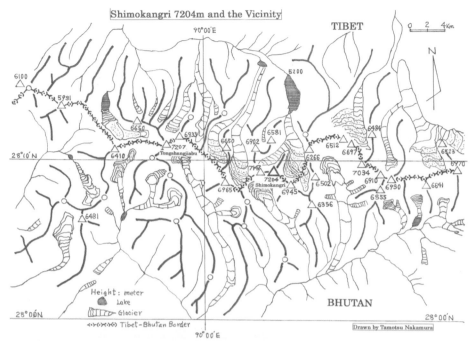

Map of Shimokangri region courtesy of Tamotsu Nakamura

On September 5, the team left Lhasa in four jeeps and a truck. In two days, they crossed an arid, 4,000m high plateau to a temporary base camp (BC) next to a lake at 5,200m. After a three-day rest, they climbed a moraine-covered glacier in bad weather and high wind, establishing an advanced base camp (ABC) at 5,400m.

On September 17, they set up C2 at 5,900m on a col just below a ridge on the Tibet-Bhutan border, while the wind continued to blow fiercely. The next day, the team began climbing a 75° snow face, ascending 1,000 meters through snow showers. On September 22 and 23, Nam Yong Mo and three others fixed ropes to 6,700m, then descended to ABC. On September 25, five climbers tried to push the route further, but had to retreat to C2 because of bitter cold wind. Snow continued to fall, then the wind got even worse, forcing them to remain at C2 for another day.

On September 27, although it was still snowing intermittently, they started up again with 20 kg loads. Exposed to avalanche and rockfall danger, the climbing was extremely difficult. By 6 p.m., they reached 6,700m and could go no further that day, so they chopped a ledge and spent an uncomfortable night on the ice. The next day, they reached the site of C3 (6,900m) at 4 p.m., pitching tents in a state of exhaustion.

They began the final push on September 29 by first climbing the north face, then moving around to a slope on the southwest ridge. They could see many peaks in Bhutan, and many highland lakes on the Tibetan side. After five hours and twenty minutes, climbing leader Nam Yong Mo and the four others reached a point just below the summit. By 10 a.m., they all stood on top of Shimokangri.

Afterword: The 1998 Gankarpunzum expedition of the Japanese Alpine Club was suddenly suspended because of a border controversy between China and Bhutan. (See *Japanese Alpine*

News, Vol. 1, October 2001). But now that a permit for Shimokangri was granted to the Korean party, perhaps other peaks on the Tibet-Bhutan border will become available for climbing (the Himalayan Association of Japan has already sent in an application for Tongshanjiabu, 7,207m).

TAMOTSU NAKAMURA, Japanese Alpine News

Mt. Everest, north face snowboarding attempt. Marc ("Marco") Siffredi, the well known 23-year-old French professional snowboarder from Chamonix, came to Mt. Everest this autumn to snowboard down two couloirs on the mountain's north side. This was to be his second descent by snowboard; his first was achieved in May last year, when he made Everest's first complete snowboard descent. His route then took him down the Great Couloir (or Norton Couloir). Now he wanted to descend a different northern route, the Hornbein and "Japanese" couloirs.

As usual, very few expeditions attempted to scale Everest this autumn. Of the five who came from France, Canada, Brazil, Japan and South Korea, only Siffredi and his three strong Sherpas were successful in reaching its 8,850m-high (29,035') summit. The Sherpas survived, but Siffredi did not.

Siffredi, Panuru Sherpa, Phurba Tashi Sherpa and Da Tenzing Sherpa arrived at the top at 2:00 p.m. Nepalese time on September 8 via the standard North Col-north ridge route. They had used artificial oxygen slogging through chest-deep snow and consumed a total of 22 bottles of it in their final push to the summit from camp 2's relatively low altitude of 7,700m (25,260') in order to keep warm. The weather at the top was fine, but Siffredi had to wait for clouds below him to disperse.

One hour later, with weather and snow conditions perfect, Siffredi launched himself for a descent that he had expected would take him just one hour to the foot of the mountain at 5,800m (19,030'), where he had pitched a camp below the Japanese Couloir. At the same time his Sherpas began their own descent on foot by the route they had ascended and reached advance base camp at 6,400m (21,000') at 10:00 p.m. that night, unaware of what had happened to Siffredi.

What had happened was that he had disappeared. With binoculars from advance base camp, he was seen starting his descent. His track in the snow was clearly visible to 8,600m (28,215'), but no trace whatsoever of him, his snowboard, or his track was visible anywhere beyond that point. One would immediately guess that he might have plunged into a crevasse, but there are no crevasses where his trail ended. No one knows what became of him. He simply vanished.

ELIZABETH HAWLEY, Nepal

Mt. Everest, snowboard descents from 2001. On May 22, 2001 I reached the summit of Mt. Everest without the help of artificial oxygen or Sherpas. As a talisman I carried a specially designed snowboard of Duotone with me and got to the very top at 3:20 (Chinese time). Half an hour later I was able to carve the first tracks in the snows below the summit.

The snow-conditions were grippy, but very hard. No powder—no fun. My plan was to ride the Norton Couloir. However, due to having no advisor via radio from the North Col at 7,050m, and feeling tired after climbing eight hours from the last camp at 8,200m, I decided not to follow my original plan. I stopped my ride below the third step at 8,650m and carried the board until 7,600m, from where I continued to descend. Shortly before ABC the ride had to be stopped because of lack of snow. My descent lasted two days. One night was spent at 8.200m.

My expedition was very successful—6 climbers out of 10 reached the summit of Mt. Everest. We followed a very unusual concept. We acclimatised in a different mountain area, north of Lhasa. In the Nyanchen Thanglha range we all climbed the Central Summit (7,117m)—myself, of course, with my snowboard. After that I realised the first ascent of the Southeast Peak of Nyanchen Thanglha (7,080m), together with my father. Then we had three rest days in Lhasa, followed by our quick ascent of Everest, in 14 days.

Our route over the north ridge was quite delicate in higher parts. Exposed traverses on rock bands like window-rims had to be accomplished at 8,500m, as well as two

Stefan Gatt riding past 7,000m under Chang La, the North Col of Everest, during his 2001 descent. *Erich Gatt*

nearly vertical rock faces of 30m in the fifth grade. Mt. Everest is the second 8,000m mountain that I have snowboarded. In 1999 I rode Cho Oyu (8,201m).

The day after I summited, Marco Siffredi made the first complete snowboard descent of Everest. Supported by a radio from the North Col to describe the conditions, a Sherpa carrying his snowboard to the top, and by the use of bottled oxygen, he rode the entire Norton Couloir and continued to my low point.

STEFAN GATT, *Austria*

Pumori north ridge. A new route was successfully forged on the Tibetan side of Everest's 7,161m (23,494') neighbor Pumori. The noted Swiss mountaineer, Erhard Loretan, led a group of nine members, all but one also Swiss, in the first attempt of its north ridge. They made their base and advance base camps at the sites of the corresponding camps for climbs on the north side of Everest and then moved west into the Pumori Glacier to pitch their first high camp here at 5,700m (18,700'). They had to climb their long, steep ridge with care, Loretan said, up a section of loose rock followed by another of powder snow. The expedition gained the summit in two parties. The first, Loretan and a Swiss member, went to the top on May 7 from their second high camp at 6,050m (19,850'), which was on the ridge itself. The next party of four more Swiss set up another camp on the ridge at 6,700m (22,000') on the 9th and summited the following day with Loretan, who had come up to their high camp early the same morning to go with them.

ELIZABETH HAWLEY, *Nepal*

Gyachung Kang, north face, second ascent of Slovenian Route. Mr. Yasushi Yamanoi and his wife Taeko were hospitalized in Tokyo for the amputation of dozens of fingers due to frostbite. Taeko and Yasushi, two of Japan's premier alpinists, climbed Gyachung Kang (7,985m) via the Slovenian Route this October. They arrived at base camp on October 5 and proceeded to an advanced base camp at the foot of the Slovenian Route. On October 6 they climbed mixed terrain (50°–60°) to 7,000m and bivouacked. On October 7 they continued climbing to 7,500m and bivouacked. On October 8 it began snowing and at 7,600m Taeko gave up climbing and decided to wait for Yasushi. Yasushi returned after reaching the summit solo, reunited with Taeko, and made another bivouac. Snow continued on October 9 and they descended to 7,200m and bivouacked. While descending in the continuous snow on October 10, Taeko was hit by avalanche, loosing her right glove and vision in her left eye. Later the same day Yasushi also lost vision in both eyes making their descent extremely difficult and forcing the pair to bivouac again. Vision in Yasushi's left eye returned the next day while Taeko had now lost vision in both eyes. They managed to descend to their advanced base camp where they found none of their support team members. A 10-hour descent on October 12 led them to a bivouac on the glacier; Taeko still had no vision. On October 13 they arrived at their base camp to learn that their support team had assumed they had disappeared and would not return. They were immediately taken to a hospital in Kathmandu and were flown to a hospital in Tokyo on October 18, where they recovered other than Yasushi's loss of toes and fingers. Gyachung Kang is located on the border of east Nepal and China (Tibet) at N 28° 06' and E 86° 45', 33 km north of Namche Bazar. The first ascent was made by a Japanese party on April 10, 1964.

TAMOTSU NAKAMURA, *Japan Alpine News*

Ngozumpa Kang II, west face, Bearzi death. Two Americans, Mike Bearzi and Bruce Miller, planned to make the first attempt on the northeast face of 7,952m (26,089') Gyachung Kang, which is on the Tibetan border between Cho Oyu and Everest. But before attacking this nearly 8,000m mountain, they did some acclimatization climbs on several peaks in Tibet very close to it. On the last of these, the two men summited Ngozumpa Kang II, 7,646m (25,085'), via its west face on May 9. As they were descending in the late afternoon, Bearzi was slowing down noticeably. At about 7:00 p.m., when Miller could see their bivouac below at 7,000m, Bearzi, who was behind him, fell at a steep place and couldn't stop himself. His death-fall ended 600m (1,900') down on the glacier west of their route. (See "An Optimistic Plan" earlier in this Journal for the story.)

ELIZABETH HAWLEY, *Nepal*

Cho Oyu ski descent and discussion of 8,000-meter ski descents. Fewer than 40 people have skied from an elevation of 8,000m or greater. In 1978 Nicolas Jaeger and Jean Afanassieff quietly made tracks into history when they strapped their skis to their feet at 8,200m on Everest and skied down. By 1999, 31 people in the world had descended from an elevation of 8,000m or greater. In 2000 the Marolt brothers from Aspen, Colorado reached what their altimeters had indicated as the shoulder or central summit of Shishapangma. Their descent marked the first from above 8,000m for anyone in the Western Hemisphere. As the fall of 2000 faded to winter, Laura Bakos of Telluride, Colorado became the first person from the Western Hemisphere to

Kris Erickson high on Cho Oyu. Erickson collection

finally ski off the summit of an 8,000m peak with her descent of Cho Oyu.

Last August John Griber, Douglas Stoup, and I left for an attempt to ski and snowboard Cho Oyu, the sixth highest peak. Our team arrived at the Cho Oyu Advanced Base Camp (18,700') on September 6. We were greeted by exceptionally calm and clear weather for the first two weeks while we established Camp I (20,950') and Camp II (23,450'). At Camp II, on the morning of September 17, three days after leaving ABC for an acclimatization trip, Griber came down with acute pulmonary edema. As we descended his condition continued to worsen, forcing Ben Marshall and me to administer Niphedipine. At one point over 22,000', where the terrain was too flat to drag Griber, Marshall carried him on his back. The rescue effort was aided when Russell Brice of Himalayan Experience ran an oxygen canister up to help with John's deteriorating condition. With oxygen and rest at Camp I, Griber was able to walk on his own accord to ABC.

Returning to make the summit on this expedition was no longer an option for John. With a small opening in the weather, Doug and I decided to try for the summit on September 21, but descended to ABC with high winds plowing over the summit and a stomach virus maligning Doug. Both John and Doug left for home, leaving me as the only member of our three-man team.

The possibility of another summit bid seemed scarce as a week of snow and high winds followed. To add to my deteriorating morale, I received word that high winds had destroyed the tents in Camp I. Remarkably, Camp I was rebuilt with new tents and most of the climbers retrieved the gear they had stashed in the tents.

On September 28, in snowy conditions, I joined the remaining members of the IMG team for our last chance at the summit. Leaving Camp III (24,800') at 3 a.m. on the night of September 30, carrying skis and using oxygen, I made a six-hour push to the summit. Conditions were calm and clear upon reaching the summit and after spending an hour resting and enjoying the outstanding views of the Himalaya, I decided to attempt the descent on skis. Standing there I watched the six others on the summit descend. With one last look over my shoulder toward Everest, I clicked my boots into the skis and started down the mountain. Rolling over the first headwall off of the summit plateau the conditions quickly improved to a chalky but firm sastrugi. Exhausted from the effort of skiing at just under 27,000', I could only link seven or eight turns before collapsing into what felt like cardiac arrest. Skiing far to the skier's right of the ascent path I bypassed Camp III and the Yellow Band on sun-crusted snow before skiing into Camp II, where I stopped using oxygen. An hour and a half had passed since I left the summit.

After resting a few hours in Camp II, I skied the best six to eight inches of Himalayan powder, was forced to rappel once over the ice cliff directly above Camp I, and finished the skiing on a great 300m section of refrozen corn before sliding into Camp I. It took an hour to ski from Camp II. A little after 7 p.m. that evening I walked into ABC tired and amazed it all came together. Twenty-four years after Jaeger and Afanassieff's descent, K2, Kangchenjunga, Dhaulagiri, Lhotse, and Manaslu still await significant descents off their faces.

KRISTOFFER ERICKSON

Kaqur-Kangri first ascent, no-trace efforts, and survey of the region. Five members of Doshisha University Alpine Club made the first ascent of Kaqur-Kangri on September 24. Located near the headwaters the Yalung Tsangpo River, Kaqur-Kangri is the highest of many virgin summits in the remote Ronglai-Kangri Range, bordering Nepal and Tibet.

The first non-native to explore this area was a Japanese priest named Kawaguchi Ekai (1866-1945), who passed through on his way to study Tibetan Buddhism. In 1900, Ekai left Marpha along Kali-gandaki, Nepal, then went along the northern side of Dhaulagiri, wandering around until he found his way to Narue via the Cang-chu River. The next visitor was Sven Hedin, the first person to go up the Cang-chu River. In 1907, he made a sketch of Kaqur-Kangri. Doshisha University Alpine Club made the first ascent of Mt. Saipal in 1963, and observed the Ronglai-Kangri Range from the summit. In 1997, Sadao Yoshinaga and the Osaka Alpine Club climbed Rongla-Kangri (6,799m), and made a reconnaissance of Kaqur-Kangri.

To avoid high avalanche danger, our eight-person team—Katsumi Nishida (climbing leader), Yusuke Ueda, Atsushi Senda, Hyosuke Tsuboi, three sherpas (Naga-Dorje, sirdar), and myself (team leader)—planned this ascent for late September or early October. We wanted to cross the Yalung Tsangpo River at New Zhongba, but when we arrived at the end of August, that unpredictable river was swollen and impassable. Instead, we had to make our approach from Laru, about three hours (by car) above Paryang, in the vicinity of the Kubi Tsangpo River. From Laru, we traveled up the Cang-chu River by yak and horseback to the Kaqur Tsangpo River. After crossing a ridge of Kaqur-Kangri, we set up base camp on the left side of the South Kaqur glacier (5,100m) on Sept. 8. Then we had to sit still for a week, waiting for the monsoon to end.

When the clouds cleared on September 14, we established advanced base camp on the lowest col of the east ridge, above the South Kaqur Glacier. But when we moved onto the East Kaqur Glacier, we encountered so many hidden crevasses that we decided to tackle the face of the east ridge instead. Because of continuing avalanche and crevasse danger, we fixed ropes to the two upper camps. High winds forced us to place Camp I (6,100m) on the leeward east side of the ridge. Then we established Camp II (6,400m) on September 20, on a large ice shelf close to the ridge.

We began our final ascent before dawn on September 24. At first we had excellent cramponing up 45° to 60° slopes, winding through crevasses near the ridge. But when we climbed over a small cornice onto the summit ridge, we encountered high winds and a steeper slope than we had expected, so we extended the fixed lines another 200m. The final corniced slope was easy. We reached the summit after only four hours of climbing on that final day.

We conducted a "no-trace" expedition, leaving only the fixed ropes near the summit (too dangerous to recover). We used portable toilets at base, and "sanita-clean" in the advance camps. All excrement was placed in plastic bags. At base, kitchen refuse and feces were mixed with a fermentation accelerating agent, then buried in a grass field. Combustibles and portable toilets were burned, and non-combustibles packed out to Lhasa. The sherpas were very cooperative in this effort .

Following our ascent of Kaqur-Kangri, we made a survey of the Ronglai-Kangri Range. Since the names of the mountains vary locally, we decided to use the Tibetan names. Kaqur-Kangri (also called Zazi-Kangri by some locals) is the main peak in center of the range. On the east side of the border ridge leading to Kaqur-Kangri are Langlung-Kangri, Surlung-Kangri, and Pakyung-Hangmu—6,000m to 6,500m virgin peaks—and the rocky, unique Galzon-Gencok. Most of the mountains trending northwest are unclimbed, but the ridge is so convoluted that it's difficult to define the border. Unlike on the Nepalese side, the glaciers are well developed and make for good routes. A well-timed approach should be relatively easy.

We also confirmed the names of the mountains extending from the source of the Yalung Tsangpo River, which branches off to the Kubi Tsampo and the Chema-Yundung Chu, west of the Ronglai-Kangri Range. These ranges are called Gorakh Himal, and the Changla Himal in Nepal. To date, only the Northwest Nepal Women's Expedition and the Climbing Team of Japan have climbed in these ranges (1983).

Impressive unclimbed mountains in the Gorakh Himal include Mukchung-Jungu, Absi, and Ngomo-dingding, which can be approached from the Kubi Tsangpo River. Local people call the main peak on the border Absi Gyablung, but the vanguard peak on the border is Absi. The main peak of the range is Mukchung-Jungu, which becomes Mukchung-Tseung in the west. The mountains called Asajyatuppa and Gorakh-Himal in Nepal correspond to Muchung-Jungu and Mukchung-Tseung, respectively.

At Langta-Chen, the Gorakh Himal turns sharply, then runs north-south. The Changla Himal are the mountains on the border. The main 6,721m peak (still unnamed) and Chema-yundung-kangri, to the east, stand out. Chema-yundung-kangri has twin peaks: one on the border, and the other inside Tibet. In Nepal, the peak on the border is known as Changla Himal (6,563m). The unnamed main peak (attempted in 1983) is called Kubi-dongdong or Dondong in Tibet. It looked to us like its summit pinnacle was bare of snow.

Finally, we tried to ascertain the source of the Yalung Tsangpo River. Local inhabitants said the Kubi Tsangpo might be its source, but others insisted the true source was the Chema-Yundung Chu. Since the Kubi Tsangpo has the greatest flow, it appeared to be the main stream, but the map shows that the Chema-Yundung Chu is longer. We had to conclude that either one could be called the source.

TOYOJI WADA, *Doshisha University Alpine Club (translated by Tamotsu Nakamura)*

Mongolia

Central Mongolia, Ulaan Bataar, The Bombadorj Arête and The Lite Path. Our five-person team pioneered a 1,600', 12-pitch route, which we believe is the hardest climb in remote Central Mongolia. My wife Heather Baer, Shawn Chartrand (our talented interpreter), Mike Strassman, Jackie Carroll, and I departed on August 11 for the "resort" in the Otgon Tengor area of Central Mongolia. After a four-day journey by van, we enjoyed natural hot springs, played chess and hacky-sack, blew bubbles, practiced gymnastics, and shot squirt guns with the friendly Mongolians. Though we had received a grant from the AAC to try for a new alpine style route on Otgon Tengor (the highest peak in Central Mongolia), it turned out to be an unappealing rubble pile. But in an adjacent valley, known locally as Brownsmoke Valley, we found an amazing golden buttress, which we decided to make our objective. After a day's rest, we left base camp at 2 a.m. and came

Central Mongolia's Temee Tower, showing the Babadorj Arête.
Steve Schneider

to a beautiful hidden lake at dawn. The approach was arduous, involving miles of grueling talus. At 9 a.m. we began climbing: Heather, Shawn, and myself formed one team, Mike and Jackie the other. After three pitches, Mike and Jackie crossed our route and eventually summited, creating a 5.10a route we called The Lite Path.

Being more stubborn, I coerced my team to push on with a more direct, harder line up the ridge. I soon encountered more difficult and more runout climbing than I had expected. By 3:00 p.m. it became obvious that we did not have enough time (nor energy) to summit and still get back down by dark. So we left fixed lines and retreated to basecamp, arriving at 11:30 p.m., after a 22-hour push. Following a few days of rest and rainstorms, we used horses to set up an advanced basecamp in Brownsmoke Valley—a beautiful place that we shared with 12 double-humped camels and their shepherd.

The next day we returned to our high point, and took several hours to hand drill five bolts on two crux pitches (5.11d), which I was able to redpoint on my first try. The second crux was an awesome splitter reminiscent of Yosemite's Red Zinger. Heather followed free in gallant style, while Shawn documented the action with photos and video. Seven more pitches in the 5.9 to 5.10 range brought us to the first of two distinct humps on the ridge. A long fourth class pitch led to the final hump of Temee Tower (Temee means camel, in Mongolian). On descent, our rope got stuck twice, and we had to re-climb almost an entire 5.8 pitch in the dark. We reached terra firma at midnight, and stumbled back to basecamp at 6:00 a.m., after a 25-hour push.

Steve Schneider sends the first ascent of Welcome to Mongolia, currently the hardest pitch in the country. Terelj, near the capital of Ulaan Bataar. Shawn Chartrand

Huiten just prior to the mountain's first winter ascent. The southeast ridge is on the left, and the real summit is hidden. Konstantin Beketov

We named the The Bombadorj Arête (V 5.11d) after our shepherd friend, who played an artful game of chess. Everyone agreed it was one of the best backcountry climbs we'd ever done— we highly recommend it. After exchanging gifts with our friends, we enjoyed a last hot tub, then reversed our epic journey back to the capital. Still glowing from our adventure in this amazing land, and thanking the Gods for keeping us safe and sound, our final week was spent sport cragging in Terelj— a cross between Joshua Tree and City of Rocks—just 90-minutes from the capital.

STEVE SCHNEIDER, *AAC*

Mongolian Altai, Huiten, first winter ascent. In winter 1998, we skied 400 km through Russia, Kazakhstan, China, and Mongolia—making the first winter ascent of Huiten (4,374m), the highest point in Mongolia, on March 3. We called our expedition the Altai–Two Mountains, because we also climbed Belukhu, the highest peak of the Altai Mountains (Huiten is the second highest). Six of us from St. Petersburg took part in this journey, carrying everything on our backs for 27 days.

The geographic literature usually identifies two ranges: the Russian Altai (the ranges in Russian territory and in Kazakhstan), and the Mongolian Altai (running north-south along the Chinese-Mongolian border). The Mongolian Altai is an unusual area with high peaks, a dry climate, and the largest glaciers of the Altai. At its southern end, the Mongolian Altai is called the Gobiskii Altai (Gobi Altai), because it abuts the edge of the Gobi desert.

Huiten is on the border between Russia and China, at the juncture of the Russian and the Mongolian Altai, in a massif called Tabyn-Bogdo-Ula ("five holy peaks"). The Tabyn-Bogdo-Ula first appeared in the scientific literature in 1905, after Russian geographer V. V. Sapozhnikov discovered the Potanina Glacier, the largest of the Altai, near the source of the Tsagan-Gol River (according to the archives of the Russian Geographical Society, Sapozhnikov named everything that bears a Russian name, in a 1905-1907 expedition).

Huiten is the mountain's old Chinese name (which means "cold"), but its Mongolian name—given during an international climbing expedition in 1970—is Nairamdal, meaning "friendship." The Tronovy brothers from Russia first tried to climb it from the Potanina Glacier in 1915, probably reaching the false summit by the southeast ridge.

On the east, in the direction of the Potanina Glacier, Huiten terminates in a steep ice wall, but two ridges provide a route to the summit. A third ridge on the north links Huiten with the peak Russkii Shater (where the boundaries of Russia, China, and Mongolia converge). This rocky ridge, beginning at the upper snowfield of the Potanina Glacier, is steeper than the others. To the west lies the basin of the Chinese Kanas River. The right-hand tributary of the Khalasi Glacier is called the Roborovsky Glacier. Through a low, wide pass, this tributary is visible from the Russian side of the Betsu-Kanas River valley. Finally, a short ridge runs south from the summit, toward the right branch of the Khalasi Glacier. Through the years, all the ridges have been traversed, but it looks like no one has ever tried to climb the south and east walls.

Besides Huiten, other peaks surrounding the basin of the Khalasi Glacier (Przheval'skii) have attracted a lot of attention. We believe that Snezhnii Tserkov' (Snowy Church) and the Krasavitsa Peak (Beauty) are still unclimbed and unexplored. They are in Chinese territory, with summits near 4,000m.

We decided to climb Huiten by the southeast ridge, from the Potanina Glacier. From our base camp on a lateral moraine, we climbed the glacier on crampons, but unroped (there were almost no crevasses). After several kilometers, at the juncture of a right-hand tributary, we began encountering crevasses, then after two more hours we ran into more snow.

From the base of the southeast ridge, the summit appeared to be a snowy cupola— but we would find out that it was actually just a narrow ridge. Since we hadn't used our skis, we left them at the base of the ridge and cramponed up 25° to 30° slopes, passing two large rock gendarmes on the right (crossing a 40° ice slope to get by the first one). It took an hour to reach a saddle on the ridge. The saddle was a flat, sheltered spot between low cliffs, with room for several tents.

On the south side (left of our route), the ridge ended in steep scree, while on our right, the east ice wall of Huiten was higher and steeper. We roped up, and continued climbing the jagged ridge, which was about 300m long. The ridge grew wider and steeper (up to 40°), and was crossed by many snow-covered crevasses. Hard ice lay beneath the surface of snow.

When we reached the south false summit, it was necessary to drop into a 25m deep, 10m wide knife-edge col, bounded by a cornice over a crevasse on the Potanina Glacier side, and a rock wall on the Chinese side. This drop was probably what stopped the Tronovy brothers in 1915. From the col, it was less than 50m to the summit marker. The ascent from the saddle had taken one hour and 30 minutes. We thought it looked like the marker was 100m south of the very highest point.

It took two hours and 30 minutes to descend to where we had left our skis. From there, those who chose to ski down reached base camp in another 30 minutes, while the rest of us who continued on foot were an hour behind them.

Although a strong wind and snowstorm, and -18°C temperatures had hampered our climb, the very next day it was sunny (but colder). March is the best month for a winter ascent of Huiten. The whole story about this skiing expedition, Altai–Two Mountains, is available in Russian on the internet at: http://www.tourism.ru/phtml/users/get_report.php?78

KONSTANTIN BEKETOV, RUSSIA, *Translated by Henry Pickford, AAC*

Siykhem Nuruu National Park, exploration and a first ascent. Our six member team from the north of England comprised Ken Findlay, Stuart Gallagher, John Given, Les Holbert, Karl Zientek, and myself. We had as our goal exploration of the area around 3,939m Ikh Turgen Uul in the Siykhem Nuruu National Park. This lies directly north of Bayan Olgi and not so far from the increasingly popular Tavan Bogd mountains. Karl and I arrived in Ulaan Baatar ahead of the others, only to find that an outbreak of foot and mouth disease had put the region of Aimag Olgi out of bounds. Our pre-booked air flights to Bayan Olgi were now useless: if we were to have flown there, we would simply have been stopped from leaving the town. Instead, when the rest of the team arrived, we moved by mini bus to Ulaangom; three days of virtually non-stop travel on non-existent roads. On our arrival we obtained permission to enter Aimag Olgi and visit Siykhem Nuruu National Park Area "B." We were directed to a base camp in the Ongorchoi Valley at the southern end of the range. This proved to be the summer grazing ground for flocks of sheep and goats owned by a group of Kazakhs. After an initial few days settling in and exploring the nearest mountains, we realized our camp was really in the wrong location. We therefore tried to get into one of the valleys further north, but unfortunately it proved impossible with the resources at hand. We therefore only explored the region that was relatively close at hand, making two main excursions: a three-day circular route climbing over two of the nearer tops, both of which were first U.K. ascents, and a more exciting five-day trip, which resulted in the first ascent of an alpine ridge (named Noodle Ridge) on the far side of the next valley north. The latter route, completed by Findlay and Zientek, took almost two days to reach. On the third day the pair traversed the ridge, climbing and rappelling rock towers to a bivouac just below the final summit. This day involved mixed climbing roughly equating to Alpine D with a harder section of steep ice up to 80°. After crossing the final and highest tower at 4,200m, the pair spent a further two days returning to base.

Although the area was interesting, it held much less snow and ice than expected, with glaciers obviously in retreat. Approaches from the north could well pay dividends, and if a party was to find a way into one of the area's middle valleys, I'm sure they would discover many alpine possibilities.

PAUL HUDSON, *U. K.*

Tavan Bogd Range, probable new route on Kowalewski, and other early repeats. The primary aim of the British Heart of Asia Expedition 2002 was to explore the Altai Mountains in the far west of Mongolia and attempt some new peaks and routes. Unfortunately, due to an outbreak of foot and mouth, we were initially forbidden from entering the region. We were effectively quarantined for 24 hours outside Bayan Olgi and subsequently fumigated and sprayed at various points in a somewhat haphazard fashion.

Instead, we visited an alternative area, the popular Otgon Tenger Uul National Park near Uliastai, then after much persistence, some bribery, and a lot of help from our Mongolian drivers and local "friends" made along the way, we were eventually allowed into the Altai Mountains.

The road head for the Otgon Tenger Uul is four days' drive from Ulaan Baatar. From here it was a day's walk to base camp located at the head of a lake (N 47°38'10.1, E 97°33'03.3). Possible new routes were climbed for acclimatization purposes on two unnamed peaks of ca 3,100m. On the first (N 47°37'40.6, E 97°31'51.2) Janet Fotheringham, Alan Halewood, Sebastian Nault, and Robert Watts climbed a pitch of British Severe up a chimney, after which the last two named climbers continued to traverse the ridge on loose rock. On the second (N.47°37'40.6, E 97°31'51.2) Michael McLaughlan and I climbed the two-pitch Platypus Crack (British VS 4a). All climbers bar myself then ascended the Normal Route up Otgon Tenger Uul (3,905m: N 47°36'32.3, E 97°33'08.7). This peak is very popular and the ascent is nothing more than a hard walk over loose scree.

We later established a base camp alongside the Potanina Glacier in the Tavan Bogd mountains of the Altai (one day's drive and a further day on foot from Bayan Olgi). From here Michael and myself made a southeast to north traverse of Huiten (4,374m), the highest summit in Mongolia. From an advanced base on the southeast flank of the mountain we traversed all five summits (Scottish II), reaching the highest point at 9 p.m., then descending via the north flank to the Potanina Glacier, where we dug a snow hole at 2 a.m. We eventually regained our tent at 10 a.m.

Seb and Rob climbed the east ridge of Snow Church (4,100m) at the head of the Alexsandra Glacier, finding the ridge mainly snow-free loose rock with a final 120m of steep ice and loose unconsolidated snow at Scottish III/IV. The overall grade was Alpine AD. Janet and Alan made an ascent of an unnamed peak of 3,900m at the head of the west end of the Grano Glacier. They traversed the mountain via the Northeast face and descent of the South ridge at Alpine PD. These two also climbed a probable new route to make the second ascent of Kowalewski (3,903m) on the southern rim of the Grano Glacier. The pair climbed a snow gully to reach the north ridge, which they followed to the summit and returned to camp in a round trip of eight hours. The overall grade was PD+. Apart from Huiten, which was climbed by a Russian-Mongolian expedition in 1956, all these other peaks were first ascended by the 1967 Polish expedition led by Witold Michalowski.

Weather conditions throughout our stay in August were usually dry, very hot, and fairly stable. However, during the last couple of weeks some electrical storms with intense rain were experienced. It also became very windy in the Tavan Bogd immediately prior to incoming frontal systems. Although most (but not all) of the principal summits in the Tavan Bogd have been climbed, many have only been ascended once or twice and often only by one route. The rock is generally loose and the glaciers fairly technical. The latter can be very hard work after mid-morning. Otherwise, the couloirs and ice fields seemed stable and there exists much opportunity for new routes at Alpine AD and above. To the south of the main range and probably accessible by foot from the Gljadien valley, a small collection of snow-covered peaks is visible and would probably repay exploration.

NINA SAUNDERS, *U. K.*

Australasia

IRIAN JAYA

Puncak Jaya, new route and first snowboard descent; Carstensz Pyramid, new route. On April 23, Corey Rich, Rob Milne, and I climbed Puncak Jaya by a new and interesting glacier route. Then I made the first snowboard descent of that peak, riding down the glacier. Counting Puncak Jaya as one of the Seven "rideable" Summits—substituting it for Carstensz Pyramid, which lacked snow—this was my sixth snowboard descent of the Seven Summits (I have not ridden Kosciusko, and don't plan to, as I don't consider it to be one of the seven). Only Everest remains, which I plan to try in summer 2003.

The following day, Rob and I climbed Carstensz Pyramid, going left of the normal route and up several pitches that were, as far as we knew, previously unclimbed. Good but sparsely protected 5.7 climbing led to the ridge on the normal route. On descent of the normal route we reset many sketchy anchors.

Two days later, Rob and I climbed Carstensz again, this time by a new six-pitch direct route on its stellar north face. We left basecamp at 5:45 a.m., began climbing at 7:00, and summitted at noon. Starting near the American Direct route, I led 5.7-5.8 climbing over clean, sharp limestone solution runnels. We simul-climbed half of the route, using Tiblocs. The crux was a sparsely protected 5.9+. At the summit, the air was buzzing with electricity. With our hair literally standing on end, we made it down to the base of the route in one hour, fighting heavy rain, lightning, and water running down the gullies.

STEPHEN KOCH, *AAC*

Stephen Koch riding the toe of Puncak Jaya's glacier, Irian Jaya. Corey Rich

OTHER MOUNTAIN ACTIVITIES

AMERICAN SAFE CLIMBING ASSOCIATION

Activity report, 1999-2002. The American Safe Climbing Association (ASCA) replaces bad bolts and anchors throughout the United States. Conceived by veteran Yosemite guide Steve Sutton in 1995, the ASCA was incorporated in 1998 by Chris McNamara, and is a 501(c)(3) non-profit. This is the second report to the *AAJ* (the first in *AAJ* 1999). In 2002 the AAC awarded the ASCA a $500 Lyman Spitzer grant; a $2,000 Lyman Spitzer grant in 1998 was one of the key factors assisting the establishment of the ASCA.

The ASCA has replaced over 3,500 bolts in the U.S. since its formation in late 1997. The original hole is almost always re-used after the original bolt is removed, and many extra bolts are removed, especially on wall climbs where bolts have proliferated. Camouflaged stainless steel bolts and hangers, coupled with rap rings instead of brightly colored webbing, reduce visual impact while restoring bolts to a standard that should not rust or require frequent replacement in the future. Replacement work is typically done on rappel where possible. However, on long routes in Yosemite, Red Rocks, Zion, and elsewhere, replacement work is usually done ground-up. Typically, the route is led on the old gear, then replaced by the follower or on rappel after the lead. Often just a few key lead and anchor bolts are replaced by a fast-moving team. More bolt-intensive routes are commonly done by a party of three, sometimes using fixed lines for multiple days of work.

Aging bolts have been replaced, in approximate order of the amount of replacement work, in Yosemite Valley, Red Rocks National Conservation Area, Tuolumne Meadows, Joshua Tree National Park, Calaveras Dome, Owens River Gorge, Little Cottonwood Canyon, Pinnacles National Monument, Indian Creek, Courtright Reservoir, Smith Rock, Tahquitz/Suicide, Mt. Lemmon, Grand Teton National Park, Rumney, Zion National Park, Tollhouse Rock, Rocky Mountain National Park, Eldorado Canyon, the Flatirons, the Needles of California, and many other local crags.

Further details on many other areas, and hundreds of replaced routes, can be found at www.safeclimbing.org. The ASCA is entirely volunteer and struggles yearly to afford top-quality stainless steel hardware used in replacing deteriorating bolts. Donations are always helpful. ASCA, PO Box 1814, Bishop, CA 93515; www.safeclimbing.org; phone: (650) 843-1473.

GREG BARNES *and* CHRIS MCNAMARA, *American Safe Climbing Association*

Kilimanjaro Porter Assistance Project

HEC porter assistance expanded to Africa and South America. On September 17, as the many climbers waited in their tents for a late season storm to pass, three porters on Mt. Kilimanjaro were not so lucky. These three porters, lacking proper clothing, were believed to have died of hypothermia. African porters on Mt. Kilimanjaro carry over 25 kilos (55 pounds) of their clients' food and gear to the high camps of the mountain, getting paid less than US$6 per day. These porters can't afford to buy the top gear that a climber brings when they climb the mountain; the porter may be wearing only cotton pants and a light jacket. Last December the non-profit Himalayan Explorers Connection established the Kilimanjaro Porter Assistance Project, modeled after the Nepal Porter Assistance Project (*AAJ* 2002, pg. 400). The HEC collects donated clothing and gear from individuals and companies such as Nike ACG, REI, Mountain Hardware, Lowe Alpine, Montrail, Patagonia, The North Face, Mammoth Mountain Ski Resort, Outdoor Research, and Thorlos. This gear is sent to the HEC offices at the base of Mt. Kilimanjaro for a clothing-lending program for porters. The offices also provide education to porters in subjects such as English, first aid, and AIDS awareness.

Back in the United States, another project is underway to work with tourists and tour operators to develop Porter Treatment Guidelines; this was in response to a recent survey of the top U.S. tour operators. The survey revealed that 90% of tour operators do not have a policy for porter treatment. This innovative program lends clothing to porters, thus allowing them to be adequately equipped for their work on the worlds highest mountains. By also educating visitors traveling to Kilimanjaro, it will make sure porters are properly cared for and outfitted. The KPAP office is located at the base of Mt. Kilimanjaro in Moshi, Tanzania. The office is open to porters, tour operators, and climbers to come in for clothing, classes, and tourist education about porter treatment.

Currently, there are Porter Assistance Project offices are in Nepal, Kilimanjaro, and opening in 2003 with partners Porteadores Inka Ñan an office in Peru. For more information about volunteering, donating equipment, or to help delivering a bag to Kilimanjaro, please contact the Himalayan Explorers Connection at info@hec.org or visit the web site at www.hec.org.

Ken Stober, *Director of International Operations, Himalayan Explorers Connection*

International Year of Mountains

What did it mean? What did it do? To most of us who read this journal, every year is a year of mountains. So you could be forgiven for thinking that the United Nations' declaration of 2002 as International Year of Mountains was, at best, a yawn and, at worst, an excuse for government-sponsored junkets to alpine resorts. Not so.

International Year of Mountains (IYM) was intended to focus worldwide attention on the value and the vulnerability of the world's mountain regions. I believe it accomplished that goal. Thousands of IYM events around the globe reached literally millions of people with messages about the importance of preserving mountain ecosystems and the value of mountain cultures. In hundreds of mountain communities, people took action to address these issues.

Mountains as a theme first made it onto the worldwide environmental radar screen at the 1992 Earth Summit in Rio de Janeiro. The Earth Summit placed the degradation of mountain environments on an equal footing with climate change, tropical deforestation, and desertification as critical issues facing the world in the late 20th and the upcoming 21st centuries. In fact, mountain ecosystems support more biodiversity than any other region on earth. They are the source of most of the world's fresh water and they are home to 767 million people—many of whom face poverty, malnutrition, disease and armed conflict. It was the country of Kyrgyzstan, whose mountain regions are threatened by war and poverty, which nominated 2002 as International Year of Mountains.

The threat that war poses to another mountain region—the Karakoram—was the inspiration behind an IYM "climb for world peace" that took place in Switzerland in August 2002. The climb was sponsored by the World Conservation Union (IUCN) and the International Mountaineering and Climbing Federation (UIAA). From August 24 to 29, a team composed of Harish Kapadia and Mandip Singh Soin from India; Sher Khan and Nazir Sabir from Pakistan; Jamie Andrew from Scotland; and Julie-Ann Clyma and Roger Payne representing the UIAA, climbed several peaks in the Swiss Alps—notably the Monch (4,099m).

One of the aims of the climb was to promote the creation of the Siachen Glacier Peace Park on the India-Pakistan border. At 6,700 meters, the glacier is the scene of the longest-running military conflict in the world. In addition to the cost in human lives, spent munitions and waste from the conflict drain from the glacier into the Indus River, threatening water supplies for millions of people. The climb marked the first time that the flags of India and Pakistan had flown together on a mountain summit. "As we unfurled our Indian and Pakistan flags together," said Mandip Singh Soin, "I felt a flutter in my heart as well. The camaraderie that existed came so strongly through the rope we were tied to that it was more like a rope of friendship, and as a climber I would have no hesitation to put my life in Sher Khan's hands, as I am sure he would have. Somehow we need to transmit and feel the goodwill that is latent in every heart of Indians and Pakistanis, for we were one once."

In Uttaranchal, India, IYM inspired the creation of the Mountain Children's Forum, with the aim of providing children in Himalayan mountain towns and villages with the skills they need to address social and economic issues in their communities. Over 400 children attended camps organized by the Forum in 2002. The Forum's Web site (www.mymountains.org) tells the story of one 15-year-old girl who, after attending a Forum camp, was inspired to successfully organize a preschool in her village and to lobby for the cleanup of the community water supply. Here in North America, education was also an IYM focus. The Mountain Institute, headquartered in Washington, D.C., launched a "Learning about Mountains" Web site (www.mountain.org/education) to provide resources for teachers and students wanting to learn about mountain environments, sports, culture, and folklore. Elizabeth Byers of the Institute says there is a real demand for these resources: "Consistently, we find that teachers have materials to introduce children to concepts of sustainability in the world's rainforests and oceans, but nothing to help them teach about mountains…. Teachers and kids living in the mountains need to be able to see themselves in the context of the wider world—as mountain people with much to offer and much to be proud of." In the first six weeks of operation, the site received over 76,000 visits.

From Scotland, Martin Price, Director of the Centre for Mountain Studies, reports, "Mountain issues were very visible during the year, in the media and through events of all sizes. Key lasting outcomes include the Land Reform Bill, which finally codifies rights of access, and Scotland's first two national parks.

In October, the American Alpine Club presented an IYM symposium on how climbers and land managers can jointly address access and conservation issues at popular climbing areas in the United States. Organized by the AAC's Linda McMillan and Jim McCarthy, the symposium was presented in conjunction with the UIAA General Assembly in Flagstaff, Arizona. It included presentations by senior managers of the National Park Service (Denali, Grand Teton, and Yosemite), the Mohonk Preserve (Shawangunk area of New York), and the Bureau of Land Management (Eastern Sierra Nevada).

Each region reported a steady growth in user visits and the associated pressures on the environment. Perhaps the most dramatic of these occurred on Bishop, California, BLM lands which, following "The Invasion of the Boulderers" (as one park manager put it), went from practically zero visits in October 1998 to over 45,000 annual visits by March 2002. As with so many IYM initiatives, education and communication were cited as the most effective means of protecting the climbing environment. Linda McMillan put it simply: "Climbers are less a part of the problem and more a part of the solution."

For someone like me, whose entire professional and private life is committed to the mountains, IYM was good news indeed. At The Banff Centre we have been focusing on mountains for more than 25 years, through programs such as the Banff Mountain Film and Book Festivals, the Banff Mountain Summits, and the Mountain Communities Conferences. IYM, however, gave us the excuse we wanted, and the momentum we needed, to try some new ideas.

To celebrate IYM we focused on three initiatives. The first was a scientific conference—Ecological and Earth Sciences in Mountain Areas—in September 2002. One outcome of the conference was to focus attention on the impact of climate change on mountain areas. Dr. David Schindler, Killam Memorial Professor of Ecology at the University of Alberta, made a chilling observation at one of the conference plenary sessions: "All of the climate models are predicting pretty close to 2 degrees centigrade warming in the next 20 years. All you have to do is pick up any scientific journal and you find that the ice sheets at high elevation are taking a real pounding.... These glaciers are going fast. In Glacier National Park—the U.S. Glacier, not the B.C. Glacier—it's predicted there won't be any glaciers in 20 years." Dr. Schindler's comments on the threats to mountain environments received national media attention here in Canada.

Our second IYM initiative was to become the new North American home of Mountain Forum (www.mtnforum.org)—a Web-based network linking over 2,700 individuals and 170 organizations in more than 100 countries. The network enables individuals and organizations concerned with mountain communities and environments to share information and resources. Since the North American node moved to Banff, the number of discussion-list participants has jumped by 80 percent to close to 800 people. Using the Forum, residents in Rockies ski towns share wildlife-savvy recycling tips with planners in Appalachian communities, and transportation coordinators in Canadian mountain parks debate regional transit options with their counterparts in Telluride, Colorado.

Our flagship IYM event at The Banff Centre was Banff Mountain Summit 2002: Extreme Landscape. The Summit explored the issues and the inspiration of the world's extreme landscapes through three days of seminars, lectures, performances and exhibitions, attracting audiences of over 2,300. One of the tangible legacies of this event was increased support for the Patagonia Land Trust—a non-profit charitable foundation that raises funds to purchase, restore and preserve lands in South America's Patagonia region. This support was inspired by presentations by Rick Ridgeway and Yvon Chouinard on how we as individuals can act to preserve the mountain environments we play in.

Another tangible result was the flurry of companies signing up to the 1% Club—Chouinard's invention—a way for individuals and companies to commit 1% of their income to environmental causes. Yet another legacy, this one artistic, was the world premiere of a stunning multimedia piece called On Earth, a combination of vertical dance and video images from the Bugaboos. Many of the Summit's presentations, including Rick's and Yvon's essays, are featured in the book *Extreme Landscape: The Lure of Mountain Spaces*, published by National Geographic (and reviewed in this Journal).

The range of Canada's IYM activities turned out to be truly astounding. Bob Sandford, chair of Canada's IYM celebrations, reports that approximately 7,000 IYM events were held in Canada, reaching approximately 4.8 million people. Sandford says that the focus of these events was to "encourage Canadians to understand human impacts on the mountains … and to involve themselves in processes and personal actions that would lead to the minimization of these impacts." Canadian IYM events were, for the most part, community-based and grass-roots—ranging from interpretive hikes about the retreat of the Illecillewaet Glacier, to centennial ascents of Mt. Columbia, to local recycling drives.

Around the world, mountain festivals expanded their offerings and audience reach during IYM. Mountain festivals in England, Italy, Canada, Austria, the U.S., Slovakia, and Scotland all featured special IYM events. Each of these festivals has become a gathering point for the global climbing community. For the most part, mountaineers pursue their passions in relative isolation, and these tribal mountain gatherings represent an invaluable opportunity for climbers to do what climbers love to do—to celebrate and to share stories and reconnect with their friends

I believe that mountain people all over the world have many things in common: their respect for the landscape, their relationship to a dramatic and sometimes tough place in which to live, their concern about alpine environmental issues and economic problems, and their sense of being inspired and nurtured by the grandeur of mountains.

International Year of Mountains was an opportunity to reflect on the huge impact mountains have on our lives—economically, recreationally, environmentally, culturally and as inspirational landscapes that fuel our creative and physical dreams. IYM was also a call to action to preserve these fragile environments. Mountains mean different things to different people. However, I believe that, at the most basic level, people go to the mountains to find their souls, and in these days, a landscape that nurtures the soul is one worth celebrating and preserving.

BERNADETTE MCDONALD, *Vice President, Mountain Culture, The Banff Centre*

THE MOUNTAIN INSTITUTE

Summary of 2002 activities. The Mountain Institute (www.mountain.org) is a non-profit organization whose mission is to conserve high priority mountain ecosystems, improve mountain livelihoods, and promote the well-being of mountain people through advocacy, education, and outreach. For 30 years TMI has served mountain people in the remotest regions in the world by helping to identify and respond to their conservation and development priorities. TMI has egional offices in the Andes (Peru, Ecuador, Bolivia), the Appalachians (West Virginia, Virginia), and Himalaya (Nepal, China, India). Other programs include Research and Education, Sacred Mountains, Sustainable Living Systems, and the Mountain Forum (www.mtnforum.org). The 400-acre Spruce Knob Mountain Center (SKMC) in West Virginia is used for mountain education courses, research, and conservation field demonstrations.

Major highlights of 2002 include the launching of a new program in Nepal and Peru entitled "Building Sustainable Mountain Livelihoods in Uncertain Times." The five-year project is focused on community capacity building, conservation, ecotourism, and conflict management with an emphasis on measuring the actual impacts of the project through sound baseline data and participatory monitoring techniques. The "Qomolangma Conservation Project" in Tibet commenced activities within its five-year workplan in conservation management, livelihood development, and cultural restoration. Partnerships and projects with five national parks were established to increase U.S. public awareness for the spiritual and indigenous cultural value of mountain landscapes within the parks. New mountain studies curriculum, teacher training courses, field research expeditions, and photographic exhibits were developed. Keynote speeches were presented by TMI staff at numerous International Year of the Mountain conferences and workshops around the world. Network membership of the Mountain Forum reached 3,600 individuals, 310 organizations from 128 countries, 13,000 email subscribers, and nearly 200,000 distinct web users.

In 2002, mountain warfare, political insurgencies, poverty, and mining-related conflicts surfaced in greater force than ever before as the key constraints facing sustainable mountain livelihoods and conservation. In response, TMI incorporated conflict reduction and management components within all field programs; placed additional emphasis on the strengthening of local communities and NGOs as the primary designers and implementors of field programs; and increased its focus on improving livelihoods through ecotourism and non-timber forest product development and promotion. An added emphasis was placed on the strengthening of its monitoring and evaluation systems so that the actual linkages between "capacity building" (e.g., training in resource management) and conservation (e.g., improvements in alpine pasture lands five years later) could be better determined. There were discussions between TMI and the AAC regarding development of joint community-based livelihood, conservation, and restoration projects in areas utilized by AAC members.

Alton C. Byers, Ph.D.

Success and Death on Mt. Everest

How the main routes and seasons compare. If you're going to climb Mt. Everest, you'll first need to choose a season and a route. Until now, you'd have had to make choices without answers to questions like: Which route has the highest success rate? Which route has the highest death rate? And what about spring vs. fall? Is the mountain safer or more dangerous than it used to be?

These questions can now be answered with data were graciously supplied by Miss Elizabeth Hawley. Starting with the American Everest Expedition in 1963, she has extensively interviewed nearly every mountaineering team passing through Katmandu (see her extensive reports in the Nepal section of this *AAJ*, and in nearly every *AAJ* for the last 40 years!). Richard Salisbury has transcribed her detailed records into an extensive computer database, which will soon be published by the American Alpine Club and The Mountaineers Books. We have now mined those data. Our goal is to help mountaineers make informed decisions when planning a climb of Everest, as well as to describe some fascinating historical trends in Everest climbing.

So, what's the surest way to reach the summit of Mt. Everest? If the past is a reliable guide to the future, then the South Col in spring offers the best chance of success. However, the North Col in spring is a close second and may even be catching up. Even so, the South Col has had the higher success in four of the past five springs. Climbers on these two routes in spring have enjoyed a remarkable 36% success rate over the past five years. That pattern does not hold on these routes in the autumn, as success rates on both routes then are strikingly reduced, especially on the North Col. Not surprisingly, climber success rates on non-main routes are relatively low, and even in spring have averaged only 12% over the past five years.

What's the best way to survive an attempt on Everest? Climber death rates are uniformly low (1% to 2%) and essentially the same on various routes and in spring or autumn. Death rates of high-altitude porters are, however, elevated in autumn relative to spring. Surprisingly, the climber death rate on "other" routes is only slightly elevated above those for the two main routes. However, the death rate on these other routes undoubtedly underestimates the danger because only relatively skilled and experienced climbers attempt these routes.

These analyses illustrate clear historical shifts in climbing on Everest. For the first decade following the first ascent, most expeditions repeated the South Col route. Beginning in 1963 (U.S. expedition to the west ridge) and lasting through the early 90s, however, many climbers on Everest attempted alternative routes. This was an era of bold climbing, with ascents on the southwest (British, Polish, Soviet), Kangshung (American, International), and northwest faces (Japanese, Australian). One in 10 climbers even went in winter!

Times have changed. In the past five years, very few climbers attempted anything other than the two main routes. Moreover, 9 of 10 climbed in spring; and only one climber went in winter. These shifts seemingly reflect an increasing conservatism on Everest, with the vast majority of climbers concentrating on the season and routes that maximize their chance of success. Indeed, 95% of all "Seven Summiters" climbed a main route on Everest.

Even many of the elite climbers are seemingly becoming more conservative. Consider the 50 climbers who have summited 10 or more of the 8,000m peaks (including Everest). Of those who first summited Everest between 1978 and 1989, 1 in 3 climbed a non-standard route; but for those who summited thereafter, 1 in 15 climbed a non-standard route. Perhaps the expanding quest for all fourteen 8000ers is encouraging even elite climbers to just "bag" Everest and get on with the remaining peaks.

Success rates on the main routes have increased the past quarter century, yet death rates have remained stable. In some ways these patterns are surprising, given the widespread belief that contemporary Everest climbers are on average less experienced and skilled than their predecessors. If that belief is accurate, then the decline in average skill and experience has been more than balanced by improved equipment and logistics, better weather forecasting, greater cumulative knowledge of the routes, and enhanced skill and experience of high-altitude porters and leaders.

RAYMOND B. HUEY, *AAC, and* RICHARD SALISBURY, *AAC*

For the complete 8-page study by Huey and Salisbury, please visit the AAJ *page on www.americanalpineclub.org for a downloadable PDF document. The historic trends, charts, graphs, and careful statistical analysis will be fascinating to anyone planning a climb of Everest.*

BOOK REVIEWS

EDITED BY DAVID STEVENSON

W.H. Murray: Evidence of Things Not Seen: A Mountaineer's Tale. W.H. MURRAY. FOREWORD BY HAMISH MACINNES. LONDON: BATON WICKS, 2002. 352 PAGES, HARDCOVER. £ 20.00.

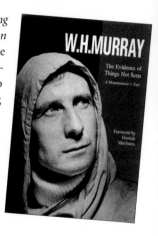

In 1947, W.H. Murray created an instant classic with his *Mountaineering in Scotland*. Four years later, he published *The Scottish Himalayan Expedition*, which remains one of the more prized books of the expedition genre. Initially, as one reads the expected British understatement and erudite observations, it would be tempting to conclude—particularly if you haven't studied Murray's wry writing or frosted-over routes—that he was another gentlemanly author from the shoulder-belaying, tweed-jacketed, and siege-styled slogs era. Yet Murray wore nylon cagoules, shortened his ice ax, and deplored large expeditions. His whimsical self-deprecation inspired and defined a whole generation of understated, sandbagging British hardmen. Then Murray came into a league all of his own by writing about soaring birds, the beauty of forests, and through unsentimental and subtly turned prose, the transformation that climbing made upon his soul.

No surprise that his recent autobiography, *The Evidence of Things Not Seen*, has won awards, right? After all, the central flaw of climbing autobiographies is that their authors are unable or unwilling to show how climbing has influenced the rest of their lives. Marriages are relegated to mere paragraphs, families—children, death of parents, and home life—are invisible behind the essential community of climbing partners, and we are often left to wonder how most climbers sew the incongruent threads of climbing into the clothing of a full life. Yet, based on The Evidence, the author succeeds in this regard.

Unlike Murray, many climbers write the so-called autobiography before midlife. The truth is that book contracts come with epic achievements crafted by authors still in their physical prime. While such books deserve a following among collectors and readers passionate about mountains, as art, the climbing autobiography remains the *enfant terrible* of the genre. Such abbreviated memoirs comprise the bulk of climbing literature, and more than a few standouts (including a few ghosted narratives) exist, but none are true autobiographies, commonly defined "as an account of a person's life." In the uncommon example of true climbing autobiographies—written when climbers become long of tooth—these memoirists earn a living through anything but writing. So by necessity the long-practiced skill of constructing a written narrative is overshadowed by career and/or climbing. Here again, Murray (author of 20 books) proves an exception.

It seems remarkable then—given the author's craftsmanship as a writer and the book's awards—that *The Evidence of Things Not Seen* is disjointed. And unless you count Murray's ironic fall, taken while fixing his roof in 1995, the disrupted narrative is not the author's fault.

The beginning of the book shows us how Murray was born into the tragedy of World War I, resulting in a national circumspection against adventure. For Murray, whose rock and ice routes would place Scotland on the map of run-out climbing, this only gave him more vertical terrain to explore.

By page 47, just as the reader has begun to piece together Murray's coming of age on the crags, a chapter from *Mountaineering in Scotland* is tacked on like an old patch on his brand new knickers. While diehard students of Murray might find this an interesting digression to the author's earlier writing style, "The Winter Ascent of Garrick's Shelf" does not fit. This chapter lacks his keen descriptions of companions, or the context of how this climb impacted his life, and the book loses narrative drive as if his otherwise capable editor (Ken Wilson, formerly of *Mountain* Magazine) had mistakenly sewn the knickers' legs shut with a patch job.

Ten pages later, the narrative recovers when Murray reluctantly enters World War II. Some scenes in Africa and the various prison camps are terribly understated—as if Murray could not fully probe these painful memories or visit some injustice on his dead companions. For instance, his platoon is machine-gunned down in front of him, while he makes a miraculous escape, but he never speaks of or any personal feelings for the men or a sense of loss. While it's easy to imagine most new millennial journalists expanding this 100-page "Fortunes of War" into a major opus of its own, Murray seems to have been gathering himself for a greater literary mission.

There's no question that he was crafting something apart from the aforementioned faulty climbing autobiography. Through his initial forebodings about war, his capture, and his internment in prisoner of war camps, *The Evidence* shows how climbing gave Murray hope and a reason to live. Through these page turning and concisely written war days, we learn of how the author spent two years finding a narrative voice while scribing *Mountaineering in Scotland* on stiffened toilet paper—wryly describing how he substituted the Red Cross volumes of Shakespeare, written on much softer paper. The Gestapo eventually found the manuscript hidden in his overcoat, interrogated Murray, then destroyed the manuscript, believing that the Scottish officer's carefully worded work about mountains had to be coded intelligence information. Over the next two years of imprisonment, Murray describes how he forced himself to rewrite the book.

The autobiography is not diminished by war's end. Murray returns to climbing and rediscovers his center—one of the most joyful and carefully delineated pieces of climbing prose ever written. A fall in the Alps kills one of his partners and fractures Murray's skull. In all of these anecdotes, the author drops in the bons mots of his carefully observed life, about how accidents are caused and the fallacy of mountains "building character" and what women give to men—conclusions that only a wise, mature man could embark upon. As if this isn't enough, his descriptions of family, home, and career illuminate a world that most climbing autobiographers have steadfastly neglected.

Here at mid autobiography, six chapters are again stitched in, this time from *The Scottish Himalayan Expedition*, along with several disparate essays that feel more like unpublished magazine articles: the pratfalls of a writing career and how Hollywood stole his biographical book about Rob Roy, a recounting of his conservation work, and chapters about more provincial Scottish climbers and places that are scarcely placed in the greater context of his life. So the promise of what Murray was up to with this beautifully initiated autobiography ended when his wife, on that roofing day in 1995, "heard a slither and a fall and found him on rocks at the edge of the loch. Not being in the habit of falling he was more concerned about this aberration than about his injuries."

There are brief passages in the latter part of the book when his narrative voice returns with full insightfulness. He wrote (obviously from old age): "The expeditions to Garwhal, Almora and Everest had convinced me that the richest Himalayan experience comes in exploratory travel and climbing, not in the siege of a big peak."

Taken as an incomplete and posthumously compiled autobiography, *The Evidence of Things Not Seen* may be without peer. Or at least less stitched together than Tom Patey's delightful *One Man's Mountains*. If a publisher in North America chooses to market this book (hopefully with a less garishly retrograde dust jacket than British publishers seem so fond of), more than a few readers will be drawn to Murray's out of print classics, deserving the anthology treatment given to that of Shipton and Tilman. Despite *The Evidence's* disjointedness, at the height of Murray's narrative powers, we see that climbing is not a thing apart, but a tapestry on which to weave a whole life.

JONATHAN WATERMAN, *AAC*

Fatal Mountaineer: The High-Altitude Life and Death of Willi Unsoeld, American Himalayan Legend. ROBERT ROPER. NEW YORK: ST. MARTINS PRESS, 2002. 306 PAGES. HARDCOVER. $25.95.

I will begin this review with a disclaimer. As far as I can remember, I never met Willi Unsoeld. Our paths might have crossed in 1967, when I went to Nepal as a correspondent for *The New Yorker*, and Unsoeld was finishing what appears to have been a not particularly successful interlude as the director of the Peace Corps there. I have also, as far as I know, never met any of the other principals in the book such as John Roskelly, Peter Lev, Lou Reichardt, and the rest. I feel obliged to say this, because this book has raised hackles among the True Believers—the Unsoelders. After reading it, I can understand why, but this may not make the portrait any less valid. Let a thousand blossoms bloom.

On the other hand, I can give my own views, including some that are purely literary. Let me start off with two. Mr. Roper belongs to the school of mountain writing that calls a turd a turd. In his account, no bowel movement goes unreported. There is no point in trying to contrast this with the writings of people like Eric Shipton or H.W. Tilman who, in 1934, were the first people to approach Nanda Devi—the mountain in the Indian Garhwal that is also a vivid character in the book. (In the name of full disclosure, I was able to study this remarkable peak from the Tibetan plateau. It is magnificent.) Reading Shipton and Tilman one would get the impression that neither of them had an intestinal tract. Shipton once told me that it was on this trip that he suggested that he and Tilman address each other by their first names—"Bill" and "Eric." Tilman agreed, adding, "But it sounds so silly!" That era is gone. There is, however, a middle ground between discretion and diarrhea.

My second literary criticism concerns Mr. Roper's dreadful habit of interrupting the narrative with pointless asides about people like Hemingway or Melville. The worst is a multi-page divagation on John Muir just at the place where he is about to describe the death of Unsoeld's daughter "Nanda Devi." It is tedious beyond belief. A firmer hand on the editorial tiller was called for.

These things aside, I think that this is a very good book. Once you start it, you will have difficulty putting it down.

As I was reading it, I kept asking myself if, had I met him, would I have liked Unsoeld and vice versa? I decided that the answer was "no." He seems to have been—this is from the book— a superannuated scoutmaster with a metaphysical carapace. Roper informs us that Unsoeld used to wake up his clients at the crack of dawn in the Tetons with a rousing rendition on the harmonica of the "Colonel Bogey March." I much preferred hearing Chamonix guides saying, under the same circumstances, "Levez vous, tas des cons!" On the metaphysics, Unsoeld was a lifelong admirer of the French obscurantist Henri Bergson on whom he wrote a thesis at the University of Washington. I have a particular animosity towards Bergson since, as an undergraduate, I had a summer job of deconstructing his views on Einstein's theory of relativity. I came to the conclusion that Bergson understood nothing, which did not stop him from writing interminably. That he won the Nobel Prize for literature in 1927, when both Proust and Joyce were overlooked, boggles the mind, as does Unsoeld's being able to extract meaning from any of this. Roper tries to explain, but it reads like a dying man grasping for breath.

Unsoeld emerges as a very intelligent, egocentric man with a considerable core of foolishness, and of course as a great climber. The book is basically an account of the 1976 expedition to climb Nanda Devi. This misbegotten adventure has been written to death and, of course, its climax was the death of Nanda Devi—a death that seems to me to have been preventable. She was clearly very ill and she should have been told in no uncertain terms to go down. Unsoeld's response when Roskelly told him that Devi had to descend—"What's a father to do?"—seems to me to have a straightforward response: Save the life of his child. We all know that this has to be done sometimes by brute force and that is what should have been applied. Both of them seem to have been caught up in some sort of spiritual nexus that is often the stuff of tragedy. Unsoeld's apparent reaction to this—to become a smiling public man for whom Devi's death became part of a lecture performance—seems to me to border on the inhuman. I think Roper disentangles this lucidly. Very likely the Unsoelders have a different take on this and I am sure they will tell us.

They may also have a different take on Unsoeld's last climb in March of 1979, on Mt. Rainier. The personnel on the Nanda Devi expedition were at least seasoned professionals— some of the best climbers in the world. The people on this ill-fated climb were in most cases beginners. The conditions were so bad that Yvon Chouinard was leaving the mountain because of his perception of the avalanche dangers. This did not stop Unsoeld. Nor did the potentially bad weather. The whole thing seems to me like sheer irresponsibility—almost suicidal. In France, where guides are sanctioned by the government, this sort of performance would have led to a trial and a probable jail sentence. As it was, it led to Unsoeld's death in avalanche along with that of a young woman whom he was guiding. That anyone survived was something of a miracle. Perhaps now you will see why I don't think I would have liked Unsoeld. He was a great mountain climber but a terribly flawed man.

JEREMY BERNSTEIN, *AAC*

Detectives on Everest: The 2001 Mallory & Irvine Research Expedition. Jochen Hemmleb with Eric Simonson. Seattle: The Mountaineers Books, 2002. 208 pages, 70 black-and-white and 13 full color photos; 3 maps, 2 appendices, bibliography, and index. Paperback. $19.95

The Second Death of George Mallory: The Enigma and Spirit of Mount Everest. Reinhold Messner. Tim Carruthers, translator. New York: St. Martin's Griffin, 2002. (Originally published in 2000 as Mallory's Zweiter Tod: Das Everest-Rätsel und die Antwort by BLV Verlagsgesellschaft mbH, Germany.) 205 pages, 37 black-and-white photos, 2 drawings, 1 map, notes, bibliography, and index. Paperback. $13.95.

Detectives on Everest is a sequel to *Ghosts of Everest,* the expedition account of the 1999 discovery of George Mallory's remains. (*Ghosts* was reviewed in AAJ 2000, pp. 403-404.) The 1999 team, largely intact and with deeper appreciation of mountaineering's grandest mystery, returned in 2001 to see what else it could find. This book, bountifully illustrated in the style of its predecessor (though in black and white), reports on the expedition's activities and examines the puzzle's remaining pieces. It also consolidates knowledge of climbing on Everest's north side in a valuable chronology and a particularly useful array of photographic and cartographic route maps. For any enthusiast of the subject, these and the bibliography will fully justify the price of the book.

Unlike 1999, there were no headlines in the spring of 2001. So is there anything new and significant to be learned here? Yes, there is, and some of it is quite surprising. This is largely because of Jochen Hemmleb, and his approach to the task. Over the years others have studied the Mallory/Irvine mystery closely, but none of them have gone about it like Jochen Hemmleb.

Hemmleb's tools and methods have come to include anything he figures could shed light—even the tiniest glimmer—on the mystery. Take, for example, his keen interest in refuse heaps. Among the discarded supplies of past high camps there might be…what? He doesn't know, but he wants to have a look at anything and everything that can be retrieved. His enthusiasm for this kind of sleuthing seems to be infectious. Even the expedition's climbers, who have to do the digging, are more than willing to chip away in frozen debris at 27,000 feet. This has a nostalgic interest of its own, as when a tin of well-preserved 1933 biscuits is found (and sampled), or when one of Norton's socks from 1924 is discovered. The yield of this scavenging has been skillfully art-directed into the book so that readers can view the relics too.

Hemmleb's use of history turns out to be more productive than the high-altitude archaeology. He looks beyond 1924 to *all* expeditions climbing via the North Col/North Ridge/Northeast Ridge, and probes for new information. We know that Irvine's ice axe was discovered by Percy Wyn-Harris on the Northeast Ridge in 1933; and that in 1979, the day before he was lost in an avalanche, Wang Hongbao told the tantalizing story of seeing an "English dead" in 1975 near Chinese Camp VI. Hemmleb wants to find out what else *may have been noticed, but not recorded,* by post-1924 climbers. This is where the investigation becomes especially fascinating. As a matter of fact, it takes Hemmleb and expedition leader Eric Simonson on a special trip to China for meetings with members of the People's Republic Everest teams of 1960 and 1975.

From the visit to China we learn that the 1999 American team was not the first to discover Mallory's body. It was the Chinese in 1975: Wang Hongbao's "English dead," lately presumed to be Irvine, must have been George Mallory. That is because—and this is *Detectives'* really big news—northeast of Mallory's resting place in a gully some 150 meters higher is another body, which could only be Sandy Irvine's. Xu Jing, deputy leader of the 1960 Chinese expedition, told Hemmleb and Simonson that he found the corpse lying face up, arms at its sides, wrapped in what he thought was a sleeping bag. As the revelation sinks in and one begins to imagine grim pictures of what may have been a bivouac, the book ends. But with the prospect of locating Irvine's body—and camera—now beckoning more insistently than ever, we may assume the story is not over.

When it comes to the enduring question of whether Everest was climbed in 1924, those who care about it seem to divide into Realists, Optimists, and Believers. Realists offer a variety of sensible reasons why Mallory and Irvine could not have made the top. Optimists point to circumstances that would have made it possible. Believers feel intuitively that the deed was done. Neither success nor failure can yet be proved. Jochen Hemmleb is definitely an Optimist, and he may be a Believer. He is also a young man. Given his methods, his tenacity, his zeal, and time, one must allow that some day he might make believers of us all.

Reinhold Messner thinks the post-1999 Mallory/Irvine industry misses the point. In *The Second Death of George Mallory*, he laments that modern climbing has lost the spirit that animated George Mallory. It has lost the spirit of amateurism, the willingness to pursue the goal with one's whole being "because it is there." Like the 1924 accident, this loss is tragic; Messner thinks of it as Mallory's "second death." And though he does not believe Mallory and Irvine reached the top, it doesn't diminish his esteem for what they did: he says their climb "overshadows all subsequent mountaineering achievements, my own included."

This remarkable salute, from the greatest Himalayan climber of the 20th century, comes early in the book. What follows is an evocation of the spirit Messner so admires, developed via an interweaving of Everest history and a selection of Mallory's own words—plus something else, which is bound to raise eyebrows.

"I felt Mallory's presence during my solo ascent of the north-face route," he writes. "Sometimes, when looking at photographs from his era, I can hear his voice. I know of course that it is my own. Yet I believe that only by trying to see events through Mallory's eyes can we truly rediscover him." Messner then explains that he has *imagined* what Mallory *might have thought* about various things and has introduced these conceptions into the book. Here they take on the voice of George Mallory. So reader beware: in *Second Death*, Mallory's actual words are in Roman type, indented; Reinhold Messner's ideas of what George Mallory would think or have thought are in italics, also indented. This visual cue is not announced in the text. For example:

…I was ready. I can still remember how my mind skimmed over the various preparations and told itself that everything was in good order, just like God after the creation.

…I do not want to make myself seem as ridiculous as my countrymen Haston and Scott who in 1975 took photographs of the aluminum tripod left by the Chinese on the summit, to convince the many critics at home that the Chinese had indeed got there before them.

…Perhaps if they searched their hearts, they might see that they do not really want to know *everything. Some things should remain untouched and unmeasured. There is no further reason to disturb me, Simonson says. But still I wonder, will they truly leave me in peace?*

More than 50 such examples occur in *Second Death*, along with 62 genuine quotations from George Mallory. It will not take a Mallory scholar to see that these represent two very different people. However, for the sake of clarity and the written record, it would have been better if Reinhold Messner had given us his own ideas straight and let George Mallory speak for himself.

Note to readers: Several discrepancies in facts will be noticed between *Second Death* and *Detectives*. Where these occur, I found that Hemmleb's version is the more careful, and in some cases has the advantage of newer information.

STEVE HUTCHINS, *AAC*

Tigers of the Snow: How One Fateful Climb Made the Sherpas Mountaineering Legends. JONATHAN NEALE. NEW YORK: ST. MARTIN'S PRESS. 2002. 336 PAGES. HARDCOVER. $26.95.

Through the lens of the repeated German attempts on Nanga Parbat between 1932 and 1953, as well as some of the early Everest expeditions, Jonathan Neale scrutinizes what can only be called the character of both Sherpas and sahibs. He provides sensitive portraits of individual Sherpas, as well as an intimate look at Sherpas' attitudes toward and experience of their work in Himalayan mountaineering. Neale clearly has enormous respect and affection for Sherpas, and the point of the book is to give them as much credit as possible for all they have done in this historic enterprise. At the same time the book is equally revealing of the Western mountaineers; Neale provides some very insightful takes on sahibs at their best and worst.

Several things contribute to the strength of *Tigers of the Snow*. First and foremost, Neale spent long periods of time in both Darjeeling (in Himalayan India) and Khumbu (the Sherpas' home region in Nepal). He made an effort to learn the Sherpa language (a dialect of Tibetan) and to get a feel for Sherpa society and culture. While the book does not add anything new to our understanding of that society and culture (nor was it meant to do so), this background work clearly helped Neale with his main objective, which was interviewing older climbing Sherpas.

The most important of these interviews were with Ang Tsering Sherpa, one of the survivors of the 1934 Nanga Parbat expedition, who was about 95 or 96 years old at the time of the interviews in 2000. Neale also interviewed about 20 other retired climbing Sherpas and sirdars, as well as in some cases their wives or widows. He was able to get people to open up to an unusual degree about their feelings with respect to climbing—the danger, the money, the sahibs. He also learned certain hitherto unknown details of Sherpa experience on the early expeditions, and especially on the 1934 Nanga Parbat expedition which is his main focus.

The other major strength of the book derives from Neale's critical perspectives on the sahibs. In the first place he has, refreshingly, no qualms whatsoever about assigning blame for accidents to specific sahibs and their bad decisions. For example, "Mallory's ambition had led to errors of judgment that killed Lhakpa, Nurbu, Pasang, Pema, Sanga, Dorje, Pemba, Shamsherpun, Man Bahadur, Sandy Irvine, and Mallory himself" (p. 57). Or: "Ten people died on Nanga Parbat in 1934 because Willy Merkl led too many men up too quickly" (p. 122). Most strikingly, Neale gives a no-holds-barred account of two of the strongest sahibs on the 1934 expedition, Erwin Schneider and Peter Aschenbrenner, abandoning several colleagues and Sherpas high on the mountain and then, because the three struggling Sherpas they were with were slowing them down, putting on their skis and skiing away from them to safety. Two of those Sherpas subsequently died on the way down.

In addition, Neale offers some interesting interpretations for why sahibs made these kinds of bad and fatal decisions. For example, he writes of the pressures Willy Merkl felt to deliver a victory to the Nazi government in Germany that was funding the expedition. He brings up as well Merkl's class background: "Most German climbers in the Himalayas, like most British and American ones, were business or professional men from comfortable homes. Merkl was not of this class"—he was raised by a single mother, went to a state technical high school rather than the more prestigious gymnasium, served in the army as a private—and, Neale suggests, felt the pressure to prove his worth (p. 93-94).

This theme of the significance of social class in understanding the sahibs' actions is illuminating throughout the book. In discussing the early Everest expeditions, Neale sees the arrogance of the sahibs largely in terms of their upper class backgrounds. Speculating about why the inexperienced Sandy Irvine was chosen to go with Mallory to the summit, Neale writes, "It was a sign of the amateurism of the British climbing world, and their class confidence, that a chap could make it to the highest camp on Everest on the word of other Oxford men who found him a useful fellow" (p. 56). In a later chapter Neale discusses the impact on the Sherpas of the French and Swiss expeditions in the early '50s. The Swiss in particular were extremely egalitarian, which made an enormously positive impression on the Sherpas, who loathed the requirements of servility vis-à-vis sahibs but of course could do nothing about them. Neale points out that virtually all of the Swiss on the Everest expeditions, and most of the French on the Annapurna expedition, were Alpine guides of peasant origins not that far in the past, and thus not all that different from the Sherpas themselves. Some Sherpas had in fact recognized this: "I asked Khansa of Namche who was the best foreigner he ever climbed with. Lionel Terray, he said ... I said that Terray was a guide, and that the grandfathers of the guides had been farmers like the Sherpas when the climbers first came. Khansa said all the Sherpas knew that, and they loved that the French had learned from their ancestors how to carry weight on the head strap" (p. 245).

Neale also relates Edmund Hillary's greatness as both a climber and a human being to his working class background: "A man of Hillary's class would not have been on a prewar expedition…Hillary worked for his father in the family beekeeping business, making a living with his muscles. He was tall, big, strong, a superb climber, deeply egalitarian, and an utterly decent man" (p. 270). Neale even has a class analysis of why the British succeeded on Everest in 1953: "After 1945, working people all over Western Europe had far more dignity and respect. Without that, Hunt would not have been able to take Hillary. Without Indian independence, and without the Swiss, he would not have been able to imagine making Tenzing a member" (272).

The weaknesses of the book revolve around its main claim, as represented in the subtitle: "How one fateful climb made the Sherpas mountaineering legend." Neale never makes a persuasive case that the 1934 Nanga Parbat expedition was in fact decisive in making the Sherpas "mountaineering legends." On the contrary, in the year before that expedition, in 1933, the British on Everest were struck with the strides the Sherpas had made since the 1920's expeditions, how much tougher and more fearless and more professionalized they had become. Something had already been happening in that decade between the early '20s and the early '30s to bring about these changes in Sherpa attitudes toward their work. My own inclination would be to look for the sources of those changes within the Sherpa community itself, perhaps in the ways in which older climbing Sherpas were passing on accounts of the '20s expeditions to their sons and other young men. But we do not really have this information.

The second major problem with the book relates to the first. Because Neale wants the 1934 Nanga Parbat expedition to carry so much weight in his account, and because all the Sherpas except Ang Tsering who had been on the expedition had either died during the climb or since, Neale simply does not have enough information to make a case for what happened on the mountain at many key points in the story. Thus he resorts to fictionalizing the thoughts and words of deceased Sherpas and sahibs who can no longer speak for themselves, most notably the thoughts and words of Willy Merkl and Gaylay during their dying hours.

Initially I found myself swept along by the fictional sections, in part because—probably like Neale himself—I wanted an unbroken and compelling narrative of what happened. But this is really not satisfactory, and I had a sort of queasy feeling afterward about the liberties Neale took with the writing in these sections.

But the book has many virtues, as I tried to indicate earlier. Thus despite these reservations I would certainly recommend this work to anyone interested in getting a much more intimate perspective on Himalayan mountaineering history, itself part of a larger and longer unfolding history of the encounter of "East" and "West."

SHERRY B. ORTNER

On High; The Adventures of Legendary Mountaineer, Photographer, and Scientist Brad Washburn. BRAD WASHBURN, WITH DONALD SMITH. THE NATIONAL GEOGRAPHIC SOCIETY, 2002. 100 PHOTOS, 240 PAGES. HARDCOVER. $40.00.

Ask Brad Washburn to sign a copy of *Among the Alps With Bradford*, the first mountaineering book he ever wrote, and you'll get more than an autograph. Washburn likes to doodle in the current year, sometimes underlined, sometimes accented with an exclamation point. I suspect he takes great pleasure in seeing today's date alongside the book's original copyright. Washburn wrote *Among the Alps* on the heels of an extraordinarily successful summer when he ticked a number of classic and coveted alpine summits including Mont Blanc, the Matterhorn, and the Grepon. In Washburn's case, however, it was all the more remarkable because he was only sixteen years old. The book was published the following year, in 1927.

Nearly 80 years later, Washburn has many more extraordinary climbs—most notably in Alaska—and a host of other books to his credit. Along the way, he and his wife Barbara have almost single-handedly built one of the world's great science museums, he's become a legend of mountain mapping and photography, and—perhaps most impressive of all—Brad and Barbara recently celebrated their sixty-third wedding anniversary. Despite Washburn's mountain of published work, *On High: The Adventures of Legendary Mountaineer, Photographer, and Scientist Brad Washburn* is the first title that attempts to put everything into context by telling the complete story of his life. As the lengthy title implies, this is an autobiography (though it reads like a biography) with many facets.

Perhaps this is why it has taken so long to get to print: Bradford Washburn is a tough character to boil down.

Washburn's early years read like scenes from a turn-of-the-previous-century New England novel: born into a loving, intellectual family, his childhood evokes idyllic images of ivy covered prep schools and rough-and-tumble summers in the rugged lake country of New Hampshire. Washburn is barely a teenager when he climbs his first mountain, writes his first book (a hiking guide to the Presidential Range), and takes his first photographs. After that it is an almost inevitable progression: his early successes with mountain adventuring and writing lead to lecturing, which generates the means and necessity for more ambitious expeditions (Alaska and the Yukon) during which Washburn's burgeoning talent for photography creates even greater opportunity for perpetuating this lifestyle.

And then Washburn makes a turn that may have modern alpine tigers scratching their heads: he marries and takes a full time job that he will work until retirement. And yet this is hardly the end. Barbara Polk Washburn is the kind of spouse every mountaineer—male or female—dreams of finding: smart, supportive, and a spirited adventurer in her own right (just three months after their wedding the couple tops Mt. Bertha in Alaska). Similarly, Washburn's new job resurrecting Boston's antiquated Museum of Science is no ball and chain. On the contrary, his museum directorship brings lasting challenge and meaning to Washburn's life (as well as opportunity for further expeditions—including his pioneering trips to Mt. McKinley, which Barbara is the first woman to summit). In fact, science and photography provide the vital path for Washburn to segue into middle age and beyond and still maintain a strong and productive connection to the mountains and the world climbing community. We should all be blessed with such luck—or, in Washburn's case, foresight.

Even Washburn aficionados familiar with his history will mine gems in *On High*. Tucked in among the well-known events and characters are a few unexpected surprises: the delightful early climbing partnership between Brad and his younger brother Sherwood "Sherry" Washburn is particularly poignant, as is the description of Brad and Barbara's first night together (in separate bunks on a railroad sleeping car!). There's even a fascinating connection between Brad and the doomed aviatrix Amelia Earhart.

If this book has a shortcoming, it is the brevity of the presentation. The publishers have clearly aimed for mass appeal—it is a classy, visually strong volume filled with impressive photos, magazine-like sidebars, and easily digested chapters. But I often found myself wishing for more—in particular, more of the stuff not already chronicled in Washburn's other books: more about the museum years, more details concerning the lives of peripheral characters and relationships (what ever happened to brother Sherry?), and more about the motivation for the zeal with which Washburn has devoted himself to debunking the mountaineering claims of Frederick Cook. And yet, in this book, it's all been so skillfully reduced—like a fine cream sauce—into such a delicious and satisfying product, that whining about the size of the portions seems an ungrateful and piggy complaint. Until the day when a truly definitive and comprehensive Washburn biography is written (as it certainly will be), *On High* can stand proudly as "the Washburn book we've all been waiting for," and provide a worthy testament to this extraordinary life.

DAVID PAGEL, *AAC*

Escape from Lucania: An Epic Story of Survival. DAVID ROBERTS. NEW YORK: SIMON & SCHUSTER, 2002. 206 PAGES. $23.00.

This is the full story of Bob Bates and Brad Washburn's first ascent of the St. Elias Range giant, Mt. Lucania, in 1937, at the time the highest unclimbed peak in North America at 17,150 feet. The ascent of Lucania is, as often, a small part of the story. The larger story is their utter isolation and necessary self-sufficiency in unknown territory. Upon dropping the men off on the glacier, bush pilot Bob Reeve found difficult snow and was just barely able to get his plane off the ground again. Thus Reeve was unable to fly in their other two partners, and even more crucial, unable to return after the climbing to pick up Bates and Washburn. They were on their own. On the way out they manage to knock off the second ascent of Mt. Steele (16,644'), but mainly they manage to find their way over 100 miles of mostly glaciated terrain and cross en route a raging Donjek River.

Throughout the book Roberts lets Bates and Washburn speak in their own voices: the trip moves forward in time but mostly without the overt use of hindsight. All three of them have tried to recreate what Bates and Washburn were thinking at the time of the climb. This strategy works well and Roberts intrudes gently with present day observations in parenthetical statements throughout, little asides from the present.

As anyone who is paying attention knows, David Roberts has a great sense of story, both what raw materials make a great story and how to tell it. In this case the story is so great a lesser writer may have succeeded in the telling. But Roberts brings a lot to the table here, most notably a 40-year mentor-protégé relationship with Washburn and a long personal resumé of climbing trips to Alaska. Though these are not the subject here, Roberts' presence in the book in the prologue and epilogue are terrific because they allow him to show Bates and Washburn in the present. In a way, their triumph on Lucania in 1937 was only the beginning—not only of their illustrious climbing careers, but of their lives as generous, graceful, and vibrant persons. Also, the reader realizes that Roberts is in a position similar to the reader: we admire these guys and wonder how we would measure up in similar circumstances.

In the prologue Roberts writes: "I felt it my duty, as I set to work on the Lucania story to dig beneath the surface of the interpersonal, to find out just what quarrels and tensions and unspoken doubts must have laced Brad and Bob's experience…."

If you know Roberts' work, you know that this is often his strategy: he wants the truth, warts and all, if they appear. He's one of the only writers I know whose work is criticized for not hiding the truth, as he sees it. His happy conclusion here is:

"In the end, however, I discovered something else: that as far as I could tell, Brad and Bob belonged o a different subspecies of human beings from myself and all the fellows my age I had climbed with." It's a very pleasing conclusion: the men you thought were gods are revealed, indeed to be gods. One of the great pleasures of reading this book is the reader's awareness that Bates and Washburn were able to collaborate extensively with Roberts, helping to get it right, and moreover that they're around to see their achievement recognized as one of the great North American mountaineering tales, as it surely is.

DAVID STEVENSON, *AAC*

The Horizontal Everest: Extreme Journeys on Ellesmere Island. JERRY KOBALENKO, NEW YORK: SOHO PRESS. 2002. 352 PAGES. PAPERBACK. $15.00.

The Horizontal Everest shows that a consummate adventurer can also aspire to illuminated historical writing. Jerry Kobalenko, a talented storyteller, is no stranger to epic sufferfests, breaking over 4,000 miles of trail on Ellesmere Island while retracing the routes of explorers or famous Mounties.

Three caveats: 1) Don't be led astray by the title of the book. Whatever marketing chutzpah or lack of poetry are created by The Horizontal Everest: Extreme Journeys on Ellesmere Island, the title works once you pick up the author's tongue-in-cheek-glance askance at the world's highest mountain.

2) The cover photograph has an unusual, almost familiar beauty that often speaks of high art—but it was inspired by a more famous photograph. Some readers will recognize the mimicry of the author jumping ice floes with Jim Brandenburg's famous 1991 photograph, from the cover of his book, White Wolf: showing that animal jumping ice floes alongside Ellesmere Island. Kobalenko even briefly introduces the reader to that wolf photographer within *Horizontal Everest*. But once you get to know Kobalenko, whose wry personality fills his book, you can imagine him chuckling in his sled's slipstream about his spoofed photo, which shows that the book is about the human—rather than the wolf—stories of Ellesmere Island. Although he has underwritten his trips to Canada's northern-most island by exposing the carefully posed photographs that appear in the book's color insert, to my eye, this adventurer's writing is his real talent. And isn't it true that most artists stand on the shoulders of giants?

3) This is an Arctic exploration rather than a climbing book. Many alpinists will agree with the author's statement that pulling a sled for weeks on end takes a different sort of athleticism than a several day push in the mountains. Historians within the 101-year-old American Alpine Club will remind us that the early membership cut their teeth in Arctic exploration, through some of the very epics that Kobalenko describes in his alluring narrative. The equipment we now accept as de rigueur, or derived from Europe's Golden Age alpinists—crampons, snow goggles, igloos, or snowshoes—actually came from the Inuit dwellers of the Arctic. The techniques and food and sponsorship campaigns of modern climbing were also refined from 19th century polar expeditions.

Even if you'll never pull a sled in the Arctic, Kobalenko's self-deprecating narrative has a way of pulling you along for a ride. Rather than focusing upon his considerable Ellesmere Island journeys, his experiences are merely jumping off points for rich tales about other northern adventurers. In what outwardly appears to be an expedition book, there is a refreshing lack of chronologically structured itinerary or first person narrative. He has an ability to cut through the macro-history hyperbole that less experienced Arctic adventurers create whole books out of, and by using his skeptical investigative eye, Kobalenko paints one of the most convincing and entertainintg portraits of northern exploration that I've ever read.

In compressed chapters, he candidly shows the reader his troubles with partners lacking motivation, unveils his polar bear encounters with refreshing and respectful candor, recounts the techniques and over-the-top sponsorships involved in North Pole expeditions (started by the lying Cook and the racist Peary), follows Krüger's disappearing trail across Ellesmere, lionizes Hattersley-Smith and the Inuit, and deftly analyzes other forgotten players of Arctic exploration. This is original ground here, and all the more stimulating because Kobalenko is no stranger to adventure.

However, the author mentions but does not properly credit the Reinhold Messner of polar travel, Børge Ousland. Kobalenko also strangely avoids using the kites that are revolutionizing sled travel in Polar regions, but his miles logged behind the sled harness against the wind probably gives him more empathy for the explorers he's following. And while the Selected Reading appendix leaves out several Arctic gems related to his stories, he lists more than a few books that could be arcane classics.

Without equivocation, Kobalenko's book deserves to be read because of its playful, yet compulsive curiosity about a landscape inhabited with rabbit herds and sailor ghosts. Through subtle turn of phrase and seamless transitions, he transports the reader to old explorers' homes, dusty Arctic museums, and back to the radiant island. "I needed the wild landscape under my feet," he writes in the beginning of the book from an icebreaker. While others "stalked about the ship with the all-consumed air of those for whom every second has meaning, I gazed through binoculars at the distant coast of Ellesmere and recalled the many times its extremes had gripped me with similar magnificent obsession."

JONATHAN WATERMAN, *AAC*

Extreme Landscape: The Lure of Mountain Spaces. EDITED BY BERNADETTE MCDONALD. NATIONAL GEOGRAPHIC PRESS. 2002. 320 PAGES. PAPERBACK. $16.00.

Anthologies are like families. You never know how the essays, all bound as one, will go. *Extreme Landscape* is a surprisingly strong collection. The subtitle of the book contains the words "mountain spaces," but the collection is a lot broader than that, encompassing everything from urban architecture to the Internet. Like most families, if you look hard enough you might discern the common threads that tie this family of essays together: spiritual quests, stories, community, and projects for the planet.

Toward the end of the last century the United Nations declared 2002 the International Year of Mountains. The Banff Centre for Mountain Culture held a summit, "Extreme Landscape: Challenge and Celebration." This book is the result of that gathering.

With climbers like Dermot Somers, Reinhold Messner, Ed Douglas, Rick Ridgeway, and Yvon Chouinard included you might expect a "we climbed—we conquered—we came back" kind of thing. Happily, there isn't a trace of that approach. To be precise, th—s is a book of ideas. And, as the ideas take hold, it becomes something more. Start with the introduction by the lyric Earth Mother of the West, Terry Tempest Williams. Mountains are inspiration and revelation. Tempest Williams insists that "we are in transition from a non-sustainable world to a sustainable one." We must honor the wild or we stand to lose it.

Beginning with Gretel Ehrlich's love story about Greenland, the book contains an overriding sense of spiritualism. The beauty of this bleak northland arrives when "the darkness came, and the ice under us became the source of light, a kind of subterranean moon." The ice is transformed into a moon in a selfless act of hope. Similarly, Ed Douglas finds a way to keep his father's spirit alive in the River Don. George B. Schaller recognizes that sacred lands exist and he makes connections between mountaineers and pilgrims. Aren't they on a similar quest? Schaller warns that "to ignore the sacred, to violate the dignity of local people, is to degrade the ethical values of a culture and diminish it." Wade Davis visits several cultures on his way to discussing Australian Aborigines' Songlines and Dreamtime. Davis explains that "should the ritual stop, the voices fall silent, all would be lost—everything on Earth is held together by Songlines, everything is subordinate to the Dreaming, which is constant but ever changing." Edwin Bernbaum argues for the sublime rather than the "extreme," referring to Buddhism, the Bible, Chinese poet Li Po, Basho, Rousseau, Goethe, Yeats, Shelley, Hemingway, and Cézanne, among others, to explain the process of attaining a sublime wisdom and transformation through the mountains. This is, in essence, what it is to be "sage." Bernard Amy writes of how the climber's quest for the vertical is both sacred and profane. It estranges the individual from the world that calls for the kind of insight that great height provides.

In "Ancient Stories, New Technologies," Chris Rainier states that "what we have lost in the West is the relevance of telling stories to our everyday lives." Rainier interestingly argues that the Internet helps expand our sense of community. A northern Cambodian village sells its arts and crafts online as do Peru's Quechua Indians. Jim Thorsell cites examples of 13 international parks to push the idea of trans-border biosphere reserves. He reminds us of Thoreau's edict about preserving the wild. Similarly, Reinhold Messner calls for an understanding of mountain ecosystems and biodiversity. This brings us back to Davis' point that we need to embrace "metaphor as we attempt to understand traditional relationships to land, history, community, and the spirit realm." There is a point mid-way through reading this collection when it seems as if each essay takes the reader in a different direction.

Then Rick Ridgeway, Barry Lopez, and Yvon Chouinard deliver the book's message with a final vision of how these spiritual quests, the stories and a sense of community connect to enact projects that sustain the planet. At one point Chouinard tells Tompkins and Ridgeway that saving Patagonia "'might be the most important thing any of us could do.... (It) makes going on these adventures seem like bullshit.'" Correspondingly, Barry Lopez argues that the human community needs to be redefined so we can merge nature "with our own nature." Chouinard tells a personal tale that turns public when Patagonia, the company, is incorporated. He talks about the illusion of sustainability, of Patagonia Inc.'s self-imposed tax for using up nonrenewable resources, and of the one-percent-for-the planet alliance. Chouinard leaves the reader with a sense of corporate redemption so vast and honorable that it makes one want to do more than just climb mountains. Read this book, and then act decisively.

DAVE BEAN

Wizards of Rock: A History of Free Climbing in America. PAT AMENT. BERKELEY: WILDERNESS
PRESS, 2002. 381 PAGES. PAPERBACK. $24.95.

Pat Ament has always been an artist, whether he is focusing on chess,
music, the martial arts, writing, or climbing. I remember a number
of years back I invited him to speak at Weber State University in
Ogden, Utah. During his stay, he taught my rock climbing class,
presented an illustrated lecture to an art class, gave a poetry reading
for the English Department, and did a public multimedia presentation, as well as knocking off several hard rock routes in Ogden
Canyon. In each setting Ament demonstrated complete confidence, the same confidence that is reflected in his life as an artist.
He founded a climbing magazine, *The Climbing Art*, that was
dedicated to climbing literature, not route descriptions. He has
tackled various literary genres in his writing, everything from
deep philosophical prose to biography, autobiography, and poetry, all of
which illustrate his confident style. He is clearly one of climbing's most prolific writers with
over 30 books to his credit.

Now Ament has turned his efforts toward history, and who better to tackle the history of
free climbing than one so steeped in it, not only as a scholar and artist, but as one who was there
pushing the standards himself.

Wizards of Rock is a historical overview of free climbing in America beginning with its
roots in early explorers like John Muir and Elkanah J. Lamb, carrying through to contemporary
climbers the likes of Tommy Caldwell, Beth Rodden, Alex Huber, and seemingly everyone in
between. Broken down in general time periods the book begins with the 1800s and gets more
and more focused as the developments in free climbing get more intense. Each period is the
story of free climbing legends, pioneers like Robert Underhill, Glen Exum, Fritz Wiessner, Tom
Frost, Royal Robbins, John Gill, Layton Kor, and Lynn Hill. The list goes on and on, as does the
list of climbs and contributions made by the aforementioned.

But what makes Ament's book even more important is his meticulous research, in which
he ferrets out lesser-known climbers who have played important roles in pushing free climbing
standards. People like Greg Lowe, Kim Miller, Beth Bennet, Barry Bates, and Jim Holloway,
to name a few. Ament is even-handed with all the personalities he features in the book, not to
mention fair in his assessment of their climbs, thus presenting a reliable history.

While *Wizards of Rock* is, in essence, an encyclopedia, the entries still reflect the skill of an
excellent storyteller. Case in point:

"Greg Lowe climbed Drop Zone, 5.11+ R, on a quartzite cliff above Ogden, Utah's east
side. This was another work of an unknown master. At every moment along the spectrum of
time, a climbing world needs a new spirit. A 'savior' is sent…. The cliffs east of Ogden were, in
the 1960s, surrealistic in their isolation, covered with ethereal orange and yellows in the setting
sun of Utah's dry light. Lowe's time was at hand…. He climbed in a clean, honest way, motivated
as much as anything by the simple desire to climb. The discovery of climbing was for him a joy,
and the style in which he implemented climbing was, undoubtedly, a natural extension of his
genius" (pp. 133-34).

Once one starts to turn its pages it's hard to stop. Pat Ament has made yet another very important contribution to the climbing canon, one that serves not only as an important reference book, but fun read as well.

MIKEL VAUSE, *AAC*

Climbing Free: My Life in the Vertical World. LYNN HILL WITH GREG CHILD. FOREWORD BY JOHN LONG. NEW YORK: W. W. NORTON, 2002. HARDCOVER. $24.95.

It has often been said that climbing can be a metaphor for life, but few books have given such thoughtful attention to the lessons each brings to the other as *Climbing Free*. Interwoven among the tales of Lynn Hill's better known accomplishments are many poignant stories of the diverse personalities, familiar and remote landscapes, and communities that influenced her growth as a climber and a person. It goes without saying that the influence went both ways.

There are plenty of anecdotes from the legendary climbs to satisfy one's taste for exciting crux moves as well, from pioneering traditional free ascents in California in the 70s; early 5.13 and 5.14 sport climbs in the East, Europe, and elsewhere; coming back from a near-fatal groundfall to championship competition climbing and sponsored travels to exotic crags in the 80s and 90s; to the untouchable free and free-in-a-day ascents of the route by which humans first climbed El Capitan, the Nose.

What sets *Climbing Free* apart are the insights into the meaning of Lynn Hill's experience. She speaks from a unique vantage point, having achieved many goals that others deemed impossible for her, or at all. Along the way, she observes the extremes of human behavior, from the most supportive to the most selfish, lifelong bonds and recurring loss of friends to the mountains, life on the road, a home abroad, working truly-odd jobs for survival during the lean years, and the different challenges of a corporate climbing team.

What shines through is the importance of maintaining a positive outlook and enjoying one's precious time playing with friends, and behaving responsibly toward the natural environment and communities upon which these moments depend.

The foreword by former Hill-boyfriend John Long is full of his characteristic warmth and humor. Greg Child has supplied the supporting material and seamless structure that have made his tales of exciting and hilarious adventures so readable. The honest voice and compassionate heart behind the book remain true to the very first drafts from many years before.

Like Lynn Hill herself, *Climbing Free* climbs free of all artificially imposed limitations. Her philosophy is best described in her own words: "No matter where I am in the world or what summit I've attained, the greatest sense of fulfillment in my life is connected to people. I am fortunate to be part of a big international family bonded by a common passion. Throughout all my experiences over the years, the sheer joy of playing on the rocks with my friends has been the underlying inspiration for my love of climbing. What started out as a simple outing on a rocky outcrop in southern California twenty-six years ago has become a vehicle for evolving as a person, learning about the world, and sharing those experiences with others."

BOB PALAIS, *AAC*

The Flame of Adventure. SIMON YATES. SEATTLE: THE MOUNTAINEERS BOOKS, 2001. 220 PAGES, WITH 8 PAGES OF COLOR PHOTOS. $16.95

What's with these Brits? They climb so well, yet drink so hard, smoke so much and hurt themselves so often you wonder how good they'd be if they ever got serious. Well, Simon Yates's book, *The Flame of Adventure*, shows that they are serious, and that the whole package— the pubs, the motorcycle wrecks, the endless cigarettes—is the point. Life is meant to be lived in a headlong tumble from hasty decision to uncertain outcome. Yates is known for his knife work in one of contemporary mountaineering's famous screw-ups (chronicled in *Touching the Void*, by Joe Simpson, 1988). This book says almost nothing about that trip with Simpson, but does give readers a fuller picture of Yates's life and, more interestingly, the life of an un-sponsored, un-wealthy, full-time climber.

There is much to like in *The Flame of Adventure*. The book tracks Yates's physical wanderings and his emotional develop-ment over five continents and ten years. His peregrinations take him from the Alps to Pakistan to India to Australia to the Soviet Union and back for longer stays in Sheffield. Yates does some beautiful climbs along the way. The north face of the Eiger, Leyla Peak in Pakistan, and Khan Tengri are all summits reached, and the list of attempts is even longer. In short, there's enough serious climbing in this book for anyone, and Yates's climbing descriptions strike a nice balance between expert terminology and layperson descrip-tion. The author, however, does not focus his narration in the detail by detail style of the "then the crack widened, but I struggled onto the ledge" school. Instead, he moves quickly from toe-holds and frosted biners to the emotional impact of the climbing and the cultures and the con-stant travel. It is, I think, in these conversations about culture and desire and adventure that this book distinguishes itself.

The Flame of Adventure follows Yates back down from mountain after mountain, and there in the valleys and the cities shows him achieving enlightenment outside climbing. It is the unusual climbing book that mentions work. In this one we get an extended description of Yates as a bicycle courier in Perth and, better, most of a chapter about his months on a London construction site. On one job Yates is accepted by the menacing workers when they hear of *Touching the Void*—they dub him "slasher." After all the altitude, working life leads Yates to some thoughtful social analysis on 1990's capitalism and climbing's popularity:

"The shift from heavy industry and manufacturing into service industries had continued unabated. Now it appeared we all sold each other pensions, holidays, insurance and cream teas to have while we were on holiday. It seemed that Britain no longer made anything…. Perhaps climbing fitted into the thinking of the time, with its emphasis on the individual and risk taking in business."

In these chapters Yates turns the climbers' gaze on modern life and reveals some things about the Western world and some things about himself.

Clearly we're not reading this book for the sociology, but Yates's fascination here is not only with hard routes, but with the way climbing changes climbers and returns them to a home now strange and therefore thought provoking. There are many places where Yates applies his experience in the developing world to the comfortable West and draws useful conclusions. For instance, the relation between comfort and stifling entitlement:

"Many people in our society…behave as if living healthily to an old age is a right, rather than good fortune. When they or their families are adversely affected by what I would consider the normal risks of being alive, of being human, they seek scapegoats through the legal system."

In *The Flame of Adventure* Yates shows that in mountaineering and in life he wants the responsibility and satisfaction of an adventurous life, and he's willing to take the risks to get it. And speaking of risks, there is a recklessness about Yates that borders on the antic. Indeed, Doug Scott shows up in the text long enough to observe, "you don't look after yourself very well lad." Let's just say that if in Pakistan you form "The Dangerous Eating Club," you get what you deserve. Injuries (just to the author!) include a foot smashed in a motorbike crash, a finger broken punching a Nepali, several untreated infections becoming septic, a sprained ankle, black eyes, dysentery and hepatitis twice.

At one point Yates wonders why he seldom summits, but the answer lies in the very lifestyle he celebrates as adventurous. But again, there is a charm to this wild ride. If you want an alternative to the culture of corporate organization and hyper-fit, hyper-prepared outdoor professionals, these impetuous Brits are for you.

There are some drawbacks to Yates's book. He summons the ghost of Shipton to bless his spirit of adventure, but a lot of his behavior distances him from that great explorer. Sometimes Yates crafts his own blinkered selfishness into the higher principles of liberation. For instance, in need of money for his Peru expedition, Yates perpetrates fraud against the local bank and leaves the country. When he returns the bank manager insists he repay the money. Here Yates treats us to a tirade about the society that oppresses freedom fighters for adventure and humanity.

"I had wanted to scream at the man and the bank he represented. They seemed to stand for everything I hated, everything that was reduced to its rightful insignificance once I was in the mountains: authority, arrogance, rules and pettiness…. I had wanted to shout at the bank manager 'What about passion? What about freedom? What about adventure?'"

What about self-examination? It is this sort of hypocrisy that gives climbers a bad name. To be self-centered and impetuous is one thing, but to dress it up as a moral imperative is at best narcissistic and is certainly a long way from Eric Shipton. That said, *The Flame of Adventure* is a good book. I liked Yates's first book, *Against the Wall*, and I like this one, too. Ultimately *The Flame of Adventure* succeeds because it examines the freedom of risk. In his epilogue he writes, "Many mountaineers struggle to come to terms with why they climb. I have never had such dilemmas. I know I climb because I love to have adventures." For Yates adventure is more than entertainment. Adventure on the peaks and in the towns is, to grasp his chosen Shipton quote, "a philosophy which aims at living a whole life while the opportunity offers." For Yates this means variety of experience, but also self-empowerment.

I feel some people recognize that by putting elements of danger, uncertainty, and challenge into their lives, they regain a feeling of freedom that they might not have even realized they had lost. Freed from the hold imposed on us by the state, employers, community, and family, people involved in an adventure can feel empowered and actually in control of their own lives.

In *The Flame of Adventure* we look back across one mountaineer's wild times, desperate effort, joy, and uncertainty. We are privileged to watch him wrestle that variety of experience into a philosophy that explains, excuses, and inspires.

JEFFREY M. MCCARTHY, *AAC*

Anderl Heckmair: My Life, Eiger North Face, Grand Jorasses and Other Adventures. ANDERL HECKMAIR. TRANSLATED BY TIM CARRUTHERS. FOREWORD BY REINHOLD MESSNER. SEATTLE: THE MOUNTAINEERS BOOKS, 2002. 304 PAGES. $24.95.

While best known for his role in the 1938 success on the north face of the Eiger, Anderl Heckmair has always embraced the classic mountaineer's lifestyle of travel, curiosity, gainful unemployment and rich experience, even extending it into his tenth decade (he was over 90 at the time of this revision and reissue of his classic memoir, *My Life as a Mountaineer*). The publisher states that this book is the first in a series of biographies in a "Mountain Masters" series; we might be curious to see what follows it, since many of the world's best-known climbers have already published an autobiography or two or three.

American audiences may have some trouble in recognizing the author's name, standing as he does in the shadow of his better-known ropemate Heinrich Harrer. Heckmair went on from the Eiger success to a life of lecturing, professional guiding, and mountaineering instruction, and continued traveling and seeking out new routes, but in a more private and less commercial fashion than many another successful climber. His one large-scale Himalayan expedition, to the Karakoram in 1953, came about as a choice between the well-known and well-funded Herrligkoffer expedition to Nanga Parbat, and a smaller one put together by some friends. He chose the smaller expedition, which turned into a series of disappointments, yet never regretted having dropped out of the more successful Nanga Parbat trip. His goal, was to have memories, not fame.

Heckmair's life has certainly left him with enough of those. One of the difficulties of climbing autobiographies lies in making them seem interesting to non-climbers. In the case of Heckmair, though, we have long discussions of learning to ski, his friendship with cinematographer Leni Riefenstahl, his resulting indirect relationship with Adolph Hitler, and, finally, some long chapters on traveling in Africa, South America, and the United States. His emphasis throughout is on adventure and satisfying his innate curiosity about the world, and it is in those sections that his personality comes through most clearly.

There are some difficulties with the tone of many passages, but it is hard to tell how much of that comes from the ordeal of translating German into English and how much is actually the result of what seems to be a very real difference in attitude towards climbing in Europe as opposed to America. Throughout the book the many references to friends and acquaintances who lose their lives climbing are brief and somehow unsatisfying, but whether that is due to Heckmair's privacy and reticence or to a more general insouciance is unclear.

For most people, the book's central appeal will come from the chance to read a new first-hand account of the Eiger Nordwand ascent, and that is certainly one of its stronger chapters. By coincidence, at the time I was reading it, *Alpinist* magazine's issue #2 came out with an article by Thomas Ulrich ("In the Footsteps of Heckmair") about a modern-day ascent of the Nordwand that was deliberately completed using original clothing and equipment. (The one exception was the hemp rope, which was given a core of nylon for safety's sake). The whole project was filmed, of course, and Heckmair was consulted for points of accuracy; but the gist of the article was the respect that the reenactment engendered for the commitment and talent of the first-ascent party.

There has never been any dispute that Heckmair was the star of the 1938 show; those who wish to know more about the man, and the charges of Nazi propagandism that haunted him for years afterwards, would do well to read this book.

RON MATOUS, *AAC*

Over the Edge: The True Story of Four American Climbers' Kidnap and Escape in the Mountains of Central Asia. GREG CHILD. NEW YORK: VILLARD. 2002. 284 PAGES. HARDCOVER. $24.95.

Over the Edge is Greg Child's fifth book. It chronicles the terror that four young American climbers underwent when Islamic militants kidnapped them for six harrowing days in August 2000. Much of the book deals with the events surrounding how the climbers made their escape when Tommy Caldwell pushed one of their tormentors off a cliff. Early on, Child gained the sole rights to their stories and so this is in some sense an exclusive for him although he has related a briefer sketch of this story earlier in *Outside* Magazine.

The book is well researched, and probes deeply into the roots of the Central Asian region and the conflict that eventually embroiled not just four American lives, but many others—from the Kyrgyzstan army, to local shepherds and villagers uprooted in the brief but violent incursion, and finally to families and friends back home in America. The last third of the book deals with the immediate aftermath and the fall-out, including the intense media scrutiny, the lasting psychological scars, and the broken relationships. But it is not all negative in the end. Child does a nice job of describing how Tommy Caldwell and Beth Rodden's relationship deepened as a result of their trials and tribulations.

Child helps us to get to know these disparate personalities: Jason "Singer" Smith, John Dickey, Tommy Caldwell, and Beth Rodden. It is Child's portrait of Caldwell and Rodden as innocents swept up in great evil that truly fascinates. Since this story takes place pre-9/11 it is all the harder for them to comprehend such evil. We cannot fault Child for coming up empty handed on the roots of this deep hatred. Many other much better known authors such as Samuel Huntington and Mark Jurgensmeyer have failed to produce any truly convincing explanations, either. In this sense, perhaps Rodden represents all of our incredulity at such loathing. How can one human being so completely hate another—one with whom they have never had a conflict and do not even know? But in spite of all that they are put through, Caldwell is truly horrified—self tortured really—over the (incorrect) thought of having killed someone. Out of such chaos both Caldwell and Rodden strike one as particularly noble individuals. Child's portraits are perspicacious and nuanced on this point. This is, in many ways, a world without moral rhyme or reason.

Eventually cracks appear in the four climbers' relationships that soon become an unbridgeable chasm. This dissension begins with the always loquacious Smith simply calling the shots as he sees them. He is unafraid and uncaring of saying whatever comes to mind. He is an individual easy to identify with. In the end this characteristic simply proves incompatible with the far more sensitive pair of Caldwell and Rodden. But the final rift occurs between the two pairs when Caldwell and Rodden hold a press conference before Smith and Dickey arrived back in the country. This is taken to be an unforgivable insult by the latter.

Besides being accomplished in his character portrayals—helping us to get to know each person intimately—Child has an interesting aside at the end of the book where he describes what seems to be John Bouchard's strange obsession with the case and his compulsion to prove the story a hoax. For whatever reasons, this narrative seems to excite disbelief in people. Bouchard has taken upon himself the cause of showing the world that such tale could never be true. This seems odd when we live in an age where terrorists hijack planes full of people and fly them into buildings full of people.

Despite its many strengths, the book is far too long, probably by about a third. There is certainly too much background on the conflict in the early part of the book that is boring and hard to follow. Then there is the seemingly endless fascination about who actually pushed their captor over the cliff. But what we really need in this book is a whole lot less of Child himself. His entire climbing resume is slipped into various parts of the book, which is disruptive at the least, and egoistic at the worst. Child even presents us with advance reviews from *Variety* breathlessly telling us that the very book we are reading is the next *Into Thin Air*. Save it for the back of the jacket cover. We also don't need to have an entire chapter (21) devoted to how the writer out-scammed everyone else for the exclusive book rights and movie rights. And then the rationalizing about why he burned *Climbing* magazine for the story and why exclusive book deals are "a simple matter of business" sounds just like, well, rationalizing. While we could have done with a whole lot less Child in the story, we could do with a whole lot more editor.

Child is a good writer already, though I believe his best book is still in him. For proof, read chapter 19—"A.K.A. Abdual"—a truly gripping account of how one of the captors was eventually killed in a hand-to-hand battle with Kyrgyzstan special forces. I can easily recommend this book. It is an incredible story, and Child does justice to the cool-headed heroism of all four Americans. Overall, it's an exciting read.

DAVID HALE

The Fall. SIMON MAWER. BOSTON: LITTLE BROWN, 2003. 370 PAGES. $24.95

The Fall is the first novel with a climbing background by a respected talent since James Salter's *Solo Faces* 20 years ago: long enough to suggest that the climbing novel is an endangered species. Ex-climber Simon Mawer wrote five novels, including his acclaimed *Mendel's Dwarf*, before drawing on his personal experiences in the pubs and crags of Wales, Scotland, and the Alps for what *New York Times* Sunday Book Review Section dubbed a "fine new mountaineering novel."

Mawer begins with a report of a fatality. Soloing a route far beyond his ability if roped, the celebrated mountaineer Jamie Matthewson, 50—he is given the status of a British Messner or Kukuczka—falls off a Welsh cliff and dies. "Why?" is the presenting problem designed to hold much of the novel together. Upon hearing the news bulletin, estranged mate Robert takes leave of career and beautiful wife and children for a *recherché du temps perdu* and Llamberis. At the memorial service, Dewar reads from Whymper's *Scrambles Amongst the Alps*.

There is more excitement in the story development than my summary conveys. Mawer is a literary conjuror with time, cryptic character, selective evidence, and non-disclosure. The second-generation story is based on Robert's recollections of his youth and relationship to Jamie. At 12, on the two boys' first experiments at climbing in a slate quarry, Jamie is captured and sodomized by a caretaker. At 16 Robert gets his sexual initiation from Jamie's glamorous Caroline over a torrid London weekend. Later the two men take up climbing avidly in Wales and Scotland. Enter Ruth the bohemian painter. At first she favors Jamie, then Robert, and one night both men together in a camper van while they wait for bad weather to clear off the face of the Eiger Nordwand.

Whereas in the boudoir Mawer descends to the conventions of the bodice-ripper, on the

Eiger his writing is almost pitch perfect. Here is a sample of the pair enduring a storm above the Traverse of the Gods:

"Powder snow avalanches spilled over the cliffs above and hissed like snakes down the ice. I stood in the stream and watched the snow course around my axes and over my boots. When the flow died away I continued climbing, through a world that was reduced to the limits of my body, a world contracted to this patch of dirty ice, this length of frozen rope, these thoughts of supplication and anger. The wind roared and stung. Beneath it was the sound of my breathing and the pain in my muffled hands."

Off-route near the exit cracks, Robert is hit by an avalanche while leading, falls, and breaks a leg. Impervious to his partner's cries not to be abandoned, Jamie solos out and away. A short break in the storm allows Robert one pathetic chance to signal distress with his flashlight, and a rescue ensues. Jamie makes it to the top, while Robert is choppered out (another well-crafted scene), and forever loses his toes, Ruth, and his will to climb. His sense of betrayal by Jamie is one of the more credible emotional moments in the book. Robert will not accept Jamie's justification that he'd climbed out to get a rescue started.

This incident is the first step for Jamie up the ladder of mountaineering fame. For the next 20 years the two rarely meet. Their last encounter follows a London lecture by Jamie to promote his biography, *In the Death Zone*—so named because, according to him, over half of all souls who've been above 26,000 feet have died. Over beers at a pub, Jamie is a burnt-out case.

"He sat back in his chair," Mawer writes. "He wasn't looking at me any longer, but at the beer in front of him, and the beads of condensation that ran like tears down the glass. He wiped them away with his finger, smiling a tight smile, the kind of smile you give when you're in pain, the kind that signifies that it hurts but that you are going to put up with it, like you put up with the headaches and the pain in the lungs, the cerebral edema, the diarrhea, the vomiting, all those things of high altitude. Then he looked me directly in the eye 'Thing is my whole life has been an escape, Rob. Escape from Guy Mattewson, from my mother, but above all'—he nodded, as though the idea had just occurred to him—'from you.' Seconds later he adds, 'The trouble is that I've been wrong all the time. I think the person I've really been trying to escape is myself. That's why it has been so difficult.'"

Right there is one of the flaws of this book: declamatory self-discovery more suitable to a play. The above excerpt is one of several moments when Jamie's fascination with Robert is inexplicable. At times Jamie seems on the point of saying the unutterable—a deeper secret even than the knowledge that his pal has poked his Mum—and then draws back. These red herrings get in the way and lead the reader on false trails: such as a possible homoerotic drive in Jamie. A similar problem is posed by Robert's character. Mawer has a number of people tell narrator Robert that he is a selfish bastard. But the reader is denied the privilege, and excitement, of finding this trait emerge from the narrative.

It may come as something of a surprise to readers of the *AAJ* that climbing and climbers are psychologically suspect. Jamie and Robert are not attractive characters. For Mawer climbing is fueled by repression, self-doubt, and the denial of reality, which in the end cleans a man out. Ruth sums up husband Jamie as follows: "Did you know that they brought him down from K2 after some kind of collapse? Cerebral edema, or something. He was weeks in hospital. I mean he's putting his mind on the line, his fucking mind, Rob. It's not just you with your wretched toes. It is his whole bloody personality that he is risking. And then I wonder, what else is there? Other than this obsession...."

Biblically the fall represents the ejection from paradise. In this story several characters at some point fall from some state of innocence, but only Jamie dies by falling, because he fails the Delphic oracle's test of "know thyself." Thus Mawer successfully answers the presenting problem of Jamie's motive for suicide. Not coincidentally, the women who don't climb end up more fulfilled than the men who do. Rich and glamorous Caroline has a prolific sex life, Diana the satisfaction of motherhood, and promiscuous Ruth has the satisfactions of becoming a successful painter besides. The *Times'* reviewer complained that sex and climbing were "compared once too often." But the moral might be (readers take note when planning your next visit to the crags) that sex is the better of the two.

The great strength of *The Fall* lies in vividness of the climbing action. For writer aspirants to The Great Climbing Novel I'd recommend Mawer's style: so fine is its tone, its rhythms, and economy of effects. His grasp of the British climbing scene is also very good. His chief defect is an over-indulgence in the machinery of suspense at the expense of the characters' density and development. Reading it a second time, I admired the consistency of the narrative and structure with the final denouement, which is revealed in a letter from Kangchenjunga. But on the first reading, the letter comes too late: for the characters Diana and Robert, and for the reader.

JOHN THACKRAY, *AAC*

Women on High: Pioneers of Mountaineering. REBECCA A. BROWN. BOSTON: APPALACHIAN MOUNTAIN CLUB BOOKS, 2002. FOREWORD BY ARLENE BLUM. 272 PAGES. HARDCOVER $22.95.

Rebecca A. Brown has given us a highly readable history of women's mountaineering. *Women on High* begins with the 1808 ascent of Mont Blanc by Marie Paradis, but focuses primarily on the Victorian era and the early decades of the 20th century, telling the stories of such fine Alpine climbers as Lucy Walker, Meta Brevoort, Elizabeth Le Blond, Mary Mummery, and Margaret Anne Jackson. In addition to describing the climbs themselves, Brown situates them within a background of evolving gender codes, climbing styles—and clothing styles (with corsets and cumbersome skirts giving way to bloomers and trousers). She also explores the varied motivations that prompted 19th-century women to climb: the desire for independence, a commitment to women's rights, the search for spiritual and personal fulfillment.

Women on High makes clear that a number of early women climbers performed at the highest standards of their day. In 1893, for example, Lily Bristow cruised the Mummery Crack on the Grepon. (Her partner on the climb was A. F. Mummery, the 19th century rock star who described his and Bristow's ascent of the iced-up Grepon "as amongst the hardest I have made.") In 1908, after several failed attempts, the American climber and feminist Annie Smith Peck finally reached the summit of 21,831-foot Huascaran Norte (and survived a harrowing descent to the Garganta). Between 1899 and 1912 another American, Fanny Bullock Workman, led six extensive expeditions in the Himalaya, reaching summits as high as 22,800-foot Pinnacle Peak in the Nun Kun range. (She was 47 years old at the time.) Yet another American climber, Dora Keen, persevering through lengthy storms that drove many of the men in the party back down the mountain, completed the first ascent of 16,000-foot Mt. Blackburn in the Wrangell Mountains of Alaska. This was in 1912, when all the major Alaskan peaks except Mt. Saint Elias remained unclimbed.

Women on High's foreword is provided by Arlene Blum, who led the first American expedition to Annapurna I in 1978 and whose *Annapurna: A Woman's Place* is required reading for anyone interested in the history of women's mountaineering. Blum notes that early in her own climbing career she knew nothing of most of the women whose stories are told in this book, adding that if she had they would have provided her "with role models, support, inspiration, and encouragement that would have made [my] own ascents easier."

DAVID MAZEL, *AAC*

Climb: The History of Rock Climbing in Colorado. JEFF ACHEY, DUDLEY CHELTON, BOB GODFREY. SEATTLE: THE MOUNTAINEERS BOOKS. SECOND EDITION, 2002. 200 B&W PHOTOS. 256 PAGES. HARD-COVER: $44.95. PAPERBACK: $29.95.

The Rocky Mountain's Front Range and the Colorado Plateau to its west make an environment conducive to rock climbing in general, and an interesting regional history and development specifically. The sandstones of the western slope desert stretch into Utah, while the gneissic and granitic composites form the Rocky's core. The swirls of the Black Canyon, the crack-infested dihedrals of Long's Peak's Diamond, the compact shatters of Eldorado Canyon's quartzite, and the steep undercut blocks of Rifle—all these create a recipe for every type of climbing practiced internationally, but also a development that historically has been set apart by its variety of rock and by the people who have explored and climbed it. Historic names (some more widely heard than others) like Layton Kor, Steve Wunsch, Dave Breashears, Billy Westbay, Duncan Ferguson, Jimmy Dunn, Tommy Caldwell, and many others, have all put their mark on standards, much of that within the confines of the eastern front of the mountains west to the towers of the Colorado Plateau. Documenting this history is no small feat.

Jeff Achey's collaboration with Dudley Chelton, who, along with Bob Godfrey, wrote the original edition, condenses the pre-seventies well, and brings the book up to speed with the fast pace of rock climbing in Colorado in the 26 years since the first edition was published. Condensing the original edition could have compromised its thoroughness, but Achey and Chelton keep the integrity and pay appropriate homage to the original masters of Colorado rock climbing. Though it is never really focused on, the theme of the book brings out the uniqueness inherent to the attitude, styles, and ethics of Colorado that are the culmination of the state's geography, geology, and the many characters that have added to the alchemy.

Achey makes it clear that this book is about rock climbing specifically, and to not have drawn that arbitrary line would have made too broad a topic upon which to give appropriate respect and coverage. And, to his credit, he avoids spreading himself thin, and ties common threads through the generations as they built upon the standards and mentorship of those before, from the era when multiple days were spent to climb a wall in the Black Canyon to the present feats of climbing the Painted Wall plus the two Chasm View walls in a day.

It is due time for this book, too. Colorado has about every type of rock offering every type of climbing, and has been a contributor to international standards for years. The layout of photos and anecdotal history make for an entertaining journey through the history of rock climbing in Colorado. The chapters are not only organized by era, but by theme and disciplines within the larger arena of rock climbing. Instead of disrupting any sort of flow, this gives the reader a sense of when and where certain aspects of the greater discipline of rock climbing were happening. Interspersed throughout are accounts from the first ascensionists, which help to not only to vary the tone of the book's dialogue, but give a personal perspective to the history.

Achey does justice to the complex and interesting history of Colorado's rock climbing past. He covers every noteworthy area in the state, and all those who were instrumental in the development of routes and standards. Along with the presentation of information, it is also apparent that all this effort came from a climber, and one who is proud of the history of his home turf.

BEAN BOWERS

The Shoes of Kilimanjaro and Other Oddventure Travel Stories. CAMERON M. BURNS. BASALT, COLORADO: HARD PRESSED BOOKS, 2002. 184 PAGES. PAPERBACK. $16.95.

The Hard Way: Stories of Danger, Survival and the Soul of Adventure. MARK JENKINS. NEW YORK: SIMON & SCHUSTER, 2002. 222 PAGES. HARDCOVER. $22.00.

Neither of these titles is strictly a book about climbing per se, but while reading them it becomes obvious that there is a lot more climbing between the lines than shows up on the page. Both writers deliver on the promise of their subtitles: Burns comes through with the "oddventure" story, the unique spin he seems to naturally find in each new locale; and Jenkins manages to live up to what at first glance seems an overhyped description: getting darned near the soul of adventure.

The opening three tales in Burns' book speak directly to climbing: trips to Kilimanjaro, the Cordillera Blanca, and Fitzroy. Burns knows we don't need to hear another, as Jeff McCarthy describes it in an earlier review: "then the crack widened, but I struggled onto the ledge" version of a climb. Instead the title story, "The Shoes of Kilimanjaro," is a humorous meditation on the footwear of his Kenyan porters: "We sat around a small fire that night, the night before our final day of the climb, eating, laughing and sipping mugs of tea. Secretly, we were regarding each other's feet." Burns then launches into a short, and again humorous, digression on the the history of footwear. This sort of a digression is a staple of most of these essays and they range widely: in an essay about sailing in the Bahamas he takes this turn: "All this Atlantis stuff started over 2,000 years ago when Plato wrote two stories called 'Critias' and 'Timaeus,' way back in 360 B.C." Or, my personal favorite, in an essay about a trip on the Ewaso Ngiro river in Kenya: "Consider the bathtub." These aren't really digressions, of course, they're just Burns putting his quirky observations into a larger context.

In his essay on Alpamayo there is an actual paragraph devoted to the climb, but Burns' meditations are directed to the social scenes at basecamp and the crowded conditions he encounters. The Fitzroy piece offers dozens of dead-on observations of our peculiar subculture: "With every patch of blue sky that floated overhead, dozens of wrists would be bared and excited consultations with barometer watches would ensue."

His piece on his attempt to dribble a soccer ball across the Elk Mountains begins with a quote from Warren Harding: "What's the sense in all this?" That line is well-chosen—there is indeed a sense that the world as seen through Burns' eyes is a kind of glorious farce. Burns writes "[Climbing trips] made me realize that there's a whole wide world out there of interesting people and cultures, mountains and geographic regions, fruits and vegetables, and international headgames involving salamis and potatoes." That's the world Burns is showing us here, but his real point is that we should see it for ourselves.

I first read most of the 23 essays collected in Mark Jenkins' *The Hard Way* as they appeared in his regular column in *Outside*. I have marveled at them over the years, read singly, wedged as they were between car advertisements and gear reviews; collected here between the covers of a book the clarity and wisdom of his words accrue for a more powerful and memorable effect. As in Burns' work, climbing appears in the background of some of the essays; In two of my favorites "What Goes Around" and "The Bike Messenger" Jenkins writes about traveling in Tibet. They contain the phrases "aborted expedition" and "failed expedition" respectively. Most writers would gladly trade a successful climb for the beauty Jenkins captures in the wake of those undescribed climbing fiascoes.

The climbing pieces as a set of about a half dozen are brilliant. They include descriptions of a first ascent on Mt. Waddington, a climb on the Matterhorn, soloing in Bolivia, ice climbing in Scotland, climbing with a stranger on Denali, and a piece on George Mallory; also, a terrific piece written as a diary composed after 17 days above 21,000 feet. In "Ego Trip" the story of his solo climb of Huayana Potosi, he writes:

"Just because I summited and managed to get down alive doesn't mean I did the right thing…. Surviving after a series of stupid moves means nothing more than that the gods took pity on you. It's nothing to brag about."

He's not bragging here, he is illuminating his (our) conflicting intellect and emotions. He knows that in considering the value of our achievements we best be honest about the line between what we've earned and the good dumb luck with which we are sometimes blessed.

Many excellent books about Mallory have been written in the last half dozen years, but in "In the Good Company of the Dead" Jenkins manages to give us a very satisfying, full portrait in a mere 10 pages.

"Wisdom" is a word I don't use lightly. Most of the wisdom Jenkins manages to get on the page is self-knowledge, what every person must figure out for him or her self. But beyond that he makes a lot of observations that might be pretty useful for the rest of us, such as, "One of the many problems with the indoor life is you start to think that all that secondhand cyberinfo you're gathering has some validity." The best advice he has comes in the essay "From the Mouths of Babes," and since it closes the book, I won't give it away here—like a lot of words to live by these are both simple and true.

Jenkins travels on foot, by ski, bicycle, and kayak. He hitchhikes, does pull-ups, climbs, skydives, rappels in holes in the earth, and plays with his kids. In his descriptions of these activities he's managed to somehow weight them equally, as if every moment is equally alive, equally capable of yielding the hard won lesson. And that's what good writers do.

DAVID STEVENSON, *AAC*

The Good, the Great, and the Awesome: The Top 40 High Sierra Rock Climbs. Peter Croft. Mammoth Lakes, CA: Maximus Press, 2002. 243 Pages. $30.00.

How would you feel, having invested in a guidebook, reading in it this? "Above looms THE corner. If you or your partner are getting whiney you better go down now, this is no place for wusses! Otherwise, remove all jewelry, roll up your sleeves and launch off into the crux." Or, as a recommendation for predawn starts: "You're all by yourself, the stars are out, and you get to see those nocturnal critters with the glow in the dark eyes that scare the crap out of you." Or "Climb fast! If you get down early you get to have french fries and beer at the Whitney Portal Café." My reaction to such playfulness depends on the author's knowledge of his mountains and the accuracy of the information he provides. The author being the foremost climber of these mountains—the Sierra Nevada—I feel I've gotten expertise, an evocation of the Sierra's beauty, and a celebration of being in the Sierra. Peter Croft's *The Good, the Great, and the Awesome* is sold as a guidebook, and is an authoritative, informative guidebook, but what I believe it really to be is a celebration.

I admit the price caused sticker shock; 75 cents a route must be a record. But this must be the first guidebook to real mountains whose author knows all the routes firsthand. And some of the routes are traverses of as many as 16 peaks (Minarets), which would be 32 routes in a normal guide. Plus the book is loaded with photos—the preponderance by Croft's close friend Galen Rowell—maps, and topos. While no more than halfway up the scale of guidebookiness on which the Ortenburger/Jackson/Secor/Yours-Truly type of scholarly tome sets the (dubious) standard, the route descriptions are as detailed, accurate, and helpful. Croft's prose may be more informative than conventional guidebookese, as when he mentions the possibility, on Mt. Russell's Fishhook Arête, of going up left, then back right: "This is what I did and it was the only part of the route that I didn't like. Everyone else that I've talked to says that straight up the arête is the way to go."

The Good, the Great, and the Awesome stands apart for its author's original thinking. Croft bases his selection of routes and his recommendations (* = good, ** = great, *** = awesome) on his own experience, not on the traditional Sierra canon. A Croft innovation is that he rates routes according to how difficult he found them. Secor seems to have taken ratings from Roper, Roper from Voge. Voge was faced with Norman Clyde's proclivity for soloing, in hobnailed boots, up to what we now call 5.6. Class 4, Croft warns, is "a grade to watch out for." He has encountered "up to 5.8 climbing on 'class 4' routes" and does some upgrading. Not even your summit snack escapes his unrestrained scrutiny. He recommends "the type of food you would eat at home," likening gorp to the Halloween candy your parents warned you not to devour en masse and, when you did, gave you a bellyache. "Environmental Concerns" is not the usual 100 feet from this and 200 feet from that, and does not contain the phrase "fragile ecosystem." It is a multiple-choice quiz, with you imagining yourself camped in your in-laws' backyard. (Would you admire the flowerbed by (a) tromping through it in lug-soled boots or (b) viewing it from the porch and complimenting "Dad" on his green thumb?)

A man who treats a traverse of nine Palisades peaks or nine Evolution peaks as one route, who solos three IVs and a V on Temple Crag—in a day—can't be expected to smell the proverbial flowers. Then what is Mt. Agassiz's class 2 Northwest Slope doing with two stars? "Although I meant to only include technical routes…I just couldn't blow this one off…. The hike…is famously beautiful and, after an easy scramble to the top, the views are just jaw dropping." Also included are two class 3 routes—the East Ridge of Mt. Russell and the East Face of Middle Palisade. "I think that Middle Pal is perhaps a bit prouder. It may be an intimidating sight from miles away but when you get there…it's even worse."

Don't worry that a man who covers as much ground as Croft expects you to do climbs car-to-car in a day. Each route description comes with the approach's mileage and uphill component ("5 miles, 3 on good trail, 1 on easy X-country, 1 on rough X-country; 2,200 ft. of elevation gain")œdata that lets you to decide for yourself, with no subliminal prodding, whether to camp or go for it in a day.

I got the sense throughout that Croft finds the Sierra beautiful, but when I searched for a passage as an example, the best I could find was "long sweeping buttresses and arêtes, swarming with face holds and studded with sudden sharp pinnacles and airy notches" (Temple Crag). Perhaps describing beauty outside the context of humans rambling through the mountains is not possible, since the only language available is that of postcard clichés. That the guy notices so much during his rambles says enough.

G, G, & A will influence my guidebook-writing; I hadn't realized how much joy it is permissible to impart. I'll never again find myself writing, "Follow the crack for 130 feet and step left," without thinking, "I remember it being more fun than that." But it is Croft's stature as a climber that allows him to be playful. If I wrote the following, people would think I was writing a parody: "Originally they called the route [Whitney's East Buttress] Peewee, which just happens to be the name of my dog. Without getting overly misty about it, I think it's a really good name." If playful is the right word: "You end up groping for fist jams behind a big detached block that PROBABLY won't fall off."

I winter in Bishop but head to Jackson Hole around June 1, intending to return by October 1 but habitually finding Wyoming's Indian summer irresistible. The highest compliment I can pay *G, G, & A* is that it has me contemplating migrating west earlier, or even forsaking Wyoming for a week in summer, to try a few Awesomes that aren't feasible when days are short and cold or approaches are snow slogs.

JOE KELSEY, *AAC*

Under the Midnight Sun: The Ascent of John Denver Peak and the Search for the Northernmost Point of Land on Earth. JOHN JANCIK, STEVE GARDINER, JAVANA M. RICHARDSON. *Colorado: Stars End Creations, 2003.* 200 PAGES, 126 COLOR PHOTOS, 4 BW PHOTOS. $29.95.

Under the Midnight Sun chronicles two expeditions by largely identical teams to find the northernmost point of land in the world and to summit unclimbed peaks in North Peary Land at the northern tip of Greenland.

The 1996 expedition sought to cross the undulating sea ice on foot and reach Oodaaq Island, a small island about 2.3 miles north of the coast believed to be the northernmost point of land in the world. Though it sounds like an easy enough proposition, Oodaaq is a 2,600-square-foot island only three feet above the mean sea level. It is easily lost among the pack ice's pressure ridges of greater height. The converging longitudinal lines this far north play with the accuracy of GPS units, making their search for a minuscule island a formidable challenge.

After one failed attempt and a 16-hour search, the group finds a small rock jutting above the flooded sea ice—Oodaaq Island, or so they think. Only as the group is about to fly in for their 2001 expedition do they learn from the Danish Polar Center that they missed Oodaaq, but found a new northernmost point of land: Top of the World Island.

Under the Midnight Sun captures the raw passion of pioneering exploration by self-described "ordinary people." While the excitement readily shows through, the book is often a cumbersome read. Three separate authors, combined with lengthy quotations from other party members, make it hard to follow the storyline. Quotes and situations repeat, and the reader often bounces between narration of unfolding events, stories about motivational moments prior to the expedition, poetry, and song lyrics. A thorough editing would cut out the extraneous clutter, leaving the kernel of explorations that is well worth reading.

Lloyd Athearn, *AAC*

Every Other Day: The Journals of the Remarkable Rocky Mountain Climbs and Explorations of A. J. Ostheimer. Edited by R.W. Sandford and Jon Whelan. The Alpine Club of Canada. 2002. 248 pages, illustrated, tipped-in map. CDN$34.95.

In 1927, 19-year-old A. J. Ostheimer pulled off a tour-de-force. In some 60 days, accompanied by the Swiss guide Hans Fuhrer and six others, he stormed around then-remote regions of the Canadian Rockies climbing most everything in sight. More precisely, he climbed 30 peaks, of which 27 were first ascents. In addition, he made such geological observations as would enable him to get school credit for this summer in the mountains! On his return, Ostheimer wrote up his journal, which may have been partly responsible for his graduating from Harvard one year early.

Previously unpublished, the journal was re-discovered by Jon Whelan. It is published by the Alpine Club of Canada "As a centennial gift to the American Alpine Club … we hope our gift will become a lasting memento of a century of shared appreciation of the glories of Canadian peaks."

I have had the good fortune to visit some of the areas and mountains that Ostheimer knew, so it was with keen interest that I read the book. And as a book, measured by the standards of such classics as James Outram's *In the Heart of the Canadian Rockies,* or Collie's and Stutfield's *Climbs and Explorations in the Canadian Rockies,* it falls short. Perhaps this is somewhat unfair, for Ostheimer wrote for private publication. A vigorous editing and sharpening of objective would help. Furthermore, he was a young lad, without the world-view of a Collie or an Outram. What remains is a look at exploratory mountaineering of a vanished era. The sheer tenacity of the man is exemplified by such notations as: "To-day we planned to ascend the first peak at 10 am; the second at 2 pm; and, if all went well, to reach the summit of the third at 6 pm. Beyond that, we had no plans." In the event they made their three first ascents. In the mode of the day, many of these climbs were no more than shale walks or snow plods. It is interesting that one of his guides was Jean Weber, who had been on the first ascent of Mt. Alberta two years before. Yet Ostheimer does not comment upon this great feat when they pass by Alberta (or if he did, it does not appear in the narrative); he seems more focused on quantity of summits than on quality of ascents. If you are a mountain history buff, or simply love a period mountain tale, this book will be attractive. But for an introduction to the exploratory era in the Canadian Rockies, I would suggest the two other books cited above.

CHRIS JONES, *AAC*

IN BRIEF

• Just before his death Galen Rowell edited a new edition of *High & Wild: Essays and Photographs on Wilderness Adventure* (Spotted Dog Press, $34.95). In his review of the first edition in the 1980 *AAJ* Charles Houston said, "It is by far his finest work and rivals any other in print; it will stand equal to Tom Hornbein's splendid *Everest: the West Ridge*. It's a book to be read again and again and to feast on in times of despair." If anything, those words are even more accurately descriptive of this new edition which features 10 new essays in addition to the original 13. As Robert Redford notes in the introduction it is the most personal of Rowell's books. Spotted Dog Press has produced a particularly elegant edition here; the color printing is excellent—in many cases an improvement on the original edition's color saturation and detail. The Preface and Photographic Notes at the end have the uncanny and heartbreaking effect of Rowell speaking to us from beyond. Charlie Houston was right about this one: we're lucky to have it.

• Many of Rowell's photographs illustrate his wife Barbara Rowell's book *Flying South: A Pilot's Inner Journey* (Ten Speed Press). Not a climbing story but definitely an adventurer's tale, it chronicles a 25,000-mile, 27-leg journey through Latin America with Galen and Doug Tompkins. Proof that marriage and adventure need not be mutually exclusive.

• *Fearless on Everest: The Quest for Sandy Irvine*, (Mountaineers, 2000; $18.95.) tells more about Sandy Irvine than has ever been told before. Written by an admiring relative, Julie Summers (his sister's granddaughter), it is by no means a disinterested treatment. Nor is it the work of a professional historian or biographer. But anyone captivated by the 1924 British Everest expedition will be thankful Ms. Summers decided to ferret out this long forgotten information.

• *When in Doubt, Go Higher: Mountain Gazette Anthology*, M. John Fayhee, editor, (Mountain Sports Press $18.95) collects together essays from 1972-'79 along with a few selections from the new *MG*, relaunched in 1999. *AAJ* readers will recognize David Roberts, Galen Rowell, Royal Robbins, and Lito Tejada-Flores, alongside such literary greats as Ed Abbey.

• *Alaska: A Climbing Guide* (Mountaineers $24.95) by Mike Wood and Colby Coombs is a noteworthy guidebook simply because it's the first comprehensive guide to 80 routes in eight great ranges in Alaska. As Brian Okonek notes in his foreword, this book should not be used as a "checklist" but as a "Springboard for your imagination."

• *Frank Smythe: The Six Alpine/Himalayan Climbing Books* (Mountaineers $38.00) is the latest in the Mountaineers series that began with the Tilman and Shipton editions. Smythe wrote 27 books; these six, written between 1920 and 1939, include The Kanchenjunga Adventure, Kamet Conquered, and Camp Six—classics all. This whole series provides a terrific service for the historian.

• *Desire & Ice: Searching for Perspective Atop Denali* (National Geographic Press $16.00) is a description of David Brill's guided climb of Denali. Well-researched and lucidly written, this is highly recommended for would-be climbers attempting the same.

CLUB ACTIVITIES

EDITED BY FREDERICK O. JOHNSON

AAC, ALASKA SECTION. The Alaska Section's members were active not only in Alaska, but around the world in the past year. Members traveled to Antarctica, the Himalaya, South America, the Continental United States, and Europe. Within Alaska, members put up many new routes and first ascents across the state, some of which appear elsewhere in this Journal.

The Section hosted a monthly slide show series in the fall of 2001 and spring of 2002 at Alaska Mountaineering and Hiking in Anchorage. Programs included Bob Jacobs discussing his trips to Everest, Kamchatka, and in the Wrangell-St. Elias Mountains. Dave Hart covered his ascent of Broad Peak just weeks before the tragic events of 9/11/01. Dave Lucey covered ice climbing in the Canadian Rockies. Gary Bocarde gave us a look back at rock climbing in Yosemite in the "early" days (first ascent of The Shield route on El Capitan, in 1972) and the Moose Antler route (another first ascent) on the southwest face of the Moose's Tooth.

After taking a break for the summer, the slide shows started again in November with a great show by Brian Okonek. Brian covered the Alaska Range near Denali and gave us a look at the first traverse of the immense Bagley icefield back in the early 1980s. In December, Siri and Charlie Sassara took us to the Dolomites and Sardinia for some warm-weather rock climbing. The slide shows will continue in 2003 on the second Tuesday each month. Featured presenters will include a video documentary of the 1963 American Everest Expedition, Dave Hart covering the big peaks on the Alaska-Canada border, Keri Meagher showing a recent Kamchatcka ski mountaineerint trip, and Roman Dial presenting his many first ascents and new routes in the Alaska Range, Chitistone Canyon, and other parts of Alaska.

On December 11, members Steve Davis, Charlie Sassara, and Danny Kost accepted the Alaska Excellence Award from the Alaska Region of the National Park Service on behalf of the Club. The AAC was honored for its support of the Clean Mountain Can project on Denali, along with the Denali Park Rangers and the Access Fund. NPS Alaska Regional Director Rob Arnsberger presented the award at a ceremony in Anchorage. The Alaska Excellence Award is given annually to "recognize the people and programs that are the best examples of leadership, stewardship, and innovation in the fields of natural and cultural resources, conservation, and education." There were 15 nominees for this award in 2002, and we are honored to have been selected.

DANNY KOST, *Chair*

AAC, CASCADE SECTION. In 2002 the Cascade Section hosted one main event and supported two others. On December 13 we had a reception and slideshow for members and guests with Carlos Buhler as our speaker. With over 160 people attending, the reception allowed members old and young to catch up with one another and tell tall tales. Outdoor Research provided the beer, always popular and drunk to the last drop, and Cascade Designs and Helly Hansen donated some excellent gear for the raffle. The slideshow and talk was inspirational and entertaining, with beautiful mountain images from Alaska, Pakistan, India, Nepal, Tibet, and Peru. Carlos selected only a few climbs from his impressive resumé to show the joy and challenge of climbing at all altitudes as low as 3,000m to the unique problems of 8,000m peaks.

On November 17 a benefit was held for Göran Kropp, organized by Helly Hansen and sponsored by the AAC and The Mountaineers. Over $1,400 was raised for charity with the showing of the late climber's epic documentary I Made It: Göran Kropp's Incredible Solo Journey to the Top of the World. Kropp died in a climbing accident near Vantage, Washington, on September 30. Ed Viesturs represented the AAC at this benefit, sharing a few of his favorite Kropp stories from the time he spent with him on Everest. The proceeds from the benefit were donated to the Göran Kropp Bishwa Darshan Primary School in Taptin, Chyangba, Solukhumbu, Nepal, which Kropp founded in 1996.

On November 14, Dr. Charles Houston gave a talk organized by Tom Hornbein and attended by many AAC members. Dr. Houston, one of our country's great gurus of the golden age of exploratory mountaineering, narrated the premier of a video he has created recounting his nearly lifelong love affair with two closely related mistresses. Introduced to mountaineering in the Alps in 1925, his first explorations occurred while a Harvard student in the '30s, notably in the remote, unexplored wilderness of Alaska and the Yukon. His film, created from still and movie footage, depicted his four great Himalayan journeys: Nanda Devi in 1936, K2 in 1938 and 1953, and the first visit to see Everest's Icefall in Nepal with Bill Tilman in 1950.

Among 2002 climbing activities reported to me by Section members are several new routes: Ade Miller with Forrest Murphy and Don Serl climbed the Passport Couloir (TD-) on Mt. Winstone in the Tchaikazan Valley, B.C., on September 22. On September 14 Mike Layton and Jordan Peters made the first ascent of Back of Beyond Buttress on the north face/buttress of Unnamed Peak 6,800 in the Kookipi Creek area near Boston Bar, British Columbia. Carlton Swan reported climbing Mt. Elbrus in Russia and Orizaba in Mexico. Daniel Mazur was very busy leading expeditions to Nojin Kansa, a 7,000m peak near Lhasa, Tibet; the Northwest face of Kangchenjunga; twice to Ama Dablam, including an attempt on the North ridge. Jim Frush and Peter Ackroyd made the first ascent of Gaugiri (6,110m) in Upper Mustang, Nepal, using the first permit issued under the new climbing regulations. Others were kept very busy on the great routes available here in the Cascades, and many other activities go unreported.

To give us all hope as we grow older, I am happy to report that on November 21 Stim Bullitt, now in his 83rd year, climbed Illusion Dweller (5.10b), a 5-star climb at Joshua Tree National Park in California. I am sure this was only one of his many hard climbs, and I know there will be many more to come!

Please visit our Web site at http://cas.alpineclub.org, and if you have questions about the Section, contact me at pdack1@attbi.com.

PETER ACKROYD, *Chair*

AAC, OREGON SECTION. Many of our members achieved noteworthy goals or honors this past year. John Harlin III was appointed Editor of the American Alpine Journal. Jill Kellog was elected President of Cascades Mountaineers. Bob Speik organized Traditional Mountaineering as a local organization with the aim of introducing people of all ages and experience levels to mountaineering in the Cascades. Greg Orton published an excellent guide covering 18 areas, Climb SW Oregon. At The Mazamas club rooms Bennett Barthelemy showed his slides of climbing in Joshua Tree National Park. His photograph of the I Can't Believe It's a Girdle traverse (5.10R) on Freak Brothers domes was featured on the cover of Accidents in North American Mountaineering-2002.

In late spring Section members, in collaboration with the Cascades Mountaineers and Traditional Mountaineering in Bend, installed the first of three rescue litters and shelters donated to Smith Rock State Park, thanks to fund raising led by Jeff Alzner. Not long after, the project was touched by tragedy. Mike Bearzi, who gave an outstanding talk on his first free ascent of Cerro Torre to benefit the Smith Rock litter project, was killed climbing in Tibet. In his honor and recognition of his contribution, the Section has dedicated the rescue litters to his memory.

The efforts of Neale Creamer and the Friends of Silcox Hut were noteworthy. In the fall they along with Timberline Lodge installed a new snow tunnel for winter access to Silcox Hut, the 1933 WPA structure at 7,000' on Mt. Hood. This provides an excellent base camp for emergency rescue on the mountain's south side.

Tom Bennett delivered a slide show at the Talkeetna Ranger Station in April on the historic 1910 Mazamas–C. E. Rusk McKinley Expedition. The slides were reproduced from the original lantern glass slides (from Mazamas archives) taken during the expedition. Rusk, who was a founding member of the AAC, went to McKinley a Cook supporter, but returned a Cook doubter. The Talkeetna Historical Society, The Mazamas, and the NPS Talkeetna rangers are collaborating on identifying locations for the Rusk images and further documenting the expedition.

New and continuing initiatives being pursued by the Section include: planning additional trail and access improvements in southern and central Oregon climbing areas; coordination with statewide groups on overall access issues and developments of interest to climbers in Oregon's many climbing venues; and raising interest in Madrone Wall, one of the state's best crags, and support for efforts to permit climbing there. A major new issue is addressing the planned expanded development of Cooper spur ski area into a destination resort and its potential impact on the wilderness of Mt. Hood's northern slopes.

June Hackett, Bill Hackett's widow, and Conrad Anker published Bill's climbing biography including exploits with the 10th Mountain Division and the 1958 K2 expedition. The book is well laid out as a historical piece with comments by Charlie Shimanski, Dee Molenaar, and Bradford Washburn. It covers Bill's expedition notes and will be an excellent reference document.

BOB MCGOWN, Chair

AAC, SIERRA NEVADA SECTION. It was an active year as usual for our members, starting with an April 6 fundraiser, complete with donated prizes from sponsors for raffle or auction, at the Berkeley Ironworks Gym. I premiered "Driven Crazy," a slide show about my recent escapades in Chile: a solo traverse of the Tower of Paine. Royal Robbins, Bob Schneider, and Brock Wagstaff were among those donating generously to the cause, and Bob even won the rope in the raffle. About 75 people attended, and we raised almost $1,500 in support of the Section's activities.

Shortly thereafter, supported by a Lyman Spitzer Climbing Grant, I had the opportunity to go exploring in Mongolia. Joining me were members Sean Chartrand and Heather Baer, my wife. We scored the first ascent of a 2000-foot granite arête in remote central Mongolia that checked in at 5.11d. We also climbed with the Mongolian national team in Terelj, a picturesque climbing area just 90 minutes from the capital city of Ulaan Bataar. We made several first ascents, both sport and trad, enjoying our time in this land of friendly people.

In May our clan gathered at Hans Florine's base camp (i.e., three-story house) in Yosemite for a barbeque, trading slander and sandbags around a slew of brews and burgers.

September brought our second (and annual?) Pinecrest weekend with climbing at the Gianelli Edges, where none other than Royal Robbins could be seen enjoying the fine granite and later hosting a shindig at his cabin on the lake. Also in September Brock Wagstaff organized a trip to Lover's Leap, an old haunt for our Section.

Our annual dinner, organized by Paul Romero, was held at Zazoo's Restaurant in Oakland, where we watched boats cruise by as we dined with our comrades. We imported Tim O'Neill from Colorado to give his program on speed climbing in Yosemite and alpine-style climbing in Patagonia. We laughed from the edge of our seats at his comic stand-up performance about his audacious climbs.

Finally, we were all saddened to lose some of our most well known members in 2002. RD Caughran passed on first, high on the slopes of Makalu. Warren Harding was the next to go, sipping wine to the finish. Barb and Galen Rowell's plane accident was so sudden, so fast. They were all great people, active in the Section over many years, and will be sorely missed.

Thanks to all who helped make our events happen, with special thanks to Paul Romero for holding us all together with his e-mails and newsletters.

STEVE SCHNEIDER, *Chair*

AAC, CENTRAL ROCKIES SECTION. The year began on a high note with the Section providing customized, limited edition embroidered jackets, vests, and hats at the AAC Annual Meeting at Snowbird, Utah. These items are sold in hopes of adding a sense of camaraderie for all members nationwide. The proceeds stay within the Section to help support local climbing issues and Section events. We also had a table at the annual meeting, where we sold mugs and cups to promote the AAC Hut System.

The CRS added two new huts during the year. The Riverside Inn in Ouray and the Colorado Mountain School in Estes Park have agreed to offer (card carrying) members a 20% discount on lodging. Some restrictions may apply; so call them directly for reservations.

In August the CRS donated $1,190 to the Grand Teton Climbers Ranch for the purchase of a new energy efficient washer and dryer. These appliances will be metered and provided to guests of the Ranch. This use of our funds is directly related to the support from local climbers and AAC members in our annual events and sales. This year the concessionaires license for the Ranch was up for review and renewal by the National Park Service, which offered it for public bidding. We are pleased to report that the AAC will retain the permit rights.

In April the CRS hosted two public meetings in Estes Park to review the proposed Environmental Assessment and changes to parking at Lumpy Ridge in Rocky Mountain National Park. For over 20 years there has been a dispute regarding use of the access road through the MacGregor Ranch. At present the NPS is doing a land appraisal, and a likely solution to the longstanding impasse would include a land swap with the ranch. This will provide additional rocks with possible climbing routes and restore previously owned water and grazing rights to the ranch. A decision is expected in early 2003.

On October 12 the CRS hosted its second annual Lumpy Trails Day at Lumpy Ridge, in Estes Park, as part of the Access Fund's Adopt-A-Crag program. Attendance at this small event has already doubled from 18 to 35 in just two years.. Volunteers have been drawn from the AAC and Access Fund memberships, the University of Colorado, the University of Denver's Alpine Club, the Colorado Mountain School, the REI Flagship store, and the National Park Service, as well as local residents. This growing turnout shows that not only are climbers good stewards and considerate users of the land, but are also proactive in their interaction with one of our country's largest land management agencies. The National Park Service gets poor press and has many awkward management tasks to balance, for which it is often unduly chastised. However, in projects like this we see that not only are NPS employees climbers themselves, but also are excited about working with climbers to improve the local climbing habitat. Another important part of this project has been the improved joint activity of the Access Fund and the AAC. These two organizations serve wide, often very diverse values for American climbers. The most important value lies is the desire of climbers to maintain access to our walls as well as to maintain a memorable historic record of our predecessors while setting precedent for the future. It would be sad if climbers didn't have both of these organizations working together to support their interests; all climbers should be members of both.

GREG SIEVERS, *Chair*

AAC, MIDWEST SECTION. The following summarizes the Section's 2002 activities. In February the Midwest Section represented the AAC at the annual International Adventure Travel and Outdoor Show on Navy Pier in Chicago. This was a fine opportunity for the Club to be "seen and heard" in the community and for us to meet current members and propagate new ones. In March the Midwest Section Dinner, hosted jointly with the Chicago Mountaineering Club, brought in over $900 for the AAC library.

In September we once again represented the Club at the International Outdoor Festival, held in Chicago's Lincoln Park. Despite the low attendance, it was a worthwhile weekend of beautiful Chicago weather and terrific slide shows and presentations.

Finally, Jacek Czyz completed a new route on Yosemite's El Capitan on November 20 after 25 days of climbing. He soloed the route of 22 pitches, 16 of which were new. Rated at A4+, this route is located between the Nose and the Salathe Wall, cutting through Muir Wall four times.

BENJAMIN A. KWETON, *Chair*

AAC, NORTH CENTRAL SECTION. The North Central Section continues to progress toward more communication, camaraderie, and interaction with the Club. Major projects for 2002 included further work on the Section Web site, clean-up days at two areas, and communicating with the Minnesota Department of Natural Resources regarding closed areas at the most popular climbing destination in the Minneapolis–St. Paul area.

Inter-State State Park lies along the St. Croix River bordering Minnesota and Wisconsin. Because of the river valley, the geological formations are spectacular. The climbs vary from 5.3

to 5.12 and are about 50 feet long. In July of 2001 a large rockfall required closing 40% of the Minnesota side. The Section continues to work with the DNR to plan for the possible re-opening of at least part of the area. Five of us had a garbage pick-up day at the park in June that included some climbing and a barbeque.

In July several of us had a clean-up day at Blue Mounds State Park in Luverne, Minnesota, near the South Dakota border. This small park has seen a big increase in climber visits in the last five years.

On October 27 the Omaha members congregated at the University of Nebraska-Omaha for a dinner/slide show, which AAC member Tyson Arp presented on Zion National Park. Organizer Matt Misfeldt also showed slides of a climb of Mt. Baker in Washington. Several non-members were present, and a few joined the Club. This event gave the Club excellent visibility, and it is hoped it will be repeated annually.

SCOTT CHRISTENSEN, *Chair*

AAC, NEW YORK SECTION. No other event has impacted the NY Section quite as severely as that which occurred on 9/11. As the year began there were constant reminders of the loss suffered by the City and so many people including our members and their families. Yet it served to bring the Section together as we all realized how fragile life is and how important are the friendships and camaraderie we make in organizations like the AAC. The Section contributed in a tangible way as well raising several thousand dollars for disaster relief at our Annual Dinner held the previous September.

The year began with a very successful get-acquainted dinner in Greenwich in January for our Connecticut members, many of whom are unable to join us at our weekday events in Manhattan. The organizer was Edgar Walsh. This was followed during the year by several slide shows and book signings here in the City arranged by Jack Reilly. Among the speakers were Ed Webster, Greg Mortensen, and Joe Blackburn. In June, thanks to David Breashears, members and their families were invited to a reception and special preview screening of his fine IMAX film "To The Roof of Africa." Later that month John Ewbank, a new member from Australia, invited us all to a slide show and party at his loft in SOHO.

With all this socializing we did some climbing, too! In January our traditional Adirondack Winter Outing, a sell-out affair, was held in ideal, almost balmy conditions in what turned out to be perhaps the best winter weekend of the year. In May a large contingent gathered at Ralph Erenzo's "Bunks in the Gunks," after a day of climbing and hiking in the Gunks, to welcome the visiting AAC Board of Directors. Our traditional Adirondack Spring Outing was carried over to late September. With the fall foliage resplendent, about 25 members and guests participated in a memorable weekend at the Ausable Club trying out some new, "black-fly free" routes in the immediate area. Bob Hall was the organizer of this event, now in its third decade. For once there was no criticism of the Chairman's wine selection, as this was professionally handled by Steve Miller, our fellow member and wine importer. Especially missed was Earlyn Dean, a longtime member and volunteer, who had passed away earlier in the year. Earlyn, a tireless volunteer, had for many years been the lady who whipped up our Sunday breakfast pancakes. Interspersed during the spring and fall were conditioning hikes in the Hudson Highlands organized by John Tiernan. Especially pleasant were the post-hike wine and cheese get-togethers at Chris and Mim Galligan's place in Garrison.

Finally, in November, our year concluded on a high note with Jim Wickwire's presentation at our Annual Black Tie Dinner. About 150 members and guests, many from out of town, were on hand for the 23rd edition of this event, which raises much needed funds to expand the Library's circulating collection. Besides Jim, two local members made short reports: John Ewbank on the rock climbing possibilities Down Under and Amy Cross on the attempt by her husband Will to ski to the South Pole. Will, a diabetic, is undertaking this 800-mile trek to raise funds for diabetes research. In his slide show Jim recounted his extraordinary life as a climber, its highs and lows and its significance to him. Only a few weeks before, tragedy once again struck on one of Jim's climbs as his partner Ed Hommer was killed by rock fall on a training climb on Mt. Rainier. Accompanying Jim at the Dinner was his charming wife Mary Lou. Finally, we introduced 20 new members and presented them with their membership pins. Doing the honors in this department was Fritz Selby, our "ace" membership recruiter. Among these talented newcomers were recent newly weds Timi and Caroline Johnstone, who had just returned from their honeymoon in Yosemite. For an old timer like me, it's refreshing to see so many interesting, varied, and competent climbers be part of this organization. And we hope to see more of you, regardless of your past experience, at our various events. Included in our outings are professionally guided clinics for all levels of experience.

Our Section Web site, http://nys.alpineclub.org, is a colorful and highly useful directory of news and other events here in the Section. Thanks go to our webmaster Vic Benes for creating and maintaining this entertaining and valuable amenity. Ours is perhaps the only one in the world of climbing with quotations from the classics. Check it out!

Meanwhile, the Section abounds in volunteer opportunities, a great way to get into the "inner circle" as well as expanding your list of potential climbing partners and friends. If you'd like to help out in any of our indoor or outdoor activities, please let us know. And we are always interested in any slide shows you may be ready to produce. You can reach me at philiperard@hotmail.com.

PHILIP ERARD, *Chair*

AAC, NEW ENGLAND SECTION. Our Section continues to grow, and in 2002 membership increased to 510 from 486 in 2001. Eighty people attended our Seventh Annual New England Section black tie event. We brought our Henderson Film Fund to $4,000, enough to begin serious work on our plans for archiving and distribution of the motion pictures of the New England technical and ice climbing made by the late Kenneth Henderson in the 1930s. Andy Tuthill of Hanover, New Hampshire, gave an elegant and humor-filled account of his 30 years of climbing from Pawtuckaway (a boulder pile in southern New Hampshire, known to all beginners) to the Karakoram (much more than a pile and experienced only by the intrepid few).

Our Rick Merritt (with Nevada's Bill Guida) climbed in Ecuador, where they reached the summits of Pasachoa, Guagua Pachincha, and North Illiniza, only later to be stormed off Cotopaxi. In the Sierra Nevada's Evolution Range Paul Dale and Rick Buirkle climbed Mt. Darwin by the northeast ridge on a 10-day outing without encountering any other member of their species. In the Khumbu region of Nepal, Tom Boydston reached 20,000 feet on Ama Dablam (22,411') as a member of a successful multinational team led by Dan Mazur of Summit Climbs. Eric Engberg and his son Zeb climbed Mt. Hood with a few days at Smith Rocks in Oregon and, back home, with many more days at our local Rumney, where Dad led an "easy," he says, 12b/c. Finally, Nancy Savickas, Trish Adams, and Dick Doucette met in Switzerland to try the Eiger's Mittelegi Ridge, but owing to generally foul weather had to be satisfied with a climb of the Monch and later the rainy day amenities over in Chamonix.

WILLIAM C. ATKINSON, *Chair, and* NANCY SAVICKAS, *Vice Chair*

THE MAZAMAS. For The Mazamas of Portland, Oregon, safety is the dominant theme in the club's numerous mountaineering endeavors. Under the highest standards of safety, the Climbing Committee conducts mountaineering education programs, schedules and supervises a wide variety of climbs, and selects and trains climb leaders. The 2002 summer schedule included 316 ascents on 79 different peaks, with the usual bad weather causing cancellation of some. The four most popular peaks were Mt. Hood, Mt. Adams, Mt. St. Helens, and Unicorn Peak (Tatoosh Range), a reflection of a mix of snow and rock climbing within easy driving distance of Portland. However, more peaks than usual with challenging routes in lesser known areas were well represented. Six leaders scheduled 18 winter climbs, but severe weather caused the cancellation of many.

The Basic Climbing Education Program enlisted 286 students in a program that includes indoor lectures, knots and belay practice, and trips to rock and snow climbing areas with groups of nine students. This program draws a majority of non-club members, who then begin Mazama membership with a sound education in safe climbing and mountain etiquette and who are well bonded with a cadre of leaders.

The Intermediate Climbing Program enlisted 45 students. It instructs seasoned beginners in higher levels of rock and snow climbing and develops and screens future climb leaders. A successful spring weekend on Mt. Hood's White River Glacier brought better conditions than January-February sessions in previous years.

The Advanced Rock Program and Advanced Snow and Ice Program enrolled smaller numbers. The Rock Review Program involved a dozen students on the basaltic walls of Rocky Butte in Portland, bolstering knowledge of knots, belaying, rappelling, and fixed-line travel. John Godino, Mazama administrative assistant, organized this program as well as a summer program, also at Rocky Butte, which took students on routes up to the 5.7 level.

The Leadership Training Program brought in six new leaders. Concerned that the leadership pool is aging, with many people having led for over 20 years, the committee concentrated on adding new leaders. All club leaders have been required to earn a Level 1 Avalanche certification by 2002.

Recipients of Mazama Climbing Awards: 15 members received the Guardian Peaks Award (Hood, St. Helens, Adams), 5 the Oregon Cascades Award (Jefferson, Three-Fingered Jack, Washington, Three Sisters); and 7 the Sixteen Major Peaks Award, for completing all-the-above peaks plus Olympus, Baker, Shuksan, Glacier, Stuart, and Shasta. David Sauerbrey received the 15-point Leadership Award, and Dean Lee the Terry Becker Award for leading the 16 major peaks.

The Outing Committee, chaired by Tracy Waechter, fielded a dozen trips in the Pacific Northwest and also abroad in Scotland and Turkey.

The Expedition Committee, chaired by Peter Aposokalis, granted funds to five expeditions: Robert Lee, Monte Smith, John Vissell, and Dave Jun for Denali's West Buttress; Robert E. Lee for a solo climb of Aconcagua; Chris LeDoux and Martin Hanson for Mt. Logan's King

Trench; Josh Wharton and Brian McMahon for The Flame spire in the Karakoram; and Pete Dronkers, Blue Eisele, and Jonas Cabiles for climbing and snowboarding on Ellesmere Island. In March the committee sponsored a slide show for 600 guests by Pete Athans, who had then climbed Mt. Everest six times. In August the committee partnered with Climb Max and Portland Mountain Rescue to sponsor Mark Twight's show on extreme mountaineering.

The Banquet Committee held its annual gala event at Portland's Jantzen Beach Double Tree Hotel, proclaiming "109 Years and Still Climbing!" After the usual award presentations with ex-president Christine Mackert as master of ceremonies, Jim Wickwire showed his slides of Reflections on a Lifetime of Climbing.

On the Executive Council David Sauerbrey succeeded Doug Wilson as President of the Mazamas. Gerry Itken was elected vice president, Brian Holcomb membership secretary, John Youngman recording secretary, and Wendy Carlton treasurer.

JACK GRAUER, *Historian*

THE ARIZONA MOUNTAINEERING CLUB. The AzMC's membership totaled 483 at year-end 2002. Given the increased popularity of rock climbing and climbing gyms, the AzMC is competing with an increasing number of climbing venues and providers. Rock climbing in Arizona has grown in popularity such that even some new master-planned communities in the Phoenix area offer rock walls as part of their amenity packages.

A core instructional program has been a mainstay of AzMC focus. This year the club graduated 81 students through its Beginning Rock Climbing School, 63 students through its Anchors and Advanced Ropework School, and 36 students through its Lead School. Students who have previously finished the Schools are invited to come back and participate as assistants. Between students and assistants the three schools generated over 1,000 user days of activity.

Snow, ice, and other alpine skills are taught in AzMC-sponsored schools. In 2002 about 70 students and assistants participated in learning and/or practicing mountaineering classes, including Glacier Travel and Crevasse Rescue, Alpine Rock, and Beginning and Advanced Ice Climbing, and an out-of-state Alpine Outing. Colorado in particular was a popular destination for AzMC ice climbers with about a dozen trips being made to the Durango, Silverton, and Ouray environs. In addition, about 20 students took a land navigation class. In total this amounted to 205 user days.

Public service projects included teaching rock climbing to at-risk kids through the Latino Police Officers Association. The twice-annual Queen Creek clean-up attracted some 70 participants and the annual Grand Canyon Clean-up drew 35 people, for 150 user days.

Much of the state was closed during the summer months owing to severe fire restrictions. The AzMC had 25 official outing leaders at the start of the year, but with the enforcement of club policy stating minimum activity levels, the number of official leaders dropped to 20 by year's end. Even so, the club offered about 20 outings with nearly 200 user days of participation.

Although there were several official club trips to nearby states, there were no outings far afield. Several parties made the inevitable trip to bag Pacific Northwest volcanoes. There were at least four groups of AzMC'ers climbing in Europe with ascents of Monte Rosa and Mont Blanc and attempts on the Matterhorn to their credit.

ERIK FILSINGER, *President*

THE MOUNTAINEERS. The Mountaineers continues to offer well-received and popular courses in fundamental to intermediate mountaineering instruction, with the same emphasis as before in the "leave no trace" wilderness ethic. Land managers give the club praise in providing manpower through our course participants to help in restoration and trail maintenance activities. Two new pilot courses were offered this past year. An aid and big wall climbing course provided instruction to advanced rock climbers through field trips and climbing on short walls leading up to multi-day climbs. Classic Yosemite techniques were learned and practiced both on local walls and in Yosemite. A small-party self-rescue seminar provided instruction in high-angle self-rescue techniques for parties of two on rock or ice. Practice was accomplished through field trips to local rock and ice climbing areas. In addition, a new bolted demonstration wall constructed on the exterior of The Mountaineers Seattle clubroom greatly facilitated instruction for the self-rescue and aid courses.

The Mountaineers have solicited detailed comments and input from mountaineering clubs and noted climbers from around the world to create a new edition of *Mountaineering: The Freedom of the Hills*. It is this extensive involvement of so many climbers from such varied backgrounds that gives authority to the principles and techniques described in this leading mountaineering text. Because they take an active role in preparing "Freedom," many climbers feel a deep sense of ownership and refer to the text as "the climber's bible." Volunteer contributors and subject matter experts under the leadership of Steven M. Cox are compiling the input in preparing the seventh edition of *Mountaineering: The Freedom of the Hills*.

The history of The Mountaineers in particular, and northwest mountaineering in general, is preserved by The Mountaineers History Committee. A current project of this Committee is preserving historic films. In 1996, Dwight Watson, a pioneer Washington skier and climber, donated to the club several high quality mountaineering and nature films made before World War II. The Committee has preserved these films on broadcast quality digital videotape and is working to acquire and preserve other professional quality films, covering rock climbing, alpine mountaineering, backcountry skiing, and wilderness conservation, most dating from the 1950s.

Lowell Skoog, a long-time Northwest ski mountaineer, is independently writing a book on the history of ski mountaineering in Washington. Lowell's project is unique in that he is conducting open research. His research findings have been published on his Web site, www.alpenglow.org/ski-history. The Web site has generated feedback and leads to make Lowell's book as complete and accurate as possible. Lowell has completed the bulk of his research and is now writing the book.

In 2002 The Mountaineers Books produced numerous titles for their outdoor readers, and the climbing community in particular. The mountaineering titles includeed *Detectives on Everest*, the sequel to the nationally recognized *Ghosts of Everest*. Written by Jochen Hemmleb and Eric Simonson, the book reveals insights into the challenges of conducting high-altitude archeological research. The Mallory and Irvine Research Expedition did not locate the body of Sandy Irvine, but discovered more clues for future detectives on Everest. The question of whether George Mallory and Sandy Irvine were the first to summit Everest remains a mystery.

DONNA PRICE, *Trustee*

IN MEMORIAM

RAYMOND DAVID CAUGHRON 1943-2002

I first met RD Caughron some 30 years ago, and knew him as a climbing and skiing companion, raconteur, advocate for Yosemite, and leading spirit of the AAC among other roles. But perhaps his greatest role was as a friend and mentor to many, many people. He liked involving people; above all he wanted to get them into the mountains.

RD Caughran in the Tetons, about 1975. Caughran collection

RD, as he was universally known, was born in San Luis Obispo, California, on May 6, 1943. He grew up in Manhattan, Kansas, graduating from Kansas State University in mechanical engineering. In 1970 RD began a new life, enrolling in the MBA program at the University of California, Berkeley, and taking up climbing. There were trips to Yosemite, the High Sierra, Tetons, and soon thereafter to Canada, Alaska, and South America. Highlights were a new route on Mt. Waddington, an early ascent of Mt. Alberta, a traverse of Denali, and Korzhenevskoy, a 7,000-meter peak in the Pamirs.

Together we made many weekend trips to Yosemite, with the usual hassles over finding a place to camp. For some years our favorite was the "Ahwahnee Annex." Being in the grounds of the hotel, it overcame the dilemma of the "out of bounds" camper: that of being given away by a parked car. Breakfasts were excellent, the washroom appreciated for shaving and general cleaning up, and we even had the occasional dinner. Coat and tie mandatory in those days.

RD worked for some years in product development at The North Face, and later for PG & E. In 1976 he married Susan Henke, from whom he later divorced; their daughter Heather was never far from his thoughts. RD was the heart and soul of the Sierra Nevada Section of the AAC, and served on the board of the national club.

RD got to know many climbers from around the world; his home in the Berkeley hills was a warm solace for many itinerant souls. One of these was the brilliant Polish climber Wanda Rutkiewicz, who he met around 1990. She enthralled him with her descriptions of Himalayan climbing, saying: "If you want you can come with us. But remember, it is dangerous." So RD now began another climbing career on 8,000 meter peaks, together with Piotr Pustelnik and his companions. In succession he climbed Gasherbrum II, attempted Nanga Parbat, ascended Dhaulagiri, and attempted K2 and Kanchenjunga. Latterly he had health problems, but in his mind this was not going to get in his way.

On April 17, 2002, RD reported from Makalu via email: "Makalu – the pictures don't show the wind which seems to gust all night long. Nothing like an evening of tent flapping and listening to Frank Sinatra in my headphones…. We are safe, in good shape, warm and in good spirits." A few days later, RD and a companion carried loads up toward Makalu La. While his companion turned around, RD continued on upward, having to make a forced bivouac. Two Swiss climbers descending from Makalu La found him the following morning. He apparently died of hypothermia.

Just a month before his departure for Makalu, RD proposed a ski trip into Yosemite's backcountry. "Can you get the maps?" I asked. "Yes, no problem" RD replied. The weather turned worse, a couple of feet of snow fell overnight, and we now had to navigate by compass in falling snow. Pretty soon we left the map quadrangle we were on. "RD—do you have the next map?" Unfazed, he whipped out the Yosemite Park tourist brochure we'd picked up at the entrance station and pointed to its ridiculous map. Needless to say we were soon hopelessly lost. We ended up close under the south face of Half Dome, and had to climb down a series of rock steps, lowering our skis and packs down as best we could. Next day, now overdue, RD hit an unseen rock, took a spill and cut his forehead. We stopped the blood, bandaged him up, and off we went. At a lunch stop the battered RD handed out smoked oysters. "This is so great" he said, grinning from ear to ear.

And so it was. Thank you RD for all the great times that so many of us have shared with you. We'll have to carry on without you now. In closing, I am reminded of a letter that Ernest Hemingway wrote to close friends on the death of a young son: "It is not so bad for Baoth, because he had a fine time, always, and he has only done something now that we all must do."

CHRIS JONES, *AAC*

EARLYN DEAN 1939-2002

Earlyn Dean died in her sleep at her winter home in Singer Island, Florida on March 31. Raised in Edmonton and Toronto, Earlyn spent most of her adult life in New York, New Jersey, and Vermont, where she was a part-owner of manufacturing businesses. She retired on January 1, 2002. In recent years she traveled extensively, including a climbing expedition to Tierra del Fuego with Olaf Sööt.

An AAC member since 1971, Earlyn will best be remembered as an indefatigable volunteer for the Club and the New York Section. Among the projects she organized and undertook was the cumulative index of the American Alpine Journal from 1929-1976, an immense and time-consuming undertaking. Each year without fail, we in the New York Section could always rely on her willingness to get up early on Sunday morning and make pancakes for a bunch of hungry climbers at our Annual Section Outing at the Ausable Club in Keene Valley.

Earlyn's climbing extended back into the 1960s: hence she knew and climbed with many of the legendary figures of Eastern climbing during those colorful decades. It was therefore appropriate that she wrote the AAJ obituaries for such Eastern luminaries as Ed Nester and Chuck Loucks, both of whom died in climbing accidents. She was part of the support team when Ted Church, her former husband and business partner, did the first ascent of the east ridge of Mount Sir Sandford in the Selkirks in 1968.

PHILIP ERARD, *AAC*

KENNETH ATWOOD HENDERSON 1907-2001

Mt. Rainier, Pinnacle Peak, Unicorn Peak, and Castle Rock in the Cascades. Yukness, Odaray, Huber, Victoria, Lefroy, Mumm, Whyte, Thompson, and The Mitre in the Canadian Rockies. In Chamonix: Aiguille de l'M by the face, Aiguille des Petits Charmoz, a traverse of the Mont Blanc massif, including an ascent of Mont Blanc du Tacul and a forced descent in bad weather to the Grands Mulets Hut. In the Zermatt district: Matterhorn, Zinal Rothorn, Unter Gabelhorn,

Monte Rosa traverse via the Dufourspitze and the
Zumsteinspitze, a traverse of the Liskamm from the Lisjoch
to the Felikjoch, the Dent Blanche by the Wandfluh, and the
Tête Blanche. The Jungfrau and the Mönch in the Bernese
Oberland. Explorations in the Wind River Range.

That's a pretty good climbing résumé, especially for
a climber of the 1920s, when a trip to the Alps was a time-
consuming affair, involving ocean-going ships. And it's even
more impressive when you realize that this is only a partial
list of the climbs that Ken Henderson submitted on his
application to join the American Alpine Club. Ken was 22 at
the time, and many of his best climbs lay in the future.

Kenneth Henderson (left) and Robert
Underhill at Billy Owen's house in Jackson, following their first ascent of the
east ridge of the Grand Teton, 1929.
William Owen

Kenneth A. Henderson passed away on September 13
at the age of 95, in Lebanon, New Hampshire. He was a
world-class climber, explorer, and film-maker. He edited
Appalachia, and wrote the first guidebook to the Wind
River Range. Henderson Peak (13,115') in the Winds is
named after him.

I spoke with Ken in June of 2000 about some of his favorite climbs. In 1926 he went to
Europe for his first Alpine season. He and his partner Percy Olton hired a guide—which was
standard practice at the time—arranging to meet in Zermatt. The guide was late in arriving,
however, and the two climbers, itching to get started, climbed the Matterhorn guideless, as a
sort of warm-up.

They did many routes that summer, but eventually Olton had to return to the States. Ken
stayed on, and decided to traverse Monte Rosa with the guide. Arriving at the hut, they encountered a group of Japanese climbers and guides. Ken said, "The Japanese of course were talking
Japanese all the time, so we couldn't understand them." Over dinner, everyone conversed in their
own versions of High German, and it turned out that one of the Japanese was Prince Chichibu,
the second son of the Emperor, and the younger brother of the man who would soon become
Emperor Hirohito. "His father told him he had to have two guides." He also had four retainers,
and they each had two guides; so the hut was occupied by two clients, four retainers, and eleven
guides. That night, Ken had the honor of sharing the top bunk with Prince Chichibu.

The next day, the whole party climbed together, and they feasted upon fresh patisserie
that the guides had hauled up from the valley. "The nice thing about climbing with the Japanese
was all that carrying power."

Before the war, Ken participated in the first ascents of a number of classic climbs, including
Standard Route on Whitehorse Ledge, Northeast Ridge of the Pinnacle in Huntington Ravine,
and the East Ridge and Lower Exum routes on the Grand Teton. He made the first ascent of Mt.
Owen, last of the high Teton peaks to be climbed.

Ken told me about that ascent of Owen. Several parties had been close to success in the late
1920s. However, the final, smooth 100-foot summit knob had turned back all attempts. In July of
1930, Ken, with Underhill, Fritiof Fryxell, and Phil Smith, made it up to the previous high point.

While his three companions discussed the difficult rock climb they faced, Ken decided he
needed a little privacy. "I had to take a crap, so I went down on the north side a little bit, and
then came back up, and I took a look over the ridge, and I could see a continuous grassy ledge.

So I went over there, walked on the grassy ledge, and there was a crack in the dome, and I walked up onto the summit standing up. No climbing at all." He stood on the summit, and looked down on his partners. "They were getting ready to put on their sneakers." After his friends had joined him on the summit, it was time for a lesson. "Bob Underhill and I and the others roped down, and we climbed the face. Neither Phil nor Fryxell had ever heard of or seen a rappel. So we introduced them to the rappel. We rappelled down to where our packs were, and we climbed the face, and made a second ascent. We did Owen up proud that day."

As he grew older, Ken shifted from putting up first ascents to mentoring younger climbers. William Putnam, who would go on to become president of the AAC and write several guidebooks to the Canadian Rockies, was an undergrad in the early 1940s. He told me, "Ken was the godfather of the Harvard Mountaineering Club. Between him and Henry Hall, we had all the guidance we could use. Ken was more practical; Henry, more theoretical. Ken took us on a number of good climbs—inspired us, cajoled us, played with us."

It was at this time that Ken shot several 16mm films of rock and ice climbs in New England. In the 20s, he had purchased a Pathé 9.5mm camera in Europe, which he used to shoot motion pictures of Zermatt. By 1938, however, he had moved up to 16mm, and he had a new idea: "I wanted to make a film which would tell a coherent story from start to finish."

The seven films that Ken made in this era are carefully shot and well-edited. Each film tells the story of a party ascending a now-classic climb, ranging from the Whitney-Gilman on Cannon to the Pinnacle Gully ice climb in Huntington Ravine.

At the beginning of World War II, the government needed a book to assist the army in its plans for the training of mountain troops. The result was what Putnam calls "Ken's greatest claim to mountaineering fame: his *Handbook of American Mountaineering*." This classic how-to book, published by the AAC in 1942, introduced American climbers to rock climbing, ice climbing, rope techniques, and outdoor survival.

Ken climbed in an era of adventure. The best available ropes were made of Italian hemp. There were no specialized rock climbing shoes. Ken said, "Once on Mt. Willard, on the upper friction slabs, we got hit by a tornado-like storm. I was wearing crepe-soled golf shoes. I took them off, tied them together, and gave them to my second, who carried them in his teeth. I felt confident that I could lead the slabs in my stocking feet."

Much has been made of Ken's elegant attire when climbing. He generally wore a coat and tie, and often a fedora. Ken said that in those early days no one had specialized athletic clothing— you simply climbed in what he called "just ordinary old clothing." He was an investment banker; hence, his old clothes were business suits. I asked Putnam about this. He allowed that everyone just climbed in their old clothes; however, he added, "I don't think I wore a tie. Didn't add a great deal to warmth or water protection."

In 1997 Craigen Bowen and Bev Boynton climbed Sulphur Peak, in the Wind River Range. Summiting on a beautiful day, they found, lying on the ground, between a couple of rocks, a small glass jar with a metal lid. They unscrewed the lid, and out fell an engraved visiting card— with no address, only a name: Kenneth A. Henderson. It had been there since 1932, when Ken made the first ascent. As far as we know, it's still there.

WILLIAM CLACK

ANDREW JOHN KAUFFMAN, II 1920-2003

One never knows how things will end in this world. How could I have known, back in 1941, when I paired up with Andy Kauffman in the ice gullies of Mt. Washington, that our teamwork would end by my writing his obituary? In Andy's junior (and my freshman) year, we met through the Harvard Mountaineering Club. With Mal Miller, then the president, the three of us became that club's nucleus for weekend rock climbs and winter forays to Mt. Washington. With a war on, that was a hurry-up period for collegiate males. Andy succeeded Mal in June of 1942, and I was elected president just before many of us went off to war at the end of the year.

Andrew Kauffman on the summit of Hidden Peak, 1958. Pete Schoening

Andy, a member of the American Alpine Club since 1941, was the son of distinguished literary parents. His mother, Ruth, and his father, Reginald, were noteworthy foreign correspondents during World War I, and well-known authors. After the war they remained in Europe, where Reggie was the League of Nations correspondent for the New York Herald-Tribune, based in Geneva. Their three children attended local schools, and this early grounding in French, until his father took the position of editor of the Bangor Daily News, served as the cornerstone of Andy's life work—analysis of the internal politics of France for the United States Department of State, where he was employed for 30 years after 1943.

Andy graduated from Harvard in January of 1943 and then sought to join me in the Mountain Troops—he even had his obligatory three letters, one each from Henry Hall, Ken Henderson, and myself. Andy, however, flunked his physical exam—some obscure form of heart murmur that never bothered him for the next 60 years. I went off to war and he wrote me dutifully, at least once a week for the next three years. In the mountains of Italy a packet of his precious letters, carefully folded deep in my knapsack, stopped a shell fragment that had my name on it.

During those war years, Andy acted as the clearing house for correspondence between Mal Miller, off in the Pacific, and myself in planning what turned out to be the 1946 Mt. Saint Elias Expedition. And it was he, when told of Ben Ferris's desire to join us, immediately ordered me: "Grab him; he's a doctor!" Andy really enjoyed that Saint Elias trip and asked that his ashes be deposited on that mountain, which will be done. Though he climbed other peaks that were higher, for him it was "the last great mountain."

Following the trip to Saint Elias, Andy returned to the Selkirk Range of British Columbia, where he, and his then wife, née Betty Conant, had spent several tortuous weeks over the previous years trying to gain access to the Battle Range. He finally got there in 1947. The next year, with Ben Ferris, Henry Pinkham, and a malamute, the four of us traversed through the northern Selkirks, making numerous first ascents and meeting with a Sterling Hendricks-led party along the way.

Andy was off to the Coast Range in 1954, where he climbed with Nick Clinch and made the first ascent of Serra IV with David Sowles. A year later he was in Peru, again with Clinch, and made the first ascent of North Pucahira. Andy's acquaintanceship with Sowles gave rise to his establishment of the American Alpine Club's prestigious Sowles Award, when David was killed a few years later in an Alpine thunderstorm.

With the ascent of Hidden Peak, for which he was later elected an Honorary Member of the Club, Andy's climbing career peaked, and he was content thereafter to join others of us on rock climbs from Seneca Rocks to the Gunks. Several times in the 1960s and 70s we took less strenuous "starvation" trips into the easier terrain (for backpacking, anyway) of the Canadian Rockies, in the course of which he became "Uncle Andy" to a number of my younger friends. During these years he served as vice-president of both the Himalayan Club and the American Alpine Club and undertook the leading role in setting to right the story of the 1939 K2 Expedition, whose leader, Fritz Wiessner, was our mentor and friend.

Andy's career as a diplomat intertwined only once with his distinguished career as an alpinist. While he was stationed as Second Secretary of the American embassy in Paris in 1958, Nick Clinch invited him to join in an attempt on Hidden Peak. Andy promptly sought the necessary leave of absence—and was told, informally, that it had been granted. Having then gone to the Karakoram and having—with Pete Schoening—been the summit party on the only first ascent of an 8,000-meter peak ever made by Americans, he then learned that his application for leave had been denied by the bureaucrats back in Washington. Then they decided that since he was so interested in things in that part of the world, he could stay there for a few years, as consul in Calcutta.

For the Department of State, Andy read through countless French newspapers every day, searching for tidbits that might have a bearing on future government actions. He was the first to predict that the return to power of de Gaulle in 1958 would bring on a spate of problems for NATO and the United States. His memo on the potential return of de Gaulle is a classic of far-sightedness.

After his three-year "exile" to Calcutta, Andy was briefly assigned to Managua before returning to Washington, where he spent his remaining years in government as one of the State Department's men at the end of the "hot line" to Moscow.

Early in our acquaintanceship, Andy instructed me that the leader's job was to pioneer the route; the followers were to carry the burdens. Thereafter, I decided it was easier to be the leader; and thereafter Andy's backpacking feats became legends of endurance. We would load him up and point him in the right direction—once even up five flights of stairs at Harvard with a 400-pound box of climbing gear strapped on his pack. He might have occasionally been slow, but he never stopped moving.

Though he did not make much of it, Andy was an excellent communicator. His letters to me—all carefully bound—take up a four-foot span of my bookcase. He starred in the line drawings for Ken Henderson's Handbook of American Mountaineering, and was the prime proofreader for that opus. Working with him on two books—The Guiding Spirit, in 1986 and K-2: The 1939 Tragedy, in 1992—were my most enjoyable literary endeavors.

Andy's last years were sad. The heart that didn't sound right to the military medics kept his body alive long after the ravages of Parkinson's Disease took his mind. He left us on December 24.

Andrew John Kauffman, II, a generous alpinist of great distinction, is survived by his estranged second wife, the former Daphne Ennis, whom he met in India, and a niece, Xenia. Ours alone, now, are the fading memories of step-chopping and snowslopes, of solid belays and freezing bivouacs, and of all the little favors that make up a lifetime of friendship and confidence. How do you say goodbye to an old friend with whom you have shared 60 years of soggy campfires and alpine crises, of grungy labor and shared misery, of mutual confidence and high adventure? It ain't easy.

WILLIAM L. PUTNAM, *AAC*

WILLIAM (BILL) HEARRELL ROBINS 1957-2002

Bill Robins, 45, died on July 7 while attempting a technical climb on the northeast face of Bolivia's 17,159-foot Pyramide Blanca of the Cerro Condoriri group.

Bill was born on July 3, 1957, in Salt Lake City, Utah to John (Jack) H. and Zelda S. Robins, and raised on a family farm in Kaysville, Utah where he hiked, rode horses, and developed an inquisitive scientific mind. He earned a bachelors degree in chemistry from the University of Utah and a degree in geology from the University of Colorado at Boulder.

Since 1988, Bill has worked as a senior research scientist at Pacific Northwest National Laboratories (PNNL) in Richland, Washington, where he contributed to the state of the art in explosives identification, for use in weapons inspections programs.

Bill made over 1,000 first ascents in Washington and Utah, and has climbed in Canada, Nepal, South America, Kyrgyzstan, and Australia. His ascents were always done in a strictly traditional way, from the ground up. In Washington, his first ascents include Pink Apes (5.11+) at the Potholes' Hall of Frustration; and Bark like a Beagle (5.11X), Chemically Adjusted Reality (5.10a), and Painted Black (5.11b) at Frenchman Coulee. In Utah, his first ascents include Angel of Fear, a WI6 ice climb in Santaquin Canyon; Upper Bridal Veil Falls, a WI5-6 in Provo Canyon; and Gates of Hell, a 2,220' 5.10d R rock climb, also in Provo Canyon.

I met Bill at Frenchman Coulee in 2002. New to the Coulee, I was eager to learn from the locals when Bill, all six feet (+) of him, walked by in a white French Foreign Legion hat and painters pants (hand-painted with colorful flowers and symbols). When I asked him to help me pick out a few routes, he enthusiastically pointed out several fine lines from a three-ring binder of carefully detailed color pictures. He knew the place intimately, as he had put up hundreds of routes there over the years. He also maintained a website (users.owt.com/wrobins/) detailing many of the Coulee's climbing areas, plus his own efforts to preserve the area through The Access Fund and the Washington State land managers.

Bill Robins had a remarkably bold, generous, and humorous spirit—he was a true character, and will be badly missed. He was deeply loved by family and friends, including Paul Certa and Leela Sasaki of Richland, and his four nieces, to whom he brought back gifts from his far away, exotic adventures.

He is survived by his parents, Jack and Zelda, his brother T. Richard Robins, his sister Ruth Ann Eldredge, his nieces Stefanie R. Christensen, Erin E. and Jessica S. Robins, and Margaret Ann White, all from Utah.

KEITH K. DAELLENBACH, *AAC, and* PAUL CERTA

ANDRÉ ROCH 1906-2002

The 20th of November saw the passing of one of the great mountaineers of our time: André Roch. Engineer, avalanche and snow expert, high mountain guide, father, oil painter, and author were some of his many accomplishments. He pioneered climbing access routes of Everest, and cut the first ski run in Aspen, Colorado. His passion for the mountains affected all he encountered.

Born in Geneva, Switzerland the 21st of August 1906 he was introduced to the mountains at a young age by his father, a professor of medicine, and quickly developed a profound love. At 96, when he departed this world, it had never grown cold.

I met André by chance on a frosty morning in early December 1973. On the outskirts of Geneva I was hitchhiking up to Chamonix for my second winter of skiing and working as a "plongeur" (dishwasher), when a rather worn, black Peugeot 404 pulled to the side of the road and I was motioned to climb in. After a brief silence I was politely asked as to my destination. When I replied, in my limited French, he must have divined my accent and inquired from what country I came. Aspen, Colorado, "Etas Unis" I replied, and upon hearing the name his blue eyes lit up. "Aspen…I have been there," he said thoughtfully. "First in 1937; I cut the first ski run on Aspen Mountain. I am André Roch."

In 1968 at the age of 19 I came to Aspen, and of course I knew of the Roch Cup downhill race, Roch run, and of André's long association with the town. I must say I was not but a little taken aback by whom I was riding with. Regretting he could not take me all the way to Chamonix, for he was due to inaugurate a new lift in the ski resort of Flaine, he promised to pay a visit to the restaurant by which I was employed. Later that winter, he did come, and the girls who owned "Tartine" could not believe André Roch would come all the way from Geneva to visit a dishwasher. He was well known in the Alps.

We stayed friends ever since and frequently corresponded. Invited to Aspen in 1987 to commemorated the 50th anniversary of the Ski Club that he founded, he predicted our first child would be a boy, and be born during his stay. He was right on both counts. During each return to Chamonix, my family has always been graciously welcomed at his home in Geneva, where a fine view of Mt. Blanc can be had from his library.

André was an amazing person, not only for his vast experiences in his long life, but for his philosophy of life itself. The positive always outweighed the negative. Once while walking together in Chamonix, I commented on how the town had changed over the years and lost much of its charm. "Peut-être…mais les montagnes sont toujours aussi attirantes" (perhaps, but the mountains are as alluring as always). The changes at the valley floor could never alter his feelings for the mountains above.

Life, however, was not always kind to André. His camp in the Himalaya was hit by avalanche, carrying the party some 1,650 feet, killing two (Kumaun, 1939). His son Jean-François was buried 45 minutes in Davos by a slide in which they were both caught. André managed to free himself and dig his son out. A head-on car crash nearly took his life. Worst of all, his daughter Suzanne and her female climbing partner fell to their deaths while climbing with André in 1962, himself saved only by the parting of the rope. Madame "Mims" Roch never shared his passion and reproached him for his frequent extended absences. She never accepted the loss of their daughter. Despite these setbacks, it never diminished André.

In 1937 he was hired by railroad magnate Ted Ryan to map the ski runs and lifts for a resort to be built in Castle Creek valley, near the ghost town of Ashcroft, approximately 12 miles from Aspen. During the winter months, André would ride a horse up the valley, skis slung over the saddle. When at a spot he wished to climb, he would dismount, turn the horse around and slap the horse's rear to send it back to the ranch. Then he would skin up to the bowls below Hayden Peak to map out the area. I recently toured in the same region, thinking of him and what amazing terrain the resort would have encompassed, had not the outbreak or WWII ended the dream.

An engineer by profession, André is most remembered for study of snow and avalanche, and to that end wrote numerous books. As a consultant he traveled world wide. He was employed for years by the Swiss Federal Institute for Snow and Avalanche in Davos. The work afforded him the pleasure of returning home by skis each evening.

As a climber and guide he has numerous first ascents to his credit; in the Alps there are

25, notably the NE face of the Triolet, and South Pillar of the Courtes in the Mt. Blanc Massif. In the Himalaya and Karakoram he is credited with 27 firsts.

André was still bouldering in his 70s, and skiing in his 80s. In his later years he continued to write technical articles. Always a landscape mountain painter, he continued avidly until his death.

I will remember his charm, wit, and unsurpassed love of the mountains, which continues to influence my own passion. I am blessed to have known and called him a friend.

ROBIN FERGUSON

GALEN AVERY ROWELL 1940-2002

In the early hours of August 11 we lost one of our most energetic and influential mountaineers and photographers when Galen Avery Rowell died in a plane crash. His wife Barbara also was killed, as was the pilot and a third passenger. The chartered flight was turning into its final approach to bringing the Rowells back home to Bishop, California, when it crashed a couple of miles short of the runway.

Galen was born in Oakland on August 23, 1940 into a family with a couple generations of experience exploring the Sierra and the world. From their home in Berkeley they started taking him at a young age onto the peaks, and in 1956 he started technical climbing in Yosemite. Three times he won scholarships to Berkeley, but three springs running he couldn't contain himself in school as the mountains called.

Galen Rowell in the Sierra, 1988.
Andy Selters

In the early 1960s he roped up with many of Yosemite's luminaries, including Warren Harding, Layton Kor, and Chuck Pratt. He started carrying a camera to record the scenes and positions he'd encounter, but for this Pratt admonished him, saying that picture-taking distracted from the climbing experience, and that the results were almost always disappointing anyway. Galen took this as a challenge, and his ensuing career might be seen as a Herculean drive to weave together the contradictory demands of both participating in and observing the mountaineering experience. During this time he also married Carol Chevez, and they had two children. By 1971 he claimed over 100 new routes in the Sierra and Yosemite.

In the 1970s he sped his pace into a legendary frenzy, supporting himself as a photographer and writer, racing to the Sierra on weekends, and taking trips north. Many of his new routes in this period were with Chris Jones, including the first ascent of the west face of North Howser Tower. He also compiled his first book, *The Vertical World of Yosemite*. The pace took a toll on his marriage, and he and Carol divorced.

In 1973 he got a huge break into the national media when he filled in for a *National Geographic* staff photographer on a feature about Yosemite. He climbed with Dennis Hennek and Doug Robinson on the first hammerless ascent of Half Dome's Northwest Face route, and Galen's pictures and writing ended up gracing the magazine with its first-ever story on technical rock climbing, and a cover photo. Galen knew that many of his climbing partners were upset at this publicity explosion for their esoteric world, but he believed that telling the world about clean climbing would bring positive, not negative effects. The following winter he joined Bishop locals for a trip he remembered fondly, the first ski traverse of California's White Mountains.

The following summer he joined David Roberts and Ed Ward to make the first ascent of Mt. Dickey's huge east face.

In 1975 his reputation as a climbing photographer landed him a spot on the American K2 expedition. Here Galen struggled to assert that he was a capable climber as well, and for him the expedition devolved into acrimonious factionalism. The book that he published from it, *In the Throne Room of the Mountain Gods*, burst onto the American scene with America's first large-format color look at the astounding Karakoram, and a disturbingly honest view of expeditionary dirty laundry. Galen met Reinhold Messner on that trip, and that meeting helped convince Galen that his longtime formula for personal adventures embodied the future for expeditions as well: wilderness objectives, with small teams of highly capable companions.

In 1977 he returned to the Karakoram with John Roskelley, Kim Schmitz, Dennis Hennek, and Jim Morrissey to make the first ascent of Great Trango. The following year, he and Ned Gillette, Alan Bard, and Doug Weins made a circum-ski of Denali, after which Galen and Ned made a one-day ascent up the West Buttress route. In 1980, Galen, Kim, Ned, and Dan Asay pulled off one of the great excursions of the modern era: a 43-day spring ski tour across the majority of the Karakoram, linking the VAST glacial systems via high passes. Hot off of that trip, Galen, Ned, and Jo Sanders went to make the first American climb in Communist China, a ski descent of Mustagh Ata.

In the 1980s Galen's whirlwind inflated into a tornado. Key to this was that in 1981 he met Barbara Cushman, Director of Public Relations at The North Face. Within a few months they married, and within a year she elevated Galen's business from a home office into a high-powered company. With her as president, *Mountain Light* would grow into a seven-figure industry.

Galen's artistic focus came to define his photography on his terms, starting with his book, *Mountain Light*. It used many of his favorite images to say that his photography was an interaction with wilderness, a balance of planning and spontaneity, and to understand the grandeur of his images one must appreciate the adventures he took to get them. His art was a quest for what he called "the dynamic landscape," photos that evoke the energetic sense of terrain and participant united in action. He had arrived to say that strenuous wilderness explorations and the camera on his chest were mutually energizing, enhancing both his experiences and his ability to photograph them. In 1984 Galen was given the Ansel Adams award for wilderness photography.

Galen then took great advantage of the fact that China was opening more of Tibet. In 1981, he was on the first modern American trek to the north side of Mt. Everest, and then he led a circumnavigation and the second ascent of sacred Amnye Machin, in northeastern Tibet. In 1983, he was leader of a team that tried Mt. Everest's west ridge, without oxygen. By the late 1980s he had visited Kailas and other areas, and he had become fed up with the Chinese line about Tibet. He contacted the exiled Tibetan leader, His Holiness the Dalai Lama, and in 1989 they compiled *My Tibet*, a book with Galen's pictures and the Dalai Lama's commentaries.

Between all this, he jammed in climbs all over the world. In 1982 he teamed with John Roskelley, Vern Clevenger, and Bill O'Connor to make the first ascent of Cholatse. In 1984 he, Jack Tackle, Gray Thompson, and Rob Milne made the first ascent of Lukpilla Brakk. In 1985, he climbed Fitzroy with Mike Graber and Dave Wilson. In Pakistan in 1986, Galen persuaded President Zia al Haq to provide him and Barbara helicopter access all over the Karakoram, and as Galen documented the Pakistani side of the Siachen war with India, he collected aerial photographs of most every corner of the range.

During the 1990s, Galen teamed up as partner and publicist for Todd Skinner and Paul Piana as that pair made bolted, first-free ascents of big walls, notably Mt. Hooker and Proboscis. Galen later told me that the sport climbing tactics on those climbs had their place, but they took away the spirit of mountaineering. In the Sierra he continued to climb as many new and difficult routes as any modern climber, and for these he always used traditional style.

Galen was endowed with an ego that turned off more than one acquaintance. Those of us who knew him well, however, got to experience him as everything from a barely contained force of wild nature, to an amazingly penetrating analyst of the world around him. I suspect that every day of his life included at least a few moments of spontaneous and infectious enthusiasm for busting out and doing something wild. I first experienced that when we worked on a river assignment together; he summoned me to escape from duty and run some rapids without a boat. Galen also developed a strong sense of philanthropy, and he was on the board of over 20 non-profit organizations.

Galen's last expedition, in the early summer of 2002, gave him some of his deepest satisfaction ever. He and Rick Ridgeway, Conrad Anker, and Jimmy Chin set out on foot, towing 200-pound loads with balloon-tired rickshaws, to find the western calving grounds of Tibet's threatened antelope. They indeed found the chiru giving birth, and the widely broadcast story is now contributing to a conservation goal of worldwide significance. *Mountain Light* is now operated under the joint ownership of Galen's son and daughter, and Barbara's brother. In March of this year, our Club bestowed Galen—already an Honorary Member—with an award for "Lifetime Achievement for Contributions to the Mountain Arts." While Galen succeeded on many climbs, his greater legacy has been to look through and beyond the summits, and this is written deeply in his photographs and essays, his hyper-alert passages across an incredible amount of our planet's wildlands, in the scores of people who got to know his impressive dynamism, and in the very way that America now looks at mountains.

ANDY SELTERS, *AAC*

HAROLD WALTON 1912-2002

Harold Walton was born in Cornwall, England and received his Ph.D. in chemistry from Exeter College in Oxford before coming to the United States to do postdoctoral work at Princeton University.

After briefly working as a research chemist, Harold became a professor at Northwestern University, leaving there in 1947 for the University of Colorado, in Boulder. He taught at CU until his retirement and chaired the chemistry department from 1962 to 1966. Harold's teaching extended well beyond CU. Fluent in Spanish, German, and French, he used his sabbaticals to teach in Peru, Venezuela, Sudan, and France. He stayed active as a professor emeritus and at the age of 83 received the University of Colorado Medal and was described as "one of the 20th century's preeminent analytical chemists in the field of ion exchange and liquid chromatography."

Harold Walton.
Walton collection

Harold had a favorite theory that an "esoteric connection exists between mountaineering and chemistry," and these two activities were major themes in his life. He was a founding member of Rocky Mountain Rescue in Boulder. His name is well known to everyone who has climbed the Maiden in the Boulder foothills and has followed the Walton Traverse on its north face. He made the first ascent of another favorite climb near Boulder, the Cussin' Crack on Castle Rock, named for the uncharacteristic outbursts of this soft-spoken man.

Harold taught at the University of Trujillo in Peru during several of his sabbaticals, and he used his fluency in Spanish in the mountains as well as the classroom. He participated in at least five expeditions to the Cordillera Blanca. The first was with Nick Clinch on the North American Andean Expedition in 1955. He led the Colorado Mountain Club expedition to Quebrada Hondo in 1963. On their numerous trips to Peru, the Iowa Mountaineers relied heavily upon Harold's fluent Spanish, his skills in dealing with Peruvian officials, and his friendships with local porters. He was a leader on at least four of their expeditions between 1961 and 1978.

A number of us climbed Huascarán with Harold in August 1972, on the last of his several ascents of that mountain, just a few days before his 60th birthday. We were with the Iowa Mountaineers on that trip, and the changing opinions of Harold were fascinating to behold. At first a few young tigers complained about having this "slow old man" along, but higher on the mountain he grew stronger and faster as the rest of us slowed down. He continued to climb actively after this trip. Five years later he made the first ascent of a peak above the Conrad Icefield in Canada, naming it Mt. Kelvin after one of Britain's greatest physicists.

Perhaps the most wonderful aspects of Harold's life in the mountains of Peru were the friendships he developed with the high-altitude porters of the Cordillera Blanca. At base camp while the rest of us climbers were clustered around our fire, Harold was often seated at the porters' fire, chatting away in Spanish. In the style of Sir Edmund Hillary, Harold looked after the welfare of the Huaraz porters for many years. To them he was "El Doctor," godfather to their children and long-time benefactor. He brought many of them and their sons to the U.S., and he helped at least one son get into the University of Trujillo.

Not often given to philosophical pronouncements, Harold did occasionally reveal that side of his character, such as in a 1979 *Trail and Timberline* article: "First ascents are only an occasional luxury, and for most of us they are not the most important part of mountaineering. Sometimes the impulse to tread untrodden peaks seems little more than the child's impulse to tread in wet cement. The real joy is to climb something beautiful and difficult, and if it has never been done before, so much the better.... In any case the days in the hills were not wasted. They were snatched from eternity, to be with us as long as we live."

KIM MALVILLE, *AAC*

NECROLOGY

GEORGE M. AUSTIN	GORAN KROPP	REINHOLD STATTIN
URSULA CORNING	ROBERT LEE	FREDDIE SNALAM
DONALD J. GARDNER	MIGNON F. LINCK	CHESTER ULLIN
WES GRANDE	SKIP MERLER	THOMAS R. WESTON
RALPH HEUMAN	JOHN H. ROSS	ROD WILLARD
ED HOMMER	BARBARA CUSHMAN ROWELL	

INDEX

COMPILED BY RALPH FERRARA AND EVE TALLMAN

Mountains are listed by their official names and ranges; quotation marks indicate unofficial names. Ranges and geographic locations are also indexed. Unnamed peaks (e.g. Peak 2340) are listed under P. Abbreviations are used for some states and countries and for the following: Article: art.; Cordillera: C.; Mountains: Mts.; National Park: NP; Obituary: obit. Most personnel are listed for major articles. Expedition leaders and persons supplying information in Climbs & Expeditions are also cited here. Indexed photographs are listed in bold type. Reviewed books are listed by title.

A

Abasraju (C. Blanca, Peru) 297-8
Achey, Jeff 67-8
Ackroyd, Peter 385-6, 464-5
Aconcagua (Argentina) 319
Adi Kailash "Little Kailash" (India) 365-6
Adi Kailash Range (India) 365-6
Africa 338-9, 342
Agua Negra (Argentina) 318
Ak-Kalpak (At-Bashy Range Kyrgyzstan) 353
Ak Saitan (Kokshaal-Too Kyrgyzstan) 350-2
Al Jil see Jabal Misht
Alaska
    Climbs and Expeditions 218-39
    Alaska Range art. 14-8; 221-31
    Brooks Range 218-20
    Coast Mts. 237-9
    Chugach Mts. 234-5
    Delta Range 221
    Hayes Range 221
    Kichatna Spires 231-3
    St. Elias Mts. 235-6
    Stikine Icecap art. 30-43, **31**
Alaska: A Climbing Guide. Mike Wood and
    Colby Coombs *(Book Review)* 463
Alaska Range (AK) art. 14-8; 221-31
Albert, Kurt 68
Alexander, P. (Borkoldoy Range Kyrgyzstan) 353-4
Alma Fuerte Peak (Argentina) 320
Alpamayo (C. Blanca, Peru) 296
Altai Mts. (Mongolia/China) 422-3, 424-5
Amelunxen, Conny 42, 259, 264
American Safe Climbing Assn. 427
Amstadter, Kyle 347-8
Ananea Group (C. Apolobamba, Peru) 312
Anderl Heckmair: My Life, Eiger North Face, Grand

Jorasses and Other Adventures. Anderl Heckmair
    (Book Review) 452
Anderson, Lynnea 315-6
Anderson, Robert 332-3
Angina (Coast Mts. CAN) 256
Anker, Conrad 332
Annapurna I (Annapurna Himal, Nepal) 384-5
Annapurna Himal (Nepal) 384-5
Antarctica 330-337
Apa Sherpa 390
Apolobamba, Cordillera (Peru) 312
Aquarius Valley (Arrigetch, AK) 218, 219
Araca Group (C. Quimsa Cruz, Bolivia) 316-7
Araujo, Rodulfo 69, 293
Argentina 318-20, 322-25
Argewicz (Coast Mts. CAN) 256
Ariel (Arrigetch Peaks, AK) 218
Arizona (U.S.) 201-2
Armstrong, Brent 212
Arniko Chuli (Mustang Himal, Nepal/Tibet) 387-8
Arran, Anne 342
Arran, John art. 76-85
Arrigetch Peaks (Brooks Range, AK) 218-20
Artesonraju (C. Blanca, Peru) 305-6
Arwa Crest (Garhwal Himalaya) art. 94-9
Arwa Spire (Garhwal Himalaya) art. 94-9, 100
    105, **100**, 369-70
Arwa Tower (Garhwal Himalaya) *art.* 94-9, **94**,
    369-70
Asgard, Mt. (Baffin Island CAN) 252
Asnococha (C. Apolobamba, Peru) 312
At-Bashy Range (Kyrgyzstan) 352-**3**
Athabasca, Mt. (Rocky Mts., CAN) 272
Athans, Pete *art.* 168-75
Athearn, Lloyd 461-2
Atkinson, William C. 470-1
Augusta, Mt. (CAN) 242

SUBMISSIONS GUIDELINES

The *American Alpine Journal* records the significant climbing accomplishments of the world in an annual volume. We encourage climbers to submit brief (250-500 words) factual accounts of their climbs and expeditions. Accounts should be submitted by e-mail whenever possible. Alternatively, submit accounts by regular post on CD, zip, or floppy disk. Please provide complete contact information, including e-mail address, postal address, fax, and phone. The deadline is December 31, through earlier submissions will be looked on very kindly! For photo guidelines and other information, please see the complete Submissions Guidelines document at the American Alpine Journal section of www.americanalpineclub.org.

Please address all correspondences to:

The American Alpine Journal, 710 Tenth Street, Suite 140, Golden, CO 80401 USA; tel.: (303) 384 0110; fax: (303) 384 0111; aaj@americanalpineclub.org; www.americanalpineclub.org